The Criminology of Criminal Law

Advances in Criminological Theory
VOLUME 8

The Criminology of Criminal Law

EDITED BY
William S. Laufer
Freda Adler

with a foreword by
Gerhard O. W. Mueller

Transaction Publishers
New Brunswick (U.S.A.) and London (U.K.)

ISSN: 0894-2366
ISBN: 1-56000-329-4
Printed in the United States of America

This book is printed on acid-free paper that meets the American National Standard for Permanence of Paper for Printed Library Materials.

Marvin E. Wolfgang

(1924 – 1998)

Editor's Note

The contributions to the first six volumes of *Advances in Criminological Theory* have generated lively discussion and comment. These comments themselves are contributing to the advance of criminological theory. There is one comment in this volume. The editors invite others to contribute to this series. Comments need not be in article form. Brief notes are equally welcome.

Contents

Part 1

Part 2

List of Figures

List of Tables

Foreword

Criminal Law and Criminology: Synergy or Allergy

G.O.W. Mueller

Years ago the editors of *Advances in Criminological Theory* decided to devote an issue to the central question of the relationship between criminology and criminal law. This question is as old as criminology itself, namely about a century. The most obvious approach might have been an invitation to submit papers on the relation or interaction between criminal law and criminology. Yet it was feared that the result might have been a melange of philosophical/doctrinal papers differing little from the positions staked out over the last 100 years: the question of dominance or subservience between the two disciplines; the issue of the possibility (or necessity) of complete integration of the two disciplines; or indeed the need for their further fragmentation. Most obvious here would be the long perceived but never enunciated trend toward further polarization along the lines: What criminology is to criminal law, criminal justice is to criminal procedure.

None of these or similar findings might have been helpful in assessing, whether in philosophical or utilitarian terms, the current relationship between criminal law (in the broadest sense) and criminology (again, in the broadest sense).

Instead, the editors decided to invite scholars, whose work had always shown an explicit or implicit involvement with the two disciplines, to submit papers of their choice. This approach, it was hoped, might permit some conclusions about the extent of synergy or allergy between the two disciplines. As it turned out, some concordant findings mark the totality of chapters in this volume of the *Advances*. Yet, whether these are of direct practicality, or whether their implications lie in the distant future, remains to be seen.

Keeping the *leitmotiv* in mind, *The Criminology of Criminal Law*, or, as reformulated in this foreword, *Criminal Law and Criminology: Synergy or Allergy*, the chapters clearly fall into two categories. There are those pointing to an existing or potential synergy (part I), and those demonstrating more allergy than synergy (although there is always hope for the future).

Part I

Part I begins with C. Ray Jeffery's "Criminology and Criminal Law: Science versus Policy and the Interaction of Science and Law." Jeffery is a scholar who has devoted a life of research and advocacy to the integration of law and criminology. He himself has impacted the crime prevention scene significantly—including by stimulating legislation, although, as Matthew B. Robinson notes in part II, Jeffery's work never had the impact it should have had. Nevertheless, Jeffery, the scholar who learned his criminology from Sutherland, his psychology from Skinner, and his law from Jerome Hall, has remained steadfast in his call for closing the gap between science, law, and politics.

Marc Riedel discusses an area virtually ignored by criminal law: stranger violence. To the extent that law has considered it (recently), it was done so without regard to scientific findings. Like lawyer-criminologist Hans von Hentig half a century ago, Riedel finds certain times and places more prone to stranger violence. Should legislation, as distinct from police deployment, endeavor to provide more protection for such times and places, as did medieval legislation of the French, English, and German kings (God's peace, King's peace), etc.? Yet, without an impact study, we would be ill advised to emulate such precedents (yet we have: drug-free school zones, etc.). Riedel is right in calling for *effective* legislation, and that means science-based legislation.

James B. Jacobs's and William S. Laufer's contributions must be assessed in conjunction with each other, as both discuss forms of criminality which have largely been ignored by criminologists. Jacobs discusses a seemingly mundane form of crime, drunk driving. Laufer calls our attention to the most horrific criminality: genocide. Why have criminologists shied away from either topic? Yet legislators—local, national and international—had to deal with both categories of criminality—unaided by research. We cannot blame legislators for devising largely ineffective, often merely ceremonious, remedies. We can only blame ourselves for not having laid the scientific groundwork for dealing with criminality beyond the penumbra of "ordinary" crimes to which criminological attention has been devoted traditionally.

Per contra, Deborah Denno provides us an example of a very successful interaction between criminal law and criminology: the emergence over the last quarter century of the criminologist as an expert witness in court. With Denno's chapter we have entered the criminal justice sphere of criminology.

Starting with the police, Carl B. Klockars and Sonya Kutnjak Inkovich offer a fascinating comparative study on the measurement of police delinquency in Croatia and the United States. Offense seriousness measurements have indeed had a pronounced impact on (mostly administrative) practice, for example, the Uniform Crime Report (UCR), though with little impact on legislation. (I only wish the authors had included questions on the use of force against "others"—especially ethnic minorities! That might have contributed to answering Laufer's unanswered question.)

Also in the law enforcement sector is Bernard Cohen's "Police Enforcement of Quality-of-Life Offending," seriously questioning the broken-windows-quality-of-life-continuum approach as productive for crime reduction, and warning of undesirable side effects such as threats to Bill of Rights protections, police abuse of force, and corruption. Here, too, criminologists have had no impact on legislation, but *considerable* influence on "the law" as administered in the streets. Desirable or undesirable? Only rigorous testing can achieve socially desirable results, as Cohen warns.

Moving from law enforcement to sanctioning, Paul E. Tracy and Kimberly Kempf-Leonard demonstrate that "the relationship between criminological research and the criminal law, and most importantly the inplications of the former on the latter, may be evidenced with respect to juvenile law." They are critical of the current trend—unsupported by research—to waive juveniles into the adult criminal justice system. Policy changes are necessary, especially with the expected increase in the juvenile population, but only if based on empirical evidence.

Edna Erez and Leslie Sebba address us with a powerful plea for reorientation of our entire approach to crime control (especially as to sanctioning) from an offender-based system toward a victim-based system of individualization, *albeit standardized individualization*. They note well that all of the massive legislation aimed at easing the lot of victims has not been conducive to victim individualization in the liberal sense. Once again, such legislative impact as criminologists may have had in the sphere of victim protection either has not reached far enough, or has been misdirected. The question remains, how do we best impact the legislatures and the courts with our research?

Concluding part I is Claire Souryal and Charles Wellford's "Sentencing Disparity and Sentencing Guidelines," a highly critical criminological evaluation of the effect of legislated sentencing guidelines. While these have gone a long way in reducing sentence disparities, legislation has not yet succeeded in ridding our system of ugly remnants of racial bias in the length and frequency of prison sentences.

Summing up the findings of part I, one can only conclude with a mixture of delight and despair. Yes, the infant science of criminology has some successes to book in terms of legislation, court procedures, and administrative application of crime prevention approaches. Yet, a true synergy has not been achieved, while the desirability and possibility of a synergy are clearly demonstrable. Is it that criminologists, as scientists, and lawyers as normative thinkers, talk different languages? The former think in terms of cause and effect, the latter in terms of syllogistic logic or precedents? What keeps us apart?

Part II

The reason, Leslie Wilkins suggests, lies far deeper than a difference in reasoning processes. In fact, he urges criminologists to give up their simplistic cause and effect thinking. As much as this linear thought process might be understandable to law makers, it rarely leads to satisfactory results and consequently produces dissatisfaction with criminology. Instead, Wilkins wants punishment policy—the nerve center of criminology—to be based on *commensurate complexity*. Thus, we should move

from	towards
search for simple cause-effect models	search for appropriate models which can accommodate commensurate complexity
concentration of power	extension of participation in decisions to all those involved in the event
symbolism, ritual, drama and display	economic analysis and use of managerial techniques with good communication,

to cite but a few of his theorems.

What Wilkins proposes cannot be accomplished overnight. It requires a whole new approach to criminology, including the training of a new generation of criminologists and, yes, of criminal law specialists and legislators. Yet, all of the papers in Part II are demonstrative of the need for commensurate complexity. Thus, Kip Schlegal and David Eitle, in *Back to the Future: A Reminder of the Importance of Sutherland in Thinking about White Collar Crime*, reject the simple (almost juridical) normatization of organized crime by some scholars, who then are able to criticize normatized white-collar crime. The issue is far more complex. White-collar crime never was intended to be a juridical, normative concept of the type to which legislators can easily address themselves. It is a scientific concept whose commensurate complexity must be recognized before it can serve as a platform from which to devise and legislate control mechanisms.

Similarly, even the law-defined concept of treason, as Vared Vinitzky-Seroussi demonstrates, is far from uncomplicated. The findings "indicate that even treason can be understood, if not accepted," and had the author extended his inquiry from Pollard to Colonel von Stauffenberg, the conclusion might have been that treason can be necessary and honorable. Commensurate complexity!

In "Technological and Other Changes: Boundary Crossings in the Control of Deviance," Bonnie Berry demonstrates that the difference between the good and the bad, the permitted and the prohibited, is anything but a static Mason-Dixon line. It is, rather, like armies of the North and South moving forward and backward, controlling this territory today and abandoning it tomorrow, thereby changing the law that governs slavery. I should not blame Berry for my civil war analogy—it simply seemed demonstrative to me, especially since, once again, it exemplifies commensurate complexity over time and space.

Yet another demonstration of commensurate complexity is Matthew B. Robinson's "Theoretical Development of CPTED" in which he showed that C. Ray Jeffery's enormous contribution to criminological theory did not have any major impact on legislation, precisely because Jeffery has always been aware of commensurate complexity—a phenomenon not resting at the level of practical implementation but rather at the preceding level of thought and research.

"Measuring Justice: Unpopular Views on Sentencing Theory," by Don M. Gottfredson, reads as if Gottfredson had read Wilkins's chapter beforehand. (He had not.) Moving away from bipolar approaches, whether they be crime-punishment, or crime-punishment-deterrence (or incapacitation), he wants us to pay attention to *precursors*, particularly the creation of quantifiable measures, and measurement itself. Similarly, David F. Greenberg argues that punishment policy is anything but a cause-effect (crime-punishment) phenomenon. Rather, it is a highly complex process, largely determined by socio-political-economic factors which aim at moving society in a given direction, e.g., from a laissez-faire society to a welfare state, or, as now, vice versa.

Included in part II which, after all, is demonstrative of more allergy then synergy, is the contribution by MacDonald and Tennenbaum, on "Justifiable Homocides by Civilians." It is a contribution which would have provided Marvin Wolfgang great pleasure, if he had occasion to read it. After all, it provides behavioral science meaning to logically cold criminal law tests of "justifiable homocide." The appearance, in part II of this volume, makes an important point: there may not be much distance between the synergy and the allergy between criminal law and criminology.

It is time to come to the one prominent intellectual thread which ties all the contributions to this volume of the *Advances* together. Who has been the persistent advocate for basing criminal law on criminology (see Jeffery's chapter); who identified stranger homicide, decades ago (see Riedel's chapter); who called for a behavioral science based concept of criminal law (see MacDonald and Tennenbaum); who first gauged the severity of crime, whether mundane (see Jacobs's chapter) or horrific (see Laufer's chapter), or juvenile (see paper by Klockars and Kutnjak Inkovich); who was the first to advocate the criminologist as expert witness in court, and served as such (see Denno'schapter); who enabled us to understand juvenile offenders within their birth cohorts (see chapter by Tracy and Kempf-Leonard); who discovered victim-precipitation and called for victim-orientation in criminal justice (see chapter by Erez and Sebba); who called national attention—and that of the U.S. Supreme Court—to racial disparities in sentencing (see chapter by Souryal and Wellford), and who is it who never embraced simplistic notions but, with the attributes of a Renaissance man, explored all cultural, historical, social, political, and economic aspects before offering criminological solutions to complex social problems (see the entire part 2)?

Marvin E. Wolfgang

Director, Sellin Center for Studies in Criminology and Criminal Law, to whom we, his associates, colleagues, former students and collaborators, dedicate this volume of *Advances in Criminological Theory*. *Ad multos annos*, Marvin!

In retrospect, our wishes were not fulfilled.
Marvin Wolfgang left us before this volume appeared in print.

Part 1

1

Criminology and Criminal Law: Science Versus Policy and the Interaction of Science and Law

C. Ray Jeffery

Marvin E. Wolfgang and American Criminology

The contributions of Professor Wolfgang to criminology will be examined in this volume and in this chapter. He continued the contributions of the Gluecks to longitudinal research focusing on the number of delinquents who went on to criminal careers. His 1972 cohort study, followed by the 1982 study (Wolfgang, Figlio, and Sellin 1972; Tracy, Wolfgang, and Figlio 1982) of delinquents in Philadelphia became a classical model for later research on criminal careers. He found that 6 percent of the cohort group committed 50 percent of the crimes. Longitudinal and experimental studies, using prospective rather than retrospective methodologies, which looked for individual differences rather than group differences, became a major research tool for many investigators such as West and Farrington (1973, 1977) who found that in England 6 percent of the offenders committed 49 percent of the offenses (Mednick Moffitt, and Stack 1987; Farrington, Ohlin, and Wilson 1986). The Gluecks (1950, 1952) studied the delinquent from an interdisciplinary approach, using biological, psychological, and social variables in the analysis, in contrast to the Chicago model of symbolic interactionism and social learning theory. Sheldon Glueck in a comment on Sutherland's theory of differential association stated that Sutherland had the sequence backwards, that is, youths became delinquents and then sought out other delinquents with whom to associate, rather than associating with delinquents and then becoming delinquents.

He called this the "birds of a feather flock together" theory (Glueck 1956). Delinquents have biological and psychological predispositions that act to determine one's associational patterns.

Wolfgang's research led to a study of the biological factors in violence as seen in his studies of violence and in the work of one of his students (Denno 1990; Wolfgang and Ferricuti 1967; Weiner and Wolfgang 1989a; Weiner and Wolfgang 1989b). He commented in volume 1 of the *Advances in Criminological Theory* (Laufer and Adler 1989: viii) that "Theory in criminology has been stagnant for decades," and he heralded the new series as a means of making theory central to criminology. In the same volume I put forth an article on criminology as an interdisciplinary science, with a plea for more psychology, more biology, and more science (Jeffery 1989). Wolfgang was very close to the origins of criminology within the Italian School of Criminology, the so-called positive or scientific school of criminology, and he helped to introduce into criminology the work of Lombroso, the M.D. who is called "the father of criminology" (Wolfgang 1972). Wolfgang also was critical of the deterrence/punishment model of criminal justice and he put forth a medical model to replace prisons and punishment (Wolfgang 1995). The failure of the criminal justice system is in need of reexamination. This means a reexamination of the relationship of criminology to criminal law, or science to law, a major theme of this chapter.

Criminal Justice versus Criminology

Two major approaches to crime and criminals dominate criminology, the classical legal approach (the criminal justice system) and the scientific positivistic approach (criminology) (Mannheim 1972). The legal approach focuses on the legal concept of *crime* as found in criminal law, based on concepts of free will and moral responsibility. The criminal justice system is reactive, that is, the police wait for a crime to be reported, the prosecutor waits for an arrest to be made, and the court waits until a criminal charge has been filed. Once a conviction has been obtained the criminal justice system acts on the basis of a medieval tradition of revenge and deterrence through punishment and prisons.

The scientific approach focuses on the study of the individual offender or the *criminal* and not the crime. The scientific approach is a result of the major paradigmatic shift in the study of human behavior that occurred in the late nineteenth century with the application of science to the study of behavior by Mendel, Darwin, and Freud, which led to the development of human genetics, behavioral psychology, neuropsychiatry, and biological psychology. Human behavior was made a part of nature to be studied scientifically (Degler 1991; Jeffery 1990; Kuhn 1962; Mannheim 1972; Wright 1994). This is the basis for criminology (Jeffery 1972).

Wolfgang (1995) discussed the development of these two approaches to crime, the failure of the retribution/just deserts approach, and the development of a scientific approach by Lombroso and others. In his article on Lombroso, Wolfgang (1972) traces the development of psychiatry in Europe and the impact of medicine on the study of behavior. "In the history of criminology probably no name has been eulogized or attacked so much as that of Casare Lombroso....one who has been called the 'father of modern criminology'" (232). Lombroso focused attention upon insanity, brain pathology, and the central nervous system, all of which are central to biological psychiatry and biological criminology today. Wolfgang quotes the statement from Sutherland and Cressey that Lombroso "delayed for fifty years the work which was in progress at the time" (288), a statement Wolfgang disputes.

Wolfgang (1995) reviews the failure and rejection of the rehabilitation model by C.S. Lewis, Robert Martinson, Francis A. Allen, Walter Bailey, the American Friends Service Committee, Andrew von Hirsch, and James Q. Wilson (see also Jeffery 1990). He notes that the National Academy of Sciences Panel on Deterrence and Incapacitation (Blumstein, Cohen and Nagin 1978) found that the evidence for deterrence is so inadequate that no definite conclusions can be drawn. He also cites the conclusions of the National Academy of Sciences Panel on Rehabilitation (Sechrest, White, and Brown 1979) that we do not know if rehabilitation efforts are at all effective. Wolfgang notes that the revival in the past twenty years of the neoclassical school has resulted in more prisons, longer and harsher prison sentences, and the decay of the juvenile court. He concludes "Deterrence, retribution, and punishment, never abandoned by the populace, have once again become acceptable to those...with the power to enforce their beliefs" (290). He goes on to state that "The empty cup of our ignorance has often been filled not with facts and knowledge but with good intentions." Wolfgang asks for a medical model in place of the just deserts model. "Within the framework...of the just deserts model, the healing arts and disciplines of knowledge...must continue. Psychiatry, psychology, psychotherapy, neurology, even endocrinology, are the medical allies...who have not flourished in the criminal justice system" (291). From the beginning criminal law and criminology have been in conflict.

Many criminologists regard the criminal justice system as ineffective (Clear 1994; Durham 1994; Gordon 1990; Murphy and Dison 1990). It is controlled by lawyers and politicians rather than by scientists, and is based on assumptions about the efficacy of revenge and punishment. Legal procedures based upon science will be discussed later in the chapter. Recent statistics show that in the United States the prison population has doubled in the past ten years and now comprises 1.6 million inmates. Most crimes are not known to the police. For example, only one of every six or seven rapes is reported. Sixty-five percent of the homicides are cleared by arrest, and this is the highest clearance rate for all crimes. Of the crimes reported, less than 20 percent result in an arrest and prosecution, and of those convicted few are sent to prisons. Of those individuals sent to prison, up to 70 or 80 percent recidivate and return to prison, while at the same time new offenders are entering the system for the first time. The result is that our prisons are overcrowded, inhumane institutions that should not be tolerated by a democratic society. Overcrowded prison conditions are forcing the early release of offenders. Recently, 445 murderers and rapists were released from the Florida prison system because of early release laws (*Tallahassee Democrat*, 26 November 1996). The juvenile justice system in the state of Florida was recently declared to be a disaster since 65 percent of the youths placed in rehabilitation programs are arrested within one year after release at a cost of $512 million this past year (*Tallahassee Democrat*, 22 June 1997). We cannot control crime by continuing to build more prisons. Today the state of Florida spends more on the construction of prisons than on higher education, and prison construction is used as a means of supporting impoverished rural communities. The criminal justice system does not protect or help the criminal, the victim, or the public. That is why crime prevention must be a critical issue in the ongoing debate over crime control policy.

A 1997 report by the National Criminal Justice Commission, *The Real War on Crime* (Donziger 1997) concluded that the war on crime was very expensive and very ineffective due to the high cost of imprisonment and the failure of deterrence and retribution. Policies such as "get tough on crime," "three strikes and your out," "truth in sentencing," and tough sentences for nonviolent drug offenders resulted in minor nonviolent offenders rather than serious offenders being sent to prison, thus creating serious prison overcrowding, prison violence, and prison brutality. The report states that 75 percent of the criminal cases involve public defenders with little financial support. Two percent of the justice budget goes for public defenders, whereas 43 percent goes for the police, and 34 percent for prison construction. Fifty percent of those in the California prison system are there for probation and parole violations and not for a new crime (Donzinger 1997: 188–93)

The report emphasized the use of fear of crime by politicians to get prisons built and to get reelected. The mass media makes crime the front-page news story, which fuels the "fear of crime" epidemic. The Department of Justice distorts criminal statistics, hides the failures of the prison system and programs such as the Drug Awareness Resistance Education (DARE) program, while at the same time we build prisons at the expense of educational and welfare programs.

The failure of the criminal justice system is matched by the failure of criminology to become a science. Sociology replaced biology and psychology in the 1920s when Lombroso and Freud were replaced by sociologists, and today criminology is not at a stage of development to replace punishment with prevention. The failure of the rehabilitation model is evidence of the problems facing sociological criminology.

Crime Prevention

Foundations of Crime Prevention

Human behavior, including criminal behavior, is a product of organism-environment interaction. The external environment in interaction with genetic processes creates the brain, since the brain is altered by environmental input. This in turn changes behavior since the brain is the organ of behavior, and behavior then changes the environment.

In order to replace punishment and rehabilitation with prevention criminology must become interdisciplinary, based on biology, neuropsychiatry, psychology, sociology, and urban planning, in interaction with the legal profession (Jeffery 1979, 1989, 1990, 1992, 1994). Any model of crime prevention must start with the fact that (1) 5 percent of the delinquents commit 50 percent or more of the serious crimes, (2) 5 percent of the urban environments experience 50 percent or more of the serious crime sites, and (3) 78 percent of the victims of serious crimes are repeat victims. To prevent crime we must concentrate on "high risk" offenders, "high risk" victims, and "high risk" environments.

Crime prevention refers to proactive measures taken before the crime occurs, rather than waiting for the crime to occur. This involves the *individual offender*, the *individual victim*, as well as the *physical envi-*

ronment where crimes are committed. The prevention approach was outlined in *Crime Prevention through Environmental Design* (Jeffery 1971, 1977, 1990). The prevention model is found in public health programs which deal with *both* the individual and the environment in terms of an epidemiological model of disease. Programs to prevent cancer and heart disease target such high risk behaviors as obesity and smoking, as well as the pollution of the environment (air and food) with lead or other toxic metals. Crime prevention should involve early intervention, treatment, and medical clinics in place of prisons, as well as restructuring our urban environment and urban growth patterns. These efforts would be based upon the new sciences of behavior as found in human genetics, psychobiology, neuropsychiatry, and urban design. The Center for Disease Control (CDC) has declared violence to be a disease to be treated as a medical problem. New knowledge of human development is now being used to prevent and treat mental disease, violence, drug addiction, deviant sexual behaviors, and other behaviors that are often under the jurisdiction of the criminal justice system. The purpose of crime prevention is to turn these developmental problems into medical problems before they become legal problems.

A recent major review of crime prevention efforts by Lawrence Sherman and the Department of Criminology at the University of Maryland (Sherman et al. 1997) found a lack of scientific evaluation and inconclusive or weak results for most of the programs. The study concluded that more rigorous research was needed, and programs must focus on the urban neighborhoods where youth violence is highly concentrated. Sherman and his associates ignored the new urban planners and architects, and they concentrated on the work of social ecologists while omitting the new ecologists and urban planners. The Sherman study also ignored the biological and psychological aspects of the individual offender.

New Ecology

Human behavior, criminal or otherwise, is a product of individuals and environments in interaction. Social ecology has been used by sociologists since the 1920s and the works of Park, Burgess, Shaw, and McKay. The new ecology is interdisciplinary and includes the physical environment as well as the social, and is a part of biology. Brantingham and Brantingham (1981) called this *Environmental Criminology*.

Ecology is defined as "the interrelationship between organisms and their environments" (Michelson 1976: 5). An ecological approach has advantages since it is an overarching concept that unites biology, psychology, sociology, urban planning, urban geography, environmental psychology, and sociology. Odum (1975) and Ehrich, Ehrlich, and Holdren (1973) regard ecology as the link between the natural and the social sciences, involving both the physical and social environments. Duncan and Schnore (1959: 134) observed that "one searches the literature in vain for more than a superficial reference to the brute fact than men live in a physical environment and employ material technology in adapting to it." They use population, organization, environment, and technology (POET) as the basic components of human ecology. Michelson (1976: 8–32) has suggested four reasons why social scientists ignore the interrelationships of the physical environment and the social: (1) the incomplete conceptualization of the environment when the sociologist studies the relationship of human beings to human beings and not human beings to the environment; (2) a fixation on concepts dealing with aggregates so as to exclude the individual; (3) the erection of barriers between sociology and other disciplines; and (4) a lack of interest in intervention in urban growth until very recently. Micklin and Choldin (1984) have also written about the separation of social ecology from human ecology, and they recommend integration of social and physical variables into a basic model of human ecology. The new ecologists, while retaining the basic concepts from ecology as found in the Chicago School of Park, Burgess, Shaw, McKay, McKensie, and Hawley, are much more interdisciplinary and go beyond sociology (Brantingham and Brantingham 1981: 12–18). A recent book, *The Social Ecology of Crime* (Byrne and Sampson 1986), did not include environmental criminology within the scope of social ecology.

Modern ecologists pay great attention to population growth and the destruction of natural resources. As Malthus predicted in 1798, population growth would exceed the food supply, resulting in famines, starvation , warfare, and epidemics (Campbell 1985; Ehrlich, Ehrlich, and Holdren 1973 ; Moran 1982; Odum 1975). The destruction of our natural resources (water, land, forest, and mineral), along with population growth, have changed the distribution and availability of resources, which in turn leads to poverty, starvation, and human health. Pollution of the environment with carbon monoxide, cadmium, mercury, and pesticides has impacted on the brain development and general health of our youth (Campbell 1985; Exline, Peters, and Larkin 1982 ; LeVine and Upton 1994; Platt, Roundtree, and Muick 1994). This destruction of the natural environment was first made prominent in *Silent Spring* by Rachel Carson (1962), followed by Colborn (1996) in *Our Stolen Future*. Colborn chronicles the destruction of our genetic systems, fertility, intelligence, and brain structures because of pollution. Several excellent books have been published recently concerning the population explosion and the assault on the natural environment, including those by Van der Ryn and Calthorpe (1986); Ornstein and Ehrlich (1989); Ehrlich and Ehrlich (1990), Ehrlich and Ehrlich (1991); Ehrlich, Ehrlich, and Dailey (1995); Meyer (1996); Van der Ryn (1996); and Wackernagel (1996). Bechtel (1997) has done an excellent job in covering the environment and behavior, including the history of environmental psychology, pollution, depletion of natural resources, energy resources, nuclear waste disposal, overpopulation, and the urban environment.

Not only is population growth a major challenge for the future, but even more so is the aging or graying of the population. The number of individuals over eighty years of age will double in the next twenty years, creating problems for Medicare and Medicaid, social security, and retirement.

The New Urbanism and Urban Sprawl

The growth of urban and suburban America since World War I, and especially since World War II, was shaped by the automobile, and this created a new urban form in contrast to the pre-automobile city studied by the University of Chicago social ecologists. The "New Urbanists" (Calthorpe 1993; Katz 1994; Langdon 1994) point to the sprawl found, for example, in Phoenix, Arizona where the suburbs are fifty miles north of the central city. Giant malls and power centers attract money and consumers from the central city, and major highways feed commuters from the suburbs to the city and back, causing rush-hour traffic jams at 8 A.M. and 5 P.M. The new urban planners place emphasis upon dense housing per acre, rather than isolated individual housing units with racial and class divisions; they want communities designed as total communities where public parks and activities are used to create shared community feelings. Streets should be designed to encourage pedestrian use and be "pedestrian friendly." Housing would face the street so as to provide "eyes on the street." To cut down on automobile use and commuting each community would be self-contained with its own housing, schools, shopping, and recreational facilities. Mass transit would be central to urban planning, connecting the central city to communities and reducing the reliance upon the automobile.

However, American's love of the automobile makes it almost impossible to encourage commuters to use mass transit transportation. Kay (1997), in the *Asphalt Nation,* discusses in great detail the destruction of urban society by the automobile. She emphasizes the destruction of villages, streets, and farm land by the development of freeways connecting downtown work and shopping centers with suburban housing developments, usually single family units on large acreage. Streets replace sidewalks, the automobile replaces walking or biking, garages replace the front porch and front door. The cost of an automobile per family per car is in the neighborhood of $6000–8000 a year, plus indirect costs of accidents, insurance, upkeep and building of roads, and on and on. She states we "must depave America," and construct "good streets that are secure streets" (Kay 1997: 330, 333). This will require mass transportation and high density urban development. A recent study found that it cost American drivers $4.7 billion a year for broken shocks and repairs to their automobiles, which is four times the $1.3 billion spent on repairs by state highway departments (*USA Today,* 17 September 1997).

Urban sprawl is well illustrated by the unmanaged growth of third world cities. There are 4.5 million automobiles in São Paulo, Brazil, more than twice the 2.1 million in New York City. In Cairo pollution from traffic jams is threatening the Sphinx, and in Bangkok, Thailand it takes three to six hours to drive to the airport (*Tallahassee Democrat,* 11 May 1997) Once farm and forest land in Tallahassee is now four- and six-laned highways twenty miles from the center of the city, and it takes over an hour to drive this distance during the traffic rushes. A recent article in *Newsweek* (25 August 1997) was devoted to the impact of the automobile on European cities, such as the traffic jams in London and the congestion and pollution of European cities. For example, Rome was closed for a week due to air pollution, and Madrid has three major beltways and anticipates 500,000 more cars in the next ten years.

Global warming in Alaska has raised the temperature over the past century, and as a result glaciers are retreating, permafrost is melting, forests are being destroyed, and huge potholes have appeared in the highways (*Tallahassee Democrat,* 14 November 1997; Overpeck 1997). A recent article on China (Hertsgaard 1997) revealed major pollution problems due to rapid industrialization and a lack of an environmental protection policy. The air is so polluted one cannot see one's finger in front of one's face, streams are filled with chlorine and are the color of motor oil, 60 to 90 percent of the rain is acid rain, the gas is leaded, the coal is unwashed, most Chinese are addicted to tobacco, and 1 of 4 deaths is from lung cancer. At the same time the population is growing, 86 million acres of farmland have been lost to suburban sprawl, the new middle class wants more food, automobiles, and air conditioning, and the official government policy is to encourage the industrialization of China at the expense of the ecological system. A major crisis is developing.

"Hot Spots" and Repeat Victimization

Two other aspects of crime prevention must be noted. Very few environments experience most of the crime, the so-called "hot spots." A study of crime rates in Minneapolis found that 50 percent of the calls to police occurred in 3 percent of the places, and only 3.6 percent of the city areas had a robbery (Sherman, Gartin, and Buerger 1989). Wikstrom (1995) found that in the central city of Stockholm 47 percent of street assaults occurred on 3 percent of the streets, and the Central Business District with 1 percent of the land area had 31 percent of the crimes. A new type of "hot spot" is the workplace where violence has become the second leading cause of death on the job, especially at social service agencies, post offices, and healthcare facilities. The Department of Labor is now involved in a study of how workplace violence can be prevented through environmental design.

Farrell (1995) found that 78 percent of all victims were repeat victims. A London study showed that 68 percent of the respondents were never victimized, whereas 2.9 percent have been victimized five times or more. Repeat victimizations occur rapidly after the first crime. For domestic burglary, half of the repeat burglaries occurred within seven days, whereas for property crimes 79 percent of the re-victimizations occurred within one month (Farrell and Pease 1993; National Board for Crime Prevention 1994).

The Individual Offender and Crime Prevention

A New Look at the Individual Offender

The fright which sociological criminologists have of biology must be overcome. As president of ASC I organized the 1978 meeting in Dallas around an interdisciplinary theme, including genetics, brain functioning, psychology, sociology, economics, political science, and law.

The biology was attacked as "neo-Lombrosian" with no place in criminology (Jeffery 1980). In addition, Ellis (1996) has written about the peril to sociology posed by biophobia.

Two major developments have occurred in psychology and psychiatry, behaviorism and psychobiology/neuropsychiatry. The behaviorism of Watson and Skinner put forth the need for a science of behavior based on experimental procedures. Behavior is based upon rewards and reinforcement, not punishment. Modern learning theory states that punishment is a most ineffective way to change behavior, and yet the criminal justice system continues to rely on punishment. We must use behavioral psychology and rewards to change antisocial behavior, and not prisons to punish undesirable behavior. There is an approach labeled "behavior modification" to alter delinquent behavior (Jeffery 1990).

Personal offenses, which make up 10 percent of the crimes, cannot be prevented in most cases by environmental design. Murder, rape, and assault usually involve people known to one another. A wife who kills her husband in the kitchen, or the husband who assaults his wife while in a drunken rage, or a date rape in an apartment cannot be prevented by locking the doors or installing security devises. Psychological and biological features of the offender must be the basis for crime prevention at the individual level.

The development of the brain sciences has led to the joining of neurology, psychiatry, and psychology. To quote two psychiatrists, "the field has shifted from the mind to the brain, one of the most exciting frontiers in biology" (Michels and Marzuls 1993: 552). The 1994 *Review of Psychiatry* declared that "the field of psychiatry has changed dramatically, and advances in knowledge about the etiology and treatment of mental illness has grown exponentially. We have become occupied with neurotransmitters, molecules, and genes, made possible by enormous advances in research" (Oldham and Riba 1994: xxiii). Pincus and Tucker (1985: 70) concluded that "If such violent acts were committed by those with evidence of abnormalities in cerebral functioning as reflected in neurological examinations, psychological testing, or electroencephalograms (EEGs), it would shift the focus of investigations into the causes of violence from the social environment to the individual brain. Is there something neurologically different about violent individuals which might explain why they are violent?"

Though the law requires medical services for delinquents, it is seldom that neurological examinations are given for brain disorders. People outside of neuropsychiatry often make decisions concerning the disposition of such trouble cases. A psychologist or social worker is the person likely to see the delinquent upon his/her arrival at a reception center, and the delinquent rarely sees a neurologist or a neuropsychiatrist (Group for the Advancement of Psychiatry, 1993) There is a division of psychiatrists into psychotherapists and neuropsychiatrists, and the two groups do not view delinquent behavior in the same way. Much more attention must be paid to the biological condition of the violent delinquent, some of which are discussed below.

Recent books devoted to neuropsychiatry and psychopharmacology include Berger and Brodie (1986), Yudofsky and Hales (1992), Oldham, Riba, and Tasman (1993), Oldham and Riba (1994), Snow and Hooper (1994), Zaidel (1994), Kalat (1992), Pincus and Tucker (1985), and Cooper, Bloom, and Roth (1992). In recent years a new group of biological criminologists has emerged using an interdisciplinary approach to human behavior based on genetics, neurology, psychology, psychiatry, sociology, and criminology. Among these are Denno (1990), Ellis (1989), Ellis and Hoffman (1990), Farrington (West and Farrington 1973, 1977; Farrington, Sampson, and Wikstrom 1993; Farrington, Ohlin, and Wilson 1986; Farrington 1992, Tonry and Farrington 1995), Fishbein (1990), Hillbrand and Pallone (1995), Jeffery (1990, 1994), Mednick, Moffitt, and Stack (1987), Moffitt and Mednick (1988), Pallone (1991), Pallone and Hennessey (1992), Raine (1993), and Walsh (1995). In a major study Masters (1997) found from ecological data that high levels of lead and manganese pollution are highly correlated with high crime rates throughout the United States.

The need to integrate the study of individual offenders with the study of environmental criminology was the topic of a recent conference in Stockholm. Studies of individual development and criminal careers would be part of crime prevention. They stated "two prominent areas of research within the field of criminology are the study of the individual development of offending (called "criminal careers research"), and socioecological studies of crime, sometimes called "environmental criminology" (Farrington, Sampson, and Wikstrom 1993: 5).

Trasler (1993: 305–22) is critical of the rational choice model of the criminal, especially when applied to the violent persistent offender, and he notes that offenders differ greatly in motivation and in the types and amount of crime they commit. Much criminal behavior is irrational and motivated by alcohol, drugs, biochemical disorders, and brain defects. Trasler uses a classical Pavlovian conditioning model to explain how individuals learn to escape from punishment by refraining from criminal acts; he states that because of brain defects criminal psychopaths lack a fear of punishment and are not deterred by punishment. The most serious part of our criminal population is not controlled by the present criminal justice system.

Pallone and Hennessy (1993), two psychobiologists, discuss criminal behavior in terms of impulsivity, thrill-seeking, head trauma, frontal lobe damage, low serotonin levels, substance abuse, and other neurological conditions of offenders. Pallone (1991) reviews the impact of mental disorders on criminal behavior, and he found that these disorders are neurological in nature, that is, 30 percent of the prisoners surveyed have gross mental illnesses, including brain damage, neurotransmitter abnormalities, and a high use of alcohol and drugs. The survey revealed that criminals had eight times the use of alcohol and nineteen times the use of drugs as non-offenders. Pallone recommended neurological and pharmacological research evidence be applied to crime prevention, including a complete neurological examination of criminals at intake into the criminal justice system. He cited studies using magnetic resonance imaging (MRI) scans which found neurological defects that were otherwise missed in a routine medical examination in 68 percent of the prisoners. Mental illness as a physical condition involving brain structure and neurochemistry conflicts with the legal view of insanity based upon free will and rational choice (Jeffery 1987; Nygaard 1996f.). Pallone and Hennessy (1996) in *Tinder Box Aggression* develop a neurological basis for sudden violence based on impulsivity and risk-taking behavior.

Tonry and Farrington (1995:10) state in the introduction to their book on crime prevention that "developmental prevention is the new frontier in crime prevention efforts." Developmental prevention, as outlined by Tremblay and Craig (1995), refers to prospective and longitudinal studies of children in order to detect "high risk" offenders. This means following the child from the prenatal period to adolescence, with investments in early childhood care to prevent later violence and aggression. Moore (1995) has outlined a similar approach to developmental prevention under the title of "Public Health Approaches to Prevention," a public health model based on prevention and treatment.

Research has determined that very few delinquents become serious habitual offenders, with approximately 5 percent committing 50 percent of the offenses (Blumstein, Cohen, Roth, and Visher 1986; Chaiken and Chaiken 1982; Farrington, Ohlin, and Wilson 1986; Wolfgang, Figlio, and Sellin 1972). Juvenile offenders have been classified in terms of those who commit minor offenses and stop by age 18 ("adolescent-limited"), as contrasted to those who continue to commit serious crimes into adulthood ("life-course persistent") (Moffitt 1993; Moffitt, Lyman, and Silva 1994; Nagin, Farrington, and Moffitt 1995). Many of the juveniles who become adult offenders end up as career criminals and end up behind bars for life or on death row, resulting in society paying billions of dollars to manage their behaviors inside institutions. Lewis and her colleagues found that fourteen out of fourteen juveniles on death row suffered from neurological defects (Lewis, Pincus, Bard, and Richardson 1988). Yeager and Lewis (1990) also found that a sample of former delinquents had a mortality rate 58 times that of nondelinquents, and all had died violent deaths. Early intervention and prevention is obviously a more humane and much cheaper alternative to the criminal justice system.

Some individuals are much more receptive to certain diseases than are others. Most individuals who have lung cancer have a history of smoking, but around 75 percent of smokers never die from lung cancer. Most criminals are male, but only a small part of the male population become criminals. Robins (1973) found that only 9 percent of the Vietnam veterans who were cocaine addicts in Vietnam were addicts after they returned to the United States. People in poverty have a high rate of crime compared to the middle class, but only some of them become criminals. Most adolescents with behavioral problems do not go on to adult criminal behavior.

There are certain "high risk" factors related to crime and delinquency. From a summary of the studies cited above we may conclude that among these are pre- and post-natal problems, lack of prenatal care, low birth weight, brain damage (especially frontal lobe damage), enuresis, nutritional deficiencies, toxic metal poisoning, drug and alcohol abuse by parents, cruelty to animals, fire setting, and attention deficit with hyperactivity disorders. As the "high risk" child grows up, he or she experiences difficulties with the family and with peers, learning difficulties and verbal deficits, poor nutrition, alcohol and drug abuse, and risky sex behavior resulting in pregnancy, which for females means families without fathers. Biological and social problems interact with one another so that by adolescence the individual is a school dropout, uneducated, unemployed, in contact with local juvenile justice and welfare agencies, and probably headed for a career in adult crime.

One of the major characteristics of criminal behavior is impulsivity, which can result from frontal lobe damage or low serotonin levels, or the use of alcohol or other drugs. Many criminals are involved in drug use, and no crime prevention program is complete without a drug prevention and treatment component. Law enforcement efforts to control the supply side of the drug problem have not been successful, and we need a new psychopharmacological approach based on neural chemistry. To give a few examples, alcohol abuse can be treated with naltrexone, buspirone, or fluoxetine, which increase the serotonin levels in the brain. Opiate addiction can be treated with naltrexone, naloxone, and buprenorphine. Cocaine addiction can be treated with such antidepressants as desipramine and lithium carbonate (Fishbein and Pease 1996).

The developmental approach to crime prevention suggests early intervention and prevention. This would include well-baby clinics and healthy start programs in our communities, requiring the cooperation of pediatricians, teachers, parents, psychologists, and neurologists. Where necessary, neuropsychological tests would be used when brain damage is suspected, and medications and nutritional remedies would be provided as indicated.

Law and Science

Law is based upon tradition, precedent, and the past. In science there are no final answers, only new questions for the future. The legal system seldom makes use of science , and when it does it is within an adversarial system where the prosecution presents evidence which the defense challenges, as occurred in the recent O.J. Simpson trial where blood and DNA evidence was challenged and disputed by experts from both sides. Lawyers for the defense battled within their group; defense lawyers challenged the prosecutors; the forensic scientists disagreed; the police challenged one another; and the judge failed to maintain control over the case (Darden 1996; Dershowitz 1996; Fuhrman 1997; Schiller and Willworth 1996; Toobin 1996). The factual innocence or guilt of Simpson was never resolved since the legal standard is "beyond all reasonable doubt," which is different from actual guilt. Guilt was not established by the prosecution, but neither was innocence established by the defense.

In the recent au pair case in Boston, Louise Woodward was convicted of first-degree murder by the jury for the murder of an infant son. The verdict was reduced by the judge to manslaughter and sentenced to time served (279 days). Both the conviction for first degree murder and the reduction of the charge to manslaughter brought major protests. The guilt of Louise Woodward was never established since conflicting scientific evidence was introduced at the trial. The prosecution argued for a "shaken baby" syndrome and injury to the neck at the time of the death, whereas the defense introduced MRI scans to show the injury was not to the neck but to the scalp, and the injuries, including a broken arm, had occurred three weeks prior to the death. The Massachusetts Society for the Prevention of Cruelty to Children wrote a letter protesting the judge's action; however these were pediatricians and not neurologists, and they had not seen the MRI evidence. Barry Scheck, the defense lawyer, asked for a review of the evidence by an panel of scientific experts (*Newsweek*, 10 Nov. 1997; 17 Nov. 1997). It is obvious that scientific evidence, such as DNA samples or MRI scans, cannot be given to a lay jury selected by lawyers to favor one side or the other.

In his *Guilty: The Collapse of Criminal Justice* Judge Rothwax (1996) raises serious questions concerning the criminal justice system. Many cases could be discussed where the criminal justice system failed to solve the case, such as the assassination of John F. Kennedy, the guilt or innocence of Sam Sheppard, the M.D. who was found guilty of murdering his family in Ohio (Cooper and Sheppard 1995), and the controversy surrounding the Jeffrey MacDonald case, the M.D. found guilty of murdering his family at Fort Bragg, South Carolina. A recent book (Potter and Bost 1995) has discovered evidence that shows it was very unlikely for MacDonald to have killed his family, and the case against him from the start consisted of false evidence, distorted testimony, and hidden evidence. At this time Dr. MacDonald is still in prison.

The recent murder of the designer Gianni Versace and the police investigation of the chief suspect Andrew Cunanan raises serious questions concerning the ability of law enforcement to solve crimes, as does the murder of JonBenet Ramsey in Boulder, Colorado. What is needed is a neutral body of experts who will evaluate the evidence and report to the court. This is similar to the French procedure of "inquisitorial justice" in contrast to the British system of "adversarial justice." In the French system the judge and not the lawyers determine the examination, collection, and evaluation of evidence with the help of expert witnesses. The prosecutor has less power in the inquisitorial system than in the adversarial system (Kadish 1983). Herbert Packer (1968) contrasted the two justice models as the crime control model and the due process model. The crime control model seeks efficiency in maintaining social order, and the major decisions are made early in the investigation and not during the trial phase, and each phase moves smoothly to the next phase. The evidence is reviewed by the magistrate before the prosecution is started. The due process model is based on preserving individual rights and each stage of the judicial process is an obstacle to be overcome within an adversarial setting. The process is designed to pit the prosecution against the defense rather than discovering what in fact happened at the crime scene.

The ability of the police to adequately use science is challenged by the U.S. Department of Justice/Office of the Inspector General (1997) report on the (Federal Bureau of Investigation) FBI crime laboratory, which made major errors in the scientific analysis of crime data in such important cases as the World Trade Center bombing and the Oklahoma City bombing. The National Association of Criminal Defense Lawyers charged the FBI with failing proficiency tests and altering evidence to aid the prosecution where DNA evidence was involved (*USA Today*, 26 Nov. 1997).

Judge Richard Posner (1990) has traced how the two philosophical traditions of idealism and empiricism have impacted jurisprudence. Law is based upon idealism, precedent, hierarchy, tradition, and authority, whereas science is based upon empiricism. Judge Posner would like to see an integration of law and science on the basis of empiricism, positivism, and legal realism as found in Holmes, Cardozo, and Pound (Jeffery, Myers, and Wollan 1991).

Judge Richard L. Nygaard, Circuit Judge, United States Court of Appeals for the Third Circuit, in a series of provocative articles outlines the need for a scientific approach to criminal law. The focus of his challenge is the foundation of criminal law upon (1) revenge, retribution, deterrence, incapacitation, and rehabilitation, and (2) free will, rationality, and moral condemnation. Assumptions regarding revenge and free will are not supported by modern science and modern neurology. He argues that the death penalty is brutal, useless, archaic, and expensive, and we would be better off using money spent on trials to find the causes of and cures for criminal behavior (Nygaard 1996a). Prisons are founded on revenge and hatred which create hardened criminals who are then released back into the community (Nygaard 1996b). Sentencing is merely an extension of revenge and deterrence, and it does not make use of scientific findings (Nygaard 1996c). He explores modern genetic research as applied to human behavior, as well as the many moral and legal implications of modern genetics. Legal concepts of free will and moral responsibility are in conflict with scientific concepts of determinism and the search for the factors involved in behavior. Judge Nygaard expresses the need for lawyers to reexamine long-standing concepts of revenge, punishment, free will, and moral responsibility in the light of behavioral genetics in order to find ways to incorporate modern genetics into the legal process (Nygaard 1996d; Nygaard 1996e)

Judge Nygaard also rejects the notion of the insanity defense, which is based upon free will and rational choice. Over time, criminal law has defined insanity as a lack of rationality and knowledge of right and wrong; behavior that is a product of an irresistible impulse; mental disease or defect; or, the inability of the accused to conform his or her behavior to the requirements of the law. These concepts of insanity are scientifically meaningless, do not make use of modern neuropsychiatric knowledge, ignore the fact that 25 percent of the population suffers from some form of mental incapacitation, and allow us to vent our hatred and revenge on individuals who are mentally ill and without control over their behavior. Judge Nygaard argues for the use of a panel of scientific experts appointed by the court to determine the physiological state of the individual; in contrast to an adversarial system of lay jurors and psychiatrists in which psychiatrists are retained by the government or the defense to support an assumption of guilt or innocence rather than acting as impartial expert witnesses (Nygaard 1996f.). The law recognizes the right of criminals to medical treatment, but we ignore this right while pursuing the right to punish them. The development of neuropsychiatry should change our sentencing procedures and our concepts of guilt and moral responsibility.

Margaret Hagen (1997), in her book *The Whores of the Court*, makes a blistering attack on clinical psychology and psychiatry for their testimony in criminal trials, repressed memory cases, and child custody cases. She labels clinical psychology a fraud, nonscientific, and in the category of astrology and not astronomy. She finds no successful clinical treatments except the behavioral therapies, clinical concepts are stated in terms that can neither be proven or disproven, clinical concepts are psychobabble and pseudoscience, and most clinical therapies are not adequately evaluated as to effectiveness. She finds it unconscionable that such testimony is allowed into the court system in criminal trials, delinquency hearings, and custody cases, and she advocates turning the criminal trial over to lay people, judges and jurors, who would decide such matters as competency and mental illness. Hagen would ban the psychological expert from the courtroom.

I agree with Hagen that much of clinical psychology is not scientifically valid (Jeffery, 1967; 1985), but I cannot agree that the analysis of human behavior must be turned over to lay people. If depression, posttraumatic stress disorder (PTSD), and mental illness do not cause behavior, as she argues, then what does? Something must? Perhaps it is the way the brain is functioning? Throughout this chapter I have argued that science must be made a part of the criminal law. As our knowledge of human behavior expands, as it has over the past twenty years, we need to make this science available to the criminal justice process. I would place emphasis on the fact that neuropsychiatry has emerged in recent years to challenge and often to replace classical Freudian couch-and-talk therapies, as is discussed above. I would have a neurological examination replace a clinical psychiatric examination for a determination of competency and insanity. Insanity is a legal, not a scientific concept, and mental illness must be redefined as a physical illness and brain disorder (Jeffery 1987; 1992). Intent and free will are concepts belonging to mentalistic psychology and not to a science of behavior. I recommended (Jeffery 1990: 441–68) that neurological examinations be given to all violent criminals, and that a major medical center be established to study the most violent of our criminals for genetic, neurological, and biochemical disorders related to violent behavior. A neurological check-up could prevent the release of prisoners who would be dangerous if released back to the community.

The late Carl Sagan, in *The Demon-Haunted World: Science as a Candle in the Dark* (Sagan 1995), pursued the theme that science is a candle in the dark. Science has not been given a proper role in society in the solution of social problems. He argued that we are governed by religious, legal, and political beliefs that cannot be falsified, and thereby we perpetuate our ignorance. The candle does not light the darkness. We are science illiterate; we lack competence in science; and in times of crisis we turn to superstition, channeling, cultism, pseudoscience, and political unrest. We do not use science to solve our major legal and political problems, and at this time Congress is considering abolishing the Office of Technology Assessment. Our politicians and legal experts are not sophisticated in science, the same argument that Judge Nygaard is making. The gap between science, law, and politics must be closed.

Summary of Issues

Crime prevention as now practiced does not give adequate attention to the individual offender; it does not prevent the first crime from occurring because we wait for crimes to be committed; it does not prevent new juvenile offenders from entering the justice system; it does not stop overpopulation, pollution, or urban sprawl; and it does not protect potential victims who move through a vast complex of environmental situations from hour to hour and day to day. We cannot deal only with individual situations such as parks or transit systems; we must take a broader perspective on urban planning.

Crime prevention and criminology must become interdisciplinary, relying on the new brain sciences, the new ecology, and on urban planning and the new urbanism in order to develop a successful crime control model. We are facing a rapidly growing adolescent population, growing problems of urban decay, dependency on the automobile, high levels of pollution, overcrowding, and child abuse, all of which will probably contribute to higher crime rates in the future. We must deal with basic problems of public health and environmental deterioration rather than building more prisons or hiring more police, as advocated by our politicians. Criminology and criminal justice programs in our universities devoted to the study of criminal justice, that is, how we do things now, should be replaced with studies of prevention to solve the crime problem. To the degree that these efforts are interdisciplinary in nature, the likelihood of successful crime prevention practice will be increased.

We must close the gap between law and science so that new concepts can replace those now found in the criminal justice system. We must make use of scientific research as found in the National Institutes of Health concerning diseases, mental illness, drug and alcohol addictions, and the role of the brain in behavior. However, we find the Department of Justice formulating policies that are in direct conflict with what the National Institutes of Health is researching.

Very little money is placed into research on crime prevention compared to building more prisons. At the same time resources are taken from education, social welfare, and medical services, which means more "at risk" children in the future to fill our new prisons. Our federal and state agencies involved in the criminal justice system do not invest heavily in brain research and violence.

Professor Wolfgang foresaw and took a prominent position in the development of many of these issues: an interdisciplinary criminology, longitudinal and experimental studies of violent habitual offenders, and the introduction of Lombroso and a scientific-medical model in place of the punitive criminal justice model. I hope his effort will bear fruit in the near future.

References

Bechtel, R.B. 1997. *Environment and Behavior.* Thousand Oaks, CA: Sage.

Berger, P. and H.K. Brodie, eds. 1986. *American Handbook of Psychiatry,* vol. 8. New York: Basic Books.

Blumstein, A. , J. Cohen, and D. Nagin. 1978. *Deterrence and Incapacitation: Estimating the Effects of Criminal Sanctions on Crime Rates.* Washington DC: National Academy of Sciences.

Blumstein, A., J. Cohen, J. Roth, and C. Visher, eds. 1986. *Criminal Careers and Career Criminals,* vol. 1. Washington, DC: National Academy Press.

Brantingham, P. J. and P. L. Brantingham , eds. 1981. *Environmental Criminology.* Beverly Hills, CA: Sage.

Byrne, J. and R .J. Sampson. 1986. *The Social Ecology of Crime.* New York : Springer-Verlag.

Calthorpe, P. 1993. *The Next American Metropolis.* New York: Princeton Architectural Press.

Campbell, B. 1985. *Human Ecology.* New York : Aldine.

Carson, R. 1962. *Silent Spring.* Boston : Houghton-Mifflin.

Chaiken, J.M. and M.R. Chaiken. 1982. *Varieties of Criminal Behavior.* Santa Monica, CA : Rand.

Clear , T. 1994. *Harm in American Penology.* Albany, NY: SUNY Press.

Colborn, T. 1996. *Our Stolen Future.* New York: Dutton.

Cooper, J.R., F.E. Bloom, and R.H. Roth. 1992. *The Biochemical Basis of Neuropharmacology,* 6th. ed. New York: Oxford University Press.

Cooper, C. and S. R. Sheppard. 1995. *Mockery of Justice.* Boston: Northeastern University Press.

Darden, C. 1996. *In Contempt.* New York: Regan.

Degler, C. 1991. *In Search of Human Nature.* New York : Oxford University Press.

Denno, D. 1990. *Biology and Violence.* Cambridge: Cambridge University Press.

Dershowitz, A. 1996. *Reasonable Doubt.* New York: Simon and Schuster.

Donziger, S.R. 1997. *The Real War on Crime .* New York: Harper-Collins.

Duncan, O.D. and L. Schnore. 1959. " Cultural, Behavioral, and Ecological Perspectives in the Study of Social Organization." *American Journal of Sociology* 3: 132–46.

Durham, A. N. 1994. *Crisis and Reform: Current Issues in American Punishment.* Boston: Little, Brown.

Ehrlich, P. H., A. H. Ehrlich, and J. P. Holden. 1973. *Human Ecology .* San Francisco: Freeman.

Ehrlich, P. H. and Anne H. Ehrlich. 1990. *Population Explosion .* New York: Simon and Schuster.

———. 1991. *Healing the Planet.* Reading: Addison-Wesley .

Ehrlich, P. R. , A. H. Ehrlich , and G.C. Dailey. 1995. *The Stork and the Plow.* New York: Putnam.

Ellis, L. 1989. *Theories of Rape.* Washington, DC: Hemisphere Press.

———. 1996. "A Disciple in Peril: Sociology's Future Hinges on Curing its Biophobia." *American Sociologist* 27: 21–41.

Ellis, L. and H. Hoffman, eds. 1990. *Crime in Biological, Social, and Moral Contexts.* New York: Praeger.

Exline, C., G. L. Peters, and R. P. Larkin. 1982. *The City: Pattern and Process in the Urban Ecosystem.* Boulder, CO: Westview.

Farrell, G. 1995. "Preventing Repeat Victimization," pp. 460–534 in M. Tonry and D.P. Farrington (eds.) *Building a Safer Society.* Chicago: University of Chicago Press.

Farrell, G. and K. Pease. 1993. *Once Bitten , Twice Bitten: Repeat Victimization and its Implications for Crime Prevention.* Crime Prevention Series Paper no. 46. London: Home Office Police Department.

Farrington, D.P. 1992. "Explaining the Beginning, Progress, and Ending of Antisocial Behavior from Birth to Adulthood," in J. McCord (ed.) *Facts, Frameworks, and Forecasts.* New Brunswick: Transaction Publishers.

Farrington, D.P., L. Ohlin, and J.Q. Wilson. 1986. *Understanding and Controlling Crime .* New York: Springer-Verlag.

Farrington, D.P., R.J. Sampson, and P.O.H. Wikstrom. 1993. *Integrating Individual and Ecological Aspects of Crime.* Stockholm: National Council for Crime Prevention.

Fishbein, D. 1990. "Biological Perspectives in Criminology." *Criminology* 28: 27–72.

Fishbein, D. and S. Pease. 1996. *The Dynamics of Drug Abuse.* Boston : Allyn and Bacon.

Fuhrman, M. 1997. *Murder in Brentwood.* Washington, DC: Regnery.

Glueck, S. 1956. "Theory and Fact in Criminology." *British Journal of Delinquency,* pp. 92–109.

Glueck, S. and E. Glueck. 1950. *Unraveling Juvenile Delinquency.* New York: Commonwealth Fund.

———. 1952. *Delinquents in the Making.* New York: Harper.

Gordon, D. 1990. *The Justice Juggernaut.* New Brunswick, NJ: Rutgers University Press.

Group for the Advancement of Psychiatry. 1993. *Psychotherapy in the Future.* Report no. 133. Washington, DC: American Psychiatric Press.

Hagen, M. 1997. *Whores of the Court.* New York: Harper-Collins.

Hertsgaard, M. 1997. "Our Real China Problem." *Atlantic Monthly* 280(5): 96–114.

Hillbrand, M. and N. J. Pallone. 1995. *The Psychobiology of Aggression .* Binghamton, NY: Haworth.

Jeffery, C. R. [1960]1972. "The Historical Development of Criminology," pp. 458–98 in H. Manheim (ed.) *Pioneers in Criminology.* Montclair, NJ : Patterson-Smith.

———. 1967. *Criminal Responsibility and Mental Disease: The Durham Rule.* Springfield, IL: Charles C. Thomas.

———. [1971]1977. *Crime Prevention through Environmental Design.* Beverly Hills, CA: Sage.

———. 1979. "Criminology as an Interdisciplinary Behavioral Science," in E. Sagarin (ed.) *Criminology: New Concerns.* Beverly Hills: Sage.

———. 1980. "Sociobiology and Criminology: The Long Lean Years," in E. Sagarin (ed.) *Taboos in Criminology.* Beverly Hills: Sage.

———. 1985. *Attacks on the Insanity Defense .* Springfield, IL: Charles C. Thomas.

———. 1987. "Criminal Law, Biological Psychiatry, and the Premenstrual Syndrome," pp. 125–47 in B. Ginsburg and B. Carter (eds.) *Premenstrual Syndrome.* New York: Plenum.

———. 1989. "An Interdisciplinary Theory of Criminal Behavior," in W. Laufer and F. Adler (eds.) *Advances in Criminological Theory,* vol. 1. New Brunswick, NJ: Transaction Publishers.

———. 1990. *Criminology: An Interdisciplinary Approach.* Englewood Cliffs, NJ : Prentice-Hall.

_____. 1992. "The Brain, the Law, and the Medicalization of Crime," in R. Masters and R. McGuire (eds.)*The Neurotransmitter Revolution*. Carbondale, IL: Southern University Press.

————. 1994. "Biological and Neuropsychiatric Approaches to Criminal Behavior," in G. Barak (ed.) *Varieties of Criminology: Readings from a Dynamic Discipline*. New York: Praeger.

Jeffery, C. Ray, Laura B, Myers, and Lauren A. Wollen. 1991. " Crime, Justice, and Their Systems: Resolving the Tension." *The Criminologist* 16: 1–6.

Kadish, S., ed. 1983. *Encyclopedia of Crime and Justice,* vol. 2, pp. 537–46. New York: The Free Press.

Katz, P. 1994. *The New Urbanism*. New York: McGraw-Hill.

Kay, J. 1997. *Asphalt Nation: How the Automobile Took Over America and How We Can Take it Back*. New York: Crown.

Kuhn, T. S. 1962. *The Structure of Scientific Revolutions*. Chicago: University of Chicago Press.

Langdon, P. 1994. *A Better Place to Live* . Amherst: University of Massachusetts Press.

Laufer, W.S. and F. Adler, eds. 1987. *Advances in Criminological Theory*, vol. 1. New Brunswick, NJ: Transaction Publishers.

LeVine, D.G. and A.C. Upton. 1994. *The City as a Human Environment*. Westport, CT: Praeger.

Lewis, D.O., J. H. Pincus, B. Bard, and E. Richardson. 1988. "Neuropsychiatric, Psychoeducational, and Family Characteristics of Fourteen Juveniles Condemned to Death in the United States." *American Journal of Psychiatry* 145: 584–89.

Mannheim, H., ed. 1972. *Pioneers in Criminology* . Montclair, NJ: Patterson Smith.

Masters, R. 1997. "Environmental Pollution, Neurotoxicity, and Criminal Violence," pp. 1–61 in J. Rose (ed.)*Environmental Toxicity*. New York: Gordon and Breach.

Mednick, S. A., T. Moffitt, and S.A. Stack. 1987. *The Causes of Crime: New Biological Approaches*. Cambridge: Cambridge University Press.

Meyer, W.B. 1996. *Human Impact on the Earth* . New York : Cambridge University Press.

Michels, R. and P.W. Marzulus. 1993. "Medical Progress: Progress in Psychiatry." *New England Journal of Medicine* 329: 552–60.

Michelson, W. 1976. *Man and His Urban Environment*. Reading: Addison-Wesley.

Micklin, M. and H. H. Choldin. 1984. *Sociological Human Ecology*. Boulder, CO: Westview.

Moffitt, T. E. 1993. "'Life-Course Persistent' and 'Adolescent-Limited' Antisocial Behavior: A Developmental Taxonomy." *Psychology Review* 100: 674–701.

Moffitt, T.E. and S. Mednick. 1988. *Biological Contributions to Crime Causation*. Dordrechts: Martin-Nyhoff.

Moffitt, T.E., D.A. Lyman, and P.A. Silva. 1994. "Neuropsychological Tests Predicting Persistent Male Delinquency." *Criminology* 32: 277–300.

Moore, M. 1995. "Public Heath and Criminal Justice Approaches to Prevention," pp. 237–62 in M. Tonry and D. Farrington (eds.) *Building a Safer Society*. Chicago: University of Chicago Press.

Moran, E. F. 1982. *Human Adaptability* . Boulder, CO: Westview

Murphy, J. W. and J. E. Dison. 1990. *Are Prisons Any Better*. Newbury Park : Sage.

Nagin, D.S., D.P. Farrington, and T. E. Moffitt. 1995. "Life Course Trajectories of Different Types of Offenders." *Criminology* 33: 111–39.

National Board for Crime Prevention. 1994. *Wise after the Event: Tackling Repeat Victimization*. London: Home Office.

Nygaard, R.L. 1996a "On Death as a Punishment." *University of Pittsburgh Law Review* 57: 825–40.

———. 1996b. "Is Prison an Appropriate Response to Crime?" *St. Louis University Law Journal* 40: 677–97.

———. 1996c. "On the Philosophy of Sentencing: Or, Why Punish?" *Widener Journal of Public Law* 5: 237–68.

———. 1996d. "Free Will, Determinism, Penology, and the Human Genome: Where's a New Leibniz When We Really Need Him?" *University of Chicago Law School Roundtable* 3:1–40.

———. 1996e. "Ten Commandments: Behavioral Genetic Data and Criminology." Paper presented at the 1996 annual meeting of the American Society of Criminology, Nov. 20–23, Chicago, IL.

———. 1996f. "On Responsibility: Or, the Insanity of Mental Defenses and Punishment." *Villanova Law Review* 41: 951–87.

Oldham, J.M, M. Riba, and A. Tasman , eds. 1993. *Review of Psychiatry*, vol. 12. Washington, DC: American Psychiatric Press.

Oldham, J.M. and M. Riba, eds. 1994. *Review of Psychiatry*, vol. 13. Washington, DC: American Psychiatric Press.

Odum, E. P. 1975. *Ecology: The Link between the Natural and Social Sciences*. New York: Holt, Rinehart and Winston.

Ornstein, R. and P. Ehrlich. 1989. *New World, New Mind* . New York: Doubleday.

Overpeck, J. et al. 1997. "Arctic Environmental Change in the Last Four Centuries." *Science* 278(5341): 1251–56.

Packer, H. 1968. *The Limits of Criminal Sanctions*. Stanford, CA: Stanford University Press.

Pallone, N. 1991. *Mental Disorders among Prisoners*. New Brunswick, NJ: Transaction Publishers.

Pallone, N. and J. Hennessy. 1992. *Criminal Behavior*. New Brunswick, NJ : Transaction Publishers.

———. 1993. "Tinderbox Criminal Violence : Impulsivity, Risk-taking, and the Phenomenology of Rational Choice," pp. 127–58 in R.V. Clarke and M. Felson (eds.) *Routine Activity and Rational Choice*. New Brunswick, NJ: Transaction Publishers.

———. 1996. *Tinder Box Criminal Aggression*. New Brunswick, NJ: Transaction Publishers.

Pincus, J.H. and G.J. Tucker. 1985. *Behavioral Neurology* . New York: Oxford University Press.

Platt, R., R. Roundtree, and P. Muick. 1994. *The Ecological City*. Amherst: University of Massachusetts Press.

Posner, R. 1990. *Problems in Jurisprudence* Cambridge, MA: Harvard University Press.

Potter, J. A. and F. Bost. 1995. *Fatal Justice*. New York: W.W. Norton.

Raine, A. 1993. *The Psychopathology of Crime* . San Diego, CA: Academic Press.

Robins, L. 1973. *A Follow-up of Vietnam Drug Users*. Washington, DC: Government Printing Office.

Rothwax, H. 1996. *Guilty: The Collapse of Criminal Justice* . New York: Random House.

Sagan, C. 1995. *The Demon-Haunted World: Science as a Candle in the Dark*. New York: Random House.

Schiller, L. and J. Willwert. 1996. *American Tragedy*. New York : Random House.

Sechrest, L., S.O. White, and E.D. Brown. 1979. *The Rehabilitation of Criminal Offenders: Problem and Prospect*. Washington, DC: National Academy of Sciences.

Sherman, L., P. Gartin, and M. Buerger. 1989. "Hot Spots of Predatory Crime: Routine Activities and the Criminology of Place." *Criminology* 27:27–56.

Sherman, L. et al. 1997. *Preventing Crime: What Works, What Doesn't.* Washington, DC: Office of Justice Programs.

Tonry, M. and D.P Farrington , eds. 1995. *Building a Safer Society: Strategic Approaches to Crime Prevention.* Chicago: University of Chicago Press.

Toobin, J. 1996. *The Run of His Life .* New York: Random House.

Tracy, P., M. Wolfgang, and R. Figlio. 1990. *Delinquent Careers in Two Birth Cohorts.* New York: Plenum.

Trasler, G. 1993. "Conscience, Opportunity, Rational Choice, and Crime," pp. 305–22 in R.V. Clarke and M. Felson (eds.) *Routine Activity and Rational Choice.* New Brunswick, NJ: Transaction Publishers.

Tremblay, R. and W. Craig. 1995. "Developmental Crime Prevention," pp. 151–236 in M. Tonry and D. Farrington (eds.) *Building a Safer Society.* Chicago: University of Chicago Press.

United States Department of Justice/Office of the Inspector General.1997. Report on the FBI Laboratory.

Van der Ryn, S. 1996. Ecological Design. Washington, DC: Island Press.

Van der Ryn, S. and P. Calthorpe. 1986. *Sustainable Communities.* San Francisco, CA: Sierra Club.

Wackernagel, M. 1996. *Our Ecological Footprints.* Gabrliola: New Society.

Walsh, A. 1995. *Biosociology: An Emerging Paradigm.* Westport, CT : Praeger.

Weiner, N.A. and M. Wolfang. 1989. *Violent Crime, Violent Criminals.* Newbury Park, CA : Sage.

———. 1989. *Pathways to Criminal Violence.* Newbury Park, CA: Sage.

West, D.J. and D.P. Farrington. 1973. *Who Becomes Delinquent.* London: Heinemann.

———. 1977. *The Delinquent Way of Life .* London: Heinemann.

Wikstrom, P.O.H. 1995. " Preventing City-Center Street Crimes," pp. 429–68 in M. Tonry and D. P. Farrington (eds.) *Building a Safer Society.* Chicago: University of Chicago Press.

Wolfgang, M. 1972. "Cesare Lombroso," pp. 232–91 in H. Mannheim (ed.) *Pioneers in Criminology.* Montclair, NJ: Patterson-Smith.

———. 1995. "The Just Deserts vs. the Medical Model," pp. 279–92 in J. McCord and J.H. Laub (eds.) *Contemporary Masters in Criminology.* New York: Plenum.

Wolfgang, M. and F. Ferracuti. 1967. *The Subculture of Violence.* London: Tavistock.

Wolfgang, M., R.M. Figlio, and T. Sellin. 1972. *Delinquency in a Birth Cohort.* Chicago: University of Chicago Press.

Wright, R. 1994. *The Moral Animal.* New York : Pantheon Books.

Yeager, C.A. and D.O. Lewis. 1990. "Mortality in a Group of Formerly Incarcerated Juvenile Delinquents." *American Journal of Psychiatry* 147:5, 612–4.

Yudofsky, S.C. and R.E. Hales, eds. 1992. *Neuropsychiatry,* 2d. ed. Washington, DC: American Psychiatric Press.

Zaidel, D.W., ed. 1994. *Neuropsychology.* San Diego, CA: Academic Press.

2

A Perspective on Stranger Violence

Marc Riedel

Strangers are an omnipresent feature of urban life. Milgram (1970) observed the following about the vast majority of people whom we personally do not know.

> In Nassau County, a suburb of New York City, an individual can meet 11,000 others within a ten-minute radius of his office by foot or car. In Newark, a moderate-sized city, he can meet more than 20,000 persons within this radius. But in midtown Manhattan he can meet fully 220,000. (1461)

Such large numbers raise several questions. First, how does interaction among people unknown to each other occur? Given that it does occur, what happens in the small proportion of violent occurrences among strangers? From a commonsense perspective, it seems that we should have more violent encounters with strangers than with nonstrangers, since we have no experience with the former. Yet, that appears not to be the case.

Also, a cursory view suggests the response to stranger violence is largely reactive. As will be described, the criminal justice process treats violent stranger offenders disproportionately more harshly than nonstrangers. Perhaps severity of sanctions is pursued more intensively because certainty and celerity are not achieved. Arrest clearances for murder, for example, have declined from 93 percent in 1961 to 65 percent in 1992 (Riedel and Rinehart 1996). While it is presumptuous to believe that most uncleared murders can be attributed to strangers, they pose a difficult problem for police investigators because of, among other factors, the absence of witnesses. Clearly, however, a system in which one-third of the most violent offenders are not arrested will have difficulties making credible claims for deterrence.

Finally, perhaps because of the lack of reliable evidence, stranger violence is the topic of media exaggeration. Estimates of stranger murder that range between 53 percent and 90 percent are surely exaggerated. The best available estimates place stranger murders between 19 percent and 25 percent of reported murders (Riedel 1996). If we assume that media reports reflect and reinforce public concerns, what characteristics of stranger violence stimulate public interest? Cases where one person is killed in a drug exchange or a husband killing a wife do not rate the media attention given to killings where the offender is believed to be a stranger.

Stranger Relationships and Stranger Violence

Robberies, assaults, and rapes involve stranger offenders although homicides have received the most empirical attention from researchers. Early research viewed strangers as an attribute of victim/offender relationships and a standard variable in the descriptions of homicide patterns in major cities (Block 1976; Curtis 1974; Hepburn and Voss 1970; Munford, Kazer, Feldman and Stivers 1976; Pittman and Handy 1964; Pokorny 1965; Voss and Hepburn 1968; Wilbanks 1984; Wolfgang 1958). As knowledge of general patterns accumulated, homicide researchers began to focus on the similarities and differences between strangers and other victim/offender relationships (Kapardis 1990; Lundsgaarde 1977; Messner and Tardiff 1985; Morgan and Kratcoski 1986; Riedel 1981; 1987; 1993; 1985; Silverman and Kennedy 1987; Zahn and Sagi 1987). Other writers have examined methodological and data problems associated with studying stranger homicides. (Decker 1994; Loftin, Kindley, Norris and Wiersema 1987; Maxwell 1989; Williams and Flewelling 1987).

While stranger violence has been a staple of empirical inquiry, there has been little conceptual development and application of theoretical concepts to the topic of stranger violence. Early treatments of stranger relationships focused on showing that what is apparently outside our social world is very much a part of it. Strangers, Simmel (1964: 402) reminded us, "are a very positive relation; a specific form of interaction." Simmel's strangers, for example, had the freedom and success of a money economy. Wood (1934) concentrated on the conditions that lead to the integration of newcomers. The difficulty is that in showing how strangers were a vital part of society, these writers also focused on the positive contributions of strangers. Beyond important fundamental assumptions, it is difficult directly to draw from their writings a concept of stranger relationships useful to explaining violence.

More recent writers, such as Goffman (1963) and Lofland (1973), recognize the pervasive presence of strangers in urban society and offer a more balanced perspective that explores the positive and negative consequences of stranger interaction. Drawing on the work of Shaler (1904), Lofland suggests that the first response we have to meeting strangers is to fit them into one or more social categories and use expectations derived from these categories to guide interaction. The interactional repertoire derived from categories is large and varied. We interact differently according to whether the other is young, old, male, female, white, African-American, Hispanic, or any combination thereof.

Of course, such interaction is shaped by our perception of how others see us. Young men interact differently, and get different responses, from young women in comparison to older men and women.

The interactional possibilities are increased by variations introduced by where the stranger is found. "I know the face, but I can't place him," is an unwitting acknowledgment of the importance of location. If, in other words, the speaker could locate the stranger in his familiar location, he or she would know something more about him. Locations are relevant cues where recollections are not relevant. Whether we see a shabbily dressed young man leaning against a building in a "bad" section of town or walking across a university campus shapes our expectations and how we will interact with the person in question.

This view of stranger relationships contrasts with a view of some nonstranger or primary relationships initially formulated by Cooley (1909): primary relationships were characterized by responses to the whole person, deep and extensive communication, and personal satisfactions received from the relationships.

The mutuality implied in primary relationships leads to a *singularity* or uniqueness. The content of interaction is configured not to a father, wife, or friend, but to *my* father, wife, or friend. As we become more intimate, we adjust our role expectations to meet the other's preferences, habits, and idiosyncracies. This process of "fine tuning" in a relationship becomes very subtle and frequently unnoticed by observers outside the relationship. For example, husbands learn that a certain glance from their wives means they have commented or are about to comment on a topic that should be left unspoken. Children learn their parents' good and bad moods to know when to present information to them that will upset or disturb them.

Interaction among strangers based on social categories and location are an instance of secondary relationships. Responses to the other are segmental, based on sharply defined roles, and communication is limited and instrumental where the other is seen as necessary to realizing a goal.

Unlike primary relationships, stranger relationships are characterized by *generalizability*. Despite the variation across types of interaction, there is a high degree of standardization of expectations and behavior for given strangers and locations.

Indeed, there is a "programmed" quality about much routine interaction with strangers. For example, consider the process of a routine purchase of many items. The interaction begins with placing the item on the counter for payment and a standard greeting from the clerk, and proceeds smoothly to picking up the paid and packaged item and leaving the store. Millions of these and similar events occur every day because both the interaction and the setting are highly standardized. The high level of standardization not only expedites the process, but insures easy participation by the largest number of people.

To be sure, there are many rules about people and settings to be applied in stranger interaction, but, once learned, they transfer more readily to a much larger number of successful encounters than is the case in nonstranger relationships. In other words, it is much easier for an unfamiliar visitor to our shores to go shopping than to make friends.

It may be that the generalizability of stranger encounters forms part of the basis for the fear of violent victimization. Because we are all involved in similar stranger encounters, it is easy to understand and vicariously identify with other victims of violent encounters. Of course, there are differences vis-à-vis social categories of victims and offenders. The fear of rape and sexual assault expressed by women is a social recognition of the differences in physical strength between males and females that may or may not be controllable in social situations. More generally, media reports of violent stranger victimization are newsworthy because they serve to remind readers of their vulnerability and similarity to victims: if *someone* with no prior relationship to the offender can be victimized, it means than *anyone* can be victimized in similar settings.

The differences between stranger and nonstranger relationships have parallels in the nature of violence and formal responses to it. One characteristic of violence between people who know one another is the demonstrated reluctance to define the behavior as an offense against the state, that is, a crime. For a very long time, violence between spouses was viewed as private matter between husband and wife. Outside agencies, such as law enforcement did little to help; friends and relatives of the battered wife did not wish to intervene or were actively discouraged from doing so. Traditionally, police officers were reluctant to arrest the abusing husband because it was a problem the couple could work out or, if an arrest occurred, the wife would frequently refuse to prosecute.

Largely due to the efforts in recent years of politically and socially active women's groups, the view of wife battering as a private matter condoned by the inaction of outside agencies is no longer tenable. Legislation to protect women, proactive law enforcement, battered women's shelters, and a massive public education effort have succeeded in curbing some of the worst forms of domestic violence (Gelles 1982).

The reluctance to define violence as a crime is also found in less intimate relationships. The underreporting of violence between people who know one another is a persistent problem for the National Crime Survey. Such underreporting is not limited to marital relationships, but includes other family members, relatives, and friends. Yngvesson (1978) suggested that conflicts between people who know one another are more likely settled informally because of social investment in the relationship. Strangers, she suggested, represent no social investment or interest to the victim and are more likely to be subject to formal sanctions. Similarly, Gove, Hughes, and Geerken (1985: 486) suggested, "...when one has a close relationship with an individual one tends, over time, to put the assault into the context of one's overall relationship with the person and as a consequence the incident becomes normalized."

The factors that lead to reluctance to define a violent act as crimes are absent in stranger violence. By definition, there is no prior relationship or emotional investment in the relationship that would encourage the victim to interpret the act in other terms. Therefore, stranger violence is better reported than nonstranger encounters, judging from the National Crime Victimization Survey. The same cannot be said for murders involving strangers, but that occurs because of reporting lags and the greater difficulty of arresting stranger offenders (Riedel 1993).

The differences between stranger and nonstranger relationships are also reflected in other parts of the criminal justice system. In comparison to nonstrangers, stranger offenders are indicted more frequently and given longer sentences (Lundsgaarde 1977), have their charges dismissed less frequently, and are convicted more often (Forst 1981; Vera

Institute of Justice 1977). In their review of discretionary decision making in criminal justice, Gottfredson and Gottfredson showed:

> The gravest dispositions are reserved continuously for events between strangers. Victims report nonstranger events less frequently, police arrest less frequently, prosecutors charge less frequently, and so on through the system. (Gottfredson and Gottfredson 1988: 259)

The Nature of Strangers and Violent Encounters

The involvement of a formal social control process is a second line of defense against predatory stranger offenders. No doubt if it were more effective, it would be used more often. The first line of defense is prevention in the form of most arrangements of public space designed to prevent the use of that space for deviant purposes. One type of control is achieved by architecture and various types of technology: locked doors, barred windows, alarms, high counters, unbreakable glass, fences, safes, keyed cash registers, posted signs, and surveillance by cameras and persons.

In areas where the latter are not available, such as public streets, there are a variety of spatial and temporal tactics to regulate our discourse with strangers. These include seeking the protection of taxis or private automobiles in traveling through "dangerous" areas; use of body language to discourage the approach of strangers in areas like airports; moving about in public areas in daylight as much as possible; traveling in groups; and avoiding isolated or unpopulated urban areas (Lofland 1973).

A recognition of the importance of prevention is a major policy implication of efforts to use location to explain criminal victimization. The lifestyle (Hindelang, Gottfredson, and Garofalo 1978) and routine activities theories (Cohen and Felson 1979) make similar predictions and some researchers, such as Sampson (1987), have treated both as a type of opportunity theory; others have focused on testing one or the other theory.

Briefly, lifestyle and routine activities theories assume a view of society in which its members mostly repetitively follow normative and structural expectations. People go to work or school, take care of a home, raise children, shop, eat, sleep, and recreate in a round of social and culturally expected activities.

Some lifestyles and variations in routine activities are seen as opportunities by offenders. Where there is a convergence in space and time of suitable targets, likely offenders, and an absence of guardians, violations occur (Cohen and Felson 1979). In exploring the ecological implications of routine activities theory, Felson and Cohen (1980:396–7) note the applicability of routine activities to stranger violence:

> Our general theoretical postulate is that the tempo of primary group activities within households varies inversely with the tempo of direct-contact predatory violations in the community. We expect this to be true because, as activities take people away from their households or their primary groups, the circumstances favorable for direct-contact predatory violations, *especially involving strangers*, will probably occur with greater frequency. (italics added)

As Cohen and M. Felson have indicated, a persistent thread in the routine activities approach is the distinction between private and public locations—where most stranger violence occurs. Some research has considered the relationship between routine activities, homicide, and victim/offender relationship in terms of social and demographic variables that imply routine activity in public locations. Messner and Tardiff (1985) found that males, those aged 16–69, and unemployed victims were more frequently killed outside their home, and more males were killed by strangers. Homicides that involved strangers were more likely to occur on weekdays while nonstranger homicides increased on weekends.

Because the elderly spend less time outside their homes, routine activities theory hypotheses that they will suffer lower victimization rates than other age groups. While this is generally true, using location and demographic variables, Kennedy and Silverman (1990) found that elderly victims were disproportionately victims of theft-based homicides by strangers. The reformulation suggested by the authors is consistent with routine activities theory and is based on two previous findings: (a) burglars select targets because of ease of entry rather than the goods within; and (b) elderly people are more likely to die of injuries than other groups. Given that elderly more often live quietly at home in areas with low daytime occupancy, their presence may not be detected by burglars selecting targets. In a subsequent confrontation with resisting victims, offenders inflict injury on persons that are less likely to recover.

There are two components that need to be added to routine activity theory to describe stranger violence. The first, addressed by Clarke and Felson (1993) and Cornish and Clarke (1986), is a concept of offender. The second is a consideration of the types of locations that describe two types of stranger violence.

The Stranger Offender

In his classic essay on the stranger, Simmel (1964) suggested that because strangers are not committed to any particular group, they acquire the attitude of objectivity. This objectivity means that strangers are not bound by commitments that would affect his or her judgment. For example, Simmel cited the practice of some Italian cities who called outside judges in to settle cases.

Another way of viewing objectivity is that strangers are capable of innovative approaches to social arrangements. In the context of routine activities, this suggests that what are viewed as commonsense preventive strategies to victims are seen as tactical challenges to stranger offenders. The ecological precautions taken to prevent stranger violence are seen as temporary obstacles by offenders.

Simmel's strangers are objective, but not detached. In his persistent use of traders as strangers, he conveys an image of a practical decision maker concerned with everyday activities. They are mobile and aware of group relations without being intimately connected. In Wood's (1934) words, they are in groups but not of them.

Such a view is consistent with a notion that offenders are decision makers who view targets and guardians in a rational and tactical way (Clarke and Felson 1993: 6). The rational choice perspective assumes that: "crime is purposive behavior designed to meet the offender's commonplace needs for such things as money, status, sex, and excitement, and that meeting these needs involves the making of (sometimes quite rudimentary) decisions and choices, constrained as these are by limits of time and ability and the availability of relevant information."

The level of rational decision making is similar to that used by the majority of people in their daily activities: rationality is bounded rather than normative. Selectiveness as an outcome of decision making characterizes many of our relationships with strangers. Routine encounters with strangers appear to have a random character because decisions about location are more important than choices about with whom we will interact at that location. The choice of gas station is dictated by fuel reserves and the location of the station in relation to other ongoing activities rather than who is working there. Which employee we interact with at airline ticket counters, post offices, and banks are determined by who is available when we reach the head of a waiting line.

But there is a measure of selectiveness in the choice of strangers with whom to interact. The use of social categories to inform our behavior also means there are opportunities to choose the strangers with whom we can interact. Not only can we behave in a manner to discourage stranger encounters, we can act in a proactive fashion to select strangers to meet goals. If we are seeking directions to a location in a large city, we approach strangers who are "open" to interaction, such as uniformed police officers (Goffman 1963). We are also more likely to obtain reliable directions from older adults than teenagers. In retail stores, we attempt to identify store employees for help by looking for identifying clothing or badges. Finally, in checkout lines, we try to identify either the shortest line or the clerk who is most efficiently processing customers.

While people going about their routine activities make efforts to regulate their interaction with strangers, they are no match for the ability of offenders to exploit locations and people for criminal and violent purposes. Offenders, Cusson (1993) suggested, have a capacity to scan many settings to find precriminal situations: circumstances "preceding and surrounding the criminal event and making the offense more or less difficult, risky, and profitable." Opportunity, he suggested, is a favorable set of circumstances.

A favorable set of circumstances includes tactics—a sequence of choices and actions by the offender to meet the goals defined in the precriminal situation. As Cusson (1993) has noted, the purpose of tactics is to neutralize the target's protection and effect escape from pursuit, identification, and punishment. For example, preferred robbery targets are small stores with one employee and times when there are few or no customers.

Categorical markers are also part of opportunity or a favorable set of circumstances. The emphasis on generalizability of stranger relationships mentioned earlier should not lead us to overlook that attributions based on social categories are important factors in the selection of targets by stranger offenders. There are three types of social markers relevant to stranger victimization. Membership in these categories represents a vulnerability to attack because the victim is less able to defend oneself and/or because others in a setting support a definition of the person as a target.

Some categorical memberships or markers are based on demographic categories. Children, women, and elderly people are more susceptible to stranger victimization because of their physical vulnerability. Because large portions of the population are members of these categories at some time, the risk of stranger victimization exists for a variety of settings.

Other categorical markers include those that reflect lifestyle or group membership devalued or despised in some settings. It is difficult to provide a concise list because viewing them as potential victims is frequently contingent on the nature of the setting. Familiar examples include gays, gang members, and winos. With the addition of a prevalent setting such as a bar, the list can be extended to include white males in African-American bars and vice-versa; supporters of opposing sports teams, college students in rural bars, and middle- class males in "biker bars."

Categorical markers that increase the probability of stranger victimization can be unwittingly acquired. For example, media reports have indicated many rental car companies in Miami have removed any indication of corporate ownership from their vehicles to prevent tourists from being victimized. Similarly, at a criminological convention in Miami located in an area where convention participants were advised not to walk around outside after dark, many participants were observed walking with their convention badges still proudly displayed. As a colleague noted humorlessly, "Yea, that's like saying, 'Here I am! Mug me!'" While it is difficult to evaluate such risks, it is worth noting that the writer and an associate were escorted by an armed guard into a restaurant outside the hotel area immediately after leaving the taxi.

To suggest that stranger offenders are rational decision makers does not imply that nonstranger offenders follow some nonrational mode. Crime is, as noted earlier, purposive behavior designed to meet a variety of different needs. At one extreme is what appears to be the epitome of a nonrational act: the battered wife who kills her husband, calls the police, awaits their arrival, and freely confesses.

Consideration of the past circumstances of many spousal murders do not make the wife's behavior as nonrational as it first appears. It is difficult to read Angela Browne's (1987) classic study of why battered women kill their tormentors without considering that the victims concluded that killing and facing prison terms was preferable to their present circumstances. For women living in constant fear of serious injury or death; bereft of the support of family and friends; economically dependent on their husbands; finding existing levels of legal intervention ineffective; and fearful that the abuse will extend to their children, killing their abusive husbands may well represent an attempt to deter, recover their identity, and/or obtain justice. Desperate circumstances make for desperate decisions that may, none the less, be rational and instrumental.

What distinguishes stranger offenders is their ability and, sometimes, their creativity, in using different types of settings to achieve their goals.

This includes how they can evaluate the circumstances of settings used by people to carry out their serious routine activities as well as those settings where people play.

Exploiting the Setting

Spatial dimensions are important with respect to interacting with strangers because, beyond categorical characteristics, there is little else available to guide our interactional expectations. Locations can be differentiated into configurations of time, space, and objects such as grocery stores, gas stations, clothing stores, parks, streets, and doctor's offices. Associated with these behavior settings are widely shared sets of beliefs about the appropriate kinds of behavior that can occur there (Barker 1968). These standing patterns of behavior describe "what activity can take place as a matter of course and without question, and for what conduct those present will be held accountable" (Cavan 1966: 3).

Much of what we do when we recreate and work with others can be distinguished by the anticipated consequences of our behavior. Most of what we do on a daily basis has serious consequences, and our job is one of the most important consequential activities. Gainful employment is fraught with serious consequences; whether we consistently report to work on time, the quality of work we do, whether such work is completed at a rate that is expected by our supervisors, the amount of cooperation that we show in working with others, the willingness to be supervised by others in the work setting are all factors that determine whether the person is retained and promoted. Such activities make it possible for us to realize our individual potential, enjoy greater prestige or greater income, or, sometimes, all three.

A much smaller amount of our daily activities is devoted to play. In her perceptive analysis of serious and unserious settings, Cavan (1966) describes unserious settings as analogous to a "time out" in sporting events where the rules of the game are suspended while coaches talk to players, walk on the playing field, change equipment, argue, and generally do things that are not permitted during the game. People who are participants in settings like bars, parties, beaches, resorts, and carnivals enter a setting where their behavior will have few consequences outside the setting.

These "play" settings involve a suspension of reality, a stepping out of the real world where the consequences of one's action are determined in the here and now. Unserious settings are places where differentials in social status are held in abeyance, and where people assume identities that cannot be maintained outside the setting. In contrast to work settings, unserious settings are where people have the freedom to initiate and terminate interaction with others, including strangers. In addition, the limits of acceptable behavior are broader and a larger variety of deviant behavior is acceptable.

Serious and unserious settings pose different problems for strangers interested in perpetrating a violent act. For serious settings such as retail outlets, behavior patterns are organized around the accomplishment of a task between two strangers. In the routine purchase of an item in a retail outlet, there is a reciprocity built upon mutual expectations that allow an encounter to go forward with a minimum of conflict. Further, these expectations guide behavior so completely that we are generally only dimly aware of the myriad rules that guide an encounter. To discover otherwise, we have only to look at small children making their first purchase to understand how difficult it is to learn not only the obvious behavior patterns, but also those expressed by body language, gestures, slang, and silence.

Imagine, if you will, what can occur if those engaged in routine interaction are wrenched from their placid exchange by the sudden appearance of an individual with a gun threatening their life if they do not comply with his or her demands. It is precisely because we are so entrenched in the expectations that guide routine activity that the onset of a robbery shocks and surprises the victim.

Unsympathetic to his or her endeavors as we may be, completing a robbery places a heavy burden on the offender. Unlike violence that involves friends and acquaintances, the stranger offender knows virtually nothing about the victim except what he or she can glean from his or her categorical characteristics. Further, while the stranger offender may be familiar with the setting, to exploit it, he or she must redefine it as a robbery site, being concerned with entrances, exits, and spatial arrangements within the setting. All of the latter must, of course, be integrated with considerations as to the best time to stage the encounter.

The latter means that the offender must convince the victim that (a) he or she is serious—this is indeed a robbery, and (b) control the victim's behavior and other elements in the setting so that the robbery can be successfully completed. The fact that victims and offenders know very little about each other increases the possibility of unpredictable behavior that may be perceived by the offender as a loss of control. Such circumstances are particularly likely to result in robbery murder.

Robberies range from personal attacks, "muggings," to robberies of commercial targets such as banks, armored cars, and jewelry stores. In considering personal attacks or "muggings," the routine nature of everyday activities makes us unwitting targets for such crimes. All of us become committed to the range of responses involved in routine activities to the point where surprise, shock, and a state of disbelief are a common response to the initial demands of a robbery offender (Lejeune and Alex 1973). Because public settings are readily accessible and because the offender can "count on" the repetitive structured behavior of the inhabitants, attacking a target may only require a momentary consideration of how the setting can be exploited to accomplish the robbery task.

In confronting their victims, robbery offenders have two major tasks. They must redefine the setting from one of routine activities to one in which a transfer of property is to occur under threat. In addition, they must control the victims during this process. Whether it involves reorienting the interaction of victims and offenders and "transforming their interaction to a common robbery frame" (Luckenbill 1981:31), "denormalizing" the setting for victims (Lejeune 1977: 137), or "declaring the crime" (Katz 1988), the consequences are similar. Even as offenders attempt to define the setting as normal for themselves, they are redefining it for the victim.

Ironically, the very elements that have made the robbery approach successful to the point of confrontation are the ones that are essential to alter if the definition of the setting as one acceptable to robbery is to succeed. Elements in the setting and behavior before the robbery that served as camouflage are the very ones that must be given a radically new meaning for the robbery to continue to completion. Thus, what is a benign, even a boring work setting, is now a dangerous one.

The process begins by taking the victims by surprise. As one of Letkeman's respondents noted, "We don't just walk in there and say, 'Well, this is a holdup, hand over the money.' We give a good bellow when we walk in." Another respondent put it more simply: "The door would fly open and the people inside, they freeze" (Letkemann 1973:108, 110).

The fear and momentary paralysis that follow is important because it gives offenders the opportunity to seize the initiative and begin to redefine the behavior that is expected in the setting. Thus, in payroll and bank robberies, the hesitation of the victims gives offenders enough time to assume their positions and back personnel away from their stations before they regain their composure and push an alarm button.

Further redefinition of the setting occurs as offenders violate the conditions of conventional serious settings. The distinctions between "front" and "back" regions are no longer applicable as offenders leap over counters, hold clerks at bay, and empty cash drawers. Persons in the setting who are ordinarily accorded deference are shoved, jostled, and threatened as readily as any other person in the setting. Even the behavior of bystanders is exploited in ways that are consistent with the new demands of the setting. Customers are forced into a position of helplessness by being made to lie, face down, on the floor.

Exploiting a setting—using settings and relationships to achieve a deviant purpose—requires the use of threat to redefine and control victims. The exclamation, "he has a gun!" is certain to play a defining role. Cook (1982:247) describes the distinctiveness and superiority of guns over other types of threats.

> A gun has several characteristics that make it superior to other readily available weapons for use in violent crime. Even in the hand of a weak and unskilled assailant, a gun can be used to kill. The killing can be accomplished from a distance without much risk of effective counterattack by the victim, and the killing can be completed quickly, without sustained effort, and in a relatively "impersonal" fashion. Furthermore, because everyone knows that a gun has these attributes, the mere display of a gun communicates a highly effective threat.

It is useful to distinguish between preemptive and reactive use of force in robberies (Lejeune 1977). Given the success of a gun as a threat, unarmed robberies pose a greater problem with respect to controlling victims and getting them to accept the robbery definition of the setting. As one robbery offender notes:

> Now, if some guy came up to me and said, "Give me your money," and all he's got is a tire iron, I'd probably beat the hell out of him. If all you got is an iron or something like that, he'd probably just laugh at you. (Luckenbill 1980: 367)

Preemptive force is used when the offender wants to define the robbery setting quickly and convincingly. Hitting, pushing, shoving and/or slapping is a way to let the victim know that the offender is serious about the robbery. Such tactics appear to be frequent in unarmed robberies. Block and Skogan (1984) in their study of stranger victimizations found that 70 percent of unarmed robberies in the National Crime Survey involved an actual attack, while only 26 percent of the armed robberies involved an attack on the victim.

Sometimes, preemptive force is used when the offender believes he or she is unable to control the victim in any other way. For example,

Lejeune (1977) gives the case of a male mugger who attacked and subdued an unsuspecting victim before robbing him because the victim was a much larger male than the offender.

Lejeune also found that younger or less experienced muggers were more likely to use preemptive force in a robbery. Because these muggers have not yet learned the most effective use of force, the tendency is to minimize the risk by using more force than would be perceived as necessary by more experienced offenders.

The reactive use of force occurs when the offender fails to obtain or loses control over the victim. Those who do not respond to the initial threats of the offender are perceived as resisting and thereby provide a justification for violent treatment. In other cases, the victim may initially comply, but at some crucial stage in the interaction refuse to continue. Such lack of cooperation justifies the use of additional force. Finally, rather than passively resisting, the victim may attempt to attack the offender to end the robbery. This also can result in the use of force by the offender, injury and possibly death for the victim.

It is unclear whether murders are a planned part of robberies or whether they emerge from the conditions of the robbery setting. There are large percentages of offenders who use alcohol and/or controlled substances immediately before the offense (Walsh 1986). Given the negative effect on the offender's judgment, injury and death of the victim can result from a misreading of victims behavior.

What makes matters worse is that robbery settings are sustained by strangers and forced compliance. Under those circumstances, it is easy for a victim's behavior to be misconstrued and a commonplace piece of behavior viewed as threatening. The following case illustrates what happened when the offender thought the victim was going for a gun.

> The victim was a nineteen-year-old white gas station attendant who was working, together with the older station manager, on the graveyard shift. The killer, a twenty-year-old black male, drove up to the station requesting a fill-up. The killer, and his companion..., left their car at the gasoline pumps and went into the station. One of them suddenly pointed a gun at the two gas station attendants. He demanded all the money in the cash register. As the younger man began to open the cash register he accidentally broke off the handle. He put the handle in his back pocket and that action was taken by the killer to mean that the attendant was going for a gun. The killer fired his .22-caliber pistol and the nineteen-year-old gas station attendant fell over dead. The killer and his companion...emptied the cash register and left the station with their haul, which amounted to $80. (Lundsgaarde 1977: 135–6)

Finally, exploitation and manipulation of people and settings for violent goals is not limited to robbery. In his study of stranger homicides in Australia, Karpardis (1990) reported instances of predatory or opportunistic homicides involving homosexuals found in public toilets, on beaches, or parks late at night. Also falling within the category of exploitative stranger violence are vulnerable victims such as chronic alcoholics or vagrants asleep in deserted public places, "thrill" killings, and the abduction and killing of women and children from public places such as shopping malls. While there is little known except for high visibility victims, the crime of "stalking" is an instance of stranger offenders using information garnered from a variety of routine settings used by the unsuspecting victim as a prelude to attack.

Confrontational Violence

While violent stranger homicides are generally believed to involve another felony, a substantial proportion do not involve felonies. Using data on stranger homicides from eight cities, Zahn and Sagi (1987) found that stranger homicides not involving felonies ranged from 33.5 percent in Newark, New Jersey to 50 percent in Oakland, California and "Ashton" (a pseudonym). For all eight cities, 160 cases, or 42.7 percent, of stranger homicides were not associated with a felony. In addition, 85 percent of stranger nonfelony homicides occurred in public space.

In contrast to Miethe, Stafford, and Long's (1987) view that routine activities theory is limited to explaining property victimization, Kennedy and Forde (1990) found support for routine activities in explaining assaults. Using data from the Canadian Urban Victimization Study and variables not available in the Miethe et al. study, the authors conclude:

> The most vulnerable groups are young, unmarried males who frequent bars, go to movies, go out to work, or spend time out of the house walking or driving around. It appears that it is this public lifestyle that creates exposure to risk and, although it may be the case that violent crime is spontaneous, the targets of violent crime are more likely to be people who are in places where conflict flares up. (143)

A characteristic of unserious places such as bars and taverns mentioned earlier is that the behavior expressed there lacked consequences outside the setting. People take positions and play roles that cannot be sustained elsewhere: employers become believers in participatory democracy, employees express depths of company loyalty they never knew they had, airline receptionists become flight attendants, and baggage handlers become airline executives, just to mention a few.

But consequentiality has a way of rearing its ugly head. While there is a consensus that claims heard in unserious settings cannot be taken at face value, that is not true everywhere always. People take exception to the behavior and remarks of others: they attribute consequences that were not meant. What a woman regards as suitable flirtatious behavior in a bar may cause a conflict with a male who attributes quite different and serious consequences to her behavior, for example.

Such confrontational conflict has been described in detail by Luckenbill (1977) as "face" contests that begins with an insult or disparaging remark on the identity of another. The other responds with negative comments that begins an escalatory process that eventuates in physical violence and death.

It is not necessary to posit personal attacks on another as a reason for violence between strangers. The wide variety of strangers that a person can interact with in bars opens the possibility that almost anything one says or does can be misunderstood or regarded as an insult by another. The range of possibilities is indicated in a study by Simmons (1969:3). He found that his 180 subjects "had called no less than 252 distinct acts and persons deviant." This, of course, does not include instances of violence between strangers who get into arguments over such weighty matters as the ownership of a can of beer or a parking place.

If aggression is goal-oriented and attempts to achieve what an actor views as justice or a favorable self-image, it seems reasonable to suppose that the views of significant others are important in a conflict. Do third parties contribute to the ongoing process of violence? Felson and Steadman (1983) found that third parties were present in 70 percent of the cases of violence studied and more often participated as antagonists than as mediators. Further, Felson (1982) and Felson, Ribner, and Siegel (1984) found that aggressive third parties increased the aggressiveness of offenders, particularly when third parties were young males or significant others. These results seem particularly relevant to nonfelony stranger violence because Zahn and Sagi (1987) found that 89 percent of the homicides were witnessed by at least one other person. By comparison, among stranger homicides involving an additional felony, 68 percent were witnessed by at least one other person.

Such settings produce violence among strangers that differs in one respect from robbery violence. It is generally true in robberies that victims are white while offenders are frequently African Americans. However, in a study of assault murders in Chicago and surrounding counties,

Przybylski (1987) found that white stranger offenders killed African-American victims somewhat more frequently than the reverse (38.4 percent versus 31.6 percent). The more equitable racial distribution of victims and offenders, in comparison to robbery murders, is consistent with the view that confrontational violence is precipitated by insults and arguments that are independent of proxy indicators of the economic value of targets.

The choice of a target for violent confrontation may take on the appearance of rationality because of the use of alcohol. Gibbs has pointed out that the consumption of alcohol can lead a person to perceive a less than complete representation of his or her environment. When a person's perceptual field is narrowed, random fluctuations in the environment can mean drastic changes in his or her perception of the setting. Actions by others may appear arbitrary and inconsistent to the perceiver because he or she has an overly simplified view of the setting. Thus, intoxicated people may be very insulted by a statement or action that others view as trivial.

There seems little doubt that bars and taverns are high-risk places for violence (Roncek and Maier 1991; Sherman, Gartin, and Buerger 1989). Bars and taverns attract young males with public lifestyles (Kennedy and Silverman 1990), deviant lifestyles, and offenders (Sampson and Lauritsen 1990). In a very real sense, strangers looking for a fight are likely to go to places where they can find one. Homel, Tomsen, and Thommeny (1992) in their study of Sydney, Australia bars found that assailants "pick their mark." Categorical markers include finding victims that are younger, smaller, and more intoxicated than the offender.

A closer examination of bars shows variation in their potential for violence. Bars and taverns vary in their decorum, kinds of customers, and behavioral expectations. Graham, La Rocque, Yetman, Ross, and Guistra (1980) studied aggression in Vancouver bars. One of the strongest explanatory factors was the barroom environment. The bars with the highest amount of physical and nonphysical aggression were characterized by loud and abusive language, lack of cleanliness, inexpensive physical surroundings, high percentages of Native Americans and unkempt patrons, patrons drinking rapidly and becoming highly intoxicated, a downtown location, tables crowded together, and unfriendly barworkers.

In their study of Sydney bars, Homel et al. (1992) found that physical violence was the outcome of interaction between aspects of patron mix, levels of comfort, boredom and intoxication, and the behavior of bouncers. The proportion of males and male groups, especially strangers to each other, were predictive of arguments and fights.

Like Graham et al. (1980), the authors found that roomy, well-ventilated places with low levels of noise had lower levels of violence. Stage entertainment, especially bands and music helped to reduce the level of boredom and violence.

High levels of intoxication and violence are encouraged by discount drinks such as "Happy Hours." In bars that provided entertainment and a cover charge, patrons frequently believed it necessary to get extremely drunk to get their "money's worth," especially if the quality of entertainment was poor.

Finally, levels of violence could be moderated by the behavior of doormen or bouncers. Homel et al. (1992: 688) note that many "bouncers seem poorly trained, obsessed with their own machismo (relating badly to groups of male strangers), and some of them appear to regard their employment as giving them a licence to assault people."

The authors conclude that the confrontational violence that appears in bars is less a matter of the relationship between the physiology of alcohol and violence and more a matter of good management, effective legislation, and police surveillance.

Summary and Conclusions

A major problem in trying to describe stranger violence is the recognition that much of it is situational. Thus, it is necessary to explain the kinds of "normal" situations in which strangers are prevalent, how these situations are changed to accommodate violence, and the characteristics of offenders. In this chapter, an attempt has been made to show how the huge number of stranger interactions in urban settings proceeds through the use of expectations based on social categories as well as locational cues. We have suggested that stranger offenders make normatively rational choices and engage in purposeful behavior ranging from obtaining money to building and reinforcing identities.

But different locations or behavior settings impose different problems for stranger offenders who attempt to achieve their purposes. The majority of settings are those in which the people in the setting are engaged in consequential activities; they are attending to social and economic processes that make it possible for the organization to deliver a product. Because much of the activity is visible, exploiting the setting requires that stranger offenders observe and plan how it can be turned to their purposes.

Precisely because unserious or play settings lack the consequentiality of work settings, stranger offenders are left to develop the confrontational components by interaction. Thus, redefinitions of situations for robberies and robbery murder occur at or near the beginning of encounters while redefinitions for assaults and murders in unserious settings develop later.

For serious settings, the consequentiality of what occurs is taken for granted; it is an element that enters into planning and behavior of the offender. It is the unanticipated event or the perception of unanticipated behavior that threatens the tenuous control maintained by the offender and leads to greater violence.

By contrast, it is the introduction of consequentiality in unserious settings that leads to conflict between strangers. The careless remark or behavior by one of the actors is given a meaning that reflects negatively on the identity of an offender and an escalation of conflicts begins.

Finally, exploitative and confrontational violence differs in the role played by third parties. For stranger offenders anticipating a robbery, the role of third parties must be minimized. For confrontational violence, audiences play a role in instigating or supporting violence.

Most stranger violence is preventable, although systematic empirical support for that statement is problematical. We avoid victimization by taking precautions: this includes not only the vast array of technology and "target-hardening" devices, but also the commonsense behavior associated with managing stranger encounters and avoiding settings where violence occurs.

Part of the genius of routine activities and lifestyle theory is a recognition of the latter and an explication of how prevention strategies might be extended and made more effective. The strategies described in situational crime prevention is one example (Clarke 1980).

The work of Felson and Cohen (1980) has served not only to highlight the ecology of places and their contribution to violent crime, but emphasizes how the management of such locations can serve to reduce violence. Homel et al.'s (1992) recommendations for reducing violence in Sydney bars is an example.

But new theories pose new problems, as they should. For example, situational crime prevention raises questions of the displacement of criminal activity which Lab (1992) suggests is not entirely resolved.

Ultimately, the routine-activities theory also raise the question of how much crime prevention can be tolerated by ordinary citizens. Crime prevention strategies involve behavior that affects the quality of life of the victim as well as the offender. Put another way, we face the problem of whether burglar bars do more to lock burglars out or inhabitants in.

Note

The author would like to express his appreciation to Marcus Felson, Rutgers University, for his helpful comments on an earlier version of this chapter.

References

Barker, R. G. 1968. *Ecological Psychology: Concepts and Methods for Studying the Environment of Human Behavior*. Palo Alto, CA: Stanford University Press.

Block, R. 1976. "Homicide in Chicago—A Nine-Year Study (1965–73)." *Journal of Criminal Law and Criminology* 66:496–510.

Block, R., and W.G. Skogan. 1984. *The Dynamics of Violence between Strangers: Victim Resistance and Outcomes in Rape Assault and Robbery*. Evanston, IL: Center for Urban Affairs and Policy Research.

Browne, A. 1987. *When Battered Women Kill*. New York: The Free Press.

Cavan, S. 1966. *Liquor License: An Ethnography of Bar Behavior*. Chicago: Aldine.

Clarke, R. V., ed. 1980. *Situational Crime Prevention: Successful Case Studies*. Albany, NY: Harrow and Heston.

Clarke, R. V., and M. Felson, eds. 1993. *Routine Activity and Rational Choice*, vol. 5. New Brunswick, NJ: Transaction Publishers.

Cohen, L. E., and M. Felson. 1979. "Social Change and Crime Rate Trends: A Routine Activity Approach." *American Sociological Review* 44: 588–608.

Cook, P. J. 1982. "The Role of Firearms in Violent Crime," pp. 173–87 in M. E. Wolfgang and N. A. Weiner (eds.), *Criminal Violence*. Beverly Hills: Sage Publications.

Cooley, C. H. 1909. *Social Organization*. New York: Charles Scribners Sons, Inc.

Cornish, D. B. and R.V. Clarke, eds. 1986. *The Reasoning Criminal: Rational Choice Perspectives on Offending*. New York: Springer-Verlag.

Curtis, L. A. 1974. *Criminal Violence: National Patterns and Behavior*. Lexington: Lexington Books.

Cusson, M. 1993. "A Strategic Analysis of Crime: Criminal Tactics as Responses to Precriminal Situations," pp. 295–304 in R.V. Clarke and M. Felson (eds.), *Routine Activity and Rational Choice: Advances in Criminological Theory* (vol. 5). New Brunswick, NJ: Transaction Publishers.

Decker, S. H. 1994. "Exploring Victim-Offender Relationships in Homicide: The Role of Individual and Event Characteristics." *Justice Quarterly* 10: 585–612.

Felson, M., and L. E. Cohen. 1980. "Human Ecology and Crime: A Routine Activity Approach." *Human Ecology* 8: 389–406.

Felson, R. B. 1982. "Impression Management and the Escalation of Aggression and Violence." *Social Psychology Quarterly* 45:245–54.

Felson, R. B., S.A. Ribner, and M.S. Siegel. 1984. "Age and the Effect of Third Parties during Criminal Violence." *Sociology and Social Research* 68:452–62.

Felson, R. B., and H. J. Steadman. 1983. "Situational Factors in Disputes Leading to Criminal Violence." *Criminology: An Interdisciplinary Journal* 21: 59–74.

Forst, B. 1981. *Arrest Convictability as a Measure of Police Performance.* Washington, DC: Institute for Law and Social Research.

Gelles, R. J. 1982. "Domestic Violence," pp. 201–35 in M.E. Wolfgang and N.A. Weiner (eds.), *Criminal Violence.* Beverly Hills, CA: Sage Publications.

Goffman, E. 1963. *Behavior in Public Places: Notes on the Social Organization of Gatherings.* New York: The Free Press.

Gottfredson, M. R., and Gottfredson, D. M. 1988. *Decision Making in Criminal Justice: Toward the Rational Exercise of Discretion*: New York: Plenum Press.

Gove, W. R., M. Hughes, and M. Geerken. 1985. "Are Uniform Crime Reports a Valid Indicator of Index Crimes? An Affirmative Answer with Some Minor Qualifications." *Criminology* 23: 451–501.

Graham, K., L. LaRocque, R. Yetman, T. J. Ross, and E. Guistra. 1980. "Aggression and Barroom Environments." *Journal of Studies on Alcohol* 41: 277–92.

Hepburn, J. and H. Voss. 1970. "Patterns of Criminal Homicide: A Comparison of Chicago and Philadelphia." *Criminology* 8: 21–45.

Hindelang, M. J., Gottfredson, M. R., and Garofalo, J. 1978. *Victims of Personal Crime: An Empirical Foundation for a Theory of Personal Victimization.* Cambridge: Ballinger Publishing Co.

Homel, R., S. Tomsen, and J. Thommeny. 1992. "Public Drinking and Violence: Not Just an Alcohol Problem." *Journal of Drug Issues* 22: 679–97.

Kapardis, A. 1990. "Stranger Homicides in Victoria, January 1984–December 1989." *Australian and New Zealand Journal of Criminology* 23:241–58.

Katz, J. 1988. *Seductions of Crime.* New York: Basic Books.

Kennedy, L. W., and D.R. Forde. 1990. "Routine Activities and Crime: An Analysis of Victimization in Canada." *Criminology* 28: 131–50.

Kennedy, L. W., and R.A. Silverman. 1990. "The Elderly Victim of Homicide: An Application of the Routine-Activities Approach." *The Sociological Quarterly* 31: 307–19.

Lab, S.P. 1992. *Crime Prevention: Approaches, Practices, and Evaluations.* Cincinnati, OH: Anderson Publishing Co.

Lejeune, R. 1977. "The Management of a Mugging." *Urban Life and Culture* 6:123–48.

Lejeune, R., and N. Alex. 1973. "On Being Mugged: The Event and Its Aftermath." *Urban Life and Culture* 2: 259–87.

Letkemann, P. 1973. *Crime as Work.* Englewood Cliffs: Prentice-Hall.

Lofland, L. H. 1973. *A World of Strangers: Order and Action in Urban Public Space*: New York: Basic Books.

Loftin, C., K. Kindley, S.L. Norris, and B. Wiersema. 1987. "An Attribute Approach to Relationships between Offenders and Victims." *Journal of Criminal Law and Criminology* 78:259–71.

Luckenbill, D. F. 1977. "Criminal Homicide as a Situated Transaction." *Social Problems* 25: 176–86.

———. 1980. "Patterns of Force in Robbery." *Deviant Behavior* 1: 361–78.

———. 1981. "Generating Compliance: The Case of Robbery." *Urban Life* 10: 25–46.

Lundsgaarde, H. P. 1977. *Murder in Space City: A Cultural Analysis of Houston Homicide Patterns.* New York: Oxford University Press.

Maxwell, M. G. 1989. "Circumstances in Supplementary Homicide Reports: Variety and Validity." *Criminology* 27: 671–95.

Messner, S. F., and Tardiff, K. 1985. "The Social Ecology of Urban Homicide: An Application of the 'Routine Activities' Approach." *Criminology* 23: 241–67.

Miethe, T. D., M.C. Stafford, and S.J. Long. 1987. "Social Differentiation in Criminal Victimization: A Test of Routine Activities/Lifestyle Theories." *American Sociological Review* 52: 184–94.

Milgram, S. 1970. "The Experience of Living in Cities." *Science* 167:1461–8.

Morgan, F., and P.C. Kratcoski. 1986. "An Analysis of the Victim-Offender Relationship in Homicide Cases." *Journal of Police and Criminal Psychology* 2(1): 52–63.

Munford, R., R. Kazer, R. Feldman, and R. Stivers. 1976. "Homicide Trends in Atlanta." *Criminology* 14: 213–31.

Pittman, D., and W. Handy. 1964. "Patterns in Criminal Aggravated Assault." *Journal of Criminal Law, Criminology, and Police Science* 55: 462–70.

Pokorny, A. D. 1965. "A Comparison of Homicide in Two Cities." *Journal of Criminal Law, Criminology, and Police Science* 56: 479–87.

Przybylski, R. 1987. *Stranger Murder in the Chicago Metropolitan Area: An Analysis of the Victim-Level Murder File,* Masters Thesis, Southern Illinois University.

Riedel, M. 1981. "Stranger Homicides in an American City." Paper presented at the annual meeting of the American Society of Criminology, Washington, DC.

———. 1987. "Stranger Violence: Perspectives, Issues, and Problems." *Journal of Criminal Law and Criminology* 78: 223–58.

———. 1993. *Stranger Violence: A Theoretical Inquiry.* New York: Garland Publishing Co.

———. 1996. "Counting Stranger Murders: A Case Study of Statistical Prestidigitation." Unpublished paper.

Riedel, M., and T.A. Rinehart. 1996. "Murder Clearances and Missing Data." *Journal of Crime and Justice* 19: 83–102.

Riedel, M., M.A. Zahn, and L.F. Mock. 1985. *The Nature and Patterns of American Homicide.* Washington, DC: U. S. Government Printing Office.

Roncek, D. W. and P.A. Maier. 1991. "Bars, Blocks, and Crimes Revisited: Linking the Theory of Routine Activities to the Empiricism of "Hot Spots." *Criminology* 99: 751–3.

Sampson, R. J. 1987. "Personal Violence by Strangers: An Extension and Test of Predatory Victimization." *Journal of Criminal Law and Criminology* 78:327–56.

Sampson, R. J., and J.L. Lauritsen. 1990. "Deviant Lifestyles, Proximity to Crime, and the Offender-Victim Link in Personal Violence." *Journal of Research in Crime and Delinquency* 27: 110–39.

Shaler, N. S. 1904. *The Neighbor.* Boston: Houghton Mifflin.

Sherman, L. W., P.R. Gartin, and M.E. Buerger. 1989. "Hot Spots of Predatory Crime: Routine Activities and the Criminology of Place." *Criminology* 27: 27–55.

Silverman, R. A., and Kennedy, L. W. 1987. "Relational Distance and Homicide: The Role of the Stranger." *Journal of Criminal Law and Criminology* 78: 272–308.

Simmel, G. [1950]1964. *The Sociology of Georg Simmel,* edited and translated by K. Wolff. New York: The Free Press.

Simmons, J. 1969. *Deviants.* Berkeley,CA: Glendessary Press.

Vera Institute of Justice. 1977. *Felony Arrests: Their Prosecution and Disposition in New York city's Courts.* New York: Vera Institute of Justice.

Voss, H., and Hepburn, J. 1968. "Patterns in Criminal Homicides in Chicago." *Journal of Criminal Law, Criminology, and Police Science* 59: 500–8.

Walsh, D. 1986. *Heavy Business: Commercial Burglary and Robbery.* London: Routledge and Kegan Paul.

Wilbanks, W. 1984. *Murder in Miami: An Analysis of Homicide Patterns and Trends in Dade County (Miami) Florida, 1917–83.* Lanham, MD: University Press of America.

Williams, K., and Flewelling, R. L. 1987. "Family, Acquaintance, and Stranger Homicide: Alternative Procedures for Rate Calculations." *Criminology* 25: 543–60.

Wolfgang, M. E. 1958. *Patterns in Criminal Homicide*: Philadelphia, PA: University of Pennsylvania Press.

Wood, M. M. 1934. *The Stranger: A Study of Social Relationships*. New York: Columbia University Press.

Yngvesson, B. B. 1978. "The Atlantic Fisherman," pp. 59–85 in L. Nader and H. F. Todd, Jr. (eds.) *The Disputing Process—Law in Ten Societies*. New York: Columbia University Press.

Zahn, M. A., and P.C. Sagi. 1987. "Stranger Homicides in Nine American Cities." *Journal of Criminal Law and Criminology* 78: 377–97.

3

Researching and Conceptualizing Drunk Driving: An Invitation to Criminologists and Criminal Law Scholars

James B. Jacobs

Introduction: Drunk Driving in the 1980s

During the 1980s, drunk driving has been pushed to the forefront of our agenda of social problems. Relentless efforts by a concerned citizens movement have captured the attention of local, state, and federal political leaders. New and human-interest stories, television dramas and public-interest advertising concerning drunk driving have become regular media fare. In 1982, President Reagan appointed a Presidential Commission on Drunk Driving.[1] Congress has enacted two provisions tying anti-drunk driving strategies to highway grants in aid, and the National Highway Traffic Safety Administration has launched a variety of programs and research projects. States and localities have passed and implemented hundreds of laws and programs.

While many systems of social control (treatment, education, private law and insurance) have been mobilized, the role of the criminal justice system has dominated. From the mid-1970s to the mid-1980s, drunk driving arrests increased by 50 percent to 1.8 million per year. This has made drunk driving the most commonly prosecuted offense in our lower criminal courts. Strong citizen concern and the enactment of implied consent laws, which pressure arrestees to provide breath samples on pain of license forfeiture, have joined with restrictions on pre-trial diversion to produce a very high conviction rate. This has posed a significant challenge to our sanctifying systems. In some states like New York, drunk drivers now constitute the largest offender category on probation. Under mandatory sentencing laws, they are also becoming an increasing presence in many jails. Moreover, recidivist drunk drivers (convicted of felonies) are appearing in state prisons in larger numbers. In Texas, for example, there are more than one thousand such prisoners.

The stepped-up attack on drunk driving is not likely to he a passing fad. In many localities and states, such as New York, anti-drunk driving efforts have become institutionalized in special-interest agencies or programs. Some initiatives like New York State's "Stop DWI Program" apply fines paid by drunk drivers to local anti-DWI (driving while intoxicated) programs, enabling them to become to some extent self-financing.

While criminal justice agencies have been highly involved in the current crusade against drunk driving, American criminologists and criminal law theorists, by contrast, have paid little attention. The subject remains on the periphery of criminological and jurisprudential writing and research. This is both regrettable and surprising, since drunk driving raises issues badly in need of clearer conceptualization. In turn, a close scholarly examination of the subject would enrich criminology and criminal law jurisprudence. It is worth asking why drunk driving has stimulated so little scholarly interest, since an understanding of the reasons for this neglect may help in the effort to formulate more effective public policy.

Lack of Criminological Interest

Research on drunk driving by highway safety and public health scholars runs at least as far back as the 1930s. This work has focused on the role of alcohol in traffic crashes, especially fatalities, and on the alcohol abuse problems of crash-involved drivers. This tradition was given a major boost by the Department of Transportation's landmark study, *Alcohol and Highway Safety,* published in 1968.

Nevertheless, drunk driving has hardly made a mark on the criminological agenda. The index to the tenth edition of the standard text by Sutherland and Cressey, *Principles of Criminology,* contains only two entries for drunk driving, each referring to no more than a brief mention of the topic. Over the last ten years (1978–87) only one article on drunk driving has appeared in *Crime and Delinquency,* a leading journal of theoretical and policy-oriented criminology. In criminal law jurisprudence the situation is no better. Although the subject presents an array of thorny theoretical and philosophical issues, a leading criminal law casebook, Kadish, Paulsen, and Schulhoffer's *Criminal Law and Its Processes,* has few references to drunk driving. In the law reviews, too, aside from a body of commentary on the implied consent laws and some articles on procedural issues like roadblocks and discovery, there is very little writing about the subject.

Six Hypotheses on Why Drunk Driving Has Not Been of Interest to Criminologists, and Arguments Why It Should Be

To try to account for the lack of criminological interest in drunk driving, six hypotheses are offered: (1) drunk driving is hard to study; (2) criminologists are uncertain about the status of drunk driving as a "real crime"; (3) criminologists are uncertain about how to classify drunk driving; (4) drunk driving does not conform to certain social and psychological images of "crime"; (5) drunk drivers do not conform to sociological images of "criminals"; and (6) drunk driving does not make a critical case either for liberal or conservative criminologists. An exploration of these hypotheses reveals much about the intellectual status of drunk driving research and contributes to our understanding of the sociology of criminology as an intellectual discipline.

Drunk Driving Is Hard to Study

The criminologist who sets out to analyze drunk driving immediately faces a data problem—the amount of offending is unknown and probably unknowable. The basic data sources on crimes, the "crimes reported to the police" contained in the FBI's Uniform Crime Report, and the "crimes reported by victims" contained in the National Crime Survey, for obvious reasons do not include many reports on acts of drunk driving. Even self-report studies are fraught with uncertainty, since a respondent frequently will not know whether he operated his vehicle in violation of the law on a particular occasion. What does it mean to operate a vehicle "while intoxicated"? How is a respondent to know whether his blood alcohol concentration (BAC) exceeded the legal limit? For these reasons, not only the overall offense rate, but also individual offender rates, are unknown and difficult to estimate.

Consequently, it is also difficult to study the impact of law enforcement measures on the rate of drunk driving. How can we tell if a particular measure has had an effect if we cannot know the incidence of drunk driving before and after its implementation? To meet this difficulty, most evaluation researchers have used single-vehicle nighttime traffic fatalities as a surrogate for drunk driving, reasoning that this category of traffic fatalities is positively correlated with the overall amount of drunk driving.

Unfortunately, there are good reasons to believe that this is not a reliable surrogate variable. First, causing fatal accidents is highly deviant behavior even for drunk drivers. Single-vehicle fatal-accident drivers are likely to be an unusual subgroup comprised of the most pathological drinkers and the most pathological drivers. They are likely to suffer disproportionately from various psychological and behavioral disorders. Second, fatal accidents are uniquely affected by increased seat belt usage and by improvements in emergency medical services which reduce fatalities but not the overall number of drunk driving injuries or frequency of drunk driving. Third, the number of single-vehicle fatalities in any one (even a relatively large) community is quite low, so that small annual fluctuations have a large impact on "rates." For these reasons, the actual rate of drunk driving could be independent of the rate of single vehicle fatalities. Rates could be falling among run-of-the-mill drunk drivers, but not among the small subgroup likely to end up in the single-vehicle nighttime fatality statistics. Until we have good data on overall driving behavior we will not be able to make confident evaluations of the impact of countermeasures.

Drunk driving countermeasures are made even more difficult to evaluate by the abundance of concurrent, relevant developments. In addition to initiatives in policing, prosecution, probation, and punishment, we have also seen a number of new treatment and education programs. At the same time, there have been changes in the legal minimum age for purchasing alcoholic beverages and in the availability of punitive tort damages and insurance surcharges. It is difficult to isolate the impact of these multiple interventions.

But while methodological difficulties do hamper empirical research on drunk driving, they do not justify ignoring or slighting the subject. Traffic safety specialists have pioneered some productive strategies, including voluntary interviews at research checkpoints. Moreover, the vast number of projects carried out in the last decade have left a residue of data about drunk drivers and drunk driving that could be profitably assayed.[2] Criminologists need to study these data and to analyze them with the same tools that they bring to bear on other criminal offenses.

Criminologists Are Uncertain about Drunk
Driving's Status as a "Real Crime"

Criminologists naturally prefer to study "serious" and "important" crimes; after all, the more important the crime, the more important the criminologist. Like other people, they have been unsure about whether drunk driving is really a crime at all, much less an important or serious one. One reason for this is that drunk driving does not appear in the criminal code, but is tucked away in the vehicle and traffic law. This throws in doubt whether the legislature meant drunk driving to be considered a full-blown criminal offense. Even during the current period of heightened commitment to prosecuting drunk drivers, no state has equated the offense with even low-level felonies like assault or burglary. DWI firmly maintains one foot in traffic law and one foot in criminal law. Furthermore, at least until recently, even those drunk drivers who killed or maimed others were often convicted of a special form of "vehicular" homicide and were not treated severely.

A second reason why criminologists might not think of drunk driving as an important crime is that it does not appear in the FBI Crime Index, which includes the eight offenses that the Bureau deems most serious. The Index tends to be equated in the popular (and perhaps the criminological) mind with "the crime rate." When Americans are told about fluctuations and trends in crime, what they are hearing about is this composite grab bag of offenses which includes burglary, larceny and car theft, but not drunk driving. When Americans ask whether the crime rate is going up or down, they are unlikely to be thinking about the frequency of drunk driving.

These reasons, of course, cannot justify lack of criminological interest. In fact, the placement of DWI in the vehicle and traffic law, and its treatment as less serious than simple assault, larceny, or burglary invite us to ask what characteristics make a crime *serious* both popularly and criminologically? What makes drunk driving less serious than some nonviolent property crimes? It is true that most drunk driving offenses do not cause injury, but the aggregate of drunk driving offenses does constitute a very serious problem. If we count their own deaths, drunk drivers may be responsible for as many deaths per year as all persons arrested for murder and manslaughter. Furthermore, they are responsible for hundreds of thousands of injuries. Perhaps our criminology (and public policy) needs a different approach to low/moderate risk behavior which, if committed on a mass basis, imposes very high social costs.

Criminological reflection on drunk driving's status as a hybrid traffic violation criminal offense would focus our attention on such questions as: (1) why does a particular society choose to criminalize certain harmful behaviors, but not others?; (2) what leads those who draft criminal codes to regard certain offenses as serious and others as trivial?; (3) what causes legislators to redefine conduct as more serious than it was previously judged to be?; (4) why and how does a nation come to define its "crime rate" in terms of the frequency of a small number of offense categories and fail to attend to trends in other offense categories?

Criminologists Are Uncertain about How to Classify Drunk Driving

Drunk driving does not fit easily under any of the standard categories for criminal offenses. It has not been regarded as a "violent" crime, since it is generally not intentional and usually does not involve physical injury. Likewise, it is not classified as a "crime against the person" since it is not directed against particular victims and it may he committed without any personal injury. Finally, drunk driving is unlikely to be classified as a victimless crime since it typically carries a threat of injury to motorists, pedacyclists, and pedestrians. Without a comfortable category in which to code it, the tendency may be to ignore it.

Social-Psychological Blinders

Like the rest of the American public criminologists have an image of the criminal that is based on deeply rooted conceptions of evil and evil doers.[3] Murderers, rapists, thieves, and swindlers play deviant roles that have been handed down to us from time immemorial, but there are no archetypical images of drunk drivers. They are newcomers to the crime scene and their exploits are not celebrated in song or legend. Our society has spawned no infamous drunk drivers to rival Jack the Ripper, Son of Sam, or Jonathan Wild. In fact, drunk drivers are often depicted as feckless and humorous rather than abhorrent and diabolical. The anti-drunk driving groups, recognizing this image problem, have striven to paint the drunk driver as a "killer drunk," but that stereotype may not have taken hold. It is likely that many members of the public still picture the drunk driver as a college student concentrating on getting home safely when he has had too much drink or as a chronic alcoholic who drives the way he lives, in a drunkenly competent manner.

In this way, drunk driving tests our capacity to overcome criminal stereotypes, and to move towards a more rational and utilitarian criminal law that condemns behavior because of the harm or risk it creates, regardless of whether it is ancient and evil or contemporary and irresponsible.

Class and Race Bias

Criminologists may also be unduly influenced by certain sociological correlates of crime. In every society, the lowest classes and racial and ethnic minority groups are disproportionately represented in prison. This reflects not only their unhappy socioeconomic predicament but also the tendency for the socioeconomically advantaged members of society to define the characteristic wrongdoings of the poor and dispossessed, but not their own, as criminal. In the United States, the lower class is disproportionately drawn from racial minorities, a phenomenon that reinforces the majority's fears and inclination to condemn. For the most part, criminology has accepted this emphasis on lower-class wrongdoing.

According to the FBI's Uniform Crime Reports, drunk driving offenders have the highest percentage of white offenders (90 percent) of any arrest group. Clearly, this is not a crime associated with the poor and dispossessed. (In fact, the lower socioeconomic groups include the largest percentage of alcohol abstainers.) Drunk driving is an offense that is often committed by members of the middle and upper classes, or is at least readily conceivable to them. It is understandable, therefore, that social condemnation of this behavior is more muted than the condemnation of "street crime."

If criminologists were to focus more attention on drunk driving, this shift of emphasis might help to break down the stereotypical image of criminals as poor blacks and Hispanics and of law-abiding people as middle- and upper-class whites. Making this point often enough might help to convince the public that criminality is extremely widespread among all social classes and racial groups. While this would not justify the wrongdoings of poor people, it might help to support and encourage more rational and restrained criminal justice politics.

Poor Fit between Ideology and Drunk Driving

Drunk driving is not an offense that makes a critical case for liberals or conservatives. It does not fit easily with such liberal explanations of crime as maldistribution of wealth, different opportunity structures, or poverty and unemployment. Nor does drunk driving resonate with the neo-conservative analysis of crime as rational economic behavior. Even traditional conservatives, who believe that the root cause of crime is "moral dissoluteness," might find drunk driving troubling because of societal ambivalence towards alcohol and alcoholic problems. The disease model of alcoholism has won great acceptance in the United States.

Focusing on drunk driving could further the development of a non-ideological criminology that would recognize the many ways that people injure others and put each other at risk.

Criminal Law Theorists Have Also Ignored Drunk Driving

Drunk driving offers a very rich subject to jurisprudentially oriented scholars. Therefore, it is surprising that criminal law theorists, like their criminological cousins, have virtually ignored this offense. Some of the concepts and issues connected with drunk driving which should whet the jurisprudential appetite are: intoxication, *mens rea*, the status of traffic law, vagueness and notice, and grading. Brief comments follow on each of these.

Intoxication

The impact of alcoholism and intoxication on criminal responsibility is a major conundrum for Anglo-American criminal law. On the one hand, intoxication poses a threat to society since it is often associated with criminality and frequently with violent crime. On the other hand, the Anglo-American jurisprudence of criminal liability posits close connection between intention and culpability. Questions therefore arise as to whether a person who commits an offense while under the influence of alcohol should have an excuse or at least have the degree of guilt mitigated.

The ambivalence of the criminal law is only one expression of a general social uncertainty about alcohol. Despite the strong temperance movement in the late nineteenth and early twentieth centuries, ours has always been a society abounding in alcohol and relatively lenient towards drunken behavior. In the 1960s and 1970s there was a major drive to decriminalize public drunkenness. Many jurisdictions began to treat public inebriates in detoxification centers rather than in the criminal courts and jails. Moreover, commentators began to question the morality and constitutionality of punishing alcoholics for their alcohol-related crimes, an argument narrowly rejected by the United States Supreme Court in *Powell v. Texas* in 1968.[4] Ironically, the criminal law seems to have become more lenient towards intoxication at the same time that it has become increasingly strict with drunk drivers.

In most jurisdictions drunk driving is defined as the operation of a vehicle while intoxicated or with a BAC of .10 or greater. It would be perverse if intoxication were accepted as a defense to a crime which, in effect, criminalizes irresponsible drunkenness. However, legal theorists need to analyze the basis of the moral responsibility of the drunk driver. Can we say that he *intended* to drive drunk? Or that he *knowingly disregarded a risk* that he might drive drunk? Or might we anchor his culpability in the act of getting drunk, or even in starting an evening of drinking? More generally, should the focus of the law be on the decision to drink or on the quality of the driving?

Confusion about Mens Rea of Drunk Driving

Since the advent of the Model Penal Code, a characteristic response to the kind of questions raised here has been to spell out the elements of the offense. More particularly, we should define the *mens rea* (guilty mind) required for conviction, and then determine how it is affected by intoxication. But, with drunk driving, both legislatures and courts have side-stepped this inquiry. Some courts have said that recklessness is required, but that recklessness can be inferred (even presumed) from the decision to drink in the first place! This hardly seems justified, unless it could be said that a person who begins drinking has, in every case, consciously disregarded a risk that he will subsequently operate a vehicle under the influence. But this would not be a reasonable assumption: maybe the drinker was quite sure that he would not get drunk or that he would not have to drive.

The majority of courts which have discussed the *mens rea* of drunk driving have concluded that it is a strict liability offense, thus requiring no proof of any *mens rea*.[5] Because of our traditional reluctance to recognize strict liability offenses this conclusion deserves close scrutiny. Moreover, if drunk driving truly justifies an exception to basic jurisprudential norms in dispensing with the requirement of subjective culpability, there is good reason to limit the severity of the punishments upon conviction.

Unclear Status of Traffic Law

One likely reason why the *mens rea* question has escaped notice is that drunk driving has been classified as a traffic offense rather than a crime, and traffic offenses have sometimes been considered an exception to the rule that requires subjective culpability. The status of traffic law itself is a difficult issue for criminal law jurisprudence. Modern criminal codes tend to define traffic law offenses as "violations," a species of criminal conduct less serious than misdemeanors. The Model Penal Code states explicitly that "violations" are not crimes and should not carry any of the stigma or indicia of true criminal offenses. Thus, the protective rules for the formulation of true crimes need not apply.

Can a rational jurisprudence accept such a labeling approach to criminal law? It might be acceptable if the labels were affixed to different ranges of sanctions. Increasingly, however, this is not so. A first DWI offense is typically defined as a misdemeanor, and a second offense as a felony, with corresponding penalties.

Vagueness and Lack of Notice

Another jurisprudential problem stems from the vagueness of the traditional DWI offense and the lack of notice provided by the more recent drunk driving per se offense (driving with a BAC over .10). It is a basic principle that criminal law should be sufficiently definite that people will not have to guess its prohibitions at their peril. Vagueness of definition also allows the police to apply the law selectively or capriciously. "Driving While Intoxicated" would seem to exemplify many of the features of a vague law. The word "intoxication" is a quality, like "pretty" or "good," which has no precise definition. In fact, some courts have held that a person who is impaired by alcohol to the slightest degree is intoxicated for purposes of the DWI statute. This would hardly conform to the public understanding of drunken driving. Other courts have held that the prosecution must prove that the DWI defendant was so substantially impaired or so intoxicated as to be unable to sign a valid will. Needless to say, neither of these formulations provides exact guidance on what is proscribed; they give the police enormous leeway to arrest anyone whom they consider impaired.

By contrast, there is nothing vague about the provision which makes it a crime to drive with a blood alcohol concentration in excess of .10. Nevertheless, it is worth asking whether such a provision gives a person a fair chance to determine whether his drinking exceeds the permissible limit. Without such an opportunity this type of statute may conflict with the due process norm requiring laws to be drafted in a manner that gives conscientious citizens a practical possibility to conform. How is a person to know that his BAC measurement has risen to the prohibited level? Perhaps it is fair to tell a person that he drinks and drives at his peril, but the occasions for driving after drinking in our society are so frequent as to make this peril considerable indeed.

The Grading of Drunk Driving Is Very Crude

In most jurisdictions, the law distinguishes only two grades of drunk driving. A first offense is a misdemeanor; while a second offense within a rather extended time period (as long as ten years) is a felony. One might ask why driving drunk many years after a first conviction warrants a felony conviction. Is it obvious that such an offender is so much greater a menace than a driver arrested for a first offense?

A better grading system might be tied to the extent of the impairment and the dangerousness of the driving. One possibility would be to create a low-grade drunk driving traffic offense consisting of an impaired effort to drive safely, where no dangerous driving and no injuries have occurred. A more serious drunk driving offense could be defined for highly intoxicated drivers, and those apprehended for driving recklessly or for causing a crash.

Criminology, Jurisprudence, and Criminal Justice Policy

The issues discussed above have significance for a variety of important policy questions surrounding the definition of drunk driving and law enforcement. More research and better conceptualization should lead to better policy making. The following policy options deserve consideration:

Should Drunk Driving Be a Crime at All?

Given the traditional ambivalence towards treating drunk driving as a serious crime, the awkward fit between drunk driving and the criminal law, and the pressures involved in processing almost two million drunk driving cases annually through the criminal justice system, it is worth exploring the option of decriminalizing drunk driving. This does not mean endorsing or legalizing drunk driving; it means, rather, shifting the first line of social control to the transportation system and assigning the lead role to Departments of Motor Vehicles. Under such an approach, the first defense against drunk driving might come through tightening the licensing system, by treating the opportunity to drive as a privilege rather than a right with stricter standards for granting a license and more liberal grounds for revocation. Suspension would still require a due process hearing, but this would be a much quicker and less expensive adjudication than a criminal trial.

If drunk driving were seen primarily as a transportation problem, it would follow that unqualified and potentially dangerous drivers should be removed from the roads. Roadblocks, for example, might be much more acceptable if they were carried out for an administrative purpose— to remove an intoxicated, or otherwise unqualified (by reason of sleepiness, illness, or whatever) driver from the roads. Neither strict liability, vague definitions, lack of notice, nor machine-tested guilt would appear as troublesome in the administrative context as they do in the criminal setting.

If attention were to shift to administrative regulation, we would have to scrutinize more carefully the effectiveness of measures designed to stop people driving. There is a pressing need for empirical research on the success of various types of license suspensions and revocations as well as vehicle impoundments. Sociologists and criminologists must investigate whether conformity with the drivers' license system would begin to break down if the system became more demanding.

Even if administrative law were assigned a more prominent part in the effort to prevent and control drunk driving, the role of the criminal law would continue to be very important. No matter what the mix of criminal and administrative laws, the police are the primary enforcement agency for the transportation system. Under an administrative law model, the institutions of criminal justice would serve as a back-up for use against those who violate the terms of their administrative sanctions. Criminal prosecution would also be appropriate as a primary measure for those who drive very dangerously while drunk and, especially, for those who cause injuries and death

If Drunk Driving Is to Be a Crime, How Should It Be Defined?

We have seen that defining the crime of drunk driving raises some difficult conceptual issues. Perhaps the threshold questions are where and how to draw the line between lawful *drinking and driving* and un-lawful *drunk driving.* How intoxicated or impaired must a driver be to merit sanctions? Does his level of driving competence have to fall below some "objective standard" of minimum competence or capacity, or is it sufficient that the driver's capacity to perform has fallen some percentage short of his personal cold sober best? Are behavioral mea-sures of intoxication (e.g., inability to walk a straight line) sufficient to establish criminal responsibility in the absence of reckless driving?

The issue is an important one. Anti-drunk driving groups have ap-plied pressure to maintain a chemical definition of intoxication and to lower the prohibited BAC threshold, thereby sweeping more people into the criminal law net. The justification for this approach is that a lower prohibited BAC level may deter people from drifting into the higher BAC ranges. A population that has internalized the message that all drinking and driving is bad, will be less likely (inadvertently, recklessly, or intentionally) to drive a vehicle in a highly intoxicated condition. But there are substantial counterarguments. The lower the threshold of law breaking, the more pressure there is on the belea-guered criminal justice system. More importantly, the broader the definition of drunk driving becomes, the less it will be viewed as morally reprehensible conduct. It will come to be seen as normal con-duct which conflicts with an unrealistic norm. A low BAC standard for violations will generate little support for criminal law enforce-ment. By contrast, the higher the prohibited BAC standard, the fewer people will be candidates for drunk driving convictions and the more deviant drunk driving will seem. The criminal law will then be more likely to be accepted as an appropriate response and vigorous en-forcement will be supported.

If Criminal Enforcement Is to Remain the Bulwark of the Response to Drunk Driving (as the 1983 Presidential Commission on Drunk Driving recommended), What Should Be the Standard Punishment?

The United States has mobilized a multifaceted response to drunk driving. Treatment for the driver, license sanctions, education, an in-creased drinking age, and deterrence through torts and insurance law all play a part. But the primary response continues to be arrest and criminal prosecution. The 1983 Presidential Commission on Drunk Driving strongly advocated the primacy of the punishment/deterrence model and even urged that diversion programs be eliminated. Since the early 1980s, the overall trend has been towards greater emphasis on more severe criminal sanctions.

Many anti-drunk driving advocates have proposed mandatory 24–48 hour jail terms for first time drunk driving offenders, and two to four weeks (or longer) mandatory minimums for recidivists. But there are several reasons to be doubtful about the efficacy of mandatory, short term incarceration as a mass response to drunk driving. First, a 24–48 hour jail sentence may serve to trivialize the offense. By suggesting that drunk driving is not really a true crime and need not be treated seriously, it delivers a message contrary to what is intended. This message is probably already understood by sheriffs and jail administrators who, as they desperately try to cope with jail crowding problems, tend to shorten drunk drivers brief jail sentences still further through various discretionary options. Some administrators segregate drunk drivers in special units or even in separate facilities so that they will not be damaged by exposure to "real criminals."

A second problem with the use of incarceration as the basic punishment for drunk drivers concerns the incomplete jurisprudence of drunk driving. Under present law, it is not necessary to prove that a defendant (even one charged with an aggravated drunk driving offense) recklessly or negligently created a substantial risk of injury. The failure of most existing laws to require any proof of culpability in this sense is incompatible with the routine use of incarceration.

The crude grading of DWI makes it difficult to determine a just and appropriate sanction. If mandatory sentences are ever appropriate, it is when the offense is a relatively homogeneous type of behavior which covers only criminal activity of approximately the same culpability and dangerousness. Since drunk driving spans such a vast range of behavior, differentiations need to be made at the sentencing stage, and a great deal of judicial flexibility is necessary.

In light of these problems with mandatory incarceration, there exists an opportunity for criminal justice scholars and strategists to experiment with alternative sanctions for drunk drivers.[6] The political obstacles here are likely to be far less formidable than with most other crimes. The American response to drunk driving has always been multifaceted. Sentences involving treatment and education have been more readily accepted when dealing with drunk drivers than when dealing with other types of offenders. Thus, the ground for creative sentencing has already been prepared.

The basic response to drunk driving should be probation, conditional on six months of home detention on weekend evenings. Since drunk driving is by far most frequent during weekend night hours, keeping drunk drivers at home during this period would have a strong incapacitative effect. House arrest would also provide an appropriate punishment. Practically everyone, especially young bar hoppers and partygoers, will feel that home confinement on Friday and Saturday nights for six months substantially inconveniences social life. Nevertheless, such a sanction is not as difficult to abide by as a full license suspension or revocation, which cuts into economic and social survival.

There will be many offenders who will not abide by this condition of probation. For home detention and other sentencing alternatives to be effective, there must be a credible risk of detection and significant punishment for violations. Electronic monitoring is an appropriate mechanism for enforcing home detention, especially if the cost can be shifted to the defendant (which is often possible with drunk drivers). Offenders who violate the conditions of their home detention should be punished with a significant jail term and a heavy fine. Otherwise, the home detention would not be a credible sanction.

Significant penal sanctions should remain for the most culpable and dangerous drunk drivers—those who have manifested their dangerousness (regardless of their level of intoxication) by driving recklessly or by causing injury. These are highly dangerous offenders who should be treated accordingly.

Conclusion

Drunk driving is not only an important subject in its own right, but it also provides a clear window for viewing general issues of criminology, criminal law jurisprudence, and social control. A close examination of the place of drunk driving in the law of crimes and the politics of crime control will help us to overcome outdated stereotypes about crime and criminals and move us toward a more mature criminology.

Focusing on drunk driving reinforces the important sociological point that the criminal law does not define a generic type of behavior, but only signals a legal response to a variety of behaviors which the political community wishes to condemn and control. For this reason, it is difficult to construct general rules about crimes. Each crime has its own distinctive etiology and patterns: to some extent, we need a separate criminology and jurisprudence for each major offense.

Finally, drunk driving offers an extremely rich subject matter for those who study the sociology of sanctions and social control. It reminds us that criminal law is only one tool in the service of social control, and one that needs to be used intelligently and sparingly.

Notes

This chapter is adapted from a lecture presented on 24 February 1988 to the Alan Fortunoff Criminal Justice Colloquium at New York University School of Law. I am indebted to David Wasserman for assistance in preparing the lecture and this paper and to Graham Hughes for his comments.

1. This was not the first spurt of federal interest. In the early 1970s Congress funded, and the National Highway Traffic Safety Administration implemented, a multi-million dollar action experiment in thirty-five localities. The purpose of this Alcohol Safety Action project was to determine whether a "systems approach" could significantly prevent or reduce drunk driving. While arrests increased dramatically, and various treatments and educational alternatives were widely implemented, evaluators could not confirm a significant effect on drunk driving and the project was terminated. The apparent failure of the "ASAPs" seems not to have dampened the enthusiasm of the initiatives in the 1980s.
2. There is a vast amount of unpublished governmental research on drunk driving. The federally sponsored research is accessible through the National Criminal Justice Reference Service, but much of the state research has to be located at the responsible state agencies. Not surprisingly, the quality of this research is very uneven. Many of the most common claims in the drunk driving literature trace back to one or another of these unpublished and usually uncritical studies.
3. Criminology has generated many classic studies on "jack rollers," embezzlers, professional fences, prostitutes, marijuana users, and armed robbers. These studies attempt to understand how a person becomes a particular type of criminal, how he learns the "craft," and the kind of rationalizations that insulate him from guilt or concern for personal safety. I know of no studies attempting to apply these methods to drunk drivers, perhaps because drunk driving is not considered a criminal activity in the same way as theft, prostitution, or drug use. Perhaps it is assumed that drunk drivers are not "committed" to their offense, do not commit it for economic or psychic gain, and do not have an image of themselves as drunk drivers.
4. 392 U.S. 514 (1988).
5. Depending upon how strict the liability is, the defendant may not even be able to plead that his intoxication was involuntary and that it occurred through no fault of his own.
6. This is already occurring to some extent. In her thorough review of alternative sentencing programs around the United States, Joan Petersilia points out that drunk drivers make up a substantial portion of the caseload in many intensive supervision probation programs and in many home detention/electronic surveillance programs. See Joan Petersilia, *Expanding Options for Criminal Sentencing*, Santa Monica, CA: The Rand Corporation (1987).

References

Gusfield, Joseph, R. 1981. *The Culture of Public Problems: Drinking-Driving and the Symbolic Order*. Chicago: University of Chicago Press.

Jacobs, James B. 1988. *Drunk Driving: An American Dilemma.* Chicago: University of Chicago Press.

Journal of Studies on Alcohol. 1985. Alcohol and Highway Safety: Proceedings of the North American Conference on Alcohol and Highway Safety Held at the Johns Hopkins Medical Institutions, 12–14 June 1984. Supplement no.10.

Laurence, Michael, Franklin Zimring, and John Snortum. 1988. *Social Control of Drunk Driving.* Chicago: University of Chicago Press.

Lender, Mark E. and James K. Martin. 1982. *Drinking in America: A History.* New York: The Free Press.

Moore, Mark H. and Dean R. Gerstein. 1981. *Alcohol and Public Policy: Beyond the Shadow of Prohibition.* Washington, DC: National Academy Press.

Presidential Commission on Drunk Driving. 1983. *Final Report.* Washington, DC: Government Printing Office.

Ross, H. Laurence. 1982. *Deterring the Drinking Driver: Legal Policy and Social Control.* Lexington, MA: Lexington Books.

United States Department of Transportation. 1968. *Alcohol and Highway Safety: Report to the United States Congress.* Washington, DC: Government Printing Office.

4

The Forgotten Criminology of Genocide

William S. Laufer

One evening in March, nearly two years ago, I joined Marvin Wolfgang and Sir Leon Radzinowicz for dinner at a wonderful continental restaurant high above Rittenhouse Square in Philadelphia. From the intellect of Thorsten Sellin to the irreverence of Richard Sparks, the conversation moved from memories of students and mentors to stories about the heavy weights and light weights of American and British criminology. A transcript of the evening's dialogue would be a revealing and provocative oral history of the discipline.

Acknowledging criminology's distinct intellectual boundaries, traditions, and scholarship, I asked why the discipline had neglected any consideration of the crime of genocide? Where were the empirical and theoretical studies of crimes waged during war and times of peace by nation-states against vulnerable ethnic and national groups? Certainly, research on criminal violence, aggression, and victimization must have considered genocide. If not, one must find this scholarship in the efforts of conflict, critical, and Marxist theorists in their explanations of organized, state-sanctioned violence and oppression. Criminologists whose life's work is crime prevention also must regularly discuss the causal factors that lead to acts of genocide.

It may be surprising, but search through every issue of *Criminology* or the *Journal of Criminal Law and Criminology* and you will find only one article on the most serious of all crimes—and that was written by Leo Alexander over forty years ago. Ask students who Polish scholar and jurist Raphael Lemkin was and they will return a blank stare (Lemkin 1944). Look in an undergraduate criminology text and you will be hard pressed to find a single reference to crimes against humanity—no less war crimes (Mueller 1987; Dinstein and Tabory 1996; Lippman 1997;

71

Bassiouni 1997). Ask criminologists about sociological, sociobiologi-
cal, and psychological theories of genocide and most too would not
rise to the challenge (Fein 1993). Why?

There is nothing wrong if answers are not immediately apparent.
Three criminologists, each with a connection to the Holocaust and World
War II, searched in vain for reasons why the scientific study of crime
and deviance as a social phenomenon had somehow forgotten the systematic decimation of one-and-a-half million Armenians by the Young
Turks during World War I (Dadrian 1989; McCormack 1997), the
planned killing of six millions of Jews, and the extermination of another five million *untermenschen,* including Gypsies, political opponents, mentally ill, retarded and other "inferior" peoples between 1941
and 1945 (Staub 1989; Bassiouni 1992). How could criminology have
neglected an examination of the crimes against humanity that resulted
in an estimated seven to sixteen million deaths over the past fifty years
since World War II? Every question asked that evening became rhetorical, and every reason offered was inadequate, revealing more than a
little confusion over the meaning of the word genocide, and its place in
both domestic and international law.[1]

Our explanations failed even though we are not dispassionate over
the deadly plight of the Tutsis and Hutus; the horrific ethnic cleansing
of Muslim Serbs; and the murderous campaign by the Khmer Rouge
that destroyed nearly a fifth of the population of Cambodia in the mid-
to late 1970s (see Harris and Kushen 1996). At that small dining room
table sat a criminologist who fought with the allied troops in World
War II, one who was displaced from his homeland as a result of the
War, and a "second generation" refugee from Nazi Germany who lost
close relatives to starvation, disease, and execution in concentration
camps in Poland and Germany. From the ethnic, religious, and nation-
alistic campaigns of death in Burundi and Uganda, to the inexplicable
killings in Paraguay and Indonesia, we were all too aware of the devas-
tation that is genocide.

In this article, I briefly revisit the unfinished business of that evening
by asking some of the same questions again. What ever happened to the
criminology of genocide? What has criminology lost by its neglect? The
answers, regrettably, remain as inadequate today as they were that evening.
Those offered say much about the almost incredible power of collective
denial, as well as the critical importance of the criminal law in setting a
boundary for the criminological imagination. Noted sociologist Zygmunt
Bauman has concluded that "the Holocaust has more to say about the

state of sociology than sociology in its present shape is able to add to our knowledge of the Holocaust" (1995: 3). Perhaps the same may be said of the state of criminology, and its disregard of genocide.

The Forgotten Criminology

Sir Winston Churchill once characterized the systematic extermination of Jews during World War II as a "crime without a name" (Freedman 1992: 11). Now that this crime has had a name for more than fifty years, it is worth asking why genocide is a crime without a criminology. Some of the more obvious and commonplace reasons are offered below.

Genocide Is a Political Act Reflecting the Will of Sovereignty

In charting the unexplored sociology of genocide, Fein (1993) stopped to observe that: "No stream of sociology or major theorist since 1945 has considered genocide focally, either to explain genocide or to consider its implications for theories of the state, of development, and of community and society. Few sociologists have studied genocide and even fewer attempted a general explanation: this is also true of anthropologists, political scientists and psychologists" (32). Unfortunately, the conventional wisdom in criminology supports Fein's observations by suggesting that acts of genocide fall well outside the boundary of our field.

Genocide, it has been said, is a political rather than criminal act most often employed to enhance the solidarity and unification of nation-states. Decisions to liquidate, exterminate, and cleanse a minority population are matters of political policy reflecting the will and ideologies of sovereignty. Genocide results from a modern, developed, state bureaucratic apparatus that moves the conception of systematic torture and killing from the criminal to the political (Horowitz 1997). The atrocities of genocide are a "...fusion of deviance to a special form of marginality..." (Horowitz 1980: 12).

The fact that acts of genocide often originate from those in sovereign power, the makers of law, the majority rule, seems to prompt a deference to sovereignty that has an immunizing effect. The immorality of genocide is tempered—almost incredibly—by a moral generosity to a sovereign's motivation. The effect of shrouding genocide in a political cloth is to see the annihilation of certain populations as something less than or different from a crime. Needless to say, such generosity is rarely accorded an individual offender.

There is more than a bit of irony here. Few know or recall that the political character of genocide was the subject of significant debate during deliberations by Committees of the United Nations over what subsequently became known as the United Nations Convention on the Prevention and Punishment of Genocide of 1948 (entered into force 12 January 1951) (Lippman 1994). The final form of the Genocide Convention specifically excludes political groups from protection under international law (LeBlanc 1984). The mass executions and inhuman atrocities of the Khmer Rouge, for example, fall outside the Convention as political persecutions.[2]

Instead, the Convention defines the crime of genocide as "acts committed with intent to destroy in whole or in part, a national, ethnical, racial, or religious group" by "killing members of the group, causing serious bodily or mental harm to members of the group, deliberately inflicting on the group conditions of life calculated to bring about their physical destruction in whole or in part, imposing measures intended to prevent births within the group, or forcibly transferring children of the group to another group" (Genocide Convention 1948: 280).[3]

No one would argue that much of the mass killings and many of the acts of genocide since World War II have been politically motivated, have a strong political character or are aimed specifically at certain political groups. For this very reason, some scholars have suggested a distinction between politicide and genocide (Harff and Gurr 1989). The question remains, however, why is it that the political nature and motivation underlying these acts are used to explain the neglect of genocide by criminologists?

Perhaps the answer rests, at least in part, with the critical distinction between the motivation behind acts of genocide and the intention of those responsible for such acts. Discussions of genocide as political, sovereign acts give priority to motive and, in doing so, obscure a consideration of genocidal intent. Acts of genocide, as noted earlier, derive from superior authority, are often clothed in terms of sovereignty and, thus, dismissed as a crime appropriate for criminologists' attention (Horowitz 1997; Chalk and Jonassohn 1990). Characterized as an offense against humanity, however, the motive, legitimate or not, is no longer at issue. In place of motive, the state's intent is material (Simon 1996). As the drafters of the Genocide Convention noted, intention is the critical difference between acts amounting to criminal homicide, and those amounting to genocide where the intention is simply to kill members of a specified group (LeBlanc 1984).

Hannah Arendt's writings about the Holocaust reveal that the intention of crimes against humanity is a violation of the very essence of what it is to be human. What makes genocide the most serious of all crimes is the intention to eliminate an ethnic or religious group—for whatever expressed or unexpressed motive or reason—by eradicating the concept of human being. As Destexhe (1995) recently acknowledged, genocide "...is not an elimination of individuals because they are political adversaries, or because they hold to what are regarded as false beliefs or dangerous theories, but a crime directed against the person as a person, against the very humanity of the individual victim." Ethnic cleansing, starvation, torture, and mass cremations can be discussed as politically motivated acts, but to do so suggests that genocide is a means to an end, rather than an end in itself (Fackenheim 1982).

Genocide as a Breach of International Norms and International Law

Several years ago two groups of victims and representatives of victims from Bosnia-Herzegovina brought an action in federal court under the Alien Tort Claims Act against the president and leader of the Bosnian Serb forces for aggravated sexual assault, forced prostitution and impregnation, various acts of extreme torture, and mass execution (*Kaic v. Karadzic*, 70 F.3d 232 [2d cir. 1995]). The case carried significant symbolic value (Isenberg 1997). Are acts of genocide torts or crimes, violations of international norms or international law? Both before and after the *Karadzic* case, the answers to these questions are far from simple.

To understand the law of genocide, one must appreciate its place in law as an international crime as well as a breach of obligations *erga omnes* (i.e., fundamental obligations toward the international community) (Hoog 1996); the many ways in which the international criminal law has been domesticated in recent years (Osofsky 1997); and how, at the same time, the international law has extended its criminal jurisdiction to acts of internal atrocities (Meron 1995). In addition, to understand the law of genocide, one must see it as both something more than and yet less than a criminal prohibition. Allegations of genocide raise far reaching and profound questions of international norms and obligations, while frustrating such basic and somewhat ministerial matters of jurisdiction and choice of law. Allegations of armed robbery or sexual assault, while some of the most serious offenses, do not engender these normative and political complexities.

Horowitz suggests that conceiving of genocide as a crime in the province of victimology or criminology will necessarily reduce its meaning. Criminologists would no doubt trivialize the political nature of genocide and focus on the victimization of innocents by society. The chances are good that criminologists would assume significant pathology in the perpetrators of genocide, even with mounting evidence of the contrary (Bauman 1985; Goldhagen 1996). These are valid concerns, but they may be well undercut by the work of critical criminologists, who already have cast much light on the oppressive nature of power; the capriciousness of state sponsored violence; and the vulnerability of certain ethnic and racial groups to this "special form of marginality" (Horowitz 1980: 12).

Genocide Is Committed by the State

The history of criminology is marked by a series of intellectual revelations that we now too often take for granted, for example, persons of high socioeconomic status commit crimes (Sutherland 1949); a small number of young chronic offenders commit a disproportionate amount of crime (Wolfgang, Figlio, and Sellin 1972). Of all the many revelations over the last fifty years, criminologists seem to have the most difficulty with the notion that an organization or entity, whether a corporation or nation state, may commit a crime. When crimes are imputed from an individual to an inanimate entity, the intellectual challenge becomes: Should an individual be blamed as well? Don Cressey's critical remarks about the fictionalizing of corporate persons, for example, reveal an all too common hostility to the notion of organizational liability and blame (Cressey 1989). This hostility is reflected in an absence of theoretical deliberation over crimes imputed or attributed to complex business organizations (cf. Paternoster and Simpson 1993). The same may not be said of theories of white collar crime (Weisburd, Wheeler, Waring, and Bode 1991). It is simply easier to theorize about individual offenders—or individuals in groups. Criminological theories of entities challenge an acceptance of anthropomorphic fiction. Scholars get mired in discussions of how and when to attribute blame; how and when to sanction; and who ultimately deserves punishment (Laufer 1994; Schlegel 1990).

Much of the same may be said of genocidal acts perpetrated by nation-states (Rosenne 1996). Our persistent equivocation with bringing those responsible for ethnic cleansing and planned mass murder can be explained, at least in part, by a resistance to the notion that individuals within a "guilty" collective may to be blame for the acts attributed to that entity (Kelsen 1948). This is true even though the common denominator between crimes against the peace; war crimes; and crimes against humanity is individual (personal) responsibility in the form of criminal liability (Dinstein 1996). This common denominator, however, is all but theoretical. From the proceedings of the International Military Tribunal at Nuremberg to the inexcusable delay in establishing a functioning international tribunal to adjudicate claims against those responsible for the killing in the former Yugoslavia and Rwanda, virtually all of the most serious offenders have gone unpunished for their acts of genocide (Lescure and Trintignac 1996; Schaf 1997; Clark and Sann 1996).

Criminologists have spent considerable time fine-tuning sentencing guidelines for state and federal offenses to the point where sanctions are precise penalties; punishments scaled in proportion to the harm done. Driven by desert based theories, the objective is simply to ensure justice. How can this work be reconciled with the failure to bring the most serious of all offenders to justice, no less the absence of any attempt to ensure proportional sanctions for those few convicted of genocide? The objectives of desert theory that now seem so well-entrenched in domestic and international criminal law continue to be frustrated.

The Magnitude of Victimization in Genocide Defies Belief

Criminological research confirms intuitive ratings of crime seriousness from multiple murder to shoplifting (Wolfgang, Figlio, Tracy, and Singer 1985). The differences in seriousness ratings for virtually all offenses are highly objective and quantifiable (Gottfredson, Young, and Laufer 1981). The extent of victimization and harm in genocide, however, strains any assessment of seriousness. Who appreciates differences in seriousness where the offense is, for example, 100,000, 250,000, or 500,000 butchered Hutus or Tutsis? Is there a difference in judgments of offense seriousness between the planned killing of six million versus seven million people?

The perceived difference in seriousness between a single homicide and a double or triple homicide is seen in multiples. Judges may double or triple an offender's sentence. To most, I surmise, the perceived difference in seriousness between six million and seven million deaths is as inconceivable as it is inconsequential. The difference is too great a challenge to one's imagination; an insurmountable challenge where and when there is a vast social distance from the victims. Commentators have noted comparable effects—genocide is "beyond the realm of possible" (Lipstadt 1986: 136); it occurs in "an unimaginable environment, one that no human mind, not even the most perverse could have conjured in fiction" (Bartov 1996: 33).

Perhaps genocide is so unimaginable—so difficult to grasp because of its magnitude—that its scientific study appears imprudent. This view would be acceptable if criminologists were no better than the empiricists of the 1800s. Over the past fifty years, however, the techniques and methods of empiricism have moved from the naïve to the scientific. Research on victimization, perceptions of crime severity, estimation of loss and harm can and should be extended to genocide. The importance of this work is underscored by the efforts of historical revisionists to further exploit the limits of human imagination (Lipstadt 1994; Butz 1980). Raising doubts about the magnitude of death plays into the hands of the perpetrators of genocide and, effectively, continues the process of dehumanization. Ignoring genocide, it can be argued, has a similar effect.

Criminology Has Little to Offer the Study of Genocide

Bauman's (1995) fascinating critique of genocide as a product of modernity raises the question as to what sociology has to offer as an explanation of the Holocaust. In dismissing the Holocaust as resulting from a breakdown of social and moral order; the result of primeval predispositions and social pathology; and an extreme example of ethnic, cultural, and racial persecution, we are offered a simple and somewhat elegant alternative hypothesis. The Holocaust resulted from the very institutions, processes, and priorities that comprise modern civilization. Those responsible for the killing were of normal mind, freely and rationally choosing self-preservation over moral duty. The lesson of the Holocaust, Bauman concludes, is that "[i]n a system where rationality and ethics point in opposite directions, humanity is the main loser" (1995: 206).

What makes Bauman's argument so interesting is how it frames the boundary of the sociology of genocide. On the one hand, there is a small, but growing body of literature that sees genocide as an extreme form of social control (Horowitz 1980), a product of personal and social pathology; failures in social structure, group and intergroup relations, as well as conflict theory (Chalk and Jonassohn 1980; Cohn 1977;

Dadrian 1974; Fein 1993; Harff and Gurr 1989; Kuper 1981; Mazian 1990; Rubenstein 1983). On the other hand, Bauman's thesis suggests that genocide, more generally, is a natural product of modern society; a product of the very institutions that criminologists claim provide the social controls that deter those prone to crime. This divergence of theory is all too familiar to criminologists; so familiar that we cannot afford to ignore this important body of work.

The Problems of Denying and Admitting Atrocity

Two prominent themes that emerge from the literature on genocide capture an ambivalence hard felt by some survivors and refugees of genocide. This ambivalence is captured in the titles of two recently published books on the Holocaust—Deborah Lipstadt's *Denying the Holocaust* (1994) and Lawrence L. Langer's *Admitting the Holocaust* (1995). Oddly enough, criminology in its neglect of genocide may have fallen prey as well.

Of course, no one would argue that criminology has embraced the rhetoric of revisionists. If there is a problem of "denial," it is collective and disciplinary. Likewise, no one would argue that there is any problem with securing an admission that acts of unspeakable horror have occurred and continue to occur. The problem of admission is with the casting of genocide as a phenomenon requiring serious study; the effects of intellectualizing mass torture and death; the packaging of the Holocaust, for example, neatly into a social science; and the elevation of genocide to a respectable academic discipline of its own, with courses that fit a core curriculum, and endowed Holocaust professorships.

Survivors, victims, and refugees resist the conscious and unconscious denial of genocide. Increasingly, all are more aware of the risks of admission; the dangers of "Americanizing" and "cleansing" the horrors of genocide so that the Diary of Anne Frank plays well on Broadway and Hollywood can sell wide-screen images of individual altruism during the Holocaust (Melnick 1997; van der Vat 1997). It is no exaggeration that genocide stands between repression and canonization (LaCapra 1994). Criminology, like all the social sciences, bears the burden and risks of both denial and admission.

Missed Opportunities

Toward the end of the dinner that memorable evening, Marivn, Sir

Leon, and I noted the distinct boundaries of criminology. What had happened to a field that was barely a century old? What had happened to a field that was still defining itself no less than a decade ago? The internal structure of criminology, we agreed, was so well-defined that its textbooks were nearly indistinguishable; its journals revisited and repackaged the same ideas and issues; and its annual conferences divided this once dynamic and changing field into generic, well-worn subject areas.

In this generation, our generation, the field of criminology had matured. Unfortunately, it has done so without considering the most serious of all crimes. Much has been and will be lost as the sociology of genocide continues to mature in spite of our neglect. Consider how the criminology of genocide would add to our knowledge of victimization, homicide, aggression, and violence. Consider, as well, how research on genocide might support the theoretical work of critical and Marxist scholars in their efforts to explain a different conception of the state in relation to crime. Most important, reflect on the contribution that criminologists could make to further our understanding as to how genocide may be prevented. Nowhere are matters of prevention more important than with the crime of genocide.

It is all too easy to say that criminology's neglect of genocide suggests a disciplinary denial; that our failure to recognize genocide implicitly contributes to the evil of revisionism; and that we should know better than to have the boundaries of our field permanently fixed by the criminal law—especially where extant law is so frail and uncertain. It is all too easy to say these things, because they are true.

Notes

This chapter is dedicated to Edith A. Laufer, whose understanding of the trauma of the Holocaust will be felt for many generations to come.

1. Lemkin derived the word in 1944 by combining the Ancient Greek word *genos* (race or tribe) and the Latin word *cide* (killing). Genocide is a crime under U.S. and international law.
2. Drafters of the 1948 Convention sought a compromise position that would effectively protect political leaders for their decisions affecting state sovereignty, e.g. the right of a nation-state to suppress internal disturbances. In fact, the effect of this exclusion was to effectively guarantee immunity to those leaders or groups who engaged in mass killings of political groups (Van Schaack 1997).
3. Due in part to the exclusion of political groups from the Convention's definition, the United States resisted its ratification for forty years. Finally, this limited and arguably inadequate definition was adopted by Congress when the United States

ratified the convention on 19 February 1986, making genocide a federal crime (18 U.S.C. §§ 1091–1093 [1988]).

References

Bartov, Omer. 1996. *Murder in Our Midst: The Holocaust, Industrial Killing, and Representation.* New York: Oxford.

Bassiouni, M. Cherif. 1992. *Crime against Humanity in International Law.* New York: Oceana.

Bassiouni, M. Cherif. 1997. *International Criminal Law Conventions and Their Penal Provisions.* Irvington-on-Hudson, NY: Transnational Publications.

Bauman, Zygmunt. 1995. *Modernity and the Holocaust.* Ithaca, NY: Cornell University Press.

Butz, Arthur. 1980. "The International Holocaust Controversy," *Journal of Historical Review* 1: 5–22.

Cressey, Donald. 1989. "The Poverty of Theory in Corporate Crime Research," *Advances in Criminological Theory* 1: 31–55.

Dadrian, Vahkan N. 1989. "Genocide as a Problem of National and International Law: The World War I Armenian Case and its Contemporary Legal Ramifications," *Yale Journal of International Law* 14: 221–334.

Destexhe, Alain. 1995. *Rwanda and Genocide in the Twentieth Century.* New York: NYU Press.

Dinstein, Yoram and Mala Tabory. 1996. *War Crimes in International Law.* The Hague: Martinus Nijhoff.

Fackenheim, Emil. 1982. *To Mend the World.* New York: Schocken.

Fein, Helen. 1993. *Genocide: A Sociological Perspective.* London: Sage.

Goldhagen, Daniel J. 1996. *Hitler's Willing Executioners: Ordinary Germans and the Holocaust.* New York: Vintage.

Gottfredson, Stephen D., Kathy Young, and William S. Laufer. 1980. "Additivity and Interactions in Offense Seriousness Scales," *Journal of Research in Crime and Delinquency* 17: 26–41.

Harris, Kenneth J. and Robert Kushen. 1996. "Surrender of Fugitives to the War Crimes Tribunal for Yugoslavia and Rwanda: Squaring International Legal Obligations with the United States Constitution," *Criminal Law Forum* 7: 561–604.

Horowitz, Irving Louis. [1980]1997. *Taking Lives: Genocide and State Power.* New Brunswick, NJ: Transaction Publishers.

Isenberg, Beth A. 1997. "Genocide, Rape, and Crimes against Humanity: An Affirmation of Individual Accountability in the Former Yugoslavia in the Karadzic Actions," *Albany Law Review* 60: 1051–79.

Kelsen, H. 1948. "Collective and Individual Responsibility for Acts of State in International Law," *Jewish Yearbook of International Law* 226.

Kuper, Leo. 1981. *Genocide: Its Political Use in the Twentieth Century.* New Haven, CT: Yale University Press.

Dominick LaCapra. 1994. *Representing the Holocaust: History, Theory, Trauma* (Ithaca, NY: Cornell University Press.

Langer, Lawrence L. 1995. *Admitting the Holocaust: Collected Essays* (New York: Oxford.

Laufer, William S. 1994. "Corporate Bodies and Guilty Minds." *Emory Law Journal* 43: 647–730.

LeBlanc, Lawrence. 1984. "The Intent to Destroy Groups in the Genocide Convention: The Proposed U.S. Understanding," *American Journal of International Law* 78: 369–85.

Lemkin, Raphael. 1944. *Axis Rule in Occupied Europe.* Washington, DC: Carnegie Endowment for International Peace.

Lescure, Karine and Florence Trintignac. 1996. *International Justice for Former Yugoslavia.* The Hague: Kluwer Law.

Lippman, Matthew. 1994. "The 1948 Convention on the Prevention and Punishment of the Crime of Genocide: Forty-five Years Later," *Temple International and Contemporary Law Journal*, 8, 1–84.

———. 1997. "Crimes against Humanity," *Boston College Third World Law Journal* 17: 171–273.

Lipstadt, Deborah. 1986. *Beyond Belief.* New York: The Free Press.

———. 1993. *Denying the Holocaust.* New York: Plume.

McCormack, Timothy L.H. 1997. "Selective Reaction to Atrocity: War Crimes and the Development of International Criminal Law," *Albany Law Review* 60, 681–770.

Melnick, Ralph. 1997. *The Stolen Legacy of Anne Frank.* New Haven, CT: Yale University Press.

Meron, Theodore. 1995. "International Criminalization of Internal Atrocities," *American Journal of International Law* 89: 554–77.

Mueller, G.O.W. 1987. "Four Decades after Nuremberg: The Prospect of an International Criminal Code," *Connecticut Journal of International Law* 499.

Osofsky, Hari M. 1991. "Domesticating International Criminal Law: Bringing Human Rights Violators to Justice," *Yale Law Journal* 107: 191–226.

Paternoster, Raymond and Simpson, Sally. 1993. "A Rational Choice Theory of Corporate Crime," *Advances in Criminological Theory* 5: 37–58.

Schlegel, Kip. 1990. *Just Deserts for Corporate Criminals.* Boston: Northeastern University Press.

Rosenne, Shabtai. 1996. "War Crimes and State Responsibility," in Y. Dinstein and M. Tabory, *War Crimes in International Law.* The Hague: Martinus Nijhoff.

Sharf, Michael P. 1997. *Balkan Justice: The Story behind the First International War Crimes Trial since Nuremberg.* Durham, NC: Carolina Academic Press.

Simon, Thomas W. 1996. "Defining Genocide," *Wisconsin International Law Journal*, 243.

Staub, Ervin. 1996. *The Roots of Evil: The Origins of Genocide and Other Group Violence* New York: Cambridge.

Sutherland, Edwin H. 1949. *White Collar Crime.* New York: Dryden.

van der Vat, Dan. 1997. *The Life and Lies of Albert Speer: The Good Nazi.* Boston: Houghton Mifflin.

Van Schaack, Beth. 1997. "The Crime of Political Genocide: Repairing the Genocide Convention's Blind Spot," *Yale Law Journal* 106: 2259–91.

Weisburd, David, Stanton Wheeler, Elin Waring, and Nancy Brode. 1991. *Crimes of the Middle Classes: White Collar Offenders in the Federal Courts.* New Haven, CT: Yale University Press.

Wolfgang, Marvin E., Robert Figlio, and Thorsten Sellin. 1972. *Delinquency in a Birth Cohort.* Chicago: University of Chicago Press.

Wolfgang, Marvin E., Robert Figlio, Paul E. Tracy, and Simon I. Singer. 1985. *National Survey of Crime Severity.* Washington, DC: U.S. Government Printing Office.

5

Criminologists as Expert Witnesses in Criminal Law Cases: The Growing Intersection between Criminology and Criminal Law

Deborah W. Denno

The current and future intersection between criminology and criminal law is aptly evidenced by the use of criminologists as expert witnesses in criminal law cases. When defense attorneys or prosecutors employ criminologists as experts, the criminal justice system acknowledges the value of criminology for deciphering the particular criminal law case at issue and also for determining future cases.

And why not use criminologists as experts, asks Donald Newman in his foreword to *Expert Witnesses: Criminologists in the Courtroom* (Newman 1987). Why restrict scientific contributions to psychiatrists and physical scientists who, unlike criminologists, "contribute little to the broader practices and policies of our criminal justice system" (ix). Patrick Anderson and Thomas Winfree recognize that criminologists' expert testimony "has formed the basis of some of the United States Supreme Court's most sensitive, far-reaching decisions" (Anderson and Winfree 1987: xvi). They emphasize that "virtually any one of these decisions has brought about more and faster change in the criminal justice system than all the various federal commissions and task forces combined" (xvi).

The criminologist's key authority for providing expert testimony is Marvin Wolfgang's heralded article, "The Social Scientist in Court" (1974). No article has ever broached the issue of the criminologist as expert with such acumen and detail in part because no criminologist before Wolfgang had ever contributed such critical in-court testimony.

In "Social Scientist," Wolfgang discusses the ethical issues and conflicts of interest he has encountered while testifying (Wolfgang 1974). He focuses in particular on the evidence he provided in federal district court in Arkansas in connection with the well known case, *Maxwell v. Bishop* (1966), which was ultimately brought before the United States Supreme Court. Wolfgang's evidence in *Maxwell* was based on a 1965 study of over 3,000 rape convictions recorded between 1945–65 in 230 counties in eleven states. The study demonstrated striking racial disparities among defendants who received the death penalty for the crime of rape. For example, black defendants convicted of raping white victims were sentenced to death about eighteen times more often than defendants representing any other racial combination of defendant and victim (Wolfgang 1974).

The *Maxwell* district court considered Wolfgang's evidence to be "more extensive and sophisticated" than any other evidence the court had viewed previously (*Maxwell* 1966: 719). Yet, the *Maxwell* court did not believe the evidence established a practice of unconstitutional racial discrimination among Arkansas juries or that the particular jury in the *Maxwell* case was racially motivated when it selected the death penalty (*Maxwell* 1966).

Looking back, the *Maxwell* court's conclusion is not surprising. The legal and political repercussions of accepting Wolfgang's results would have been highly unpredictable. Moreover, the criminal justice system rarely initiates change, even when change is warranted. Regardless, the fact that the *Maxwell* court allowed Wolfgang's testimony to provide the central focus of such an important case was, given the political circumstances, a stunning sign of progress.

The *Maxwell* court's evidentiary openness also spurred the start of several remarkable trends demonstrating the intersection between criminology and criminal law: (1) courts' increasing acceptance of criminological research as evidence in criminal law cases (the *Maxwell* court could have excluded Wolfgang's testimony and evidence altogether); (2) courts' growing recognition of criminologists as experts in criminal law cases (Wolfgang's qualifications to testify in *Maxwell* were "established" and never questioned); and (3) courts' recognition that criminological research could potentially demonstrate that some aspects of the criminal justice system are unconstitutional. These trends also prompted the concept of the "criminologist as expert" in criminal law cases, illustrated by Anderson and Winfree's compilation of the testifying experiences of "the best, brightest criminologists" (Newman 1987: x).

The in-court experiences of Wolfgang and other testifying criminologists have extended way beyond *Maxwell*, although the unconstitutional practices of the death penalty remain a major focus (Baldus, Woodworth, and Pulaski 1990; Radelet 1987). Other areas of criminology that have influenced criminal law doctrine include research on police use of deadly force, prison deprivations and the survival techniques of inmates, criminal homicide, jury decision making, DNA evidence, past criminal record as a predictor of crime, plea bargaining, the different syndromes (e.g., rape trauma, child sexual abuse), and eyewitness identification. The hypothetical list is endless.

Relative to other professionals, then, criminologists typically do not view themselves as potential expert witnesses, although it is well time they should. Those criminologists who have testified have achieved a marked impact on the development of the criminal law. Criminal law doctrine in turn helps direct research in the field of criminology. "[A]s findings from social and behavioral sciences become increasingly relevant to the resolution of legal issues...the number of cases employing this disciplinary mix should increase" (Wolfgang 1974: 247). Without question, this "disciplinary mix" will be all for the betterment of both criminology and criminal law.

Note

I am most grateful to Jorene Robbie for research assistance.

References

Anderson, P.R., and L.T. Winfree, Jr. 1987. "Prologue," in P.R. Anderson and L.T. Winfree, Jr. (eds.), *Expert Witnesses: Criminologists in the Courtroom*. Albany, NY: State University of New York Press.

Baldus, D.C., G.G. Woodworth, and C. Pulaski, Jr. 1990. *Equal Justice and the Death Penalty: A Legal and Empirical Analysis*. Boston: Northeastern University Press.

Maxwell v. Bishop. 1966. 257 F. Supp. 710.

Newman, D.J. 1987. "Foreword," in P.R. Anderson and L.T. Winfree, Jr. (eds.) *Expert Witnesses: Criminologists in the Courtroom*. Albany, NY: State University of New York Press.

Radelet, M.L. 1987. "Sociologists as Expert Witnesses in Capital Cases: A Case Study" in P.R. Anderson and L.T. Winfree, Jr. (eds.) *Expert Witnesses: Criminologists in the Courtroom*. Albany, NY: State University of New York Press.

Wolfgang, M.E. 1974. "The Social Scientist in Court." *The Journal of Criminal Law and Criminology* 65: 239–47.

6

The Measurement of Police Delinquency

Carl B. Klockars and
Sanja Kutnjak Ivkovich

Introduction

How serious is acceptance of a bribe by a police officer? How serious is acceptance of a free meal or holiday gifts? How serious is excessive use of force by police officers? In more general terms is theft more serious than assault? As Wolfgang et al. (1985: v) argue,

> Implicit judgments about the severity of crime are imbedded in our social institutions. Requiring the death penalty for certain crimes designates them as the most serious that can occur in this society. Crimes labeled felonies are considered more serious than those labeled misdemeanors. Crimes that can incur life sentences are more serious than those that receive prison sentences of only a few years.

However, as Wolfgang et al. (1985) further describe, relying on legal categories may be problematic. Some jurisdictions may criminalize certain actions, while other jurisdictions may not even consider these same actions to be illegitimate (e.g., marital rape). Even when the same action is criminalized in various jurisdictions, the penalties prescribed may vary. Furthermore, the actual enforcement of legal norms and the punishments may differ from judge to judge. In addition, the prescribed punishments may change over time in the same jurisdiction (e.g., adultery, drug use, driving under the influence). How do the criminal law punishments compare with the disciplinary punishments for the members of a particular profession? Is a prison sentence a more or less lenient punishment than revoking a medical license?

Interest in criminal statistics has existed for a long time, but the first systematic means of supplying the basic data for the measurement of criminality started with the collection of judicial criminal statistics in the 1820s in France and was soon followed in other countries (Sellin and Wolfgang 1964). Official classifications of crime, that is, arrest data, judicial statistics, typically rely on legal categorizations and labels, which, as was pointed out earlier, may be problematic. Sellin and Wolfgang (1964: 19) described various problems associated with official measures of crime and Sellin proposed that "[t]he value of a crime rate for index purposes decreases as the distance from the crime itself in terms of procedure increases." Furthermore, they were among the first to illustrate that some types of offenses may be more likely to be affected by police activity than other types, and that, consequently, official statistics on crime are likely to vary considerably more for some types of crimes than for others. Because Sellin and Wolfgang (1964: 1) concluded that police statistics did not provide an adequate basis for the scientific measurement of criminality, they undertook a task of designing an instrument that would "measure or provide an index to the degree and the nature of changes in delinquency over a period of time in a population exposed to the preventive activity."

They determined that both the frequency of crimes and the seriousness of crimes must be used in the design of a weighted index—an alternative to the traditional way of indexing offenses. They wrote (1964: 42) that

A more useful classification of offenses for the purposes of measurement would be one based on their relative seriousness in terms of injury caused to the victim's person or property...and on the degree of public disapproval of an offense, as determined by a sampling of public opinion or by a grading of official measures taken for its repression.

In the search of such evaluations of relative seriousness or the seriousness scale of delinquent acts, Sellin and Wolfgang (1964) distributed questionnaires containing up to thirty descriptions of offenses. In the context of the current paper it is interesting to highlight two groups of their respondents. They distributed questionnaires to undergraduate students arguing that they had middle-class values and were, consequently, very important as respondents because "the definition of crime and the administration of criminal justice are institutionalized expressions of the normative structure of the dominant middle class in American society" (1964: 250). Furthermore, the questionnaires were also distributed to police officers, who exhibited an interesting combination of characteristics. They were perceived to belong to the lower stratum based on their education, occupation, and income, while, at the same time, as a part of their job, they needed to enforce the legal rules which embody middle-class values.

The seriousness of the offenses about which these and other groups were surveyed was evaluated by them either on an eleven-level category scale or on an unrestricted magnitude scale. Finally, the "primary index scale" was created based on the original twenty-one descriptions of the offenses, and Sellin and Wolfgang (1964: 268) concluded that

> [t]he most strongly supported conclusion on the basis of the data at hand is that all the raters, although unconstrained in their use of the magnitude scale assignments, tended to so assign the magnitude estimations that the seriousness of the crimes is evaluated in a similar way, without significant differences, by all the groups...A pervasive social agreement about what is serious and what is not appears to emerge, and this agreement transcends simple qualitative concordance; it extends to the estimated numerical degree of seriousness of these offenses.

Sellin and Wolfgang (1964: 275) also compared the results for various groups both in terms of the absolute values and ratios, and they wrote that, based on the responses on the unrestricted magnitude scale,

> although absolute numerical scores varied among rating groups, with the police scores generally higher, the inherent ratio quality of the magnitude judgments means that the numbers used by the raters are not particularly relevant and that the only fact of real importance is the ratios of offense seriousness which are preserved intact.

This ground-breaking study by Sellin and Wolfgang (1964) spurred a waive of interest among social scientists. In the wake of their pioneering effort, other researchers began examining whether the same scale might be used in other cultures, whether different groups within one country share the same understanding about the seriousness of offenses, whether the characteristics of the victims and offenders make a difference in terms of estimated seriousness, and how to improve the methodology and analysis used in the study.

Sellin and Wolfgang (1964) did not appear to be much concerned about the different voices either in the same societies or across societies because their goal was finding common elements. As Wolfgang et al. (1985: 7) explained:

> Unlike light or loudness, crime severity is a culturally determined entity...the very existence of a crime depends on one's culture defining an event as such. Thus it would be expected that, across the spatio-temporal boundaries of different

cultural and subcultural groups, the perceptions of the relative severity of crime would change...Sellin and Wolfgang were concerned primarily with the construction of an instrument which would provide another kind of indicator of crime trends in addition to the presently used UCR index. As such, they focused on the consensual aspects of the scale by assuming that variation in seriousness perception surrounding a given event constitutes error or "noise" and that true point-estimates are provided through calculation of geometric means.

Researchers studying the application of the scale crossculturally wanted to determine whether there is a common, shared understanding of crime severity so that the cultural elements can be really treated as "noise," or whether these cultural elements have a much greater impact on the severity scores and should be, consequently, appropriately taken into account. Starting from the first replication project conducted in Canada (Normandeau 1966), the results of that and the later studies (e.g., Velez-Diaz and Megargee 1971; Hsu 1973; Kvalseth 1980) pointed that there is, indeed, a high degree of shared understanding across cultures in terms of offense seriousness. Using the same or very similar methodology, researchers typically found that correlations of U.S. data with data from other countries, especially the Western cultures, were very high (Pearson correlation coefficient typically around or even above .80), while a smaller slope coefficient is reported for crosscultural comparisons (.60 in Hsu's study, 1973; .62 in Kvalseth's study [1980] for the comparison with the Canadian data and .60 for the comparison with the U.S. data) than for comparisons within a country. Hsu (1973) suggests that "noise" may have an impact and explained that these differences were a consequence of a culture of the Taiwan society which tended to be quite different from the American or Canadian cultures.

Similarly, studies comparing the severity estimates by various groups belonging to the same society suggest the same pattern. It seems that there is a general understanding shared by the majority in the society, but cultural differences may exist and influence the estimates of seriousness. In two of the studies (Velez-Diaz and Megargee 1971; Figlio 1975) the researchers compared the estimates of seriousness provided by convicted offenders to the estimates provided by non-offenders and concluded that there was a high degree of similarity in terms of relative seriousness, but the range of absolute values varied across groups (Figlio 1975) as did the distances among offenses (Figlio 1975). A comparison of the ratings of the offenses by police officers and students in the study by Kelly and Winslow (1970) yielded no significant differences and, therefore, provided support for the assumption that seriousness of crimes may be a widely shared understanding.

The influence of demographic characteristics of the respondents was examined in several other studies. Rossi et al. (1974) found that there was a presence of a strong consensus among groups of respondents. When ratings for various groups were compared to the overall sample ratings, they yielded high correlation coefficients (equal to or above .86). However, they also reported that there were differences among groups in terms of seriousness estimates. African-Americans and women evaluated offenses as being more serious than did Caucasians and men respectively. In a subsequent study, Rossi et al. (1985) also reported differences between the estimates of seriousness by the African-American respondents (more severe in the judgment about the property, victimless, and white-collar crimes, but less severe in the cases of crimes against persons) to those by the Caucasian respondents. Even the later national study of crime seriousness conducted by Wolfgang et al. (1985) provided similar results. Wolfgang et al. (1985: vi) wrote:

> In general, people tend to agree about the severity of specific crimes. A few differences appear, however, when the scores of different groups are examined. For example, blacks and members of other racial groups in general assign lower scores than whites. Older people found thefts of large amounts to be more serious than people in younger age brackets. Men and women, however, did not differ in any significant way in their overall scoring pattern. As might be expected, victims assign higher scores than nonvictims.

Even the demographic characteristics of the offenders and victims included in the descriptions of the cases may influence people's judgments of severity. For example, the respondents in the study by Wolfgang et al. (1985) evaluated a scenario describing a man stabbing and killing his wife as more serious than an identical scenario describing a wife stabbing and killing her husband. Similarly, Rossi et al. (1985) reported that there were significant differences in evaluation of the offenses with respect to the gender of the offender, whereas, with respect to the race of the offender, differences were limited to certain types of crimes.

Some researchers proposed a more detailed descriptions of the crimes to be used in the subsequent research, especially in terms of the characteristics of the offenders and victims (e.g., Parton et al. 1991) and also questioned the additivity of the scale of offense seriousness developed by Sellin and Wolfgang (e.g., Gottfredson et al. 1980).

Measuring Police Delinquency

In the spirit of the research conducted by Sellin and Wolfgang, we examined the estimates of seriousness of scenarios describing a rarely studied subset of delinquency—police delinquency. We describe cases of police corruption, involving typical forms of corruption, such as theft, bribes, and kickbacks, as well as some forms of behavior that may not necessarily be criminal but may be a violation of departmental policy (e.g., acceptance of free meals and holiday gifts). Furthermore, we also included a scenario describing a use of excessive force by police officers. We compare the seriousness of these forms of police misconduct based on the estimates of seriousness from two groups of respondents with no experience in policing (students) and those with a great deal of experience in policing (active police officers). In addition, we also provide a crosscultural comparison of these issues using questionnaires from police officers and students in two countries—the United States and Croatia.

The Research Design

In April of 1995 we designed and pretested a questionnaire that sought to accomplish three goals. First, we sought to obtain the estimates of the seriousness of a variety of cases of police delinquency and compare them across groups of respondents which differ with respect to their experience in policing and with respect to their cultural background. Our second aspiration in designing our questionnaire was to do so in a manner that would permit its administration crossculturally. This aspiration presented some interesting design problems that we shall discuss below. Third, we wanted the questionnaire to be designed in such a way as to assist in providing answers in a systematic, standardized, quantitative manner to two questions that are crucial to both an organizational/occupational-culture theory of police corruption and practical police administration: (1) What is the level of knowledge of organizational rules governing corruption?; (2) How strongly does the occupational culture condemn the behavior that those rules prohibit?

To accomplish these ends we designed a questionnaire that presented eleven brief scenarios (figure 6.1) describing practices that would be recognizable to police in any modern, industrial society. Included in these eleven scenarios were nine that described behavior generally regarded as corrupt, one that described an incident of intentional use of excessive force, and another that described a behavior—conducting an off-duty, security system business—that is permitted by policy in some police agencies and prohibited in others. The order in which the scenarios appear in the questionnaire was random.

We did not attempt to describe in these eleven case scenarios the full range of possibilities of police corruption or police delinquency. Our major concerns in the design of the scenarios were to offer scenarios that would/could be described briefly, represented a range of severity, and would constitute a believable temptation to patrol officers to abuse their office. We intentionally excluded corruption scenarios that involved high level administrators, special units, sting operations, and other areas and types of policing that we could not be confident were common to the experience of all of our respondents. There were no different conditions in the scenarios; all of the respondents read the same eleven case descriptions.

Respondents were asked seven questions about each of these scenarios (figure 6.2). Questions 1 and 2 ask about *seriousness*; question 3 asks whether or not the described behavior constitutes a *violation of official policy*; questions 4 and 5 ask about appropriate and expected *discipline;* and questions 6 and 7 ask about the Code or *willingness to report* misconduct.

The question about the respondent's own evaluation of the seriousness contained a five-point category scale. Consequently, and unlike the magnitude estimation scale used in Sellin and Wolfgang's work (1964), this type of scale limits the respondents in the range of values they can assign or select. Therefore, instead of just focusing on the relative scores, we will also examine the differences in absolute numbers.

Issues in the Crosscultural Measurement of Corruption

Because we sought to use this questionnaire in a fairly large number of crosscultural applications, special attention was given to creating case scenarios that were as near as possible culturally neutral in the sense that they would describe situations familiar to citizens and represent equivalent acts in any modern industrial society.

The first problem that a study of corruption (a form of police delinquency or police abuse of authority *for gain*) faces in achieving cultural neutrality of this kind is the different meaning of money in different cultures. A bribe of U.S.$50 has a clearly different meaning to a U.S. police officer who earns $30,000 per year and an Eastern European police officer who earns the annual equivalent of U.S.$4,000. Conversion of U.S. currency to the currency of some other nation at prevailing exchange rates does not solve this problem as the stimulus of a U.S.$50 bribe will be different in the economic life of each officer.

FIGURE 6.1
Corruption Case Scenarios

Case 1	A police officer runs his own private business in which he sells and installs security devices, such as alarms, special locks, etc. He does this work during his off-duty hours.
Case 2	A police officer routinely accepts free meals, cigarettes, and other items of small value from merchants on his beat. He does not solicit these gifts and is careful not to abuse the generosity of those who give gifts to him.
Case 3	A police officer stops a motorist for speeding. The officer agrees to accept a personal gift of half of the amount of the fine in exchange for not issuing a citation.
Case 4	A police officer is widely liked in the community, and on holidays local merchants and restaurant and bar owners show their appreciation for his attention by giving him gifts of food and liquor.
Case 5	A police officer discovers a burglary of a jewelry shop. The display cases are smashed and it is obvious that many items have been taken. While searching the shop, he takes a watch, worth about two days pay for that officer. He reports that the watch had been stolen during the burglary.
Case 6	A police officer has a private arrangement with a local auto body shop to refer the owners of the cars damaged in the accidents to the shop. In exchange for each referral, he receives a payment of 5 percent of the repair bill from the shop owner.
Case 7	A police officer, who happens to be a very good auto mechanic, is scheduled to work during coming holidays. A supervisor offers to give him these days off, if he agrees to tune-up his supervisor's personal car. Evaluate the SUPERVISOR'S behavior.
Case 8	At 2 A.M. a police officer, who is on duty, is driving his patrol car on a deserted road. He sees a vehicle that has been driven off the road and is stuck in a ditch. He approaches the vehicle and observes that the driver is not hurt but is obviously intoxicated. He also finds that the driver is a police officer. Instead of reporting this accident and offense he transports the driver to his home.
Case 9	A police officer finds a bar on his beat which is still serving drinks a half hour past its legal closing time. Instead of reporting this violation, the police officer agrees to accept a couple of free drinks from the owner.
Case 10	Two police officers on foot patrol surprise a man who is attempting to break into an automobile. The man flees. They chase him for about two blocks before apprehending him by tackling him and wrestling him to the ground. After he is under control both officers punch him a couple of times in the stomach as punishment for fleeing and resisting.
Case 11	A police officer finds a wallet in a parking lot. It contains the amount of money equivalent to a full day's pay for that officer. He reports the wallet as lost property, but keeps the money for himself.

FIGURE 6.2
Case Scenario Assessment Options

---

1. How serious do YOU consider this behavior to be?
   Not at all serious   Very serious
       1   2   3   4   5

2. How serious do MOST POLICE OFFICERS IN YOUR AGENCY consider this behavior to be?
   Not at all serious   Very serious
       1   2   3   4   5

3. Would this behavior be regarded as a violation of official policy in your agency?
   Definitely not   Definitely yes
       1   2   3   4   5

4. If an officer in your agency engaged in this behavior and was discovered doing so, what if any discipline do YOU think *SHOULD* follow.
   1. NONE   4. PERIOD OF SUSPENSION WITHOUT PAY
   2. VERBAL REPRIMAND   5. DEMOTION IN RANK
   3. WRITTEN REPRIMAND   6. DISMISSAL

5. If an officer in your agency engaged in this behavior and was discovered doing so, what if any discipline do YOU think *WOULD* follow.
   1. NONE   4. PERIOD OF SUSPENSION WITHOUT PAY
   2. VERBAL REPRIMAND   5. DEMOTION IN RANK
   3. WRITTEN REPRIMAND   6. DISMISSAL

6. Do you think YOU would report a fellow police officer who engaged in this behavior?
   Definitely not   Definitely yes
       1   2   3   4   5

7. Do you think MOST POLICE OFFICERS IN YOUR AGENCY would report a fellow police officer who engaged in this behavior?
   Definitely not   Definitely yes
       1   2   3   4   5

Pease et al. (1975) suggested that a better way to express losses from crimes would be to find a measure that relates to the purchasing power in the country, rather than to the absolute dollar values. Following this logic, in the scenarios we created that involved monetary gain we attempted to resolve this problem by expressing the gain in terms of some local value equivalent. In Case 3 we describe the value of a bribe for ignoring a speeding violation as worth one half the value of the fine. In Case 5 we describe the value of a watch taken in an opportunistic theft as worth about two days pay. Similarly, we describe in Case 6 an auto-repair kickback scheme as producing a reward for the officer of 5 percent of the value of the repair.

In addition, in Case 4 we avoided specific mention of occasions that in the United States and some other cultures are occasions for gift-giving to police. Instead of "Christmas" we used "holiday" on the assumption that respondents in nations without a dominant Christian tradition (e.g., Israel, Turkey) may still have holidays on which gift-giving to police is not uncommon.

While the above modifications in our scenarios attempted to make them, as near as possible, "culturally neutral," we found that even our best efforts at picking culturally common opportunities came up short. For example, we found that in attempting to translate our scenarios for distribution to a sample of police officers in India, both Case 7 and Case 8 had to be modified to reflect the fact that virtually no line police officers in India earned enough to own a car. (We substituted motorbikes.) Similarly, in Poland, bars are not subject to closing hours. In our Polish survey we changed the offense from a late closing to serving underage drinkers—an offense that is taken quite seriously in Poland though it is widely ignored elsewhere in Europe.

The Survey Samples

The Sample of Croatian Police Officers

The sample of Croatian police officers is a stratified national sample that includes a substantial proportion of police officers in the entire country. Because we were interested in the occupational culture of policing in different locations, instead of sampling a fraction of police officers in all police stations, we selected forty-one police stations nationally and surveyed all police officers assigned to each of them. The stations were selected in a manner that reflected as closely as possible the national distribution of police by region, size, type, and district.

The questionnaire was sent by courier to each of the police stations. Each questionnaire contained a cover letter from the researchers. In addition, the chief of each agency received a letter from the Office of the Minister of the Interior inviting the chief and police officers to participate in the study. Police officers received the questionnaire in a sealed envelope and were instructed to place it in another sealed envelope before returning it to the person in charge of questionnaire distribution.

The survey yielded a sample of 1649 respondents. The vast majority were full-time sworn Croatian police officers, but a few were civilians who held administrative or technical positions within the Croatian police. Most of the police officers in the study (74 percent) had been police officers for less than five years, and most (85 percent) had worked at their present police station for less than five years. About 19 percent of the respondents are employed in supervisory ranks. Most of the police officers reported performing patrol (41 percent) or traffic (21 percent) assignments. Most work in small (25–75 officer) or medium-sized (75–200 officer) police agencies.

The Sample of Croatian College Students

Our sample of Croatian college students included 504 University of Zagreb students. The questionnaire was distributed during class hours. The questionnaires were distributed at four different schools: the School of Educational Studies (44.6 percent), the School of Physical Education (31.0 percent), the School of Electrical Engineering (11.9 percent), and the School of Veterinary Medicine (12.5 percent).

Thirty-nine percent of the students were either first-year or second-year students. None of the students had previous experience as police officers and only very few students (1.4 percent) reported that they were planning to become police officers.

The Sample of U.S. Police Officers

We have surveyed sworn officers in thirty police agencies in the United States. Unlike the Croatian sample, which was a systematically selected, stratified national sample, the U.S. sample was selected by contacting persons in leadership positions with whom we had previous relationships. Thus, the U.S. sample is a convenience sample.[1]

In each agency we relied upon the efforts of a liaison officer to distribute the questionnaires and collect those that had been completed. In some agencies this was done by distributing the questionnaires to all agency personnel through the agency's internal mail system and having officers return the questionnaires directly to the liaison officer. In other agencies the questionnaires were distributed to unit or division supervisors and they assumed responsibility for distributing and collecting them within their units or divisions. In still others, an officer assumed direct responsibility for distributing and collecting the surveys and did so personally, visiting shifts, and standing by while officers completed the surveys.

The survey yielded a sample of 3,235 respondents. Only one in four police officers in the study (27 percent) had been a police officer for less than five years. Approximately one in five respondents (19.8 percent) are employed in supervisory ranks. Most police officers (63.1 percent) reported performing patrol assignments. The majority of the police officers in our sample (59.9 percent) work in very large agencies (over 500 sworn officers).

The Sample of U.S. College Students

Our sample of U.S. college students consists of 375 students enrolled in sociology and criminal justice classes at the University of Delaware. The questionnaire was administered during class hours. The majority of the students (56.8 percent) were either freshmen or sophomores. Furthermore, approximately one-half (53.1 percent) were criminal justice majors though only a few (12.8 percent) planned to become police officers.

The Results

In table 6.1 we have summarized the results of the portion of the questionnaire in which respondents were asked to evaluate the seriousness of the behavior described in each of the eleven scenarios. A visual inspection of table 6.1 illustrates that our respondents, students and police officers from two countries, believed that the scenarios presented to them covered a rather wide range of seriousness. We will first examine the differences in absolute values by comparing the mean values. We will then turn our attention to the relative numbers—the ranks—and will compare the scale(s) of seriousness based on the ranks of the means provided by the U.S. students, U.S. police officers, Croatian students, and Croatian police officers.

The Absolute Mean Differences between U.S. and Croatian Police Officers' Perceptions of Seriousness of Misconduct

In table 6.1 we compare the mean value of the responses of U.S. and Croatian officers with respect to their own estimates of offense seriousness. The first finding to which we may call attention is that there is

TABLE 6.1

Reports of Their *Own* Perceptions of Offense Seriousness by Croatian Students, Croatian Police Officers, U.S. Students, and U.S. Police Officers

Case No. and Description	Croatian Students			Croatian Police Officers			U.S. Students			U.S. Police Officers			F-value (d.f.)
	—	ST. DEV	RANK	—	ST. DEV	RANK	—	ST. DEV	RANK	—	ST. DEV	RANK	
Case 1—Off-Duty Security System Business	2.12	1.29	2	2.57	1.52	2	1.37	.72	1	1.46	.94	1	330.20* (3;5343)
Case 2—Free Meals, Discounts, on Beat	2.50	1.27	3	3.01	1.49	4	2.05	1.00	3	2.60	1.34	2	60.57* (3; 5321)
Case 3—Bribe from Speeding Motorist	3.89	1.20	9	4.47	1.06	9	4.12	.90	9	4.92	.37	10	403.28* (3; 5337)
Case 4—Holiday Gifts from Merchants	1.83	1.16	1	2.13	1.34	1	1.81	1.01	2	2.84	1.38	3	182.22* (3; 5321)
Case 5—Crime Scene Theft of Watch	4.57	.87	11	4.72	.83	11	4.69	.60	11	4.95	.32	11	108.55* (3; 5333)
Case 6—Auto Repair Shop 5 percent Kickback	4.10	1.26	5	3.86	1.36	7	3.34	1.11	5	4.50	.90	7	6.27* (3; 5329)
Case 7— Supervisor: Holiday for tune-up	3.71	1.15	7	4.09	1.26	8	3.10	1.14	4	4.18	1.04	6	119.51* (3; 5330)
Case 8—Cover-up of Police DUI Accident	3.45	1.31	6	2.79	1.47	3	3.43	1.27	6	3.03	1.39	4	38.80* (3; 5321)
Case 9—Drinks to Ignore Late Bar Closing	3.38	1.32	4	3.85	1.26	6	3.73	1.09	7	4.54	.90	8	278.31* (3; 5323)
Case 10—Excessive Force on Car Thief	3.82	1.28	8	3.03	1.53	5	3.99	1.14	8	4.05	1.23	5	193.19* (3; 5319)
Case 11—Theft from Found Wallet	4.31	1.03	10	4.55	.97	10	4.15	.90	10	4.85	.54	9	172.33* (3; 5344)

*p<.001

a difference between Croatian and U.S. samples in the mean values for all eleven cases and this difference is statistically significant in all eleven cases. Given the very large size of the combined samples, this is by no means surprising. Therefore, although these differences were statistically significant, we do not regard all of them as substantively important. In evaluating whether a statistically significant difference in mean seriousness scores also signaled a real and meaningful difference of opinion, we used a rather arbitrary standard of at least a 0.50 difference in the mean scores. Employing this standard we consider the mean differences in five cases (Case 1—Off-Duty Security System Business; Case 4—Holiday Gifts from Merchants; Case 6—Auto Repair Shop 5-percent Kickback; Case 9—Drinks to Ignore Late Bar; and Case 10—Excessive Force on Car Thief) to be important in substantive terms. We may, however, point out that in nine out of eleven cases the mean differences reflect higher levels of seriousness evaluations by U.S. than by Croatian officers, although the differences were found to be quite small in some of the cases.

The seriousness of running an off-duty security system business. The first case, Case 1, concerns an officer who runs an off-duty, security system business. This is one out of only two cases in which the means of the responses provided by Croatian police officers are higher than the means of the responses provided by U.S. police officers, indicating that the Croatian respondents, on average, evaluated this case as more serious. The difference in this case is large; it is 1.08 on a five-point scale.

Interestingly, two-thirds of the U.S. police respondents reported that such behavior was definitely not a violation of policy in their agency. While such behavior is prohibited in some U.S. police agencies, in Croatia it is specifically prohibited for all police officers by national law. Consequently, we were not surprised when Croatian police officers in our sample estimated this scenario to be of a greater seriousness than did the U.S. police officers in our sample.

The seriousness of accepting holiday gifts from merchants. U.S. police officers reported that accepting holiday gifts from merchants was, in their own opinion, an offense of 2.84 seriousness on a five-point scale. By contrast, Croatian officers' mean seriousness score for their own opinion was 2.13.

It is interesting to relate answers provided on this particular question of seriousness to the answers our respondents selected when asked whether accepting holiday gifts constituted a violation of official policy.[2]

The U.S. police officers, the majority of whom (67.0 percent) evaluated this case as a violation of the official policy, evaluated this case to be more serious than did the Croatian police officers, majority of whom (66.4 percent) evaluated this case as not violating the official policy. Although accepting such gifts is prohibited by policy in Croatia, this difference may reflect a degree of Croatian cultural support for it; giving holiday gifts to police officers may be understood as an extension of a wider practice of giving Christmas gifts.

The seriousness of a 5-percent kickback deal with an auto body shop. The mean difference in the U.S. and Croatian evaluations of the seriousness of a police officer participating in a 5-percent kickback arrangement with an auto body shop is .64 for officer's own perceptions of seriousness. Although this substantial difference might be understood as, in part, reflecting cultural differences in expectations toward gift giving, it is a behavior that is simply regarded as less serious by Croatian than U.S. police officers.

The seriousness of accepting free drinks to ignore late bar closing. The mean difference between the U.S. and Croatian evaluations of the seriousness of a police officer accepting free drinks to ignore a late bar closing is .69 for officer's own perceptions of seriousness. Responses from the Croatian sample indicate that this behavior is sometimes defended by Croatian officers as helpful to the cultivation of bar owners as informants. It may also reflect, in part, a difference between U.S. and Croatian attitudes toward alcohol consumption and regulations that control it.

The seriousness of the use of excessive force on a car thief after a foot pursuit. After Case 1—the off-duty security system business scenario that reflected a substantial difference in U.S. and Croatian law and policy—Case 10 (describing the use of excessive force on a car thief after a foot pursuit) reflected the largest differences in mean seriousness scores between U.S. and Croatian officers. The difference was 1.02. It is clear that Croatian officers regard this behavior as substantially less serious than U.S. officers do.

The use of excessive force on resistant perpetrators has, at least historically, been customary in many U.S. police agencies and is still strongly supported in some of the U.S. agencies we surveyed. Although we have no systematic evidence to support such a speculation, it may be that this difference is magnified by the recent public outcry following a number of high profile use of excessive force incidents in the United States. Whether that difference in attitude is temporary or has changed general U.S. police norms for the long term remains to be seen.

The Absolute Mean Differences between U.S. and Croatian Students' Perceptions of Seriousness of Misconduct

There are even fewer differences in the mean scores for Croatian and U.S. students that we consider to be of substantive importance than there are for mean scores for Croatian and U.S. police officers; in three cases mean differences were not even statistically significant despite the large sample sizes. The only two cases with substantial (i.e., greater than 0.50) differences were Case 1 (Off-Duty Security System Business) and Case 7 (Supervisor: Holiday for Tune-Up).

The difference between the means of the responses by the U.S. and Croatian students in Case 1 was the largest for all eleven cases (.75), but it still somewhat smaller than the difference between the means by the U.S. and Croatian police officers (1.08). For both the police officers and students, the means of the responses provided by the Croatian respondents were higher than the means provided by the U.S. respondents.

The second case with substantive differences involves another case where the Croatian students tended to evaluate the case as more serious, Case 7 (Supervisor; Holiday for Tune-Up) is the only case that describes the behavior of a supervisor and not a behavior of a line officer. Interestingly, although the differences between the means for the U.S. and Croatian police officers are rather small (.09), the difference between the means for the U.S. and Croatian students were large (.61). This gap in the student assessments of seriousness may reflect the lack of work experience of U.S. students and influence their appreciation of corrupt behavior on the part of supervisors.

The Absolute Mean Differences between Students' Perceptions and Police Officers' Perceptions of Seriousness of Misconduct

When we examine the differences between the mean scores for students and police officers from the same country two findings of note emerge from those examinations. First, we find that the differences between the mean scores for police officers and students from the same country tended to be more frequent and of a larger magnitude for the U.S. respondents than for the Croatian respondents. In seven of the eleven cases for U.S. police and U.S. students respondents mean seriousness scores differed by 0.50 or more. Croatian police and student respondents differed in their mean seriousness scores by 0.50 or more in only four cases. Moreover, the differences in mean scores exceeded 0.80 in four cases for the U.S. respondents while none of the cases reflected a difference of that magnitude for the Croatian respondents.

Our second finding of note is that in the vast majority of cases, the mean scores for police officers exceeded the mean scores for students from the same country (there is only one exception for the U.S. respondents and two exceptions for the Croatian respondents).

Differences in Mean Seriousness Scores of
U.S. Students and U.S. Police Officers

Police officers tended to evaluate cases as more serious than did students. In ten out of eleven cases the means of the police officers' answers were higher than the means of the students' answers, although these differences were small in two cases (Case 1—Off-Duty Security System Business; Case 10—Excessive Force on Car Thief). In seven cases (Case 2—Free Meals, Discounts on Beat; Case 3—Bribe from Speeding Motorist; Case 4—Holiday Gifts from Merchants; Case 6— Auto Repair Shop 5-percent Kickback; Case 7—Supervisor: Holiday for Tune-Up; Case 9—Drinks to Ignore Late Bar Closing; and Case 11—Theft from Found Wallet) these differences were large (above .50) and in three cases exceeded 1.00 difference on a five-point scale. In general terms, the U.S. police officers in our sample tended to evaluate these cases as being of greater seriousness than did the U.S. students in the sample.

The single case U.S. students evaluated as more serious than U.S. police officers was Case 8, involving the cover up of a drunk driving offense and minor accident by a police officer. The difference of 0.4, while statistically significant, did not reach the standard we employed for determining a meaningful difference in responses.

Differences in Mean Seriousness Scores of Croatian
Students and Croatian Police Officers

The mean scores for the Croatian police officers' estimates of seriousness were higher than were the mean scores for the Croatian students' estimates of seriousness on nine out of eleven cases; the two cases in which the mean scores for students were higher were Case 8—

Cover-up of Police DUI Accident, (the same case which reflected a higher U.S. student than police score) and Case 10—Excessive Force on Car Thief. The two cases for which the means were higher for the students were two out of the four cases in which the differences between the means were equal to or exceeded .50.

The finding that in both the U.S. and Croatian samples officers, with only a very few exceptions, rated the behaviors described in the scenarios as more serious than did student respondents bears some emphasis. This finding goes against popular stereotypes found in hard-boiled and cynical portraits of police. It suggests instead that police may have a greater investment in their reputation for integrity than citizens, as well as a stronger opinion of the consequences of misconduct on their own reputations.

The Relative Similarities and Differences between U.S. and Croatian Police Officers' Perceptions of Seriousness of Misconduct

Another way to analyze the results is to provide not an *absolute* but a *relative* measure and compare the results across the groups. We ranked the mean scores for each of the groups (U.S. students, U.S. police officers, Croatian students, and Croatian police officers) from the least serious to the most serious. The ranks are shown in table 6.1 and analyzed in table 6.2.

The Spearman's correlation coefficients (table 6.2) of the rank ordering of the seriousness of the offenses were all above .80. This suggests that there exists, in a manner consistent with the *Measurement of Delinquency* tradition, a shared understanding among police officers and students in both countries of the hierarchy of the seriousness of the various types of police delinquency described in our questionnaire. The correlation was especially strong (above .90) when the rankings were compared for the groups within the same level of experience in policing (e.g., police officers) from two countries. Similarly, the correlation of the rankings of students from the two countries was also high (above .90). Furthermore, the correlation coefficients exceeded .87 when the rankings of the two groups of respondents from the same country were compared.

Conclusion

In summary, in the spirit of the ground-breaking study by Sellin and Wolfgang (1964), we examined estimates of seriousness of eleven sce-

TABLE 6.2
Spearman Correlation Coefficients—Rank Ordering of Own
Views of Seriousness by Croatian Students, Croatian Police Officers,
U.S. Students, and U.S. Police Officers

	Croatian Students: OWN View of Seriousness	Croatian Officers: OWN View of Seriousness	U.S. Students: OWN View of Seriousness	U.S. Officers: OWN View of Seriousness
Croatian Students: OWN View of Seriousness	1.000			
Croatian Officers: OWN View of Seriousness	.873 p<.001	1.000		
U.S. Students: OWN View of Seriousness	.909 p<.001	.809 p<.01	1.000	
U.S. Officers: OWN View of Seriousness	.809 p<.01	.909 p<.001	.882 p<.001	1.000

narios describing police delinquency. Samples of police officers and students from the United States and Croatia evaluated the seriousness of a range of cases of police misconduct. The differences in absolute scores revealed not only that U.S. police officers tended to rank the misconduct described in the case scenarios as more serious than did Croatian police officers, but that police officers from both countries tended to regard most of the incidents of misconduct as more serious than did the student respondents. Despite the fact that differences in absolute seriousness ratings existed, relative, rank-order seriousness correlations were very high. This stability of the rankings of our cases across cultures (U.S. and Croatian) and across at least two levels of police experience (no experience among students and a substantial amount of experience among active police officers) suggests that a hierarchy in the structure of offense seriousness that was first discovered in its general form by the pioneering efforts of Sellin and Wolfgang (1964) is shared by both police and citizens with respect to police misconduct.

Notes

This study was supported by grant no. 95-IJ-CX-0058 from the National Institute of Justice. The opinions expressed in this report are those of the authors and do not necessarily reflect the policies or positions of the National Institute of Justice or of the United States Department of Justice. We would also like to acknowledge the financial and logistic support given by the Croatian Ministry of the Interior.

1. We are aware of some systematic biases that may be reflected in our sample. It includes, for example, no state police agencies, only one sheriff's agency, and only one county police agency. Thus it overrepresents municipal police agencies. While our sample also overrepresents police agencies from the northeastern United States, it does contain agencies from the South, Southeast, and Southwest, but none from West Coast, Northeastern, or Midwestern cities.
2. The question was worded as follows: "Would this behavior be regarded as a violation of official policy in your agency?" The possible answers ranged on a five-point scale from 1 ("definitely not") to 5 ("definitely yes").

References

Figlio, R. M. 1975. "The Seriousness of Offenses: An Evaluation by Offenders and Nonoffenders." *Journal of Criminal Law, Criminology and Police Science* 66: 189–200.

Gottfredson, S. D., K. L. Young, and W. S. Laufer. 1980. "Additivity and Interactions in Offense Seriousness Scales." *Journal of Research in Crime and Delinquency* 17: 26–41.

Hsu, M. 1973. "Cultural and Sexual Differences on the Judgment of Criminal Offenses." *Journal of Criminal Law, Criminology and Police Science* 64: 348–53.

Kelly, D. H. and R. W. Winslow. 1970. "Seriousness of Delinquent Behavior: An Alternative Perspective." *British Journal of Criminology* 10: 124–35.

Kvalseth, T. O. 1980. "Seriousness of Offenses." *Criminology* 18: 237–44.

Normandeau, A. 1966. "The Measurement of Delinquency in Montreal." *Journal of Criminal Law, Criminology and Police Science* 57:172–77.

Pease, K., J. Ireson, and J. Thorpe. 1975. "Modified Crime Indices for Eight Countries." *Journal of Criminal Law, Criminology and Police Science* 66: 209–14.

Parton, D. A., M. Hansel, and J. R. Stratton. 1991. "Measuring Crime Seriousness." *British Journal of Criminology* 31: 72–85.

Rossi, P. H., C. E. Bose, and R. E. Berk. 1974. "The Seriousness of Crime: Normative Structure and Individual Differences." *American Sociological Review* 39:224–37.

Rossi, P. H., J. E. Simpson, and J. L. Miller. 1985. "Beyond Crime Seriousness: Fitting the Punishment to the Crime." *Journal of Quantitative Criminology* 1: 59–90.

Sellin, T. and M. E. Wolfgang. 1964. *The Measurement of Delinquency.* New York: Wiley.

Velez-Diaz, A. and E. I. Megargee. 1971. "An Investigation of Differences in Value Judgments between Youthful Offenders and Nonoffenders in Puerto Rico." *Journal of Criminal Law, Criminology and Political Science* 61: 549–53.

Wolfgang, M. E., R. M. Figlio, P.E. Tracy, and S.I. Singer. 1985. *The National Survey of Crime Severity.* Washington, DC: U.S. Government Printing Office.

7

Police Enforcement of Quality-of-Life Offending: A Critique

Bernard Cohen

Introduction

Critical issues have recently arisen concerning increased efforts on the part of police departments in major American cities to enforce rigorously quality-of-life offenses. Although the majority of offenses defined as "quality-of-life" rarely result in direct physical harm or loss of property for an individual, these behaviors are regarded as violating the sensibilities of ordinary citizens and the community as a whole by creating a sense of fear, insecurity, and despair. Offenses that fall within this rather sweeping category include panhandling, illegal peddling, street prostitution, gambling in public, defacement of property, public intoxication, dangerous mental illness, excessive noise, disorderly behavior, minor drug dealing, and using drugs in public areas. Strict zero tolerance quality-of-life policing is based upon the *broken window* theory, which suggests that unaddressed neighborhood disorder, including run-down, deteriorated conditions of both public and private property, signal that no one is concerned with community decay. Community apathy and failure to act invites further neighborhood disorder and decline. Eventually, according to the *broken window* theory, hardened violent criminals and others with criminal lifestyles are attracted to these areas, resulting in a complete downward spiral of the entire community (Kelling and Coles 1996; Wilson and Kelling 1982; Skogan 1990).

Recently, several cities have introduced a zero tolerance policy—rigorous police enforcement to relentlessly combat minor infractions in public places that involves a unique strategy. Because quality-of-life offenders often conduct business during predictable hours at stable and visible street locations, zero tolerance policing ostensibly is a practical, convenient and sensible enforcement strategy. Offenders such as prostitutes, panhandlers and low-level drug dealers can easily be detected, apprehended, and arrested. While seemingly a simple enough agenda, this shift in policy signals a necessary change in the behavior and attitudes of the officers involved, as similar tactics are generally not feasible for most predatory crimes which long have been the focus of law enforcement such as armed robbery and burglary which are sudden, short-lived and concealed. Traditional methods used in detecting potentially violent criminals are inappropriate for the goal of policing quality-of-life offenders. Coercive enforcement tactics designed primarily for apprehension of seasoned criminals are ill-suited for routine encounters that include nonthreatening persons. After years of indifference, officers are now expected to enforce rigorously quality-of-life infractions, yet generally no meaningful training has been designed specifically for this purpose.

Impact Policing

Strict enforcement of quality-of-life offenses is in a sense an innovative and novel style of policing because this strategy identifies *beforehand* the percentage crime reduction it aspires to achieve. This places police management, and indeed all personnel involved at great risk, because its performance will be called into question should the organization fail to achieve its goal. Coercive enforcement is far more intensive than *reactive 911 incident policing* where officers primarily *respond* to crimes that already have been committed, and usually even more intensive than *proactive community policing* where officers seriously attempt to *apprehend* criminals and search for *solutions* to *deter* and *prevent* crimes prior to their *occurrence*. Strict enforcement of quality-of-life policing incorporates crime response, proactive apprehension, deterrence and prevention. But it also involves a more radical concept, where law enforcement agencies and individual officers, working in concert with clearly defined communities, *strive to alter or impact the relationship and balance between criminal acts and law-abiding behavior in a targeted community, by actively setting goals that have a direct impact on reduction of crime, including diminution of quality-of-life offenses.* This form of means-end goal setting, referred to here as

TABLE 7.1
Police Enforcement Approach

	Function		
	Crime Response— Reaction	Crime Prevention— Strict Enforcement	Crime Reduction— Impact
Policing Style			
Reactive 911 Incident Policing	+	−	−
Proactive Community Policing	+	+	−
Impact Policing	+	+	+

impact policing, of which *zero tolerance* of quality-of-life offending is but one example, is where law enforcement agencies, primarily police departments, set *goals* and develop *means* for attaining a measurable reduction impact on crime and quality-of-life offenses. Table 7.1 illustrates the features of *impact policing* which encompasses all three aims including reactive 911 incident enforcement, proactive community policing and *crime reduction.*

A widely held belief, increasing in popularity, is that application of *impact policing* to quality-of-life offending results in substantial reduction in a community's criminal activity. New York City's recent shift to this style of policing, and its concurrent decrease in crime, is used as a prime example of its effectiveness. Doubts have arisen, however, about whether its presumed crime reduction benefits actually outweigh the consequences of an expected increase in abuse and crime by police officers enforcing this policy, including the severe abridgment of individual freedom and constitutionally protected civil and human rights. *Impact policing* of quality-of-life offenses invariably magnifies the number of situations or incidents where police infractions may arise, such as unnecessary force, abuse of authority, racism, discrimination, illegal "sweeps," entrapment, corruption, etc., because this style of policing by definition involves highly alert, energized, and *aggressive* patrol tactics. Many officers may experience pressure to effect arrests regardless of circumstances and tactics, in order to achieve the demanding crime reduction goals preset by the department.

In some cities official counts of civilian complaints may have remained steady or even decreased since implementation of strict enforcement of quality-life-offending (Kelling and Coles 1996). But the intervals examined are much to short for definitive conclusions. Moreover, the *number* rather than the *seriousness* of complaints was reported. Also, many complaints may not have been filed due to loss in confidence, as the public discovered that rarely were officers seriously disciplined for misconduct, although over the years many departments had imposed increasingly severe penalties. Rather than reporting complaints to the civilian complaint review board, many complainants have decided to bring lawsuits seeking expensive settlements or judgments especially for serious police misconduct.

It may very well be that in some communities where impact policing has been implemented the *ratio* of civilian complaints to arrests has decreased steadily over the last few years. Regardless, an overall *volume* increase in incidents involving abuse and unnecessary force associated with increased arrests, means more individuals have been attacked, assaulted and victimized. A "successful" mathematical ratio is virtually meaningless to victims, especially if incidents of police misconduct increase and are ever concentrated against specific ethnic groups and communities. Even supposing strict enforcement does indeed impact quality-of-life-offenses, as suggested by many police managers, politicians, criminologists, and journalists (Skogan 1990; Silverman 1996; Kelling and Coles 1996), setting aside *crime displacement* from targeted to other areas and time periods and the influence of intervening variables, still, little *concrete* evidence based upon rigorous research exists to support the policy that coercive tactics actually reduce more serious crime (Moran 1998; Lardner 1997; Walker 1984).

Measurement of Quality-of-Life Offenses

The efficacy of police strategies related to crime reduction derived from the *broken window* theory has not been demonstrated, and cannot be, without a reliable and valid *index* of quality-of-life offenses that can provide accurate information on the incidence of these behaviors. While a national index for measurement of serious crimes has been established (*Uniform Crime Reports)* and even a national means for estimating harm to victims (*The National Crime Victimization Survey),* no similar *national* index for behavior characterizable as quality-of-life offenses has been developed. *Measurement* of quality-of-life offenses, including techniques for estimating its qualitative and quantitative impact (Sellin and Wolfgang 1964), is an essential and critical task that requires a *national* research and implementation effort. This research should first define precisely what are considered quality-of-life offenses. What concrete behaviors violate these laws? How many of these crimes occur? How harmful is this behavior? How are police contacts and interaction with quality-of-life offenders defined, captured, and measured? How is quantity and quality of harm determined? What are the legal precedents for enforcement? What are the relevant legal issues and court cases?

Integration of Criminology and Criminal Law

Integration of criminal law and criminology is crucial for the construction of a national index to measure quality-of-life offenses and the evaluation of high-profile, impact policing. Criminalization of most predatory acts of violence are based on a societal *consensus* because of the personal harm and victimization characterizing these offenses. Criminalization of most quality-of-life offenses may be attributed primarily to powerful and often small groups who have the influence and authority to *construct and enforce* laws. It is not necessarily derived from societal consensus. Therefore, intricate knowledge of legal theory, laws, court cases, criminological theory and research methodology are particularly relevant for examining empirical issues related to quality-of-life offenses. Legal issues pertaining to high-profile impact policing include arrest, search and seizure, due process, probable cause, unreasonableness, particularity, field interrogations, stop and frisk, investigatory stops, and consent searches. These issues form the core of constitutional amendments, including the First, Fourth, Eighth and Fourteenth, dealing with freedom of speech, unreasonable searches and seizures, probable cause, cruel and unusual punishment, deprivation of life, liberty, or property without due process of law, and equal protection under the law. Numerous court cases are pertinent to these legal and substantive issues including *United States v. Watson* (1976, arrest), *Terry v. Ohio* (1968, stop and frisk), *Adams v. Williams* (1972, investigatory stops), *Brown v. Texas* (1979, pedestrian investigatory stops), *Kolender v. Lawson* (1983, loitering), *Shuttlesworth v. City of Birmingham* (1965, "loitering for the purpose of"), *Powell v. Texas* (1968, vagrancy laws) (Champion 1997; Way 1980). Obviously, much of the stepped-up, high-profile enforcement of quality-of-life offenses involves an increased focus on behavior, on both the part of the officer and his/her target, that falls under the protection of the United States Constitution.

Towards the Twenty-first Century

Issues raised by strict enforcement of quality-of-life offenses are particularly appropriate for a volume devoted to integration of criminal law and criminology, especially one dedicated to Marvin E. Wolfgang, a distinguished mentor, unsurpassed world-class criminologist and gentleman. Wolfgang's life-work, that of his outstanding mentor Thorsten Sellin, and that undertaken by their numerous students have been devoted to examination of the underlying controversies raised by high-profile quality-of-life policing, including discrimination, racism, inequity, and abuse by government authorities. Wolfgang and Sellin's brilliant and groundbreaking work on the measurement of delinquency provides a superb starting point and model for construction of a national index for quality-of-life offenses (Sellin and Wolfgang 1964). Professor Wolfgang's unique contribution, extending over much of the last half of the twentieth century, provides a solid infrastructure and blueprint for integrated criminological research for well into the twenty-first century.

Topics pertinent to police enforcement of quality-of-life offenses should be broadened to include research on similar issues relating to the criminal justice system. While examples abound about abuse, discrimination and racism by the police, courts, jails and prisons, no comparable body of research exists on systematic discrimination in the application and management of probation, parole, and other aspects of the criminal justice system.

The next section explores and *critiques* several issues related to high-profile *impact policing* of quality-of-life offenses including imprecise definitions, corruption, police abuse and brutality, racism and discrimination, illegal "sweeps," entrapment, enforcement strategies, enforcement impact, and depletion of resources. These issues raise important questions concerning the most efficient and effective strategies for an aggressive order maintenance program for controlling quality-of-life offending, a crucial task for ensuring the vitality and protection of citizens and communities. Although much of the rationale behind strict enforcement of quality-life-offenses has been derived from the *broken window* theory, alternative means for impacting this behavior, also potentially derivable from this theoretical perspective, may produce superior results. Attacking symptoms or searching for "root solutions" of social disorder alone, cannot fully succeed without also addressing the root causes of each category of quality-of-life offending.

Scenarios on *impact policing* obtained through *field observation* and *media accounts* in *Los Angeles* and *New York* are provided throughout the text as illustrative examples of issues explored by this chapter. Most studies, evaluations and experiments involving disorder rely on surveys of participants' opinions before and after introduction of an "intervention." The present research suggests how field data may be utilized to measure visible disorder. The observation methods are derived from sociologist Max Weber's concept *verstehen* (Weber 1949, 1978), or putting oneself in a situation in order to comprehend the dynamics taking place. I refer to this method as *research vérité*, because the data were derived from field observations of *actual* behavior involving quality-of-life offending and high-profile police operations. Agency access or permission was not required, nor was there reliance on *official* data. Traditional techniques of participant and non-participant observation of government organizations usually require agency approval and agreement. That in itself may tend to mitigate validity, unlike *research vérité* where agency authorization and cooperation are not necessary (Goffman 1961). There is no harm to human subjects because all research is conducted in public places and anonymous. Moreover, the researcher is merely reporting or otherwise disposing of information derived from street observations witnessed routinely by citizens (Cohen 1980). *Research vérité* ought to be applied to other criminal justice organizations that partially operate in public view, including prosecutorial and judicial agencies. Integration of field observations derived from *research vérité* with data from official records, media, interviews, surveys, and other sources, creates an eclectic perspective referred to as *ethnometrics*, which is an optimal methodological approach (Cohen 1980).

Obstruction of Field Research

Researchers who engage in independent field studies *(research vérité)* may be subject to stops, searches, interrogations, and arrests, during enhanced enforcement of quality-of-life offenses. Uncertainty concerning local laws and police enforcement policies, and absence of "street smarts" regarding quality-of-life offenses, may not only result in faulty research, but also lead to arrest. Although this issue pertains only to a small group of investigators willing to navigate rough streets and public areas where police and citizens are likely to collide, it nevertheless is consequential because researchers play a vital role in uncovering significant social facts and patterns beneficial to citizens (Ferrel 1997).

Recent legislation establishing anti-loitering and vagrancy laws coupled with strict police enforcement practices makes the conduct of street research especially difficult and dangerous. Police officers in many jurisdictions are now required to stop, interrogate and arrest persons believed to be *loitering* for the *purpose* of committing a crime. Inquiring about the price of drugs or sex may technically violate the law and could result in a researcher's arrest. Researchers conversing with street criminals, asking information or merely situated in a targeted area conducting observations may be perceived as law violators, especially when viewed by the police as "outsiders," e.g., a white person in a Latino neighborhood; an African American in a white neighborhood; a middle-class stranger in a poor neighborhood. Vulnerability for arrest increases as well during certain "unlikely" hours, for example, between midnight and early morning when "decent folks" ought to be home asleep. Individuals conducting research on quality-of-life offending must be fully informed in criminology and criminal law, not only for intellectual and scholarly pursuits, but also for personal safety.

Several years ago arrest was not a serious concern, because in many American cities, quality-of-life offending was winked at, or virtually ignored by the police. Police activity was reserved for serious crimes because departments with limited resources could not afford to have officers tied up in station houses and courts, often on overtime, for minor offenses viewed by the police as social work. Moreover, officers on routine patrol were discouraged from making quality-of-life arrests because of corruption. In New York City special public morals units were mainly responsible for enforcement of quality-of-life offenses. Usually, aggressive prostitutes, drug dealers, vagrants, and other persons clearly engaged in visible criminal lifestyles were arrested and charged. However, greater police resources, including enhanced budget, increased personnel, strengthened corruption controls, improved supervision and a conviction that quality-of-life offenses are a prelude to serious crime, contributed to a major shift in policy. Currently (1997), officers assigned to routine patrol amongst the Department's some 38,000 sworn members, are encouraged to make arrests for quality-of-life offending.

Critique of Strict Enforcement of Quality-of-Life Policing

The critical propositions, hypotheses and "statements" that follow aim to stimulate fresh debate and research on high-profile impact policing pertaining to quality-of-life offending, while searching for alternative control strategies *that do not incorporate the negative consequences of coercive enforcement tactics.* They intend to raise more questions than solutions. Many issues pertaining to these statements have been discussed adroitly by several scholars including Skogan (1990) and Kelling and Coles (1996), but not solely within the context of quality-of-life police enforcement. Vigorous data accrual and verification of these propositions are essential for development of a meaningful, effective and efficient theoretical perspective and enforcement program focusing on "quality-of-life."

Imprecise Definitions

Proponents of strict enforcement of quality-of-life offending tend to assemble extremely *diverse behaviors* into one all encompassing category and view them as a single offense. Advocates of the *broken window-quality-of-life policing* perspective tend to lump a variety of illegal acts involving extremely diverse behaviors into a single comprehensive category. These behaviors usually involve different substantive and legal elements and ought not be grouped into one category encompassing other quality-of-life offenses. A john soliciting a street prostitute, a college student purchasing marijuana from the corner drug dealer, panhandling, scrawling graffiti or playing loud music, differ in intent, circumstances, and consequences. These acts incorporate common elements in that all may annoy and frighten community residents; nevertheless, each behavior is distinct with diverse *etiologic* and *enforcement* prerequisites. Grouping individual quality-of-life offenses as a single form of offending not only impedes research on quality-of-life-offenses, but also it obstructs the search for causes, enforcement remedies, and treatments. Moreover, this oversight obfuscates and misconstrues the debate on processes of criminalization, decriminalization, and legalization.

Etiologic Explanations

Typical theories on crime and delinquency cannot explain the etiologic criminal dynamics of quality-of-life offenses or their relationship with the criminal justice system due to the distinct and unique motives and behavioral patterns that characterize each of the actions in this category. No theoretical perspective yet offered successfully explains as a group the key determinants of such varied offenses as prostitution, loud noise, illegal drugs, street gambling, panhandling, or scrawling graffiti. Unemployment, poverty, inferior education, inequality, blocked opportunities, controls and subcultures do not readily explain these forms of deviance. Traditional theoretical concepts may partially uncover the reasons why people commit armed robbery, burglary, aggravated assault and battery, or rape, but they are not pervasive explanations for quality-of-life offending, notwithstanding the frustrations that emanate from these social conditions that may contribute partially to a quest for "release." Employable, educated, successful, and otherwise "upright" citizens, including police officers themselves, at times engage in behavior characterizable as quality-of-life offending, but usually refrain from more serious crime. Predatory acts however, are more likely to be inflicted by individuals who exhibit criminal lifestyles and are poor, disenfranchised, disconnected and discredited.

Sociological and even psychological theories designed to uncover the etiology of predatory acts do not alone explain all forms of quality-of-life offending, because actions of persons who use drugs, visit prostitutes, illegally gamble or tend to be intoxicated involve pleasure derived directly from patently physical acts intrinsic to the infractions (e.g., euphoria, "rush," thrill) that directly impact body chemistry or functions. Therefore, physical factors are relevant to crimes involving drugs, sex, gambling, and drunkenness even more so than to most predatory acts, although social as well as psychological factors play a major role in each of these behaviors. *Integrated theory* is a *sine qua non* not only for explaining predatory crime, but also for understanding behavior characterizable as quality-of-life offending.

Quality-of-life offending also differs substantially from predatory crime in the amount and intensity of harm inflicted on the community. Homicide, rape, robbery, aggravated assault and battery, burglary, larceny-theft and arson are acts perceived as evil in themselves (*mala in se*) because they cause tangible harm to others. Many quality-of-life offenses are *mala prohibita,* a result of laws based more on *morality* and *nuisance.* Injury, loss and damage resulting from predatory acts usually are personal, involving clearly identifiable victims, while victimization from quality-of-life offending in many instances is directed at the *community.* A form of personal victimization ultimately may be experienced, as members of the community alter their habits out of a sense of fear due to quality-of-life offending. But these experiences, even when cumulative, are not as drastic or traumatic as the fear of being robbed of a week's or a month's pay, or experiencing serious physical injury. The victimization impact of quality-of-life offenses on the community may virtually disappear when quality-of-life offenses occur unobtrusively or behind closed doors. Predatory acts including rape, robbery, and aggravated assault and battery, regardless of location, always involve definite and definable victimization. It may very well be that those who participate in quality-of-life offending are victimized by themselves or others participating in the event (e.g., the customer is denigrating the prostitute or other women). This argument may be valid, but similar logic can be applied to law-obeying behavior such as different or radical sex styles, divorce proceedings, lying, extreme rudeness, consuming diet pills with unknown side effects, overeating, insufficient sleep, and overwork, which are not the focus of stepped-up police activity.

Predatory acts are universally condemned, unlike quality-of-life offenses such as smoking marijuana, prostitution, and gambling, that are acceptable to many individuals and are legal or winked at in certain communities or circumstances. Smoking marijuana may be less harmful than smoking cigarettes or consuming alcoholic beverages or gambling, yet it is illegal, while smoking tobacco, consuming alcohol, and gambling are not in themselves law-violating behaviors. Are all behaviors currently targeted by impact policing more harmful to a community's quality-of-life than other behaviors that are universally accepted as legal? Does marijuana use cause more destruction to a community's fabric than excessive drinking? Criminologists and scholars suggest a national debate be convened to consider various harm-reduction strategies including partial and even full decriminalization or legalization of marijuana (Reinarman and Levine 1997: Zimmer and Morgan 1997). *The sharp differences described above require formulation of distinct etiologic statements for various forms of quality-of-life offending and predatory acts.*

Proponents of strict enforcement of quality-of-life offending lump many different forms of behavior into a *single legal category*. Not only do proponents of the *broken-window-theory-quality-of-life-policing* perspective group together many different forms of deviant behavior, they also tend not to differentiate among distinct behaviors encompassed by a single legal category. *Prostitution*, for example, includes prostitution on the streets, "in-house" visits by call girls, in massage parlors, by escort services, and "body rubs." Sale, possession, and use of different drugs in varying amounts including marijuana, heroin, cocaine, and crack involve vastly different behaviors with a wide range of consequences. Each action may require a distinct enforcement response, and even perhaps a unique explanatory mode. While street prostitution certainly qualifies as a quality-of-life offense, doubts arise concerning prostitution by call girls or escort services, especially where outcalls occur and the prostitute meets the customer at a hotel often in an upscale high-quality-of-life neighborhood. Similar arguments, can be applied to drug transactions or illegal gambling discreetly conducted behind closed doors, where community order and security may not be threatened and thus raise issues regarding the crime's "quality-of-life" distinction. Imprecise definitions make it extremely difficult to legislate laws and establish guidelines for controlling these infractions.

Police Misconduct

Strict enforcement of quality-of-life offenses tends to increase the quantity and seriousness of complaints regarding *corruption, unnecessary force,* and related expensive *settlements and verdicts* due to *lawsuits.*

Corruption

The presumed crime reductions, order restoration, and neighborhood resurgence that is thought to be achieved through rigorous impact policing of quality-of-life offenses may be partially neutralized by increases in acts characterizable as corruption and police brutality. Rigorous enforcement of quality-of-life offenses subjects officers to greater temptation, due to increased contacts with petty criminals including prostitutes, gamblers, and drug dealers. Recent events in several New York City precincts that involved systematic corruption, documented by the Mollen Commission (Commission to Investigate Allegations of Police Corruption 1994) lends credence to these arguments. Similar events were recorded by the Knapp Commission (Commission to Investigate Allegations of Police Corruption 1972) in New York City some twenty-five years ago when corruption involved substantial numbers of officers from virtually all ranks and assignments (Mass 1973). Rigorous enforcement of quality-of-life offending devoid of carefully designed safeguards could produce a recurrence of widespread and pervasive corruption.

Unnecessary Force

Incidents of abuse and unnecessary force and related litigation are also likely to increase due to strict enforcement of quality-of-life offending. Current hearings by New York City Council members on allegations of police misconduct (1997), and its decision to establish an independent review board only 2–3 years after implementation of a coercive order maintenance program for quality-of-life offending, attests to the seriousness of these problems. An officer who unnecessarily shoves, strikes, kicks, chokes, shoots, or otherwise manhandles a suspect is committing criminal assault. Homicide charges could be brought against the officer should the suspect die. Since 1987, personal injury lawsuits based upon alleged brutality by the New York City Police Department increased by 80 percent. Over the past fiscal year, through 30 June 1997, New York City attorneys settled 503 police misconduct claims (*The New York Times*, 17 September 1997, p. B5). Strict enforcement of quality-of-life offending is likely to intensify an upward spiral on future lawsuits. Several notable lawsuits have recently been brought against New York City and/or its Police Department, illustrating how complaints of unnecessary force arise during periods when quality-of-life offending is rigorously enforced.

In the South Bronx, a New York City police officer was charged with strangling to death a young Latino man because a football he was playing with was mistakenly bounced off the hood of the police vehicle (Tomasky 1997). The officer was terminated from the force and convicted in court on a second complaint that he tried to choke another Latino male for illegally driving a go-cart on city streets. (*The New York Times*, 30 September 1997, p. B2)

In Queens, New York, a twenty-seven-year-old Haitian college student was tackled and beaten by the police for allegedly drinking a bottle of beer in public. An angry crowd assembled and a public riot nearly ensued. The student was acquitted of all charges brought against him by the police. (*The New York Times*, 2 October 1997, p. B1)

In New York City when a woman called the police about the barking of a neighbor's dog, the woman caller, not the owner of the dog, was arrested and charged with harassment and disorderly conduct. When her seventy-year-old husband protested the arrest and handcuffing, he was thrown to the ground by officers whereby his hip was fractured and required surgery. (*The New York Times*, 4 September 1997, p. B3)

A Manhattan resident was handcuffed, arrested, and strip-searched by the police, and held in custody for more than five hours because his dog drank from a public drinking fountain in Central Park. The "offender" admitted using a pejorative term when addressing an officer. (*Daily News*, 10 October 1997, p. 8)

On 9 August 1997 at 4 A.M. according to newspaper accounts, several officers of the NYPD responded to a disturbance call outside the Club Rendez-Vous in Brooklyn, New York. Mr. Abner Louima, a thirty-year-old Haitian immigrant employed as a security guard, with no criminal record, was arrested, handcuffed, taken into custody and booked on misdemeanor charges by two white officers, one twenty-five years old and the other in his early thirties. At the 70th Precinct station house, in the public lobby, Mr. Louima was stripped naked from the waist down ostensibly to search for contraband and then he was taken handcuffed into the station house bathroom. In the bathroom it was alleged at least one officer restrained Mr. Louima while another officer thrust a blunt instrument, some claim a toilet plunger, into his rectum causing severe internal injuries. He then shoved the stick into Louima's mouth breaking several teeth. After the attack, one of the officers emerged from the bathroom in plain sight of other officers, confident that the code of silence would prevail. Also, several young white cops, including the arresting officer, were charged with taking Mr. Louima to a deserted street while on the way to the precinct station house and beating and pummeling him in the patrol car with fists and a police radio. Only two officers at the time of this writing have been known to come forward with information. Other officers in the station house at the time of the incident apparently have refused to cooperate, adhering to the blue code of silence. (*The New York Times*, 19 August 1997, p. A1)

These incidents of alleged police brutality corresponded to the period of the dramatic increase in coercive enforcement of quality-of-life offenses, and were experienced by citizens whom one would classify as nonthreatening. It may very well be that the more authority (not discretion) vested in police officers to enforce quality-of-life offenses, the greater the incidence and seriousness of complaints, especially regarding acts characterizable as unnecessary force. Officers encouraged to arrest ordinary citizens for minor offenses often develop an exaggerated sense of power and authority, where levels of coercion and force are utilized that cross over into illegitimate behavior. Forceful tactics against ordinary citizens and petty offenders which previously were reserved for hardened criminals would seem inevitable, as these are the primary tactics taught in police training programs. Current police training in *verbal judo* alone, is inadequate preparation, although a positive initial step where nonthreatening citizens are involved. Can officers as currently trained, draw distinctions between various levels of offending and offenders where verbal coercion or other alternatives may be more effective than physical force? Quality-of-life offending, as previously stated, involves mostly minor or trivial infractions where the suspect frequently is not a habitual offender and may hold a full-time job, have a family and be an upstanding, or at least nonthreatening, member of the community. Arrestees may believe their actions are in accordance with the law, and thus do not deserve to be stopped, searched, questioned, arrested, handcuffed, strip searched and placed in a cell with "real" criminals, often for more than twenty-four hours, especially for an infraction that eventually will result in, at most, a token fine. This may be the offender's first criminal encounter with the law. Not having prior experience with law enforcement, commands by officers to stop, wait, or remain silent often are ignored or misunderstood. This apparently was what happened in the Louima incident. Officers claimed they encountered "back talk" and that Louima tried to walk away from the fracas after officers ordered him to stand still.

Quality-of-life policing can be confusing for all involved parties, when officers confront ordinary citizens who commit trivial infractions. Policies regarding encounters with serious criminals still apply in these situations, and it appears the ambiguities and complexities of this type of policing have not been resolved. Are these persons, even when indeed caught committing minor illegal acts, "real" criminals or dangerous until proven otherwise? When is police force acceptable in certain instances, excessive in others? At which point does legitimate force evolve into unnecessary force? When does necessary force escalate into assault, aggravated assault, and even homicide? A distinct, intensive law enforcement training program must be developed to provide officers with the necessary knowledge and skills on how to enforce, properly, laws prohibiting quality-of-life offending. Optimally, this training will be offered before officers are ordered to enforce these regulations. Equally crucial, is that community members become informed about quality-of-life enforcement programs so all involved will know what to expect and how to behave and react in public spaces.

Police personnel and performance issues must also remain a top priority for the nation's police departments because of the complexities related to coercive enforcement of quality-of-life-offending. What are the likely background characteristics of officers who tend to use unnecessary force? Which personality types are not able to differentiate between the response necessary in policing a predatory act at one moment, and a relatively minor quality-of-life offense the next? Can an officer whose on-the-job behavior is acceptable in response to criminals involved in predatory acts modulate his behavior in enforcing quality-of-life offenses? How many complaints within a specified time period must an officer accumulate before official intervention? What level of training and supervision is required to ensure lawful behavior? In what other ways can injurious behavior be prevented? These selected police personnel issues must be addressed in order to suppress abuse and ensure proper police performance.

Broken Windows and Police Misconduct

One strategy for controlling abuse and brutality, *that does not share the same excesses experienced by ordinary citizens due to impact policing*, is application of the *broken window theory* to police misconduct. According to advocates of the broken window theory, just as strict enforcement of lessor offenses may result in a reduction of serious crime, so may highly energized and assertive enforcement of minor police misconduct including discourteous behavior, offensive language, excessive but non-injurious body contact, and adherence to the "code of silence," result in a decrease in more serious and harmful acts of unnecessary force. Abuse, brutality, and other excesses are potential hazards for ordinary citizens, but pose no similar risks for police officers charged and disciplined for minor misconduct.

Racism and Discrimination

Strict enforcement of quality-of-life offenses tends to increase patterns of *racism* and *discrimination*. Rigorous, high-profile quality-of-life offense enforcement tends to increase an officer's vulnerability to charges of racism and discrimination. Police officers must draw conclusions as to what a person's intent is in waiting or standing in the street, whether that individual is engaged in aggressive panhandling or soliciting prostitutes, or purchasing marijuana, or participating in other forms of illegal activity once relatively ignored, but now being heavily monitored by impact policing. Racism, both conscious and unconscious, may play a key role in an officer's decision-making process. Racism and discrimination are significant concerns in prosecution and sentencing as well, but prosecutors and judges conduct much of their business in public view, under greater scrutiny and supervision. They are not required to make instant "street" decisions. Therefore, it is more difficult for police officers to learn how to manage effectively and lawfully behavior characterizable as quality-of-life violations. Issues related to discrimination and racism were clearly discernible during field observations in Los Angeles.

> In downtown East Los Angeles numerous situations were observed where white officers, who comprise much of the LAPD, stopped, questioned, and searched Latino or African-American males of all ages, although most appeared to be under thirty-five years. These "suspects" often were handcuffed behind their backs, spread-eagled and ordered to face a wall. Sometimes, suspects were forced to

their knees, heads down, with hands cuffed behind their backs, only to be released after several minutes. Blacks and Latinos were treated in this manner, especially in areas where large numbers of "illegals" tended to congregate. However, Caucasian suspects were almost never forced to their knees by the police even in rundown neighborhoods where young, white, disheveled, and disoriented males were plentiful, as in deteriorated sections of Hollywood Boulevard in West Los Angeles. In more affluent areas of Los Angeles like Park-La Brea, Hancock Park, or Beverly Hills, where white, middle-class males were exhibiting behavior clearly defined as loitering, none were stopped, handcuffed, frisked, and questioned in this demeaning manner. Nor were women, regardless of the socioeconomic area observed, forced to their knees, although several were handcuffed and freed after questioning by the police.

Sweeps

Strict enforcement of quality-of-life offenses tends to increase police *sweeps* where innocent and guilty alike are arrested. This tactic is likely to increase the number of persons arrested and stigmatized. In New York City this often takes the form of police vans cruising specific areas, targeting suspected prostitutes, drug dealers, and vagrants, indiscriminately picking up anyone perceived as potential criminals. Suspected johns and even male prostitutes are less likely to be targeted by sweeps compared to female prostitutes. Nevertheless, this tactic tends to over-stigmatize individuals from the working- and under-classes because sweeps usually are carried out in declining neighborhoods. Persons with lower incomes tend to be vulnerable to sweeps because they are more likely to reside in areas utilized by prostitutes, drug dealers, and other minor offenders.

Data from field observations in Los Angeles revealed that suspected female street prostitutes, who were standing or sitting at bus stops at the intersection of Alverado and Ninth frequently were arrested, especially where a mobile police unit was operating. The mobile arrest unit consisted of a trailer and several marked and unmarked police vehicles parked on a designated street, in a high crime area. The police trailer was equipped to process large numbers of criminals who either were caught in the act or suspected of engaging in behavior characterizable as quality-of-life violations. Signs were placed on the streets indicating that the area had been targeted for anti-prostitution and narcotics enforcement, warning potential offenders to stay away or face arrest. Usually, more alert criminals, including prostitutes, drug dealers, chronic users, and experienced johns avoided the area until the police crackdown ended, leaving only the most decrepit, unhealthy, disheveled, drug-addicted prostitutes, users, dealers, and unaware johns in the clutches of the police. Dozens of Latino males loitering at or near the same bus stops intending to pick up prostitutes and accompany them to nearby motels were almost never arrested. Similarly, a few blocks east at Olympic Boulevard and Georgia Street, one block north of the convention center in downtown East Los Angeles, prostitutes loitering near several rundown motels were harassed and arrested in police sweeps but johns in the same area seemed immune from similar tactics. Enforcement tactics utilized for transvestite and transsexual prostitutes echoed that of female prostitutes. However, male prostitutes operating in full public view on the stretch of Santa Monica Boulevard between Highland and Fairfax Avenues in West Hollywood, a major location of street prostitution, were rarely targeted by police sweeps.

Prostitution arrests resulting from sweeps by the Los Angeles Police Department appeared to be influenced by gender. Similar sweeps by the New York City Police Department in the Hunts Point section of the Bronx, a neighborhood somewhat analogous in ethnicity and socioeconomic status to "Alverado and Ninth" in Los Angeles, appeared to target females as well, while males observed at the same street locations were usually disregarded.

Entrapment

Strict enforcement of quality-of-life offenses encourages *entrapment*. Entrapment involves tactics by law enforcement personnel that lure individuals into committing crimes that otherwise would not have occurred (Champion 1997). Coercive enforcement practices aimed at curbing quality-of-life offenses are likely to result in an unusually high incidence of arrests that could be interpreted as entrapment. Practices of entrapment can lead to other serious violations as officers commit perjury to conceal illegal tactics. Only rigorous training, supervision, and command accountability can ensure that officers operate in accordance with the law. The following field observation illustrates marginal actions taken by the police that could lapse into entrapment.

On a Thursday night at approximately 9:30 P.M. in East Los Angeles, a lone Caucasian woman dressed provocatively in tight pants and a halter top was standing on the northeast corner of Ninth and Beacon. Several cars passed the corner and the female smiled, gesticulating with her hands and finger for the driver to stop. The woman called out to him "Do you want a date? How about a good time?" One man stopped his car, and the female approached the driver's side window, engaging him in conversation. She then signaled and two young male police officers parked a block away on Union Avenue raced over to the corner location and positioned their police cruiser in front of the suspected john's car, successfully blocking its movement. The two officers exited the police cruiser, ordered the john out of his car, and pushed him up against the wall. The officers then handcuffed, searched, questioned and placed the john in the police vehicle under arrest. The female police decoy disappeared during this time, hiding so as not to reveal her identity to other potential johns. After the arrest the decoy officer resumed her position at the corner of Ninth and Beacon and waited for the next john.

Enforcement Strategies

A policy of strict enforcement of quality-of-life offenses and offending virtually eliminates police *discretion*. Police tactics, devised for seasoned criminals, have been extended to encompass routine encounters with nonthreatening persons. Intensive programs need to be designed to *train* and *educate* the police and the public on mutual expectations and responsibilities of a strict "quality-of-life" enforcement program.

Current tactics of police zero-tolerance enforcement of quality-of-life offenses makes little or no distinction among different types of violators or lawbreaking behaviors. Since these acts range from drug dealing to panhandling and involve public disturbances by persons not necessarily leading a defined criminal lifestyle, police enforcement tactics should be tailored to fit each particular incident. Police reaction and resolution should be based upon severity of the violation, the suspect's behavior and prior criminal status. The following scenario, describing a demonstration in New York City protesting police brutality, highlights the importance of differentiating among varying forms of offending, and between citizens with and without criminal lifestyles.

> On 29 August 1997 about four hundred persons, who were taking part in a rally protesting police brutality and the torture of Abner Louima in a Brooklyn precinct station house were met by over one hundred police officers, many on horseback and equipped with riot gear. More than one hundred demonstrators were arrested and handcuffed by the police and charged with disorderly conduct, obstruction of governmental administration, unlawful assembly or other minor charges. Many were fingerprinted and jailed overnight. Demonstrators claimed aggressive action by the police precipitated the confrontation, including slowing the marchers down and ultimately preventing their movement. Many demonstrators asserted the police attacked them without cause or provocation, while the police countered that the marchers ignored their commands. Demonstrators claimed they did not hear the orders issued by the police. Thirteen of the demonstrators were later released without charges. (*The New York Times*, 31 August 1997, p. 27)

The routine, daily behavior of the majority of citizens who participated in this march does not appear to contribute to the decline of a city or neighborhood, as does the behavior and lifestyle of street prostitutes or low-level drug dealers who day after day occupy the same street locations and consistently violate the law. Distinctions ought to be made among varying individuals, groups, and actions based upon intent, purpose, and degree of criminal lifestyle. Yet many demonstrators were arrested, handcuffed, charged, detained and otherwise treated like ordinary criminals, although the police may have only been following official guidelines. Individual officers should not be punished for honest mistakes, but only for a pattern of poor performance. Persistent application of impact policing of quality-of-life offending will increase substantially the number of persons arrested and stigmatized. Prevalent exercise of this strategy risks establishing an *over-criminalized population* where a substantial number of citizens possess criminal records. *Treatment of citizens in this manner, could tend to increase quality-of-life offenses, serious crime, and even public disturbances as citizens take a reactionary, us-against-them stance opposing those who ostensibly are there to protect and serve them.* Confidence in the LAPD and the NYPD has diminished sharply since the Rodney King and Abner Louima incidents. A recent poll revealed that over the past year-and-a-half, confidence in the NYPD decreased from 61 to 48 percent, a 13-percent drop in the approval rating. Moreover, 54 percent of New Yorkers believe that the police break the law or lie to ensure convictions, and 62 percent think that the police discriminate against blacks (*The New York Times*, 3 October 1997, p. B7).

Alternative enforcement strategies already exist for policing typical nonthreatening citizens without arresting, handcuffing, strip searching, fingerprinting, and charging them, although more imaginative and effective techniques still need to be devised, as for example, property *forfeiture* and *abatement* programs. Persons or suspects involved in minor infractions or quality-of-life offenses for the first time, who have valid identification, a permanent address, no outstanding warrants, and who appear in control of themselves, should be warned and allowed to leave the area without being placed under arrest. Issuance of a summons at the location, as with a traffic violation, may be appropriate for some individuals or behaviors after these conditions have been verified. A desk appearance ticket should be issued at the station house for those persons whose identification and warrant status require further verification. The police can still determine the presence of handguns or other weapons using these tactics. Suspects should be questioned on the street or at the station house about other crimes and criminals which now is common practice. Handcuffing, fingerprinting, and spending several hours and even days in police transport vans and holding cells with hardened criminals and dangerous mentally ill persons is cruel and unnecessary, especially for first-time offenders who neither appear dangerous nor whom exhibit a criminal lifestyle. Rough coercive tactics devised for dealing with dangerous offenders and persons with criminal lifestyles should not be employed routinely with nonthreatening individuals. Police officers should strive to avoid confrontations when no apparent danger exists, especially in police initiated incidents where civilian complainants are not present.

An intensive and innovative law enforcement training, supervision, and accountability program must be devised to instruct police personnel from patrol officers on up through supervisors and commanders, on how to recognize and enforce different forms of "quality-of-life" offending, without stigmatizing large segments of the population or brutalizing the suspect. Several issues and questions need to be addressed. Under what circumstances is discretion legal or justified? Under what conditions is it a crime for a law enforcement officer to ignore suspicious street behavior? At what point is standing around or frequenting an area infested with drugs or prostitution, or even conversing with drug dealers or prostitutes probable cause for loitering for the purpose of prostitution or for drug dealing or purchasing? Does the officer have to inquire as to the reason the suspect was present at the scene? Should the officer be required to admonish the individual prior to making an arrest? Must the officer inform the violator of all rights in precisely the same way as if a serious offense had occurred such as rape, armed robbery, and so forth? What if such warnings were not forthcoming? Should there be laws of this kind altogether? Should a suspect be given a chance to exit the area without incident? What alternative means are available for dealing with these infractions?

A program of education developed for the public ideally should be initiated prior to implementation of a rigorous "quality-of-life" enforcement policy. The program should inform members of the community exactly what are quality-of-life offenses, how they are to be enforced and what is expected of the community. Specific instructional items should include, but not be limited to media campaigns, advertisements, distribution of printed materials, and presentations at schools and community gatherings so that children and adults will be aware of mutual obligations and responsibilities. A brief trial period limited to warnings, except for extremely serious violations or clearly visible threatening behavior, or persons with outstanding warrants, should precede full implementation of rigorous "quality-of-life" enforcement.

Enforcement Impact

Strict enforcement of quality-of-life offenses may contribute to stabilization, restoration, enhancement and an increased sense of security in targeted neighborhoods, but its precise *impact* on serious crime remains unknown. Police executives, politicians and criminologists defend strict enforcement of quality-of-life offending arguing that high-profile impact policing has resulted in substantial decreases in crime in communities that are livable, whereas acts of proven racism, discrimination, brutality and entrapment are rare occurrences (Kelling and Coles 1996; Silverman 1996). However, no cumulative body of empirical evidence based upon rigorous research exists that can demonstrate these claims (Moran 1998; Walker 1984). Skogan's (1990) pathbreaking and resourceful work linking disorder, fear, urban decay, and crime, summarizes evidence of community stabilization, improvement, and disorder reduction due to increased enforcement efforts, including the widely discussed Houston and Newark field experiments. But these original and imaginative efforts did not properly account for displacement effects and key intervening factors. Moreover, the time intervals were too short to draw definitive conclusions. Also, the criterion for evaluation consisted of participants' opinions assembled by survey, rather than counts of disorder incidents, or number of persons engaged in this behavior. Nevertheless, based upon field observations from the present research, zero tolerance of quality-of-life offending, at least during periods of rigorous enforcement, appears to have *accompanied* enhanced community restoration, business resurgence, morale, and the public's sense of security, while at the same time achieving a reduction in the level of fear in *targeted communities*. Determination of an *overall* reduction in quality-of-life offending, requires control of key variables and cognizance of crime *displacement effects* from the targeted neighborhood to other areas and time periods (Cohen 1980).

The presumed benefits of strict enforcement of quality-of-life offenses were observed on the Upper West Side of Manhattan, between Fifty-ninth and Ninety-sixth streets. This community has been widely regarded as showing improvement over the last few years for many reasons, for example, economic, demographic, reduction in the level of drug use, etc., but strict impact policing quality-of-life offenses accompanied these social changes and may have influenced neighborhood ambiance, stabilization and resurgence. Field observations from 1987–97, and evidence from everyday life (ask any long term resident) revealed that deviant street behavior did decrease over this period on the Upper West Side.

Drugs

During the period 1987–94, on a typical evening, a dozen or so drug dealers solicited potential customers in the open, on Amsterdam Avenue between Eighty-third and Ninety-fifth streets. Observations conducted in mid-1997, about three years since implementation of quality-of-life enforcement by The New York City Police Department, revealed that the area was usually free of obvious drug transactions although several scattered street dealers were still discreetly present.

Prostitution

From 1987–94, at least a dozen or so prostitutes openly worked Broadway and West End Avenues between Eighty-sixth and Ninety-second streets soliciting potential customers from around 9:00 P.M. until morning. As of mid-1997, two or three relatively unobtrusive prostitutes strolled along this same stretch of Broadway early evening, while four or five prostitutes, similarly discreet, "worked" West End Avenue, but only from about 1 A.M. until the first hint of early light.

Panhandling

Panhandlers virtually "controlled" nearly every block on Broadway between Fifty-ninth to Ninety-sixth Street during the day and early evening hours between 1987–94. Coercive police enforcement nearly brought panhandling to a complete halt. After a new local law allowed non-aggressive begging, about a quarter of the panhandlers that previously worked the streets reappeared on the same stretch of Broadway between Fifty-ninth and Ninety-sixth streets.

A decrease in petty crime on the Upper West Side, including car break-ins which previously had occurred on a regular basis at an alarming rate, also accompanied rigorous enforcement of quality-of-life offenses. Street parking is considerably safer today (1997) than several years ago. Streets that were filled with litter, discarded newspapers, trash and debris are much cleaner, partly due to an innovative workfare program introduced over the past year. During the approximate period of impact policing by the New York City Police Department (1995–97) the streets have been crowded with pedestrians and shoppers as never before in recent memory. People appear more relaxed, comfortable and secure in public places than in previous years.

The precise impact on neighborhood enhancement and crime due to increased enforcement of quality-of-life offenses in New York City's Upper West Side still remains to be determined not only because of intervening social, demographic, and economic factors as well as increased rates of incarceration, but, several other police policies that were introduced at about the time as the quality-of-life order maintenance program. In New York City these include: *Compstat*, (considered a highly effective police program of sophisticated crime-mapping techniques and command accountability, involving frequent meetings hosted by top commanders where primarily middle-level managers and supervisors must justify local anti-crime programs), community policing, and a substantial increase in police manpower and resources. Virtually no data exist establishing the nexus between a reduction in quality-of-life offenses and tactics involving zero tolerance in New York City streets, taking into account other police policies. Similarly, the connection if any, between the city's record decrease in serious crime and impact policing of quality-of-life offenses requires verification.

Depletion of Police Resources

Strict enforcement of quality-of-life offenses tends to *deplete* police resources. Limited police resources utilized for more serious crimes may be spent on enforcement of quality-of-life offenses. *Although demands to curb these activities are justified because of inherent citizen rights, individual responsibility, and community interests,* officers may be lured to quality-of-life policing due to the minimum effort required for detection and arrest and a high level of excitement, as illustrated by the following street observation.

> One afternoon in mid-May at Hunts Point in the Bronx, two young women stood at the corner of Burnet Place and Barry Street, in an isolated industrial area gesticulating for car drivers to stop. They would often ask "do you want a date?" After some time, a car stopped and one female approached the driver of what appeared to be an aging Oldsmobile. After a brief conversation, the female bent over and appeared to be massaging or scratching her leg. She successfully signaled several police officers waiting nearby in two patrol cars, a police van and three unmarked vehicles. The police vehicles surrounded the car that had stopped. Approximately twelve officers, six in plainclothes, spent about ten minutes at the scene many grinning and joking, while one officer questioned, arrested and handcuffed the suspect and then placed him in the police van. The suspect was arrested for soliciting a prostitute who in fact was one of the two female decoy officers, both of whom disappeared and hid during this time so as not to blow their cover. The two decoy officers returned to the same corner location several minutes later to await the next "suspect."

In addition to potential police misconduct due to rigorous enforcement of quality-of-life offenses, wasted or squandered police resources remains a major problem. Fourteen officers (including the two female decoy cops) certainly were not required to arrest suspected johns. Field observations in Los Angeles revealed fewer officers were required for similar street "activities." For example, in a street encounter described previously, only three officers were utilized for "prostitution" arrests (26).

Conclusion

The benefits of rigorous high-profile police enforcement on "quality-of-life" and on serious crime remains unknown, although this strategy, at least for the moment, has *accompanied* increased community stability, restoration and order in many targeted neighborhoods. It has not yet been determined whether criminal activity returns to an area after an interval of time. Intervening factors and effects due to *crime displacement* still need to be examined, optimally by specially devised field experiments, to determine the *overall* contribution of coercive *impact policing* to community renewal and crime reduction. Quality-of-life offenses need be clearly defined and an *index* must be constructed for its accurate measurement. Field observations, optimally *research vérité*, analysis of official data, interviews, surveys, and other research techniques must be undertaken to determine the dynamics and consequences involved in policing relatively minor infractions. Individuals conducting field research should be provided protection or immunity so long as their work is in accordance with the law. An integrated, eclectic approach marrying varying perspectives from criminology and criminal law is essential for research, as well as for developing original and inventive concepts regarding the root causes and the most effective control mechanisms for quality-of-life offenses.

It may very well be that perceived benefits of rigorous, high-profile quality-of-life offense enforcement as currently practiced, do not outweigh its potential negative consequences (e.g., police abuse, corruption, racism, discrimination, entrapment, wasteful resources and excess punishment, and so forth). An overcriminalized citizenry especially concentrated in selective neighborhoods and communities, a tarnished police force, and mutual distrust not only vitiate immediate gains from zero-tolerance police tactics, but also undermine the respect and legitimacy for the criminal justice system. Safe and secure streets are achievable without reliance on arresting nonthreatening individuals, alienating substantial portions of the population and brutalizing the police.

Specialized and thorough training must ideally precede *impact policing* of quality-of-life offenses and be offered on an ongoing basis for officers of all ranks and assignments. This instruction must include creative and imaginative tactics for dealing with minor, nonthreatening, first time quality-of-life offenders that go beyond warnings, summonses, fines, community service, and drug, alcohol, and gambling treatment programs, which in the long run, may prove more effective than zero tolerance police enforcement as currently practiced. Educational programs should also be developed to socialize members of the community concerning mutual expectations and obligations required by strict high-profile "quality-of-life" enforcement.

The arguments against coercive, high-profile enforcement of quality-of-life policing raise doubts concerning its efficiency and efficacy. Therefore, testing and evaluation should be initiated to determine the costs-benefits associated with this enforcement perspective. It appears that locking-up virtually *everyone suspected* of such offenses is not an optimal policy, socially, psychologically, or economically.

Note

I wish to express my gratitude to Professors Paul Blumberg and Lauren Seiler for extremely useful, perceptive, and imaginative comments. Also, James Kenney's excellent editing skills greatly enhanced this work.

References

Adams v. Williams, 407 U.S. 143, 92 S Ct. 1921 (1972).
Brown v. Texas, 443 U.S. 47, 99 S Ct. 2637 (1979).
Champion, Dean. 1997. *The Roxbury Dictionary of Criminal Justice.* Los Angeles: Roxbury Publishing Company.
Cohen, Bernard. 1980. *Deviant Street Networks: Prostitution in New York City.* MA: Lexington Books.
Daily News. 1997. 10 Oct., p. 8.
Ferrel, Jeff. 1997. "Criminological Verstehen: Inside the Immediacy of Crime." Northern Arizona University. *Justice Quarterly* 4:1.
Goffman, Erving. 1961. *Asylums.* New York: Doubleday and Co.
Kelling, George L., and Catherine M. Coles. 1996. *Fixing Broken Windows: Order and Reducing Crime in Our Communities.* New York: Martin Kessler Books, The Free Press.
Knapp Commission Report on Police Corruption. Commission to Investigate Allegations of Police Corruption and the Cities Anti-Crime Procedures. 1972. Commission Report.

Kolender v. Lawson, 461 U.S. 352 (1983).

Lardner, James. 1996. *Crusader: The Hell-Raising Police Career of Detective David Durk*. New York: Random House.

Lardner, James. 1997. "Can You Believe the New York Miracle." *The New York Review of Books*, 14 Aug., pp. 54–8.

Mass, Peter. 1973. *Serpico*. New York: Viking Press.

Mollen Commission. Commission to Investigate Allegations of Police Corruption and the Anti-Corruption Procedures of the Police Department. 1994. Commission Report.

Moran, Richard. 1998. "Community Policing Strategies Do Little to Prevent Crime," pp. 104–7 in *Crime: Current Controversies*. San Diego: Greenhaven Press.

Powell v. Texas, 392 U.S. 514 (1968).

Reinarman, Craig and Harry G. Levine, eds. 1997. *Crack in America*. California: University of California Press.

Sellin, Thorsten and Marvin E. Wolfgang. 1964. *The Measurement of Delinquency*. New York: John Wiley and Sons, Inc.

Shuttlesworth v. City of Birmingham, 382 U.S. 87 (1965).

Silverman, Eli B. 1996. "Mapping Change: How the New York City Police Department Re-engineered Itself to Drive Crime Down." *Law Enforcement News*, 15 Dec., pp. 10–12.

Skogan, Westley G. 1990. *Disorder and Decline*. New York: The Free Press.

Terry v. Ohio, 392 U.S. 1, 88 S Ct. (1968).

Tomasky, Michael. 1997. "The Brutal Truth." *New York Magazine*, 8 Sept., pp. 36–7.

United States v. Watson, 423 U.S. 411, 96 S Ct. 820 (1976).

U.S. Department of Justice. Federal Bureau of Investigation. 1996. *Crime in the United States. Uniform Crime Reports*. Washington, DC: U.S. Government Printing Office.

———. Bureau of Justice Statistics. 1997. *National Crime Victimization Survey. Changes in Criminal Victimization*. NCJ-162032. Washington, DC: Criminal Justice Reference Center.

Walker, Samuel. 1984. "Broken Windows and Fractured History: The Use and Misuse of History in Recent Police Patrol Analysis." *Justice Quarterly* 1: 57–90.

Way, Frank H. 1980. *Criminal Justice and the American Constitution*. MA: Duxbury Press.

Weber, Max. 1949. *The Methodology of the Social Sciences*. New York: The Free Press.

———. 1978. *Economy and Society*. New York: The Free Press.

Wilson, James Q., and George L. Kelling. 1982. "Broken Window: The Police and Neighborhood Safety." *Atlantic Monthly* (Mar.): 29–38.

Zimmer, Lynn, and John P. Morgan. 1997. *Marijuana Myths, Marijuana Truths*. New York: Lindesmith Center.

8

Sanctioning Serious Juvenile Offenders: A Review of Alternative Models

Paul E. Tracy and
Kimberly Kempf-Leonard

The relationship between criminological research and the criminal law, and most importantly, the implications of the former on the latter, may be evidenced with respect to juvenile law. Juvenile justice reform, including transferring juveniles to adult court for criminal prosecution, has become increasingly important as research forecasts a new crisis of escalating rates of delinquency, and particularly, juvenile violence. It has become nearly an everyday occurrence to read or hear that the juvenile justice system needs reform if not a radical overhaul. Such comments are often made by public officials and media professionals, but now also are coming from the general public who, despite a lack of relevant information and a reliance instead on distorted facts and images, have become increasingly dissatisfied with the current system of responding to juvenile crime. This dissatisfaction among the public carries a significant risk that juvenile justice reform may proceed on a reactionary basis rather than from a position of informed commentary and debate.

The present situation surrounding a new wave of delinquency and escalating juvenile violence is such that legitimate concern seems warranted. That is, while overall crime rates, as reported by the FBI, have declined during the past three years, the same cannot be said about youth crime and violence. In fact, the forecasts for the next so-called wave of juvenile violence may not be just another erroneous prediction that never comes to pass. These forecasts are now offered by informed researchers, and their predictions seem to provide scientific confirmation for previous media speculation.

We offer below the recent comments of Blumstein (1995a; 1995b), Snyder and Sickmund (1995), and DiIulio (1995); commentaries which constitute chilling forecasts of the juvenile crime problem, especially juvenile violence, that await us in the not so distant future. Importantly, these authors are not merely speculating, but rather, are offering a research-based prognosis for the future of juvenile crime. Such a prognosis and the concomitant necessity for a responsive public policy, clearly demonstrates the implications of criminological research on criminal law generally, and sanctioning models for juveniles in particular.

Blumstein (1995a) noted that, despite recent trends showing a leveling off of crime, disaggregating crime by age reveals disturbing distinctions. Following a long period (i.e., 1965–85) of relative stability in the rates of juvenile violence, the data since 1985 indicate that, "the rate of homicides committed by young people, the number of homicides they committed with guns, and the arrest rate of nonwhite juveniles for drug offenses all *doubled*" (Blumstein 1995a: 3, emphasis added).

Similarly, Snyder and Sickmund (1995), in a thorough and comprehensive analysis, made all the more definitive because it reviews both FBI arrest data and National Crime Survey data, showed that juvenile violence increased sharply between 1988 and 1992 after more than a decade of relative stability. Snyder and Sickmund also made projections using a "constant rate" assumption in which violent crimes by juveniles between the years 1992 and 2010 would increase by 22 percent, as well as an "increasing rate" model in which the rates of juvenile violence would increase as they have prior to 1992. Under their increasing rate assumption, the number of juvenile arrests for violent crime would double by the year 2010, with an increase of 145 percent for murder (1995: 7).

DiIulio (1995) recently commented on the apparent effectiveness of select law enforcement, prosecutorial, and correctional programs to reduce overall crime rates in specific locations across the country. He noted that "Americans are sitting on a demographic crime bomb" because current projections indicate that by the year 2000, we will have an additional 500,000 persons in the crime prone age group of 14-17 (1995: 15). The consequence of this according to DiIulio is that, "in five years we will have 30,000 more young murderers, rapists, and muggers on the streets than we do now" (1995: 15). DiIulio's prognosis is alarming:

> This crime bomb probably cannot be defused. The larger population of seven to ten-year old boys, now growing up fatherless, Godless, and jobless—surrounded

by deviant, delinquent, and criminal adults—will give rise to a new and more vicious group of predatory street criminals than the nation has ever known. We must therefore be prepared to contain the explosion's force and limit its damage. (1995: 15)

The current teenage cohort responsible for the majority of the recent increases in juvenile violence is a small cohort, in contrast to the much larger cohort of youth aged five to fifteen who will be moving into the crime prone years in the near future (Blumstein 1995a: 3). This phenomenon provides additional evidence of the demographic stimulus to the expected rates of future violence. Moreover, the population of fifteen-to-nineteen-year-old males who is responsible for the most crime, will increase by some 30 percent between 1995 and 2010, and many of them will have grown up in poverty to single mothers. Consequently, in the absence of strategic public policy changes, the crime wave of the early 1990s which broke national homicide rate records will be nothing but a small taste of what is to come (Blumstein 1995b: 10).

Whether one accepts the extrapolated projections of DiIulio, or the empirical estimates generated by Blumstein and Snyder and Sickmund, the future of juvenile crime appears to be a "growth industry." It also is clear from numerous studies that the majority of adult offenders are products of juvenile police recognition and juvenile court processing. Thus, juvenile delinquency causation must be thoroughly investigated, both theoretically and empirically, and appropriate measures taken. Large resource allocations will be necessary for research and implementation. We need to know more about the causal processes that induce delinquency.

The majority of eventual adult criminals can be first addressed while they are still juveniles; therefore, the arena of juvenile justice must be accorded greater primacy in the battle against crime. We cannot ignore that our past response to that small cadre of serious juvenile offenders has not been effective. We have demonstrated elsewhere that chronic delinquents have continued their delinquency careers and most have made the transition to adult crime without missing a step (Tracy and Kempf-Leonard 1996). Thus, we must heed the research literature and the accumulating evidence that provides a cautiously optimistic response to the famous question—what works?

We are poised at a crossroads. Most juvenile proceedings still operate primarily within a traditional treatment orientation aimed at serving the best interests of minors while vocal public opinion argues that public safety concerns are not being met and juvenile offenders are being coddled. As a consequence, juvenile crime and justice reforms are now a frequent topic of debate and a myriad of changes are being initiated by legislatures across the country. All too often, these reforms are conceived too quickly and with inadequate consideration of their likely consequences. It is critical that we move beyond knee-jerk reactions and develop juvenile justice policy that is substantively grounded and is likely to provide effective solutions. The situation is particularly acute at present, because the time to implement effective strategies is now while the current cohort of five-to-fifteen-year-olds are still young enough for policy changes to produce results.

The purpose of this article is to review the historical development of juvenile justice sanctions with particular emphasis on the waiver or transfer method of addressing the problem of the very serious and very violent juvenile offender. In this context, we also review a unique hybrid model for sanctioning juveniles, used in Texas, which constitutes a "just deserts" approach within the juvenile court as opposed to transfer or waiver to adult court. The Texas statute provides an excellent comparative basis to examine differential approaches to the pressing policy problem surrounding violent and serious delinquency.

Foundations

One of the significant features of the criminal justice system in the United States is the existence of a bifurcated, or two-track, justice system that determines court jurisdiction on the basis of the age of the offender. There is one court system, with attendant policies and procedures, specifically designed to handle young offenders and an entirely different court system for adult criminals. While there is some variation across the states concerning the statutory upper age limit for the jurisdiction of juvenile or family courts, the majority of states use ages sixteen or seventeen as the cutoff point for delinquency and juvenile justice jurisdiction.

Despite the lack of a uniform age for the boundaries of juvenile and adult justice, there is considerable consistency surrounding the philosophy, goals, procedures, and thus, the *raison d'être* of juvenile justice. Since its inception in 1899 in Cook County, Illinois, juvenile or family courts have been easily distinguishable from their adult court counterparts. Fundamentally, juvenile courts are guided by a *parens patriae* doctrine, by which the court acts as a surrogate parent for the welfare of the child, and the judicial action is guided by the principle of "the best interests of the child."

This *parens patriae* doctrine has resulted in a particular form and substance for juvenile justice. By tradition, if not by statute, juvenile courts are: (1) informal and not adversarial; (2) guided by a philosophy of nonintervention; (3) oriented towards the least restrictive sanction, usually community-based treatment rather than custody; and (4) concerned with the rehabilitation of the delinquent and the prevention of subsequent delinquency. On the other hand, adult courts are characteristically more "crime control oriented," and consequently, adult courts and the criminal justice system are (1) formal and adversarial; (2) intrusive; and (3) focused on punishment, incapacitation, and deterrence.

From its origins in 1899, the basic rationale for such a vastly different court philosophy and procedure was the belief that the phenomenon of delinquency is quite dissimilar from that of adult crime. Not only have delinquent acts been considered distinct from adult crimes, but also juvenile offenders have been viewed as different from adult criminals. The typical delinquent is presumed to be young and immature and his/her misbehavior is generally presumed to be infrequent and not serious. Most important, the "condition" of delinquency is assumed to be fleeting and temporary and is thus susceptible to remediation through appropriate (and usually *limited*) court interventions. This "typical" delinquent is seen as requiring a very different justice model from his/her adult counterpart.

A host of commentators (see, e.g., Hackler 1978; Ohlin 1983; Hufstedler 1984; Rubin 1985; Schwartz 1989; Bernard 1992; and Albanese 1993) have noted that the image of the prototypical delinquent, as well as both the appropriateness and effectiveness of the "benign hand" of juvenile justice, have been seriously questioned. There is growing recognition that many juvenile offenders do not fit the prototype described above, and in fact, these offenders are indistinguishable from adult criminals except for the fact that they are younger. Consequently, the validity and usefulness of juvenile justice is being challenged by the accumulation of contrary evidence that has prompted many jurisdictions to reevaluate juvenile justice philosophy and procedures.

The first, and perhaps the most definitive, evidence of the existence of the serious juvenile delinquent came from several major studies published in the 1970s. These studies—*Delinquency in a Birth Cohort* (Wolfgang et al. 1972), *The Violent Few* (Hamparian et al. 1978), and Shannon's (1978, 1980) research on three cohorts in Racine, Wisconsin—showed conclusively that a very small proportion of juvenile offenders was responsible for the majority of delinquent acts, including the most serious acts of delinquency. These studies further indicated that this small group of "chronic" delinquents began their careers very early (by age thirteen or fourteen), and that their careers continued well into the adult years, despite prior adjudications by juvenile courts.

Recent research has confirmed that the chronic delinquency syndrome, first discovered by Wolfgang (1972), Hamparian (1978), Shannon (1978, 1980), and their associates, was not a passing phenomenon. Tracy et al. (1990) reported that the chronic offender effect was replicated in the 1958 Philadelphia birth cohort and this effect was even stronger than in the previous study. Tracy et al. (1990) noted specifically that although the 982 chronic male delinquents in the 1958 cohort comprised only 7 percent of the cohort, they were responsible for 61 percent of the 15,258 acts of delinquency, and committed almost 75 percent of the serious acts of violent delinquency, including homicide, rape, robbery, and aggravated assault.

More importantly, Tracy and Kempf-Leonard (1996) completed an investigation comparing continuity and discontinuity in the transition from the juvenile career to the adult criminal career for all 27,160 subjects in the 1958 cohort. They found that the single best predictors of adult arrest status are: (1) a prior record of chronic juvenile delinquency; (2) overly lenient juvenile court dispositions early in the chronic delinquent's career; and (3) a delay in the imposition of potentially effective sanctions. The latter finding obviates the value of sanctions in reducing delinquent recidivism and thereby preventing adult crime.

The second piece of contrary evidence concerned the very rapid increases in juvenile crime, especially violent juvenile crime, exhibited in the 1970s and into the 1980s. Serious and violent juvenile crime, as recorded by the FBI, rose steadily every year from 1974 through 1981. Many critics of the juvenile justice system have pointed to these alarming increases in juvenile crime as definitive evidence that the rehabilitative philosophy and procedures maintained by juvenile courts have been highly ineffective in controlling serious delinquents.

Juvenile Justice Reform

The presumed ineffectiveness of juvenile justice centers on three main issues:

1. sanctions in juvenile courts are neither certain enough nor severe enough to deter serious delinquents from continually committing serious crimes;

2. the rehabilitative techniques used by juvenile courts have not sufficiently reduced recidivism; and,

3. the preponderance of noncustodial sanctions (such as probation), or the very short institutional sanctions that are applied allow delinquents to pose a continued and severe risk to public safety.

Following growing concern over the ineffectiveness of juvenile courts, and the general decline of the rehabilitative ideal and the rise of a more punitive model of criminal justice, there has been an observable punitive trend in juvenile justice in recent years. This occurred despite the absence of contemporaneous empirical data to support these changes in juvenile justice policy. Schwartz referred to this evolution as the "winds of change" that characterized juvenile justice policy developments beginning in the 1970s:

> While the federal agenda and the voices of reformers were calling for deinstitutionalization and the emptying of the training schools, an entirely different agenda was emerging in the states. Public outrage over the juvenile crime problem was generating tremendous pressures on state and local politicians, juvenile court judges, prosecutors, and others to take corrective action. The result was an avalanche of "get tough" policies and practices that were implemented throughout the mid and late 1970s and early 1980s. (1989: 7)

Ohlin (1983) similarly noted that the shift in juvenile justice policy reflected a strong conservative reaction to the liberal policies that had been advocated by the President's Commission on Law Enforcement and Administration of Justice (1967). In Ohlin's view, the growing fear of crime and increasing demands for repressive action led to more punitive sentencing and to a rapid escalation of incarcerations and the length of sentence to be served (1983: 231). Ohlin further argued that the just deserts approach began spreading to the juvenile system as well. He writes:

> In many states we see increasing incarceration even as delinquency rates decline. Juvenile reform legislation now calls for more mandatory sentencing and more determinate sentences for juveniles, lowering of the upper age of juvenile jurisdiction, greater ease in obtaining waivers to adult court for juvenile prosecution, and greater access to juvenile records. (1983: 231)

Zimring specifically noted that these attempts to reform sentencing practices in juvenile courts were "efforts to lead sanctioning models away from the jurisprudence of treatment and towards concepts of making the punishment fit the crime" (1981: 884). Indicative of the fact that the punitive approach has persisted, Feld recently observed that, "the influence of just deserts principles for sentencing adults has spilled over into the routine sentencing of juveniles as well" and that "despite persisting rehabilitative rhetoric, treating juveniles closely resembles punishing adult criminals" (1993: 263).

The consequences of the more punitive approach have been well documented. Krisberg and Austin argued that, "The increase [in the proportion of young people processed through the juvenile court and juvenile corrections systems between 1980 and 1990] was due to more formal punitive juvenile justice policies that produced more court referrals and expanded use of detention and juvenile incarceration" (1993: 171). Schwartz (1989) also showed that between 1977 and 1985 the rates of juvenile detention increased by more than 50 percent and the rates of juvenile incarceration in training schools increased by more than 16 percent.

Criminalizing Delinquency

The trend to criminalize the handling of serious delinquents has several manifestations.

First, some jurisdictions have adopted initiatives—generally referred to as "habitual offender" programs—in juvenile courts that are designed to identify, prosecute, and punish or incapacitate the serious juvenile offender. These programs are in sharp contrast to the *parens patriae* philosophy that has characterized juvenile justice heretofore and represents the adoption of adult career criminal prosecution procedures that are used for the serious and high-rate adult criminals.

Second, many states have adopted new procedures, or have revised their existing procedures, to remove the juvenile from the jurisdiction, care, and custody of the juvenile court in favor of processing and prosecution in adult courts for the purpose of subsequent incarceration in adult prisons. These transfer procedures are fostered by two basic assumptions:

1. The juvenile system is fundamentally unable to curb chronic juvenile recidivism; and
2. Because adult courts are more likely to impose severe sanctions (especially long prison sentences), the criminal court is a more suitable, and potentially more effective, venue in which to handle the serious and chronic juvenile delinquent.

There are several distinct procedures by which the transfer of a juvenile can be accomplished. These procedures generally are as follows:

1. To lower the maximum age of juvenile court jurisdiction so that juveniles become eligible for adult court prosecution earlier in their careers;
2. To exclude certain offenses from the jurisdiction of the juvenile court and instead require by statute that these offenses (e.g., homicide or rape) must be prosecuted in adult court;
3. To allow the prosecutor by statute to file a case in either adult court or juvenile court when a juvenile commits a very serious offense; and
4. To waive, certify, or transfer certain juveniles to adult court using a combination of such selection criteria as age, prior record, severity of instant offense, and amenability to treatment.

By far the most prevalent type of transfer method is the "waiver" process. This method is not only the most prevalent, but also is the most problematic, and the most in need of review and evaluation. Commonly, there are two principal types of waiver procedures—judicial and legislative. In judicial waiver, an individual juvenile court judge makes a determination that a particular juvenile should or should not be transferred to adult court using criteria which were established in the landmark U.S. Supreme Court case, *Kent v. the United States*. On the other hand, legislative waiver is not unlike the actuarial models used by the insurance industry. That is, under legislative waiver, all juveniles who fit a certain profile are mandated by statute to be transferred to adult court.

These two procedures are quite different and engender distinct problems. With judicial waiver there is the problem of allowing the judge too much discretion in determining which juveniles should be transferred. There also is the problem of ensuring that judges apply the waiver criteria correctly in each individual case. With legislative waiver there is the problem of the validity of the profiles that guide the decisions. That is, most prediction research in criminal justice shows a large number of incorrect predictions when using profiles. There are a considerable number of "false positives," or cases that were predicted to be dangerous but in actuality were not, and "false negatives" which are cases that the profile labeled as not dangerous but actually turned out to be dangerous recidivists.

Thus, regardless of whether transfer occurs under judicial waiver or legislatively mandated waiver, the process may mislabel many juveniles by using inappropriate or ineffective criteria concerning the dangerousness of a particular child. The grave consequence of these procedures is that some juveniles will be waived incorrectly and will be unnecessarily and unfairly exposed to the punitiveness of adult court and perhaps adult prison. Other juveniles will escape waiver even though they would have turned out to be dangerous, which unnecessarily exposes the public to potential harm.

Waiver of Juveniles

Juvenile waiver policy is the epitome of the current controversy about juvenile crime and justice. The juvenile codes in most states have traditionally specified that waiver hearings should determine the minor's amenability to treatment within the juvenile system. Youths judged as lacking such amenability are to be remanded to criminal courts for processing. Typically, however, waiver is seldom invoked. Whether called waiver, transfer, certification, or remand, the process of shifting authority over a minor from juvenile justice to criminal justice traditionally has been reserved for a few exceptional cases (Sickmund 1994). Once jurisdiction is waived, the accused youth acquires adult arrest status. The process has seemed relatively straightforward and has not posed much controversy. Aside from clarifying due process guidelines for waiver hearings, which the Supreme Court provided in the 1966 landmark *Kent* case, minimal attention has been given to the objectives, criteria, or processes used to transfer youths to criminal court.

In an interesting turn of events, both the number of transfer hearings and the prevalence of certification to criminal court have notably increased in recent years. Several reports have charted a growth in the number of waiver hearings and the corresponding increase in the number of actual youths transferred to criminal courts (Bishop et al. 1989; Champion 1989; Hamparian et al. 1982; Krisberg et al. 1986; Nimick et al. 1986). On the national level, it has been estimated that 5 percent of the more than two million juvenile arrests in 1990 were filed directly in criminal courts (Snyder 1992), and that the total number of juvenile cases processed in criminal courts that year was as high as 200,000 (Office of Juvenile Justice and Delinquency Prevention 1993). Further, Butts, and his colleagues (1995) showed that between 1988 and 1992 the percentage of cases waived out of juvenile courts increased by 68 percent.

Perhaps most importantly, legislatures across the country today have made waiver a political "hot button" issue in their efforts to respond to public concern about juvenile crime (Sontheimer and Volenick 1995). A bill introduced in the spring, 1995, legislative session of the U.S. House of Representatives to lower the minimum age for certification on a violent offense from fifteen to thirteen, suggests that waiver is even a federal concern. This, however, is largely symbolic because federal prosecutors do not bring many juveniles to trial.

The political debate centers on what is the best mechanism to transfer youths to criminal court. There are various themes among the reform efforts, and some represent unique strategies. Most plans expand the list of offenses and lower the minimum age of youths eligible for waiver consideration. Reform advocates also promote various strategies to limit the discretion of juvenile court judges. Some proposals restrict juvenile court involvement and rest the decision-making authority with the prosecutor by making waiver presumptive or by granting concurrent jurisdiction in the criminal court for certain types of cases. Other plans legislatively mandate certification for some offenses or accumulated prior record.

It is a time of lively debate, sometimes uniting crime control conservatives and due process liberals who both favor a greater use of waiver in opposition to the *parens patriae* advocates of traditional juvenile justice. Dispute over punishment, treatment, deterrence, and incapacitation is reflected in diverse opinions about the objective of transferring youth from juvenile court to criminal court jurisdiction, as well as in notions about which youths should be processed and the preferred method to do so.

Unfortunately, the rhetoric belies the absence of actual knowledge about which mechanisms of transfer are the most effective vehicles of crime control, which forms of intervention are the most efficient use of resources to assure public safety, and which juveniles are the most preferred candidates for transfer to criminal justice. These omissions are critical in the policy arena as progress in the social response to juvenile offenders can never be achieved unless reasonable people have accurate information to help them distinguish sentiment and image from proven effectiveness.

Existing Knowledge about Juvenile Waiver

Before discussing the hybrid juvenile processing model used in Texas, it is fundamentally important to discuss the current state of knowledge on the topic of transfer. The literature helps to identify why the objectives, assessment criteria, outcomes, and procedures of waiver are now at the center of legislative policy debate on juvenile crime.

Objectives. There is some indication that juvenile justice often responds to youth with a punitive approach rather than the traditional treatment orientation (Ohlin 1983; Krisberg et al. 1986; Schwartz 1989; Wizner 1984). This philosophical shift is also evident among waiver statutes which have cast aside traditional amenability to treatment objectives in favor of public safety goals (Kempf and Fagan 1989). However, the public safety rationale for waiver has been examined (Gasper and Katkin 1980), labeled ill defined (Alers 1973), and its effectiveness questioned (Hamparian et al. 1982).

Public interest shifting away from rehabilitation in favor of just deserts may not be the only explanation for changes in the purpose of certification. The goal may simply be preserving scarce juvenile court resources. From this pragmatic view, Rubin (1985: 26) argues that "waivers are public-placating escape valves used to rid juvenile courts of chronic recidivists, regardless of the insignificance of their offenses." Alternately, the objective of expanded transfer may reflect desperate political maneuvering to preserve the very future of a separate juvenile justice system. This argument of political scapegoating is advanced by Bortner:

> In evidencing a willingness to relinquish jurisdiction over a small percentage of its clientele, and by portraying these juveniles as the most intractable and the greatest threat to public safety, the juvenile system not only creates an effective symbolic gesture regarding protection of the public but it also advances its territorial interests in maintaining jurisdiction over the vast majority of juveniles and deflecting more encompassing criticisms of the entire system. (1986: 69–70)

Whether the result of strategic politics or growing public demand for punitive action, the rationale for transfer of youths to criminal courts is definitely undergoing change and is in urgent need of clarification.

Correlates of Waiver

In this context of befuddled objectives, the criteria used to determine transfer might help to explicate the process. Fortunately, several studies have tested the amenability and public safety criteria and have identified some correlates of traditional judicial waiver. While amenability could logically be judged by several factors, Feld (1987) noted that the criteria routinely considered are the age of the minor, particularly the time remaining until he or she reaches the legal age of majority, history of juvenile court interventions, and available juvenile justice resources. Houghtalin and Mays (1991) found that lack of amenability equates to age when minors are nearly at adult status. In the only study to examine the adequacy of juvenile justice resources (Singer 1996), transfer decisions were found to be motivated in large part to available funding at the local level. The issue of cost savings may now be an even more pressing concern because treatment preferences include smaller, more expensive, facilities and fewer large facilities remain in use. Amenability has almost without exception been measured by prior record.

Moreover, the findings relating transfer and prior juvenile justice intervention are mixed. Some research found that chronic offenders with lengthy records of treatment were more likely waived (Nimick et al. 1986), but other studies report likely transfers among those without prior institutionalization (Houghtalin and Mays 1991; Lemmon et al. 1991). Poulous and Orchowsky (1994) report that despite chronic behavior, nonserious offenders were not likely to be transferred in Virginia. They also note that receiving mental health treatment in the past is actually interpreted as the definition for amenability to treatment; the fact that a juvenile had not received mental health treatment made him or her more likely to be transferred Poulous and Orchowsky (1994). Once mandatory waiver for felonies with capital and life sentence options was implemented in Florida and the pool of cases eligible for transfer decisions were constrained, prior record became the sole criterion of transfer (Bishop et al. 1989).

In terms of assessing public safety, criteria should include prior violence, level of violence, threat, premeditation, and offense seriousness (Kfoury 1987). However, public safety criteria may not dictate waiver as often as perceived. Rather than violence, alleged property offenders constitute the largest group transferred to criminal court (Bortner 1986; Feld 1987; Hamparian et al. 1982; Lemmon et al. 1991; Nimick et al. 1986), and their proportionate representation increased by 1988 (Champion 1989). Other research suggests that the offense profile continued to change between 1988 and 1992 with person offenses contributing a greater share (Sickmund 1994).

In their research on correlates associated with waiver, Gillespie and Norman (1984) concluded that public safety was neither enhanced nor alternative juvenile treatments exhausted. Even after efforts were made to control discretionary decisions through presumptive guidelines, Osbun and Rode (1994) concluded that transfer decisions in Minnesota were primarily subjective. Finally, Bortner admonished that:

(A)dvocates of remand assume that the decision-making process provides for the identification of the most dangerous and intractable delinquents...But, traditional rhetoric notwithstanding, there is little evidence to suggest that those

juveniles remanded are, in fact, the most dangerous or intractable delinquents.
(1986: 58–9)

Outcomes

Thus far our review of the literature has suggested that the goal of
certification to criminal court is unclear and that even the most likely
criteria used to authorize such transfer are not systematically used.
Before concluding that transfer is a haphazard process devoid of routine policy or procedure, we must concentrate on the results of waiver.
Even if this is a situation in which small numbers of cases preclude
empirical classification, or that each case requires individualized consideration, the results may indicate that the youths transferred were
appropriate for such processing. For example, regardless of the waiver
objective we would expect transferred minors to receive criminal court
processing. We also would anticipate that most transferred youths would
receive significant criminal justice intervention, albeit treatment or
punishment perceived as unavailable within juvenile justice.

Regrettably, even research on the criminal justice experiences of transferred youths show dissimilar results. Houghtalin and Mays (1991) reported the outcomes anticipated; the majority of the transferred youths
were prosecuted, convicted, and sentenced to prison. But, elsewhere many
youths who are transferred to criminal courts have their charges dismissed
or reduced significantly when they almost definitely would have been
institutionalized by the juvenile courts (Sagatun et al. 1985). The results
of several studies indicate that juvenile sanctions were more certain than
those in criminal courts (Fagan et al. 1987; Rudman et. al. 1986). Waived
cases also appear to take a lot longer to prosecute than those processed in
juvenile courts (Rudman et. al. 1986; Lemmon et al. 1991).

The assumption that criminal justice provides harsher punishment receives support in cases involving violent offenders (Barnes and Franz
1989; Thomas and Bilchik 1985). With the exception of violent offenders, however, the opposite is often true (Barnes and Franz 1989; Bishop
et al. 1989; Gillespie and Norman 1984; Lemmon et al. 1991). A conviction does not assure incarceration (Sagatun et al. 1985), although Greenwood (1986) argues that incarceration for some crimes occurs as often
for chronic juvenile offenders as for those from any other age group.
Most youths who are sentenced receive probation (Feld 1987), although
a slight increase in use of prison and intermediate punishments was also
noted (Champion 1989). Sontheimer, co-author of a Pennsylvania waiver

study, is quoted as saying, "There may be some symbolic content in an adult record,...but if the goal of waiving kids to adult court was to incapacitate them for longer than the juvenile court could have done, in most cases it wasn't accomplished" (*Tallahassee Democrat*, 1994). Bortner (1986) concludes that if protection equates to incarceration, the waiver data demonstrate a failure to assure public safety.

Even explanations for the tendency toward greater leniency in criminal justice differ. Greenwood and his colleagues (1980) contend that when transferred youths are not incarcerated it is because they are objectively less serious offenders than adults. In contrast, Feld (1987) explains that the leniency is due to different perceptions about youths and adults who commit similar offenses.

The literature also offers other arguments pertaining to the consequences of transfer. Feld (1984: 275) argues that generally youths treated as adults have a greatly reduced probability of surviving adolescence with their life chances intact than their juvenile justice counterparts. Bishop and her colleagues (1989) warn specifically that transfer removes protection from publicity and the attendant personal status degradation and blocked opportunities that accompany criminal justice experiences. They note the Supreme Court's 1988 ruling in *Thompson v. Oklahoma,* which restricted the death penalty to offenders convicted for crimes committed at a minimum age of sixteen, and the report by Robinson and Stephens (1990) identifying twenty-eight such youthful offenders for which capital sentences were imposed.

The preponderance of the evidence seems to imply that traditional waiver proceedings have failed to operate as intended, or even very well regardless of their intent. Indeed, we might realistically discuss the transfer of youths from juvenile court to criminal jurisdiction as being arbitrary and capricious. The potential significance of this apparent lack of a waiver policy is underscored by findings of geographic disparity (Poulos and Orchowsky 1994; Singer 1996), and racial disparity that results in making minorities more often transferred to criminal court than similarly situated white youths (Bortner 1986; Eigen 1981; Fagan et al. 1987; Bishop and Frazier 1988).

Procedures. Given the evidence that transfer to criminal courts now exists in the absence of clear focus, specific criteria, and intended outcome, it is to be expected that debate should center on the appropriate form for remanding youth to adult jurisdiction. Here, however, noted scholars have offered various ideas but previous work still provides little guidance.

The lack of structured criteria to guide judicial discretion over waiver has been criticized frequently (Bishop and Frazier 1991; Feld 1978, 1987; Zimring 1991). Consistent with rational policy guidelines, Gottfredson and Gottfredson (1980) offer some basic principles to initiate substantive and procedural changes, but concedes their difficulty. Even when guidelines exist, subjective criteria have been found to dictate transfer decisions (Osbun and Rode 1984). Most recently, Simon and Feeley (1995) admonish that actuarial models and those who use them to classify offenders merely emphasize population management without concern for either punishment or treatment of the individual, do not reflect public interest, and are, in fact, devoid of the concept of humanity.

Of course, as a result of frustration with traditional judicial waiver decision processes, transferring decisions to prosecutors has gained prominence. This popularity is explained, at least in part, by the view that prosecutor involvement provides an element of punishment that the public may not perceive exists among juvenile court judges (Rosett and Cressey 1976). It is not surprising that the National District Attorneys Association endorses greater involvement of prosecutors with accused juveniles (Shine and Price 1992).

The influx of prosecutors, and concomitantly attorneys in general, is likely to change the handling of all juvenile cases (Sanborn 1993). Proponents argue that attorneys will provide assurances of greater due process for youths (Feld 1988). Opponents argue that regardless of the venue, legal counsel cannot work effectively with minors (Guggenheim 1984). Most of these arguments are speculative, however, there are three reports on the effects of prosecutorial waiver in Florida and these reports offer valuable commentary on its implementation (Bishop et al. 1989; Bishop and Frazier 1991; Thomas and Bilchik 1985).

More than a year after the law took effect, most prosecutors had no policy directing how transfer cases should be handled (Bishop et al. 1989). However, survey results showed that Florida prosecutors favored the new policy, thought their jurisdiction should extend to younger people and more offenses, and saw no conflict between the prosecutor waiver and juvenile justice objectives (Bishop et al. 1989). Thomas and Bilichik (1985) concluded that the potential for abuse by prosecutors exceeded that previously available to judges because their decisions occur outside of public scrutiny and without routine review. Bishop and her colleagues later concluded that this policy represents a fundamental shift in justice philosophy and poses a threat to the very existence of a separate justice system for juveniles (1989: 181).

Perhaps it doesn't really matter who makes the transfer decision within juvenile justice. According to Rubin (1985), decisions against waiver are proportionately few among the outcomes of transfer hearings. Thus, a waiver hearing essentially equates to waiver, and, if the outcome is a foregone conclusion, perhaps the court work group environment (Walker 1994) operates simply and prevails over policy and procedure. For example, in her interview of professionals throughout juvenile justice, Bortner (1986) found that while they all expressed initial confidence in the system's ability to identify appropriate juveniles for transfer, their responses differed when asked more specifically to compare transferred youth with similar counterparts retained within the juvenile system. In addition, in the Florida studies cited above initial increases in transfer decisions were subsequently curtailed in response to the increased workload for prosecutors and vocal attack was made by the Florida judiciary over the large number of cases (Bishop et al. 1989; Thomas and Bilchik 1985).

The proposals for change of juvenile proceedings extend the entire spectrum from revitalizing traditional therapeutic goals to complete abolition in favor of criminal justice. Calls for a hybrid approach also exist. For example, concerned about due process limitations and what he calls "criminalizing the juvenile court," Feld has been a vocal advocate of uniting elements of juvenile and criminal court and served on a task force which recently initiated such a reform in Minnesota (1993; 1995). There is no systematic evaluation of direct criminal justice processing of youths, although Bernard (1992) provides persuasive argument based on historical evidence that serious difficulties may also exist with this format. Hirschi and Gottfredson (1993) meanwhile contend that only one justice system should exist and the juvenile court model is the best.

The current state of knowledge concerning the who, where, when, and how best to process serious, violent, and chronic juvenile offenders is lacking. Criminology must work to remedy this shortcoming, and we must work quickly to be of use to policymakers who are now confronting this problem.

Juvenile Justice Reform in Texas

Owing to changes in the juvenile code in 1987 and again very recently in June 1995, Texas offers a unique opportunity to examine the comparative effects of choosing either a juvenile justice or a criminal justice management approach to particularly serious, violent, and/or chronic juvenile offenders. The 1987 legislation and the 1995 revisions were passed in an attempt to respond to a juvenile crime problem that was increasing significantly. Despite declines in the overall crime rate in the 1990s, the juvenile crime rate in Texas had increased every year since 1989. More significantly, the violent crime rate among juveniles has increased approximately 175 percent over the past five years and the juvenile murder rate has increased 291 percent over the past decade. Between 1992 and 1993 the number of juveniles arrested doubled from 83,695 to 152,379, and 16,000 were arrested for violent felonies. These statistics bear witness to the scope of the juvenile crime problem in Texas and form the backdrop against which the state has recently developed new initiatives in juvenile justice.

Texas's Determinate Sentencing Act of 1987

In 1987, the Texas legislature passed the Determinate Sentencing Act (see, Texas Family Code 1987; see also, Dawson 1988) to provide what Dawson (1990) has called a middle ground between the two usual alternatives—either juvenile court handling of a case or transferring the case to adult court. The Texas Determinate Sentencing Act of 1987 is a prime example of how reforms have been instituted in the juvenile justice system to accommodate concerns that traditional juvenile justice is inadequate to handle the problem of serious delinquency. The determinate sentencing law is a punitive, or just deserts, approach to serious delinquency in every conceivable way. The significant features of the 1987 law are displayed in table 8.1.

First, the Determinate Sentencing Act applies to all juveniles within the statutory jurisdiction of the juvenile court (i.e., ages ten through sixteen) who are charged with any of six specific felony offenses: (1) capital murder; (2) attempted capital murder; (3) murder; (4) aggravated kidnapping; (5) aggravated sexual assault; and (6) deadly assault on a police officer or court participant.

Second, the prosecutor is given the discretion to file the case in three different ways: (1) in juvenile court for normal delinquency processing; (2) seek a transfer to adult court; or (3) invoke determinate sentencing. If determinate sentencing is invoked, a petition must be filed and heard by a county grand jury. If the petition is sustained by the grand jury (with at least nine of the twelve jurors sustaining the indictment), the juvenile has a trial in juvenile court and is entitled to a twelve-

TABLE 8.1
Texas's Determinate Sentencing Act, 1987

Eligibility:

Age	juveniles, 10–16 years of age
Offenses	1. capital murder;
	2. murder;
	3. attempted capital murder;
	4. aggravated kidnapping;
	5. aggravated sexual assault; and
	6. deadly assault on a law enforcement officer or court participant;

Petition:

Step 1	prosecutor has discretion to file case:
	a. in juvenile court;
	b. seek a transfer to adult court; or
	c. invoke determinate sentencing procedures;
Step 2	if determinate sentencing is invoked, the prosecutor files a petition in juvenile court;
Step 3	prosecutor then presents petition to county grand jury;
Step 4	petition must be sustained by a vote of at least nine of the twelve-person grand jury;

Juvenile Court:

Phase 1	juvenile has a trial in juvenile court and is entitled to a twelve-person jury;
Phase 2	if adjudicated, either the jury or the juvenile court judge may sentence the juvenile;
Phase 3	juvenile may be sentenced to probation or any incarceration sentence up to thirty years in prison;

Commitment and Release

Stage 1	juvenile is first committed to the custody of the Texas Youth Commission (TYC);
Stage 2	Texas Youth Commission may petition the juvenile court at any time for a parole hearing;
Stage 3	if the juvenile has not been released on parole from TYC by the age of seventeen and one-half years, a mandatory hearing is then held in juvenile court;
Stage 4	the juvenile court then determines whether to:
	a. recommit the juvenile to TYC without a determinate sentence;
	b. transfer the juvenile to the Texas Department of Criminal Justice (TDCJ) for incarceration in an adult facility; or
	c. parole the juvenile from TYC;
	if released on parole from TYC, the juvenile will remain under supervision until:
	a. the full sentence is served;
	b. the age of twenty-one is reached; or
	c. a discharge is ordered by the juvenile court;
Stage 5	upon transfer to TDCJ at approximately age seventeen and one-half, the juvenile is treated as an adult offender for purposes of parole eligibility and subsequent supervision.

person fact-finding jury. If adjudged to be delinquent, either the jury or the juvenile court judge may sentence the juvenile to probation or any incarceration sentence up to thirty years.

Third, the juvenile is first committed to the custody of the Texas Youth Commission (TYC). The TYC may petition the juvenile court at any time for a discharge hearing. If the juvenile has not been released on parole from TYC by the age of seventeen-and-one-half years, a mandatory hearing is then held in juvenile court. The juvenile court then determines whether to: (1) recommit the juvenile to TYC without a determinate sentence; (2) transfer the juvenile to the Texas Department of Criminal Justice (TDCJ) for incarceration in an adult facility; or (3) parole the juvenile from TYC.

Fourth, if released on parole from TYC, the juvenile will remain under supervision until: (1) the full sentence is served; (2) the age of twenty-one is reached; or (3) a discharge is ordered by the juvenile court.

Fifth, upon transfer to TDCJ at approximately age seventeen and one-half, the juvenile is treated as an adult offender for purposes of parole eligibility and subsequent supervision.

Evaluation of the "Old" Determinate Sentencing Act

Dawson conducted an empirical assessment of case processing under the determinate sentencing system for the first sixteen months (1 September 1987–31 December 1988) of its operation. Dawson noted his expectations of the evaluation as follows:

> I imagined that the statute would be invoked very selectively—that it would be reserved for only the most aggravated cases within the limited category of very serious offenses covered by the law. I also imagined that once a prosecutor sought to invoke the statute, the case could be pursued with vigor due, in part, to the very selectivity that marked the decision to invoke the statue. Finally, I imagined that in those cases in which the respondent was adjudicated of having committed a covered offense, the sentences imposed would be very long, again because of the selectivity in administering the law. (1990: 1935)

Dawson's evaluation of thelaw's effect after sixteen months, however, showed that there were many unintended and surprising results. For example, in the absence of criteria to structure the decision-making, prosecutorial practices varied markedly. Determinate sentencing was pursued in Dallas County for any case which fit the offense criteria. As a result, 87 percent of all the state's grand jury cases were from

Dallas, including twenty-five cases of aggravated sexual assault. In Harris (Houston) County, where the prosecutor perceived many aggravated sexual assault charges to be "completely consensual," use of determinate sentencing was more conservative. Patterns of case attrition helped Dawson to infer that prosecutors also used the statute to enforce their positions in plea-bargaining situations. Differences in sentencing between judges and grand juries were also noted, which Dawson interpreted as judicial preference to retain control over the youths at the TYC without permitting their transfer to the Department of Corrections (1990, 1989).

Although Dawson's 1990 evaluation was constrained by the availability of only fifty-three cases, and thus, the results were preliminary and lacked generalizability, his analysis helps highlight interesting empirical questions regarding policies, procedures, and practices in the handling of serious, violent, and chronic juvenile offenders in Texas. The important consequences of these decisions, including a strong likelihood of subsequent incarceration as an adult, underscore the need to address these issues. In addition, there are consequences for correctional administrators, as research on the effects of incarceration of juveniles in adult facilities in Texas showed that juveniles pose more discipline problems and are more often held in restrictive custody (McShane and Williams 1989).

New Juvenile Justice Reform in Texas

Texas's Revised Determinate Sentencing. Concerns seemingly abound that the problem of serious youth crime in Texas and across the country has reached the crisis stage. Such concern usually spawns a host of suggestions for reform and the present situation is no exception. In 1987, Texas instituted the *Determinate Sentencing Act* to augment the handling of serious juvenile offenders in juvenile court. Against a backdrop of rising juvenile violence in 1992 through 1994, the new governor, George Bush, took office in January 1995. He fulfilled a campaign promise to the electorate by signing into law in June 1995, a new family code which instituted widespread revisions to the Texas juvenile justice system and to determinate sentencing in particular. These revised particulars of determinate sentencing are shown in table 8.2.

The 1995 revisions affected important changes in the processing of serious offenders within juvenile court. First, the new code significantly expanded the list of offenses for which determinate sentencing is pos-

TABLE 8.2
Texas' Determinate Sentencing Revisions, 1995

Eligibility:

Age	juveniles, 10–16 years of age
Offenses	1. capital murder;
	2. murder;
	3. aggravated robbery;
	4. aggravated assault;
	5. aggravated kidnapping;
	6. aggravated sexual assault; or sexual assault;
	7. felonious injury to a child, elderly person, or disabled person
	8. felony deadly conduct including discharge of a firearm
	9. aggravated controlled substance felony;
	10. criminal solicitation;
	11. criminal solicitation of a minor;
	12. indecency with a child; and
	13. criminal attempt of offense numbers: 1, 2, 3, 5, 6, 12

Petition:

Step 1	prosecutor has the discretion to file a case:
	a. in juvenile court;
	b. seek a transfer to adult court; or
	c. invoke determinate sentencing procedures;
Step 2	if determinate sentencing is invoked, the prosecutor files a petition in juvenile court;
Step 3	prosecutor then presents petition to twelve-person county grand jury;
Step 4	petition must be sustained by a vote of at least nine members of the grand jury;

Juvenile Court:

Phase 1	juvenile has a trial in juvenile court and is entitled to a twelve-person jury;
Phase 2	if adjudicated, either the jury or the juvenile court judge may sentence the juvenile;
Phase 3	the juvenile may be sentenced to probation or any incarceration sentence up to forty years in prison;

Commitment and Release

Stage 1	the juvenile is first committed to the custody of the Texas Youth Commission (TYC);
Stage 2	the TYC may petition the juvenile court at any time for a parole hearing;
Stage 3	if the juvenile has not been released on parole from TYC by the age of seventeen and one-half years, a mandatory hearing is then held in juvenile court;
Stage 4	the juvenile court then determines whether to:
	a. recommit the juvenile to TYC under a determinate sentence until the age of 21, at which time, either "b" or "c" below apply;
	b. transfer the juvenile to the Texas Department of Criminal Justice (TDCJ) for incarceration in an adult facility; or
	c. parole the juvenile from TYC, (but such parole shall be under the authority of the TDCJ.
Stage 5	upon transfer to TDCJ at approximately age seventeen and one-half, the juvenile is treated as an adult offender for purposes of parole eligibility and subsequent supervision.

sible. The original list of six offense categories authorized by the 1987 act clearly represented by all accounts a set of very serious violent offenses. However, under the 1995 legislation, the list expanded to include the following thirteen offenses: (1) capital murder; (2) murder; (3) aggravated robbery; (4) aggravated assault; (5) aggravated kidnapping; (6) aggravated sexual assault or sexual assault; (7) felonious injury to a child, elderly person, or disabled person; (8) felony deadly conduct including discharge of a firearm; (9) aggravated controlled substance felony; (10) criminal solicitation; (11) criminal solicitation of a minor; (12) indecency with a child; and (13) criminal attempt to commit any offense in preceding offense groups numbered 1, 2, 3, 5, 6, and 12.

Thus, juveniles are at-risk for determinate sentence processing for over twice as many offenses as before, and the new set of offenses includes a much wider band of severity, ranging from violence to drug and weapon offenses. Further, under the new list, juveniles face the possibility of determinate sentencing even when their offense is only an attempt to commit a serious crime. As with the 1987 Act, there are still no applicable statutory criteria associated with the juvenile's amenability to treatment, just his/her risk to public safety objectives as the basis to proceed with determinate sentencing. Indeed, as before, prosecutors have sole and complete discretion whether to proceed on cases with a determinate sentence indictment. Clearly, the number of times such an option can be pursued has increased substantially due to the increased number of offenses eligible.

Second, in an effort to introduce further punitiveness into the new code, determinate sentencing extends the maximum incarceration period from thirty years to a maximum of forty years. Like before, the sentencing procedure allows either the juvenile court judge or the jury to commit the juvenile for a period of incarceration under the jurisdiction of the TYC. After a mandatory judicial review in juvenile court prior to age eighteen, a possible transfer to either the institutional or pardons and paroles divisions of the TDCJ is possible.

Third, however, the revised code tightens up the release options so that a juvenile cannot be released by the discretion of TYC staff. That is, the new code provides that the juvenile court may at the first statutorily required hearing, either recommit the juvenile to TYC under a determinate sentence (which keeps the youth under the jurisdiction of the court), or transfer the youth to the adult corrections system. Further, even if the youth is neither recommitted nor transferred, but is paroled instead, such parole is administered through the adult pardons and parole division of TDCJ rather than under TYC authority.

Thus, under the new code, there are still three distinct ways that minors accused of serious, violent, or chronic offenses can be handled. Authority is granted to prosecutors in deciding which option to pursue. One method is the traditional juvenile court hearing for which the most serious sanction available is commitment until age nineteen to the TYC. A second option is juvenile court waiver to criminal court from which convictions can result in lengthy sentences, a life sentence, or even capital punishment. This waiver option is available in cases involving: (1) youths aged fourteen through sixteen who are accused of a crime designated as a capital felony, an aggravated controlled substance felony, or any first degree felony; or (2) youths aged fifteen or sixteen who are accused of felonies in the second or third degree or state jail felonies. The law directs judges to invoke a waiver decision based on probable cause, the seriousness of the offense alleged, or background of the child. Once a minor is certified as an adult, juvenile court jurisdiction is permanently removed. The last option is determinate sentencing as discussed above.

Texas's progressive sanctions guidelines. In addition to the revisions surrounding determinate sentencing, the legislature attempted to standardize the dispositions given to juvenile offenders under the *Texas Family Code* by implementing for the first time a set of specific guidelines under the title of "Progressive Sanctions" (Title 3, *Juvenile Justice Code*, chapter 59). The intended purposes of the Progressive Sanctions Guidelines are to:

1. Ensure that juvenile offenders will face uniform and consistent consequences and punishments that correspond to the seriousness of their current offense, prior delinquent history, special treatment or training needs, and effectiveness of prior interventions;
2. Balance public protection and rehabilitation while holding juvenile offenders accountable for their conduct;
3. Permit flexibility in the decisions made in relation to the juvenile offender to the extent allowed by law;
4. Consider the juvenile offender's circumstances; and
5. Improve juvenile justice planning and resource allocation by ensuring uniform and consistent reporting of disposition decisions at all levels (see *Texas Family Code*, chapter 59).

The Progressive Sanctions Guidelines provide specific procedures by which sanction levels are to be assigned. Following the child's first commission of delinquent conduct or conduct indicating a need for supervision, the probation department may or the juvenile court may in a disposition hearing, assign the child one of seven sanction levels according to the child's conduct. The seven sanction levels are displayed in table 8.3.

The seven sanction levels generally follow the following set of offense characteristics:

1. For conduct indicating a need for supervision, other than a Class A or B misdemeanor, the sanction level is one;
2. For a Class A or B misdemeanor, other than a misdemeanor involving the use or possession of a firearm, or for delinquent conduct under Section 51.03a(2) or (3), the sanction level is two;
3. For a misdemeanor involving the use or possession of a firearm or for a state jail felony or a felony of the third degree, the sanction level is three;
4. For a felony of the second degree, the sanction level is four;
5. For a felony of the first degree, other than a felony involving the use of a deadly weapon or causing serious bodily injury, the sanction level is five;

TABLE 8.3
Texas's Progressive Sanctions Guidelines, 1995:
Sanction Levels and Associated Offenses

Sanction Level	Offense Classifications
One	Conduct indicating a Need for Supervision other than a Class A or Class B Misdemeanor
Two	a. Class A or Class B Misdemeanor, other than a misdemeanor involving the use or possession of a firearm; b. Violation of a juvenile court order; Violation of a justice or municipal court order (contempt);
Three	a. Misdemeanor involving the use or possession of a firearm; b. State Jail felony; c. Third Degree felony;
Four	Second Degree Felony;
Five	First Degree Felony, other than a felony involving the use of a deadly weapon or causing serious bodily injury;
Six	a. First Degree Felony involving the use of a deadly weapon or cuasing serious bodily injury; b. Aggravated Controlled Substance Felony;
Seven	a. Determinate Sentencing for a First Degree Felony involving the use of a deadly weapon or causing serious bodily injury; b. Determinate Sentence for an Aggravated Controlled Substance Felony; c. Capital Felony.

6. For a felony of the first degree involving the use of a deadly weapon or causing serious bodily injury or for an aggravated controlled substance felony, the sanction level is six or, if the petition has been approved by a grand jury under Section 53.045, seven; or
7. For a capital felony, the sanction level is seven.

In addition to these instant offense criteria, the progressive sanctions program also includes provisions for assigning escalating sanction levels. These provisions cover subsequent offenses regardless of whether they represent increased severity over the previous offense. The particulars of the seven sanction levels are given in table 8.4.

Generally speaking, the escalation in sanction level is based upon the delinquent engaging in additional delinquent conduct—which itself may be grounds for a higher sanction level because of recidivism per se, or because such recidivism represents and increase in the severity of the delinquent conduct. These principles surrounding sanction level increases are given below.

1. If a child refuses to comply with the restrictions and standards of behavior established by the parent or guardian and the court, a parent or guardian may notify the court of the child's refusal to comply, and the court may place the child at the next level of sanction;
2. If the child's subsequent commission of delinquent conduct, or conduct indicating a need for supervision, involves a violation of a penal law of a classification that is the same as, or greater than, the classification of the child's previous conduct, the juvenile court may assign the child a sanction level that is one level higher than the previously assigned sanction level (unless the child's previously assigned sanction level is seven which is already the highest level);
3. If the child's previously assigned sanction level is four or five and the child's subsequent commission of delinquent conduct is of the grade of felony, the juvenile court may assign the child a sanction level that is one level higher than the previously assigned sanction level;
4. A juvenile court or probation department that deviates from the guidelines under this section shall state in writing its reasons for the deviation and submit the statement to the juvenile board; and
5. A probation department may extend a period of probation specified under sanction levels one through five if the circumstances of the child warrant the extension and the probation department notifies the juvenile court in writing of the extension and the period of and reason for the extension.

Implications of the Texas Hybrid Model

The latest juvenile code reforms in Texas—the *Determinate Sen-*

TABLE 8.4
Texas' Progressive Sanctions Guidelines, 1995:
Sanction Levels and Associated Sanctions

Sanction Level	Recommended Sanctions
One	1. require counseling for the child regarding the child's conduct; 2. inform the child of the progressive sanctions that may be imposed on the child if the child continues to engage in delinquent conduct or conduct indicating a need for supervision; 3. inform the child's parents or guardians of the parents' or guardians' responsibility to impose reasonable restrictions on the child to prevent the conduct from recurring; 4. provide information or other assistance to the child or the child's parents or guardians in securing needed social services; 5. require the child or the child's parents or guardians to participate in a program for services under Section 264.302; 6. refer the child to a community-based citizen intervention program approved by the juvenile court; and 7. release the child to the child's parents or guardians.
Two	1. place the child on court-ordered or informal probation for not less than three months or more than six months; 2. require the child to make restitution to the victim of the child's conduct or perform community service restitution appropriate to the nature and degree of harm caused and according to the child's ability; 3. require the child's parents or guardians to identify restrictions the parents or guardians will impose on the child's activities and requirements the parents or guardians will set for the child's behavior; 4. provide the information required under Level One nos. 2 and 4; 5. require the child or the child's parents or guardians to participate in a program for services; 6. refer the child to a community-based citizen intervention program approved by the juvenile court; and 7. if appropriate, impose additional conditions of probation.
Three	1. place the child on probation for not less than six months; 2. require the child to make restitution to the victim of the child's conduct or perform community service restitution appropriate to the nature and degree of harm caused and according to the child's ability; 3. impose specific restrictions on the child's activities and requirements for the child's behavior as conditions of probation; 4. require a probation officer to closely monitor the child's activities and behavior; 5. require the child or the child's parents or guardians to participate in programs or services designated by the court or probation officer; and 6. if appropriate, impose additional conditions of probation.
Four	1. require the child to participate as a condition of probation for not less than three months in a highly intensive and regimented program that emphasizes discipline, physical fitness, social responsibility, and productive work; 2. after release from the program, continue the child on probation supervision for not less than six months or more than twelve months;

TABLE 8.4 (continued)

3. require the child to make restitution to the victim of the child's conduct or perform community service restitution appropriate to the nature and degree of harm caused and according to the child's ability;
4. impose highly structured restrictions on the child's activities and requirements for behavior of the child as conditions of probation;
5. require a probation officer to closely monitor the child;
6. require the child or the child's parents or guardians to participate in programs or services designed to address their particular needs and circumstances; and
7. if appropriate, impose additional sanctions.

The juvenile court shall discharge the child from the custody of the probation department on the date the provisions of this section are met or on the child's eighteenth birthday, whichever is earlier.

Five

1. require the child to participate as a condition of probation for not less than six months or more than nine months in a highly structured residential program that emphasizes discipline, accountability, physical fitness, and productive work;
2. after release from the program, continue the child on probation supervision for not less than six months or more than twelve months;
3. require the child to make restitution to the victim of the child's conduct or perform community service restitution appropriate to the nature and degree of harm caused and according to the child's ability;
4. impose highly structured restrictions on the child's activities and requirements for behavior of the child as conditions of probation;
5. require a probation officer to closely monitor the child;
6. require the child or the child's parents or guardians to participate in programs or services designed to address their particular needs and circumstances; and
7. if appropriate, impose additional sanctions.

The juvenile court shall discharge the child from the custody of the probation department on the date the provisions of this section are met or on the child's eighteenth birthday, whichever is earlier.

Six

a. For a child at sanction level six, the juvenile court shall commit the child to the custody of the Texas Youth Commission, and:
1. require the child to participate in a highly structured residential program that emphasizes discipline, accountability, fitness, training, and productive work for not less than nine months or more than twenty-four months unless the commission extends the period and the reason for an extension is documented;
2. require the child to make restitution to the victim of the child's conduct or perform community service restitution appropriate to the nature and degree of the harm caused and according to the child's ability, if there is a victim of the child's conduct;
3. require the child and the child's parents or guardians to participate in programs and services for their particular needs and circumstances; and
4. if appropriate, impose additional sanctions.

b. On release of the child under supervision, the Texas Youth Commission may:

TABLE 8.4 (continued)

	1. impose highly structured restrictions on the child's activities and requirements for behavior of the child as conditions of release under supervision; 2. require a parole officer to closely monitor the child for not less than six months; and, 3. if appropriate, impose any other conditions of supervision. c. The Texas Youth Commission may discharge the child from the commission's custody on the date the provisions of this section are met or on the child's nineteenth birthday, whichever is earlier.
Seven	a. For a child at sanction level seven, the juvenile court shall sentence the child to commitment to the Texas Youth Commission and the commission may: 1. require the child to participate in a highly structured residential program that emphasizes discipline, accountability, fitness, training, and productive work for not less than twelve months or more than ten years unless the commission extends the period and the reason for the extension is documented; 2. require the child to make restitution to the victim of the child's conduct or perform community service restitution appropriate to the nature and degree of harm caused and according to the child's ability, if there is a victim of the child's conduct; 3. require the child and the child's parents or guardians to participate in programs and services for their particular needs and circumstances; and 4. impose any other appropriate sanction. b. On release of the child under supervision, the Texas Youth Commission parole programs may: 1. impose highly structured restrictions on the child's activities and requirements for behavior of the child as conditions of release under supervision; 2. require a parole officer to monitor the child closely for not less than twelve months; and 3. impose any other appropriate condition of supervision.

tencing Act and the Progressive Sanctions Guidelines were stimulated by the belief that recent juvenile crime is somehow more frequent or at least more serious (violent) than in the past, even the recent past. At first glance, this may seem just another example of a cycle that continues unabated—increases in juvenile crime or just the perception that juvenile crime is increasing necessitates reforms, and after such reforms are instituted and no apparent effect on juvenile crime is evidenced, the cycle begins anew. However, the latest reforms in Texas followed extensive debate during the fall election in 1994 and legislative deliberation throughout the spring of 1995, which pointed to statutory failures in the juvenile code as the cause of the inability of the juvenile system to respond to serious juvenile crime.

These latest reform efforts in Texas, therefore, have been guided by a comprehensive analysis not of the nature and extent of juvenile crime, but rather, by an effort to remediate the peculiar problems which confront the juvenile justice system in its attempt to respond to juvenile criminals. The reforms in Texas suggest two main perspectives.

First, there is a manifest attempt to increase the likelihood that the most severe cases of violent delinquency can be administered through procedures which handle the case within the province of the juvenile court system, rather than merely transferring the case out and relying upon the adult court and adult correctional system to "do something" with the juvenile through the waiver process. As we have seen above and as we will argue below, waiver is a process that is fraught with problems. By relying on determinate sentencing options in juvenile court, Texas is providing for a just deserts approach to serious delinquents without engaging in the prediction fallacy that often characterizes waiver procedures. The determinate sentencing provisions of the new *Texas Family Code* thus represent a unique and innovative effort to respond to serious delinquency.

Second, with the implementation of its Progressive Sanction Guidelines, Texas is also attempting to instill a high degree of consistency and predictability in the dispositions that are given to delinquents at their first offense and throughout their delinquency career as they accumulate more offenses. This guidelines policy has enormous potential to enable the juvenile justice system to respond in a timely and structured way, and more important, one which is consistent across all juveniles similarly situated with respect to offense rank and offense severity.

Conclusion

There are many possible ways to address the problem of serious and violent juvenile crime. There are historical precedents that guide present juvenile justice policies, and likewise, there are theoretical and philosophical underpinnings that shape different responses to juvenile and adult offenders. Boland and Wilson (1978) argued that one of the primary reasons for the ineffective processing of serious juvenile offenders is the historically based two-track system of justice. In their view, the procedure of handling juvenile and adult offenders in separate and different justice systems, without the benefit of coordinated criminal history record-keeping, is ineffective and can lead to undesirable sentencing practices. First, the manifestly rehabilitative and preventive philosophy of juvenile courts allows lenient—or at least less punitive—interventions. Consequently, severe sanctions and punishment for the serious and habitual offenders must wait until they progress to adult criminality. Second, because a juvenile's record is often unavailable—sometimes by statute, more often by practice—to adult authorities, the person in effect begins anew in criminal court and may be treated as a first-time offender, in spite of a possibly lengthy juvenile career. This process of starting over in terms of one's criminal history can seriously delay more appropriate punitive actions by the courts that the chronic offender seems to warrant.

The juvenile justice system seems poised for further policy developments to respond to the "coming crisis" of juvenile violence. At this juncture, it is crucial that change within the juvenile justice system be guided by relevant and accurate information about the extent, character, and complexity of juvenile crime and the particular role of the violent or chronic offender. We suggest that the improved handling of offenders within the juvenile justice system is, at least for now, preferable to the increasing tendency to remove juveniles from the juvenile justice process by certifying them as adults for prosecution and transferring the case to the adult authorities. We suggest that the certification or waiver process is fostered by the legislative assumption that the juvenile system has failed to curb recidivism and that adult courts hold a better promise of severe sanctions. This initiative to remove juveniles from the province of juvenile court may not only be premature, but may also be based on false assumptions.

First, the rationale for waiver is based on the notion that more severe penalties are not only available in criminal court, but will in fact be applied to the certified youth. The available evidence on this issue does not show that juveniles who have been referred for prosecution, with the exception of juvenile murderers, generally receive harsher treatment by criminal courts. In many instances, these juvenile offenders actually receive more lenient sanctions than comparable offenders retained by juvenile courts.

Second, the waiver procedure assumes a degree of efficiency in predicting dangerousness—usually expressed as the likelihood of an additional serious offense—that is not supported by available evidence. Most waiver statutes specify that age of the accused, in combination with current offense and prior record are legally permissible factors that predict future misconduct, and thereby, may be legitimately used as waiver criteria. However, the accumulation of research on this issue does not identify a unique set of factors with such predictive validity. Most studies instead show a considerable percentage of "false positives," or youths who were predicted as becoming recidivists but who remained law abiding. There also are several observations of "false negatives," in which the criteria predicted that the youths would desist from offending, but they in fact continued their criminal careers.

Waiver processes that rely on such faulty prediction criteria will mislabel many offenders with potentially grave consequences. Some will be misidentified as "dangerous" and will be waived to criminal court. They will face adult procedures and, if convicted, may face harsh imprisonment with adult felons. Some offenders, who will continue to offend, will be labeled as likely desisters and will encounter benign and ineffective dispositions.

Thus, expanded juvenile waiver is arguably a faulty policy initiative and at best, it is premature. Juveniles can, and should, be dealt with in a serious manner when their behavior and prior record warrant such action. Although juvenile justice operates in accord with objectives of judicious nonintervention and the least restrictive means standards, those who implement this system can revise their thinking and expectations consistent with the severity of the offender. The chronic juvenile offenders, for example, are unique and require special handling. They need not be waived to criminal court before efforts are made to improve the juvenile justice procedures for handling them. Waiver is no substitute for sensible juvenile justice policy, and may even provide an excuse for not developing such a policy.

We have identified two key innovative features of the *Texas Family Code* that are singularly unique. The determinate sentencing process provides for three very different approaches to the processing and sanctioning of serious, violent juvenile offenders and the progressive sanction guidelines maintain a strategic and measured response to juvenile offenders as their careers progress. These features of the *Texas Family Code* underscore the need for more states to move beyond the typical process of implementing crime control policies, especially for juveniles, that are based on widespread beliefs that it is preferable to handle the serious juvenile outside, rather than within, juvenile or family courts. We have shown the fatal flaws that may ultimately befall the easy and popular reform approach represented by the waiver process.

Juveniles can receive effective punishment within the juvenile court instead of waiver to the adult venue. The new *Texas Family Code* appears to hold high promise in this regard because of its unique procedures, particularly determinate sentencing and progressive sanctions. Of course, these new procedures for handling juvenile offenders in Texas are quite new, and because they did not take effect until 1 January 1996, it would be premature to gage their effectiveness. However, the point remains that Texas has adopted innovative methods of responding to juvenile crime which maintain jurisdiction of the case in the juvenile court system where such cases belong.

Our concern here has been to suggest that other jurisdictions might benefit from using the *Texas Family Code* as a guide. It is important that when new policies are considered, juvenile policy development should proceed, not merely to assuage an emotional public and without clear objectives, viable alternatives, and adequate information on which to base new policies. We must move beyond rhetoric, the assigning of blame for past policy failures, and acquiescing to the public's demand that the juvenile system be bypassed in favor of the adult court alternative. There can be no real progress in controlling serious and chronic juvenile offenders until those with the authority to implement policies move beyond knee-jerk reactions and benefit from the lessons of innovative policy development.

References

Albanese, Jay S. 1993. *Dealing with Delinquency: The Future of Juvenile Justice.* Chicago: Nelson-Hall Publishers.

Alers, M. 1973. "Transfer of Jurisdiction from Juvenile to Criminal Court." *Crime and Delinquency* 19: 519–26.

Barnes, C.W. and R.S. Franz. 1989. "Questionably Adult: Determinants and Effects of the Juvenile Waiver Decision." *Justice Quarterly* 6:117–35.

Bernard, Thomas J. 1992. *The Cycle of Juvenile Justice.* New York: Oxford University Press.

Bishop, Donna and Charles E. Frazier. 1988. "The Influence of Race in Juvenile Justice Processing," *Journal of Research in Crime and Delinquency* 25:242–63.

Bishop, Donna and Charles E. Frazier. 1991. "Transfer of Juveniles to Criminal Court: A Case Study and Analysis of Prosecutorial Waiver," *Notre Dame Journal of Law, Ethics, and Public Policy* 5: 281–302.

Bishop, Donna, Charles E. Frazier, and J.C. Henretta. 1989. "Prosecutorial Waiver: Case Study of a Questionable Reform," *Crime and Delinquency* 35 (2): 179–201.

Blumstein, Alfred S. 1995a. "Violence by Young People." In *National Institute of Justice Journal.* Washington, DC: National Institute of Justice.

———. 1995b. "An Interview with Professor Alfred Blumstein." *Law Enforcement News,* 422, 10–13.

Bortner, Margaret A. 1986. "Traditional Rhetoric, Organizational Realities: Remand of Juveniles to Adult Court," *Crime and Delinquency* 32(1): 53–73.

Butts, J., H. Snyder, T. Finnegan, A. Aughenbaugh, N. Tierney, D. Sullivan, R. Poole,

M. Sickmund, and E. Poe. 1995. *Juvenile Court Statistics 1992.* Washington, DC: Office of Juvenile Justice and Delinquency Prevention.

Champion, Dean J. 1989. "Teenage Felons and Waiver Hearings: Some Recent Trends, 1980–1988," *Crime and Delinquency* 35(4): 577–85.

Dawson, Robert O. 1988. "The Third Justice System: The New Juvenile-Criminal System of Determinate Sentencing for the Youthful Violent Offender in Texas," *St. Mary's Law Journal* 19: 943–1015.

———. 1990. "The Violent Juvenile Offender: An Empirical Study of Juvenile Determinant Sentencing Proceedings as an Alternative to Criminal Prosecution," *Texas Tech Law Review* 21: 1897–1937.

DiIulio, John J. 1995. "Arresting Ideas." *Policy Review* 74: 12–16.

Eigen, Joel P. 1981. "Punishing Youth Homicide Offenders in Philadelphia," *Journal of Criminal Law and Criminology* 72: 1072–93.

Fagan, Jeffrey, M. Forst, and T.S Vivona. 1987. "Racial Determinants of the Judicial Transfer Decision: Prosecuting Violent Youth in Criminal Court," *Crime and Delinquency* 33:259–86.

Feld, Barry C. 1978. "Reference of Juvenile Offenders for Adult Prosecution: The Legislative Alternative to Asking Unanswerable Questions," *Minnesota Law Review* 62: 515–618.

———. 1983. "Delinquent Careers and Criminal Policy: Just Deserts and the Waiver Decision," *Criminology* 21:195–212.

———. 1984. "The Decision to Seek Criminal Charges: Just Deserts and the Waiver Decision," *Criminal Justice Ethics* (Summer/Fall): 27–41.

———. 1987. "Juvenile Court Meets the Principle of Offense: Legislative Changes in Juvenile Waiver Statutes," *Journal of Criminal Law and Criminology* 78: 471–533.

———. 1988. "In re Gault Revisited: A Cross-state Comparison of the Right to Counsel in Juvenile Court," *Crime and Delinquency* 34: 393-424.

———. 1992. "Criminalizing the Juvenile Court: A Research Agenda for the 1990s," pp. 59–88 in I. Schwartz (ed.) *Juvenile Justice and Public Policy.* New York: Lexington Books.

———. 1993. "Juvenile (In) justice and the Criminal Court Alternative," *Crime and Delinquency* 39 (4): 403-24.

———. 1995. "Violent Youth and Public Policy: A Case Study of Juvenile Justice Law Reform," *Minnesota Law Review* 79 (5): 965-1128.

Flicker, B. 1981. "Prosecuting Juveniles as Adults: A Symptom of a Crisis in the Juvenile Courts," pp. 351–77 in J.C. Hall et al. (eds.) *Major Issues in Juvenile Justice Information and Training.* Washington, DC: Department of Justice.

Gasper, J. and D. Katkin. 1980. "A Rationale for the Abolition of the Juvenile Courts' Power to Waive Jurisdictions," *Pepperdine Law Review* 7: 937–51.

Gillespie, L. K. and M.D. Norman. 1984. "Does certification mean prison: Some preliminary findings from Utah." Juvenile and Family Court Journal 35: 23–35.

Gottfredson, M.R. and D.G. Gottfredson. 1980. *Decision-Making in Criminal Justice: Toward the Rational Exercise of Discretion.* Cambridge, MA: Ballinger.

Greenwood, P. 1986. "Differences in Criminal Behavior and Court Responses among Juvenile and Young Adult Defendants," in M. Tonry and N. Morris (eds.) *Crime and Justice: An Annual Review of Research,* vol. 7. Chicago: University of Chicago Press.

Greenwood, P., J. Petersilia, and F.E. Zimring. 1980. Age, Crime and Sanctions: The Transition from Juvenile to Adult Courts. Santa Monica, CA: Rand.

Guggenheim, Martin. 1984. "The Right to be Represented but Not Heard: Reflections on Legal Representation for Children," *New York University Law Review* 59: 76–155.

Hackler, J.C. 1978. "The Need to Do Something," *The Prevention of Youthful Crime: The Great Stumble Forward.* Toronto: Methuen Press.

Hamparian, D.M., R.S. Schuster, S. Dinitz, and J.P. Conrad. 1978. *The Violent Few: A Study of Dangerous Juvenile Offenders.* Lexington, MA: D.C. Heath.

Hamparian, D., L.K. Estep, S.M. Muntean, R.R. Priestino, R.G. Swisher, P.L. Wallace and J.L. White. 1982. *Youth in Adult Courts: Between Two Worlds.* Washington, DC: Department of Justice.

Hirschi, T. and M.R. Gottfredson. 1993. "Rethinking the Juvenile Justice System," *Crime and Delinquency* 39 (2): 262–71.

Houghtalin, M. and G.L. Mays. 1991. "Criminal Dispositions of New Mexico Juveniles Transferred to Adult Court," *Crime and Delinquency* 37(3):393–407.

Hufstedler, S.M. 1984. "Should We Give Up Reform?" *Crime and Delinquency* 30 (3):415–22.

Kempf, K. and J.A. Fagan. 1989. "An Empirical Typology of Statutory Approaches to Waiver of Juveniles to Criminal Court," Presented at the Annual Meetings of the American Society of Criminology.

Kent v. United States. 1966. 383 U.S. 541

Kfoury, P.R. 1987. *Children before the Court: Reflections on Legal Issues Affecting Minors.* Boston, MA: Butterworth.

Krisberg, B., I.M. Schwartz, P. Litsky, and J. Austin. 1986. "The Watershed of Juvenile Justice Reform," *Crime and Delinquency* 32: 5–38.

Krisberg, B. and Austin, J.F. 1993. *Reinventing Juvenile Justice.* Newbury Park, CA: Sage.

Lemmon, J., H. Sontheimer, and K. Saylor. 1991. A Study of Pennsylvania Juveniles Transferred to Criminal Court in 1986. Pennsylvania Juvenile Court Judges' Commission, Harrisburg, PA.

McShane, M.D. and Frank P. Williams, III. 1989. "The Prison Adjustment of Juvenile Offenders," *Crime and Delinquency* 35 (2): 254–69.

Mylniec, W. 1976. "Juvenile Delinquent or Adult Convict: The Prosecutor's Choice," *American Criminal Law Review* 14: 29–57.

Nimick, E., L. Szymanski, and H.S. Snyder. 1986. *Juvenile Court Waiver: A Study of Juvenile Court Cases Transferred to Criminal Court.* Pittsburgh: National Center for Juvenile Justice.

Ohlin, Lloyd. 1983. "The Future of Juvenile Justice Policy Research." *Crime and Delinquency* 29: 463-89.

Office of Juvenile Justice and Delinquency Prevention. 1993. *A Comprehensive Strategy for Serious, Violent, and Chronic Juvenile Offenders, Program Summary.* Washington, DC: U.S. Department of Justice.

Osbun, L.A. and P. Rode. 1994. "Prosecuting Juveniles as Adults: The Quest for 'Objective' Decisions," 22 *Criminology* 2.

Poulous, T.M. and S. Orchowsky. 1994. "Serious Juvenile Offenders: Predicting the Probability of Transfer to Criminal Court," *Crime and Delinquency* 40 (1): 3–17.

Robinson, D.A. and O.H. Stephens. 1990. "Patterns of Mitigating Factors in Juvenile Death Penalty Cases." Paper presented at Academy of Criminal Justice Sciences.

Rosett, A. and Donarld.R. Cressey. 1976. *Justice by Consent.* New York: Lippincott.

Rubin, H. Ted. 1985. *Behind the Black Robes: Juvenile Court Judges and the Court.* Beverly Hills, CA: Sage Publications.

———. 1985. *Juvenile Justice: Policy Practice and Law.* New York: Random House.

Rudman, C., E. Hartstone, J. Fagan, and M. Moore. 1986. "Violent Youth in Adult Court: Process and Punishment," *Crime and Delinquency* 32: 75–96.

Sagatun, I., L.L. McCollum, and L.P. Edwards. 1985. "The Effect of Transfers from Juvenile to Criminal Court: A Loglinear Analysis," *Journal of Crime and Justice* 8:65–92.

Sanborn, J.B. 1993. "Philosophical, Legal, and Systemic Aspects of Juvenile Court Plea Bargaining," *Crime and Delinquency* 39 (4): 509–27.

Schwartz, Ira M. 1989. *In (Justice) for Juveniles: Rethinking the Best Interests of the Child.* Lexington, MA: D.C. Heath.

Shannon, Lyle W. 1980. *Assessing the Relationship of Adult Criminal Careers to Juvenile Careers.* Washington, DC: U. S. Government Printing Office.

———. 1988. *Criminal Career Continuity: Its Social Context.* New York: Human Sciences Press.

Shine, J. and D. Price. 1992. "Prosecutors and Juvenile Justice: New Roles and Perspectives," pp. 101–33 in I. Schwartz (ed.) *Juvenile Justice and Public Policy.* New York: Lexington Books.

Sickmund, M. 1994. *How Juveniles Get to Criminal Court.* Washington, DC: U.S. Department of Justice.

Simon, Jonathan and Malcolm Feeley. 1995. "True Crime: The New Penology and Public Discourse on Crime," in Thomas G. Blomberg and Stanley Cohen (eds.) *Punishment and Social Control: Essays in Honor of Sheldon Messinger.* New York: Aldine-de-Gruyter.

Singer, Simon. 1996. *Recriminalizing Delinquency: Violent Juvenile Crimes and Juvenile Justice Reform.* Cambridge: Cambridge University Press.

Snyder, Howard S. 1992. *Arrests of Youth 1990.* Washington, DC: U.S. Department of Justice.

Snyder, H.N. and M. Sickmund. 1995. *Juvenile Offenders and Victims: A Focus on Violence.* Washington, DC: Office of Juvenile Justice and Delinquency Prevention.

Soler, Mark. 1988. "Litigation on Behalf of Children in Adult Jails," *Crime and Delinquency* 34: 190-208.

Sontheimer, Henry and A. Volenik. 1995. "Tough Responses to Serious Juvenile Crime Includes Waiver to Adult Court—But Is That the Best Answer?" *Juvenile Justice Update* (February) 1: 1–10.

Tallahassee Democrat. 1994. "Adult Trials for Juveniles Can Backfire on Public." 25 April.

Thomas, Charles W. and Shay Bilchik. 1985. "Prosecuting Juveniles in Criminal Courts: A Legal and Empirical Analysis," *Journal of Criminal Law and Criminology* 76: 439–79.

Thompson v. Oklahoma. 1988. 108 S.Ct. 2687.

Tracy, P.E., M.E. Wolfgang, and R.M. Figlio. 1990. *Delinquency Careers in Two Birth Cohorts.* New York: Plenum Press.

Tracy, P.E. and K. Kempf-Leonard. 1996. *Continuity and Discontinuity in Criminal Careers: The Transition from Delinquency to Crime.* New York: Plenum Press.

United States v. Bland. 1972. D.C. Cir. 472 F.2d 1329.

Wizner, S. 1984. "Discretionary Waiver of Juvenile Court Jurisdiction: Arbitrariness," *Criminal Justice Ethics* (Summer/Fall): 41–50.

Wolfgang, M.E., R.M. Figlio, and T. Sellin. 1972. *Delinquency in a Birth Cohort.* Chicago: The University of Chicago Press.

Zimring, F.E. 1991. *The Changing Legal World of Adolescence.* New York: The Free Press.

9

From Individualization of the Offender to Individualization of the Victim: An Assessment of Wolfgang's Conceptualization of a Victim-Oriented Criminal Justice System

Edna Erez and
Leslie Sebba

Introduction

In his keynote address at the Third International Symposium on Victimology in Munster/Westfalia, Germany in 1979, Marvin Wolfgang launched the concept of victim individualization and proposed it as a beacon for legal reform and the framing of penological policy (Wolfgang 1982). According to Wolfgang, "The principal point is that a variety of victim attributes and characteristics relative to the harm inflicted on the victim might be taken into account not only in scientific research but in statutory provisions and in the adjudication and offender sentencing process" (Wolfgang 1982: 48). Wolfgang also noted that "although some statutory provisions exist which recognize the specificity of some victims, legislative recognition has been minimal, perhaps because of a vague sense of democratization of victims of similar crimes so as not to acknowledge a hierarchy of differences, perhaps out of a fear of retrogression to an earlier stage of social evolution" (Wolfgang 1982: 48). He suggested that more crimes might be defined and sanctions provided on the basis of specific attributes of the victimization process.

Wolfgang supported his arguments with an extensive array of examples from the norms and practices of penal systems from ancient times to the present, referring, inter alia, to differentiated penalties where the victim was a nobleman under the Code of Hammurabi, and to the special protection of "masters and Christians" under early American colonial codes. He also mentioned differentiations occasionally made in the modern law,[1] for instance, in relation to children or police officers as victims. He proceeded to consider a number of areas in which victims 'variables might be taken into consideration, under the headings "age, sex, and time," "injury severity," "emotional trauma and economic loss," "victim-offender relationship" and "multiple victim variability" (Wolfgang 1982: 50–4).

These proposals should be seen not only in the context of prevailing approaches to penal philosophy and the victims, but also as the culmination of a line of research and scholarship in which Wolfgang had been engaged over a long period of time. Wolfgang's interest in the victims of crime dates from his early research on homicide, in the context of which he coined the concept of *victim precipitation* (Wolfgang 1958). Ironically, however, this approach, together with its extension by Amir (1971) and the earlier classifications of Mendelsohn (1974) led to the perception that victimologists were concerned with "blaming the victim" (Ryan 1971) rather than with the development of a new penal philosophy. Thus, this early research seems to have been less influential in formulating the ideas expounded in Wolfgang's 1979 keynote address than his methodologically pioneering study of *The Measurement of Delinquency* (Sellin and Wolfgang 1964), developed initially in conjunction with Thorsten Sellin, although this latter work was in its early stages conceptually unrelated to victim research and policy.

The research on the measurement of delinquency, it will be recalled, was developed as the basis of a new system of criminal statistics. Criminal events were to be recorded not just in terms of their numbers and legal or police classification, but also in terms of their seriousness. The main objective of the research was to develop a weighting system for measuring the seriousness of criminal events, based on pubic perceptions of such events. The scales that were developed through the use of psychological scaling techniques, reflected two main dimensions of seriousness: (1) the type of harm inflicted by the offense—injury, theft or damage to property, and (2) the amount of such harm. The purpose of this sophisticated exercise was to facilitate both the "indexing of delinquency" on a macro scale and the monitoring of changes in the delinquency rates of a group exposed to a particular type of treatment (Sellin and Wolfgang 1964/1978: ch. 18 and p. 1).

By 1976, however, in his contribution to the *Festschrift* in honor of Henry D. McKay, Wolfgang (1976) suggested that the seriousness scales that Sellin and he had developed could be applied to the formulation of criminal justice policy, in relation to juveniles. It was perhaps a natural step when, on being invited to address the International Symposium on Victimology three years later, he chose to develop the concept of a seriousness-scale based criminal justice policy, reorienting it towards the victim. Moreover, the applicability of the ideas was no longer to be confined to juvenile justice policy.

By this time Wolfgang and his colleagues had embarked on a much more comprehensive seriousness-scaling survey based on a national sample of respondents, which could provide a more meaningful data-base for criminal justice policies. When the results of this survey were published (Wolfgang et al. 1985), the final chapter of the accompanying text dealt with the applications of the scale, including its use in the context of sentencing. The policy discussion referred to the "just deserts" movement, but did not discuss the role of the victim, and there was no direct support for a victim-oriented sentencing policy. As indicated, however, the results, and the selection of items included, provided a sophisticated infrastructure for the development of such a policy. [2] In his 1979 keynote address, in which the victim individualization theme was developed, Wolfgang used illustrations from the data collected in the survey, as well as from injury scales developed by medical- and automobile-related organizations.

In the two decades since the 1979 keynote address was delivered, the theme of victim individualization in statutory law, adjudication, and sentencing has been explored and applied on several fronts. Not only have we witnessed the proliferation of legislative acts taking into account victim attributes (e.g., federal legislation sanctioning fraud committed against the elderly), but the U.S. Supreme Court has taken a close look at whether, to use Wolfgang's terminology, retrogression resonates from considerations of victim attributes and the acknowledgment of hierarchy of differences (*Booth v. Maryland*). The issue seems subsequently to have been resolved in favor of victim specification and individualization (*Payne v. Tennessee*), in apparent accordance with the approach advocated by Wolfgang. (The implication of these cases in this context will be further considered below.)

This chapter surveys and evaluates the way in which Wolfgang's ideas about "victim individualization" have been manifested in recent legislative developments and justice practices. It analyzes the prevailing penological philosophy (just deserts) and considers how this philosophy may be conceptually and practically linked to the individualization of the victim. It then surveys areas of the criminal justice system in which a victim role has gained recognition, and discusses the theoretical obstacles to a victim orientation. Further, drawing upon empirical research conducted by Erez and her colleagues (Erez et al. 1994; Erez and Rogers, forthcoming), it identifies the accommodations made by the justice system's agents to incorporate or circumvent such victim-oriented norms. Both theoretical and empirical analyses are found to converge around two alternative concepts of victim individualization. The chapter concludes with a consideration of the ramifications of these developments for victimological theory and research.

Background Developments

As noted, Wolfgang's writings in this area coincided with the emergence of two ideological movements related to criminal justice: the justice or "just deserts" movement and the victims' rights movement.

The "Just Deserts" Movement

The "just deserts" movement developed primarily as a result of dissatisfaction with the rehabilitation model of individualized justice, which was perceived as arbitrary and unprincipled (American Friends Committee 1971; Fogel 1975). It favored the replacing of the almost unfettered discretion possessed by criminal justice decision makers, including, indeed especially, the sentencing decision, by a structured system of norms. Sentences were to be "commensurate" with the offense, that is, the punishment was to fit the crime rather than the needs of the offender (von Hirsch 1976: Wolfgang 1979). This emphasis on proportionality seemed to echo the philosophy of the eighteenth-century Classical School; but the rationale was now retribution (proportionality for its own sake) rather than deterrence. Proportionality-based sentencing has increasingly been adopted both in the United States and elsewhere, by means of sentencing guidelines and other techniques (Ashworth 1992).

The preceding analysis makes no reference to the victim, who indeed barely earned a mention in "desert" advocacy, and discussion in the academic literature linking desert theory with the status of the victim has been sparse (but see Cavadino and Dignan 1993: Sebba 1996: ch.7). Analytically, however, such linkage is warranted. The principle of proportionality meant that the punishment should reflect the seriousness of the crime, and the seriousness of the crime was seen to be reflected primarily (if not solely) in the extent of the harm or suffering inflicted upon the victim. There was a clear potential here for using the Sellin-Wolfgang scale, measuring seriousness in terms of injury, theft and damage caused to the victim.[3] However, the applicability to sentencing of the Sellin-Wofgang scale and, indeed, of the victim orientation expounded by Wolfgang in his 1979 address, would partly depend on at least three issues with which desert theorists are faced. These issues relate to (1) the components of seriousness, (2) the harm elements, and (3) the philosophical and methodological base of the seriousness scale.

Components of seriousness. According to von Hirsch, the leading advocate of desert sentencing (see von Hirsch 1976; 1985), seriousness has two components: culpability and harm. While the harm element in the offense is inextricably related to the victim's experiences, culpability focuses on the degree of intentionality and moral turpitude attributed to the offender when perpetrating the prohibited act. These aspects of seriousness tended to be omitted from the original Sellin-Wolfgang scale (cf. Sebba 1980), and were only marginally addressed in the nationwide replication.[4]

The concern with culpability, however, would tend to derogate from the absoluteness of the correlation between seriousness and victim harm and suffering. Thus the infliction of harm which was not foreseen by the offender (and certainly the harm which was unforeseeable) should not be taken into account under culpability principles (cf. .Singer 1979: 26–7). Other elements of the offense, such as the choice of "vulnerable victims" or the employment of "deliberate cruelty" might perhaps be seen as aggravating the harm as well as culpability. While all such factors could be taken into account by a seriousness scale which related to culpability as well as harm, aspects of culpability relating to the viciousness or other characteristics of the offender's conduct are clearly unrelated to the victim.

Finally, insofar as the offender's previous record is to be taken into consideration (and not all desert theorists believe it should, see Fletcher 1978: 461–3), this too would detract from the victim focus of the sentencing tariff.

The harm element. Harm is a complex topic that has been widely discussed in the legal literature (see e.g., Feinberg 1984: Schulhofer 1974). In the present context, however, the main question is whether the harm on which the seriousness scale would be based, and the offender accordingly punished, is that actually suffered by the particular victim in the instant case, or that *typically* caused in the average case. Only the first meaning of harm would constitute a basis for the individualization in the full sense. Some desert theorists, however (e.g., von Hirsch 1985), have expressed the view that a sentencing tariff should reflect the appropriate sentence for the level of seriousness of the offense in the typical case. Individualization of the victim would be lost here, except insofar as the tariff were highly calibrated to take into account a wide variety of offense situations and victim experiences. Alternatively, individualization of the victim could be expressed in the form of *departures* from the sentencing tariff, insofar as these were permitted; this is the approach adopted by von Hirsch (1985: 70) illustrated by the case in which the finger broken in the course of a crime belonged to a concert pianist.

Philosophical and methodological base. As noted, the philosophy behind the desert orientation is retributive rather than consequentialist. The penalties are to be selected not for any practical goals they are intended to achieve, but for their intrinsic appropriateness, or justice. This approach assumes that there is some known yardstick for determining the appropriate penalty for any particular offense. However, since the initial statement of the just desert philosophy (von Hirsch 1976), it has been clear that there is no agreed basis for the development of a sentencing tariff. As a practical solution, legal systems which have followed the path of standardized sentences, have tended to use current sentencing practice as the basis for the new tariff (U.S. Sentencing Commission 1994: 3). The focus here is likely to be on traditional offense categories, which generally lacked an orientation to the victim.

To base the sentencing tariff on public perceptions of crime seriousness, employing the Sellin-Wolfgang scale, would increase the victim orientation of such scales. This possibility was noted by von Hirsch in *Doing Justice* (von Hirsch 1976:78). However, seeking an "objective" measure of (typical) harm, von Hirsch, following Sparks, considered that the use of victimization studies as a basis for determining seriousness would be preferable (von Hirsch 1985: 65–6), but eventually opted for a scale based upon Feinberg's theory of interests (von Hirsch 1985:67–71). In a later work with a colleague he developed a measure based on the degree to which the offense constitutes an invasion of the "living standard" (von Hirsch and Jareborg 1991). While most of these proposals have a victim orientation, the extent of victim individualization varies among the models, as well as with the precision of their implementation.

The Victim Movement

The victim movement emerged in the 1970s to alleviate the crime victim's plight in the criminal justice system, particularly victim neglect, mistreatment, and their lack of voice in proceedings. Activities on behalf of victims resulted in legislation which mandated rights of compensation from the state, restitution from the offender, support and counseling services, and victim participation rights (Erez 1989). The latter guarantees to victims input into sentencing and other offender-related decisions such as parole release. In most jurisdictions that have adopted this reform, the right to input into sentencing is known as a *victim impact statement*: a vehicle to inform the judge of any physical or psychological harm, or any loss or damage to property, suffered by the victim as a result of the crime. Some jurisdictions have gone further and allowed victims to make *statements of opinion* concerning the offender's sentence (McLeod 1986).

By 1984 a Bureau of Justice Statistics survey found that victim-related legislation in the United States alone covered nearly 1500 pages. The National Victim Center (1996: 1) recently reported that its legislative database includes "more than 27,000 statutes concerning victims' rights and related interests." An Addendum to its publication following the November 1996 elections noted that twenty-nine states had amended their constitutions in order to guarantee victims' rights therein, while a proposed amendment to the U.S. Constitution has gained considerable support (NOVA 1996). The combined effect of the just desert and victim movements is well manifested in the shift toward individualization of the victim.[5]

A Critique of Victim Procedural Rights

Attempts to provide victims with rights have met with much resistance in the legal community. The objections to allowing victims a voice have involved several issues. A major argument is that providing victims a role in proceedings challenges the conception of crime as a violation against the state and not the individual victim (e.g., Ashworth 1993). Objections also raised possible detrimental effects that a victim's voice might have on criminal justice processes and outcomes: it will constitute unacceptable pressure on the court (Rubel 1986) and may result in substitution of the victim's subjective approach for the objective approach presumably practiced by the court (Victorian Sentencing Committee 1988). The latter may introduce outcome disparity, as similar cases would be disposed of differently, depending upon the availability or thoroughness of the input victims provide (Hall 1991), or "the resiliency, vindictiveness or other personality attributes of the victim" (Grabosky 1987: 147; see also infra).

In academic circles, the victim's right to input has been criticized for its presumed alliance with, or exploitation by, the "law and order" campaign. Opponents have argued that victims' anguish has been mistranslated into support for the conservative ideology, and that the attempt to integrate victims into the process may be a way to accomplish the goal of harsher punishment (e.g., Henderson 1985; Hellerstein 1989).

Other objections pertain to the presumed adverse effects of victim input on the criminal justice process. Concerns were raised over delays, lengthier proceedings, and additional expenses for an already overburdened system, if victims are allowed to have a voice (e.g., Australian Law Reform Commission 1987; Miers 1992). Because consideration of impact material by the court may increase the severity of punishment, the offender must be given the right to challenge the input: specifically, to dispute causes, extent of harm, and prognosis. This, some argue, may result in longer trials (with mini-trials on the veracity or accuracy of the input) and in victims being subjected to unpleasant cross-examination (Victorian Sentencing Committee 1988). Some also argue that victim input would add very little useful or novel information which is not already available to the court (Australian Law Reform Commission 1987) or taken into account in definitions of offenses and mitigating or aggravating circumstances (Ashworth 1993).

Supporters of victim participation in proceedings have argued that victim input will provide a recognition of victims' wish for party status (Hall 1991) and individual dignity (Henderson 1985). It will also remind judges, juries, and prosecutors that behind the "State" is a real person with an interest in how the case is resolved (Kelly 1987). They suggest that information on victim harm will enhance proportionality and accuracy in sentencing rather than punitiveness (Erez 1990), and increase fairness for victims by providing them with equal right to be heard by the court (Sumner 1987). In the United States, the President's Task Force on Victims of Crimes (1982) summarized the need for victim input into sentencing by reference to fairness, justice, and penalogical concerns, suggesting that "a judge cannot evaluate the seriousness of a defendant's conduct without knowing how the crime has burdened the victim. A judge cannot reach an informed determination of the danger posed by the defendant without hearing from the person he has victimized" (76–7).

The debate surrounding victim voice in the criminal justice process highlights three major tensions in the practice of criminal law, tensions that have been resolved in ways that are not conducive to victim individualization. First, the tension between the preservation of traditional conceptions of the adversary legal system and the provision of victim participatory rights. In this context, one legal scholar has predicted that efforts to define a role for the victim would meet great resistance from the principal actors in criminal processing—the prosecutor, the defense counsel, and the judge. To them, attempts to integrate victims would only "formalize a relationship with the victim which already exists, or which prosecutors and judges have decided for good reason should not exist" (Goldstein 1984: 242).

The second related tension is created by attempts to accommodate victim rights within an emerging ideology of "managerial justice" (Douglas et al. 1994), the "new penology" (Feeley and Simon 1992) or "actuarial justice" (Feeley and Simon 1994), which puts a high premium on speed and efficiency and prefers to deal with aggregates over individuals. This ideology of administrative rationality and technocratic justice (O'Malley 1984) has transformed the courts into modern business-like administrative agencies concerned with productivity and cost-effectiveness in the delivery of their "services" (Heydebrand and Seron 1990). Concerns about adverse effects of victim integration on criminal justice efficiency, and whether benefits of victim voice would outweigh its presumed costs are common objections raised by the legal profession.

Lastly, a tension emerges between the demands to provide victims with a voice, and the movements to increase sentence uniformity and reduce its severity. These two movements, the victim movement and "just deserts" may, in fact, pull in different directions. Uniformity, for instance, can be disrupted by consideration of unique victim reactions. In regard to the effect of victim input on court outcomes, there is a disagreement between the liberal and conservative camps about the likely effects of victim input on sentence severity and defendants' rights, the former suggesting increased punitiveness and potential for violations of the accused's procedural rights. The remainder of this chapter will consider legislative and other criminal justice developments calculated to promote this victim-oriented model of justice, and will report on some field studies designed to examine how, and how far, such legislative reform is implemented.

Individualization Outside the Criminal Justice System

One of the main dilemmas of the victims' rights movement has been the question of whether responsibility towards the victim lies primarily with the state and the community, with an emphasis on remedies *outside* the criminal justice system, or whether it lies primarily with the offender, in which case the emphasis may be rather on the victim's participatory rights in that system (see Sebba 1996 and forthcoming).[6] Nearly all systems, however, have supported the establishment of state-run victim compensation schemes for the victims of violent crimes, and of victim support schemes or victim assistance services (cf. Parent et al. 1992; Roberts 1990).

While Wolfgang did not focus on these developments in the works previously referred to, the quotation from his 1979 lecture cited in our opening paragraph does refer to "statutory provisions" as an entity distinct from "the adjudication and offender sentencing process." We draw attention to these institutions here, not only in view of the prominent role they play in the victim movement, but because they give maximum expression to the concept of the individualization of the victim, or at least, have the potential to do so. For if a compensation board calculates the precise amount of harm inflicted upon the victim, in order to assess the amount of compensation due,[7] or if a victim support professional or volunteer worker endeavors to ensure that the victim's practical and/or psychological needs are met, this will constitute a level of individualization and, indeed, victim rehabilitation beyond even that provided for the defendant under the defunct positivist model.

Needless to say, the services actually provided to victims fall short of the objectives cited here.[8] Moreover, conceptually, individualization of this type insofar as it occurs, need not replace individualization of the offender. Indeed, as argued by Sebba (1982; 1996), the two policies are consistent with a model whereby the state, as part of its welfare and social control functions, has direct responsibility for both offender and victim. This, however, is a different kind of individualization from that envisaged by Wolfgang, and will therefore not be discussed further.

For the remainder of this chapter we will focus upon individualization of the victim in a criminal justice context.

Individualization in Substantive Criminal Law

While discussion of victim-related reforms in the criminal justice system generally focus on procedural reforms and sentencing, one should also note reforms in the criminal law itself. Such (mainly legislative) reforms may be classified into three types: (1) Primary normative reforms, which create new offenses or expand the definition and scope of existing offenses (examples of this are stalking and marital rape)[9] ; (2) Secondary normative reforms, which are designed to add further protection to victims of offenses already in existence (an example of this is the offense of failing to report child abuse, or the duty to assist a person in distress); and (3) Amendments to sentencing provisions, creating new sub-categories of offenses in order to impose heavier penalties[10] (examples would be increased penalties for offenses of violence committed against children or the elderly).

In what sense can the above-mentioned reforms be construed as pertaining to the individualization of the victim? Two aspects may be noted in this connection. In the first place, such legislation changes the emphasis of the criminal law from an *offender* orientation to a *victim* orientation. Offenses have traditionally been defined in terms of the offender's conduct and mental state (e.g., breaking and entering with intent), with reference to the victim being the exception (such as the age of consent for sexual relations). The new offenses, on the other hand, tend to place express emphasis on the object of this conduct—the victim. Secondly, and more significantly in the context of the present analysis, the references in such legislation to specific categories of victim, such as the elderly, the institutionalized, and so forth, are directly analogous to the examples employed by Wolfgang in his 1979 address for the purposes of illustrating the individualization theme. While his terminology suggests an intention to place the focus on the *individual* victim, Wolfgang's illustrations, both historical and contemporary, cited in support of his approach deal with *categories* and *sub-categories* of victims rather than with individuals.

Individualization in Criminal Procedure and Evidence

Much of the victim-related legislation is concerned with the procedural rights of victims, whether at the pre-trial stages (in particular the decision to release on bail, and the decision to charge), during the trial process (e.g., the right to be present), and following the trial, especially at parole hearings.[11] The focus of some of the states' constitutional amendments, as well as the current proposal for an amendment to the U.S. Constitution, has been on a general right to be heard at all relevant stages of the criminal process (Lamborn 1995:220).

Other legislation has been designed to alleviate victims' hardships experienced in their capacity as witnesses, often involving the reform of the laws of evidence. In particular, efforts have been made to reduce the trauma for victims of sex offenses in general, and child victims in particular, by limiting the scope of the defense's cross-examination when such victims testify, for example, by "rape shield" statutes, and by making provision for video testimony, to obviate the need for the victim to face his or her alleged abuser directly (Spencer and Flin 1992).

Many of these provisions, especially the constitutional amendments to criminal justice procedures, are directed at crime victims in general, and thus lack the element of individualization. Again, however, there are two senses in which this feature is found here, too. First, as indicated, some of these special arrangements are designed for particular categories or sub-categories of victim (e.g., victims of sexual assault under a certain age). Secondly, under some provisions, use of the special provisions is discretionary. Thus, under an Alabama statute, the victim may be excused from testimony in the pre-trial proceedings where there is a fear of intimidation directed at the victim or the victim's family.[12] The enabling norm in such cases is intended to be used only where the particular circumstances of the case warrant its application. These circumstances may include consideration of the likelihood of prejudicing the rights of the defendant, but will focus mainly on the vulnerability of the individual victim. Moreover, the discretionary dynamic here is, again, reminiscent of the procedures which were applied to offenders under the rehabilitation model, to which the victim individualization model was being compared by Wolfgang.

Individualization in Sentencing

Three aspects of individualization of the sentence will be considered here:

(1) sentences bringing direct benefit to the victim, that is, restitution; (2) sentencing with a symbolic message for the victim (desert or tariff)[13]; and (3) procedural and evidential aspects.

1. Court sentences have been traditionally concerned with punishing or rehabilitating the offender. Ordering the offender to pay restitution to the victim was, in common-law jurisdictions, generally a secondary and sparsely used sanction (Sebba 1996: 168). In the wake of the ascendancy of victims' rights, this disposition, which is calculated to bring direct material benefit to the victim, has greatly increased in popularity. Section 3553 (a)(7) of Title 18 of the U.S. Code requires the court in determining the particular sentence to be imposed, to consider the need to provide restitution to any victims of the offense, and if the court does not order restitution to any victims of the offense, or orders only partial restitution, it must state its reasons for doing so (U.S. Sentencing Commission 1994: 285). Sixteen states now provide for restitutional rights in their constitutions (National Victim Center 1996: table 2-I and Addendum), while twenty-nine states have provisions similar to those cited above (ibid.: 300).

How far are courts able to adapt the amount of the restitution orders to reflect the loss inflicted on the individual victim? In many states the information required to assess the loss forms part of the victim impact statement (National Victim Center 1996: 301). Further, estimate of loss is no longer confined to such as is incurred by way of injury or direct economic loss, but may include expenses resulting from psychological treatment, HIV testing, lost profits, moving and meal expenses, as well as burial costs (ibid.: 300).

Such individualized restitution may be modified, however, by the need to take other factors into account, such as the financial sources of the defendant. A federal provision seeks to balance this possibility by the provision of an alternative: the possibility of ordering the offender to perform services for the benefit of the victim (U.S. Sentencing Commission 1994: 285).

Arguably, an individualized restitution system is an effective form of desert sentencing or retribution: the offender is literally "paying back" for the harm inflicted.[14] On the other hand, conventional desert theory would have the sanction reflect the offender's culpability, as well as the degree of injury inflicted. This would detract from the individualization of the victim, since it would generally reflect offender-related characteristics. Another view would support the *enhancement* of the restitutional payment in criminal cases, in order to distinguish them from civil cases (Thorvaldson 1990; Sebba 1996: 330–5), and to reflect the added value of the moral opprobrium. However, insofar as the premium was proportional to the loss inflicted, the principle of individualization would be maintained.

2. Desert sentencing is more generally thought to be reflected in the structuring of the traditional sanctions imposed upon offenders (such as prison terms and fines), by such means as guideline tariffs. Some of the issues of principle related to the development of such tariffs were considered above. As was noted there, tariffs are oriented primarily towards the amount of victim harm inflicted, although also incorporating measures of offender culpability. Here we will consider examples from the Federal Sentencing Guidelines, focusing in particular upon victim-related variables.

Robbery, an offense against both property and the person, has a base score of 20 (33–41 months for a first offender). If bodily injury is inflicted, however, the score is increased by two, four, or six levels (up to 78 months for first offenders), depending on the extent of the injury. A further increase of between one and seven levels is posited where the loss inflicted exceeds $10,000, the extent of the increase, again, depending upon the amount involved (U.S. Sentencing Commission 1994: 60). The Guidelines also make general provision, applicable to all types of offense, for "victim-related adjustments." These specify sentencing enhancements where the offense is committed against certain types of victims, namely, vulnerable victims (owing to age, or physical or mental condition), or official victims (offenses committed against government employees, when motivated by the victim's status, as well as assaults on police and correctional officers). An adjustment is also provided when a victim was physically restrained in the course of the offense. (These situations enhance the sentence by two or three levels.) These examples are a reflection of the type of victim-oriented fine-tuning referred to by Wolfgang in his seminal address.

In addition to these victim characteristics, which may give rise to specified sentencing enhancements, the Guidelines also provide for (open-ended) departures from the assigned levels (U.S. Sentencing Commission 1994: 6, 308ff.). The scheme envisages that such departures may be for grounds unforeseen in the Guidelines, but one section of the Guidelines seeks to aid the court by identifying some of the factors that the Commission has not been able to take into account fully in formulating the guidelines (ibid.: 309). This section specifies physical injury and extreme psychological injury. Theses provisions reflect a much stronger concept of victim individualization in two respects: first, their application is predicated not simply upon objective information about the case, or the type of case, but upon precise information on the extent of the trauma inflicted. Second, the extent of the sentence enhancement is open-ended and may be in some sense commensurate with the extent of the trauma inflicted in the particular case, however severe (subject only to any maximum laid down for the offense).

The same section of the Guidelines also provides for sentence *reduction* (again open-ended) when the offense was provoked by the victim (ibid.: 313). This form of victim individualization forms a link between the present topic and Wolfgang's early research on victim precipitation (cf. also Wolfgang 1988).

3. Sentencing procedures: the procedural and evidentiary aspects of sentencing are (or should be) calculated to implement the prevailing sentencing objectives. Thus under the rehabilitative model, evidence was put forward at this stage—usually through the good offices of a probation officer—of the defendant's character and life history, and the circumstances which led him or her to commit the offense. This evidence was not subject to the constraints of the adversarial rules of proof (cf. *Williams v. New York*) since the objective was purportedly not punitive but to identify the optimal solution for the individual concerned.

The new system of guideline or tariff sentencing did not totally abandon the above type of procedure, since some consideration of the offender's needs or personality is still permitted in determining the precise sentence[15]; but clearly such individualized procedures have become much less significant. On the other hand, the introduction of victim-impact statements and victim's opinion statements have resulted in complementary procedures designed to adduce evidence related to the victim. This includes information as to the impact of the offense upon the victim, descriptions of the victim's character and attributes, and the victim's views (or those of the victim's survivors) on the appropriate sentence (National Victim Center 1996: 231–2). This information, too, may be channeled through a probation officer, or alternatively through a police officer (for instance in Canada or South Australia) or directly by the victim. The degree to which such evidence may be challenged by the defendant is variable (ibid.: 232). These provisions import a degree of symmetry between the status of the victim and the defendant respectively, with an increasing emphasis on victim-related provisions.[16]

Expressions of Individualization

In terms of sentencing philosophy, the procedural and evidential aspects of victim-oriented sentencing may have less significance than the *nature* and *content* of the victim-related input. Individualization of the victim at the sentencing stage (and, *mutatis mutandis*, at the other stages of the criminal justice system) may, in terms of its content, be expressed in at least three different ways. The victim-related input may be concerned with (1) the nature and degree of suffering inflicted upon the victim and the victim's family as a result of the crime; (2) the personal attributes of the victim; or (3) the views of the victim and/or the victim's family regarding the offender and the sentence to be imposed.

The relevance to and admissibility in sentencing proceedings of these elements of victim individualization were considered by the U.S. Supreme Court in a series of cases (referred to in the introduction) in which victim-related information was presented to the court at the sentencing stage.[17] These were capital cases in which, following the presentation of the victim-related testimony, the defendants were sentenced to death.

Booth v. Maryland, decided in 1987, involved the robbery and murder of an elderly couple in their home. The victim-impact statement, based on interviews with family members, included a description of the emotional and personal problems suffered by family members following the murders, an account of the outstanding qualities of the victims, and the views of the surviving children as to the appropriate social response. The Supreme Court held that such evidence was inadmissible and quashed the conviction. In *South Carolina v. Gathers*, decided two years later, a self-proclaimed preacher was murdered in a chance encounter with some youths in a park. The prosecutor alluded to the victim's religious inclinations and his good citizenship. The Supreme Court held such statements regarding the personal characteristics of the victim as inadmissible.

The Supreme Court's approach underwent a radical change in *Payne v. Tennessee*, decided in 1991.[18] In that case, a mother and two-year-old child were murdered while the mother was attempting to resist the defendant's sexual advances. Her three-year-old son survived. At the sentencing stage, the grandmother testified as to how the boy missed his family, and the prosecutor commented on the boy's presumed expectations in terms of the appropriate penalty. Reversing their previous decisions, the Court held that evidence of the emotional impact of the crime on victims or survivors, and evidence relating to the personal characteristics of the victim, were admissible. No decision was reached on the admissibility of victims' views as to the appropriate sentence.

Insofar as the *impact of the crime on the victim* can be both objectively measured and foreseen by the offender, it will be legitimate to include this in a desert-based sentencing tariff, on the condition that the information is consistently provided in all cases; this may also apply to emotional impact. This approach would seem to illustrate victim-individualization in Wolfgang's sense of fine-tuning the tariff, while retaining the principles of culpability. Under these principles unforeseen (and especially unforeseeable) impacts should not be taken into account; but the Supreme Court's views on these issues were ambivalent (Sebba 1996:160).[19] This reservation applies with even greater force when such testimony, somewhat random in its presentation, will determine whether the defendant will be executed.

The issue of *victim attributes* is somewhat different. Here, too, culpability considerations require that these characteristics of the case, in order to be taken into account in determining the penalty, must be known to the perpetrators. Generally speaking, however, unlike in the social contexts from which Wolfgang's historical examples were drawn, such attributes will no longer be considered relevant under contemporary desert principles. It is surely inappropriate for the law to engage in "moral accounting" in order to differentiate the sentence according to the relative worth of the victim.[20]

Finally, while there may be therapeutic or other grounds for providing victims or survivors an opportunity to voice their *views as to the severity of the sentence*, these views are likely to be unpredictable and thus inappropriate, for considerations of culpability, in a formal criminal trial (in contrast to, for example, an informal or mediated proceeding). Moreover, taking account of such a variable input may result in a substantial deviation from the type of individualization envisaged by Wolfgang, in that it could actually *weaken* the correlation between the sentence and the degree of harm inflicted by the crime; a vindictive victim may request a severe sentence for a relatively minor harm (cf. Graboski 1987). Here, in particular, measures designed to achieve individualization of the victim in a literal sense—as indeed seem to have been indicated by the *rhetoric* of Wolfgang's argumentation—raise serious problems for a desert-based criminal justice system which constituted his point of departure. Thus, some of the recently adopted victim-oriented procedures and in particular those providing for the expression of victim views—apart from raising problems in relation to the culpability principle—may be quite inconsistent with the type of tariff envisaged by Wolfgang and reflected in his illustrations.

In order to determine the extent to which the individualization of the victim was being implemented in practice, whether in the spirit of Wolfgang's examples (i.e., of a fine-tuned tariff) or in a more literal sense—by adapting the criminal justice system to the individual victim—empirical research on court practices has been conducted by one of the authors. The following sections will describe this research, its findings, and the implications for victim individualization.

Implementation of Victim Individualization in Sentencing

Studies of the effect of victim integration on criminal justice outcomes and processes found that the majority of court officials favored the principle of considering victim voice in sentencing decisions, and that few officials believed that it would create or exacerbate processual problems. Indeed, most judges and prosecutors believed that victim input improved the quality of justice by influencing restitution awards or by having some impact on the length and type of sentence (Hillenbrand and Smith 1989; Erez et al. 1994). Yet, despite sympathy for the victims and in the desire to give them a voice in criminal justice, research indicates that legal professionals mostly paid lip service to victim input (Henley et al. 1994). Legal professionals, by and large, intimated that victim input needs to be taken with "a grain of salt" (Erez et al. 1994).

Research suggests that two major factors limit the criminal justice system's ability to individualize victims: first, the prevailing legal culture, and second, organizational forces and "work groups" (Eisenstein and Jacob 1977) dynamics operating in the court.

Legal occupational culture provides several mechanisms for excluding individualization based on victim input. One mode of thinking identified in research is typification or the "normal" victim. Similar to other situations in which elements of criminal cases are processed (e.g., Sudnow 1965; Frohman 1992), the processing of victim harm is subject to typification. In the course of routinely adjudicating criminal cases with victims who suffer various types of harm, prosecutors and judges become acquainted with the typical features of cases and their associated types of harm. In fact, knowledge of the properties of "normal" victim harm, i.e., the typical or familiar victim reactions to crime categories, constitutes the mark of any given attorney's or judge's competence.

Research indicates that legal professionals can cite the "normal" effects of various offenses that they have tried, and exhibit an expert knowledge of the repertoire of symptoms associated with various crimes. Likewise, they become familiar with typical categories of victims. Rape victims, for example, are commonly young women, not babies or grand-mothers, and the typical injuries associated with this offense for this category of victims is known (Erez and Rogers, forthcoming.

But legal practitioners not only become familiar with the typical man-ner in which various kinds of offenses affect victims, they also begin to expect it. "Normal victims" are persons whose typical features of harm are known and expected by professionals when they invoke specific laws defining the appropriate sentence. The individual crime victim ceases to be an individual, with idiosyncratic responses to his/her experience, but is reduced to the victim of the specific crime category with its concomi-tant injuries. The focus is no longer on the individual victim but on the characteristics of victimization according to offense types, for instance, the kinds of harm rape victims suffer, symptoms characteristic of abused children, or the way burglary victims react.

The transformation of typical and familiar victim reactions into the "normal" victim, and the way this construct is used in sentencing think-ing and practice, is evidenced in the way legal professionals distinguish and apply the difference between the "normal" and exceptional charac-teristics of the case. In a "normal" crime, harm is viewed as built into sentencing. It is commonly not noticed: it is assumed. Only in a minority of cases, labeled by some legal professionals as the "celebrity cases"—extraordinary and unusual victimizations which attract high media cov-erage and public attention—does the harm suffered by the victim receive special recognition in sentencing (Erez and Rogers, forthcoming).

Yet, the "normal" victim is also a yardstick against which judges and other legal professionals evaluate victims and the veracity of their impact statement. In the routine handling of felonies, legal practitio-ners use their knowledge regarding typification of harm, that is, "nor-mal" victims' physical, emotional, and psychological reactions to violations of property and person, in assessing the truthfulness of vic-tims' input, and the credibility of their testimony. Victim reactions that are not perceived as typical are often viewed as exaggerated, illogical, and unbelievable by all legal professionals, and particularly by defense attorneys (Erez and Rogers, forthcoming).

Research suggests that although a few highly experienced practitio-ners can recognize variations in "normal" victim reactions, the major-ity of legal professionals are willing to accept only a short range of "normality" in victim harm, and are unwilling to tolerate a victim's apparently extreme or excessive reaction to a crime. Overall, the bulk of the accumulated "typical" victim experiences serves to reduce professionals' preparedness to accept as genuine or truthful a reaction that is out of the "normal" or expected range of experience. This typification phenomenon has contributed significantly to professionals' ignoring victims' input and rejecting individual reactions to crime (Erez and Rogers, forthcoming). This tendency was evident even in jurisdictions (such as South Australia) which passed explicit laws requiring judges to consider harm suffered by the particular victim (Erez et al. 1994).

Another feature of practitioners' occupational culture invoked by legal professionals when they approach victim input and individual reactions is "objectivity." Objectivity is the legal apologetic that defends against the use or acknowledgment of affect or standpoint in the perception and construction of legal events or decisions (Creedon 1993). It is both a strategic presumption and ritual that protects judges from charges of bias toward a particular party interest. Objectivity is a normative ideal in law, and the legal literature is filled with exaltations of judges' capability to be objective, to apply this principle in everyday practice and thereby produce "just" legal decisions (e.g., Naffine 1990: ch. 1). Judges claim, and are presumed, to examine cases that come before them in a "clinical" fashion, detached from any emotional baggage that the human stories in the criminal cases they try often carry, and to dispose them objectively (Rogers and Erez, forthcoming).

Despite a growing recognition that objectivity is elusive and problematic in the interpretation and application of legal rules (for gender, see for instance, Naffine 1990; for race, Higginbotham 1978), judges, in fact, all legal professionals, describe their routine case dispositions as "objective." The belief in the feasibility of "objective" application of law in sentencing decisions allows judges to define unusual victims' stories of crime impact as "subjective," hence irrelevant (Erez and Rogers, forthcoming).

Research suggests that legal professionals feel a compelling need to examine victim voice carefully, and to disregard what is perceived as "subjective" input. They often reiterate the importance of applying the standard of "objectivity" to the content of victim input. Invoking the principle of "objectivity" allows judges to consciously and completely ignore any victim voice which appears to them "out of the ordinary," exaggerated, unbelievable, or outside the legal professionals' routine experience with this crime. Practitioners who mention the importance of objectivity often offer the apologetic that victims have various mo-

tives, or built-in incentives, to lie or exaggerate: the penalty the offender would receive (victims were presumed to be vindictive), and
financial gain or the size of a compensation order a victim would be
awarded (victims were presumed greedy) (Erez et al. 1994). Yet, research suggests that perceptions of "objectivity" held by legal professionals are very subjective. They are influenced by factors such as
political positioning, professional role, proximity to victims, or experiences prior to serving on the bench (Rogers and Erez 1997).

A related feature of legal occupational culture is the practice of "retelling" facts in legal documents—the presentation of victim voice in a
mode acceptable for legal consumption, which commonly eliminates
idiosyncratic elements of individual victims. The "retelling" of victim
harm in court documents by reporters other than the actual victim, often "sterilizes" (see Delgado 1989) and flattens the report, and takes
the power out of the victims' stories. The effect of "retelling" harm
utilizing a "clinical" approach to victim harm results in the suppression
of individualized attributes of victim harm, and result, according to
one judge, in "a generous understatement of victim harm" (Erez and
Rogers, forthcoming).

Another theme, which leads to practitioners' resisting individualization of victims, is organizational concerns. One commonly mentioned
reason judges ignore or assign little weight to a victim's individual
harm was a concern with appeals of sentences. The organizational concern with "downstream consequences" (Emerson and Paley 1994),
namely attracting appeals of sentences if they are higher than the tariff,
or reversal of sentences by a higher court, has militated against individualization of harm in sentences. For judges, a reversal or modification of a sentence is not a desirable career event; they do not routinely
risk a reversal. Defense attorneys know that judges are concerned about
appeals and reversal of sentences. They use this knowledge to benefit
their clients, a practice to which judges respond and keep sentences "in
line" (Erez and Rogers, forthcoming).

Lastly, resisting victim individualization is a natural outcome of a
"managerial" or "actuarial justice" approaches. The meager resources
allocated to provide victims a voice in an overburdened criminal justice system staffed with overly busy court officials, result in "paying
only lip service" to victim individualization (Erez et al. 1994). The
ubiquitous bureaucratic pressure to move cases along, or clear courts'
dockets, commonly results in victims' voices being unheard or ignored
(Davis and Smith 1996; Erez et al. 1994).

Legislation providing victims a voice has nonetheless resulted in a small number of situations in which victim individualization does take place. In some jurisdictions, victim input provides a source for quotes, which can be included in sentencing remarks. Research suggests that judges often cite victim statements in their sentencing remarks, in order "to bring home to the offender the effect of his act on the victim" (Erez and Rogers, forthcoming). Although most legal professionals feel this practice reflects mostly a cosmetic change in sentencing decisions, a minority thinks that using victims own words may not be benign, and may affect sentencing outcomes (Erez et al. 1994). Also, some legal professionals in jurisdictions that mandate a definition of harm to the particular victim (for instance, South Australia) felt that this practice allows for more individualization of victims. However, they agreed that the impact was at best confined to a very limited number of cases (Erez et al. 1994), and stressed that the particular harm was subordinate to criminal law principles of culpability, and that only foreseen and expected consequences should be considered in sentencing (see Ashworth, 1993 above).

Legal professionals who were asked to provide specific instances in which they thought a sentence was changed or reconsidered based exclusively on victim input offered examples suggesting that victim individualization may lead to both more severe and more lenient sentences. Particularly cruel crimes, or violations which caused prolonged suffering to victims, or long-lasting consequences, led to more severe sentences, whereas complete recovery, a forgiving victim, or circumstances which suggest that the offense harm was misperceived by observers led to more lenient outcomes (Erez and Rogers, forthcoming).

The minimal role victim input plays in sentences is also evidenced in the limited extent of its impact on court schedules and proceedings. Allowing victims a voice has neither resulted in longer trials, or mini-trials on the content of impact statements, nor has it led to challenges of victim input. At most it has added a few minutes to sentencing, as "it takes only few minutes to read the impact materials" or "it takes two to three minutes to digest the statements" (Erez and Rogers, forthcoming).

In sum, the tensions inherent in attempts to individualize victims and balance conflicting and paradoxical demands of the movements to increase "justice" in sentencing while providing victims a voice have been resolved in ways that are not conducive to victim individualization in the liberal sense. The criminal justice system's modes of adaptation to these paradoxical expectations has been mostly ritualistic, with only minor adjustments in courtroom procedures, time schedules, routines, and outcomes. Legal occupational culture, in interaction with organizational concerns jointly combine to exert restrictions on the ability of the system to accommodate individual victims. For sentencing outcomes, attempts to individualize have increased proportionality rather than punitiveness in a small minority of cases.

Conclusion

Penological theory was dominated until recent times by a rehabilitationist philosophy, the key concept of which was the individualization of the offender. This approach was predicated upon the vesting of wide discretionary powers in the hands of sentencing courts and/or the correctional agencies, applying their subjective judgment to meet the needs of the case as they interpreted it. The "just deserts" approach that replaced this philosophy was designed to achieve "objectivity" and consistency by narrowing the discretion of the law enforcement authorities, and by specifying in advance the sanctions applicable to any given offense (or sometimes offender) category.

In principle, Wolfgang's proposals were consistent with the "just deserts" approach . Following upon his research on the scaling of offenses, he suggested that the offense categories for which the sanctions were to be prescribed could be more closely defined (or fine-tuned) according to the nature and extent of the harm and the characteristics of the victim. He referred to this fine-tuning as "the individualization of the victims." However, unlike the individualization of the offender under the rehabilitation model, the victim-oriented model, in fact, presupposed an intense structuring of sentencing policy, and a minimum of discretion.

Recent victim-oriented developments have moved beyond the destination indicated by Wolfgang, in the direction of individualization of the victim in a more literal sense— in the subjective, personalized sense in which the term was previously applied to the offender. This development may have the advantage of producing a historical symmetry, and even to give rise to a sense of justice on the part of some victims, survivors and victim advocates. Yet it is also subject to precisely those criticisms which were leveled at the earlier offender-oriented philosophy; it may result in sentences which are unpredictable, arbitrary, and ultimately unfair.

However, the empirical research presented above shows that this policy is modified at the implementation stage by the criminal justice decision makers. These agents, by standardizing or typifying the case in practice, adopt a policy much closer to that envisaged by Wolfgang, in the same way as these officials tended to standardize cases when the system was offender-oriented. Thus, at the end of the day, it seems that it is Wolfgang's concept of individualized justice, more firmly rooted in principles of predictability (and thus ultimately also of culpability), that prevails.

Notes

This paper was presented at the conference, "Integrating Victim Perspective in Criminal Justice" York, England, July 1998, in a session dedicated to Dr. Marvin Wolfgang. Carol Gregory and Brian Kale helped with the use of electronic mail and word processing applications necessary for co-authoring an article from both sides of the Atlantic.

1. Wolfgang noted, however, that "criminal law has regressed since the Hammurabi code by compressing degrees of harm into few categories..." (Wolfgang 1982: 54).
2. Moreover, in 1978, Wolfgang and a colleague showed how the methodology employed in the measurement of delinquency research could be applied for the purpose of victim classification: see Wolfgang and Singer (1978).
3. Indeed, this possibility was referred to in a footnote in the pioneering statement of the just-desert theory in *Doing Justice* (von Hirsch 1976).
4. The authors of the replication study relied on the findings of Riedel (1975) that "inferences of intent are unimportant factors in the perception of the seriousness of criminal events" (Wolfgang et al. 1985: 7); but see Sebba (1980).
5. The move toward individualization, of which victim individualization is only one of its sites (O'Malley 1996), has been attributed to various causes: social movements such as the women's and the victim's movements (Erez 1989); the "feminization of social control" (Erez and Laster 1994); or, to broader development of the law, such as the reassertion of emotionality in formal legal institutions (Laster and O'Malley 1996). The rise of these forces have helped victims regain a meaningful place in the criminal justice process while the state, the former representative of society, is taking a back seat. This trend is well expressed in the move toward restorative justice. Our chapter aims merely to evaluate the manifestation and practices of the move toward victim individualization rather than analyze its causes.
6. Thus, for example, the English victim support organization has generally objected to victim participation in the process, see *Victim Support* (1995). For a discussion of the differences in the ideologies of American and British victim advocates see Mawby and Gill (1987).
7. In this context it may be noted that Britain recently moved away from a compensation scheme based upon individualized assessments (akin to civil law damages) towards a standardized tariff; see Duff (forthcoming).
8. See Elias (1983 and 1993) and Fattah (forthcoming).
9. Another route for the expansion of the protection of the victim is by narrowing the scope of a defense, e.g., by refusing to recognize infidelity on the part of a spouse as justification for homicide, or even as a grounds for reducing the severity of the charge.
10. Penalty provisions are commonly dealt with as though part of *criminal procedure*, but in fact have a substantive character. Moreover, amendments such as

those considered here are sometimes adopted by means of additions to the substantive sections of the law, see for instance, Israel's provisions on "vulnerable
victims" (Article F1 of the Penal Law, 1977).

11. Sentencing procedures could be included here, but will be dealt with separately
    below.
12. See National Victim Center (1996: 339; see also ibid:101)
13. The theoretical aspects of this topic were considered above. Here we will con-
    sider some applications.
14. For different views on the relationship between restitution and retribution, see
    Barnett (1977), Zedner (1994) and Sebba (1996: 187ff.)
15. Thus, under the federal sentencing guidelines, the court, in selecting a sentence
    within the permitted range, is called upon to consider "the nature and serious-
    ness of the conduct, the statutory purposes of sentencing and the *pertinent of-
    fender characteristics*" (U.S. Sentencing Commission, 1994: 269; emphasis
    added). Moreover, a *departure* from the guidelines based on offender consider-
    ations, although possible, would be rare (ibid.: 310).
16. Cf. the sentencing guidelines referred to above. Moreover, the victim role is
    additional to the traditional "adversary" of the defendant, viz., the State, is ap-
    parently weighting the scales against the defendant. In practice, however, the
    extent to which the system is being transformed by the umption of a victim
    orientation may be more limited than indicated by the formal norms: see the
    empirical findings presented below.
17. These cases have been analyzed by one of the authors in greater depth else-
    where (Sebba 1994).
18. Changes in the composition of the Supreme Court resulted in the erstwhile mi-
    nority view becoming the view of the majority; see Sebba 1994.
19. The Federal Sentencing Guidelines originally held to the culpability principle in
    sentencing, but now defined as relevant "all harm that resulted from the acts and
    omissions specified" (U.S. Sentencing Commission 1994: 16). J. Souter in *Payne
    v. Tennessee* resolved the issue by attributing to the offender knowledge "that
    the person to be killed probably has close associates, survivors, who will suffer
    harms and deprivations from the victim's death" (cf. Sebba 1996: 160).
20. Chief Justice Renquist, for the majority in *Payne v. Tennessee*, claimed that the
    purpose of such evidence was merely "to show...each victim's 'uniqueness as a
    human being'"(ibid.: 734).

References

American Friends' Service Committee. 1971. *Struggle for Justice*. New York: Hill
    and Wang.
Amir, M. 1971. *Patterns of Forcible Rape*. Chicago: University Press.
Ashworth, A. 1992. "Sentencing Reform Structures." *Crime and Justice* 16: 55–98.
———. 1993. "Victim Impact Statements and Sentencing." *Criminal Law Review*,
    pp. 498–509.
Australian Law Reform Commission. 1987. *Sentencing*. Report No. 44. Australian
    Government Publishing Service, Canberra.
Booth v. Maryland 482 U.S. 496 (1987).
Cavadino, M. and J. Dignan. 1993. "Reparation, Retribution, and Rights." *Interna-
    tional Review of Victimology* 4: 233–53.
Davis, R. D. and B. Smith. 1994. "The Effect of Victim Impact Statements on Sen-
    tencing Decisions: A Test in an Urban Setting." *Justice Quarterly* 11(3): 453–69.
Delgado, R. 1989. "Storytelling for Oppositionists and Others: A Pleas for Narra-
    tive." *Michigan Law Review* 87: 2411–41.

Douglas, R., K. Laster, and N. Inglis. 1994. "Victims of Efficiency: Tracking Information through the System in Victoria, Australia." *International Review of Victimology* 3: 95–110.

Duff, P. (forthcoming). "The Measure of Criminal Injuries Compensation: Political Pragmatism or Dog's Dinner." *Oxford Journal of Legal Studies.*

Eisenstein, J. and J. Jacob. 1977. *Felony Justice.* Boston: Little, Brown and Company.

Elias, R. 1983. *Victims of the System.* New Brunswick, NJ: Transaction Publishers.

———. 1993. *Victims Still: The Political Manipulation of Crime Victims.* Newbury Park, CA: Sage.

Emerson, R.M. and B. Paley. 1994. "Organizational Horizons and Complaint Filing," in K. Hawkins (ed.) *The Uses of Discretion.* Oxford: Oxford University Press

Erez, E. 1989. "The Impact of Victimology on Criminal Justice Policy." *Criminal Justice Policy Review* 3(3): 236–56.

———. 1990. "Victim Participation in Sentencing: Rhetoric and Reality." *Journal of Criminal Justice* 18:19–31.

Erez, E. and K. Laster. 1994. "Naming, Blaming, and Claiming: The Vicissitudes of Feminist Victimology." Paper presented to the American Society of Criminology Annual Meeting in Miami, November.

Erez, E., L. Roeger, and F. Morgan. 1994. *Victim Impact Statements in South Australia: An Evaluation.* Series C, no. 6. Adelaide: Office of Crime Statistics, South Australian Attorney General's Department.

Erez, E. and L. Roeger. 1995a. "Crime Impact v. Victim Impact: Evaluation of Victim Impact Statements in South Australia." *Criminology Australia* 6: 3–8

———. 1995b. "The Effect of Victim Impact Statements on Sentencing Outcomes and Dispositions: The Australian Experience." *Journal of Criminal Justice* 23: 363–75.

Erez E. and L. Rogers. (forthcoming). "Victim Input and Sentencing Processes and Outcomes: The Perspectives of Legal Professionals." Paper presented at the Law and Society Annual Meeting in St. Louis, May.

Fattah, E. A. (forthcoming). "From a Handful of Dollars to Tea and Sympathy: The Sad History of Victims Assistance," in J. Van Dijk, R.I. Van Kaam, and J.A. Wemers (eds.) *Caring for Victims.* Monsey, New York: Criminal Justice Press.

Feeley, M. and J. Simon. 1992. "The New Penology: Notes on the Emerging Strategy of Corrections and its Implications." *Criminology* 30: 449–74.

———. 1994. "Actuarial Justice," in D. Nelken (ed.) *The Futures of Criminology.* Newbury Park, CA: Sage.

Fletcher, G. 1978. *Rethinking Criminal Law.* Boston: Little, Brown.

Fogel, D. 1975. *We are the Living Proof... The Justice Model for Corrections.* Cincinnati: W.H. Anderson.

Froham, L. 1992. "Discrediting Victims' Allegations of Sexual Assault: Prosecutorial Accounts of Case Rejections." *Social Problems* 38(2): 213–26.

Goldstein, A.S. 1984. "The Victim and Prosecutorial Discretion: The Federal Victim and Witnesses Protection Act of 1982." *Law and Contemporary Problems* 47:225–48.

Grabosky, P.N. 1987. "Victims," pp. 143–57 in G. Zdenkowski, C. Ronalds, and M. Richardson (eds.) *The Criminal Injustice System* (vol. 2). Sydney: Pluto Press.

Hall, D.J. 1991. "Victim Voices in Criminal Court: The Need for Restraint." *American Criminal Law Review* 28: 233–66.

Hellerstein, D.R. 1989. "Victim Impact Statement: Reform or Reprisal?" *American Criminal Law Review* 27: 391–430.

Henderson, L.N. 1985. "The Wrongs of Victims' Rights." *Stanford Law Review* 37: 937–1021.

Henley, M., R.C. Davis, and B.E. Smith. 1994. "The Reactions of Prosecutors and

Judges to Victim Impact Statements." *International Review of Victimology* 3: 83–93.

Heydebrand, W. and C. Seron. 1990. "Rationalizing Justice: The Political Economy of Federal District Courts." New York: State University of New York Press.

Hillenbrand, S.W. and B.E. Smith. 1989. Victim Rights Legislation: An Assessment of its Impact on Criminal Justice Practitioners and Victims. Report of the American Bar Association to the National Institute of Justice.

Higgenbotham, A. L., Jr. 1978. *In the Matter of Color: Race and American Legal Process.* New York: Oxford University Press.

Kelly, D. P. 1987. "Victims." *Wayne Law Review* 34: 69–86.

Kelly, D.P. and E. Erez. 1997. "Victim Participation in the Criminal Justice System." In R.C.Davis, A.J. Lurigio, and W. Skogan (eds.), *Victims of Crime.* Thousand Oaks, CA: Sage.

Laster, K. and P. O' Malley. 1996. "New Age Sensitive Laws: The Reassertion of Emotionality in the Law." *International Journal of Sociology of Law* 24: 21–40.

McLeod, M. 1986. "Victim Participation at Sentencing." *Criminal Law Bulletin* 22: 501–17.

Mawby, R. and Gill, M.L. 1987. *Crime Victims: Needs, Services, and the Voluntary Sector.* London: Tavistock

Mendelsohn, B. 1974. "The Origin of the Doctrine of Victimology," pp. 3–11 in S. Drapkin and E. Viano (eds.), *Victimology.* Lexington, MA: Lexington Books.

Miers, D. 1992. "The Responsibilities and the Rights of Victims of Crime." *Modern Law Review* 55: 482–505.

National Victims Center. 1996. 1996 Victim's Rights Sourcebook: A Compilation and Comparison of Victim's Rights Legislation. Arlington, VA.

Naffine, N. 1990. *The Law and the Sexes: Exploration in Feminist Jurisprudence.* Boston: Allen and Unwin.

NOVA. 1996. Newsletter, vol. 17, no. 9.

O'Malley, P. 1984. "Technocratic Justice in Australia." *Law in Context: A Socio-Legal Journal* 2: 31–49.

———. 1996. "Post-Social Criminologies: Some Implications for Criminological Theory and Practice." *Current Issues in Criminal Justice* 8 (1): 26–38.

Parent, D.G., B. Auerbach, and K. E. Carlson. 1992. *Compensating Crime Victims: A Summary of Policies and Practices.* Washington, DC: U.S. Department of Justice.

Payne v. Tennessee 111 S. Ct. 2597 (1991).

President's Task Force on Victims of Crime. 1982. *Final Report.* Washington, DC: U.S. Government Printing Office.

Reidel, M. 1975. "Perceived Circumstances, Inferences of Intent and Judgments of Offense Seriousness." *Journal of Criminal Law and Criminology* 66: 201–8.

Roberts, A. 1990. *Helping Crime Victims.* Newbury Park, CA: Sage.

Rogers, L. and E. Erez. 1997. "The Contextuality of Objectivity in Sentencing among Legal Professionals in South Australia." Paper presented at the American Society of Criminology Annual meeting in San Diego, Nov.

Rubel, H.C. 1986. "Victim Participation in Sentencing Proceedings." *Criminal Law Quarterly* 28: 226–50.

Ryan, W. 1971. *Blaming the Victim.* New York: Vintage.

Sebba, L. 1980. "Is Mens Rea a Component of Perceived Offense Seriousness?" *Journal of Criminal Law and Criminology* 74:124–35.

———. 1982. "The Victim Role and the Penal Process: A Theoretical Orientation." *American Journal of Comparative Law* 30: 217–40.

———. 1996. *Third Parties: Victims and the Criminal Justice System.* Columbus, OH: Ohio State University Press.

————. (forthcoming). "Victim's Rights—Whose Duties?" in J. Van Dijk, R.I. Van Kaam, and J.A. Wemmer (eds.) *Caring for Victims*. Monsey, NY: Criminal Justice Press.

Sellin, T. and M.E. Wolfgang. [1964]1978. *The Measurement of Delinquency*. Montclair, NJ: Patterson Smith.

Singer, L. 1979. *Just Deserts: Sentencing Based Equality and Desert*. Cambridge, MA: Ballinger.

Spencer, J.R. and R.H. Flin. 1993. *The Evidence of Children: The Law and the Psychology*, 2d ed. London: Blackstone.

South Carolina v. Gathers 480 U.S. 805 (1989).

Sudnow, D. 1965. "Normal Crimes: Sociological Features of the Penal Code in a Public Defender Office." *Social Problems* 12:255–77.

Sumner, C. J. 1987. "Victim Participation in the Criminal Justice System." *Australian and New Zealand Journal of Criminology* 20: 195–217.

Talbert, P.A. 1988. "The Relevance of Victim Impact Statements to the Criminal Sentencing Decisions." *U.C.L.A. Law Review* 36: 199–232.

Thorvaldson, S.A. 1990. "Restitution and Victim Participation at Sentencing: A Comparison of Two Models," pp. 23–36 in B. Galaway and J. Hudson. (eds.) *Criminal Justice, Restitution and Reconciliation*. Monsey, NY: Criminal Justice Press.

U.S. Sentencing Commission. 1987. Sentencing Guidelines and Policy Statements. Washington, DC: U.S. Sentencing Commission.

————. 1994. Guidelines Manual. Washington, DC: U.S. Sentencing Commission.

Victorian Sentencing Committee. 1988. "Sentencing: Report of the Committee," Attorney-General's Department, Melbourne, Australia.

Victim Support. 1995. The Rights of Victims of Crime.

Von Hirsch, A. 1976. *Doing Justice: The Choice of Punishments*. New York: Hill and Wang.

————. 1985. *Past or Future Crimes: Deservedness and Dangerousness in Sentencing of Criminals*. New Brunswick, NJ: Rutgers University Press.

Von Hirsch, A. and A. Ashworth, eds. 1992. *Principled Sentencing*. Boston: Northeastern University Press.

Von Hirsch, A. and N. Jareborg. 1991. "Gauging Criminal Harm: A Living Standard Analysis." *Oxford Journal of Legal Studies* 11:1–38.

Williams v. New York 337 U.S. 241 (1969).

Wolfgang, M. E. 1957. "Victim-Precipitated Criminal Homicide." *Journal of Criminal Law, Criminology and Police Science* 48: 1–11.

————. [1965]1975. "Victim Compensation in Crimes of Personal Violence," pp. 116–29 in J. Hudson and B. Galaway (eds.), *Considering the Victim*. Springfield, IL: Charles C. Thomas.

————. 1976. "Seriousness of Crime and a Policy of Juvenile Justice." in J.F. Short (ed.) *Delinquency, Crime and Society*. Chicago: University of Chicago Press.

————. 1982. "Basic Concepts in Victimological Theory: Individualization of the Victim," pp. 47–58 in H.-J. Schneider (ed.), *The Victim in International Perspective*. Berlin: De Gruyter.

————. 1989. "Victim Precipitation in Victimology and in the Law," pp. 133–42 in Z. P. Separovic (ed.) *Victimology: International Action and Study of Victims*.

Wolfgang, M.E., R.M. Figlio, P.E. Tracy, and S.I. Singer. 1985. The National Survey of Crime Severity. Washington, DC: U.S. Department of Justice.

Wolfgang, M.E. and S.I. Singer. 1978. "Victim Categories in Crime." *Journal of Criminal Law and Criminology* 69: 379–94.

Zedner, L. 1994. "Reparation and Retribution: Are They Reconcilable?" *Modern Law Review* 57: 228–50.

10

Sentencing Disparity and Sentencing Guidelines

Claire Souryal and
Charles Wellford

Introduction

A major purpose of structured sentencing schemes is to reduce unwarranted sentencing disparity. In contrast to indeterminate sentencing where judges and parole boards maintain wide discretion in determining criminal punishment, structured sentencing schemes (e.g., voluntary/descriptive sentencing guidelines, statutory determinate sentencing, presumptive/prescriptive sentencing guidelines) limit or structure the discretion of the judiciary in imposing criminal sanctions (Tonry 1993:268).

Structured sentencing schemes are explicitly crafted to take into account legal characteristics pertinent to the sentencing outcome (e.g., prior record, offense seriousness). Sentencing disparity that springs from such legal characteristics is considered warranted disparity. Unwarranted sentencing disparity arises when extra-legal factors, say, race, class, or gender, influence the sentencing outcome.

Examination of the influence of extra-legal factors (particularly race/ethnicity) on criminal justice processing in general has a long history in criminological research (Wolfgang 1973). The impact of extra-legal factors on the *sentence* outcome in particular has received special attention due to the highly visible and symbolic nature of the sentencing decision (Blumstein et al. 1983:39). Despite the salience of the issue to the criminal justice system and the multitude of studies devoted to understanding the relationship between race and sentence outcome, consistent research findings have not emerged.

Nonetheless, the balance of research does not suggest a pattern of systemic or *overt* discrimination with regard to race in sentence outcomes. More subtle effects of race on sentence outcomes cannot be discounted, however. There is some evidence to suggest that in certain contexts, race influences the incarceration decision such that black defendants are more likely than white defendants to receive a sentence of incarceration (Sampson and Lauritsen 1997:355). However, race/ethnicity does not appear to directly influence sentence length contingent upon incarceration. In addition, there is evidence to suggest that the effect of race on the incarceration decision may operate indirectly through mediating variables such as pretrial release, plea-bargaining practices, or work history. Although the implementation of structured sentencing schemes (most commonly presumptive sentencing guidelines) appears to have reduced unwarranted racial sentencing disparity as intended, evidence of racial disparity under such schemes persists (Tonry 1993:168–9).

The following study will examine unwarranted sentencing disparity with respect to race/ethnicity in the state of Maryland under Maryland's voluntary sentencing guidelines system.[1] Specifically, it will assess whether an individual's race/ethnicity influences the probability of incarceration (i.e., the decision whether to incarcerate), and contingent upon incarceration, the length of sentence (adjusting for legal characteristics). In addition, it will explore whether the effect of race/ethnicity is equally likely to influence the sentence outcome among sentences that are *consistent* (or inconsistent) with the sentencing guidelines. The sentence outcome of roughly 81,000 individuals convicted in Maryland Circuit Courts between January 1987 and September 1996 will be analyzed.

Literature Review

Racial Disparity in Sentencing

The overrepresentation of minorities in prison populations relative to their percentage of the U.S. population clearly raises the possibility of unwarranted sentencing disparity.[2] Whether the observed disproportionality in prison populations stems from disproportional involvement of minorities in crime and/or to disparate or discriminatory treatment by the criminal justice system has been the subject of considerable debate (e.g., Crutchfield 1994:166–7).

While the vast majority of sentencing research examines the corre-lation between race/ethnicity and sentencing outcome at the individual level, another approach assesses disproportionality in *imprisonment* by comparing aggregate Uniform Crime Report (UCR) arrest statistics and imprisonment rates by race. For example, Blumstein (1982) compared official UCR arrest statistics and imprisonment rates at the *national* level and found that 80 percent of the racial disproportionality in pris-ons in 1974 and 1979 appeared to be explained by disproportional in-volvement of minorities in crime.

Crutchfield et al. (1994:173) replicated Blumstein's approach using data collected in 1982 and found that 90 percent of the racial disproportionality in prisons nationwide may be attributed to dispro-portional minority involvement in crime. Crutchfield et al. (1994:175) then extended the analysis one step further by examining state-level statistics. The state-level analysis revealed considerable variation in patterns of imprisonment. In some states, for example, racial disproportionality in imprisonment appeared to be entirely explained by disproportionate involvement in crime (i.e., arrest rates), whereas in other states less than 60 percent of the disproportionality in imprison-ment was similarly explained. The Crutchfield et al. (1994:175) analy-sis revealed that approximately 66 percent of the imprisonment disparity in the state of Maryland in 1982 was explained by differences in rates of arrest for Whites and Nonwhites.

The most common form of sentencing disparity research examines the relationship between race/ethnicity and sentence outcome at the individual level. However, distinguishing the unique effect of extra-legal factors such as race on sentencing outcomes has proven to be a formidable methodological task. Research efforts suffer from omitted variable bias or measurement error (where variables relevant to the explanation of the sentence outcome which are also associated with race are either excluded from explanatory models or inadequately mea-sured, thereby biasing the effect of race on the sentence outcome) (Blumstein et al. 1983:16). Sample selection bias also presents a prob-lem in estimating the effect of race on sentence outcome when unob-served, nonrandom screening processes which occur at earlier decision-points in the criminal justice process (e.g., arrest or charging decisions) and are also associated with race are not taken into account (Klepper et al. 1983:64–5).

Over the last sixty years, four "Waves" of this line of sentencing research have been identified (distinguished mainly by methodological advances) (Zatz 1987:71–81). The earliest research (Wave I) on the relationship between race and sentencing revealed that race exerted a significant effect on sentence outcome. Wave 1 research (1930s–mid-1960s), however, is suspect because it generally failed to control for relevant legal factors associated with the sentencing outcome (e.g., prior record). The second wave of research (late 1960s–1970s) employed controls for legal factors such as prior record. Reviews of Wave II research (e.g., Hagan 1974; Kleck 1981) suggested that the apparent effect of race on sentencing outcome was largely an artifact of the failure in prior research to control for legally relevant variables (in particular, prior record). Thus, Wave II research appeared to advance what has been dubbed the "no discrimination thesis" (NDT), although it did in fact draw attention to the possibility of indirect or interactive effects of race on sentence outcome.

Wave III research (1970s–1980s) is characterized by the use of more sophisticated statistical techniques intended to adjust for "selection bias" and "omitted variable bias." Wave III research also explored the possibility of indirect effects of race on sentencing (e.g., race affects pre-trial release status which in turn influences sentence) or interaction effects (e.g., the effect of race on sentencing varies depending on whether an individual has a prior record). Such research, for example, suggested that blacks in some jurisdictions may be less likely to plead guilty which in turn affects the incarceration decision (Welch et al. 1985:73). Although Wave III research did not yield consistent findings, importantly it called the NDT into question. As Sampson and Lauritsen (1997: 348) explain, it suggested that "there is *some* discrimination, *some* of the time, in *some* places."

Wave IV research began in the 1980s and continues into the present. Wave IV may be distinguished from Wave III not necessarily by methodological advances but by the advent of structured sentencing. By enacting structured sentencing systems, discretion shifted from judges to decision makers earlier in the process, chiefly, the prosecutor. Studies of the impact of race on prosecutorial decision making became more prevalent. Wave IV research also became increasingly cognizant of the importance of macrosocial context (e.g., influence of urbanization or poverty) (Sampson and Lauritsen 1997:349). For example, Chiricos and Crawford's (1995) review of thirty-eight studies revealed that black defendants were more likely to receive a sentence of incarceration in particular contexts. As the authors explain, "We have shown that black defendants are significantly more disadvantaged than whites at the point of incarceration in the South, in places where blacks comprise a larger percentage of the population and where unemployment is relatively high" (Chiricos and Crawford 1995:300). Race did not influence sentence length in their study, however. Contextual research may be the key to understanding and explaining seemingly inconsistent or anomalous research findings (Peterson and Hagan 1984:56).

In short, the preponderance of the evidence does not support the thesis that the sentencing decision is marred by a pattern of systemic racial disparity. Racial disparity in *imprisonment* appears to be largely explained by disproportional involvement of minorities in crime at the national level (although there appears to be substantial variation at the state level). Research findings at the individual level also seem to be sensitive to specific contexts, time periods, or locations (i.e., rural versus urban location, poverty level, population composition), such that findings from one jurisdiction or time period may not generalize to another. Wave III and Wave IV sentencing research certainly call the NDT into question. There is evidence to suggest that black defendants are more likely to receive a sentence of incarceration than white defendants in certain contexts (Chiricos and Crawford 1995:300; Spohn et al. 1981:86). Evidence also suggests that race may have an indirect effect on the incarceration decision.

Sentencing Guidelines and Racial Disparity in Sentencing

Structured sentencing schemes were implemented in response to the growing disillusionment with indeterminate sentencing in the late 1970s and 1980s. Disillusionment with indeterminate sentencing sprang from a number of sources including, for example, the desire to limit discretion and demand accountability from public officials, the shift from utilitarian to retributivist philosophies, growing skepticism regarding the efficacy of rehabilitation programs, and findings of racial disparity (Blumstein et al. 1983: 61–6). As Blumstein et al. (1983:61) report between 1975 and January 1982, "eleven states abolished parole release for the majority of offenders, seventeen states established administrative rules for release decisions (e.g., parole guidelines), more than thirty states passed mandatory minimum sentence laws, and, in almost every state, judges experimented with guidelines to structure their own sentencing decisions."

Voluntary sentencing guidelines were one of the forerunners of structured sentencing schemes (Tonry 1988: 276). As the name suggests, judges are not required by law to comply with voluntary sentencing guidelines and as a consequence defendants do not possess a right to be sentenced according to the guidelines. Generally instituted by judges, voluntary sentencing guidelines are by and large descriptive in nature. In other words, they are expected to serve as a model of past sentencing behavior (Blumstein et al. 1983:135). Presumptive sentencing guidelines, on the other hand, possess legal authority since they are mandated statutorily and are subject to appellate sentence review. Judges are expected to sentence according to the guidelines or provide an explanation for noncompliance. Presumptive sentencing guidelines are generally considered prescriptive in nature because they seek to institute new sentencing policies (Blumstein et al. 1983: 135).

Research on the effect of sentencing guidelines (particularly voluntary sentencing guidelines) on racial disparity is sparse. Several state sentencing commissions (Minnesota, Washington, and Oregon) examined the impact of presumptive sentencing guidelines on unwarranted disparity with regard to race and gender (Tonry 1993:168–71) . By and large, the implementation of presumptive sentencing guidelines appeared to reduce although not eliminate sentencing disparity. Tonry (1993:168) summarizes the Minnesota sentencing commission findings as follows:

> The Minnesota's commission's three-year evaluation concluded that racial differences in sentencing declined under guidelines; nonetheless, minority defendants were likelier than whites to be imprisoned when the presumptive sentence prescribed non-state imprisonment, minority defendants received longer sentences than similarly categorized whites, and men received longer prison sentences than similarly categorized women.

Similar findings emerged in Washington and Oregon. Despite a reduction in racial disparity in Washington, white defendants appeared to be more likely to benefit from the use of mitigating provisions (e.g., for first-time offenders). In Oregon, "whites were slightly less likely than minority defendants to receive upward dispositional departures, slightly more likely to receive downward dispositional departures, and much more likely to benefit from an 'optional probation' alternatives program" (Tonry 1993:169).

Miethe and Moore's (1985:358) study of sentencing disparity before and after the implementation of Minnesota's guidelines revealed that although the direct effects of social variables (e.g., gender, marital status, race) on compliant sentences diminished subsequent to the implementation of the guidelines, such variables still influenced the sentence outcome indirectly through case processing characteristics. The effect of race on sentence outcome was mediated by prior record and the use of a weapon.

In another study of unwarranted sentencing disparity under Minnesota's presumptive sentencing guidelines, Stolzenberg and D'Allessio (1994) employed an interrupted time-series design to assess the presence of unwarranted disparity with regard to the incarceration decision (Yes/No) and sentence length decision between 1980 and 1989. Unwarranted disparity was defined as disparity in the sentence outcome that did not stem from legally mandated factors (thus it is not specific to race). The results of the study suggested that although the guidelines initially reduced disparity with regard to the incarceration decision (Yes/No), the reduction in disparity was not sustained over the long-term. The sentencing guidelines appeared to substantially reduce disparity in sentence length throughout the course of the study (Stolzenberg and D'Allessio 1994:306).

Research assessing the impact of voluntary or descriptive sentencing guidelines on unwarranted disparity is less common (Tonry 1988:279). What evidence is available suggests that voluntary sentencing guidelines did not appear to substantially reduce sentencing disparity. For example, an evaluation of voluntary sentencing guidelines within multiple jurisdictions in Maryland and Florida suggested that unwarranted sentencing disparity was generally not reduced (one of four jurisdictions in Maryland seemed to be an exception to the rule, however) (Tonry 1988:280). Commentators speculate that it is the voluntary nature of the guidelines which seemed to limit their effectiveness (Tonry 1988:282; Miethe and Moore 1985:341).

In short, while sentencing disparity appears to have decreased with the implementation of presumptive sentencing guidelines, it has not been eliminated. Even under presumptive sentencing guidelines, white defendants appear to be more likely to benefit from sentencing alternatives.

Methods

Data

In order to investigate the possibility of unwarranted sentencing disparity under Maryland's voluntary sentencing guidelines, the population of persons (N=80,608) convicted of a single offense in a Maryland Circuit Court between January 1987 and September 1996 were analyzed. The database was provided by the Maryland Administrative Office of the Courts to the University of Maryland Center for Applied Policy Studies. The data were extracted from courtroom worksheets which are routinely completed by court clerks at each circuit court. The accuracy of the database was verified using random samples drawn from the total database.

The database contains attributes of the offense and offender, as well as case-processing characteristics. Offender attributes include basic demographic characteristics such as sex, race/ethnicity, and age as well as an offender score summarizing an individual's prior record. Offense attributes include offense type and an offense seriousness score. Offenses are categorized into person, property, or drug offenses since a separate sentencing matrix is used for each crime category. Case processing characteristics include mode of disposition and Circuit Court. Mode of disposition consists of the following: (1) plea agreement; (2) plea, no agreement; (3) jury trial; and (4) court trial.

Variables specific to the Maryland sentencing guidelines include the offense score and the offender score. These variables are of particular importance to the study since prior research indicates that offense seriousness and prior record are the most influential factors in determining sentence outcomes (Blumstein et al. 1983:11). The *Offense* score provides a measure of the seriousness of the offense. The *Offender* score provides a summary measure of an individual's prior record.

The database also contains the sentence outcome for each individual. Data describing the sentence outcomes included, for example, whether an individual received a sentence involving incarceration and the length of that sentence (e.g., incarceration time, suspended time, actual time). If an individual was not sentenced to incarceration, the length of the probation term and whether a fine was imposed were also available. Lastly, data regarding whether the sentencing judge complied with the sentencing guidelines were documented.

Missing-data values. Missing-data values did not pose a serious problem. Missing-data values were most prevalent among demographic variables. The percentage of missing-data values for each variable, however, did not exceed 3 percent. For example, 2.3 percent of the sample were missing age, 2.0 percent were missing race, 0.7 percent were missing sex. The most commonly missing case processing variable was disposition type (1.2 percent). As a consequence, missing-data values were assumed to be "missing at random" and cases with missing-data values were excluded from the analyses. Missing-data values are considered to be missing at random if the probability that they are missing is independent of the true value of the incompletely observed variable (Little 1992:1229).

Sample characteristics. Roughly, 81,000 individuals had been convicted of a single offense between 1 January 1987 and 30 September 1996 in one of eight Maryland circuit courts. Descriptive statistics are shown in table 10.1. The percentage of persons convicted of an offense each year was similar over the course of the evaluation although a slightly smaller percentage of the sample had been sentenced during calendar year 1986 (8 percent) or 1987 (9 percent), as compared to calendar years 1988 through 1995 (11 percent). Over half of the defendants had been processed in three of the eight Maryland Circuits: (1) Circuit three (13 percent); (2) Circuit seven (23 percent); and (3) Circuit eight (33 percent).[3]

Convicted defendants were twenty-nine years of age on average. Roughly 87 percent were male. Sixty-five (65 percent) of the defendants were black, 34 percent were white, 1.3 percent were Hispanic, and 0.5 percent had been classified as "other."

The most common mode of disposition was a plea agreement (74.3 percent) followed by a plea without agreement (16.9 percent), and either court or jury trials (8.9 percent). Just over half of the sample had been convicted of a drug offense (52.1 percent). Conviction of a violent offense was second most common (28 percent) followed by a property offense (20 percent).

Approximately, 69 percent of the sample received a sentence involving a term of incarceration. The average length of incarceration (actual sentence) was 34 months (median of 12 months). Approximately, 55 percent of the sentences imposed were consistent with the Maryland sentencing guidelines. Among sentences that were not consistent with the guidelines, 38 percent fell under the guideline recommendation and 8 percent exceeded the guideline recommendation.

Analytic Strategy

A sentence outcome consists of two separate decisions: (1) the decision whether to incarcerate; and (2) the decision as to the length of incarceration. As noted above, prior research suggests that the factors that influence each decision are not necessarily synonymous. Therefore, each decision will be analyzed separately here.

Logistic regression models will be estimated to examine the effect of legal and extra-legal factors on the incarceration decision (Yes/No). Logistic regression is commonly used to analyze the relationship between a set of explanatory variables and a binary outcome. Logistic regression is based on the cumulative logistic probability function which relates probabilities of the dependent variable to the explanatory variables (Hanushek and Jackson 1977:187). The logistic transformation of the dependent variable represents the logarithm of the odds of an event occurring (Pindyck and Rubinfeld 1991:259). Ordinary least squares (OLS) regression will be used to assess the influence of legal and extra-legal factors on sentence length (among individuals who have been sentenced to a term of incarceration). Since each person included in the model has a non-zero sentence length, the dependent variable will be truncated at zero.

Regression models will be estimated first using the total sample. Since the Maryland sentencing guidelines utilize separate matrices for each crime type and the offense seriousness measure (a primary determinant of sentence outcome) varies slightly across crime categories, a crime-specific approach will also be adopted whereby separate models will be estimated for person, drug, and property offenses. The crime-specific approach will allow us to assess whether there is an interaction between crime type and race. That is, whether sentencing disparity with regard to race is more or less likely within certain categories of crime.

Lastly, additional models will be estimated in order to determine whether the effect of race differs depending on whether the imposed sentence was *consistent* or *inconsistent* with the sentencing guidelines. Models will be estimated to assess the effect of race on both the incarceration decision and sentence length among only those sentences that were *consistent* with the sentencing guidelines. Similarly, models will be estimated to examine the effect of race among only those sentences that were *inconsistent* with the sentencing guidelines.

The regression analyses rest on the assumption that the regression model has been correctly specified— that is, that all relevant variables associated with the sentencing decision are included in the model. It also rests on the assumption that key constructs such as offense seriousness have been adequately measured. To the extent that our models exclude variables that affect the sentencing outcome or provide only partial measures of such constructs, they may be vulnerable to omitted variable bias or measurement error. If the omitted variables (or inadequately measured variables) are associated with both race and the sentencing outcome, the estimate of the effect of race on sentencing may be biased. As a consequence, the results of the analyses must be interpreted with caution.

Measures

Dependent variables. The first dependent variable of interest will be whether an individual received a sentence that involved a term of incarceration independent of the length of sentence. A binary indicator will be created whereby an individual receives a code of 1 if they are sentenced to a term of incarceration and a 0 otherwise.

The second dependent variable will consist of the length of incarceration measured in months contingent on being sentenced to prison. Therefore only individuals who receive a term of incarceration will be included in the analysis. Length of incarceration represents the actual time an individual is expected to serve (i.e., total sentence length less suspended time).

Independent variables. The independent or explanatory variables included in the regression models are shown below. Variable attributes are illustrated in table 10.2: age, race, sex, type of offense, mode of disposition, offense score, offender score, and circuit court.

Explanatory variables have been constructed as follows: (1) age is measured in years as a continuous variable; (2) race is measured as a set of binary indicators (coded 1 or 0) for each race/ethnicity (black, white, Hispanic, and "other"); (3) sex is represented by a binary measure (male=1; female=0); (4) disposition type consists of binary measures coded 1 or 0 for each disposition type (plea agreement, plea without agreement, court trial, and jury trial); and (5) circuit consists of a set of binary measures coded 1 or 0 to represent each circuit.

The measure of offense seriousness varies across crime categories since it was specifically created for use with the person offense matrix of the sentencing guidelines. For person offenses, it combines the seriousness category of the offense (which is statutorily determined) with three indicators of the nature of the offense (i.e., whether the victim was injured, whether a weapon was used, and whether the victim was especially vulnerable). The Offense score ranges from 1 to 15 (15 is the most serious offense score). Since information regarding victim injury, etc. is not generalizable to drug and property offenses, the seriousness category of each offense was used as a measure of offense seriousness. The seriousness category is one component of the offense score for person offenses. Thus, it is a comparable, though not identical measure.[4]

The offender score provides a summary measure of an individual's prior record. It consists of the following factors: (1) whether the individual was involved with the criminal justice system at the time of the instant offense (0=no/1=yes); (2) juvenile record (0=not more than one finding of delinquency; 1=two or more findings without commitment or one commitment; 2=two or more commitments); (3) prior adult record (0=none, 1=minor, 2=moderate, 3=major); (4) prior adult parole/probation violations (0=no, 1=yes). The offender score ranges from 0 to 9 with a score of 9 representing the most serious offender score.

Results

The Incarceration Decision

Logistic regression models were estimated to examine the effect of legal and extra-legal factors on the incarceration decision using the SAS System (SAS, 1990). The results of analyses using the total sample are shown in table 10.3.

Adjusting for the influence of legally relevant factors race exerted a positive and statistically significant effect on the incarceration decision. Both black and Hispanic offenders were more likely to receive a sentence of incarceration than white offenders. The predicted probability of incarceration is shown in figure 10.1 (see end of chapter). The predicted probability of incarceration for white defendants with mean/median values on all other explanatory variables included in the model was $\pi=0.56$. In comparison, the predicted probability of incarceration for black defendants was $\pi=.65$ and the predicted probability of incarceration for Hispanic defendants was $\pi=0.77$. Figure 10.2 illustrates the predicted probability of incarceration when black, Hispanic, and individuals classified as "other race" are combined into one category. The predicted probability of incarceration for white defendants is $\pi=0.56$, whereas the predicted probability of incarceration for nonwhite defendants is $\pi=0.65$. Due to the relatively small sample size of Hispanic and "other" individuals, the predicted probabilities mirror the predicted probabilities of white and black offenders when each race/ethnicity is modeled separately.

As expected, both the offense score and offender score exerted a strong, positive effect on the incarceration decision. The more serious the offense or the more serious an individual's prior record, the greater the probability of an incarceration sentence. Figures 10.3 and 10.4 illustrate the predicted probability of incarceration for each level of the

TABLE 10.1
**Descriptive Statistics of Individuals Sentenced between 1 January 1987
and 30 September 1996 for Single Count Offenses**

Variable	Total Sample N=80,608
Age (X, SD)	28.66 (8.74)
Median	26.75
Male (N, percent Yes)	69,727 (87.1)
Race (N, percent Yes)	
Black	51,050 (64.6)
White	26,590 (33.6)
Hispanic	1,020 (1.3)
Other	376 (0.5)
Mode of Disposition (N, percent Yes)	
Plea Agreement	59,157 (74.3)
Plea, No Agreement	13,423 (16.9)
Court Trial	3,505 (4.4)
Jury Trial	3,546 (4.5)
Crime Type (N, percent Yes)	
Violent	22,183 (27.5)
Drug	41,970 (52.1)
Property	16,454 (20.4)
Circuit (N, percent Yes)	
One	4,529 (5.6)
Two	2,852 (3.5)
Three	10,251 (12.7)
Four	2,933 (3.6)
Five	7,900 (9.8)
Six	6,824 (8.5)
Seven	18,518 (23.0)
Eight	26,801 (33.2)
Offense Score (X, SD)	3.588 (2.197)
Median	3
Offender Score (X, SD)	1.986 (2.162)
Median	1
Incarcerated (N, percent Yes)	55,766 (69.2)
Sentence Length (X, SD)	34.44 (62.17)
(In Months) Median	12.01

offender score (0–9) and each level of the offense score (1–15), with all other explanatory variables held constant at their mean or median value.[5] As illustrated in figure 10.3, the predicted probability of incarceration for an individual with an offender score of zero equals $\pi=0.5$. As the offender score approaches 9, the predicted probability of incarceration is virtually $\pi=1.0$. Similarly, the predicted probability of incarceration for an individual with an offense score of one and mean or median

TABLE 10. 2
Research Variables and Variable Attributes

Sex	1= Male	
	0= Female	
Race	1=Black;	0=Other
	1=White;	0=Other
	1=Hispanic;	0=Other
	1=Other Race;	0=Other
Age	Age in Years	
Mode of Disposition	1=Plea;	0=Other
	1=Plea w/o Agreement;	0=Other
	1=Court trial;	0=Other
	1=Jury trial;	0=Other

Circuit   Circuit:
1= Dorchester, Somerset, Wicomico, Worcester Counties
2= Caroline, Cecil, Kent, Queen Anne's, Talbot Counties
3= Baltimore and Harford Counties
4= Allegany, Garrett, Washington Counties
5= Anne Arundel, Carroll, Howard Counties
6= Montgomery, Frederick Counties
7= Calvert, Charles, Prince George's, St. Mary's Counties
8= Baltimore City

Crime Category	1=Person;	0=Other
	1=Drug;	0=Other
	1=Property;	0=Other

Offense Seriousness Person Offense: Seriousness Category (1, 2, 3, 4, 5, 6, 7)*
Category   +   Victim Injury: 0= No injury
(varies by crime type)   1= Injury, Non-permanent
                                        2= Permanent Injury or Death

            +   Weapon Usage
                                  0= No weapon
                                  1= Weapon Other than Firearm
                                  2= Firearm or Explosive

            +   Special Vulnerability of Victim
                                  0= No
                                  1= Yes

Drug Offense: Seriousness Category (2, 3, 4, 5, 7)*
Property Offense: Seriousness Category (2, 3, 4, 5, 6, 7)*

*Seriousness category is converted to a point score ranging from 1 to 10. The higher the point score, the more serious the offense.

TABLE 10. 2 (continued)

Offender Score	Relationship to CJ System at time of offense:		
	+	0=	None or Pending Cases
		1=	Court or Other Criminal Justice Supervision
	Juvenile Delinquency		
		0=	Not More Than One Finding of Delinquency or Over Age 25
	+	1=	Two or More Findings, None or One Commitment
		2=	Two or More Commitments
	Adult Record		
		0=	None
		1=	Minor
	+	3=	Moderate
		5=	Major
	Prior Adult Parole/Probation Violations		
		0=	No
		1=	Yes
Sentence Involving Incarceration	Incarceration	0=	No
		1=	Yes
Sentence Length	Sentence Length in Months		
Compliance	Compliance with Sentencing Guidelines:		
		1=	Within guidelines
		2=	Under guidelines
		3=	Above guidelines

value on all other variables included in the model is less than $\pi=0.5$. The predicted probability of individuals with an offense score of 6 or more exceeds $\pi=0.8$ (see figure 10.4). Examination of other variables included in the model suggested the following: (1) males were significantly more likely to be incarcerated than females; (2) older individuals were less likely to be incarcerated than younger individuals; and (3) individuals who were convicted subsequent to a plea agreement, or plea without agreement, or a court trial were significantly less likely to be incarcerated than individuals who were convicted by means of a jury trial.

Crime category-specific approach. In addition to the total analysis, the effect of race on the incarceration decision was examined within each crime category. The results are shown in tables 10.4–10.6. By and

TABLE 10.3
Logistic Regression Estimates Predicting the Incarceration Decision between
January 1987 and September 1996 Using Single Count Data (N=75,959)

Variable	b	s.e.	X^2
Constant	−1.788	0.076	—
Male	0.659	0.026	664.81***
Age	−0.012	0.001	127.90 ***
Black	0.374	0.021	325.80***
Hispanic	0.958	0.086	123.91***
Other Race	0.101	0.124	0.67
Property Offense	0.218	0.030	53.87***
Drug Offense	−0.071	0.023	10.08**
Plea Agreement	−0.246	0.053	21.58***
Plea, No Agreement	−0.342	0.056	37.21***
Court Trial	−0.243	0.068	12.83**
Offense Score	0.330	0.006	3348.26***
Offender Score	0.493	0.006	7061.79***
Circuit 1	1.739	0.048	1337.85***
Circuit 2	1.527	0.056	734.16***
Circuit 3	−0.080	0.030	7.39**
Circuit 4	1.371	0.055	625.98***
Circuit 5	−0.215	0.034	40.21***
Circuit 6	0.342	0.035	95.15***
Circuit 7	1.543	0.028	3020.38***
Log-likelihood	−36260.56		

* p <.05   **p<.01   ***p <.0001

large, the effect of race on incarceration did not vary dramatically among crime categories. The magnitude of the effect did appear to be stronger among individuals convicted of drug offenses.[6] The only other notable difference among the models was related to disposition type. Disposition type did not appear to influence the incarceration decision among property offenders.

Sentence Length

OLS regression models were estimated to assess the influence of race on sentence length. Regression estimates using the total sample are shown in table 10.7. Overall, the results of the analysis were similar to the logistic model predicting the incarceration decision. Notably, however, race did not exert a statistically significant effect on sentence length.

TABLE 10.4
Logistic Regression Estimates Predicting the Incarceration Decision
between January 1987 and September 1996 among Individuals Convicted
of a Person Offense Using Single Count Data (N=20,780)

Variable	b	s.e.	X^2
Constant	−1.001	0.135	—
Male	0.846	0.059	208.49***
Age	−0.025	0.002	195.85 ***
Black	0.242	0.040	36.03***
Hispanic	0.454	0.143	10.07**
Other Race	0.155	0.211	0.538
Plea Agreement	−0.497	0.092	29.01***
Plea, No Agreement	−0.498	0.101	24.51***
Court Trial	−0.439	0.124	12.60**
Offense Score	0.319	0.009	1282.08***
Offender Score	0.520	0.012	1821.50***
Circuit 1	1.279	0.094	184.96***
Circuit 2	0.751	0.111	46.04***
Circuit 3	−0.457	0.055	67.92***
Circuit 4	1.028	0.108	91.22***
Circuit 5	−0.146	0.069	4.44*
Circuit 6	−0.035	0.070	0.26
Circuit 7	0.944	0.054	303.50***
Log-likelihood	−9241.03		

* $p < .05$ ** $p < .01$ *** $p < .0001$

Offense effect score and offender score exerted a positive and statistically significant on sentence length. Males received longer sentences than females. Here, however, older individuals received longer sentences than younger individuals. Individuals who were adjudicated by means of a plea agreement, plea without agreement, or court trial received shorter sentences than individuals who were adjudicated by means of a jury trial.

Crime category-specific approach. The OLS regression models were estimated separately within each crime category. The results of the analyses are shown in tables 10.8–10.10. Examination of the effect of race on sentence length within each crime category revealed that race exerted a significant effect among persons convicted of *drug* offenses only. Race did not influence sentence length among persons convicted of person or property offenses.

TABLE 10.5
**Logistic Regression Estimates Predicting the Incarceration Decision
between January 1987 and September 1996 among Individuals Convicted
of a Drug Offense Using Single Count Data (N=39,761)**

Variable	b	s.e.	X^2
Constant	−2.221	0.110	—
Male	0.569	0.034	283.08***
Age	−0.008	0.002	25.72***
Black	0.456	0.030	224.31***
Hispanic	1.380	0.131	110.88***
Other Race	0.032	0.213	0.02
Plea Agreement	−0.254	0.083	9.26**
Plea, No Agreement	−0.383	0.087	19.42***
Court Trial	−0.085	0.105	0.65
Offense Score	0.363	0.008	1914.12***
Offender Score	0.466	0.008	3135.40***
Circuit 1	2.248	0.072	978.82***
Circuit 2	2.229	0.087	649.73***
Circuit 3	0.161	0.044	13.69**
Circuit 4	1.921	0.083	534.16***
Circuit 5	−0.149	0.048	9.76**
Circuit 6	0.664	0.049	185.08***
Circuit 7	1.962	0.040	2382.47***
Log-likelihood	−18935.12		

* $p < .05$ **$p < .01$ ***$p < .0001$

Variables that exerted statistically significant effects on sentence length across all three crime categories included the offense score, offender score, and disposition type. While males were more likely than females to receive longer sentences in person and drug offenses, male and female property offenders appeared to receive sentences of equal lengths. Lastly, while older individuals were more likely to receive longer sentences among person and property offenses, an individual's age did not influence sentence length if convicted of a drug offense.

Racial Disparity among Consistent and Inconsistent Sentences

The total sample was divided into two subsamples: individuals who received sentences that were consistent with the sentencing guidelines and individuals who received sentences that were inconsistent with the

TABLE 10.6
Logistic Regression Estimates Predicting the Incarceration Decision between January 1987 and September 1996 among Individuals Convicted of a Property Offense Using Single Count Data (N=15,418)

Variable	b	s.e.	X^2
Constant	−2.003	0.154	—
Male	0.818	0.056	217.22***
Age	0.002	0.002	0.63
Black	0.324	0.042	60.15***
Hispanic	0.841	0.215	15.31***
Other Race	0.008	0.220	0.001
Plea Agreement	0.045	0.106	0.18
Plea, No Agreement	−0.023	0.113	0.04
Court Trial	−0.187	0.136	1.89
Offense Score	0.308	0.022	191.72***
Offender Score	0.507	0.012	1934.62***
Circuit 1	1.159	0.093	154.80***
Circuit 2	0.916	0.108	72.43***
Circuit 3	−0.395	0.064	37.63***
Circuit 4	0.598	0.107	31.14***
Circuit 5	−0.582	0.073	63.32***
Circuit 6	−0.112	0.078	2.05
Circuit 7	1.173	0.064	339.40***
Log-likelihood	−7699.15		

* $p < .05$ ** $p < .01$ *** $p < .0001$

sentencing guidelines (either above or below the suggested range). Fifty-five percent of the total sample received sentences that were consistent with the sentencing guidelines. Logistic and OLS regression equations were then estimated to assess the effect of race on the incarceration decision (Y/N) and sentence length within each subsample. If adherence to the sentencing guidelines reduces sentencing disparity by race, the effect of race in this subsample would be expected to be negligible. Due to the relatively small sample size of Hispanic and "other" defendants and to the inclusion of interaction effects, race/ethnicity was collapsed into white versus nonwhite (black, Hispanic, and "other").

Consistent subsample. A logistic regression equation was estimated to assess the impact of race/ethnicity on the incarceration decision among individuals who received sentences that were consistent with the sentencing guidelines. The full set of explanatory variables were

TABLE 10.7
Ordinary Least Squares Regression Estimates Predicting Sentence
Length in Months between January 1987 and September 1996
Using Single Count Data (N=52,627)

Variable	b	s.e.	t
Constant	−25.993	1.687	−15.41***
Male	3.983	0.754	5.28***
Age	0.117	0.026	4.50***
Black	0.315	0.501	0.63
Hispanic	0.771	1.838	0.42
Other Race	6.313	3.377	1.87
Property Offense	17.677	0.725	24.37***
Drug Offense	−11.290	0.505	−22.35***
Plea Agreement	−39.288	0.962	−40.86 ***
Plea, No Agreement	−35.407	1.070	−33.09***
Court Trial	−33.893	1.387	−24.43***
Offense Score	16.104	0.112	144.29***
Offender Score	8.282	0.100	82.92***
Circuit 1	24.525	0.909	26.99***
Circuit 2	34.819	1.155	30.15***
Circuit 3	9.261	0.783	11.82***
Circuit 4	30.650	1.189	25.78***
Circuit 5	3.043	0.905	3.36**
Circuit 6	4.824	0.848	5.69***
Circuit 7	11.808	0.563	20.97***
R²=0.396			

* p <.05   **p<.01   ***p <.0001

included in the model in addition to race-by-crime-category interaction effects. Race-by-crime interaction effects were added because prior analyses suggested that the effect of race may vary by crime type.

The parameter estimates are shown in table 10.11. The results reveal that race exerted a significant effect on the incarceration decision even among *consistent* sentences. The interaction effect between race and crime category (particularly the drug crime category) also exerted a strong statistically significant effect on the incarceration decision, suggesting that the effect of race on the incarceration decision varied by crime category.

In order to further explore the suggestion of a race effect and a race-by-crime type interaction effect, the percentage of white and nonwhite defendants who fell within each cell of the *drug* offense matrix and

TABLE 10.8

Ordinary Least Squares Regression Estimates Predicting Sentence Length in Months between January 1987 and September 1996 among Individuals Convicted of Person Offenses Using Single Count Data (N=15,112)

Variable	b	s.e.	t
Constant	−53.587	4.351	−12.32***
Male	11.694	2.539	4.61***
Age	0.261	0.065	3.98***
Black	1.229	1.352	0.91
Hispanic	−4.664	5.230	−0.89
Other Race	6.413	7.992	0.80
Plea Agreement	−53.276	2.282	−23.35 ***
Plea, No Agreement	−46.601	2.656	−17.54***
Court Trial	−47.666	3.549	−13.43***
Offense Score	21.570	0.213	101.41***
Offender Score	9.417	0.271	34.73***
Circuit 1	28.131	2.592	10.85***
Circuit 2	40.542	3.562	11.38***
Circuit 3	7.257	2.026	3.58**
Circuit 4	26.139	3.197	8.18***
Circuit 5	−2.306	2.365	−0.97
Circuit 6	0.944	2.453	0.38
Circuit 7	8.500	1.585	5.36***
R^2=0.455			

* p <.05   **p<.01   ***p <.0001

were incarcerated was examined (see tables 10.12 and 10.13). Table 10.12 contains the percentage of white individuals who fell within each cell of the drug offense sentencing matrix and received a sentence of incarceration. Table 10.13 contains the percentage of nonwhite individuals who fell within each cell of the drug offense sentencing matrix and received a sentence of incarceration. Comparison of the percentage of white and nonwhite individuals within each cell of the drug offense sentencing matrix revealed that when judges were given the option to impose either probation or a short term of incarceration, nonwhite offenders were more likely to receive a sentence involving incarceration than white offenders. For example, 36 percent of white offenders who were convicted of a drug offense with a seriousness category of four who had an offender score of zero received a term of incarceration, whereas 49 percent of nonwhite offenders who fell within the same cell of the sentencing matrix received a sentence of incarceration. Thus,

TABLE 10.9

Ordinary Least Squares Regression Estimates Predicting Sentence Length in Months between January 1987 and September 1996 among Individuals Convicted of Drug Offenses Using Single Count Data (N=27,589)

Variable	b	s.e.	t
Constant	−4.574	1.435	−3.19**
Male	3.352	0.584	5.73***
Age	−0.037	0.023	−1.60
Black	4.082	0.458	8.92***
Hispanic	9.807	1.473	6.66***
Other Race	15.541	3.445	4.51***
Plea Agreement	−29.345	0.890	−32.99***
Plea, No Agreement	−27.833	0.973	−28.61***
Court Trial	−23.855	1.238	−19.26***
Offense Score	7.106	0.120	59.04***
Offender Score	7.983	0.087	91.89***
Circuit 1	18.623	0.770	24.19***
Circuit 2	28.970	0.958	30.25***
Circuit 3	7.535	0.730	10.32***
Circuit 4	29.906	1.034	28.92***
Circuit 5	0.380	0.824	0.46
Circuit 6	3.500	0.699	5.00***
Circuit 7	8.578	0.463	18.52***
R^2=0.355			

* p <.05   **p<.01   ***p <.0001

race appeared to influence the incarceration decision even among sentences that were consistent with the guidelines. The magnitude of the effect was particularly strong for drug offenses. Notably, among sentences that were consistent with the guidelines, mode of disposition did not exert a significant influence on the incarceration decision.

With regard to sentence length among consistent cases, race appeared to have a slight direct effect on sentence length (see table 10.14). The interaction effect between race and drug crime category also exerted a statistically significant effect on sentence length. Examination of the mean and median sentence length within each cell of the *drug* offense matrix for white and nonwhite defendants did not reveal substantively large differences, however.

Inconsistent subsample. Logistic regression models were also estimated to examine the impact of race among the subsample of individuals who received sentences that were *inconsistent* with the sentencing

TABLE 10.10
Ordinary Least Squares Regression Estimates Predicting Sentence Length in Months between January 1987 and September 1996 among Individuals Convicted of Property Offenses Using Single Count Data (N=9,926)

Variable	b	s.e.	t
Constant	−3.423	2.452	−1.40
Sex	0.347	1.143	0.30
Age	0.161	0.039	4.12***
Black	−0.216	0.663	−0.33
Hispanic	1.099	3.166	0.35
Other Race	−0.025	4.383	−0.01
Plea Agreement	−18.279	1.506	−12.14 ***
Plea, No Agreement	−15.518	1.640	−9.46***
Court Trial	−13.744	2.084	−6.59***
Offense Score	6.328	0.318	19.93***
Offender Score	7.488	0.144	52.10***
Circuit 1	13.710	1.321	10.38***
Circuit 2	13.734	1.619	8.48***
Circuit 3	12.905	1.095	11.79***
Circuit 4	14.968	1.741	8.60***
Circuit 5	0.228	1.275	0.18
Circuit 6	1.406	1.292	1.09
Circuit 7	7.158	0.914	7.83***
R^2=0.285			

* $p < .05$ ** $p < .01$ *** $p < .0001$

guidelines (see table 10.15). Again, the direct effect of race on the incarceration decision was statistically significant. Inclusion of race-by-crime category interaction effects failed to reveal a significant interaction between race and drug crime category. The effect of race on sentence length among sentences that were not *inconsistent* with the sentencing guidelines was marginal (see table 10.16). The interaction effect between race and drug crime category was not statistically significant among sentences that were inconsistent with the guidelines.

Summary

In summary, examination of the effect of race on the incarceration decision using logistic regression models suggested that race affects the probability of incarceration in a nontrivial manner adjusting for the effect of legal characteristics. The predicted probability of incarcera-

TABLE 10.11

Logistic Regression Estimates Predicting the Incarceration Decision between January 1987 and September 1996 Using Single Count Data among Sentences *Consistent* with the Sentencing Guidelines (N=41,610)

Variable	b	s.e.	X^2
Constant	−4.661	0.137	—
Male	0.558	0.044	162.75***
Age	−0.011	0.002	38.33***
Nonwhite	0.292	0.061	23.32***
Property Offense	1.210	0.067	331.25***
Drug Offense	0.276	0.060	21.26***
Nonwhite*Property	0.071	0.084	0.72
Nonwhite*Drug	0.871	0.079	122.59***
Plea Agreement	0.035	0.086	0.16
Plea, No Agreement	−0.038	0.092	0.17
Court Trial	−0.079	0.113	0.49
Offense Score	1.145	0.015	5577.55***
Offender Score	1.469	0.023	4162.15***
Circuit 1	1.449	0.072	408.81***
Circuit 2	1.195	0.087	186.78***
Circuit 3	−0.486	0.055	77.05***
Circuit 4	0.749	0.088	72.02***
Circuit 5	−0.336	0.062	29.45***
Circuit 6	0.015	0.063	0.06
Circuit 7	1.628	0.050	1062.80***
Log-likelihood	−12159.697		

* p <.05   **p<.01   ***p <.0001

tion for white offenders holding all other explanatory variables constant at their mean/median is π=0.56, whereas the predicted probability of incarceration for nonwhite offenders is π=0.65. The influence of race on the incarceration decision does not appear to vary by crime type. '

OLS regression models were used to examine whether race influences sentence length contingent upon incarceration. Using the total sample, race did not appear to influence sentence length adjusting for the effect of legally relevant variables (e.g., offense score, offender score, crime type). However, the crime category-specific approach appeared to uncover an interaction between crime category and race. Specifically, race appeared to influence the sentence length of individuals convicted of drug offenses, but not the sentence length of individuals convicted of person or property offenses.

TABLE 10.12

Comparison of Incarceration Decision (Y/N) among *White* Defendants Convicted of Drug Offenses and Sentenced in Compliance with the Sentencing Guidelines

Seriousness Category	Offender Score							
	0	1	2	3	4	5	6	7+
2	n=9*	n=3	n=1	n=1	—	—	—	n=1
	n=9**	n=3	n=1	n=1				n=1
	100%	100%	100%	100%	5Y-8Y	6Y-10Y	8Y-15Y	100%
	1Y-4Y***	2Y-5Y	3Y-6Y	4Y-7Y				15Y-25Y
3	n=589	n=403	n=177	n=128	n=135	n=98	n=69	n=31
	n=585	n=400	n=177	n=128	n=135	n=98	n=69	n=31
	99.3%	99.3	100%	100%	100%	100%	100%	100%
	6M-3Y	1Y-3Y	18M-4Y	3Y-7Y	4Y-8Y	5Y-10Y	7Y-14Y	12Y-20Y
4	n=1,379	n=551	n=103	n=74	n=38	n=17	n=20	n=10
	n=500	n=290	n=103	n=74	n=38	n=17	n=20	n=10
	36.3%	52.6%	100%	100%	100%	100%	100%	100%
	P-12M	P-18M	6M-18M	1Y-2Y	1.5Y-2.5Y	2Y-3Y	3Y-4Y	3.5Y-5Y
5	n=766	n=463	n=81	n=79	n=80	n=40	n=27	n=44
	n=181	n=193	n=81	n=79	n=80	n=40	n=27	n=44
	23.6%	41.7%	100%	100%	100%	100%	100%	100%
	P-6M	P-12M	3M-12M	6M-18M	1Y-2Y	1.5-2.5Y	2Y-3Y	3Y-4Y
7	n=599	n=152	n=59	n=46	n=44	n=15	n=7	n=9
	n=2	n=0	n=1	n=15	n=17	n=8	n=7	n=9
	0.3%	0%	1.7%	32.6%	38.6%	53.3%	100%	100%
	P	P	P	P-1M	P-3M	P-6M	3M-6M	6M-12M

*The first n equals the total number of individuals who fell within a particular cell.
**The second n represents the number of individuals who received a sentence involving incarceration, followed by the%age of the total.
***Denotes the sentencing guidelines for each cell where P=Probation, M=Months, and Y=Years.

The total sample of individuals was then subdivided into those individuals who received sentences that were consistent with the sentencing guidelines and those individuals who received sentences that were inconsistent with the sentencing guidelines. The results suggested that race influenced the incarceration decision among consistent *and* inconsistent sentences. A significant interaction effect between race and drug crime category further revealed that the magnitude of the effect of race on the sentencing decision was greater among individuals convicted of drug offenses and sentenced in compliance with the sentenc-

TABLE 10.13

Comparison of Incarceration Decision (Y/N) among *Nonwhite* Defendants Convicted of Drug Offenses and Sentenced in Compliance with the Sentencing Guidelines

Seriousness Category	Offender Score							
	0	1	2	3	4	5	6	7+
2	n=81*	n=16	n=5	n=6	n=4	n=4	n=4	n=1
	n=80**	n=16	n=5	n=6	n=4	n=4	n=4	n=1
	98.8%	100%	100%	100%	100%	100%	100%	100%
	1Y-4Y***	2Y-5Y	3Y-6Y	4Y-7Y	5Y-8Y	6Y-10Y	8Y-15Y	15-25Y
3	n=3,615	n=1,729	n=978	n=671	n=804	n=506	n=342	n=172
	n=3,609	n=1,729	n=978	n=671	n=804	n=506	n=342	n=172
	99.8%	100%	100%	100%	100%	100%	100%	100%
	6M-3Y	1Y-3Y	18M-4Y	3Y-7Y	4Y-8Y	5Y-10Y	7Y-14Y	12-20Y
4	n=801	n=402	n=86	n=70	n=68	n=38	n=32	n=26
	n=389	n=253	n=86	n=70	n=68	n=38	n=32	n=26
	48.6%	62.9%	100%	100%	100%	100%	100%	100%
	P-12M	P-18M	6M-18M	1Y-2Y	1.5-2.5Y	2Y-3Y	3Y-4Y	3.5Y-5Y
5	n=1,494	n=769	n=212	n=164	n=185	n=87	n=67	n=86
	n=590	n=428	n=212	n=164	n=185	n=87	n=67	n=86
	39.5%	55.7%	100%	100%	100%	100%	100%	100%
	P-6M	P-12M	3M-12M	6M-18M	1Y-2Y	1.5-2.5Y	2Y-3Y	3Y-4Y
7	n=271	n=60	n=27	n=26	n=25	n=13	n=10	n=3
	n=0	n=0	n=0	n=10	n=13	n=7	n=8	n=3
	0%	0%	0%	38.5%	52.0%	53.8%	80%	100%
	P	P	P	P-1M	P-3M	P-6M	3M-6M	6M-12M

*The first n equals the total number of individuals who fell within a particular cell.
**The second n represents the number of individuals who received a sentence involving incarceration, followed by the%age of the total.
***Denotes the sentencing guidelines for each cell where P=Probation, M=Months, and Y=Years.

ing guidelines. Under this scenario, nonwhite offenders convicted of drug offenses were substantially more likely to receive short terms of incarceration (rather than probation) than white offenders. The direct effect of race on sentence length was small among both consistent and inconsistent sentences.

Conclusion

The results of the present study are largely consistent with prior research. Offense seriousness and prior record were the most power-

TABLE 10.14

Ordinary Least Squares Regression Estimates Predicting Sentence Length in Months between January 1987 and September 1996 among Sentences *Consistent* with the Sentencing Guidelines Using Single Count Data (N=29,153)

Variable	b	s.e.	t
Constant	−55.553	2.051	−27.09***
Sex	−1.672	0.882	−1.89
Age	0.165	0.031	5.39***
Nonwhite	1.972	0.999	1.97*
Property	21.233	1.214	17.49***
Drug	−7.955	1.096	−7.26***
Nonwhite*Property	−1.607	1.467	−1.10
Nonwhite*Drug	−7.981	1.283	−6.22***
Plea Agreement	−24.195	1.079	−22.42 ***
Plea, No Agreement	−21.925	1.211	−18.11***
Court Trial	−22.512	1.579	−14.25***
Offense Score	21.000	0.135	155.89***
Offender Score	12.913	0.124	104.49***
Circuit 1	13.537	0.995	13.61***
Circuit 2	20.896	1.393	15.01***
Circuit 3	3.751	0.914	4.10***
Circuit 4	13.697	1.464	9.36***
Circuit 5	5.604	1.090	5.14***
Circuit 6	5.737	1.021	5.62***
Circuit 7	10.390	0.650	15.98***
R^2=0.588			

* $p<.05$ ** $p<.01$ *** $p<.0001$

ful predictors of sentence outcome. Race was found to influence the incarceration decision net of legal factors in the *total* sample, but not sentence length. Notably, the effect of race on sentence length varied by crime category. Black and Hispanic defendants convicted of drug offenses were more likely to receive longer sentences than white defendants. Furthermore, race influenced the incarceration decision regardless of whether the sentence was consistent or inconsistent with the sentencing guidelines. The magnitude of the effect of race on the incarceration decision was particularly strong among individuals convicted of drug offenses and sentenced in *compliance* with the sentencing guidelines.

These findings are also consistent with the emerging research on the effects of sentencing guidelines. While such systems seem to reduce racial disparity in sentencing, they do not eliminate it. When structured

TABLE 10.15
Logistic Regression Estimates Predicting the Incarceration Decision
between January 1987 and September 1996 Using Single Count Data
among Sentences *Inconsistent* with the Sentencing Guidelines (N=34,348)

Variable	b	s.e.	X^2
Constant	−0.484	0.121	—
Male	0.556	0.038	219.97***
Age	−0.006	0.002	16.33***
Nonwhite	0.291	0.058	25.53***
Property Offense	−0.478	0.070	46.59***
Drug Offense	−0.413	0.058	51.40***
Nonwhite*Property	0.172	0.088	3.85*
Nonwhite*Drug	−0.115	0.069	2.80
Plea Agreement	−0.383	0.083	21.22***
Plea, No Agreement	−0.465	0.087	28.45***
Court Trial	−0.339	0.103	10.74**
Offense Score	0.077	0.008	97.09***
Offender Score	0.344	0.007	2458.01***
Circuit 1	2.327	0.102	522.87***
Circuit 2	2.185	0.107	416.53***
Circuit 3	−0.117	0.041	8.05**
Circuit 4	2.056	0.100	421.77***
Circuit 5	−0.227	0.046	24.19***
Circuit 6	0.504	0.050	102.46***
Circuit 7	1.464	0.042	1191.49***
Log-likelihood	−18064.562		

* $p < .05$ ** $p < .01$ *** $p < .0001$

sentencing systems allow a choice between prison and an alternative to prison, black defendants are more likely to receive a prison sentence. In order to eliminate this form of disparity, sentencing patterns will have to be constantly monitored. In addition, it may be necessary to minimize the opportunity for judges to make such choices.

Notes

The research in this chapter was conducted for the Maryland Commission on Criminal Sentencing Policy. The Commission is not responsible for any of the results or interpretations.

1. The voluntary sentencing guidelines have been in effect in Maryland since 1 July 1983. The guidelines were revised in January 1987.

TABLE 10.16
Ordinary Least Squares Regression Estimates Predicting Sentence
Length in Months between January 1987 and September 1996
among Sentences *Inconsistent* with the Sentencing Guidelines
Using Single Count Data (N=23,473)

Variable	b	s.e.	t
Constant	−5.705	2.798	−2.04***
Sex	7.846	1.174	6.69***
Age	0.146	0.040	3.65**
Nonwhite	2.602	1.332	1.95*
Property	17.599	1.698	10.37***
Drug	−6.597	1.464	−4.51***
Nonwhite*Property	−2.801	2.088	−1.34
Nonwhite*Drug	0.336	1.703	0.20
Plea Agreement	−48.271	1.589	−30.37***
Plea, No Agreement	−43.249	1.746	−24.77***
Court Trial	−39.497	2.238	−17.65***
Offense Score	11.712	0.170	68.83***
Offender Score	4.908	0.153	32.11***
Circuit 1	32.545	1.584	20.55***
Circuit 2	42.313	1.736	24.37***
Circuit 3	11.513	1.226	9.39***
Circuit 4	40.071	1.750	22.90***
Circuit 5	−0.465	1.358	−0.34
Circuit 6	3.087	1.262	2.45*
Circuit 7	9.941	0.905	10.98***
R^2=0.252			

* $p < .05$ **$p < .01$ ***$p < .0001$

2. A prison sentence is clearly the culmination of a series of criminal justice system decisions.
3. Circuit court three consists of Baltimore and Harford counties. Circuit court seven consists of Calvert county, Charles county, Prince George county, and St. Mary's county. Circuit court eight consists solely of Baltimore city.
4. Note that for drug and property offenses, the seriousness category as converted to a point score identical to the point score conversion used for person offenses.
5. Note that due to the skewed distribution of the offense score and offender score, the median value was used instead of the mean. The logistic regression function was used to calculate the predicted probability of incarceration (King 1989: 104–5). The predicated probability of incarceration refers to a hypothetical individual characterized by average levels of all explanatory variables in the model except offense score or offender score (which were allowed to vary over their range).
6. Note, however, that race-by-crime type interaction effects did not contribute significantly to the total model.

FIGURE 10.1
Predicted Probility of Incarceration for a Hypothetical Individual
with Mean Values on All Variables except Race

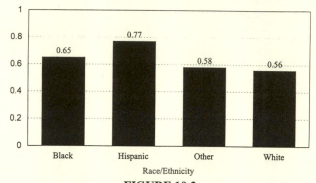

Race/Ethnicity

FIGURE 10.2
Predicted Probability of Incarceration for a Hypothetical Individual
with Mean Values on All Variables except Race

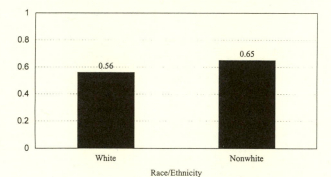

Race/Ethnicity

FIGURE 10.3
Predicted Probability of Incarceration for a Hypothetical Individual
with Mean Values on All Variables except Offender Score

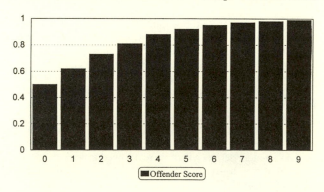

FIGURE 10.4
Predicted Probability of Incarceration for a Hypothetical Individual
with Mean Values on All Variables except Offense Score

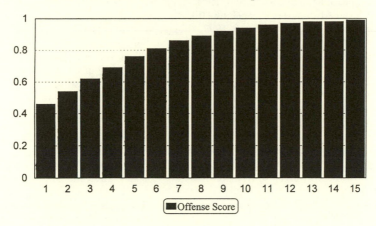

References

Blumstein, A. 1982. "On the Racial Disproportionality of the U.S. States' Prison
    Populations." *Journal of Criminal Law and Criminology* 73(3):1259–81.
Blumstein, A., J. Cohen, S.E. Martin, and M. Tonry, eds. 1983. *Research on Sentenc-
    ing: The Search for Reform*, 2 vols. Washington, DC: National Academy Press.
Chiricos, T.G. and C. Crawford. 1995. "Race and Imprisonment: A Contextual As-
    sessment of the Evidence," in D. Hawkins (ed.) *Ethnicity, Race, and Crime: Per-
    spectives across Time and Place*. Albany: State University of New York Press.
Crutchfield, R.D., G.S. Bridges, and S.R. Pritchford. 1994. "Analytical and Aggre-
    gation Biases in Analyses of Imprisonment: Reconciling Discrepancies in Studies
    of Racial Disparity." *Journal of Research in Crime and Delinquency* 31(2):166–
    82.
Hagan, J. 1974. "Extra-legal Attributes and Criminal Sentencing: An Assessment of
    a Sociological Viewpoint." *Law and Society Review* 8:357–84.
Hanushek, E.A. and J.E. Jackson. 1977. *Statistical Methods for Social Scientists*. San
    Diego: Academic Press, Inc.
King, G. 1989. *Unifying Political Methodology: The Likelihood Theory of Statistical
    Inference*. Cambridge: Cambridge University Press.
Kleck, G. 1981. "Racial Discrimination in Criminal Sentencing: A Critical Evalua-
    tion of the Evidence with Additional Evidence on the Death Penalty." *Criminol-
    ogy* 46:783–805.
Klepper, S., D. Nagin, and L. Tierney. 1983. "Discrimination in the Criminal Justice
    System: A Critical Appraisal of the Literature," in A. Blumstein, J. Cohen, S.E.
    Martin, and M. Tonry (eds.) *Research on Sentencing: The Search for Reform*. 2
    vols. Washington, DC: National Academy Press.
Little, R.J.A. 1992. "Regression with Missing X's: A Review." *Journal of the Ameri-
    can Statistical Association* 87(420):1227–37.
Miethe, T.D. and C.A. Moore. 1985. "Socioeconomic Disparities under Determinate
    Sentencing Systems: A Comparison of Preguideline and Postguideline Practices
    in Minnesota." *Criminology* 23(2):337–63.

Peterson, R.D. and J. Hagan. 1984. "Changing Conceptions of Race: Towards an Account of Anomalous Findings of Sentencing Research." *American Sociological Review* 49:56–70.

Pindyck, R.S. and D.L. Rubinfeld. 1991. *Econometric Models and Economic Forecasts.* 3d ed. New York: McGraw-Hill.

Sampson, R.J. and J.L. Lauritsen. 1997. "Racial and Ethnic Disparities in Crime and Criminal Justice in the United States." In M. Tonry (ed.) *Ethnicity, Crime, and Immigration: Comparative and Cross-National Perspectives, Crime and Justice: A Review of Research* (vol. 21). Chicago: The University of Chicago Press.

SAS Institute. 1990. *SAS/STAT User's Guide.* Cary, NC: SAS Institute.

Spohn, C., J. Gruhl, and S. Welch. 1981–2. "The Effect of Race on Sentencing: A Reexamination of an Unsettled Question." *Law and Society Review* 16(1):71–88.

Stolzenberg, L. and S.J. D'Alessio. 1994. "Sentencing and Unwarranted Disparity: An Empirical Assessment of the Long-Term Impact of Sentencing Guidelines in Minnesota." *Criminology* 32(2):301–9.

Tonry, M. 1988. "Structured Sentencing," in M. Tonry and N. Morris (eds.) *Crime and Justice: A Review of Research*, vol. 10. Chicago: The University of Chicago Press.

———. 1993. "Sentencing Commissions," in M. Tonry (ed.) *Crime and Justice: A Review of Research*, vol. 17. Chicago: The University of Chicago Press.

Welch, S., C. Spohn, and J. Gruhl. 1985. "Convicting and Sentencing Differences Among Black, Hispanic, and White Males in Six Localities." *Justice Quarterly* 2:67–79.

Wolfgang, M.E. and M. Riedel. 1973. "Race, Judicial Discretion, and the Death Penalty." *The Annals of The American Academy of Political and Social Science* 407:119–33.

Zatz, M. 1987. "The Changing Forms of Racial/Ethnic Biases in Sentencing." *Journal of Research in Crime and Delinquency* 24:69–92.

Part 2

11

Punishment Policy and Commensurate Complexity

Leslie T. Wilkins

This project began with an examination of published data on the wide variations in the use of prison in different jurisdictions. I will not here work up any new data but merely make brief references to accepted findings, and then offer a theoretical explanation.

There had been considerable comment in the press regarding the very large variations in incarceration rates, and the rate for England and Wales was said to be the highest in Europe.[1] I could find explanation for these differences neither in the levels of seriousness nor the amounts of recorded crime. So I searched elsewhere for correlates.

For the countries I was able to study, no substantial correlations could be found in any statistical series deriving from the criminal justice systems. I widened my search to other data sets. Among those available were several economic series. As Pease and others[2] had earlier noted, there were high correlations between the uses of prison and several economic indices. Briefly, the strong associations were not between economic factors and measures related to crime itself but between measures related to how the criminal justice system *reacted to* criminals. For example, there was only a low correlation between reported crime and unemployment, but a far higher correlation between unemployment and the severity of punishment. Again, confirming Pease's data I found that the propensity to use imprisonment was greatest where income distribution was most disproportionate. Prison use varied directly with the percentage of the country's income going to the extremely wealthy. (The highest correlation was between prison use and the percentage of income going to top 5 percent of the population). I do not think it is necessary to repeat here the details of these findings, which are illustrative of the general patterns found by research on this topic in the "Western world."[3] Rather than elaborate these kinds of data, it is my purpose here to set forth some hypotheses which may help in the search for explanation.

Crime Policy and Economic Policy

It seems to be a simple fact that a country's criminal justice policy and its economic policy go together. But in what ways? I examined some political indices. Of course, different political parties proclaim different policies to deal with crime (or, more usually, with "criminals"). To demonstrate this fact would be trivial. In democracies political power is believed to reflect voting behavior. Voting behavior, in turn, may be partly a reaction to economic conditions such as unemployment. Certainly behind political power is voter power. The connection between economic and judicial issues, should, then more appropriately be sought in data on those public attitudes which incline voters to vote or not to vote in particular ways.

Perhaps voters are attracted to party platforms which advocate related policies for crime control, taxation and other economic strategies. In which case, the same people— those in the legislatures— make both crime policy and economic policy and are elected to office by persons who make the same connections. This would be a direct but again a rather inconsequential explanation of the observed correlations. So, after a brief look at voting behavior, I turned my attention to data on value preferences, attitudes and beliefs, namely, to data relating to "public opinion" on various ethical issues such as abortion, the death penalty, and religious involvement.

Psychologists have explored this area and proposed different definitions for values, opinions, beliefs, and attitudes. Opinions and beliefs express assumptions about the world. Attitudes are considered to be indicators of probable future action: if a trigger is released, action takes place in the direction indicated by the "attitude." It is not of great importance here to complicate the discussion by careful discrimination of these differences. In any event, the classifications are not generally agreed.

Packages of Political and Other Attitudes

Opinion research has established that moral values (beliefs, or opinions) are held in "packages." If one knows an individual's views on crime/criminals, many more moral and political positions may be guessed with a high likelihood of correctness. Studies carried out in many cultures all show "high density correlation patterns" among ethical, religious, political, and other opinions/attitudes.[4] Various theories have been put forward to explain the patterns. Some have suggested that "dimensions of personality" are indicated by the clusters of values. We can, definitely, be certain of the non-random nature of the associations between held values, and this feature itself is challenging. It is, however, unnecessary and probably unsound to read into the observations of non-random collections of opinions any systemic structure—such as may be represented by vectors in space.[5]

While it is interesting to use these data to support concepts of "types of personality" (as does Eysenck, Cattell, and many others), it is possible, for present purposes, to avoid these kinds of inferences. (Occam's razor principle would suggest that whether or not they are factually correct, inessentials should be omitted). Certainly we cannot observe "dimensions," though, as with longitude and latitude (which also we cannot see!) it may be useful for specific purposes to postulate them.

Perhaps it is not surprising that the "packages" of values (high correlation densities) held by individuals are similar to the packages which form political platforms, but they also have strong similarities with religious doctrines. I began to think that, rather than sort out values for themselves, people "buy" packages already wrapped and presented by organizations that attract their loyalty or promise to satisfy some of their needs. There is no doubt of the strict analogy between the selling of political platforms and the sale of any other packaged commodities: precisely the same selling techniques are used and are equally effective. Some may resent the suggestion that religious evangelism is also a package-selling activity. But is not a creed as much a package as a political manifesto?

Cognitive Dissonance?

This interpretation may seem cynical and is at best only a partial explanation of the patterns of associated values. There is a theory termed "cognitive dissonance"[6] which holds that individuals seek to "harmonize" their views of the world. Does this theory offer an alternative explanation? If it does, the fit of the observations is neither direct nor self-evident. No shared pattern can be detected among the items in typical packages. What common logic, for example, could explain the extremely high correlation between beliefs held under the label of "right to life" and the demand for capital punishment? Similarly other high correlations (packaged sets) could not be explained in terms of any direct tendency to put together items so as to avoid logical conflict or obvious "dissonance."

Despite my skepticism as to the interpretation of the "packages" in terms of traits or dimensions, the challenge of the data remains. Data can neither be destroyed nor deified by any process of analysis. But whether the non-random "packages" might be regarded as logical, emotional, or other kinds of "clusters" or "dimensions" of personality or something else is not agreed. I think that obstacle can be avoided and that no clarification is necessary.

Learning of Values and Learning Language

There is some support for a hypothesis which I found attractive, but confess that it is from a branch of study where my knowledge is more than usually restricted, namely that the explanations are to be found in child development. The idea may, nonetheless, serve as an illustration of a possible direction for inquiry. However, I think it is more useful to see the "packages" of value preferences as more akin to the structures of grammars than to simple mathematical dimensions or space.

Whether this model is useful or not, it nonetheless seems reasonable to postulate that values are learned at much the same time in life as language is being learned, and that these experiences are not totally independent of each other. Surely a young child exposed to continuous flows of profanities will not only adopt different linguistic styles, but also rather different value perspectives from another child undergoing early learning in a household which uses language with rather more precision. The work of Basil Bernstein[7] provides a sophisticated analysis of the variety of aspects of verbal control of infants. His work seems to me to reinforce the idea of learned values in association with language learning. Also concordant with this suggestion are the results of my own work in relation to delinquent age cohorts reported in Delinquent Generations. In my study of juvenile cohorts[8] I found (contra to Bowlby's popular thesis of maternal deprivation) that excess criminality was associated with periods of social disturbance such as the 1939–45 war and the 1930 depression. However, the critical age for the impact of these events, identified by my macro-analysis, was around three years: the time of early social experience. Similar results were found in Poland, and several other countries where the analysis was replicated. I am, of course, conscious of the fact that whenever precisely similar methods produce exactly similar results, the possibility remains that these could be due to the methods rather than to the data.

I may now ask whether it is reasonable to assume that the undeniable tendency for people to operate with "packages" of value-preferences is explained by reference to early learning? Children must be given simple moral rules, and these may seldom subsequently be challenged. Then, as parents the same rules are passed on to the next generation. But the correlation between parental opinions and the opinions of their grown children is difficult to establish. While it may be true that many attitudes, value preferences, or moral stances derive from parental instruction, this cannot be the case for all. I would note that there is a well recognized tendency for offspring to reject parental values, and certain topics cannot be appreciated by the very young. Views about abortion, crime and punishment, for example, may be adopted views, but they are not the result of language/value early learning in any direct way. Yet the connections between these opinions tend to be stronger than those which might more likely have been derived from childhood experiences or early learning. The early learning hypothesis is clearly inadequate as an explanation of the "packaging." Some better theory is needed. Because it is the link between economic policy and incarceration rates, clearly the "packaging" evidence has to be dealt with before we can move on.

Ways of Thinking—Styles of Thought Processes

I found a major difficulty in that none of the existing theories seemed adequately to distinguish the structure from the content. Indeed those who advocate a "dimensional" model use the content to infer the structure. At this point in my inquiries it began to seem unlikely that more data would provide the solution to the difficulty (i.e., the high-density correlation packages). One alternative was to consider the settings in which the data are generated.

Individuals not only keep thoughts, as it were, in a store, but they also process information. Research into memory deals mainly with the former. Research into information processing (decision making) is a different area of investigation. When asked to express an opinion one might expect the response to be one retrieved from "the store," rather than the outcome of on-the-spot information processing. However, in many cases the honest (if not the given) reply to a question asking individuals what they think about a current topic would be, "Frankly until you asked me, I had not given the matter a moment's thought!" But that is a different point. I have asked people (including many who would be thought to be highly intelligent), "How do you think?" and invariably got the rejoinder, "How do I think about what?" It was difficult to get my respondents to focus upon the processes of thought independently of the content of the thought. Nonetheless it seems reasonable to assume (and indeed research has shown) that different people adopt different processes for thinking about values as well as adopting different value packages.

It seemed important for me to get some idea of how people operated with information within themselves. Put another way, I was interested in how people "represented" problems—what paradigms they tended to employ or, in my terms, what kinds of models they used. The introspection stimulated by my questioning proved unhelpful. All too frequently claims were made to use operating procedures which have been demonstrated to be impossible for the human intelligence! Clearly decision makers are operating with "models" of situations, but they cannot describe the intuitive model-building process. Judges and members of Parole Boards, for example, were insistent that they took into account *all* the relevant information before sentencing![9] The concept of information overload was totally foreign to them, and, indeed to most of those I questioned. It seemed likely that this rather specific research had much wider significance and that opinions and values, in general, are similarly based on somewhat shadowy constructs.

The Demand for Certainty

Only one feature appeared dominant, namely, the demand for certainty. It was, it seemed, impossible for most individuals to consider a decision to be rational unless, as they would say, they were "certain of the facts." I would strongly disagree—rationality does not require the assumption of certainty. Indeed the quest for certainty is in itself irrational. Our currently best models of the world are probabilistic. However, though probability in relation to values was a problem, all but a very few of my informants were able quite easily to assume subjective certainty about their values. Most were quite willing to claim certainty for all data surrounding their moral and religious positions and indeed much more.

Opinions on abortion, the death penalty, crime, and punishment were particularly characterized by the quality of subjective certainty. (Some might think that it is necessary to believe that the accused is truly guilty of murder before carrying out the death penalty.[10]) But, it is not merely "opinion" about the death penalty which is of relevance in our concern about high-density correlation patterns among values, but the underlying "structural" feature of thought processes. I would claim that attitudes towards abortion and the death penalty, and indeed most moral positions, especially those encoded into religious, fundamentalist beliefs tend to be held together because they have the same structure. It is not what is thought but the nature of the way of thinking. In particular it is the idea of certainty, often linked with simplicity, which underlies all of these viewpoints.

Deference for Authority

The individual tendency to seek certainty is amplified by social structure in that there is a tendency to accord more respect to those who claim to dispense certainties. Usually the less forceful the claim to know what was right, the less the deference accorded. Those claiming authoritative knowledge are all too often assessed at their own self-evaluation. This was particularly the case with those who looked to religions, but it also applied to many whose orientation was towards science.[11] The quality of note is that of respectfulness or deference. Or, as has been said elsewhere, "I don't know, but I know a man who does!"

Selling and the Market for Moral Values

People everywhere have a strong emotional need to feel subjectively certain. Those who claim to be able to be certain have a large market for their product! If the package they offer also seems simple, the market is probably greater. It is not, then, surprising that those who claim to be able to dispense this product "get the business." This, I think, is at the root of the "packages" of values—people have bought them and shared them, often with their children who never challenged the package served up with their baby food.

Certainty is "bought" and "sold" in the courts, the churches, and indeed sometimes even in the learned journals.[12] It is so nice to feel reassured. Why should that pleasant warm feeling be rejected? For the powerless, it can do no harm. For the powerful it has only the desired consequences—they can manipulate it. There is little incentive to make life more complicated. That is to say, there is no incentive for all but a minority to model problems in complex forms. But this results in frequent mismatches between the mental representations and the world as we now know it. I have discussed in some detail elsewhere[13] the consequences of simplifying the problem of crime to the problem of the offender: "if the criminal did not do it there would be no crime!" Clearly a desirable simplification for some. It is tempting to believe that this useful viewpoint is consciously adopted to serve merely as a means of avoiding collective responsibility. But perhaps it is more reasonable to assume that this and any similar statements are no more than simplifications and the rhetorical excesses of eccentric political extremists.

Be that as it may, there remains unexplained the lopsided development in our social and political institutions. We have invented extensions to our hands (machines and tools of all kinds), we have invented extensions to our legs (transport of all kinds), and we have invented extensions of our voices, but we have invented few extensions to our mental equipment, which remains much as it was centuries ago. We are, indeed, still dominated by many value positions derived from authorities of that time. The computer is a doubtful claimant to be an aid to our mental abilities. It is much faster than the human mind in many tasks, but it has neither radically transformed nor increased the "tool kit" of mental analyses. True it has made it possible to solve problems which could not previously be solved, but it has helped but little with the more important task of formulating the important questions.

Perhaps we need to find a language in which, in exactly the same terms, we can consider and communicate both desirabilities and probabilities, both values and descriptions of the universe? Is there any reason why ethics cannot develop a means to cope with uncertainty without linguistic or mathematical transformation?

Relevance to the Practical Policy Question of Punishment

But the question with which I began still remains. Even should my arguments as to value packages and the demand for certainty seem sound, variations in penal policy are not much enlightened thereby, so it may help to take the line of thinking somewhat further. I might ask how it is that claims to certainty are so appealing? What are its attractive qualities? Perhaps certainty is so attractive because it is less complex than probability? But what makes simplicity attractive? There is, of course, a principle of least effort! If a problem is simplified, then dealing with it requires less mental endeavor. But simplicity is not justified because it appeals to those who are lazy!

There is clearly more to it than that. If certainty is unchallenged as a basic concept, we can get by with two dimensional concepts; a two-value system of logic; a person is either guilty or not guilty; a proposition is either true or false; something is "there" or it is "not there," and so on. It is, by this means, possible to reduce the number and level of abstractions which would otherwise be called for. In a world of subjective certainty we have a world in which simple (or mentally lazy) people feel that they can cope! Perhaps the model of such a world was quite adequate for a nomadic or hunting and gathering peoples, but it is not adequate today. Nonetheless it seems that most people have little difficulty in accepting value packages put together when the "flat earth" was accepted as true. But we know that a "flat earth" model suffices only for very restricted travel (such as walking around a city like Cambridge). But surely value positions built up in flat earth times (or earlier!) are of very restricted merit today?

Commensurate Complexity

Human activity has added to the environment much complexity and our models must reflect that complexity if we are to make sense and provide practical strategies for decision makers. In *Punishment, Crime and Market Forces*[13] I pointed out that, analogous with Ashby's Law of Requisite Variety,[14] simplified statements, descriptions, or models have limits beyond which any further reduction of complexity results in unacceptable distortion. Communication theory supports this viewpoint. Shannon's tenth theorem, for example, means that a communication channel must be of sufficient capacity to resolve ambiguity in the transmitted signals. And Ashby's Law, in his own words, states "only variety can destroy variety."

In addition to the requirement of commensurate complexity (no excessive simplification) there is a need to distinguish carefully between macro and micro models. The reason why, for example, the analogy of the grocery store is inappropriate as a model for a nation's economy is not merely its degree of simplification but the fact that the former is correctly represented by micro models whereas the latter requires macro models. Many outside economics find this a difficult, limited, or trivial distinction. An interesting example is to be found in the concept of the "independence of the judiciary." The independence of the judiciary (macro) does not mean the right of every individual judge (micro) to do precisely what seems right, but rather refers to the independence of structures. Indeed, the essential democratic feature of the independence of the judiciary may well be prejudiced by too great an exercise of idiosyncrasies of individual judges. Thus, in this example, the micro is directly opposed to the macro interpretation of the concept.

It is self-evident that the level of complexity which is necessary to provide an explanation (or afford control) of any situation is a direct function of the purposes sought. If I wish to have a guide to help me to find my way around the streets of Cambridge, a two-dimensional map will suffice and, indeed, be preferable to one which accommodates altitudes; if my city was, say, San Francisco I would find three dimensions useful; if I would travel in space, I need four dimensions (and a few other things as well!). The "truth" of the situation is not the relevant issue, but that which I wish to achieve: not the "whole truth," but "sufficient truth" to represent the situation I need to comprehend. In short "my purpose" is all-important. I do not, however, wish to suggest that there are no useful generalities, and that each purpose has to be considered separately.

Connecting up the Ideas

I have now reached a point where the various factors noted can be tied together and related to the original problem. If complexity is reduced to a minimum, we arrive at the simple dichotomy, the resolution into true versus false, right versus wrong, guilty versus innocent, known versus unknown, us versus them...But it will be recalled that I distinguished what is thought from how it is thought about. If it is consciously adopted for a specific purpose and retained under control, a two-value dichotomy may usefully summarize a variable. But it should be obvious that division of a variable into two is not the same as employing a dichotomy as a basic classification. The results of both operations look deceptively the same. Furthermore, there are qualitatively different categories of dichotomies. Compare, for example, "true versus false," "us versus them," "right" versus "wrong" and "black" versus "white."

Some dichotomies include more of the available information than others (e.g.: male/female versus dark/light). In other cases dichotomies may be the lowest level of complexity, achieved by considering only extremes of variables. It is unsafe to assume, without testing, that a dichotomy of a variable includes sufficient information to satisfy a particular purpose. Too often verification is dispensed with. For one topical example, only extremely unusual cases are referred to the Court of Appeals, yet it is assumed that their decisions provide "guidelines" for sentencing in general!

In the simplified specification of issues, and particularly of values and opinions expressed as dichotomies we have the avoidance of essential complexities. The simple description dispenses with all but the polarities—true/false, right/wrong, them/us.... they are the only values counted (which are seen to "count"). This is "extremism."

Extremism as a General Feature of Thinking

The identification of "extremism" (as defined here in nonjudgmental terms) provides an explanation of many problems. Among these is the problem with which I began my inquiries, namely the high variation in the uses of imprisonment in different countries. It sorts out also the apparent lack of logical connection between the advocacy of the death penalty simultaneously with that of the right to life. Both positions are perceived in terms of reduced complexity and treated as unrelated to each other. A person who takes another's life has by that act forfeited the right to life. Neither "life" nor "death" are seen as variables. The extreme penalty is that of death, and the extreme criminality is taking a life, therefore these extremes go together! Similarly a "child" is a "child," and it also is either alive or dead; there is no perception of a variable in terms of becoming or ceasing to be a human being. A dichotomy takes over. Thus it seems that the "packages" of value preferences which we observe are due to the processes of thinking. It is a failure to accommodate commensurate complexity, in general. It has nothing to do with the specific subject matter of that thought.

Many persons demonstrate general thought patterns which show a propensity to think in simple, extremist (low complexity) terms. Unfortunately among these are politicians, some (such as the one-time British minister of education) are proud of this, pointing out that the Bible endorses that view.[15] Typical of all fundamentalist sects is the endorsement of absolute values and claims to certainty by revelation. Acceptance of this perspective provides a structure (or euphoric state!) which permits the formulating of moral and value problems in low complexity paradigms. My analysis leads me to claim that these models (generally thought to provide foundations for contemporary value systems) are far too constrained.

But it is not only those who are usually recognized as fundamentalists who adopt such models of the world. Others avoid complexity and uncertainty by other means—by genuflection towards other authorities. This is the style of thinking which tends to accept the value package which includes endorsement of : capital punishment for murder, severe punishment as "just desert," anti-abortion laws, calls for religious education in schools and "discipline in the home." The good deserve reward: the bad their punishment, and it is a simple matter to distinguish this dichotomy. This structure of thought may be defined as the basis of "extremism." One result is that what are seen as correct rewards or punishments escalate as the center ground is attenuated.

One task for reformers (or for evolution itself?) is to upgrade the ways in which people think. A more difficult task, perhaps, than seeking to change what they think. More dimensions must be added to the models, and uncertainty accommodated within sound ethical principles.

We cannot look backward to earlier philosophers, prophets, or gods. The language of those times does not "map" on to the current problems of human survival. We have evolved to a point where we can cause technology to function, but we have frozen the evolutionary development of values by employing constricted thinking styles and religious "imperatives." To give but one example: Death used to be simple to define and the moral positions implicit in mortality were straightforward. (Life and death were reasonably dealt with as dichotomies—two dimensions were enough). Now we have difficulty in defining precisely when human life ends as, similarly, we have with when "human" life begins. Decisions are made ad hoc in the courts or by rules of procedure set down in statutes. These provide a rag-bag of practices and few principles are clearly stated.

It is my view that the time and space dimensions and the physical constraints upon information which permitted the simple statements of values in earlier times no longer apply. These moral positions must be updated. A more controversial example of this general point may be given. When "Christian" morality was being developed, information as to the plight of the poor was restricted to information derived from personal contact. The Good Samaritan saw the victim and his compassion was commensurate with his information and he had the means to put this into action. Then it was easy to discuss personal responsibility—the problem as presented was commensurate with the action an individual might or might not make. That is to say, the underlying general feature of such thought processes was correctly in terms of micro models. We need to revise this concept of responsibility to fit with the essential macro models that now relate to contemporary information flow.[16] We might conclude that individual, private, personal charity is, today, a form of response ill-adapted to the complexities of modern society.

If my perception of these issues is anywhere near reasonable, there is a very challenging task ahead. I can leave this only as a stated challenge at this point. Our civilization has refined the language of description but stills lack a contemporary logic of prescription. We can say *what is*, and our claims can be tested, but when we discuss *what ought to be*, the quality of our discourse deteriorates to little more than assertions. Many minds are required to be applied to the task of developing ethical concepts and political policies which will be adequate to guide the development of technology and the sociopolitical activity of our time.

Notes

1. The incarceration rate is taken up in the press when it has some topical interest. See, for example, the *Daily Telegraph* (10 Oct. 1988, p. 4) under heading UK TOPS PRISONS LEAGUE TABLE. It is not clear whether the implication was that it was good to be top in something!
2. L.T. Wilkins L.T. and K. Pease (1988), "Public Demand for Punishment Issues in Contemporary Criminology," *International Journal of Sociology and Social Policy* 7(3):16.
3. A cursory reference to abstracts will provide more than adequate data in support of this general tendency, and the fact that different indices tend towards similar findings adds, rather than detracts, from the challenge to look further into the likely linkages between economic data and crime data. More similar data will be less useful than the setting up of somewhat different hypotheses which will expand the ranges of data that might be relevant.
4. G. Newman et al. (1974) "Authoritarianism, Religiosity and Reactions to Deviance," *Journal of Criminal Justice* 2: 249–55.
5. H. Eysenck (1947) "Primary Social Attitudes," *International Journal of Opinion and Attitude Research* 3 (49); R.B. Cattell (1947) *Description and Measurement of Personality* (New York: World Book Co.). The methods whereby the "dimensions of attitudes, opinions and moral values were 'discovered' were precisely similar to the methods used to measure 'intelligence.'" (See, for example, L.L. Thurstone [1936] *Vectors of Mind*, Chicago: University of Chicago Press.) It was, therefore, not surprising that all other similarities tended to be assumed and some emphasized hereditary factors (e.g., C. Burt [1940] *Factors of the Mind*, London: University of London Press). Certainly the "dimensions" had an aura of the scientific. However, it was possible that the results obtained (dimensions) derived more from the methods of analysis than from that which was analyzed. Usually any matrix (intersecting set) of correlations can be resolved into three dimensions which will "explain" most of the variance—with or without rotation of the axes.
6. L. Festinger (1957) *A Theory of Cognitive Dissonance* (Stanford, CA: Stanford University Press).

7. B. Bernstein (1990) "Elaborated and Restricted codes; Overview and Criticism," ch 3 in *The Structuring of Pedagogical Decisions,* vol 4 (London: Routeledge).
8. L.T. Wilkins (1960) "Delinquent Generations," *Home Office Research Report* (London: HMSO).
9. D. Gottfredson et al. (1978) *Guidelines for Parole and Sentencing,* Appendix A (Lexington, MA: Lexington Books).
10. A minority of the public say they are prepared to take the risk of carrying out the death penalty on innocent persons and a similar minority deny that errors could ever take place is sentencing. The member of Parliament, R. Gale, who introduced a Bill for the return of capital punishment argued that more lives would be saved than lost and that this trade-off justified the death penalty for murder.
11. I remember a discussion with Sir Leon Radzinowicz in which he said that while he recognized the quality of my work, few people understood it. For this reason, he said, it was necessary for me show that I valued it most highly, because then it would be taken at that evaluation. I fear that he was right!
12. Even Steven Hawking in his *Brief History of Time* makes a gesture of this kind in his reference at the end of his book to "the mind of God."
13. L.T. Wilkins (1991) *Punishment, Crime and Market Forces* (Brookfield, VT: Dartmouth, Aldershot).
14. R. Ashby (1952) *Design for a Brain* (New York: Wiley).
15. "Patten Links Hell and the Rise of Crime," *The Independent*, 18 Apr. 1992, p. 19, letter signed Alan Bennett.
16. Of course, the printing press added to the quantity of information available, but the value system disseminated was mainly that which might be inferred from the Bible, and set down around 2000 years previously.

12

Measuring Justice:
Unpopular Views on Sentencing Theory

Don M. Gottfredson

Theories of Sentencing

Attempted sentencing reforms are rarely based on a consensus of views on sentencing philosophy or on any coherent theory. Each of the traditional aims of sentencing—retribution, general deterrence, incapacitation, and treatment—is tossed into the legislative pot, seasoned with rhetoric about getting tougher, giving criminals the punishment they deserve, and controlling crime. Stirred into a theoretically inconsistent mass, the result has something for everybody but pleases few. The effects of the reforms are difficult to evaluate, in part because the change is not tied to any internally consistent theory.

Examples are found in many state criminal codes and in the federal system. For example, the Sentencing Reform Act of 1984 (Title II of the Comprehensive Crime Control Act of 1984) that established the United States Sentencing Commission provided for the development of guidelines "...that will further the basic purposes of criminal punishment: deterrence, incapacitation, just punishment, and rehabilitation" (United States Sentencing Commission 1993: 1). The rationale of the Congress, as described by the Commission, included the aims of combating crime by achieving an effective, fair sentencing system, uniformity in sentencing, and proportionality—imposing "appropriately different sanctions for criminal conduct of differing severity" (United States Sentencing Commission 1993: 2).

Sentencing philosophies provide an extraordinary example of an intertwining of normative and scientific outlooks. A coherent sentencing theory consistent with the normative position accepted and also informed by science may be desired; if so, then attention to fundamental measurement problems, which can clarify the meanings of central concepts of prevailing sentencing philosophies, may be helpful. This chapter will identify the central ethical issues, suggest three contrasting sentencing views, and assert that each of these positions can be clarified and better assessed by needed attention to measurement.

Deontological versus Teleological Theories

A central issue in sentencing is whether retributive and utilitarian objectives both may be achieved within a coherent ethical position. The ethical positions that undergird these aims, reflecting Kantian (Kant 1797a) versus utilitarian views, contrast sharply and are inconsistent with one another. They reflect differing views *of* ethics and also opposed views *in* ethics. Ethics may concern, on the one hand, how persons ought to behave in general, not as a means to any end. Or, the main topic may be value, with an emphasis on what is desirable or good in itself. In the deontological view, duty is prior to value; in the teleological outlook, our only duties are related to ends and are to produce value (Lacey 1986: 66–7). Oversimplifying grossly, one may say that the fundamental conflict between retributive (deontological) and utilitarian (e.g., Mill 1863; Hume 1751) (teleological) views is whether what is right is good or whether what is good is right (Prichard 1955). The debate has continued for more than 2,000 years (Plato 350–340 B.C.).

These divergent orientations are metaphysical: first principles are asserted *a priori*, with origins in religious perspectives. Ethical debates about sentencing are yet little informed by science. The interesting question whether they *should* be is not addressed in this chapter. Rather, my purpose is to show that methods of definition and measurement in science can assist in the clarity of meaning of concepts and may be necessary for implementation of any sentencing perspective with fidelity to the theory advocated.

The utilitarian orientation (a variety of consequentialism [Smart 1973]) includes the concepts of deterrence, treatment, and incapacitation. Each looks forward to some good to follow from punishment: warn others, rehabilitate offenders, or isolate those likely to commit future crimes. Each seeks the reduction of crime. Utilitarianism is not concerned only with what is useful or works best to control crime. A more general view would be given by Locke's statement that "The end of government is the good of mankind" (Locke 1690). The utilitarian theory is that the best course or act is the one that makes for the best whole (that results in the greatest good or the least dissatisfaction). Punishment, by definition a harm, must be avoided unless outweighed by the good to follow. The traditional utilitarian position rests also on a premise of natural determinism.

"Act-utilitarianism" provides the rationale for the traditional sentencing aims of deterrence, incapacitation, and rehabilitation. This is the view that the rightness of an action is to be judged by the goodness of the consequences of the action. This is contrasted with "rule-utilitarianism," which is the view that the rightness of an action is to be judged by the goodness of the consequences of a rule that everyone should perform the action in like circumstances (Smart 1969: 9). Punishment, defined as the deliberate infliction by the state of pain or suffering on one convicted of a crime, must be regarded as a harm unless it can be shown that benefits to the greater good outweigh the harm done by the punishment itself. The right action is that which will result in the least harm.

Desert theory, distinct from but related to retribution,[1] is not future-oriented. It looks only to the past harm done. Those who choose to do crimes are blameworthy and should be punished. The perspective rests heavily on the concepts of free will and individual responsibility.

Since people are ordinarily responsible for their acts, they ordinarily ought to be given their just deserts. Following Kant rather than Beccaria (1764) or the utilitarians, this theory emphasizes that punishment *must* be given if (but only if) it is deserved.

Contemporary advocates, such as von Hirsch (1976) stress that punishment should be proportional to the gravity of the harm done. This is Beccarian rather than Kantian, since Kant believed in the *lex talionis*. Beccaria emphasized proportionality but also would have imposed the least severe sanction possible under the circumstances.[3] Kant's ethical objection to utilitarianism rests on his dictum that a human being never can be manipulated as a means to someone else's purposes; one must act so as to treat humanity always as an end and never as a means only (1797b).

To the extent that an offender is to be punished according to the blameworthiness of an act—and only that—utilitarian objectives of crime control, treatment of the offender, incapacitation, or deterrence have no bearing; these aims have no standing from the ethical theory of deserved punishment. The fundamental flaw of utilitarian perspectives, from the Kantian viewpoint, is the failure to honor the principle (stated previously) that is stressed as the hallmark of moral behavior: that one must act so as to treat persons always as ends and never as means only. The most offensive attribute of sentencing or correctional decision making in pursuit of utilitarian aims, it is argued, is a willingness to manipulate people as if they were objects, disrespecting their dignity, autonomy, and humanity in a manner starkly lacking in the humility that should characterize rendering judgments or power over other human beings.

From these few principles arise basic conflicts for ethical positions on sentencing. Punishment is demanded, as deserved; but forgiveness is required (and punishment forbidden), unconditionally or as is necessary for learning to do better. We must consider only the harm done, and punish accordingly; yet, we must look to the future, to see what good may be done. Punishment must be based only on the crime done, and never on one merely expected; but it must serve as an example to others, teach a lesson, and restrain the offender from future crimes. Punishment must be done; but we must turn the other cheek. The person must not be used as a means to an end; but it may be necessary to punish the individual for the greater good of society. We must only look back to the crime for the justification of punishment; but since the past is gone, we must only look ahead.

Desert theory recently has gained increased acceptance, yet to some philosophers it "seems to be the bald, unexplained assertion that crime simply does deserve punishment" (Mackie: 10). Certainly, all those who have tried to justify retributivism without circularity and without recourse to consideration of any consequences have met with difficulty. It is a paradox that while "...a retributive principle of punishment cannot be explained within a reasonable system of moral thought,...such a principle cannot be eliminated from our moral thinking," and "...it in vain condemns the gratification of the very desire from which it sprang" (Westermarck 1932: 86). Thus is the retributive impulse condemned in much of society's criminal law while that law nevertheless demands a retributive response by society.

When the utilitarian attitude is applied to criminal justice sanctions, debate often centers on whether future crime can best be prevented by hurting and controlling identified offenders, by threatening and scaring potential offenders, or on the best means of hurting, controlling, threatening, or scaring; or it focuses on the best means of treatment or help to reduce the probability of further offending.[3]

Recent attempts to resolve the fundamental conflict between the perspectives of desert and utility include Morris's (1976), limiting principle acceptance of that position by O'Leary and Clear (1985: 354), and the contrary position of von Hirsch and his colleagues (1989) that collective incapacitation strategies (or substitute sanctions) may be used consistently with a desert perspective only when principles of proportionality and equity are not violated (von Hirsch 1986).

Varieties of Retributivism

At least three types of retributive principles may be defined, with different consequences for the implementation of both retributive and utilitarian perspectives and for "hybrid" orientations. These are: negative retributivism, positive retributivism, and permissive retributivism (Mackie 1982). The first asserts that one who is not guilty must not be punished. The second states that one who is guilty ought to be punished. The third posits that one who is guilty may be punished. One may think that negative retributivism is noncontroversial, yet it is precisely one point of criticism by the desert theorist of the incapacitative purpose that under some proposed utilitarian strategies of sentencing (such as incapacitation) some persons expected to do crimes will be punished for offenses not yet done and which might not ever be done. Permissive retributivism has considerable appeal for those of a consequentialist orientation, giving room for a seeking of utilitarian aims that might be defeated by punishment, and for those who wish to support concepts of forgiveness or mercy; and it may have appeal to those who, with Morris, would regard deserved punishment only as a "limiting" principle.

Positive retributivism may be more controversial when correlative principles are added, as in desert theory. What is at issue is the assertion that one who is guilty ought to be punished in proportion to that guilt, with rejection of permissive retributivism on the grounds that otherwise the principles of equity and proportionality will be violated.

Science and Utility

Conflicting views of ethics and morality do not exhaust the sources of advice given to those who would make sentencing theory or policy. Claims are made also about the best means of achieving utilitarian (usually crime prevention) goals. These give rise to further ethical questions and present issues of evidence and thus of science.

Changes in sentencing policy in the United States over the last twenty years have reflected shifting values but have been based in part on opinions that are thought to be based on evidence of effectiveness. These changes have been toward increased determinacy, decreased discretion, and a greater emphasis on deserved punishment rather than utilitarian aims (Harris 1975; M. Gottfredson and D. Gottfredson 1988). Thus, the changes have been partly related to ethical views and partly to questions of science.

During this same period, two panels of the National Research Council of the National Academy of Science carefully and thoroughly examined the scientific evidence on the efficacy of deterrence, incapacitation, and rehabilitation (Blumstein et al. 1978; Sechrest et al. 1979). After searching inquiry, the panels had informative, still apt, comments on the efficacy of each of these major traditional crime control aims of sentencing.

Deterrence

For the panel on deterrence, Nagin reviewed more than twenty analyses directed at testing the deterrence hypothesis for non-capital sanctions. Then he cautioned that

> despite the intensiveness of the research effort, the empirical evidence is still not sufficient for providing a rigorous confirmation of the existence of a deterrent effect. Perhaps most important, the evidence is woefully inadequate for providing a good estimate of the magnitude of whatever effect may exist.
>
> This is in stark contrast to some of the presentations in public discussions that have unequivocally concluded that sanctions deter and that have made sweeping suggestions that sanctioning practices be changed to take advantage of the presumed deterrent effect.... Policymakers in the criminal justice system are done a disservice if they are left with the impression that the empirical evidence, which they themselves are frequently unable to evaluate, strongly supports the deterrent hypothesis. (Nagin 1979)

The National Research Council panel as a whole offered a similar caution, stating

> In summary...we cannot yet assert that the evidence warrants an affirmative conclusion regarding deterrence. We believe scientific caution must be exercised in interpreting the limited validity of the available evidence and the number of competing explanations for the results. Our reluctance to draw stronger conclusions does not imply support for a position that deterrence does not exist, since the evidence certainly favors a proposition supporting deterrence more than it favors one asserting that deterrence is absent. The major challenge for future research is to estimate the magnitude of the effects of different sanctions on various crime

types, an issue on which none of the evidence available thus far provides much useful guidance. (Blumstein et al. 1979)

We cannot prove it (yet, the panel said), but deterrence *may* work to some degree. With whom, under what circumstances, with what degree of effect, we cannot tell. Certainly, there is in the scientific literature no strong policy guidance for an escalation of punishments in order to reduce crime by means of deterrence.

Research continues to support the contention that the certainty of punishment is a more important consideration for crime control than is the level of severity. Blumstein states, "research on deterrence has consistently supported the position that sentence 'severity' (that is, the time served) has less of a deterrent effect than sentence 'certainty' (the probability of going to prison) (citation omitted). Thus, from the deterrence consideration, there is a clear preference for increasing certainty, even if it becomes necessary to do so at the expense of severity" (Blumstein 1995).

Incapacitation

The panel was somewhat more positive about incapacitation effects, But on this topic, too, the panel was cautious, stating

Models exist for estimating the incapacitative effect, but they rest on a number of important, and as yet untested, assumptions. Using the models requires estimates of critical, but largely unknown, parameters that characterize individual criminal careers. (Blumstein et al. 1979)

A selective use of incapacitation has been proposed (Greenwood 1982). A distinction has been made also between selective and collective incapacitation (Cohen 1978) with important ethical implications. Under a selective strategy, the sentence would be based at least in part on predictions that particular offenders would commit crimes at a high rate if not incarcerated. Under a collective strategy, all persons convicted of a designated offense would receive the same sentence. The selective incapacitation proposed by Greenwood has been criticized on both ethical and scientific grounds (Cohen 1983; von Hirsch and Gottfredson 1983–84; S. Gottfredson and D. Gottfredson 1985).

The use of prediction methods in a strategy of selective deinstitutionalization also has been proposed (S. Gottfredson and D. Gottfredson 1985). Offenders selected on the basis of the risk of future offending and the societal stakes thereby at risk would be selected for deinstitutionalization. No offenders would be punished more than believed to be deserved—that is unless they were punished as a result of misclassification. Some offenders, however, would be punished less than that. The ethical theory implied is a permissive retributivism.

Rehabilitation

It has become popular among academics, legislators, and the press to discuss the "demise of the rehabilitative ideal," and unpopular to continue to advocate rehabilitation as a sentencing aim. Legislators have removed the purpose from the criminal code sections on sentencing purposes; academics have accepted the null hypothesis, and politicians have tended to support "getting tough." Much of this marked change in attitudes and values has been attributed to findings of science; and many people now seem to believe that it now has been demonstrated that, when it comes to rehabilitating offenders, "nothing works." But the evidence does not support the notion that treatment programs have been adequately tried and found irredeemably unproductive (Sechrest et al. 1979).

The rehabilitative balloon, having been vigorously inflated in the 1940s and 1950s, popped after a series of widely publicized reviews and extensive research projects summarized the generally negative evidence on the efficacy of rehabilitation efforts (Bailey 1966; Kassebaum et al. 1971; Lipton et al. 1971; Martinson 1974). A report of a thirty-year follow-up study of the Cambridge-Summerville Youth project summarized the evidence that the treatment group did worse than the controls, not better (McCord 1978). As the balloon deflated, so did enthusiasm, probably contributing to the increased acceptance of deserved punishment as the fundamental, or sole, aim of the criminal sanctioning system. Some advocates of desert theory were quick to cite the generally negative evidence of rehabilitation effects, little bothered by the inconsistency of use of a utilitarian argument after rejecting the utilitarian premise. But a scientist, after examining the evidence, may wonder why the hopes for rehabilitation were abandoned so easily. The evidence from evaluation research does not support such a policy of abandonment. If the aim is given up, it will have to be on normative, not yet on scientific, grounds.

The 1979 report of the National Academy of Sciences' National Research Council panel on rehabilitation research concluded

There is not now in the scientific literature any basis for any policy recommendations regarding rehabilitation of criminal offenders. The data available do not present any consistent evidence of efficacy that would lead to such recommendations.

and also

The quality of the work that has been done and the narrow range of options explored militate against any policy reflecting a final pessimism...The magnitude of the task of reforming criminal offenders has been consistently underestimated. (Sechrest et al. 1979)

One member of the panel stated

Because there is so little evidence that credible treatments have been implemented with fidelity, and because so much of the evaluation research done so far has been inefficient or defective in other ways, we have no compelling experimental evidence for the contention that powerful, theoretically defensible, and faithfully executed interventions hold no promise.

Good evaluation research does not focus solely on the outcomes of programs, strategies, or reforms. It should assess also the operation and implementation of the program or reform. If the rehabilitative ideal has failed, it is in a failure to *implement* interventions with realistic prospects of preventing future delinquent or criminal behavior. Feeble, ineffectual interventions would not be expected to work; and there is little evidence that potent interventions have been tested. (G. Gottfredson 1979)

Later work often has supported the contention that some well planned and implemented programs can and often do reduce recidivism (Andrews and Bonta 1994; Andrews, Bonta, and Hoge 1990; Cullen and Gendreau 1985; Gendreau and Andrews 1990; Gendreau and Ross 1979; Gottschalk, Davidson, Mayer, and Gensheimer 1987; Izzo and Ross 1990; Lipsey 1992; Palmer 1992; Gendreau, Cullen, and Bonta 1994).

Ethical Theories and the Role of Science

Thus, the two major orientations (the desert and utilitarian perspectives) are fundamentally opposed. And, the three main utilitarian methods aimed at crime control—deterrence, incapacitation, and treatment—lack scientific evidence of effectiveness sufficient to provide clear guides to policy formulation. If a choice must be made, as it logically must, it must be on the basis of the ethical justifications for the contrasting normative positions. The ethical debate cannot be resolved by scientific methods, but both the implementation and evaluation of the theories depend upon clarity of definitions; and some of the issues raised depend upon evidence. Some of the concepts can be clarified by use of methods of definitions common in science. An increased clarity is required also for determinations of the degree to which any of the prevailing theories is implemented in practice.

We must be aware of the ethical choices that must be made. Moreover, even if it is assumed that normative theories do not require empirical support, there is a responsibility to be guided by the evidence when questions of fact are at issue. The central purpose of sentencing and corrections either should be the reduction of harm, hence the reduction of crime; or else it should be the imposition of deserved punishment. Some partial accommodation to the fundamental conflict, however, may be sought. If a "hybrid" of the contrasting normative positions is desired, it may be asked whether it can be created within an internally consistent theory.

Methods of science can provide a greater clarity of definitions and improved measurement of concepts. Thus, their application can contribute markedly to debates about sentencing policy and should be used. After considering some of the measurement issues inherent in the debate, three theoretical models will be defined in the terms next to be discussed: the desert model, a utilitarian model, and a "hybrid" model.

Measurement Issues

The measurement topics central to desert theory concern the seriousness of harm, the severity of the sanction, the equivalence of sanctions, and proportionality. Concepts basic to utilitarian aims include these and, in addition, constructs related to assessments of risk, societal stakes, and consequences. Fundamentals of measurement impose rather strict demands in respect to these topics.

A few quite noticeable but usually neglected facts about the sentencing behavior of judges should be described, because they have provided a starting point for the methods to be used. These facts concern habits, numerical preferences, and characteristics of human perception and judgment. They are independent of the sentencing theory invoked to justify particular sentences.

Sentencing Preferences [4]

Sir Francis Galton noted a peculiarity of the distributions of punishments when he studied the sentences of males imprisoned in England more than a century ago (Galton 1895). He commented on his plots of these data (shown in figure 12.1) as follows:

The extreme irregularity of the frequency of the different terms of imprisonment forces itself on the attention. It is impossible to believe that a judicial system acts fairly, which, when it allots only 20 sentences to 6 years' imprisonment, allots as many as 240 to 5 years, as few as 60 to 4 years, and as many as 360 to 3 years. Or that, while there are 20 sentences to 19 months, there should be 300 to 18, none to 17, 30 to 16, and 150 to 15.... Runs of figures like these testify to some powerful cause of disturbance which interferes with the orderly distribution of punishment in conformity with penal deserts. Sentences of 3, 5, 7, and 10 years appeared to be preferred to the values between. (Galton 1895)

Generally the same result was found (as seen in figure 12.2) with sentences in Essex County, New Jersey Courts in 1976–77, before a revision of the criminal code, when judges had somewhat wider discretion than they now have. A similar pattern was discerned. Sentences were preferred at 6 or 18 months or at 1, 3, 5, 7, 10, 12, 15, and 20 years.[5]

Similar patterns were noticed by Pease and Sampson in a study in England of sentences at the same time (1977). Studying sentences of up to 4 years, they found sentences to 6 or 12 months to be common; but there was no sentence to 5 months and none to 13 or 14 months. Similarly, sentences to 18, 24, 30, 36 and 48 months often were imposed.

FIGURE 12. 1
Number Chosen in Sentencing to Years in Prison, England, 1893

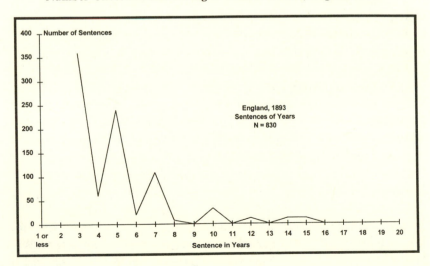

Source: Data from Galton, as cited in E. Banks (1964).

FIGURE 12.2
Number Chosen in Sentencing to Jail and Prison,
Essex County Court, 1976–1977

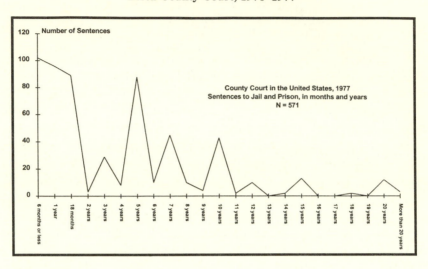

Source: D.M. Gottfredson (1984).

The Sentencing Judge as a Measuring Instrument

The judge has not often been seen as a measuring device. Yet, it is his or her business to make an assessment of the seriousness of the crime, the culpability of the offender, the needs of the offender, victims, and the society at large, and to choose a sentence that is both fair and effective.

It was noticed by Pease and Sampson that the gaps in the distribution representing unused sentence lengths increase as sentence length increases. Although they (like Galton) discussed the idea of preferred numbers, they turned first to a well known concept in psychophysics—that of a "just noticeable difference" (jnd) to account for the increase in the size of the gaps as the length of sentence increased. The early psychophysicist Weber had shown that there seemed to be a definite law governing the relation between the intensities of stimulation and the ability to distinguish which stimulus was greater (for example, in judging weights). The "just noticeable difference" was, according to Weber, a constant fraction of the stimulus that is set as the standard for comparison.

Twenty-five years after Galton's observations of sentence distributions, Fechner noticed that:

> the intensity of sensation does not increase in a one-to-one correspondence with an increasing stimulus, but rather in an arithmetical series which may be contrasted with the geometrical series which characterizes the stimulus. If one bell is ringing, the addition of a second bell makes much more impression on us than the addition of one bell to ten bells already ringing; if four or five candles are burning, the addition of another makes a scarcely distinguishable difference, while if it appeared with only two its psychic effect would be considerable. The effects of stimuli are not absolute, but relative; relative, that is, to the amount of sensation already existing. (as cited in Murphy, 1930)

If, for each sense modality, there is a certain increase in the stimulus that would produce a certain intensification of the sensation, then we might say that sensations increase arithmetically according to a formula including the constants that determine the rate of geometrical progression for the different senses. Thus, Fechner stated the law:

$$S = k \log C$$

where S is the sensation, k is a constant for each sense modality and C is the stimulus. We have used different letters than is usual for this formula, because, in analogy, S may be read as "sanction" and C may be read "crime."

Measurement of Proportionality

Recall that the principle of proportionality is central to the desert theory of sentencing. Thus a length of imprisonment (taken as a presumptive measure of severity of punishment) must be in some way proportional to harm done and the culpability of the offender. With this in mind, Fitzmaurice and Pease turned to an examination of its meaning. As they point out aptly, the relation (over all cases) between judgments of seriousness and sentence lengths chosen is at issue; and "If the prescription of that relationship is not possible, the possibility of justice in retributive terms does not exist" (Pease and Sampson:106). As they describe also, there may be an infinite number of proportionalities; and the nature of the precise relationship is not defined in retributive sentencing theories. As they say,

> For example, there can be a proportionality where, as one thing increases, (e.g., a person's weight), another decreases (e.g., his chance of surviving until 70). There can be types of proportionality where as one variable increases, so does another,

but at a different rate. To talk about proportionality as if it described sentencing behavior is not helpful.... [and]...although the proportion...is certainly one in which sentences increase as culpability increases, the precise relationship is left for individual judges to decide. (Pease and Sampson 1977)

Among other possibilities, they chose (for reasons they describe) to investigate a well known principle in psychophysics known, after its originator, as Stevens' power function (Stevens 1975). This can be written:

$$S = kC^\beta$$

where S again is the sensation magnitude (read "sanction"), which increases as a power function of the stimulus magnitude, C (read "crime"). The exponent (b) reflects the relative rate of increase along the two scales. Thus, it is a proportionality measure. In the language of sentencing, it indicates that an increase in offense seriousness corresponds to a geometric increase in sanction severity. When transformed to logarithms,

$$\log S = \log C + \log k$$

or

$$\log \text{ sanction severity} = \log \text{ offense seriousness} + \log k$$

it describes a straight line relating offense seriousness to punishment, with b indicating the slope of the line (figure 12.3). The data from each of these studies show that there is not a one-to-one correspondence of sanction severity to crime seriousness. That is, whatever proportionality in sentencing means, it does not seem to mean a simple incremental increase in sanction given an increase in seriousness. Clarification of the nature of the proportionality intended is central to the meaning of desert. The equation shown is one way that proportionality can be defined. It may be noted that the slope (b) is critical to that definition and that it may vary over individual judges or jurisdictions, and over offense, ethnic, or gender groups. Thus, the definition of the slope (b) is a critical sentencing theory and policy decision.[6] Also, it may provide a measure of variation not implied by the particular normative theory (i.e., unwanted disparity).

Measurement of General Severity of Sanctions

Another critical policy decision concerns the value of k. This is the

FIGURE 12.3
Schematic Representation of Relation between
Sanction Severity and Offense Seriousness

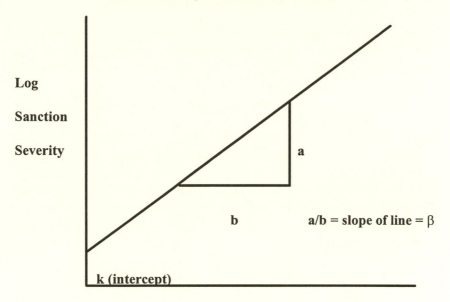

Adapted from Fitzmaurice and Pease (1982).

intercept value (figure 12.3), which may be taken to represent the seriousness of the crime appropriate for the least serious sanction. It could be regarded as a general measure of leniency or severity. The intercept value, like that of the slope, could be expected to vary among judges, or among judges for various types of cases, or among jurisdictions, or among various classifications of offenders such as ethnic or gender groups (indicating unwanted disparities associated with those classifications of persons).

The generality of the formulation may be illustrated also for the strictly utilitarian theory of D. Gottfredson and colleagues (1989). In that conceptualization, appropriate sanctions are related to the interaction of measures of "societal stakes" and offender "risk" (predictions of any offending).

As used commonly in criminal justice, "risk" is defined as the probability of re-offending (or a similar criterion, often dichotomous). The concept of "stakes," familiar to gamblers, also is important to decisions made under uncertainty, such as sentencing. This is obvious in games such as roulette, when not only the odds of winning or losing a bet (risk) but also the amount of the wager—the stakes—are considered by the prudent gambler. Thus, the expected value of a given bet may be taken as the product of the probability of winning and the amount at risk (the wager).

If the concept of risk is limited to some assessment of the probability of a dichotomous criterion, then analyses of decisions such as those made at sentencing may fail to consider the concept of stakes. If, for example, sentencing decisions have an incapacitative intent, then information should be sought that is relevant to the likelihood of new offenses (risk), the nature of the harm expected if new offenses are committed (stakes) and the combination of these (i.e., the conditional probabilities of risk and stakes).

These concerns of risk and stakes are conceptually separate, and measures of them may be relatively independent. Perhaps the reader can easily conceptualize offenders expected to be "high risk–low stakes" or "low risk–high stakes." As an example of the former, consider the chronic shoplifter. There is a high risk—that is, a high probability of recidivism. The stakes, however, could be considered to be low (more shoplifting). An example of the latter could be the spouse killer with no prior record. Such offenders typically do not reoffend; but if they should, we might consider the stakes to be high.

Thus, the analogous formula for policy description on this theory would substitute a term for this interaction for the offense seriousness assessment of the desert formulation. Since the log of a product is the sum of the logs of the factors, we would have

$$\log S = (\log SS + \log R) + \log k$$

where

$$SS = \text{societal stakes and } R = \text{risk.}$$

In this way, any judge's or group of judges' sentences—or sentencing policies as carried out in practice—could be examined to determine the degree of fit of sanctions imposed to the contrasting orientations. In one sample of sentences, both judges' assessments of risk and a measure of stakes (based on other offender attributes and judicial ratings) accounted for substantial variation in the decision to incarcerate. Time to be served in confinement also was related substan-

FIGURE 12. 4
Schematic Representation of Relation between
Sanction Severity and Log Stakes X Risk

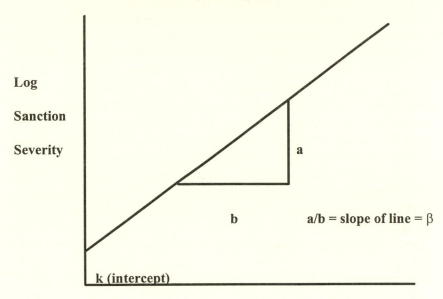

tially to stakes, risk, and their interaction (D. Gottfredson, S. Gottfredson, and Conly 1989).

In this model, the sanction imposed should be proportional to the combination of empirically determined stakes and risks (figure 12.4). The sanction should be selected pragmatically. Punishment is not precluded, but, consistently with a utilitarian perspective, punishment, which causes misery, is bad because an important goal is the reduction of misery. Since crime causes misery, the right balance must be struck: the right action is that which will result in the least misery.

Scaling Issues

Various types of scales of measurement have different properties that determine their usefulness in sentencing frameworks such as those of the theories discussed. These are important for considering how both offense seriousness and sanction severity are to be measured. They are critical to any attempt to establish "alternative punishments," and—fundamentally for theoretical concerns—to the clarification of the meaning of concepts such as proportionality, offense seriousness, stakes, risk, and equivalent sanctions. The four main types of measurement scales have been described by Stevens (1951).

If numbers are assigned to objects (or persons or offenses or sanctions) only to distinguish those that are alike from those that are different, as in a zip code or a penal code section, the resulting scale is called a nominal scale. The numbers may not be used additively.

If numbers are assigned to objects or persons is such a way that they are ranked in order according to some quality or magnitude, the scale is called an ordinal scale. Criminal codes often group offenses into categories that are ranked in presumed seriousness. The scale gives no information about the sizes of intervals along the scale, which are not necessarily equal, so differences between the numbers are not meaningful. Thus, if we have offenses arranged in an ordinal scale, we can say that (in some sense) one is more serious than another, but not how much.

An interval scale is one in which the differences between numbers may be regarded as equal. This is important for the use of many statistical procedures, because the differences between numbers have some meaning. Common measures of averages, variability, and correlation require at least this level of measurement.

A scale in which equal ratios may be regarded as equal (called a ratio scale) has the properties of each of the other scales but also a non-arbitrary zero point. Ratio scales ordinarily are required for determinations of proportionality.[7]

Measures of harm or of punishment could be regarded as having a zero point if no harm was done (no offense) or if no sanction was imposed. If one wishes to discuss proportionality, the aim minimally should be to establish that measures of seriousness of offense (or of stakes or of risk) and severity of sanction are made using scales with intervals as equivalent to one another as possible; and if possible, the scales should have a zero point. The attribute of a non-arbitrary zero point (hence, a ratio scale) is necessary for determination of proportionality, because it must be shown that equal ratios may be regarded as equal, a characteristic not found in other scales.

These issues can be studied empirically. In order to examine the models suggested, representative samples of any offense groups could be studied. For example, to examine the fit of sentences with the desert theory, data would be required on estimates of seriousness by judges and on the severity of the sentence. Length of confinement imposed (maximum or minimum penalty) could be taken, for example, as a presumptive measure of sanction severity. The log of the mean sentence length and the log of the geometric mean magnitude estimate of offense seriousness could be calculated and plotted. This would replicate, with actual judges' judgments, a pilot study done by Fitzmaurice and Pease on the basis of students' judgments. They found a substantial relation as indicated by the model.

Difficulties, however, are presented by the lack of a common metric for sanction severity, such that the values of alternative sentences (which are quite diverse) can be assigned scores that can be used to examine the severity and proportionality issues over all sentenced cases. Because the various types of scales of measurement have different properties that determine their usefulness in such an examination, these are important for considering how both offense seriousness and sanction severity are to be measured. They are critical to the establishment of equivalence of sanctions in order to provide the common metric that is desired, and they are important also for determination of proportionality. Some such work has been done for the scaling of offense seriousness and some progress has been made also on the scaling of sanctions. Problems of measurement of both offense seriousness and sanction severity are complex; but in both instances a substantial body of literature is informative.

Measuring Offense Seriousness

Crime seriousness measurement, first accomplished by Thurstone, has a long history (Thurstone 1927; Sellin and Wolfgang 1964; Rossi, Waite, Bose, and Berk 1974; S. Gottfredson, Young, and Laufer 1980; S. Gottfredson, Warner, and Taylor 1988). Most scales of offense seriousness provide at best ordinal measurement (as in legal codes defining categories of offenses with differing levels of punishment) or (better, but ordinarily used only for research, if at all) interval scales such as provided by Thurstone and by Sellin and Wolfgang. Even with the scaling improvement provided by these authors, most scales of seriousness rest on questionable assumptions of unidimensionality, additivity, and linearity (S. Gottfredson, Young, and Laufer 1980). Each of these issues is critical to the assessment of proportionality.

Much more attention should be given to the problem of scaling the seriousness of offenses and the probable multidimensionality of this concept. Suppose you are presented with a bundle of sticks randomly gathered in the woods and asked to order them in terms of "bigness" and to consider also the distances between sticks (that is, to provide an interval scale).[8] You might reasonably protest: some are longer, some shorter; some are thick, others thin; some are heavy, others light. Your complaint would be essentially that the concept "bigness" has more than one dimension, which makes it difficult to place the sticks on just one scale, particularly without losing information in the process. If there are different dimensions to offense seriousness— i.e., different kinds of harms each varying in degrees of harm, then it will be very difficult to define "proportionate" sanctions in relation to one dimension of seriousness. If it is argued that a certain amount of "thickness" is equivalent to some amount of "longness," then it must be asked how the transformation of thickness to length has been established.

Measuring Sanction Severity

A number of studies have explored the problem of measurement of sanction severity or have developed severity scales (Hamilton and Rotkin 1976; Sebba 1976; Erickson and Gibbs 1979; Buchner 1979; Stipak and McDavid 1983; Hamilton and Rytina 1980; Sebba and Nathan 1984; Allen and Anson 1985; Tremblay 1987; Ouimet 1990). For example, Ouimet developed a continuous scale of sanction severity enabling a translation (based on severity estimates of his survey respondents) of any of the various types of sanctions (included in his survey) to an equivalent in any other type. "Penal equivalents" based on responses from a general public sample and from a court practitioner sample permitted a translation of the punishment value of any penalty to any other. "Penal equivalents" could be found using graphs, the use of which he described as follows:

> To know the equivalency of, say, one year of probation for the public, you find the intersection between 365 days and the curve for probation, and you go horizontally to the point where the same intensity of perceived gravity joins the curve for the prison sentence. At this intersection, you have the equivalency in days of prison for one year of probation, namely, about 33 days. (Ouimet 1990)

One may, as does von Hirsch, contest the use of such scales on the grounds that people's unsupported opinions are not necessarily a good measure of actual harm, culpability, or discomfort. He proposes the alternative that severity of sanctions be measured by the normative importance of the personal interests compromised by the penalty. Thus, the more basic are the interests infringed upon, and the greater the extent of infringement, the more severe would be the penalty. Various penalties could be ranked in order of relative intrusiveness according to the extent to which a penalty affects a person's liberty, autonomy, or comfort.

The same complaint—that people's opinions are not necessarily a good measure of actual harm—is levied against measures of offense seriousness. There may be good reasons for measuring the actual harm done by offense behavior, rather than perceived harm, and for measuring actual harm done by punishment. The possibility of combining the normative and survey approaches was suggested by von Hirsch, Wasik, and Greene (1989). Judgments, however, still will be required to be made by someone to arrive at the normative importance of the interests infringed and to permit even the ordinal scaling proposed. For the proportionality assessment wanted, ratio scales are needed. And, the argument implies that the personal interests compromised by a penalty are multidimensional. If so, measurement is not precluded, but scaling within the categories of personal interests is needed.

The problems of an assumption of unidimensionality (and of additivity and linearity) are inherent in the measurement of sanction severity, just as in the case of offense seriousness. In the latter case, the problem is measurement of harm to the victim or, in addition, to society. As with harm to victims, harms to offenders may come in a variety of forms—perhaps with different dimensions of deprivations of liberty, physical and psychological pain, or other damages. At least, the assumption of a unidimensional scale of severity of punishment is unwarranted without further study. And, if different dimensions are found, the rules for transformation should be provided if a single dimension is to be considered.

Measuring Risk

Assessment of the differential risk (for new offenses, violation of probation or parole, and like criteria) also has a long history (Gottfredson and Tonry 1987; S. Gottfredson and D. Gottfredson 1988a; S. Gottfredson and D. Gottfredson 1993). Such assessments are important for a variety of research purposes and practical applications, and a technology is available for measuring risk with relatively reliable and valid results when appropriate procedures are followed. Sentencing philosophies emphasizing incapacitation, and particularly those relying on selective incapacitation, are dependent upon assessments of risk.

In considering any selective incapacitation strategy, it must be remembered that there are four potential consequences to any predictive selection decision with an uncertain dichotomous outcome. Two types of errors and two types of correct predictions will be made: We will predict that some persons will fail (e.g., commit new crimes) who in fact succeed. These errors usually are called "false positives." We will predict some persons to succeed who in fact will fail (errors usually called "false negatives"). We will predict some persons to fail who will fail (correct predictions). And, we will predict some persons to succeed who will succeed (correct predictions).

For a given failure rate, the total number of errors (the sum of false positives and false negatives) will be the same with any method of prediction whether we select a smaller or a larger group as predicted to fail. We may have fewer or more of either type of error by changing the proportion selected (i.e., by changing the "cutting score") as predicted to fail. For example, if we select fewer persons to fail, we will make fewer mistakes of the first kind (false positives). But then we will make more mistakes of the second kind ("false negatives"). Thus, by changing the proportions selected for incapacitation, we can increase or decrease either false positives or false negatives, but this always is at the expense of more errors of the other kind. The total number of errors cannot be manipulated in this way; only the relative proportions of the two kinds of errors may be changed. The only way to change the total number of errors is to increase the accuracy of the prediction method. There is no other way around the problem: The total number of errors can be decreased only by increasing the value of the statistic measuring the relation between some combination of the predictors and the criterion.

There are only two ways to increase the accuracy of the prediction method. The first is to increase the dependability of the prediction measure by finding items that consistently are better predictors. The other is to increase the dependability of the criterion measure—that is, the measure of new crimes, by more careful definition, better record keeping, or more efficient law enforcement.

Because we can predict only modestly well with data that now are collected, any presently available method of prediction will result in large numbers of false positive and false negative errors. This is true whether the prediction is made by a human judgment (as by a judge) or by using an objective, empirically derived, prediction device. False positives—persons kept in confinement because of a mistaken prediction of failure—would be criticized by philosophers from the ethics of

desert, by inmates treated unfairly, by correctional administrators dealing with overcrowded prisons, and by economists for the waste of money.
False negatives—persons released because of a mistaken prediction of
success who do in fact commit new crimes—would be criticized by
philosophers from the ethics of utility, by members of the press, by the
general public, and certainly by the citizen who had no wish to be set
upon by a false negative.

Because we never can expect to be able to predict perfectly, the utility of incapacitation as a crime control strategy always will be constrained by our ability to predict.[9]

Measuring Stakes

We do not yet have adequate measures of the concept of stakes. If a
fundamental purpose of the criminal law is assumed to be condemnation, that concept may include the seriousness of the offense and the
culpability of the offender. Unlike a strict desert theory, it may include
attributes of the prior criminal record of the offender, for several reasons. First, the prior record, as well as the present offense, may provide
evidence of the nature of expected harms, should these occur. Second,
the stakes of the decision maker, or the institution represented, may be
higher should repeated serious offenses occur in a context of prior similar
offense behavior. Third, the prior record may be relevant to the assessment of culpability.

On the first issue, prior record, the presently available evidence suggests caution in stressing the nature of either the present offense or of
prior offenses as clues to the next offense committed, should one occur.
The issue is the extent to which offenders "specialize" such that repeated offenses of the same kind may be expected. The evidence suggests that there is modest specialization but that repeated offenders are
largely "generalists," and that the criminal history does not provide
much information about the next offense to be expected if one in fact
occurs (S. Gottfredson and D. Gottfredson, 1992, 1994).

The second issue, stakes, is important, but its measurement is yet
rudimentary. If a serious offense occurs which, it is thought, could have
been prevented by a different action of the criminal justice functionar-
ies involved (e.g., judges or parole board members) there often is a
serious threat to the maintenance of the criminal justice institution involved or to continuation of some of its programs. Issues of how stakes
may be scaled empirically, (a scientific question) and how they ought

to be scaled (a normative question), are both important ones to consider in sentencing theory development.

The third issue, culpability, also is in need of measurement development. Despite the centrality of the concept for both desert and utility theories, tools and procedures for its measurement remain to be developed. Concepts of fault, indifference, recklessness, and intent must be inferred from behavior, and resulting judgments of culpability may be scaled.

Reliability and Validity in Sentencing

The judge has not often been seen as a measuring device. Yet, it is the judges' business to make assessments of the seriousness of the crime, the culpability of the offender, the needs of the offender, victims, and the society at large, and to choose a sentence that is both fair and effective. It is surprising, given the importance of this decision, that so little is known about how it is made and that even less is known about its consequences. The increasingly prominent theory of deserved punishment cannot be regarded as possible to implement if the meaning and measurement of proportionality is not clear. Similarly, an evaluation of penal laws specifying that punishments shall be proportional to the harm done or the seriousness of the offense of conviction cannot be done reasonably unless the meaning of proportionality is clear. The same is true for the contrasting utilitarian theory relating sanctions to the interaction of stakes and risk. In either case, the application of the fundamental measurement concepts of reliability and validity could be most informative.

Reliability refers to consistency in measurement, in this case referring to either within judge, between judge, or between jurisdiction variability. Hence, the reliability problem is that usually discussed under the heading of "disparity" (more specifically, "unwarranted disparity") in sentencing. Although usually measured otherwise (such as analyzing the variance within and between judges or courts) it may be measured by differences in the intercept values, slope values, and variability or degree of fit (e.g., R^2) in the formulation shown as figure 12.1. This would at the same time provide a measure of fidelity with the theoretical sentencing orientation providing the basis for the analysis. One theorist's unwarranted disparity may be another theorist's fidelity to the theory.

Validity refers to the ability of the measuring instrument (in this case, the judge) to measure what is intended to be measured or to permit a correct inference. The available means for assessment of validity differ for the two contrasting orientations of desert and utility. In the case of desert, the degree of fit of a judge's judgments to the deserved punishment model would provide a measure of construct validity within that theory (Cronbach and Meehl 1955). Similarly, the fit with the utilitarian model would provide a measure of construct validity of that model. If there are utilitarian aims, the follow up of offenders to determine outcomes of sentences is required for measures of criterion validity (Nunally 1978). Criterion validity for the desert model would require measures of the punishment actually experienced. If the intent of the judge at the time of sentencing is known, then measures of the effectiveness of incapacitative and rehabilitative aims may be assessed through an examination of the subsequent behavior of the offender. (If the aim is general deterrence, this would not apply.) Such analyses are complex, because simplifying experimental designs are rarely feasible; but if adequate data are available, "quasi-experimental" methods may be used that can provide "strong ignorability" of potentially biasing selection factors in the comparisons or outcomes implied (Berk 1987).

Whether a retributive (just desert) orientation to sentencing makes a practical difference in respect to utilitarian aims is beside the point to the pure desert theorist (Singer 1987). But those more inclined toward utilitarian aims nevertheless will want to measure and assess the consequences of implementations of desert theory—for example, with respect to crime control purposes. Unless we are content with an ethical analysis positing a normative theory, unadulterated by knowledge of the consequences of its implementation, efforts to implement a desert oriented sentencing theory also should, as with other perspectives, be monitored and evaluated in terms of a broad range of potential consequences. Despite the justification of the desert policy on nonconsequentialist grounds, the ways in which punishments are administered, the values of k and of b, and attributes of the punishments administered may have consequences for specific and general deterrence, for rehabilitation, and for other outcomes. Thus, the advocates of desert may be asked to join the consequentialists in advocating also the systematic evaluation of results of attempts to implement their proposals.

The effectiveness of sentences, according to legislative or judicial intents, in respect to incapacitative or rehabilitative aims, can be examined by the framework suggested. Moreover, the model may enable the classification of judges according to the fit of their sentences with the desert or utilitarian models, and the consequences of this fit in respect to crime control. A general question (rarely examined) is whether the ethical positions or stated sentencing purposes are relevant to the longer-range consequences of the sentence.

Application of the models proposed could inform the philosophic debate on sentencing purposes and provide methods for assessment of reliability and validity of sentencing structures. The conceptualization provides ways to assess sentencing policies and to inform policymakers about choices now implicitly made and about the potential consequences for sentencing structures. At the same time, it provides methods not previously available for the examination of discrimination and unwanted disparity in sentencing. We might then have some new methods for examining the growth of prison populations, which appear to be coming about nationally by an increase in the value of k, the sanction origin, or the slope, b, or both.

Three Sentencing Theories

Models of the Desert and Utility Theories

Models of two contrasting theories (of desert and of utility) are summarized by the conceptualizations of figures 12.3 and 12.4. The desert theory is summarized by the statement that the log of the severity of the sanction ought to be proportional, given a specified value of b, to the log of offense seriousness, as adjusted for culpability. The utilitarian theory is summarized by the statement that the log of the severity of the sanction ought to be proportional, given a specified value of b, to the log of the product of stakes (including but not limited to offense seriousness, adjusted for culpability) and risk. The critical values requiring measurement, without which specific policies cannot be formulated clearly, implemented, or tested, are offense seriousness, culpability, stakes, risk, sanction severity, and proportionality. Both theories are silent about the value of k, which is an independent policy decision. It would be determined empirically in the utility theory, but it is not addressed in the desert theory. Neither theory specifies the value of b, except for the requirement of utility in the consequentialist perspective and the implication that it is positive in the desert view.

One may seek to formulate, so far as possible, a policy position based on a coherent ethical theory that can meet desert theory requirements while incorporating utilitarian values when that can be done without inconsistency within the theory (Robinson 1988). The retributive impulse persists in our culture, enjoying strong emotional support, despite the claimed difficulties in its ethical justification. So too does the utilitarian aim of seeking the greatest good have wide appeal. There is nothing in the desert theory that prohibits the seeking of utilitarian aims so long as the requirements of desert, proportionality, and equity are not violated and so far as the integrity, individuality, and autonomy of the individual are not, either. In seeking an internally consistent "hybrid" model, either the deontological or teleological position could be accepted as primary. Most criminal codes now have moved from the latter position to the former, so in exploring the concept of a hybrid model the assumptions of desert will be accepted as fundamental to the theory for the purpose of discussion. One could proceed alternatively to develop a hybrid model on the basis of the primacy of utility.

A "Hybrid" Model: Seeking a Path from Desert to Utility

As noted previously, the desert theory does not specify a beginning level of severity of sanctions (k) nor does it specify slopes (b) or kinds of punishments. This means that, consistently with the desert theory, k and b, as also noted, are policy decisions that must rely either on some other theory or on an elaboration of the desert theory. Also, the desert theory is silent on the kinds of punishments to be included as sanctions, except for one important point: the severity of punishments of different kinds, by implication of the theory, must be measured on the same scale or else on scales that may be transformed one to the other. Otherwise, the proportionality and equity requirements of the theory cannot be met.

Concerning overall punishment severity (reflected in the values of both k and b) and the form of punishment, the hybrid model may rely generally on utility. [10] Currently available evidence (concerning deterrence, incapacitation, and treatment) suggests, from the utilitarian perspective, frugality in policies with respect to the value of both k and b. The burden of proof of effectiveness should be placed on those wishing to increase the general level of severity of punishment; the presumption is in favor of lesser punishments. Governmental intrusions into the lives of citizens must be justified by showing the evidence that such intervention is necessary to the achievement of a legitimate governmental purpose aimed at the greater good and that no lesser intrusion will serve as well. The available evidence does not support a "get tougher" position; rather, it supports one of parsimony in the application of costly punishments.

The policy prescription of k, the least serious offense to be sanctioned, typically is set in criminal codes. It is noteworthy that a sanction is associated already with any criminal conviction, regardless of the sentence imposed subsequently by the court, because the conviction itself means that the offender is certified and proclaimed publicly, authoritatively, decisively, and enduringly to have done blameworthy harm to an innocent victim (Weiller 1974). As Weiller points out, and although it often is overlooked, this stigmatization of an offender inflicts "not only a damaging, but also one of the most enduring, sanctions that the state can mete out." Rarely is this sanction seen as sufficient, however, and the value of k represents the beginning point on the offense seriousness scale for the imposition of additional sanctions.

The policy prescription of b, the slope of the line defining proportionality, also might rely on considerations of utility, besides desert. The desert theory requires that the slope be positive; its value can be informed by utility. The rate of increase in sanction severity associated with increases in offense seriousness could be defined as a partly empirical question dependent upon the evidence of study of the consequences of its variation.

Kinds of punishments acceptable may be defined in utilitarian terms, so long as the principles of proportionality and equity are not violated. The desert model specifies a need for proportionality, but neither its amount nor form. If confinement in jail or requirements of intensive supervision in the community, for example, both are punishments (because both infringe upon liberty) one may ask how much intensive supervision with particular characteristics is equivalent to a day in jail. Given the measurement work that is requisite to informed decisions about such questions, the code, or the code and the judge, may assign "punishment units" or "sanction units" as a first step in sentencing, the judge then determining the specific punishment (perhaps including treatment, restitution, fines, house arrest time, drug testing, etc.) thought useful in respect to utilitarian purposes.[11] So long as a good case can be made that the sanctions applied to persons with similarly serious offenses and culpability are equally punitive and the proportionality principle is not violated, the desert requirements have been met. The assumptions of unidimensionality of the punishment scale may not be warranted; this complicates the measurement problem but does not defeat the logic of possible equivalence.[12]

None of the available sentencing theories is adequate to the task of specifying the precise punishments, and their forms, to be used for every offense. None, except a simple minded *lex talionis* claim to do so. For this reason and because of the complexity of offense behavior, some discretion in sentencing is desirable and should be provided. It should be structured to provide a clear and explicit sentencing policy, as for example with sentencing guidelines. Within the area of discretion provided by such a policy, there is room for the application of programs aimed at crime reduction, including rehabilitation and incapacitation, consistently with the desert theory when the punishment required already has been determined. There is room also for a partial permissive retribution, suggesting that the least harmful sanction not inconsistent with proportionality be applied.

Conclusions

Normative theories of sentencing emphasizing deserved punishment and those stressing consequences are fundamentally opposed. Scientific methods cannot resolve basic conflicts in ethical or normative theories but can better inform the debates about sentencing theory and resulting law and practice. Retributive theories of deserved punishment cannot be implemented or evaluated unless the meanings of the central concepts of offense seriousness, sanction severity, and proportionality (of seriousness and sanction) are clear and measurable. Utilitarian theories including those of deterrence, incapacitation, and treatment have similar requirements. The consequences of adoption of either sentencing perspective, or a "hybrid" are apt subjects for scientific study.

When the major constructs of contemporary sentencing theories have been identified, some attendant measurement problems are apparent. Similar methods may be used to examine the logical structures of the contrasting theories. Despite the opposed perspectives of these theories, a theoretically internally consistent "hybrid" theory, which requires particular attention to problems of measuring the punitive values of differing sanctions, may be examined in a similar way.

Statistical models informed by prior studies using psychophysical methods may be defined according to the conflicting theoretical orientations to sentencing. The models provide ways to assess sentencing practices in terms of fidelity to the theoretical orientations discussed, the impact of the orientations on consequences for crime control (regardless of the sentencing aim), and methods for analyses of sentencing disparity within the frame of reference of a particular sentencing theory.

Regardless of the normative orientation accepted, the importance of attention to problems of measurement is urged as a precursor to advances in sentencing theory.

Recent reform measures typically have presented a "laundry list" of traditional purposes of sentencing, but fundamental conflicts among them are ignored and priorities are not indicated. As a result, little guidance in structuring sentencing policy or in making sentencing decisions is provided. Attempting to satisfy everyone may result in a politically viable document (code or policy) but one that ignores problems of internal consistency of the underlying, if implicit, theories and may exacerbate rather than cure the sentencing ills thought to be addressed.

The psychometrician troubled by the present inadequacy of measurement of the central concepts would be correct to be concerned, and my intent is to argue that measurement must be improved. Yet, it must be admitted that all measurement is relatively inaccurate and the psychometrist may be advised to consider the value of small gains in measurement when considered in the light of usual sentencing behavior. The current degree of precision in sentencing still may be seen as reflected in the spiked distributions described long ago by Galton. Measurement must be improved, but perhaps even roughly improved measurement can help improve rough justice.

The need for increased clarity in sentencing theory formulation is apparent and is brought into better focus when measurement requirements are considered. Besides a more adequate specification of the basic postulates of any particular theory, and increased attention to the need for logical consistency, there is a need for definition of the central concepts of these postulates permitting their operational definition. This can allow more careful examination of the logical coherence of the parts of the theory, and the testing of hypotheses that may be derived from the basic assumptions. Internal consistency is possible in a desert theory, in a utilitarian theory, or in a hybrid theory. The more serious attention to measurement issues can, regardless of the ethical position taken, help clarify policy debates, contribute to increased fairness and effectiveness, and provide advances in sentencing theory.

Notes

1. Some writers consider desert to be one variety of a class of positions called retributivism Cottingham (1979) listst nine theories of repayment, desert, pen-

alty, minimalism, satisfaction, fair play, placation, annulment, and denunciation. Concepts of revenge and of retaliation also should be distinguished from all of these.

2. This is a permissive retributivism, unlike Kant's positive retributivism, as to be explained in the next section.

3. Such an emphasis only on crime control aims does violence to the much more general utilitarian perspective. If the essence of utilitarianism is to assert that the best course or act is the ne that makes for the best whole—that is, that results in the greatest good or the least dissatisfaction, the ethic is not limited to the reduction of crime.

4. Portions of this section are adapted from M.R. Gottfredson and D.M. Gottfredson (1988).

5. Galton accounted for his results "by the undoubted fact that almost all persons have a disposition to dwell on certain numbers, and an indisposition to use others," he remarked, "Theses trifles determine the choice of such widely different sentences as imprisonment for 3 or 5 years, 5 or 7, and of 7 or 10 for crimes whose penal deserts would otherwise be rated at 4, 6 and 8 or 9 years, respectively."

6. The intercept value and the exponent in the equation relating offense seriousness and sanction severity serve functions that are different from but not inconsistent with sentencing guidelines ads now used in a number of jurisdictions. This formulation should not be confused with the concept f sentencing guidelines. The intercept indicates an overall degree of severity demanded; the exponent defines proportionality. (As k increases, the line depicting the slope moves up on the chart, so all offenses are affected—not just the least serious.) Guidelines can serve as a further means of explication of the sentencing policy wanted, as an additional means of reduction of unwanted disparity, as a means of institutional population control, and as a system for monitoring and revising the application of policy (M.R. Gottfredson and D.M. Gottfredson 1984).

7. Stevens, however, has shown the power function to be applicable at other levels of measurement (Stevens 1971).

8. This example is due to W. Toregson, Department of Psychology, The Johns Hopkins University.

9. Besides the scientific evidence, there are ethical reasons–pointed up in the desert theory—to be wary of the current emphasis on incapacitation. When a person is punished out of proportion to the harm done, in order to restrain that person from crimes that he or she has not done and might not do, that is not only costly; from the perspective of deserved punishment, it is also unfair.

10. This is a simplifying assumption, because some punishments could have demonstrable utility but may be rejected widely on moral grounds—e.g., flogging, public humiliation as with stocks, or dismemberment usually are now rejected in our culture without regard to expected utility. Similarly, punishments seen as excessive (i.e., undeserved) would be regarded as unacceptable, so it is questionable whether desert considerations can be wholly excluded. Also, a hybrid model might rely on an elaborated desert theory or on other normative principles.

11. This concept originated in a Committee of the Supreme Court of New Jersey, called the "Sentencing Pathfinders Committee." Nothing in this chapter, of course, implies agreement or endorsement by that Committee or by the Supreme Ocurt of New Jersey.

12. If sanctions are equivalent, may the offender be offered a choice? Can a judge end a sentence with a proposition?

References

Allen, R. B. and R. H. Anson. 1985. "Development of a Punishment Severity Scale: the Item Displacement Phenomenon." *Criminal Justice Review* 10: 2: 39–44.

Andrews, D. A, J. Bonta, and R. D. Hoge. 1990. "Classification for Effective Rehabilitation: Rediscovering Psychology." *Criminal Justice and Behavior* 17: 19–52.

Andrews, D. A., and J. Bonta. 1994. *The Psychology of Criminal Conduct*. Cincinnati, OH: Anderson.

Bailey, W. C. 1966. "Correctional Outcome: An Evaluation of 100 Reports." *Journal of Criminal Law, Criminology, and Police Science* 57: 153–60.

Banks, E. 1964. "Reconviction of Young Offenders," *Current Legal Problems* 17:74, 74– 6.

Beccaria, C. [1764]1963. *On Crimes and Punishments*. Reprint. Indianapolis, IN: Bobbs-Merrill.

Berk, R. A. 1987. "Causal Inference as a Prediction Problem," in D.M. Gottfredson and M. Tonry (eds.) in *Prediction and Classification: Criminal Justice Decision-Making*. Chicago, IL: University of Chicago Press.

Blumstein, A. 1995. "Prisons," pp. 408–9 in J.Q. Wilson and J. Petersilia (eds.) *Crime*. San Francisco, CA: Institute for Contemporary Studies.

Blumstein, A., J. Cohen, and D. Nagin, eds. 1978. *Deterrence and Incapacitation: Estimating the Effects of Criminal Sanctions on Crime Rates*. Washington, DC: National Academy of Sciences.

Buchner, D. 1979. "Scale of Sentence Severity." *Journal of Criminal Law and Criminology* 70: 2: 182.

Cohen, J. 1973. "Incapacitating Criminals: Recent Research Findings." *Research in Brief*. Washington, DC: National Institute of Justice. December.

———. 1978. "The Incapacitative Effect of Imprisonment: A Critical Review of the Literature," in A. Blumstein et al. (eds.)*Deterrence and Incapacitation*.

———. 1983. "Incapacitation as a Strategy for Crime Control: Possibilities and Pitfalls," in M. Tonry and N. Morris (eds.) *Crime and Justice: An Annual Review of Research*, volume 5. Chicago: University of Chicago Press.

Cottingham, J.G. 1979. "Varieties of Retribution," *Philosophical Quarterly* 29, as cited in J. L. Mackie, "Morality and the Retributive Emotions." *Criminal Justice Ethics* (Winter/Spring 1982): 3–10.

Cronbach, L. J., and P. E. Meehl. 1955. "Construct Validity in Psychological Tests," *Psychological Bulletin* 52: 281–302.

Cullen, F. T., and P. Gendreau. 1989. "The Effectiveness of Correctional Rehabilitation: Reconsidering the 'Nothing Works' Debate, pp. 23–44 in L. Goodstein and D. MacKenzie (eds.) *American Prisons: Issues in Research and Policy*. New York: Plenum Press.

Erickson, M. L. and J. P. Gibbs. 1979. "On the Perceived Severity of Legal Penalties." *Journal of Law and Criminology* 70(1): 102–16.

Galton, F. 1895. "Terms of Imprisonment." *Nature* (letter to the Editor). June 20. 174–6.

Garrett, C. J. 1985. "Effects of Residential Treatment on Adjudicated Delinquents: A Meta-analysis." *Journal of Research in Crime and Delinquency* 22: 287–308.

Gendreau, P. and Andrews, D. A. 1990. "Tertiary Prevention: What the Meta-analysis of the Offender Treatment Literature Tells Us about 'What Works." *Canadian Journal of Criminology* 32: 173–184.

Gendreau, P. and R. R. Ross. 1979. "Effective Correctional Treatment: Bibliotherapy for Cynics." *Crime and Delinquency* 25: 463–89.

Gendreau, P., F. T. Cullen, and J. Bonta. 1994. "Intensive Rehabilitation Supervision: The Next Generation in Community Corrections?" *Federal Probation* 58(1): 75.

Gottfredson, D. M. 1984. *The Effects of Criminal Sanctions,* Report to the National Institute of Justice, U. S. Department of Justice. Newark, NJ: Rutgers University School of Criminal Justice.

Gottfredson, D. M. and S. D. Gottfredson. 1988. "Stakes and Risks in the Prediction of Violent Criminal Behavior." *Violence and Victims* 3(4): 247–62.

Gottfredson, D. M., and M. Tonry, eds. 1987. *Prediction and Classification: Criminal Justice Decision Making,* volume 9 of *Crime and Justice: A Review of Research,* Chicago: University of Chicago Press.

Gottfredson, D. M., S. D. Gottfredson, and C. H. Conly. 1989. "Stakes and Risk: Incapacitative Intent in Sentencing Decisions." *Behavioral Sciences and the Law* 7(1): 91–106.

Gottfredson, G. D. 1979. "Penal Policy and the Evaluation of Rehabilitation," remarks prepared for a symposium titled "Evaluating the Rehabilitation of Criminal Offenders," meeting of the American Society of Criminology, November.

Gottfredson, M. R. and D. M. Gottfredson. 1984. "Guidelines for Incarceration Decisions: A Partisan Review." *University of Illinois Law Review* 2: 291–317.

———. 1988. *Decision Making in Criminal Justice: Toward the Rational Exercise of Discretion,* 2d ed. Cambridge, MA: Ballinger, 155–69.

Gottfredson, S. D. and D. M. Gottfredson. 1985. "Selective Incapacitation?" *Annals of the American Academy of Political and Social Science* 478: 135–49.

———. 1988b. "Violence Prediction Methods: Statistical and Clinical Strategies." *Violence and Victims* 3(4): 303–24.

———. 1993. "The Long Term Validity of the Base Expectancy Scale." *Howard Journal of Criminal Justice* 32: 276–90.

———.1992. *Incapacitation Strategies and the Criminal Career.* Sacramento, CA: California Department of Justice, EIC Monograph Series, Edition 8, December.

———. 1988a. "The Accuracy of Prediction," in *Criminal Careers and "Career Criminals,"* edited by A. Blumstein, et al. Washington, DC: National Academy Press.

———. 1994. "Behavioral Prediction and the Problem of Incapacitation." *Criminology* 32(3): 441–74.

Gottfredson, S. D., B. D Warner, and R. B. Taylor. 1988. "Conflict and Consensus in Justice System Decisions," in N. Walker and M. Hough (eds.) *Sentencing and the Public.* Cambridge Series in Criminology. London: Gower.

Gottfredson, S. D., K. L. Young, and W. S. Laufer. 1980. "Additivity and Interactions in Offense Seriousness Scales." *Journal of Research in Crime and Delinquency* 17: 26–41.

Gottschalk, R., W. S. Davidson, J. Mayer, and R. Gensheimer. 1987. "Behavioral Approaches with Juvenile Offenders: A Meta-analysis of Long-term Treatment Efficacy," pp. 399–422 in E.K. Morris and C.J. Braukman (eds.) *Behavioral Approaches to Crime and Delinquency: A Handbook of Application, Research, and Concepts.* New York: Plenum Press.

Greenwood, P. W. with A. Abrahamse. 1982. *Selective Incapacitation.* Santa Monica, CA: Rand Corporation.

Hamilton, V. L. and L. Rotkin. 1976. "Interpreting the Eighth Amendment: Perceived Seriousness of Crime and Severity of Punishment," in H.A. Bedau and C.M. Pierce (eds.) *Capital Punishment in the United States.* New York: AMS Press.

Hamilton, V. L. and S. Rytina. 1980. "Social Consensus on Norms of Justice: Should the Punishment Fit the Crime?" *American Journal of Sociology* 85 (5): 1117–44.

Harris, M. K. 1975. "Disquisition on the Need for a New Model for Criminal Sanctioning Systems." *West Virginia Law Review* 77: 663 *et seq.*

Hume, D. [1751]1927. *An Enquiry Concerning the Principles of Morals,"* pp. 194–252 in C.W. Hendel, Jr. (ed.) *Hume Selections.* New York: Charles Scribner's Sons.

Izzo, R. and R. R. Ross. 1990. "Meta-analysis of Rehabilitation Programs for Juvenile Delinquents: A Brief Report." *Criminal Justice and Behavior* 17: 134–42.

Kant, I. [1797a] 1965. *The Metaphysical Elements of Justice: Part I of the Metaphysics of Morals*, translated by J. Ladd. Indianapolis, IN: Bobbs-Merrill, 100.

Kant, I. [1797b] 1959. *Foundations of the Metaphysics of Morals*, translated by L. W. Beck. Library of Liberal Arts, no. 113. New York: Liberal Arts Press, 39.

Kassebaum, G. D. A. Ward, and D. M. Wilner. 1971. *Prison Treatment and Parole Survival*. New York: Wiley.

Lacey, A. R. 1986. *A Dictionary of Philosophy*, 2d ed. London: Routledge, 66-67.

Lipsey, M. W. 1992. "Juvenile Delinquency Treatment: A Meta-analytic Inquiry into the Variability of Effects, " pp. 83–127 in T.D. Cook, H. Cooper, D.S. Cordray, L.V. Hartmann, L.V. Hedges, R.J. Light, T.A. Louis, and F. Mosteller (eds.) *Meta-analysis for Explanation*. New York: Russell Sage Foundation.

Lipton, D., R. Martinson, and J. Wilks. 1975. *The Effectiveness of Correctional Treatment: A Survey of Treatment Evaluation Studies*. New York: Praeger.

Locke, J. [1690]1928. *Treatise in Civil Government*. In S.D. Lampert (ed.) *Locke Selections*. New York: Charles Scribner's Sons.

Martinson, R. 1974. "What Works? Questions and Answers about Prison Reform," *Public Interest* 10.

McCord, J. 1978. "A Thirty Year Follow Up of Treatment Effects." *American Psychologist* 33: 284–89.

Mill, J. S. [1863]1931. *Utilitarianism*. London: J. M. Dent and Sons, Everyman's Library.

Morris, N. 1976. "Punishment, Desert, and Rehabilitation," in United States Department of Justice, *Equal Justice Under the Law*, Bicentennial Lecture Series. Washington, DC: U. S. Government Printing Office.

Murphy, G. 1930. *An Historical Introduction to Modern Psychology*. New York: Harcourt, Brace and Co.

Nagin, D. 1978. "General Deterrence: A Review of the Empirical Evidence," in Blumstein et al. (eds.) Panel on Research on Deterrent and Incapacitative Effects. Washington, DC: National Academy of sciences.

Nunnally, J. C. 1978. *Psychometric Theory*. New York: McGraw-Hill.

O'Leary, V. 1985. "Reshaping Community Corrections." *Crime and Delinquency* 31(3): 354.

Ouimet, M. P. 1990. "Tracking Down Penal Judgment: A Study of Sentencing Decision-making Among the Public and Court Practitioners." unpublished Ph.D. diss., Rutgers University.

Palmer, T. 1992. *The Reemergence of Correctional Intervention*. Newbury Park, CA: Sage.

Pease, K. and M. Sampson. [1977]1982. "Doing Time and Marking Time," *Howard Journal* 16: 59–64, as cited in C. Fitzmaurice and K. Pease "On Measuring Distaste in Years," in J. Gunn and D.P. Farrington (eds.) *Abnormal Offenders, Delinquency, and the Criminal Justice System*. New York: John Wiley and Sons.

Plato. [350–340 B.C.] 1980. *The Laws*, translated by T. J. Saunders. New York: Penguin Books.

Prichard, H. A. [1912]1955. "Does Moral Philosophy Rest on a Mistake?" *Mind* 21. Reprinted in A. I. Melden, *Ethical Theories: A Book of Readings*, 2d ed., pp. 469–81. Englewood Cliffs, NJ: Prentice-Hall.

Robinson, P. H. 1988. "Hybrid Principles for the Distribution of Criminal Sanctions." *Northwestern University Law Review* 19.

Rossi, P. H., E. Waite, E. Bose, and R. Berk. 1974. "The Seriousness of Crime: Normative Structure and Individual Differences." *American Sociological Review* 39: 224–37.

Russell, B. 1962. *Unpopular Essays*. New York: Simon and Schuster.

Sebba, L. 1976. "Some Explorations in the Scaling of Penalties." *Journal of Research in Crime and Delinquency* 15(2): 247–65.

Sebba, L. and G. Nathan. 1984. "Further Explorations in the Scaling of Penalties." *British Journal of Criminology* 23(3): 221–49.

Sechrest, L., S. O. White, and E. D. Brown, eds. 1979. *The Rehabilitation of Criminal Offenders: Problems and Prospects*. Washington, DC: National Academy of Sciences.

Sellin, T., and M. Wolfgang. 1964. *The Measurement of Delinquency*. New York: John Wiley and Sons.

Singer, R. 1987. As cited in F.N. Dutile and C.H. Foust, *The Prediction of Criminal Violence*, p. 56. Springfield, IL: Charles C. Thomas.

Smart, J. J. C. 1973. "An Outline of a System of Utilitarian Ethics," in *Utilitarianism: For and Against*. Cambridge: Cambridge University Press.

Stevens, S. S. 1951. "Mathematics, Measurement, and Psychophysics," in S.S. Stevens (ed.) *Handbook of Experimental Psychology*. New York: John Wiley and Sons.

———. 1971. "Issues in Psychological Measurement." *Psychological Review* 78, 426–50.

———. 1975. *Psychophysics: Introduction to its Perceptual, Neural, and Social Prospects*. London: John Wiley and Sons.

Stipak, B., and J. C. McDavid. 1983. "Statistical Procedures for Analyzing Factors Affecting Judicial Sentences using Simultaneously Derived Crime Seriousness and Sentence Severity Scales." *International Journal of Comparative and Applied Criminal Justice* 7: 1.

Thurstone, L. L. 1927. "The Method of Paired Comparisons for Social Values." *Journal of Abnormal and social Psychology* 21: 384–400.

Tremblay, P. 1986. "On Penal Metrics: Pursuing Erickson and Gibbs' Hypothesis." Paper presented at the 1986 meetings of the American Society of Criminology. Revised draft dated August, 1987.

United States Sentencing Commission. 1993. *Federal Sentencing Guidelines Manual, 1994 Edition*. St. Paul, MN: West Publishing Company, 1.

von Hirsch, A. 1976. *Doing Justice: The Choice of Punishments*. New York: Hill and Wang.

———. 1986. *Past vs. Future Crimes: Deservedness and Dangerousness in Sentencing*. New Brunswick, NJ: Rutgers University Press.

von Hirsch, A. and D. M. Gottfredson. 1983–84. "Selective Incapacitation: Some Queries about the Research Design and Equity." *New York Review of Law and Social Change* 12: 1.

von Hirsch, A., M. Wasik, and J. Greene. 1989. "Punishments in the Community and the Principles of Desert." *Rutgers Law Journal* 20(3): 595–618.

Weiler, P. C. 1974. "The Reform of Punishment," p. 107 in *Studies on Sentencing*. Ottawa, Canada: Law Reform Commission of Canada.

Westermarck, E. 1932. *Ethical Relativity* (London: Kegan, Paul, Trench, Trubner and Co., Ltd.), p. 86, as cited in J.L. Mackie, "Morality and the Retributive Emotions." *Criminal Justice Ethics*, Winter/Spring, 1982.

13

Punishment, Division of Labor, and Social Solidarity

David F. Greenberg

Introduction

A long-standing sociological tradition considers the type of social control measures utilized in a society to be determined by its more fundamental features. For Durkheim (1933, 1992), it is the division of labor in a society and the degree of absolutism of its government that determine collective responses to violations of social rules. To social scientists inspired by Marx, the mode of production in a society, the demand for exploitable labor, and the kinds and intensity of class conflict are fundamental determinants (Rusche and Kirchheimer 1939; Fine 1980; Melossi and Pavarini 1980; Miller 1980; Williams 1980; Adamson 1984). In recent years Donald Black (1976) and his followers (Horwitz 1990) have been extending this research program by positing the influence of a number of social characteristics on levels and styles of social control.

At best, the insights furnished by this approach have been partial. One need not reject those insights to recognize that some recent developments in crime control policy cannot be fully understood in these reductionist terms. Without abandoning it altogether, I want to explore a different way of thinking about criminal sanctions by suggesting that some features of punishment policy and practices can be understood as components of political strategies for *changing* a society. It is an intended *future* social structure and culture, not its current condition, that shapes the strategies. These strategies are not directed to crime alone, but also to an array of other social issues, such as welfare, education, and immigration. They rely on assumptions about the way society functions, or could function. Their ability to attract wide support rests in part on their congruence with popular conceptions of justice, and beliefs about the way society operates.

Tough Punishment

Until the early 1970s, American prison populations rose and fell over the decades, yet remained within bounds, without any long-run trend (Blumstein and Cohen 1973; Blumstein, Cohen and Nagin 1976). After declining appreciably for much of the 1960s, incarceration rates began to rise, and have been outpacing population growth steadily ever since. At the end of 1996, more than 1.6 million people were in prison or jail, and another 3.5 million were on probation or on parole. This is the population of a large city. Not content with this expansion, some politicians and policy analysts call for further expansion (e.g., DiIulio 1995).

A clearer picture of carceral growth can be had by examining trends in rates. In 1972, there were 93 sentenced prisoners per 100,000 residents in state and federal institutions (Maguire and Pastore 1996:556); at the end of 1995, there were 409 (Gilliard and Beck 1996:3). This is the highest incarceration rate in the industrialized world. Many of those committed to prison have been convicted of relatively minor offenses[1] (Austin and Irwin 1991).

This enormous increase is all the more remarkable in that it has come at a time when governments have been facing strong pressures to cut budgets.[2] The punishment system appears to have spun out of control. Predictions made a decade ago that the growth in prison populations "will taper off before long" for demographic reasons have failed the test of time (Blumstein 1987). Whatever the factors were that kept prison populations within limits in previous generations, they are no longer operating (Blumstein 1988). Prisons are being built and filled for political reasons, not because of demographic considerations.

Prison expansion is only one of many ways punishment policy has been toughening. Increasingly, states are adopting legislation allowing juveniles to be tried as adults, and are removing the confidentiality of juvenile court records (Butterfield 1996a). A number of states have started to hold parents responsible for offenses committed by their children (Kotlowitz 1994; Applebome 1996; Torbet et al. 1996). Educational programs for prison inmates are being eliminated in budget cuts (Kunen 1995). Federal legislation has excluded some addicts from Social Security benefits and from welfare payments. "Three strikes" legislation adopted by some states provides life sentences without parole for felons with two prior felony convictions, no matter how long ago, and sometimes without regard to the seriousness of the earlier offenses[3] (Shichor and Sechrest 1996). In 1995, Alabama restored the chain gang (Bragg 1995), a form of penal servitude long regarded as an instrument of racial oppression. After a moratorium on executions between 1967 and 1977 while the U.S. Supreme Court was considering the constitutionality of the death penalty, executions have resumed; the number of prisoners currently awaiting execution now exceeds 3000. In another decision, the Supreme Court ruled that judges can legitimately extend someone's sentence on the basis of charges of which the defendant has been acquitted.

In addition, public funding to finance appeals of death sentences brought by indigent defendants has been eliminated. The U.S. Senate has approved legislation limiting the rights of state prisoners to argue in the federal courts that they were unconstitutionally convicted or sentenced. This restriction on the right of *habeus corpus* would prevent a federal judge from stopping the execution of a state prisoner sentenced to death, even if new evidence is uncovered indicating that the prisoner is probably not guilty, or if the conviction was obtained through an incorrect ruling in the state trial court (Lewis 1995). Another bill limits the power of judges to turn the supervision of prison conditions over to a court-appointed special master.

Explaining Toughening

How to explain these developments? Homicide rates, considered the most accurate of all reported crime statistics, have changed little since 1980. Reported rates for other offenses did rise, but since victimization surveys show no parallel increase during the 1970s and 1980s, the increase in reported rates may reflect nothing more than an increased willingness of victims to notify the police (Orcutt and Faison 1981; O'Brien 1996).

That increases in reported crime rates do not necessarily lead to higher incarceration rates is demonstrated by the drop in prison populations during the late 1960s while reported crime rates were rising (at least partly for demographic reasons); and they are rising now, even though reported crime rates have been falling for five years in a row.[4]

The inability of crime rates to account fully for trends in prison populations is equally evident when considering trends comparatively. Since

1950, rates of reported serious crime have risen virtually in parallel in the Netherlands and in England/Wales; yet trends in prison populations have been quite different. The Dutch prison population was about the same in 1990 as in 1950, while in England and Wales it doubled (Downes 1988: 7, 34).

A court can sentence to prison only those offenders who are actually brought into the criminal justice system. Could it be that more people are being imprisoned because the police are arresting more criminals? In 1972, the arrest rate for index offenses per 100,000 population was 883.4; in 1995 it was 1132.7[5] (FBI 1973:126, 1996:209). This increase of 28 percent can hardly explain a more than four-fold increase in the incarceration rate.

A very large increase in arrests on narcotics charges has certainly contributed.[6] But imprisonment rates have increased for other offenses as well. Many states have adopted legislation mandating longer sentences for convicted criminals, and restricting or eliminating parole. Judges have been ladling out prison sentences more generously, and parole authorities have been revoking parole more readily (Shane-Dubow, Brown and Olsen 1985; Tonry 1988; Pillsbury 1989; Langen 1991; Wicharaya 1995; Marvell and Moody 1996). As a result, prison populations have grown at an historically unprecedented rate (Blumstein 1988; Langan 1991; Zimring and Hawkins 1995).

This trend is clearly inexplicable within the framework of Durkheim's (1933) model of legal evolution. That model sees the basis for social solidarity gradually shifting from "mechanical" to "organic" solidarity. In societies with mechanical solidarity, similarity in occupations and life circumstances is supposed to lead social members to identify strongly with one another, and to punish any infraction of social norms passionately, vigorously, and harshly. Societies with organic solidarity are supposed to be based on complementarity of function in a complex division of labor. Here demand for punishment is supposed to be milder, ameliorated by humanitarian sentiments; and social control places increased emphasis on restitution, less on retribution. Order is secured primarily through market exchanges rather than forcibly secured similarity, although punishment does not disappear.

It has long been known that long-term trends do not fit this model (Barnes 1965; Sheleff 1975; Spitzer 1975), and it clearly furnishes no insights that would help us to understand increased punitiveness now. Though the division of labor in contemporary United States is complex, the demand for severe punishment is high. Between 1972 and 1978, the percentage of respondents in a national survey saying that the courts were not harsh enough toward criminals rose from 66 percent to 85 percent (Hindelang, Gottfredson, and Flanagan 1980:196–7) and then leveled off. Support for the death penalty has risen over the past generation[7] for reasons that are not related to changes in the division of labor, at least not in the way Durkheim envisioned. It is not because American society is becoming less differentiated that it is becoming more punitive.

Increased punitiveness might, however, be explained by increasing inequality. Generalizing from diverse literatures, Donald Black (1976), has proposed that punishment will be more intense the higher the degree of economic inequality in a society, and that it will be harsher the lower the financial status of the person being punished.

A crossnational study of prison populations based on a global sample has found them to be larger where economic inequality is higher[8] (Killias 1986), consistent with this proposition.[9] Because political conditions in the less-developed countries are often quite different from those in the developed world, a crossnational study based on a globally representative sample of nations runs the risk of mixing apples and oranges, possibly obscuring patterns that may be distinct to the developed nations. Yet it is patterns for the developed world that might help us to understand recent American developments.

To determine whether the results Killias found hold for the developed world, I collected data for the nations[10] defined by the World Bank as having "high income," and computed the correlation between the imprisonment rate and economic inequality.[11] It is evident from figure 13.1 that there is a moderately strong positive relationship between imprisonment rates and economic inequality; the correlation between these two variables is 0.47. When the United States, which is clearly an outlier, is deleted from the sample, the correlation rises to 0.69. The correlations are quite similar if one measures punitiveness by the ratio of the imprisonment rate to the crime rate rather than by the imprisonment rate.

This correlation is not due to countries with high inequality having high crime rates and hence more people in prison: with the United States deleted from the sample, the correlations between inequality and the homicide and burglary rates are small and statistically insignificant. Only the auto theft rate[12] has a non-trivial correlation with inequality (0.28). Moreover, the crime rates are virtually unrelated to the level of imprisonment. Although a number of crossnational studies of crime rates have found higher rates to be associated with economic inequal-

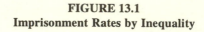

FIGURE 13.1
Imprisonment Rates by Inequality

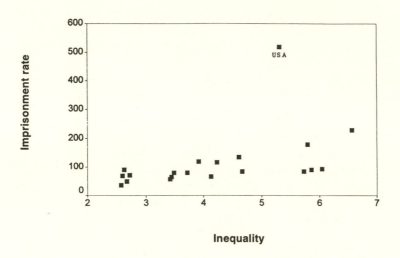

ity, this relationship is not found among the "high income" nations[13] (see figures 13.2, 13.3, and 13.4). Though the United States is among the more stratified nations in this sample, its overall crime rate is not unusually high.[14]

Nor does the relationship between punishment and inequality arise because highly unequal societies are also unusually wealthy, and therefore better able to afford the cost of building and maintaining prisons. Statistical controlling for gross national product (GNP) per capita hardly changes the correlation between inequality and the imprisonment rate.[15] Nor does it appear that the international differences can be wholly explained by differences in the kinds of crime the countries face. For specific kinds of crime, such as robbery, some countries imprison much more readily than others and for longer periods (Downes 1988:36–40; Downes 1990; J. Lynch 1988; Muncie and Sparks 1991).

Economic trends in the United States are consistent with a positive relationship between income inequality and prison population. Over the past two decades, as the prison population has risen, the distributions of income and wealth have become appreciably more skewed[16] (Winnick 1989; Burtless 1990; Phillips 1990:3–31; Karoly 1992, 1993; Krugman 1992, 1994; Danziger and Gottschalk 1993; Bradsher 1995; Westergaard 1995; Wolff 1995a, 1995b; Head 1996).

FIGURE 13.2
Homocide Rates by Inequality

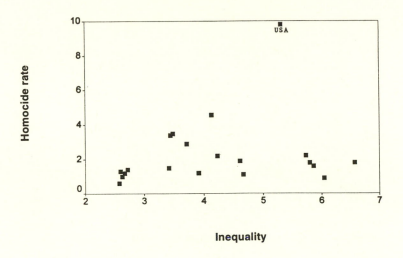

This skewing reflects two simultaneous trends: the rich have grown a good deal richer, while the poor have become somewhat poorer. The trends are the same when income is measured by earnings alone and by incomes from all sources. Between 1977 and 1988, incomes of the upper 1 percent of the population grew by 49.8 percent in constant dollars, while incomes of the bottom 80 percent fell, with the highest drop—14.8 percent—sustained by the bottom tenth (Phillips 1990:17). Between 1973 and 1995, average weekly earnings of "production and nonsupervisory workers," adjusted for inflation, fell by 18 percent, while "the real annual pay of corporate chief executives increased by 19 percent, and by 66 percent after taxes" (Head 1996). Between 1977 and 1989, average family income for the bottom quintile dropped by 9 percent; for those in the top 5 percent, it rose by 24 percent, and for those in the top 1 percent, it rose by 103 percent (Krugman 1992).

Children have been especially hard hit by this drop (Lichter and Eggebeen 1993): according to a report issued recently by Columbia University's National Center for Children in Poverty (1997), the number of children under age six living in poverty grew from 3.5 million to 6.1 million between 1979 and 1994. One in four children in that age bracket now live in poverty, a higher percentage than in other Western democracies.

FIGURE 13.3
Burglary Rates by Inequality

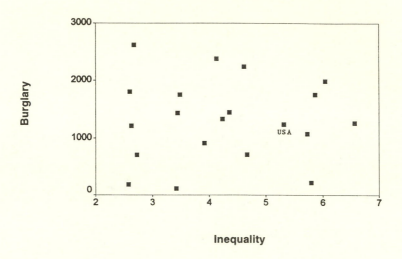

Inequality

Trends for punishment and inequality are thus consistent with a cross-sectional relationship between inequality and punishment levels among the nations. Yet it is equally apparent from figure 13.1 that the relatively high level of economic inequality alone cannot explain why the United States dishes out punishment so generously. Its prison population is far larger than can be explained by economic inequality alone.

Moreover, sentencing research does not entirely support the expectation that low-income defendants are punished more harshly. Though British judges are more likely to incarcerate defendants convicted of minor crimes when they are unemployed (Crow et al. 1989); in the United States, employment status appears to have little effect on this decision (Klein et al. 1990).

It is possible, of course, that punishment will be harsher where inequality is greater even if low-income defendants are not punished more severely than defendants with higher incomes. It could be that in less egalitarian societies, everyone is punished more severely, though it is unclear from Black's writings just why this should occur. He himself does not offer any explanation as to why this relationship should be found.[17]

Others have offered explanations, but they can hardly be called satisfactory. Instrumental Marxists have argued that the ruling class in

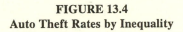

FIGURE 13.4
Auto Theft Rates by Inequality

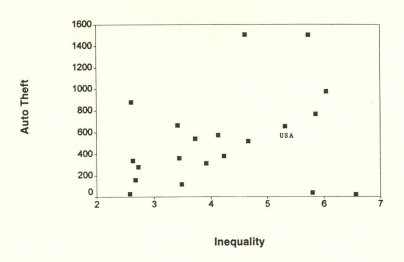

Inequality

highly stratified societies must punish criminals harshly to prevent exploited and impoverished workers from rebelling against poverty and exploitation (Chambliss and Seidman 1980; Quinney 1977:131–34). The positive correlation found in time series and panel analyses between unemployment and the size of prison populations[18] in a number of market economies[19] (Greenberg 1977a; 1989; Jankovic 1977; Box and Hale 1982, 1985, 1986; Hale 1989; Inverarity and Tedrow 1987; Laffargue and Godefroy 1989; Sabol 1989; Yeager 1979; Wallace 1981; Cappell and Sykes 1991) is consistent with this explanation. Yet the instrumental Marxist answer does not strike one as adequate in nations where the courts operate with a good deal of institutional independence from capitalist control, in which judges are not necessarily drawn from the capitalist class themselves, and in which the poor are not rebelling.

Moreover, the Marxist model, which attributes an expansive penal policy to a small ruling class, fails to account for the widespread belief among the American public that judges and parole boards are too lenient (Warr 1995). In the 1991 General Social Survey[20] (a nationally representative survey covering many issues), only 3.2 percent of 1326 respondents disagreed with the statement that lawbreakers should get stiffer sentences. 83.9 percent thought that the courts are too lenient, only 2.8 percent that they are too harsh. In a recent survey of Texas residents, 76.9

percent favored building more prisons; 93.2 percent disagreed with sentences being made shorter; 87.3 percent disagreed with the greater use of probation; 88.0 percent favored death for murder; and 50 percent favored death for rape (Farnworth, Bennett, and West 1996).

The extent of this support for severe punishments, however, does little to explain variability in the level of punishment across space and time. Why does the United States imprison so much more readily than other nations? Why so much more now than a quarter-century ago?

At first glance, it might seem that another of Black's generalizations could conceivably be relevant: it is that punishment will be greater when there are large differences in status and culture between those who punish and those who are punishing. One would expect the dominant groups in society—those who make and enforce the laws—to punish those they regard as unlike them more harshly. Where groups are ranked hierarchically in prestige or moral repute, those in lower ranked groups should be more vulnerable to imprisonment.

In many countries, minority populations are disproportionately represented in arrest, conviction, and prison statistics (Home Office 1990; Carr-Hill 1987; Biles 1986; Albrecht 1987; Junger 1988; Hudson 1993; Tonry 1993, 1997; Chiricos and Crawford 1995; Jackson 1995). Those who make and enforce American laws are white and have relatively high incomes; those who are punished are disproportionately nonwhite[21] and have low incomes. Well-off white citizens can endorse tough law enforcement measures, confident that they will not be subjected to police abuse, unfair and discriminatory prosecutorial and judicial procedures, long sentences, and harsh prison conditions. Perhaps the United States has so much larger a prison population than the other high-income nations because the others do not have comparable racial-ethnic or class divisions.

Studies of sentencing in the criminal courts might be construed as failing to give consistent support to this idea. A number of statistical studies of criminal sentences have found that on average, the race of the defendant has little or no impact on the outcome (Hagan 1974; Kleck 1981; Blumstein, Cohen, Martin, and Tonry 1983; Wilbanks 1987). On the other hand, other research has found evidence for invidious racial discrimination at various stages of criminal justice processing, unmitigated by the introduction of sentencing guidelines intended to eliminate prejudice (Chiricos and Crawford 1995; Jerome Miller 1996:78). With prosecution and sentencing decisions decentralized, practices are likely to vary with jurisdiction. Generalization on the basis of data from a single jurisdiction should probably be avoided.

The existence of discrimination in the criminal justice system, however, is not central to Black's proposition. In a hypothetical world in which no discrimination whatsoever takes place, knowledge that the recipients of harsh punishment are unlikely to be people like oneself could still lead to support for harsher punishment. This may be as much so in a world where disproportionate minority presence in the ranks of the punishment is due to their high levels of involvement in crime rather than to discrimination within the criminal justice system. Less-punitive nations like Denmark, Sweden, the Netherlands, and Japan are ethnically more homogeneous than the United States.[22]

Research showing that racial prejudice is associated with support for the death penalty (Vidmar and Ellsworth 1974, R. Young 1991; Barkan and Cohn 1994) suggests that greater prejudice may explain America's unusual punitiveness. However, this punitiveness is not required by difference alone. The significance attached to ethnic, racial, and cultural differences is culturally variable. Racial, ethnic, and cultural differences need not preclude solidarity or empathetic identification.

American punitiveness need not be related to cultural difference. Cultural differences between whites and blacks—as measured by educational attainment, for example—have diminished with time. They are surely less now than they were in 1970, making it doubtful that the repression of cultural difference could, by itself, explain why American penal policy has become tougher since then.

Leslie Wilkins (1984:72–73) has proposed a cultural explanation of the relationship between penal practices and income differentials based on the observation that the dispersion of incomes in a society establishes a scale for rewarding valued behavior. In societies where valued performances are rewarded with relatively high salaries, the scale for translating value into monetary awards is more extended than in societies where remuneration is more equal. This same scale should apply when behavior that is disvalued and condemned is punished. Where income inequality is especially high, one should also find draconian penaltes for disvalued behavior. Wilkins thus predicts a positive association between the severity of penal sanctions and income inequality. Insofar as longer sentences tend to produce higher prison populations, one would also expect a positive correlation between the size of prison populations and income inequality. This is just what we found.

Some caution is in order with regard to Wilkins' implicit assumption that in each society there exists a broad consensus about rewards and punishments, or that public opinion determines the distributions of incomes and punishments.[23] One cannot conclude from the mere existence of a high degree of inequality in income that the population as a whole accepts this inequality as just. Growing economic inequality in the United States has been deplored by some commentators[24] (Phillips 1990; Wolff 1995b; DeParle 1996a; David Gordon 1996). Moreover, it is unclear from Wilkins's analysis why the scale for rewarding American performances (positively and negatively) has changed so dramatically in the space of a single generation.

If inequality is to be understood as a direct cause of the imprisonment rate, then it is immaterial why some nations are more unequal than others. Whatever the factors responsible for high inequality, it leads to more punishment. However, the relationship can be understood as something other than simply and directly causal. To consider this alternative possibility it becomes relevant to ask why inequality has grown in the United States. In considering this question, it is relevant to note that inequality has not grown in some of the other "high income" industrial nations such as England and France (Wolff 1994:21–26). It is not an intrinsic feature of a technologically advanced economy.

Various factors have been invoked to explain the growth of inequality in the United States after some decades in which it declined or remained stable: increased returns to education and to nonsalary sources of income such as stocks, bonds, and real estate investments; the loss of blue-collar jobs as corporations have shifted investment abroad; increased competition among blue-collars workers resulting from immigration; a decline in union membership; reductions in welfare benefits; a decline in the real minimum wage; and higher rates of divorce— which can leave mothers and small children in poverty. Researchers are still assessing the precise contributions of these and other factors (Wilson 1987; Moffitt 1990; Levy and Murnane 1992; Danziger and Gottschalk 1993, 1995; Juhn, Murphy and Pierce 1993; Borjas 1994; Freeman 1993; Krugman 1994; Bluestone 1995; Card and Krueger 1995: ch. 9; Borjas, Freeman and Katz 1996; DiNardo, Fortin and Lemieux 1996; David Gordon 1996; Mishel and Schmitt 1996; Tilly 1996; Nielson and Alderson 1997; McCrate 1997); they need not concern us here.

What is critical is that disposable incomes depend not just on extragovernmental social and economic factors, but also on the distribution of the tax burden and of governmental subsidies, including direct transfer payments and tax benefits. Constant exposure to condemnations of welfare for the poor makes it easy to forget that there are large (and largely unpublicized) subsidies to middle- and upper-income groups. Income tax deductions for interest paid on home mortgages are as much a subsidy as the provision of public housing. The federal government currently spends $66 billion a year on tax deductions for property taxes and interest paid on mortgages, quadruple the amount spent on low-income housing. According to DeParle (1996a), "more than two-thirds of it goes to families with incomes above $75,000." Bailouts for failing businesses are as much subsidies as unemployment compensation (Glasberg and Skidmore 1997). Federally guaranteed student loans, and payments to farmers for not planting their fields, are as much subsidies as unemployment compensation and AFDC (aid to families with dependent children) payments. Subsidies to business add up to $85 billion a year (Fischer et al. 1996:145). In addition to direct subsidies, such state interventions as minimum wage laws, tariffs, import quotas, and immigration policies affect economic outcomes indirectly through their effects on supply and demand for labor and commodities.

According to one estimate, in 1991, American households with incomes under $10,000 received a total of $5,690 in tax benefits and direct transfer payments, while households with incomes over $100,000 received $9,280—almost twice as much. Were indirect subsidies and the provision of public goods and services that largely benefit middle- and upper-income households to be taken into account, the figures would change but the disparity would almost surely be even larger (Beeghley and Dwyer 1989).

This disproportionality has increased over time. Between 1980 and 1991 federal outlays to households with incomes under $10,000 dropped by 7 percent in constant dollars, while those to households with incomes over $200,000 doubled (Howe and Longman 1992). If incomes are becoming more unequal, we may infer not only that some forms of income-producing activity have become more lucrative than others, but also that the government has not intervened effectively to compensate for this trend. In many ways, the government exacerbates it. No political movement has mobilized effective opposition to this exacerbation.

Income distributions, then, are as much an outcome of "politics" as of "economics." The direction and extent of state intervention to increase or reduce economic inequality may be taken as a measure of the degree to which a concern for the well-being of low-income strata has been made a goal of public policy. These policies thus indicate the extent to which a state is a class state. Formally, that is, in law, the United States does not have a class state. Eligibility to vote and to hold public office are not restricted by class, and at least in principle, citizens of all classes are protected equally by law. Still, the benefits of citizenship are very unequally distributed.

Some economists have argued otherwise. In the long run, they contend, redistributive welfare policies do a disservice to the poor. By reducing the incentive to invest in physical or human capital, and by reducing the supply of potentially productive labor, high minimum wage laws and generous welfare policies supposedly slow economic growth (Gilder 1981; Alesina and Rodrik 1994; Henderson 1997). In the long run, they prevent the pie that feeds all classes from expanding.

Unlike the subsidies to the rich, those that benefit the poor are denounced as being especially pernicious. According to anthropologist Marvin Harris (1981:131), in providing aid to families of dependent children, "the federal government places its stamp of approval on both the fatherless inner-city family and the pursuit of crime as the solution to black men's unemployment problems."

Consistent with this anti-welfare position, the more egalitarian European countries have higher levels of unemployment and lower levels of new job creation than the less egalitarian United States. In our sample, the correlation between inequality and GNP per capita is 0.31. Yet, a more systematic analysis of the evidence does not seem to support the antiredistribution argument. One reason the European countries have higher unemployment rates than the United States is that the United States more readily imprisons its unemployed, and prisoners are not counted in unemployment statistics (Western and Beckett 1997). Higher levels of inequality reduce nations' economic growth for reasons unrelated to redistribution (such as making education unaffordable to those in low-income brackets). In some circumstances, redistributive policies can enhance economic growth, or at least have no detrimental impact (Blank 1994; Chang 1994; Persson and Tabellini 1994; Fischer et al. 1997; Bénabou, forthcoming).

Just as a society's concern for those with little money is manifested in its welfare policy, its willingness to execute and to imprison readily and for long periods indicates the extent to which the well-being of criminal offenders figures into governmental response to violations of the law. Many of those punished for law violation are drawn from low-income brackets, and so concern for the well-being of one group is not unrelated to concern for the other.

One may thus see the comparative leniency of the Dutch and Scandinavian criminal justice systems and their low degree of economic inequality (which is substantially a product of their generously funded

welfare systems[25]) as manifestations of a high degree of empathic identification and concern for the well-being of others. Where this identification and concern are high, citizens will tend to support social-demo-
cratic measures that partly detach economic well-being from fate in the
marketplace. They will think that a member of the polity is entitled to
an adequate standard of living simply by virtue of being a member of
society, independently of any individually earned or inherited merit.
Market outcomes themselves will be seen as the product of multiple
contingencies, such as fluctuations in labor market conditions, that lie
outside an individual's control and that should not play too large a role
in determining someone's life chances. Principles of redistributive justice moderate commodification of labor in a market economy.

Citizens in the more collectively oriented societies will also tend to
identify with criminals, not just with their victims. They will tend to
see criminal conduct as stemming in part from social, economic, and
familial conditions over which law violators exercise little control.
Operating on the principle, "there but for the grace of God go I," citizens will be less prone to insist on harsh punishment for those who
break the law. In arguing that identification with victims in homogeneous societies will lead to harsh punishment, Durkheim neglected to
consider that identification with perpetrators who are members of the
same society would tend to mute punitiveness.

Recent trends in American penal practices reflect changes in the level
of this identification. In the mid-1960s, civil rights legislation gained
the support of a substantial fraction of the white population, and the
president launched a war on poverty. Both developments signal increased
empathetic identification with minority and low-income populations.
In the same years, prison populations dropped appreciably and support
for the death penalty fell, even as reported crime rates and arrest rates
were rising.

The significance of both trends may be highlighted by recalling one
of the critical insights of Durkheim's discussion of organic solidarity.
Market exchanges, Durkheim observed, are not self-enforcing. Where
they occur as part of an ongoing relationship, fairness may need no
external guarantees because each partner will find it advantageous to
retain the good will of the other. But in a complex market economy,
many business dealings do not occur in the context of an ongoing relationship. And the informal pressures and constraints that might operate
in a small-scale band or tribal society, or in a small town in a capitalist
society into which the impersonality of the market has not fully pen-

etrated, cannot be counted on to uphold transactions or ensure fairness. Thus parties may succumb to the temptation to back out of an earlier agreement, or to exploit or cheat others when it is advantageous. Hence the state may be needed to enforce contracts, and to ensure that contracts meet standards of fairness. This insight can be generalized more broadly. In the complex conditions of modern society, distributional fairness is not something that market institutions can be counted on to supply. It requires the intervention of the state. However, as we have seen, state intervention does not necessarily bring about distributional equality or fairness. On the contrary, it can itself give rise to, or exacerbate, inequality and unfairness.

In Durkheim's model of social evolution, a complex division of labor is not created by the state; it occurs when unsuccessful competitors in existing occupations devise new occupations. However, the origins of modern market economies cannot be understood through this model of social evolution. An alternative model can be constructed by drawing on Durkheim's discussion of what he calls "abnormal forms" of the division of labor.

Abnormal Forms of the Division of Labor

Writing broadly of France at the end of the nineteenth century, Durkheim (1933:354–88) maintained that the division of labor brought about by the industrial revolution was neither mechanical nor organic. Instead, it was "abnormal." The growth of industry had been so rapid that new norms to govern industry had not had time to evolve; hence the division of labor was "anomic"—unregulated. In the absence of economic planning, investment decisions were vulnerable to miscalculation, triggering economic crises. The scale of business enterprises had grown to the point where communication between workers and employers had broken down. Instead of cooperation, the classes fought.

In traditional society, people were, according to Durkheim, satisfied with the station in life into which they were born. Now no longer willing to stay in their customary place, they were nevertheless excluded from many career lines. Where there were no formal barriers, obstacles such as lack of educational qualifications and financial assets could still prevent them from taking up certain occupations: "Even today among the most cultivated peoples, there are careers which are either totally closed or very difficult to be entered into by those who are bereft of fortune" (Durkheim 1933: 378).

When individuals cannot choose their occupations on the basis of their interests and talents, roles are allocated inefficiently, and the division of labor is "forced." Inequalities of wealth also open the door to exploitation. Rewards are incommensurate with efforts. If one social class is obliged, in order to live, to offer its services at any price, while the other can do without them, thanks to the resources at its disposal, which are not however necessarily due to any social superiority, the second unjustly dominates the first. In other words, there cannot be rich and poor at birth without there being unjust contracts (Durkheim 1933:384).With an abnormal division of labor, "only an imperfect and troubled solidarity is possible."

Although several sociologists have stressed the theoretical importance of Durkheim's discussion of the abnormal forms of the division of labor (Taylor, Walton, and Young 1973; Pearce 1989), Durkheim's failure to incorporate the abnormal forms into his model of legal evolution has allowed sociologists to ignore them when explicating Durkheim's analysis of law.[26]

Though deeply indebted to Marxian critiques of capitalism, Durkheim's decision to refer to the division of labor characteristic of his own day as "abnormal" suggested—contrary to Marxian analyses—that irrationality and exploitation were transient and ephemeral features of industrial capitalism, rather than essential to it (Schwendinger and Schwendinger 1974). They were, in other words, the result of an adaptive lag. Industrialization had taken place so rapidly that society had not had time to develop the institutions and norms needed to cope with the unprecedented problems it created. Hoping that the state would take up the challenge of these new problems, Durkheim did not need to incorporate them into his model charting long-term trends in legal evolution. It is, however, not difficult to do so.

As Durkheim argued, early human societies had a relatively low division of labor, but that does not mean cooperation and mutual dependence was absent. Because every member of a small-scale society is important to the survival of the collective, and because members are linked to one another in long-lasting multiplex relationships that extend cooperation and dependence across different social functions (work, ritual, reproduction, socialization), dispute resolution tends to emphasize conciliation and restitution. Harsh punishment is rare because it would rupture these relationships and alienate those punished from the group, along with their families, friends and allies. Solidarity in such societies is based in part on interdependence (organic solidarity), but affiliation to kinship groups within a tribe (lineage or clan, for example) is also an important source of identity and loyalty, and strongly influences responses to norm violations. Culturally mandated redistributive processes may prevent stratification from destroying this solidarity. Such societies combine some of the features Durkheim links with organic solidarity with some of those he associates with mechanical solidarity.

As human societies become more productive, and as the size of the group increases, the division of labor becomes more complex. Inequalities of stratification and power appear, and with them the state forms as a specialized social agency[27] (Engels 1942). States try, and often succeed, to establish their own authority and gain new sources of revenue by replacing retaliatory and conciliatory dispute-processing procedures with compulsory, punitive procedures under their own control.[28] They may give formal recognition to such social cleavages as castes and estates, and limit mobility between them through legal proscriptions. Class divisions based on the forcible extraction of surplus from slaves or serfs define the division of labor as forced and exploitative.

In societies where a forced division of labor is formally recognized in law, punishment will typically be harsher than in the more egalitarian small-scale primitive societies. The enlarged scale of the group means that individual norm violators may be considered expendable. The death penalty may be applied far more generously than in a band or tribal society. Punishment may also entail assignment to a degraded social status and to forced labor, e.g., penal slavery (Sellin 1976; French 1997).

In the usual case, offenses committed by individual members of the lower orders against their social superiors will be treated more harshly than vice versa, but this is not always the case. Elites may be expected to adhere to higher standards of conduct, and may be punished more heavily when they violate them. In the ancient Hindu Laws of Manu, for example, Brahmins are punished more harshly for certain infractions than members of other castes.

Where the state is not too powerful, many rule violations may be punished privately rather than publicly. A citizen head of household, for example, may hold the authority to punish members of his household, including slaves as well as wives and children. Even where the household head has the authority to kill his dependents—as the Roman *pater familias* did in certain cases—his interest in not losing an heir, or the services of a wife or slave, or the political support of his wife's family, might induce him to overlook an offense or to chastise the offender mildly. In the antebellum South, for example, slave-holders disciplined their slaves by whipping them, but had an incentive not to kill or incapacitate them. After the slaves were emancipated, their former masters, now their employers and landlords, had no such incentive. According to William E. Strong, Inspector General of the Freedmen's Bureau:

> The freedmen are in a worse position than they ever were as slaves. When they were held in bondage they were, as a rule, treated well; cases of extreme cruelty were very rare.... Now it is quite different, they have no interest in them, and seem to take every opportunity to vent their rage and hatred upon the blacks. They are frequently beaten unmercifully, and shot down like wild beasts, without any provocation.... (O. Howard 1866, quoted in Simon, 1991)

In many societies characterized by politically formalized abnormal divisions of labor, social movements developed to eliminate the formal distinctions between classes or estates. On the whole they have enjoyed striking success. Throughout most of the world feudalism and slavery have been abolished. In many countries, labor movements and socialist movements mobilized to reduce or abolish the exploitative class relationships implicated in the forced division of labor, with varying degrees of success.

Law has played a critical role in the transition toward a society in which occupational choice is unrestricted, and in which the conditions of work are not exploitative. It was through legal enactments that feudalism and slavery were abolished, and legal impediments to the employment of certain categories of people (such as women or members of religious and racial minorities) ended. Through legislation prohibiting discrimination in employment on the basis of race, sex, religion, and national origin, the state acted to remove long-standing public and private barriers to participation in the market economy.

In the United States, further legal steps were taken to remove the most glaring obstacles to full participation in social and political life.[29] Voting rights were extended to blacks and women, and equality of citizens before the law was established as a constitutional principle. The Supreme Court struck down state legislation prohibiting racial intermarriage. The segregation of schools, public transportation, public facilities, and housing was ended. Public higher education expanded to give opportunities to classes of students who did not have them previously.

Minimum wage laws were adopted to prevent exploitation at the workplace. Numerous legal measures, including hours restrictions, child labor laws, and occupational safety and health regulation, were adopted to protect the physical and mental well-being of workers. Unemployment compensation, compensation for on-the-job injuries, and grants to parents of dependent children were instituted to give workers and their families a source of financial support independent of employment. Regulations were put in place to protect consumers against fraud, unsafe products, and oligopolistic or monopolistic pricing practices. When first proposed, many of these steps were resisted, sometimes violently. Some of them were sought because they offered advantages to capitalists rather than workers or consumers. Nevertheless, the long-run trend has been one of eliminating particularistic barriers to full social participation, and of providing limited shelter from the vicissitudes of the capitalist market economy.

All these steps can be seen as elements of a broad trend to move society from one with an abnormal, forced division of labor to one more closely approximating Durkheim's description of organic solidarity. In recent years this trend continued with the establishment of affirmative action programs in employment and education, and minority set-asides for government contracts, justified by the belief that in a society with a centuries-long history of legally enforced white supremacy, mere formal legal equality would not suffice to bring about equal outcomes or genuine organic solidarity in any reasonable time period.

Though these efforts have not brought about full parity of the races or sexes, though they have not removed all obstacles to freedom of occupational choice or advancement, or fully protected workers, they have had partial success. Welfare programs, denounced by conservatives for fostering dependency and sanctioning immorality, have made major inroads on poverty. Crossnational research shows that the higher the welfare benefits in a nation, the greater the ability of recipients to escape poverty (Duncan et al. 1993). A recent evaluation of such American welfare programs as food stamps, housing assistance, school lunch programs, the earned-income tax credit, Social Security, and Aid to Families with Dependent Children, based on Census Bureau data, concluded that: "federal and state antipoverty programs have lifted millions of children out of poverty. Many of those who remained poor were significantly less poor than they would have been without government assistance" (Primus et al. 1996:1; also see Ozawa 1995). Open admissions to the City University of New York, begun in 1970, enabled thousands of students who would otherwise have been excluded from higher education, to obtain bachelors' degrees and better jobs (Arenson 1996a).

Between 1971 and 1985, the black-white gap in high school completion narrowed dramatically—from 23 to 6 percentage points (with a slight widening—to 7 points—after that) (National Center for Education Statistics 1995:72–73). The black middle class is now substantially larger than it was a generation ago (Landry 1987) and larger than it would have been in the absence of such programs as subsidized loans for higher education, affirmative action, and federal civil rights legislation (Lavin and Hyllegard 1996; "A Small Ripple" 1996). The number of marriages between blacks and whites, though low, has risen appreciably, pointing to increased social interaction, and growing acceptance of intermarriage (Kalmijn 1993; Holmes 1996a). Black representation in Congress, and in state and local government, has grown. Even though black arrest rates are substantially higher than white rates, over time the gap has narrowed.[30]

Equally dramatic gains have been made in relation to gender equality. All the Western democracies have extended the right to vote to women. Though the Equal Rights Amendment to the U.S. Constitution, intended to give authoritative backing to the equality of the sexes, was defeated, women have entered the labor force in large numbers, and many are pursuing careers in the professions, government, and the business world. The gap in wages between women and men has gradually narrowed (Kemp 1994:175). According to government figures, the number of women and racial minorities in corporate management has tripled over the last thirty years (Myerson 1997).

Durkheim argued that as the division of labor became more complex, the collective conscience would weaken, ameliorating punitive impulses. Humanitarian movements would seek to reclaim the criminals who were being destroyed in public exhibitions of power. Arguably, these movements developed only at the point where the expansion of the market economy made it appear practical to deal with large numbers of offenders without killing them or sending them into exile (Rusche and Kirchheimer 1939). Moreover, penal reformers' motivations were not exclusively benevolent and altruistic. The reformers who campaigned to replace executions, penal slavery and transportation to overseas penal colonies with prison sentences, half-way houses, and job-training programs were often alarmed by lower-class criminality, and threatened by the prospect of lower-class radicalism. However, their agenda of instituting more effective control over criminals, workers, and immigrants (Platt 1969; Foucault 1977; Ignatieff 1978: 58; Humphries and Greenberg 1981; Garland 1985; Polsky 1991; Simon

1993) does not necessarily mean that "humanitarian" concerns were altogether absent. Regardless of the complex factors that made it possible, the transformation of sentiment occurred.

Consider John Howard, the Bedfordshire sheriff who documented the filth and squalor of eighteenth-century English and continental jails. At a time when degrading jail conditions were widely known but considered inevitable—and perhaps desirable as a deterrent—Howard (1780) argued that the indiscriminate mixing of inmates exposed the innocent and the novice to the influence of hardened criminals, thereby promoting crime. Clean, orderly, disciplined jails, he contended, could reform criminals. This was a pragmatic argument, not an appeal to humanitarian sentiment. Yet, following a religious conversion, Howard also felt acutely that he was as much a sinner as were the prisoners, and shared with them a common humanity. Writing in an unpublished manuscript, he thanked God for making "such a worm" as himself "the Instrument of alleviating the miseries of my fellow creatures and to connect more strongly the social bond by mutual exertions for mutual relief" (quoted in Ignatieff 1978:56). There is little reason to think Howard was being hypocritical when writing this private document. In the previous generation, the Anglican priest John Wesley also felt a common sense of humanity with prisoners, but confined his efforts on their behalf to preaching sermons for them at the gallows (Ignatieff 1978:55). Whereas Wesley sought to save lost souls for the world to come, Howard wanted to lead them to a more virtuous life in this world, through better jail conditions (and stricter discipline within them).

In the following century, when novelist Charles Dickens sent letters to the *Daily News* arguing for the abolition of capital punishment, he insisted that abolition was "for the advantage of society, for the prevention of crime, and without the least reference to, or tenderness for any individual malefactor whatever." Yet in one of those letters he also wrote that after he and his friends had witnessed the hanging of a murderer, one whose treachery they detested:

> if any one among us could have saved the man (we said so, afterwards, with one accord) he would have done it. It was so loathsome, pitiful, and vile a sight, that the law appeared to be as bad as he, or worse; being very much the stronger, and shedding around it a far more dismal contagion. (quoted in Collins 1968:226)

Dickens' public disavowal of sentimentality probably reflected his defensiveness in the face of Thackeray's attacks on death penalty abolitionists for being effeminate.

Similar themes appear in the writings of American penal reformers. The Constitution of the Philadelphia Society for Alleviating the Miseries of Public Prisons (1787) announced that the obligations of benevolence, "founded on the precepts and example of the author of Christianity, are not canceled by the follies or crimes of our fellow-creatures" and called for the extension of compassion to suffering prisoners (Pillsbury 1989). They and like-minded reformers had an assimilationist agenda; they sought to incorporate wrong-doers into the social body rather than to expel them. It is true that the incorporation did not usually challenge class inequality in any fundamental way. Thus Elizabeth Fry, the Quaker who brought solace to women prisoners in early nineteenth-century England, and lobbied for prison reform, wrote about her servants that "We are not their familiars or equals in the things of life, for we have reason to believe that difference in our status is ordered by a wiser [one] than ourselves" (Simeral 1916:154). Reformed punishment could, indeed, be considered a more sophisticated and effective instrument of class rule than the cruder methods relied upon previously.

It is also true that the incorporation was to be on the reformers' terms, that it required assimilation to their culture, and that it was to be implemented coercively. Their moralism and their concentration on helping individuals while failing to change social-structural sources of marginalization doomed many of their efforts to uplift the poor and steer criminals to the straight-and-narrow. All this has had major implications for the character of the programs reformers proposed and implemented. Nonetheless, their agenda was premised on a humanity that controllers and controlled shared.

Though some penologists and criminologists of the late nineteenth and twentieth centuries openly embraced doctrines of racial inferiority (Lombroso 1871, 1876) this was never a prominent element in the reformist agenda. In the last half-century reformers have generally endorsed the goal of full citizenship and participation of those being reformed. This democratic goal is radically different from those sought by state punishment systems and their defenders in early modern Europe (Foucault 1977; Langbein 1977; Spierenberg 1984, 1991).

As with measures to benefit workers and consumers, the reformers' agendas were rarely implemented in full, but over the past two centuries much was accomplished. Fines, imprisonment, probation, and parole became the primary state sanctions, largely replacing execution, exile, and corporal punishment. Rehabilitative programs were introduced into the prison, albeit on a very modest scale. Juvenile courts and reformatories were established, and juvenile arrest records were sealed to protect juveniles from the stigma of a conviction.

To protect the innocent and to ensure fairness, the Supreme Court extended due process protections to suspects and defendants in criminal cases. To prevent punishment from disrupting ties to family and community, and to facilitate offender "re-integration," reformers argued for the creation of "alternatives to incarceration" located in the community (Alper 1974; Perlstein and Phelps 1995). Concerned that prosecutors and judges were discriminating invidiously against blacks and other minorities, reformers proposed restrictions on the exercise of judicial discretion in sentencing (American Friends Service Committee Working Party 1971).

The toughening of criminal justice policy reverses a number of these trends, just as reversals of incorporative trends are taking place on policies not directly related to crime, where the state has been promoting a transition from a forced division of labor toward organic solidarity. Consider regulation, which, ever since the Progressive Era, has been a major instrument for the protection of workers and consumers. President Ronald Reagan established a Task Force on Economic Competitiveness charged with the elimination of regulatory measures that imposed excessive costs on business. Under President George Bush, its successor, the Council on Competitiveness, made numerous changes in regulations drafted by the Environmental Protection Agency, many of them taken directly from documents prepared by the companies being regulated. The Council eliminated a proposed ban on incinerating lead batteries, and recycling provisions for new incinerators. It speeded up the Food and Drug Administration's approval procedure for new medical drugs, blocked attempts to regulate genetically engineered microbes, drugs and foods, and sponsored a bill to end all laws regulating the environment as infringing on property rights protected by the constitution (Tokar 1992).

Limits on welfare benefits for the poor and for immigrants have been enacted into law, with support from both major political parties. The federal income tax schedule has been made more regressive. Democratic and Republican politicians call for further tax cuts for the middle and upper classes, while ignoring the greater need of low-income citizens. Federal legislation has barred lawyers in federally financed Legal Services offices from handling class action suits on behalf of the poor (Greenhouse 1996). City governments have repressed begging in public places, and used zoning regulations to stop religious institutions from operating soup-kitchens to feed the homeless (Kress 1994).

Legislatively imposed budget cuts have forced retrenchment in public higher education. At a time when the stock of low-income rental housing has shrunk, federal funding for subsidized housing has been cut back sharply (O'Flaherty 1996; DeParle 1996b). In response to court decisions curbing preference programs, minority set-aside programs intended to help minority contractors obtain government contracts have been dismantled, resulting in the closing of large numbers of minority-owned businesses (Pear 1990; Hinds 1991; Holmes 1996b).

In California, a referendum calling for an end to affirmative action programs in state institutions passed in a popular vote, and has now gone into effect after surviving a court challenge. Though legal protection against discrimination in employment remains in effect, staff cuts at the Equal Employment Opportunity Commission ostensibly made for budgetary reasons have led to a large and growing backlog of unresolved cases[31] (Kilborn 1994). In much the same way, lack of enforcement of sanitation rules for farm workers—including requirements that employers provide toilet facilities and fresh drinking water—have effectively nullified the protections nominally provided by the Occupational Safety and Health Act (Noble 1988).

Collectively, these measures represent a withdrawal from public commitment to transform society from an abnormal division of labor to one based on organic solidarity. Where regulatory enforcement is weakened, businesses operate anomically; the interests of consumers in purchasing safe and reliable products, of employees in working in a safe work environment, and of all residents in an environment that is not dangerously polluted, are sacrificed to profit maximization.

In principle, injured parties can still seek remedies through private law suits, but long backlogs in the courts and the high cost of litigation make this remedy impractical, if not unattainable, for many potential plaintiffs.[32] To avoid the costs of litigation and the risk of losing law suits, many businesses are requiring as a condition of employment that employees sign away their rights to bring court cases alleging discrimination (Myerson 1997).

The fall in real wages that many workers have experienced over the last two decades, paralleled by rising productivity and growth in profits, and increases in wealth and income for the rich, indicates that capitalist firms are becoming more exploitative. Ostensibly, some of the new measures—such as the lifetime limit on welfare imposed by federal legislation in 1996—are intended to encourage those who now lie outside the division of labor to enter it by removing disincentives to job-seeking. There is, however, little reason to think that millions of new jobs for new workers with limited skills and work experience will be created quickly. The gap between needs and the welfare support to be withdrawn is far in excess of what private charities can conceivably supply. In New York City alone, almost 470,000 adults were on welfare in August, 1996. Under the new federal law just signed, at least 80 percent of these will lose welfare benefits within five years. Labor market specialists assert that the paid labor market is capable of absorbing only a small fraction of this number when their eligibility for welfare ends[33] (Finder 1996).

To the extent that welfare recipients do seek employment, they will exert downward pressure on wages, increasing the number of working poor with incomes below the poverty line, and intensifying exploitation. The denial of further benefits to welfare mothers who bear additional children, which some states have adopted, may or may not reduce out-of-wedlock births, but will surely leave families into which such children are born even more impoverished. The exclusion of children of illegal immigrants from public schools—a proposal not yet enacted into law—is more likely to create a new generation of illiterates and innumerates than it is to curtail illegal immigration. Work requirements for welfare, supposedly intended to prepare recipients for jobs, are interfering with recipients' efforts to earn the college degrees that will help them achieve upward mobility (Arenson 1996b).

For many of those who do not inherit substantial wealth, education is crucial to upward mobility. Rapid rises in college tuition at a time when federal loans for college are being cut are making it more difficult for prospective students to attend college, and force them to choose colleges on the basis of financial considerations, rather than for educational reasons (Geraghty 1997). Escape from the lower class through education is becoming more difficult.

On average, poor children do not perform as well in school, and independently of their performance and talents, are less likely to attend college (Sewell and Shah 1967; Persell 1977; Hill and Sandford 1995; Alexander and Entwisle 1996). In the absence of outside intervention, the children of the lower classes will largely remain in their class of origin. With reduced intergenerational mobility, the United States will more closely approximate a caste system, one sustained not by formal barriers between castes, but by *de facto* barriers arising from differences in the advantages that accrue to current class positions.[34]

The developments in criminal justice and those concerning welfare and inequality feed on one another. Prisons are expensive to build and to operate. The billions spent on police and prisons have created a "prison-industrial complex" that lobbies for further spending increases (Christie 1993; Lilly and Knepper 1993; Donziger 1996:85–96). At a time when politicians are loath to raise taxes or to increase deficit spending, a vast expansion in prison costs implies a corresponding contraction in the availability of funds for welfare or education.[35] Funds spent building new prisons are unavailable for opening new colleges that might admit students who believe they are being deprived of a college education by affirmative action programs.

The ban on the use of Pell grants to enable prison inmates, many of whom have serious educational deficits, to take college courses, which was put in place by the 104th Congress, will make it harder for ex-convicts to repair these deficits while in prison. A criminal record can further damage prospects for future employment and lawful earnings.[36] Trying juvenile offenders in criminal courts and imprisoning those convicted will enlarge the pool of people who have limited prospects of improving their returns in lawful labor markets. Given current arrest and imprisonment patterns, this labor market damage will impinge very disproportionately on black and Latino males.

Where prospects for lawful remunerative stable employment and upward mobility are restricted, the incentive to acquire income illegally through theft, prostitution, and the sale of narcotics is enhanced;[37] and—leaving aside the effect of "repeat offenders" legislation—those with a criminal record have less to lose from a subsequent arrest or conviction.

High crime rates in a neighborhood discourage business investment, and provide incentives for current residents and businesses who can afford to relocate to do so, increasing the spatial segregation that high economic inequality tends to promote. Because jobs are often found through contacts with those who already have them, these developments further reduce economic opportunities for local residents who cannot move (Bénabou 1993).

Individually and in the aggregate, levels of violence rise with poverty (e.g., Eberts and Schwirian 1968; Loftin and Hill 1974; Braithwaite 1979; Braithwaite and Braithwaite 1986; Messner 1980, 1982; Kick and LaFree 1985; Blau and Blau 1982; Bailey 1984; Simpson 1985;

Avison and Loring 1986; Krahn, Hartnagel and Gartrell 1986; Rosenfeld 1986; Peterson and Bailey 1988b; Maume 1989; Unnithan and Whitt 1992; Reiss and Roth 1993:130–31), and are reduced by government support for the poor (DeFronzo 1983; Rosenfeld 1986). Poverty increases the incidence of child abuse and domestic violence (Elmer 1967; Gil 1970; Gelles 1974; Maden and Wrench 1977; Straus and Gelles 1990; Straus, Gelles, and Steinmetz 1980). Thus, a decline in the economic well-being of the lower classes can be expected to increase levels of violence.[38] To the extent that the prevention of victimization is a reason or a pretext for more punishment, the new anti-welfare policies will help to keep violence and victimization at appropriately high levels.

It could be objected that the deteriorating economic circumstances of the lower classes did not lead to large increases in theft and violence in the recent past. Apart from a modest increase in violence in the late 1980s, almost certainly related to the crack trade, homicide rates were quite stable between 1970 and 1990. The illegal drug market undoubtedly made it possible for many nominally unemployed individuals to avoid stealing, and the expansion of the prison system took many criminals out of circulation. Just how much prison expansion contributed to keeping crime rates from getting out of hand is not entirely clear, but it may have done a good deal through deterrence and incapacitation of prospective law violators (Marvell and Moody 1994; Spelman 1994; Wicharaya 1995; Levitt 1996). The argument often made by opponents of further prison construction—that the stability of crime rates in the face of an enormous expansion in the prison population proves the ineffectiveness of imprisonment at stopping crime—neglects the possibility that crime rates might have grown a great deal for reasons having to do with the state of the economy, had the prison populations not risen.[39]

Why the Backlash?

Social trends do not halt or reverse automatically. It is often easier to continue or expand an effort than to turn it around. Yet government crime policy did reverse course. While punishment was a major component of crime policy during the 1960s, it was not the only component of the crime-fighting strategy that Presidents Kennedy and Johnson were devising. Even while fashioning new law-enforcement initiatives, they also proposed an anti-poverty program as another important element of their strategy. In the interests of fairness, they proposed to give defendants more rights in court. As U.S. Attorney General, Robert F.

Kennedy proposed that the federal government should make it possible for indigent defendants to be represented by attorneys in court (Calder 1982; Steel and Steger 1988). The Kerner Report, issued in the aftermath of large-scale rioting, proposed new initiatives to improve black employment prospects, education, housing and welfare, and to prevent abusive behavior on the part of the police (National Advisory Commission, 1968). Yet, once Richard Nixon took office in 1968, strategies for reducing crime that tried to alter its "root causes" no longer had presidential backing, and criminal justice proposals originating in the White House entailed strengthening, not weakening, enforcement capabilities. This reversal, alongside a reversal of welfare policy, calls for explanation.

Ask someone who supports the abandonment of egalitarian social policies and favors more punitive penal strategies why ameliorative policies lost favor, and you will be told that the old policies were obviously failing. Billions of dollars had been spent in the War on Poverty, yet welfare rolls rose,[40] and so did crime. Instead of helping recipients to become self-supporting, welfare undermined the work ethic. Instead of bringing about integration, mandatory school bussing hastened "white flight," leaving schools segregated and cities deprived of tax revenues (Coleman, Kelly, and Moore 1975; Henig 1994:102). Liberal elitist judges were flouting the will of the people on such issues as school prayer, school desegregation, and abortion rights. Minimum wage laws and pollution control cost jobs. The breakdown of traditional morality, and Supreme Court decisions favoring criminals, were leading to promiscuity, illegitimacy, drug use and violence. Programs to rehabilitate criminals did not work. The public became aware of these difficulties, and demanded that politicians reverse course (Gilder 1981; Murray 1984; Van den Haag 1975; Wilson 1975; Mead 1992).

Many of these claims do not withstand close scrutiny. Efforts to reduce poverty and eliminate discrimination accomplished much, and would have accomplished more had more resources been devoted to implementation and enforcement. There is little evidence that overly generous welfare provisions increased welfare rolls, discouraged recipients from seeking jobs, or increased teenage pregnancies (Wilson 1987; Moffitt 1990; Hacker 1992; Jencks 1992; Tonry 1995:12–17; Luker 1996). Some research suggests that the minimum wage law, criticized by economists for increasing youth unemployment, does not in fact do so (Card and Krueger 1995; Blinder 1996). The bussing of school children probably had little impact on white flight (Rosell 1975–1976;

Pettigrew and Green 1976). Many government initiatives and regulatory interventions have demonstrably improved public health and safety, and have benefitted the public in other ways (Kuttner 1996).

Although conservative critics denounced the Supreme Court for handcuffing police by requiring that defendants be informed of their rights, that indigent defendants be given attorneys, and that illegally obtained evidence could not be introduced in trial, these decisions did little to hinder law enforcement (Fyfe 1983; van Duizend, Sutton, and Carter 1984:91; Gordon 1990:34–36). The attacks on the Supreme Court were made without any basis in research whatsoever.

Changes in incarceration policy were not required by clear research results, and some of them were made notwithstanding experts' serious reservations about their consequences (Pillsbury 1995). The flat assertion that "rehabilitation doesn't work" (Robison and Smith 1971; Martinson 1974) was quickly seen to be an overstatement. Some treatment evaluations did show signs of effectiveness, though many did not (Ross and Gendreau 1980; Jenkins and Brown 1988; Cullen and Gendreau 1989; Whitehead and Lab 1989, 1990; Andrews et al. 1990a, 1990b). A research report claiming that the death penalty was a powerful deterrent of homicide (Ehrlich 1975) was promptly shown to rely on questionable statistical procedures (Passell and Taylor 1975; Bowers and Pierce 1975; Klein, Forst and Filatov 1978; Bowers 1988).

Studies showed that city crime rates were unresponsive to increases in the size of the police force (Greenberg, Kessler, and Logan 1979, Greenberg and Kessler 1982; Rich, Lineberry, and Jacob 1982), making the hiring of more police a dubious way to reduce crime. Cost-effectiveness assessments asserting that imprisonment was a good investment because it prevented losses greatly in excess of its costs (Zedlewski 1985, 1987) were shown to rest on equally dubious assumptions (Zimring and Hawkins 1988; Greenberg 1990). It appears that early intervention programs such as training parents of children at risk for delinquency, and providing incentives to discourage early school-leaving, would be far more cost-effective than mandatory prison sentences for repeat offenders (Greenwood 1996).

Of course, just because doubts have been raised about conservative, hard-line claims does not mean that they are entirely lacking in substance. One need not be a conservative to recognize that some regulatory agencies were captured by the industries they were supposedly regulating, or that they failed to protect the public (Fellmuth 1970; McAvoy 1976; Wilson 1981). Introspection will convince most people that the threat of punishment has some deterrent value, and common sense indicates that when active law-breakers are confined behind bars, some crime is prevented by virtue of their incarceration. Surely some people who could work exploit the welfare system. Yet, even if all the liberal efforts had been failures, failure need not require the abandonment of an enterprise. If an intervention is considered worthwhile, failure can be met with further experimentation. In some circumstances it may indicate the need for more far-reaching intervention.

It is an oversimplification to assert, as James Q. Wilson (1975) has, that politicians were forced to take tough stands because leniency was failing, and that the public was frightened by rising crime. Some hard-line proposals—notably narcotics control measures—retain their popularity with politicians and public despite failures that have been noted by critics over and over again. Popular support for gun control has not swayed politicians who fear retribution from the National Rifle Association. Moreover, public opinion, though increasingly punitive in recent years, has not been univocal. When the newly elected President Reagan announced in 1980 that "the public wants criminals clobbered, and that is what we are going to do" (quoted in Steel and Steger 1988), he was distorting what opinion polls showed the public to want. Alongside support for the death penalty and less leniency, substantial support for preventive and rehabilitative programs remained (Duffee and Ritti 1977; Riley and Rose 1980; Warr and Stafford 1984; Cullen, Clark and Wozniak 1985; Gottfredson and Taylor 1987; Cullen, Cullen, and Wozniak 1988; Skovron, Scott, and Cullen 1988; Cullen, Skovron, Scott, and Burton 1990; McCorkle 1993).

Still, this does not mean that popular feelings about an issue have been irrelevant. Politicians may exaggerate the punitiveness of their constituents, perhaps because constituents who are most fearful or most sanguinary are the most likely to communicate their convictions to their government representatives. However, in one of the studies demonstrating politicians' exaggeration of public punitiveness (Gottfredson and Taylor 1987), only a third of the respondents opposed new prison construction. There is no substantial constituency in favor of less punishment, whose existence is unknown to the politicians.[41]

Critics of the argument that politicians had to respond to public concern note that when conservative politicians began to call for expanded law enforcement capabilities and the nullification of Supreme Court decisions on defendants' rights, few citizens identified crime as the nation's most important problem when surveyed (Chambliss 1994,

1995). In fact, the percentage identifying crimes or drugs as the most serious problem is quite volatile; it rises sharply when news media highlight instances of horrendous violence, and when politicians harp on the perils of rising crime rates in their speeches, quite independently of any changes in levels of reported crime[42] (Alderman 1994; Beckett 1994; Chambliss 1994, 1995; Flanagan 1996).

Yet this measure is an imperfect indicator of public concern about crime,[43] and does not demonstrate the absence of spontaneous concern based on personal experience and the experience of one's associates. Nor does it prove that demands for punishment are irrational. Between 1960 and 1970, the numbers of each of the seven index offenses rose by factors of two to three. Ordinary citizens are not criminologists, and do not necessarily pay close attention to each and every fluctuation in crime rates. But when theft and violence increase regularly year after year for more than a decade, chances of victimization climb, and awareness of the increases diffuses through the population.

Increases of this magnitude and regularity could hardly have failed to make an impact on levels of fear, and on assessments of the seriousness of crime as a social problem. In the same years that index crime rates climbed, American cities were wracked by riots,[44] and major public figures, including a president, were assassinated. These events are often overlooked by scholars who try to refute the existence of any "objective" basis for fear of crime by examining crime rates for the years after the early 1970s, when the crime rates had leveled off.

More critical than the existence of concern are the implications that follow from that concern. One response to the riots following the assassination of Rev. Martin Luther King, Jr. was to prevent crime by "getting at its cause; slums, unemployment, run-down schools and houses" (Hubert Humphrey, quoted in Chambliss 1995). Another was that of the conservative senators and congressmen who sponsored the Omnibus Crime Control and Safe Streets Act allowing wiretapping without a court order, and exempting law enforcement agencies from the Civil Rights Act of 1964 (Chambliss 1995). These were measures, it might be noted, that had no conceivable relevance to the prevention of riots or more common kinds of crime. To the extent that the wiretapping provision had a policy goal, its goal was to strengthen federal capacity to deal with organized political opposition, of which there was then a great deal.

What is true for politicians is equally true for the public at large. It does not follow from the mistaken public view that crime has been increasing steadily that support for rehabilitation should have declined, while support for more punishment rose (Gerber and Engelhardt-Greer 1996).

That the brief and modest trend toward leniency in criminal justice policy and toward incorporation and reduced social inequality should have evoked some opposition is hardly surprising. When social change injures the interests of a sector of the population, or they believe that it does; and when it challenges the principles on which the old order is based, countermovements opposed to the change emerge calling for a return to "the good old days," or if that appears impractical, for an attainable alternative. The precise nature of the backlash, and the interests that are at stake, are of some interest.

To understand the increased punitiveness of the last twenty-five years we must consider both the politicians who call for punitive measures and the responsiveness of the public to these calls. Before doing so, though, we must note that for some backers of a hard-line approach this was nothing new. When civil rights measures were adopted in the 1960s, a substantial fraction of the country strongly opposed them. Many congressmen, including George Bush, voted against the 1964 Civil Rights Act. Their later opposition to affirmative action is easily understood as a continuation of their earlier opposition to formal racial equality. When a politician who opposed the legal equality of the races in 1964 now condemns affirmative action as "reverse discrimination," a violation of the principle that governments should treat all citizens equally, one must suspect that the condemnation really stems from long-standing opposition to government measures that will help blacks, not from commitment to formal legal equality. Public opinion has simply changed to the point where the earlier racist sentiment cannot be voiced in public. Having lost the battle to maintain white supremacy openly, they seek to preserve it covertly, in the name of the formal equality that they had long opposed. Likewise, a significant fraction of the population approved highly punitive penal methods all along, and opposed restrictions on law enforcement. As early as 1966, New York City voters defeated an all-civilian police board by a large margin in a referendum in which the Patrolmen's Benevolent Association led the opposition (Viteritti 1973); and a proposal for community control of the police lost even in Berkeley, one of the most liberal of all American towns.

One must also keep in mind that many people have not abandoned "liberal" positions. Ameliorative and redistributive programs still enjoy support in some quarters. College administrators still tend to favor affirmative action in admissions (Lederman 1996a, 1996b), and many public figures have condemned the new welfare provisions as ill-advised. Surveys show majorities in favor of affirmative action by spreads of 10 to 15 percentage points[45] (Harris 1995). In a referendum held in Houston in the fall of 1997, voters approved affirmative action programs by a majority of 54 to 46 percent. The city's business leaders and politicians had all supported the programs[46] (Verhovek 1997a). When asked whether the government needs to make a greater effort to try to rehabilitate criminals who commit violent crimes, or to punish them and put them away, 32 percent say "rehabilitate" and another 8 percent say "both equally" (compared to 49 percent who say "punish").[47]

Initially, it was conservative Republican and Southern Democratic politicians who campaigned for tougher law enforcement measures. They attacked the Supreme Court for favoring criminals by upholding or extending defendants' rights, possibly to discredit the Court for its invalidation of legislation upholding segregation. The conservatives called for preventive detention, longer sentences for narcotics offenses and for the use of a weapon in a crime, for limiting bail and the insanity defense, and for permitting wire-taps.

By contrast, in 1968, Democratic Presidential candidate Hubert Humphrey called for redistributive programs and equal rights for all citizens as a way to deal with crime. In 1972, the Democrats opposed the death penalty, and called for prison reform and a ban on hand-guns. Candidates like Hubert Humphrey, George McGovern, and George Dukakis, who held the more "liberal" positions, all lost. Although their defeats were surely not due to their stands on crime issues alone, it is quite understandable in light of this history that in his first term, President Bill Clinton protected his reelection bid by introducing a crime control act providing funds for 100,000 more police. A more principled liberal opposition to hard-line proposals might have left their proponents vulnerable to accusations of lacking empathy for crime victims.

In advancing the conservative agenda at a time when the public appears not to have been overly concerned about routine crime, politicians sought votes by linking conventional illegality with cultural and political developments that worried many voters. Republican Barry Goldwater's 1964 presidential campaign ran television ads conflating civil rights demonstrations with street crime and riots. In 1967, Vice President Spiro Agnew (1969:40) returned to this theme by lambasting "muggers and criminals in the streets, assassins of political leaders, draft evaders and flag burners, campus militants, hecklers and demonstrators against candidates for public office and looters and burners of cities." By rhetorically associating political opposition to American participation in the War in Vietnam with conventional crime, Nixon and Agnew were able to discredit the opposition and make the threat of crime appear larger and more worrisome. This threat was then used as the basis for arguing that the repressive capacities for the state had to be strengthened.

Similar campaigns have been conducted on economic issues. Proponents of free markets have long argued against state interference with market transactions, contending that government can best promote economic efficiency and growth by not interfering with private choices. Taxes and subsidies, the free-marketers contend, should not be used to alter distributions of income produced in competitive marketplaces; doing so merely introduces inefficiencies by discouraging productive activity. Government bureaucracies, they say, impose burdensome costs on businesses, making it difficult for them to compete in a global economy; and often fail to protect the public. Opponents of affirmative action programs charge them with failing to reward merit, heightening group consciousness, damaging the self-esteem and career prospects of those they try to help, and illegally discriminating on the basis of race and sex (Sowell 1975; Capaldi 1985; Eastland 1990; F. Lynch 1989; Steele 1990; Carter 1991; Yates 1994). Under the Reagan and Bush presidencies, the critics of liberal policies became more vocal and gained broader influence on public policy.

Representations—or misrepresentations—of crime in the mass media helped to make the public more receptive to the claims of politicians that crime rates were soaring (Antunes and Hurley 1977; Fishman 1978, 1981; Ericson, Baraneku, and Chan 1991; Surette 1992; Beckett 1994; Chambliss 1994, 1995; Schlesinger 1994; Chernak 1995; Murphy and DeStefano 1996). Television and film dramas—both in fiction and in news reporting—exaggerate the extent to which crimes involve violence, and through their "realism," leave viewers feeling threatened and insecure. Television and film depict due process constraints on law enforcement only as obstacles in apprehending and punishing criminals, not as protections for "honest" citizens (Crew 1990). One reason that many Americans have believed that crime rates have been growing rapidly is that television networks have devoted more time to crime news (Donziger 1996:69). Active criminals and ex-convicts are poorly positioned to oppose these representational distortions.

We need not assume that politicians who rail against "welfare queens," who wax with indignation at the supposed unfairness of affirmative action, and who ask a rival candidate for public office how he would feel were his wife to be raped, actually believe the myths they circulate, feel the emotions they display before audiences, or expect much from the programs they advocate; some of them may have adopted conservative positions opportunistically. Without believing what they say about welfare, race or crime, the hard-liners know that they can use these issues to further their prospects in the next election. If voters can be made to fear violence and resent immigrants and welfare recipients, they will vote for politicians who support longer sentences, and restrictions on immigrants and welfare.

Politicians' proposals for dealing with crime, however, suggest that more may be at stake than career promotion. Jacksonian-era figures who sponsored the building of penitentiaries and asylums saw them as small-scale models of the ideal society—hierarchical, authoritarian, disciplined. They hoped that once the success of the prison, mental asylum, and poor house had been demonstrated, the model would be adopted by other institutions in "free" society, such as the family and the school (Rothman 1971). The same may be true today. Conservative politicians' agenda is to shore up threats to authority and inequality. The criminal law appeals to them as a way of gaining consent. It entails one class of people—those who hold government office—telling other people what to do, threatening disobedience, and punishing those who fail to conform. The criminal justice system is designed to gain compliance through coercion from those who will not conform on the basis of the law's legitimacy, or on the basis of positive incentives. When a policy analyst proposes to increase the number of police in the United States from half a million to five million (Walinsky 1995), one may suspect that the proposal does not reflect a rational strategy for protecting lives, but a fascination with the idea of government by armed men wearing uniforms.

Through its punishment rituals, criminal law validates the moral superiority of those who make and administer the rules. Due process constraints on law enforcement are a symbolic challenge to this superiority. In allocating rights to suspects, they undercut this moral hierarchy. Similarly, state-mandated welfare implies—as private charity does not—that recipients have a right to a certain standard of living independently of their submission to the authority of an employer. The conservatives hope to create a world in which rights play a less important role in society, and coercion and legitimate authority play a larger role.

The conservatives have been able to gain exposure to their views on issues like taxes, welfare, and regulation because business corporations provide massive funding to conservative foundations and think-tanks, which in turn promote books and newspaper articles that advance the conservative agenda (Blumenthal 1986; Miller 1996). Possibly because left-wing critics of welfare and treatment programs had advertised their control functions so persistently (Piven and Cloward 1971; Platt 1969; American Friends Service Committee Working Party 1971), liberals did not take the strong stands against the backlash they might otherwise have made. The rich have been less active in promoting repressive criminal justice policies than in lobbying for the deregulation of business, probably because policing and prisons have less relevance to their class interests than taxation and regulation.

Some of the support these measures receive from the public can be attributed to simple self-interest. It is quite rational for people who feel threatened by violence to suppose that they will be safer with more people in prison. If tax-payers are being squeezed by declining real incomes, cuts in welfare programs and taxes might sensibly be seen as offering relief. Part of the white opposition to affirmative action programs stems from the belief that they or their children are being denied access to good jobs and elite schools (Bobo and Kluegel 1993). It is advantageous to this constituency to argue that affirmative action programs discriminate against whites, and that college admissions and financial aid decisions should be made on the basis of "merit," not on the basis of allegedly irrelevant criteria such as race and ethnicity.

In the last two decades, middle-income voters have faced job insecurity and a gradual decline in real wages. As corporate "down-sizing" jeopardized white middle-class jobs (Newman 1988), whites became increasingly concerned with preserving their own class position, and less concerned with helping others. Thinking only of themselves and of the immediate short-run implications of admissions and hiring practices while forgetting the long-run social consequences, they have been less willing than before to foster upward mobility for the poor, and more vigorous in seeking tax cuts. Given this stance on social issues, it would be quite rational to want to put more criminals in prison. If redistributive and preventive measures are to be excluded, what else can one do?[48]

This reasoning, however, overlooks the high costs of the hard-line approach. Once these are figured in, it is not likely that the tough approach is rational when viewed in a purely material light. While self-interest may explain some opposition to welfare payments and affirmative action, it fails to account for the low-income citizens who oppose welfare, and those blacks who oppose affirmative action. Nor does it explain why some middle- and upper-class people have supported welfare, civil rights, and affirmative action. In the absence of support that extended beyond the beneficiaries, these measures would never have been adopted.

The rational actor model overlooks the emotional loadings that accompany positions on all these issues. For many people, crime policy, welfare policy, race relations policy, all touch on fundamental beliefs and values, and are heavily weighted with emotion. Attempts to understand public responses to these issues that neglect their emotional and often irrational dimensions may be doomed to fail.

Chancer and Donovan (1996) have recently attempted to explain the moral outrage over crime and the demand for stringent punishment by arguing that "the general insecurities" of a middle-class anxious "about its own economic precariousness, status, and general life situation" are critical in gaining mass support for retributive policies. The aggression provoked by these insecurities is channeled toward criminals, whose open hostility toward authority make them unconscious objects of fascination and admiration.

This analysis focuses too narrowly on the lower middle-class, which is no more punitive than other classes. In two studies, support for retributivism was not significantly related to socioeconomic status (Warr and Stafford 1984; Grasmick et al. 1992). In the 1991 General Social Survey, however, respondents whose total family income is high have significantly higher support for stiffer sentences, though the effect is small. Those whose financial circumstances had recently improved were more likely to think the courts were not harsh enough, and that criminals deserve stiff punishment, but these differences were also small.

Chancer and Donovan's focus on economic anxiety may be misplaced. Neither anxiety over one's status, nor economic difficulty, nor punitiveness, is a monopoly of the middle class. Rossi, Simpson and Miller (1985) found punitivism to be little affected by respondents' race, sex, income, and household income. Those who had experienced a negative life event such as unemployment, serious illness, or a death in the family were significantly more likely to be punitive, suggesting that anxiety or frustration from multiple sources might lead to punitive feelings. However, it is unclear how much this anxiety is due to economic restructuring under conditions of uncertainty.

If economic declines produce punitive feelings, one would have an explanation for the relationship between the business cycle and rates of admission to prison found in several capitalist countries, as well as the emotional appeal of punishments. The low sentences found in Scandinavia, the Netherlands, and Japan may reflect a lower popular demand for punishment in societies whose economic systems do not engender high levels of insecurity. In Scandinavia or the Netherlands the welfare system is relatively generous (de Haan 1990; Downes 1992), and in Japan unemployment is very low and jobs are often assured for life.

A direct test of this reasoning would require comparable data about levels of economic insecurity in different societies, and such data are not currently available. However, to focus too exclusively on fears about one's job or income may be to slight the process through which fears and anxieties are directed toward particular issues by politicians and the mass media. The emphasis they have given to crime, welfare, and affirmative action has focused anxiety on those issues, rather than—for example—on the military budget, or defects in the economic system.

In trying to explain why American prison populations soared, while those in West Germany declined modestly over the same years. Joachim Savelsberg (1994) has argued that politicians and the mass media play an important role in structuring popular beliefs about crime and crime control. Savelsberg notes that countries vary in the extent to which politicians and newspapers highlight crime as a social problem and call for harsher measures to deal with it. In the more corporatist societies, different political factions or bodies are formally recognized and represented politically. Attempts are made to accommodate their interests through explicit bargaining and concessions.

Politicians in such societies should be less likely to try to win support through inflammatory campaign rhetoric that exaggerates the magnitude of social problems. Because all the major parties share in the responsibility for dealing with these problems, they will not have strong incentives to misrepresent them. For the same reasons, they will refrain from attacking the existing policies as being outrageously misguided. Publics in these societies are not as fearful of crime, and are less likely to make demands on the state for more stringent penalties.[49]

Differences in political arrangements make sense not only of the contrast between West Germany and the United States, but also of the low levels of incarceration in the Netherlands during the decades in which its "pillarized" political system was in place. In that system,

major political decisions were made through behind-the-scenes agreements between the major political parties (Downes 1988; de Haan 1990).
As this system has weakened in recent years, Dutch prison populations
have risen, though not to the extent that they have in the United States.

A test of the importance of corporatism in structuring social responses
to crime can be conducted using our sample of data for the affluent
nations. When the per capita prison population is regressed on inequality, GNP, the crime rate, and a measure of corporatism measuring the
extent to which different sectors of society engage in explicit bargaining and compromise agreements, (Pampel, Wiliamson, and Stryker
1990), corporatism is found to reduce the prison population significantly, while inequality no longer has a significant influence (see table
13.1). The more corporatist societies are less punitive. The United States
is the second least corporatist society in the entire sample, and the most
punitive.[50] Were the Democrats and Republicans to work out the main
outlines of punishment policy behind closed doors, it is unlikely that
Presidential candidate George Bush would have run television advertisements taxing his opponent George Dukakis for the crime Willie
Horton committed on prison furlough (Anderson 1995).

Of course, the United States would also have ranked low on cor-

TABLE 13.1
Multiple Regression of Incarceration Rates*

Variable	Standardized Regression Coefficient**	
Corporatism	−.80	−.78
	(2.15)	(2.20)
GNP	.63	.58
	(2.08)	(1.99)
Inequality	.00	.05
	(.00)	(.14)
Homicide Rate	−.08	
	(1.03)	
Total Crime Rate	−.193	
	(1.06)	
R^2	.65	.68
adjusted R^2	.52	.56

*Pairwise deletion, United States deleted from sample
**Figures in parentheses underneath regression coefficients are Student's t statistics.

poratism three decades ago, when the incarceration rate was far lower than it is now, and declining. In itself, a culture of individualism and a more competitive political system need not lead to panics about crime, or to punitive policies. Crime became a public issue because racial conflict, radical political challenges, cultural changes including wider use of recreational drugs, the rise of feminism, and the weakening of sexual restrictions were occurring at the same time reported crime rates were rising rapidly.

Social changes of this magnitude would surely have elicited concern and opposition from substantial sections of the population even in the absence of political exploitation. They posed a challenge to the values, moral and political beliefs and familiar ways of life of many. The fear and anger aroused by cultural change and political opposition became joined to the fear aroused by crime and riots through framings posed by conservative politicians and amplified by misrepresentations on the part of those same politicians, and by depictions in the mass media.

Other countries encountered many of the same problems. In May 1968, the French New Left came close to toppling the government. The New Left in Germany and Italy was much more violent than in the United States. But politicians in those countries did not turn these threats into a general war against crime. Where repression took place, it was more narrowly focused on the political threat.

The more corporatist societies are not only less punitive; they are also more egalitarian and have more far-reaching redistributive policies. In our sample, the correlation between the corporatism score and inequality is $-.66$.[51] Welfare policies in the corporatist societies enjoy stronger public support. When asked whether the government should provide everyone with a "guaranteed basic income," support was far higher in Britain (59 percent), the Federal Republic of Germany (51 percent), and the Netherlands (48 percent) than in the United States (20 percent) (Smith 1990).

Obviously, these correlations pose a chicken-and-eggs problem. Corporatist political arrangements are not distributed among the nations at random, and they cannot necessarily be treated as exogenous to economic equality. It is in societies where it is considered important to accommodate diverse interests, including those of workers and people who cannot support themselves, that corporatist political arrangements tend to be found. The culture that gives rise to corporatism, and in turn to greater tolerance of deviance, shows a good deal of stability over time. The Netherlands had a lower rate of execution than England in the eighteenth through nineteenth centuries, and abolished capital punishment much earlier (Downes 1988: 69). English society has been exceptionally individualist for hundreds of years (Macfarlane 1979); France has been known for its identification of the people and the centralized state. Possibly there is something about the cultures of some countries that make them more amenable to corporatism and to egalitarian economic policies.

However they come about, once corporatist political arrangements are in place, they tend to perpetuate themselves. Just as politicians will tend to refrain from demonizing criminals, they will tend to avoid attacks on welfare recipients, and citizens will recognize that, despite its costs, it benefits them. In Norway, where welfare benefits are extravagant by American standards, and taxes to pay for them are equally high, businesses support the welfare state because they value the social peace it has brought them[52] (Ibrahim 1996). Making sure that a minimum standard of living is maintained, if necessary through the welfare system, becomes part of the national identity, valued for its own sake, just as "individualism" comes to be valued as an element of Americans' political identity.

On the other hand, sometimes political culture changes. For the first half of this century, the Netherlands had a higher incarceration rate than England and Wales, even though it had less crime (Downes 1988). Between 1968 and 1971, the value placed on social equality rose in national surveys of the American people; then in the 1970s it fell relative to such personal values as having a comfortable life, a sense of accomplishment, and excitement, possibly because awareness grew that equality came at a price. When real incomes began to fall, those costs came to be seen as unacceptable by a substantial fraction of the white population (Rokeach and Ball-Rokeach 1989).

Punitive Attitudes, Models of Society, and Principles of Justice

Because penalties for crime are imposed very disproportionately on members of minority groups, some observers have argued that the war on crime is really a war on blacks and Latinos (Miller 1996). It is, however, difficult to reconcile this argument with surveys showing that support for integration and equal treatment of the races has been growing gradually over the decades (Schuman et al. 1985; Firebaugh and Davis 1986; DiMaggio, Evans, and Bryson 1996; Quillian 1996).

Only limited support for the "war on blacks" thesis can be found in survey research. In the 1991 General Social Survey, respondents who supported residential racial segregation and who said that they would not vote for a qualified black presidential candidate nominated by their party were more likely to believe that the courts are not harsh enough, but the differences were tiny: for segregation, 81.8 percent versus 80.9 percent; for the presidential vote, 87.5 percent versus 84.1 percent. Whites were more likely than blacks to think the courts not harsh enough, but here too the differences were small (84.7 percent versus 79.8 percent).

Support for the death penalty was more strongly influenced by racial attitudes: 91.6 percent of strong supporters of racial segregation supported the death penalty for murderers, compared to 68.6 percent of strong opponents. 83.7 percent of those who would not vote for a black candidate favored capital punishment compared to 74.5 percent of those who would. The differences among the races were also stronger: 58.9 percent of black respondents supported the death penalty compared to 77.5 percent of whites.

These results suggest that one source of support for harsh punishment may be racist feelings, but it is clearly not the only one. A majority of blacks favor it. A large majority of blacks support stiffer punishment for criminals, as do a large majority of racists and nonracists. The percentage of the population endorsing strongly racist views is relatively small. Few Americans now advocate legal segregation of neighborhoods and public schools. Even were racists' views on punishment to be more distinctive than they are, those who endorse explicitly racist views would contribute relatively little to overall sentiment regarding punishment. Even in their absence, public sentiment for tough punishment would be strong—strong among blacks, and strong among those who reject racism. If it is not credible to suppose that blacks are supporting a war on blacks, perhaps another view of white support for the war on crime is called for.

Because a disproportionate percentage of blacks—approximately 28 percent—receive means-tested welfare support—it might be suspected that opposition to welfare could be motivated by antipathy to blacks. However, the race of the welfare mother has been found unrelated to views of welfare spending (Gilens 1996). A substantial majority of whites (69 percent) thinks that most welfare recipients are not truly needy, but are taking advantage of the system; so do a majority of blacks (62 percent). More whites than blacks think welfare for low-income families should be kept, but the difference is not large (55 percent versus 46 percent) (Gallup 1995:38).

The emphasis on explaining differences in the standard social-science statistical procedures provides limited insights when it is a pattern of similarity one seeks to explain. In attitudes toward punishment and welfare, the most striking feature is not that there are some modest differences between the races, or between those holding different views of race relations, but the similarities. There is strong support for stiff punishment and cuts in welfare budgets among all groups. Some insights into the sources of this support can be gleaned from the rhetoric that is deployed on behalf of penal policy positions.

Many factors surely contribute to the attitudes people hold about crime, punishment, and welfare. Yet the texts in which policy stances on these issues are defended reveal the common themes, suggesting that greater punitiveness may be one component of a larger policy shift toward an anomic and forced division of labor. It would be too much to say that individual views on crime, welfare, affirmative action, and other social policies always appear in tandem. The positions people hold on social policy issues are not always logically coherent and consistent. Sometimes they are idiosyncratic. Policy stands are correlated in predictable ways, but imperfectly. It is the common themes on which I focus here.

The notion that the courts are justified in punishing convicted criminals proportionately to the wrongfulness of their crimes has won a wide following among penological theorists in recent decades. Wrongdoers, they argue, should be punished because they deserve to be punished on the basis of what they have done. In so arguing, "just deserts" theorists do not contend that these principles are optimal for preventing crime, but rather that justice requires them. It is the wrongfulness of criminal acts, not social utility, that should govern the severity of punishment (Frankel 1972; Fogel 1975; Twentieth Century Fund 1976; von Hirsch 1976, 1985; Gross 1979).

Ordinary citizens rarely elaborate the subtle distinctions to be found in the essays of the just deserts theorists, but they too draw on conceptions of justice. Consider the recent letter to the editor of the *New York Times* that complained of "convicts wearing prison-supplied Nikes while watching cable television and exercising in gyms that surpass many high school facilities," indulgences that lead the author to wonder "if there is a punitive element in America's penal system" (Brennan 1997). Brennan's grievance is not that it is wrong to watch cable television or that public safety will be jeopardized by turning prisoners into couch potatoes. He fumes because he thinks that prisoners do not deserve to live so comfortably.

The same concern with justice figures prominently in reasons that supporters of the death penalty give to explain their support. "Murderers deserve punishment," they say; "an eye for eye; a life for a life" (Lotz and Regoli 1980; Finckenauer 1988; Steel and Steger 1988). Many of those who say they favor capital punishment to protect the public also say that they would not withdraw their support were evidence that it failed to deter homicide to emerge (Vidmar and Ellsworth 1974; Ellsworth and Ross 1983; Longmire 1996). Their belief that capital punishment deters may be a consequence of their belief that murderers deserve to die rather than a cause of their belief.[53]

Debates over affirmative action are also phrased in the vocabulary of deserts. Opponents argue that students with high grades and test scores deserve to be admitted to the best colleges. Admitting students with lower grades and test scores over those who are better qualified because they are classified as minority group members unjustly confers a benefit on the basis of what ought to be irrelevant. As Michael Levin (1989) put it, "it is *unfair* to bypass white males...who are not themselves responsible for the plight of blacks and women" (emphasis added). The laws should not set out to disadvantage anyone on account of their race. The current cohort of students did not create the historic pattern of segregation whose consequences affirmative action seeks to overcome; they should not be punished by the adoption of remedial measures that impair their life chances.

Though opponents of affirmative action point to what they contend will be long-term pernicious consequences of affirmative action (racial polarization, stigmatizing of minority students and job-holders, inefficiency in the use of educational resources), they also argue that college admission should be a reward for individual achievement or ability, not an instrument for improving society.

Overlaps between populations thought unworthy result in stereotypes through which a deficiency in relation to one activity sphere discredits those in other activity spheres. The belief that poor people are lazy discredits the claim that they turn to crime from necessity, not maliciousness; and reduces white support for welfare spending (Gilens 1996), presumably because of the belief that a large proportion of welfare recipients are black,[54] perhaps criminal. Conscious and unconscious prejudice against blacks can stigmatize all criminals, and all welfare recipients through a contamination of categories with overlapping membership.

All of these stands—those on punishment, those on welfare, those on affirmative action—rest on assumptions about questions of fact that do not withstand close scrutiny, and on the applicability of particular normative framings. A desert-based punishment scheme based on criminal behavior alone assumes that it is equally easy for everyone to comply with the law.[55] To the extent that this assumption is rendered false by the existence of discrimination and structured inequality not chosen by a defendant, equal proportional punishments no longer correspond to equal desert.[56] Just deserts theorists have long been aware of this difficulty (von Hirsch 1976:143–51), but have found no way to resolve it. Sentencing reform was potentially attainable through advocacy and lobbying; economic redistribution was not. Better to lobby for what is attainable even if the result falls short of standards that supposedly justify the scheme.[57]

Opponents of affirmative action in college admissions assume that grades and test scores adequately measure aptitude, and that restitution for past discrimination, compensation for inferior education and cultural devaluation or familial disadvantage should not be taken into account. Presumably better study habits could have raised grades and test scores, independently of a child's life circumstances. Or if one rejects this farfetched notion, one might simply accept continued racial stratification as a consequence of the formal equality. By that logic, universities and governments should not take accidents of birth into account, even though the continuing consequences of slavery, racial discrimination and economic disadvantage will ensure that individuals' life chances are greatly influenced by historical events over which they have no control.

Views of welfare also rest on assumptions about the recipients. Those who think welfare mothers are lazy, and believe that most people are poor because "they don't try hard enough to get ahead" are less sympathetic to welfare spending than those who think that people are poor "because they don't get the training and education they need"[58] (Gilens 1996).

Contrary to claims made by critics of welfare policy and affirmative action, class origin has a large influence on tests that supposedly measure intellectual ability (Fischer et al. 1995:79–88), and expensive coaching can improve test scores substantially. Class and race have large influences on someone's chances of being arrested, prosecuted, and convicted of crime. The suggestion that a better substitute for affirmative action in college admissions and in employment would be an upgrading of the public schools and the reconstitution of the black family (Sullivan 1995) is made without any realistic plan for accomplishing these goals.

The assumption in many discussions of affirmative action that in the absence of special programs a "level playing field" exists runs counter to evidence about discrimination in hiring and promotion (Kilborn 1995). The important role of friends and relatives in obtaining jobs is overlooked. A suggestion made by Shelby Steele (1990) that stepped-up prosecutions against discriminators could make affirmative action in hiring unnecessary ignores the higher standards of proof required in a criminal trial and the small likelihood that significant prosecutorial resources will be devoted to the prosecution of discriminating employers.

The critics of these programs hold a utopian view of American society. In the absence of state intervention, conscientious parents will raise children who will buckle down, overcome any and all obstacles, and triumph over adversity. Employers will always want the best-qualified employees, and therefore will avoid prejudicial discrimination. Those who do not will be driven out of business by their competitors. No shortage of adequately remunerative jobs stands in their way; or if there is a shortage, it is a product of minimum wage laws that make it too expensive for employers to hire marginally productive job applicants.

This is a world of wishful thinking. Would that all these interventions were unnecessary! Much money and much effort could be saved. Violation of appealing abstract principles of formal equality could be avoided. If the substantial efforts already undertaken have not yet brought a fair world into being, how much easier to persuade oneself that it has already done so. To acknowledge that it does not exist might impose burdensome moral obligations that many might prefer not to have to shoulder.

This fantastic utopianism lends a peculiar quality to the move toward a more "abnormal" division of labor. In earlier historical eras, people's placement in the stratification system was attributed to divine will. The secularization of culture made it impossible to sustain gross inequalities of wealth and power on this basis. Explanations of stratification as resting on innate differences in virtue and talent offered an alternative legitimation, one which held a good deal of appeal in the age of imperialism. The power of this explanation to legitimate hierarchy was almost completely nullified in the course of the twentieth century by its association with colonial rule and genocide (Arendt 1951). Though attempts have been made to revive it (Michael Young 1958; Herrnstein and Murray 1994), the strength of democratic egalitarian ideology has limited the influence of these attempts. The sway of doctrines of racial inferiority in the United States is now largely limited to politically impotent, marginal white militias.

In contemporary discussions of crime policies and allocation controversies one rarely encounters genetically-based arguments.[59] In contrast to early twentieth-century criminological writings, almost all contemporary criminologists agree that inherited traits at best play a minor role in explaining differences among individuals in illegal behavior (Katz and Chambliss 1991), and do not explain differences in racial and ethnic involvement. Differences between the races in unemployment and poverty are widely understood to reflect social and cultural factors, not racial differences in aptitude. Debates on immigration policy revolve around issues of language, the labor market and tax burdens, not on the issues of racial or national inferiority. When claims of intrinsic racial difference have been introduced into analyses of crime and economic inequality (Herrnstein and Murray 1994; Wilson and Herrnstein 1985; Rushton 1990, 1995a, 1995b), they have been very widely, even vitriolicly, attacked (Fraser 1995; Jacoby and Glauberman 1995).

We have then, not a push toward the reestablishment of a society based formally on racial or class distinctions. The opponents of affirmative action do not propose a return to Jim Crow law; whether honestly or hypocritically, they endorse legal equality, while opposing those measures that could make this equality more than formal. They see no inconsistency in this advocacy because they believe that remedial measures are no longer necessary.[60]

If, as all indicators suggest, this view is mistaken, the result will be to leave in place a division of labor that is *de facto* forced, costumed as an organic division of labor based on complementarity. One of the very few tools left in such a society for managing the strains of actual inequality is punishment. Other options would require an acknowledgment that the Eden of equal possibility has not yet arrived, potentially undermining the legitimacy of many social arrangements.

With this conjunction of a culture of formal legal equality and social structure of high and stable inequality, the proportion of the population processed by the state punishment system expands, and the intensity of punishment increases. Inequality of social outcomes persists or increases, secured through legislation that appears to apply equally to all, but impacts differentially on different social strata; and through the discriminatory exercise of police, prosecutorial and judicial discretion. Packaged and promoted as a "war on crime," escalation in punishment of the magnitude the United States has seen in the past quarter-century is the mark of a society at war with itself.

Particular conceptions of justice make such a war widely acceptable. There is nothing in any given policy domain to determine the
framing that makes a particular justice scheme applicable. In the com-
munes of medieval Italy, crimes involving interpersonal violence were
routinely managed through compensatory and conciliatory cash payments to injured parties or their families, not through state-imposed
retribution. Poverty was the basis for a reduction in the compensation
paid[61] (Blanshei 1981, 1982). Today everyone takes for granted that the
state should punish violent offenders.

A hundred years ago, positivist criminologists urged the abandonment of Enlightenment-era formal equality in punishment based on the
seriousness of the offense on the grounds that it represented an anach-
ronistic survival of metaphysical thinking. Scientific advances, they
contended, undercut the epistemological basis for attributing responsibility to offenders, and thus made considerations of justice irrelevant to
the disposition of criminal cases (Ferri 1900:87–8; Parmalee 1908:190;
Lombroso 1911:361–3, 379–84). The interests of crime prevention, they
thought, could be served best by ignoring questions of justice, and focusing instead on utilitarian concerns, which could be advanced through
incapacitation and rehabilitation of offenders. In recent years dissatisfaction with some of the consequences of this utilitarian framework
(American Friends Service Committee Working Party 1971) have motivated a return to older "metaphysical" principles of retributive justice.

A hundred years ago the courts handled civil suits involving on-the-
job injuries within a legal system that required the establishment of
blame for the accident. The unpredictability of jury awards stimulated
the replacement of intent-based procedures and standards with a no-
fault system (Friedman and Ladinsky 1967), that in recent years has
been extended to automobile insurance.

Supporters of affirmative action have likewise argued for the irrel-
evance of merit. "Admission to graduate school is not a reward for the
meritorious. It is—or ought to be—a method of selecting students who
will do the most good for the population at large" (Henkin 1989). The
purpose of affirmative action is not to affirm an abstract principle of
formal equality, but to remedy an intolerable situation in which distinct
sectors of the population are seriously underrepresented in the more
prestigious and lucrative occupations because of a long history of discrimination. Perhaps prizes in piano competitions and golf contests
should go to the competitors who play best, but for the supporters of
affirmative action it isn't obvious that this principle should determine

who goes to college. A consistent moral justification for programs to widen college attendance should not be attempted, because none can be given (Fish 1996).

Whatever one thinks of Fish's argument, his hope that beliefs about justice and fairness can be dropped from a debate at will is probably as vain as was the hope of the Italian positivists that they could be abandoned in the criminal sphere. For policies to be based on a judgment as to what distributional outcomes are socially useful rather than on earned "desert," whether positive or negative, would require the acceptance of a logic that is at odds with the justifications given for disparate outcomes in a market economy. If it is not worrisome that competition of differently equipped and differently motivated individuals in a formally equal labor market gives some people higher incomes than others, then why should it be a cause for concern if the number of minority students attending the better universities and professional schools drops dramatically,[62] so long as the drop results from a race-blind policy?

To a limited extent it has been possible to depart from principles of universalism. No one has ever mounted a media campaign denouncing the violations of universalism that occur when owners of businesses preferentially hire and promote members of their own family, or colleges give preference to applicants who are children of alumni ("legacies"). In these cases, the violations benefit groups who are not tainted by the stigma of laziness, dependence, and criminality; and they tend to reproduce, rather than challenge, the existing stratification order.

Some departures from market principles and from retributive punishment have also been introduced even when the beneficiaries are stigmatized in this way, for example, when welfare payments are made on the basis of need, and when juvenile delinquents are sentenced on the basis of supposed treatment considerations. However, these departures are insecurely grounded and are proving vulnerable to attack. This vulnerability has increased as the proportion of blacks among the recipients of welfare and the children brought into juvenile court has increased. It is the familiarity and acceptability of allocating goods on the basis of needs and social utility in the Dutch and Scandinavian welfare systems that enables those nations to distribute "bads" in a manner that relies less on a retributive logic. It is not merely that the scale for rewarding and punishment behavior is compressed in these countries, as Wilkins has suggested, but that less weight can be given to the logic of rewards and punishment.

The belief that harsh penalties will effectively deter—held by many proponents of tough punishment—is also the logic of the market. Employers attract employees by outbidding other employers. Entrepreneurs induce investors to invest capital by promising profits on their investment. The greater the inducement, the stronger its motivating force. This is the flip side of the logic of crime deterrence. The appeal of harsh punishment, notwithstanding its high cost and its inefficiency, is its consistency with the logic that works every day in the business world.

Change or Stability

Will current trends continue? The political strength of those sectors of the population most damaged by highly punitive crime policies is weakened by the disenfranchisement of convicted felons and by poor voting turn-outs in low-income neighborhoods.[63] As both major political parties increasingly frame their policies to appeal to wealthy campaign contributors, low-income voters, who are also the least punitive, are less and less likely to think that their vote will make a difference.

A culture that attributes success to individual virtues builds in psychological satisfactions for better-off sectors of the population, to supplement the material benefits they receive. Those who are doing well receive cultural confirmation that their success is due to their own virtues. Those who do not can preserve their egos by attributing their failures to affirmative action programs, however modest and limited their impact.

Empirically, affluence is positively associated with the belief that society is fair (Jackman and Jackman 1983; Jackman 1994), and white Americans are more likely to think society fair than black Americans (Schuman, Steeh, and Bobo 1985; Kluegel and Smith 1986; Sigelman and Welch 1991). Such beliefs are psychologically satisfying because they imply that those who have done well have done so by their own merits. By implication, those who have not done as well are less meritorious. Ward Connerly, a black businessman and regent of the University of California, justified his opposition to affirmative action in higher education by claiming, "Nobody ever gave me any race or sex preferences when I came into the cold world fifty-six years ago, and I made it anyway—high school, college, my own big business, important friends. If I could make it, anybody can...." (Ayres 1996). Since "anybody" isn't making it, his own accomplishment is magnified. Connerly's assumption that if one person can do something, there are no structural obstacles to everyone doing so, is of course a fallacy. Likewise those whose good luck or good behavior enable them to avoid being arrested can have their virtue confirmed through the moral downgrading of those who are punished. The wretched living conditions of those eking out a subsistence on welfare, or who will be deprived of welfare support altogether, only confirm the virtues of all the Connerlys, indeed, of all those who are not at the very bottom. When changes in the economy make it more difficult for many people to feel that they are being validated by their occupational successes, validation by degrading others may offer compensatory satisfactions.

Could moral outrage stir those who gain materially and psychologically from current trends? In principle this is possible. However, some of the most forceful expressions of outrage in recent years have been provoked only by the victimization of someone in the same subgroup. It was blacks and Latinos who rioted after the acquittal of white Los Angeles police officers accused of beating black motorist Rodney King. The beating was widely perceived to be a manifestation of pervasive police mistreatment of black civilians.[64] The acquittal of the officers charged with the beating, following a trial in which a videotape of the beating was introduced as evidence, was understood as a refusal to convict officers responsible for brutality toward blacks, no matter what the evidence. The rioting was fueled by anger toward long-standing abusive police practices toward which the Los Angeles police department had proved indifferent, and against which the courts had provided no protection—not just by the verdict in a particular case (Koon 1992; Gooding-Williams 1993; Ogletree et al. 1995).[65] It was not the population at large, but gays, who rioted in San Francisco after Dan White was convicted on a lesser charge for killing Mayor George Moscone and Supervisor Harvey Milk, who was one of the gay community's most visible, popular, and powerful political leaders (Shilts 1982; Koon 1992; Gooding-Williams 1993).

The belief that these episodes did indeed exemplify systemic injustice rather than individual aberrancy was not universal. Whites, for example, were more likely than blacks to think that the beating of Rodney King was justified, and to believe O.J. Simpson guilty of murder. Whites and blacks differ in attitudes toward capital punishment and toward police use of deadly force (Gallup 1994:213–16, 241–42, 1995:113–16; Cullen et al. 1996).[66] These differences are rooted in the differing histories and experiences of blacks and whites with the police and courts that shape not just abstract principles of justice, but their application to events of the day[67] (Skolnick 1995).

These limited responses are what is expected when the division of labor is forced. Outrage based on similarity—the response Durkheim suggested associated with a low division of labor—continues to occur when the division of labor is complex. But when that complexity embodies systematic disadvantage, exploitation, discrimination, and exclusion, empathetic identification is substantially restricted to members of the group with whom one identifies. That identification may be on the basis of any sort of group membership, not necessarily occupational similarity. Victimization of an out-group member will elicit no reaction, or a much weaker reaction.

The attenuation of outrage when out-group members are victimized is, of course, not total. Many whites were distressed by the Rodney King beating, but they did not respond with the same emotional intensity; their identification with King was reduced. Their outrage does not appear to have been as widely shared or as intense as when black civil rights demonstrators in the South were beaten, shocked with electric cattle prods, set upon by police dogs, and killed in the early 1960s. A generation of anger at crime, welfare recipients, and supposed beneficiaries of preferential hiring, and their ideational linkage with blacks, weakened the sympathy white liberals had for civil rights demonstrators in the 1960s.

Perceptions of the social exclusion and cultural disparagement that accompany forced divisions of labor generate defensive counter-ideologies deprecating dominant groups and affirming the worth, sometimes even the superiority, of the excluded groups. Within these groups, as among dominant groups, solidarity is felt largely with other group members, not with outsiders, who may be viewed with hostility and rejected as allies. In the mid-1960s the appeal of separatism and the growth of anti-white and anti-Jewish sentiment among blacks, followed by similar responses in other groups (e.g., lesbian separatists) created additional barriers to the building of a coalition that might reverse current trends (Gitlin 1995).

Eventually, of course, the cost of new prison construction will prove unsustainable. The vast sums allocated to the military budget during the cold war, however, show that a great deal of room remains for further expansion as long as the population believes it is in danger. With levels of violence and theft falling dramatically, fear may moderate, and enthusiasm for expansion may slacken. However, it is not clear that this will happen as long as politicians and the mass media shape perceptions of crime. In the absence of major changes in American political life, it is difficult to envision a change in the role they play.

Appendix A
Data Sources for the High-Income Nations Sample

Homicide rates are for 1989–92, and are taken from United Nations (1995:484–503) except for Israel, Denmark and Switzerland, whose homicide rates are taken from Interpol (1992). Burglary and auto theft rates are taken from Interpol (1992). I have used 1990 rates except where unavailable. The Australian auto theft rate is from Clarke and Harris (1992). The Australian auto theft rate is for 1987/8; the burglary rate for New Zealand is for 1984, and for Belgium is for 1983. Income data represent income after taxes and transfer parents, and are from World Bank (1994:221). GNP per capita is for 1990, and taken from World Bank (1995). Imprisonment rates are taken from Mauer (1995b) except for Norway, whose rate is taken from Young and Brown (1993). The Israel prison population includes approximately a thousand Israeli "security prisoners," but excludes more than 3000 from the occupied territories.

Notes

Parts of this paper were presented to the 1996 meeting of the Eastern Sociological Society. I am grateful to Lynn Chancer, Robert Stanley, Valerie West and Leslie T. Wilkins for comments on that paper, and to Slawomir Redo for assistance in finding data.

1. Just under half of state prisoners in 1993 were committed for an offense involving interpersonal violence of any sort (Snell 1995:11), while only 28.5 percent of new court commitments were for violent offenses (Gilliard and Beck 1994:10). As the number of drug offenders sent to prison has risen the percentage of violent offenders has fallen dramatically; in 1980, it was 48.2 percent.
2. In 1992, state governments spent $18.75 billion on corrections, up from $4.26 billion in 1980 (Maguire and Pastore 1995:13). Notwithstanding this large increase, the percentage of the population that thinks more should be spent has risen slightly (Maguire and Pastore 1995:161). Scull (1977) argued that the fiscal crisis of the state was leading to decarceration for criminals and psychiatric patients. However, the large-scale deinstitutionalization of psychiatric patients that may have been motivated by cost considerations has not been paralleled by comparable deinstitutionalization for prisoners.
3. In Great Britain the Tories have introduced similar legislation calling for a mandatory life sentence on a second conviction for an offense involving sex or violence.
4. Between 1961 and 1968, U.S. prison populations fell from 220,149 to 182,102 (Maguire and Pastore 1995:540). Index crimes known to the police increased over that period from 2,087,500 to 4,477,200 (Federal Bureau of Investigation 1972:61). Diana Gordon (1990) also notes the inability of crime rates to explain trends in prison populations. In the Netherlands, Australia, England and West

Germany there were also periods when prison populations dropped while crime rates rose (Downes 1988; Savelsberg 1994).

5. To preserve compatibility between the 1972 and 1995 figures, I have deleted arrests for arson from the 1995 rates. With arson included, the 1995 rate is 1140.3 per 100,000.

6. Arrest rates for drug violations rose from 9.5 per 100,000 in 1965 to 317.3 in 1974, falling after that to 147.3 in 1992 (Maguire and Pastore 1995:413). Between 1980 and 1993, the number of inmates in state prisons for drug offenses rose from 19,000 to 186,000—almost a tenfold increase (Snell 1995:11).

7. Support for the death penalty has increased from its lowest point—less than 45 percent—in 1966, to about 79 percent in 1987, its highest in this century (Bohm 1991; Warr 1995; Longmire 1996).

8. Prison populations are not an ideal measure of punitiveness (J. Lynch 1988). They depend on both the number of people sentenced and the length of time they are imprisoned; and are not normed for the number of offenders eligible for imprisonment. Our analysis is limited by the information available about prison populations in different countries.

9. Similar findings are also reported by Wilkins and Pease (1987) and Gottfredson and Clarke (1990:119–25).

10. The nations are New Zealand, Israel, Spain, Hong Kong, Singapore, Australia, United Kingdom, Italy, the Netherlands, Canada, Belgium, Finland, France, Germany, United States, Norway, Denmark, Sweden, Japan, Switzerland. United Arab Emirates was deleted from the sample because it does not publish statistics for crime rates or the distribution of income.

11. Inequality is here measured by the ratio of the disposable income received by the upper 10% to that received by the bottom 20 percent. Sources for the data used in the analyses based on this sample are listed in Appendix A.

12. One might be concerned that rates of auto theft should not be computed on the basis of a country's population, but on the number of automobiles. However, this may not make much difference. Clarke and Harris (1992) give auto theft rates for 19 high-income nations in 1987/8 per 1000 people, and per 1000 cars. I computed the correlation between these two rates; it was 0.905. Earlier studies that found a relationship between inequality and homicide rates computed inequality on the basis of income before taxes and transfer payments, while it is income after taxes and transfer payments that would appear to have the greater theoretical relevance. We have used the latter.

13. These results are based on reported crime rates, and must therefore be considered uncertain. There is no good reason for supposing rates of reporting and recording crimes to be similar in different countries. A number of the countries with rates of reported crime that are higher than those in the United States have rates of reported victimization that are lower than those in the United States, suggesting that reporting and recording rates may vary crossnationally (Van Dijk, Mayhew and Killias 1991).

14. The "crime rate" is defined as the sum of the homicide rate, the burglary rate and the auto theft rate. It is dominated by the two property offense rates, which are not exceptionally high in the United States. Rates of violence, however, are unusually high in the United States. Michalowski and Pearson (1990) and Ouimet and Tremblay (1996) have found homicide rates to be good predictors of imprisonment rates of the U.S. states in cross-sectional analyses. Changes in U.S. homicide rates, however, are essentially unrelated to changes in imprisonment rates.

15. Van Dijk and Mayhew (1992), Young and Brown (1993) and Mauer (1995a, 1995b) reach a similar conclusion.

16. According to the annual report on the state of the economy of the President's Council of Economic Advisors, this trend halted and slightly reversed in the years 1993–1995, as the lowest-income wage-earners gained disproportionately to others. The report attributes this gain to rising employment, the earned-income tax credit, and legislation specifying a higher minimum wage. However, reports issued in 1996 by the University of Michigan and by the Census Bureau show the gap between rich and poor to be widening (Hershey 1997). Data collected by the Federal Reserve Board suggest that income growth between 1992 and 1995 occurred disproportionately in middle-income brackets (Wessel 1997). In the face of these discrepant findings, it is not clear what the most recent trends are.

17. It is the absence of any specification of mechanisms or processes linking one variable to another in Black's writings that leads critics to contend that his ideas, whatever their validity, do not constitute a theory (Greenberg 1983; Hunt 1983). *Felix qui potuit rerum causas cognoscere!*

18. This relationship has become controversial. Galster and Scaturo (1985) and Parker and Horwitz (1986) find no evidence for the existence of a relationship between unemployment and prison admissions among the American states, in panel analyses for short time spans (1974–1979 for Parker and Horwitz), once common trends are removed from the data. However, six years is a short time-span over which to assess the existence of such a relationship. More damaging, Jacobs and Helms (1996) find no support for a relationship between unemployment or inequality and prison admissions between 1950 and 1990, contrary to Black's (1976) proposition. Chiricos and Delone (1992) survey a number of studies, finding the evidence to be mixed. For several reasons, unemployment statistics are less than ideal as indicators of a threatening population. They fail to count many who are not working, e.g., those who have given up on finding work, and they may count some who are working "off the books." Many of those who are unemployed are not a threat, e.g. middle- and upper-class workers who have savings, a network of family and friends who can help out, and options for other sources of employment. If prison admissions respond to a perceived threat, overall unemployment figures may be a poor measure of it.

19. This correlation is not found in non-market economies, such as Poland in the decades after the Second World War (Greenberg 1980), or in the Netherlands, where a generous welfare system has been in place (de Haan 1990).

20. All analyses of the 1991 General Social Survey reported here have been carried out by me.

21. In 1992, 54.3 percent of the new court commitments to prison in thirty-eight states in 1992 were black (Maguire and Pastore 1995:553). Nationally, approximately almost 7 percent of black men are in prison on any given day, (New York Times 1995) and 25 percent of black American men between the ages of twenty and twenty-nine are under correctional supervision (Mauer 1990). In some states and age-brackets the percentages are much higher: in California, almost 40 percent of black men in their twenties are in prison, on probation or parole (Butterfield 1996b). In addition, between 1977 and 1993, 121 white prisoners and 87 black prisoners were executed (Stephan 1994:11).

22. Insofar as ethnic homogeneity is a source of identification and solidarity based on similarity, one might expect greater punitiveness in such societies on the basis of Durkheim's analysis of mechanical solidarity. The observed pattern is just the opposite.

23. In a private communication, Wilkins assures me that his current thinking on this issue does not assume the existence of societal consensus on rewards and punishments.

24. Aggregating data from 1985, 1990 and 1993 from the General Social Survey I find that 45 percent of the respondents who expressed an opinion thought that the government should *not* redistribute income, while 31.8 percent that the government should. These were the only three years in which the question was asked. No trend is evident in the responses.

25. Higher rates of child poverty in the United States compared to other industrialized nations reflect differences in transfer payments and wage structures (Rainwater 1995).

26. They are not mentioned, for example, by Inverarity, Lauderdale and Feld (1982:148), who say, "Durkheim distinguished between two forms of social solidarity, which he called mechanical and organic," or by Treviño (1996).

27. Much effort has been invested in developing alternative models of state formation (Carneiro 1970; Service 1975). Whatever the details, the relationship between stratification and state formation is empirically sound.

28. In the early stages of this transition, the logic of compensation may be preserved. Payment is made to the state (as well as to a private injured party) to make amends for "the breach of the king's peace" (Goebel 1976; Knepper 1991).

29. A parallel account, differing only in detail, could be provided for European countries.

30. The ratio of black to white arrests declined from 3.13 in 1965 to 2.34 in 1992 (Maguire and Pastore 1995:378).

31. In the year ending 30 September 1996, the Equal Employment Opportunity Commission handled 160 bias cases, compared to 643 in 1990 (Myerson 1997).

32. Supreme Court decisions of the 1980s increased the difficulty of proving discrimination and of bringing a class action suit. However, the Civil Rights Act of 1991 made it easier to prove discrimination, and increased the size of a potential award. In response, the number of class action suits alleging discrimination has risen. Nevertheless, discrimination is often difficult to prove, and in many cases it remains difficult to find an attorney willing to bring a complaint (Myerson 1997).

33. A further problem is that many welfare recipients already do work. In one study, 43 percent of a nationally representative sample of AFDC recipients earned income by working an average of thirty-four hours a week. They worked in spurts because continuous employment was not continuously available, or was impractical because of life circumstances such as illness and family responsibilities. Had the recipients worked full-time, their wages would not have been high enough to raise a family of three over the poverty line (Spalter-Roth 1994; Edin 1991).

34. It is very likely the higher degree of economic inequality found in the United States that accounts for its exceptionally low mobility between generations. In a study of intergenerational mobility in Britain, Canada, Finland, Germany, Malaysia, Sweden, and the United States, Björklund and Jäntti (1997) found that the United States and Britain had the lowest rates.

35. A Rand Corporation study of the likely impact of California's new "Three Strikes" legislation projected that it would add between $4.5 billion and $6 billion to the state budget. With new taxes politically impossible, the study noted that the funds would most likely come from higher education, parks, environmental preservation, and other regulatory agencies (Pillsbury 1995).

36. It might be argued that because many of those who acquire criminal arrest, conviction, and imprisonment histories have limited job prospects for reasons unrelated to their criminal records (educational deficits, shortage of jobs), a criminal record cannot have much impact. However, the criminal justice system casts its net widely, especially in minority communities. One study found that two-thirds of nonwhite adult males in California had been arrested before reaching the age

of thirty (Tillman 1987). There is evidence that a criminal record reduces labor market prospects for some individuals (Lott 1990, 1992; Waldfogel 1994a, 1994b; Grogger 1992, 1995), and increases rates of recidivism in the current and subsequent generation (Hagan and Palloni 1990; Laub and Sampson 1993).

37. An econometric analysis based on data from the National Longitudinal Survey of Youth concludes that the level of lawful income available to a youth strongly influences a youth's decision to desist from crime (Pezzin 1995; see also Votey 1991).

38. Research findings regarding the effects of unemployment on crime are less consistent. For time series research using aggregate data, see Cantor and Land (1985), Chiricos (1987), Hale (1991), Hale and Sabbagh (1991) and Land, Cantor and Russell (1995). A panel study by Parker and Horowitz (1986), using aggregate data, also failed to find evidence for an effect of unemployment on criminality. However, unemployment data are notoriously poor. Moreover, many of those who are unemployed are not in serious economic difficulty. They have left one job to seek another; they have savings and financial support from family. Moreover, these studies focus on the instantaneous effects of marginal changes in the unemployment rate. The effects of long-term unemployment and destitution are quite another. Studies of individuals have yielded mixed results. Gottfredson (1985) concluded that juvenile employment had little or no effect on involvement in crime. On the other hand, several other studies found that employment did reduce adult involvement in crime (Rossi, Berk, and Lenihan 1980; Berk, Lenihan, and Rossi 1981; Jurik 1983; Thornberry and Christenson 1984; Votey 1991).

39. Prisons are, of course, not the only element of law enforcement that can potentially contribute to crime prevention. Police officials have maintained that the drop in crime rates of the past five years is due to newly aggressive policing. It may have contributed, though crime rates have also dropped in cities like Los Angeles, where aggressive policing is nothing new (Karmen 1996; Barrett 1997). The possible contribution of employment gains in an economy that has been expanding since 1991, when homicide rates began to drop, has received little attention in this discussion, but may also have played a role.

40. Between 1965 and 1975, AFDC monthly caseloads went from 1 million to 3.5 million, and the number of food stamp recipients from 0.4 million to 17.1 million (Moffitt 1990).

41. In a national survey conducted in 1972, only 10 percent of the respondents said that they would be less likely to vote for a candidate who advocated tougher sentences for lawbreakers, compared to 79 percent who said that they would be more likely. In a Harris poll conducted in 1970, 64 percent thought the courts dealt too leniently with criminals, compared to 3 percent who thought them too severe (Hindelang et al. 1975:206–297). Convicted felons, who might tend to favor lenient policies, are disenfranchised; politicians can safely ignore their policy preferences. Low-income and minority groups, who are somewhat less punitive, are also less likely to vote.

42. The percentages indicating that crime and violence were the most important problem facing the country in the Gallup poll rose from 2 percent in March of 1991 to 5 percent in March of 1992, to 9 percent in January of 1993, to 37 percent in January of 1994, to 52 percent in August of 1994, and then fell to 27 percent in January of 1995. The number of index crimes reported to the police fell steadily over these years. Similarly, the percentages indicating that drugs and drug abuse were the most important problem facing the country rose from 2 percent in January of 1985 to 38 percent in November of 1989, and then fell to 6 percent in January of 1993 (Maguire and Pastore 1995:140).

43. The proportion of respondents identifying crime as the most important problem can change even when public concern about crime is highly stable, because concern about other issues, such as war and unemployment, have declined.

44. By one count, 673 riots occurred in American cities between 1961 and 1968, with 141 taking place in 1968 alone (Spilerman 1971).

45. When the policy implications of the text of the California Civil Rights Initiative, which passed in November, 1996, were explained to survey subjects a year before the vote, many withdrew their support for the measure (L. Harris 1995).

46. A week later, a similar program maintained by the county in which Houston is located, was declared unconstitutional by a Federal judge (Verhovek 1997b).

47. There is more support for attempting to lower the crime rate by spending money on social and economic problems (52 percent) than for spending money on police, prisons, and judges (39 percent) (Maguire and Pastore 1995:171).

48. This question has occurred even to hard-liners. John DiIulio (1996) has recently argued that with welfare being cut back, even the prisons will not be able to stop black crime. The solution, he thought, must come from the black churches. This is surely an instance of a drowning man grasping at straws.

49. In special circumstances, crime may remain off-limits for ideological reasons even when the political system is not corporatist. Ajzenstadt (1996) notes that in the hotly contested national elections just held in Israel, crime was not made an issue by any of the political parties because both embrace a Zionist ideology of inclusiveness. This ideology provides the basis for social work and assimilative efforts directed toward delinquency, which is believed to occur disproportionately among immigrant youth.

50. Even when its low level of corporatism is taken into account, the United States remains an outlier in this regression so long as the analysis is restricted to linear terms in the independent variables.

51. The correlation between corporatism and rankings for redistributiveness, based on data for income taxes, indirect taxes, social service expenditures and redistributive effects taken from Hewitt (1977), is 0.74.

52. High revenues from oil exports have enabled Norway to pay for its welfare state without putting too large a crimp in middle- and upper-class lifestyles. Global competition has placed pressure on other nations to cut back on welfare benefits.

53. This would explain why people resist new knowledge that challenges their attitudes toward capital punishment. It is their attitudes toward the death sentence that is fundamental, not their belief about its effectiveness (Lord, Ross and Lepper 1979).

54. In a national survey, the median guess for the percentage of poor people who are black was 50 percent; the correct figure is 28 percent (Gilens 1996).

55. The impact of these beliefs on popular views of punishment can be seen in the 1991 General Social Survey 9.4 percent of those who believed that people cannot change the course of their lives agreed that the courts are too harsh, compared to 2.8 percent of those who strongly disagreed. The figures for strongly agreeing that law-breakers deserve stiff punishment were 41.5 percent and 48.3 percent.

56. There is a strong relationship between social class and involvement in crime (Braithwaite 1981), suggesting that the assumption of equal ease of compliance is far from valid.

57. Von Hirsch argued that deserts-based sentencing, even if not fully just, would be better for blacks than highly discretionary sentencing systems. In the intervening years, the proportion of prisoners who are black has risen. This may

reflect the structure of the penalties built into the new sentencing schemes. Federal sentencing guidelines, for example, penalize the sale of crack cocaine much more heavily than the sale of the powder form, even though the U.S. Sentencing Commission recommended an equalization. In 1994, just 3.5 percent of federal crack defendants were white, compared to 29.7 percent of the defendants charged with selling powdered cocaine (Jones 1995).

58. In the 1991 General Social Survey, 23.8 percent of those who strongly agree that people can't change the course of their lives strongly support government action to help the poor, compared to 15.One percent of those who strongly disagree.

59. Nelkin and Lindee (1995) point to passages in popular and academic discourse that explain crime genetically, but do not show that they are common or increasing. Perhaps policymakers and analysts give limited attention to research in this area because it offers so little in prevention or control strategies that could be implemented now or in the near future.

60. In a 1995 national survey, 62 percent of whites said that affirmative action programs are no longer needed to overcome discrimination, compared to 11 percent of blacks. Whites were more likely than blacks to think that black children have as good a chance as white children to obtain a good education (85 percent versus 64 percent) and to find a job for which they are qualified (75 percent versus 52 percent) (Gallup 1996:44).

61. When it came to power in thirteenth-century Bologna, the *popolo*, or popular party, was able to introduce state-administered punishment, probably in order to reduce political violence instigated by the feudal magnates, but the new legislation was weakly enforced and eventually abandoned.

62. Linda Wightman has estimated that if law school admissions were to be made only on the basis of grades and test scores (the main criteria for white applicants), the percent of admissions who are black would fall from 26 to 3. Asian-American admissions would fall from 26 to 15 percent, Mexican-American admissions from 32 to 9 percent, and Puerto Rican admissions from 24 to 6 (Strosnider 1997). Restrictions on the use of affirmative-action criteria in admissions decisions at the University of California system imposed in the aftermath of the passage of Proposition 209 in November of 1996, and at the University of Texas Law School following a federal court decision in the Hopwood case have already led to dramatic reductions in the number of black and Hispanic students admitted to law school at UCLA, the University of California at Berkeley, and the University of Texas (Higginbotham 1988; Rosen 1998).

63. According to one recent study, 14 percent of black men cannot vote because they are in prison or have a felony conviction (Butterfield 1997).

64. The belief is empirically well justified (Skolnick and Fyfe 1993; Ogletree et al. 1994).

65. Residents of South Central Los Angeles, where the riot occurred in 1992, were not as moved in 1997 when O.J. Simpson was convicted in a civil trial of causing wrongful death. The large differences in wealth and lifestyle between Simpson and the great majority of black Angelenos reduced their identification with him and muted their response (Goldberg 1997).

66. The racial differences in beliefs about the Rodney King case were smaller than in the O.J. Simpson case, no doubt because the videotape evidence left less room for interpretive maneuver.

67. These differences in experience are also manifesting themselves on juries in criminal trials. There are persistent reports of black jurors who are skeptical of testimony by police officers, and will not vote to convict black defendants even when the evidence is persuasive (Butler 1995; Rosen 1977).

References

Adamson, Christopher. 1984. "Toward a Marxian Penology: Captive Criminal Population or Economic Threats and Resources." *Social Problems* 31:435–58.

Agnew, Spiro T. 1969. *The Wisdom of Spiro T. Agnew*, New York: Ballantine.

American Friends Service Committee Working Party. 1971. *Struggle for Justice: A Report on Crime and Punishment in America.* New York: Hill and Wang.

Ajzenstadt, Mimi. 1996. "Social Control and the Welfare State: Discipline and Regulations in Israel, 1930–1970." Paper presented to the International Conference on Law and Society, Glasgow, Scotland.

Albrecht, Hans-Jorg. 1987. "Foreign Minorities in the Criminal Justice System in the Federal Republic of Germany." *Howard Journal* 26:272–86.

Alderman, J. 1994. "Leading the Public: The Media's Focus on Crime Shaped Sentiment." *The Public Perspective* 5:26–28.

Alesina, A. and D. Rodrik. 1994. "Distributive Policies and Economic Growth." *Quarterly Journal of Economics* 109:465–90.

Alexander, Karl L. and Doris R. Entwisle. 1996. "Early Schooling and Educational Inequality: Socioeconomic Disparities in Children's Learning," pp. 63–79 in J. Clark (ed.) *James S. Coleman.* London: Falmer Press.

Alper, Benedict S., ed. 1974. *Prisons Inside-Out: Alternatives in Correctional Reform.* Cambridge, MA: Ballinger.

Anderson, David C. 1995. *Crime and the Politics of Hysteria: How the Willie Horton Story Changed American Justice.* New York: Times Books.

Andrews, D. A., Ivan Zinger, Robert D. Hoge, James Bonta, Paul Gendreau and Francis T. Cullen. 1990a. "Does Correctional Treatment Work? A Clinically Relevant and Psychologically Informed Meta-Analysis"? *Criminology* 28:369–404.

———. 1990b. "A Human Sciences Approach or More Punishment and Pessimism: A Rejoinder to Lab and Whitehead." *Criminology* 28:419–29.

Antunes, George and P. Hurley. 1977. "The Representation of Criminal Events in Houston's Two Daily Newspapers." *Journalism Quarterly* 54:756–60.

Applebome, Peter. 1996. "Parents Face Consequences As Children's Misdeeds Rise." *New York Times* (April 10):A1, B8.

Arendt, Hannah. 1951. *The Origins of Totalitarianism.* London: Thames and Hudson.

Arenson, Karen W. 1996a. "Study Details CUNY Successes from Open-Admissions Policy." *New York Times* (May 7):A1, B4.

———. 1996b. "Workfare Rules Cause Enrollment to Fall, CUNY Says." *New York Times* (June 1):A1, A25.

Austin, James and John Irwin. 1991. *Who Goes to Prison?*. San Francisco: National Council on Crime and Delinquency.

Avison, William R. and Pamela L. Loring. 1986. "Population Diversity and Cross-National Homicide: The Effects of Inequality and Heterogeneity." *Criminology* 24:733–49.

Ayres, B. Drummond, Jr. 1996. "Fighting Affirmative Action, He Finds His Race an Issue." *New York Times* (April 18):A1, A19.

Barkan, Steven E. and Steven F. Cohn. 1994. "Racial Prejudice and Support for the Death Penalty by Whites." *Journal of Research in Crime and Delinquency* 31:202–9.

Barnes, J. A. 1965. "Durkheim's Division of Labour in Society." *Man* N.S. 1:158–75.

Barrett, Wayne 1997. "Not So Magic Stats: Did Rudy Cut the Murder Rate Himself?" *Village Voice* (January 14):15.

Beckett, Katherine. 1994. "Setting the Public Agenda: 'Street Crime' and Drug Use in American Politics." *Social Problems* 41:425–47.

Beeghley, Leonard and Jeffrey W. Dwyer. 1989. "Income Transfers and Income Inequality." *Population Research and Policy Review* 8:119–42.

Bénabou, Roland. 1993. "Workings of a City: Location, Education, and Production." *Quarterly Journal of Economics* 108:619–51.

———. forthcoming. "Inequality and Growth." *NBER Macro Annual.*

Berk, Richard A., Kenneth J. Lenihan and Peter H. Rossi. 1980. "Crime and Poverty: Some Experimental Evidence from Ex-Offenders." *American Sociological Review* 45:766–86.

Black, Donald. 1976. *The Behavior of Law.* New York: Academic Press.

Blau, Judith R. and Peter M. Blau. 1982. "The Cost of Inequality: Metropolitan Structure and Violent Crime." *American Sociological Review* 47:114–29.

Bailey, William C. 1984. "Poverty, Inequality and City Homicide Rates." *Criminology* 22:531–50.

Biles, David. 1986. "Prisons and Their Problems." In D. Chappell and P. Wilson (eds.) *The Australian Criminal Justice System, the mid-1980s.* Sydney: Butterworths.

Björklund, Anders and Markus Jäntti. 1997. "Intergenerational Mobility of Economic Status: Is the United States Different?" Paper presented to the American Social Sciences Association.

Blank, Rebecca. 1994. "Does a Larger Social Safety Net Mean Less Economic Flexibility?" pp. 157–87 in R. Freeman (ed.) *Working under Different Rules.* New York: Russell Sage Foundation.

Blanshei, Sarah Rubin. 1981. "Criminal Law and Politics in Medieval Bologna." *Criminal Justice History: An International Review* 2:1–30.

———. "Crime and Law Enforcement in Medieval Bologna." *Journal of Social History* 16:121–38.

Blinder, Alan S. 1996. "The $5.15 Question." *New York Times* (May 23): A27.

Bluestone, Barry. 1995. "The Inequality Express." *The American Prospect* 20 (Winter):81–93.

Blumenthal, Sidney. 1986. *The Rise of the Counter-Establishment: From Conservative Ideology to Political Power.* New York: Basic Books.

Blumstein, Alfred. 1987. "Sentencing and the Prison Crowding Problem," pp. 161–78 in S.D. Gottfredson and S. McConville (eds.) *America's Correctional Crisis.* New York: Greenwood Press.

———. 1988. "Prison Populations: A System Out of Control?" pp. 231–66 in M. Tonry and N. Morris (eds.) *Crime and Justice: A Review of Research,* vol. 10. Chicago: University of Chicago Press.

Blumstein, Alfred and Jacqueline Cohen. 1973. "A Theory of the Stability of Punishment." *Journal of Criminal Law and Criminology* 64:198–207.

Blumstein, Alfred, Jacqueline Cohen, Susan E. Martin, and Michael Tonry, eds.1983. *Research on Sentencing: The Search for Reform,* vol. 1. Washington, DC: National Academy Press.

Blumstein, Alfred, Jacqueline Cohen, and Daniel Nagin. 1976. "The Dynamics of a Homeostatic Punishment Process." *Journal of Criminal Law and Criminology* 68:317–34.

Bobo, Lawrence and James R. Kluegel. 1993. "Opposition to Race-Targeting: Self-Interest, Stratification Ideology, or Racial Attitudes." *American Sociological Review* 58:443–64.

Bohm, Robert M. 1990. "American Death Penalty Opinion, 1936–1986: A Critical Examination of the Gallup Polls," pp. 113–45 in R.M. Bohm in *The Death Penalty in America: Current Research.* Cincinnati: Anderson.

Borjas, George B. 1994. "The Economics of Inequality." *Journal of Economic Literature* 32:1667–1717.

Borjas, George B., Richard B. Freeman, and Lawrence F. Katz. 1996. "Searching for the Effect of Immigration on Labor Markets," *American Economic Review* 86:246–51.

Bowers, William G. 1988. "The Effect of Executions is Brutalization, Not Deterrence," 49–89 in K.C. Haas and J.A. Inciardi (eds.) *Challenging Capital Punishment: Legal and Social Science Approaches*. Newbury Park, CA: Sage.

Bowers, William G. and Glenn L. Pierce. 1975. "The Illusion of Deterrence in Isaac Ehrlich's Research on Capital Punishment." *Yale Law Journal* 85:187–208.

Box, Stephen and Chris Hale. 1982. "Economic Crisis and the Rising Prison Population." *Crime and Social Justice* 18:20–35.

———. 1985. "Unemployment, Imprisonment, and Prison Overcrowding." *Contemporary Crises* 9:209–228.

———. 1986. "Unemployment, Crime and Imprisonment, and the Enduring Problem of Prison Overcrowding," pp. 72–96 in R. Matthews and J. Young (eds.) *Confronting Crime*. London: Sage.

Bradsher, Keith. 1995. "Widest Gap in Incomes? Research Points to U.S." *New York Times* (Oct. 27): D2.

Bragg, Rick. 1995. "Chain Gangs to Return to Roads of Alabama." *New York Times* (Mar. 26):I.16.

Braithwaite, John. 1979. *Inequality, Crime, and Public Policy*. Boston: Routledge and Kegan Paul.

———. 1981. "The Myth of Social Class and Criminality Reconsidered." *American Sociological Review* 46:36–57.

Braithwaite, John and Valerie Braithwaite. 1986. "The Effect of Income Inequality and Social Democracy on Homicide." *British Journal of Criminology* 20:45–53.

Brennan, Mark G. 1997. "Lax Punishments." *New York Times* (Jan. 9): A20.

Burtless, Gary. 1990. "Earnings Inequality over the Business and Demographic Cycles," pp. 77–122 in G. Burtless (ed.) *A Future of Lousy Jobs?*. Washington, DC: Brookings Institution.

Butler, Paul. 1995. "Racially Based Jury Nullification: Black Power in the Criminal Justice System." *Yale Law Journal* 105:677–725.

Butterfield, Fox. 1996a. "States Revamping Laws on Juveniles as Felonies Soar." *New York Times*, Section 1 (May 12):1, 24.

———. 1996b. "Study Examines Race and Justice in California." *New York Times* (Feb. 14): A12.

———. 1997. "Many Black Men Barred From Voting." *New York Times* (Jan. 30): A12.

Calder, James B. 1982. "Presidents and Crime Control: Kennedy, Johnson and Nixon and the Influences of Ideology." *Presidential Studies Quarterly* 12:574–89.

Cantor, David and Kenneth C. Land. 1985. "Unemployment and Crime Rates in the Post-World War II United States: A Theoretical and Empirical Analysis." *American Sociological Review* 50:317–23.

———. 1991. "Exploring Possible Temporal Relationships of Unemployment and Crime: Comment on Hale and Sabbagh," *Journal of Research in Crime and Delinquency* 28:418–25.

Capaldi, Nicholas. 1985. *Out of Order: Affirmative Action and the Crisis of Doctrinaire Liberalism*. Buffalo, NY: Prometheus.

Cappell, Charles L. and Gresham Sykes. 1991. "Prison Commitments, Crime, and Unemployment: A Theoretical and Empirical Specification for the United States, 1933–1985." *Journal of Quantitative Criminology* 7:155–99.

Card, David and Alan B. Krueger. 1995. *Myth and Measurement: The New Economics of the Minimum Wage*. Princeton, NJ: Princeton University Press.

Carneiro, Robert. 1970. "A Theory of the Origin of the State." *Science* 169:733–38.

Carter, Steven L. 1991. *Reflections of an Affirmative Action Baby*. New York: Basic Books.

Chambliss, William J. 1994. "Policing the Ghetto Underclass: The Politics of Law and Law Enforcement." *Social Problems* 41:177–94.

———. 1995. "Crime Control and Ethnic Minorities: Legitimizing Racial Oppression by Creating Moral Panics" pp. 235–58 in D.F. Hawkins (ed.) *Ethnicity, Race, and Crime: Perspectives across Time and Place*. Albany: State University of New York Press.

Chambliss, William J. and Robert Seidman. 1990. *Law, Order, and Power*, 2d ed. Reading, MA: Addison-Wesley.

Chancer, Lynn and Pamela Donovan. 1996. "A Mass Psychology of Punishment: Crime and the Futility of Rationally Based Approaches." *Social Justice* 21:50–71.

Chang, Roberto. 1994. "Income Inequality and Economic Growth: Evidence and Recent Theories." *Economic Review* (Federal Reserve Bank of Atlanta) 79:1–10.

Chernak, Steven. 1995. *Victims in the News: Crime and the American News Media*. Boulder, CO: Westview Press.

Chiricos, Theodore G. 1987. "Rates of Crime and Unemployment: An Analysis of Aggregate Research Evidence." *Social Problems* 34:187–212.

Chiricos, Theodore G. and Charles Crawford. 1995. "Race and Imprisonment: A Contextual Assessment of the Evidence," pp. 281–309 in D.F. Hawkins *Ethnicity, Race, and Crime: Perspectives Across Time and Place*. Albany: State University of New York Press.

——— and Miriam Delone. 1994. "Labor Surplus and Punishment: A Review and Assessment of Theory and Evidence." *Social Problems* 39:421–46.

Christie, Nils 1993. *Crime Control as Industry*. London: Routledge.

Clarke, George R. G. 1995. "More Evidence on Income Distribution and Growth." *Journal of Development Economics* 47:403–27.

Clarke, Ronald V. and Patricia M. Harris. 1992. "Auto Theft and Its Prevention," pp. 1–54in M. Tonry (ed.) *Crime and Justice: A Review of Research*, vol. 16. Chicago: University of Chicago Press.

Coleman, James S., S. Kelly, and J. Moore. 1975. *Trends in School Segregation, 1968–1973*. Washington, DC: The Urban Institute.

Collins, Philip. 1968. *Dickens and Crime*. Bloomington: Indiana University Press.

Crew, B. Keith. 1990. "Acting Like Cops: The Social Reality of Crime and Law on TV Police Dramas," pp. 131–42 in C.R. Sanders (ed.) *Marginal Conventions: Popular Culture, Mass Media and Social Deviance*. Bowling Green, OH: Bowling State University Press.

Crow, I., P. Richardson, C. Riddington and F. Simon. 1989. *Unemployment, Crime, and Offenders*. New York: Routledge.

Cullen, Francis T., Liqun Cao, James Frank, Robert H. Langworthy, Sandra Lee Browning, Renée Kopache, and Thomas J. Stevenson. 1996. "'Stop Or I'll Shoot': Racial Differences in Support of Police Use of Deadly Force." *American Behavioral Scientist* 39:449–60.

Cullen, F. T., G. A. Clark, and J. F. Wozniak. 1985. "Explaining the Get Tough Movement: Can the Public Be Blamed?" *Federal Probation* 49:16–24.

Cullen, F. T., J. B. Cullen and J. F. Wozniak. 1988. "Is Rehabilitation Dead? The Myth of the Punitive Public." *Journal of Criminal Justice* 16:303–17.

Cullen, Francis T. and Paul Gendreau. 1989. "The Effectiveness of Correctional Rehabilitation." In L. Goodstein and D. L. MacKenzie (eds.) *The American Prison: Issues in Research Policy.* New York: Plenum.

Cullen, F. T., S. E. Skovron, J. E. Scott, and V. S. Burton, Jr. 1990. "Public Support for Correctional Treatment: The Tenacity of the Rehabilitative Ideology." *Criminal Justice and Behavior* 17:6–18.

Danziger, Sheldon and Peter Gottschalk, eds. 1993. *Uneven Tides: Rising Inequality in America.* New York: Russell Sage Foundation.

DeFronzo, James. 1983. "Economic Assistance to Impoverished Americans: Relationship to Incidence of Crime." *Criminology* 21:119–36.

DeParle, Jason. 1996a. "Class Is No Longer a Four-Letter Word." *New York Times Magazine* (March 17):40–43.

———. 1996b. "Slamming the Door." *New York Times Magazine* (Oct. 16):52–57, 68, 94, 105.

DiMaggio, Paul, John Evans and Bethany Bryson. 1996. "Have Americans' Social Attitudes Become More Polarized?" *American Journal of Sociology* 102:690–755.

DiIulio, John J., Jr. . 1994. "The Question of Black Crime." *The Public Interest* 117:3–32.

———. 1995. "White Lies about Black Crime." *The Public Interest* 118:30–44.

———. 1996 "Black Youth Crime: Churches Are the Answer." New York University. Fortunoff Colloquium.

DiNardo, John, Nicole M. Fortin and Thomas Lemieux, "Labor Market Institutions and the Distribution of Wages, 1973–1990: A Non-Parametric Approach," *Econometrica* 64:1001–1044.

Donziger, Steven R. 1996. *The Real War on Crime: The Report of the National Criminal Justice Commission.* New York: HarperPerrenial.

Downes, David. 1988. *Contrasts in Tolerance: Post-War Penal Policy in the Netherlands and England and Wales* Oxford: Clarendon Press.

———. 1990. "The Case for Going Dutch: The Lessons of the Post-War Penal Policy." *Political Quarterly* 63:12–24.

Duffee, David and R. Richard Ritti. 1979. "Correctional Policy and Public Values." *Criminology* 14:449–60.

Duncan, Greg J., B. Gustaffson, R. Hauser, G. Schmauss, M. Messenger, R. Muffels, B. Nolan and J. C. Ray. 1993. "Poverty Dynamics in Eight Countries," *Journal of Population Economics* 6:215–34.

Durkheim, Émile. 1933. *The Division of Labor in Society.* Trans. George Simpson. New York: Macmillan.

———. 1992. "Two Laws of Penal Evolution." Tr. T. Anthony Jones and Andrew T. Scull. Pp. 21–49 in M. Gane (ed.) *The Radical Sociology of Durkheim and Mauss.* New York: Routledge.

Eastland, Terry. 1990. *Ending Affirmative Action: The Case for Colorblind Justice.* New York: Basic Books.

Eberts, Paul and Kent P. Schwirian. 1968. "Metropolitan Crime Rates and Relative Deprivation." *Criminologica* 5:43–52.

Edin, Kathryn. 1991. "Surviving the Welfare System: How AFDC Recipients Make Ends Meet in Chicago." *Social Problems* 38:462–74.

Ehrlich, Isaac. 1975. "The Deterrent Effect of Capital Punishment: A Question of Life and Death." *American Economic Review* 65: 397–417.

Ellsworth, Phoebe and Lee Ross. 1983. "Public Opinion and Capital Punishment: A Close Examination of the Views of Abolitionists and Retentionists." *Crime and Delinquency* 29:116–69.

Elmer, E. 1967. *Children in Jeopardy: A Study of Abused Minors and their Families.* Pittsburgh: University of Pittsburgh Press.

Engels, Frederick. 1942. *The Origins of the Family, Private Property and the State.* New York: International Publishers.

Ericson, Richard Victor, Patricia M. Baranek, and Janet B. L. Chan. 1991. *Representing Order: Crime, Law, and Justice in the News Media.* Toronto: University of Toronto Press.

Farnworth, Margaret, Katherine Bennett, and Vincent M. West. 1996. "Mail vs. Telephone Surveys of Criminal Justice Attitudes: A Comparative Analysis." *Journal of Quantitative Criminology* 12:113–33.

Federal Bureau of Investigation. 1996. *Crime in the United States—1995.* Uniform Crime Reports, Department of Justice. Washington, DC: USGPO.

———. 1973. *Crime in the United States—1972.* Uniform Crime Reports, Department of Justice. Washington, DC: USGPO.

Fellmuth, Robert C. 1970. "The Regulatory-Industrial Complex." In B. Wasserstein (ed.) *With Justice for Some.* Boston: Beacon.

Ferri, Enrico. 1905. *Socialism and Positive Science (Darwin, Spencer,Marx).* Edith C. Harvey, trans. London: The Socialist Library.

Finckenauer, James O. 1988. "Public Support for the Death Penalty: Retribution as Just Deserts or Retribution as Revenge?" *Justice Quarterly* (March):81–100.

Finder, Alan. 1996. "Welfare Clients Outnumber Jobs They Might Fill," *New York Times* (Aug. 25):1, 46.

Fine, Bob. 1980. "The Birth of Bourgeois Punishment," *Crime and Social Justice* 13 (Summer):19–26.

Firebaugh, Glenn and Kenneth E. Davis. 1988. "Trends in Anti-black Prejudice, 1972–1984: Region and Cohort Effects." *American Journal of Sociology* 94:251–72.

Fischer, Claude S., Michael Hout, Martín Sánchez Jankowski, Samuel R. Lucas, Ann Swidler and Kim Voss. 1996. *Inequality by Design: Cracking the Bell Curve Myth.* Princeton, NJ: Princeton University Press.

Fish, Stanley. 1996. "When Principles Get in the Way." *New York Times* (Dec. 26):A17.

Fishman, Mark. 1978. "Crime Waves as Ideology." *Social Problems* 25:531–43.

———. 1981. "Police News: Constructing an Image of Crime." *Urban Life* 9:371–94.

Flanagan, Timothy J. 1996. "Public Opinion and Public Policy in Criminal Justice," pp. 151–158 in T.J. Flanagan and D. R. Longmire (eds.) *Americans View Crime and Justice: A National Opinion Survey.*Thousand Oaks, CA: Sage.

Fogel, David. 1975. *"...We Are the Living Proof...": The Justice Model for Corrections.* Cincinnati: W. H. Anderson.

Foucault, Michel. 1977. *Discipline and Punish: The Birthday of the Prison.* Trans. Alan Sheridan. New York: Pantheon.

Frankel, Marvin E. 1972. *Criminal Sentencing: Law Without Order.* New York: Hill and Wang.

Fraser, Steven, ed. 1995. *The Bell Curve Wars: Race, Intelligence, and the Future of America.* New York: Basic Books.

Freeman, Richard. 1993. "How Much Has Deunionization Contributed to the Rise in Male Earnings Inequality?" pp. 100–21 in S. Danziger and P. Gottschalk (eds.) *Uneven Tides: Rising Inequality in America.* New York: Russell Sage Foundation.

French, Howard W. 1997. "The Ritual Slaves of Ghana: Young and Female." *New York Times* (Jan. 20):A1, A5.

Friedman, Lawrence M. and Jack Ladinsky. 1967. "Social Change and the Law of Industrial Accidents." *Columbia University Law Review* 7:50–82.

Fyfe, James J. 1983. "The NIJ Study of the Exclusionary Rule." *Criminal Law Bulletin* 19:253–60.

Gallup, George, Jr. 1994. *The Gallup Poll: Public Opinion 1993*. Wilmington, DE: Scholarly Resources.
————. 1995. *The Gallup Poll: Public Opinion 1994*. Wilmington, DE: Scholarly Resources.
————. 1996. *The Gallup Poll: Public Opinion 1995*. Wilmington, DE.: Scholarly Resources.
Galster, G. A. and L. A. Scaturo. 1995. "The U.S. Criminal Justice System: Unemployment and the Severity of Punishment." *Journal of Research in Crime and Delinquency* 22:163–89.
Garland, David. 1985. *Punishment and Welfare*. Aldershot: Gower.
Gelles, Richard J. 1974. *The Violent Home*. Beverly Hills, CA: Sage.
Geraghty, Mary. 1997. "Finances Are Becoming More Crucial in Students' College Choice, Survey Finds." *Chronicle of Higher Education* (Jan. 17): A41.
Gerber, Jurg and Simone Engelhardt-Greer. 1996. "Just and Painful: Attitudes toward Sentencing Criminals." *Americans View Crime and Justice: A National Public Opinion Survey*. Thousand Oaks, CA: Sage.
Gil, David. 1970. *Violence against Children: Physical Child Abuse in the United States*. Cambridge, MA: Harvard University Press.
Gilder, George F. 1981. *Wealth and Poverty*. New York: Basic Books.
Giles, Martin. 1996. "'Race Coding' and White Opposition to Welfare." *American Political Science Review* 90:593–604.
Gilliard, Darrel K. and Allen J. Beck. 1994. *Prisoners in 1993*. Bureau of Justice Statistics Bulletin. U.S. Department of Justice. Office of Justice Programs.
————. 1996. *Prison and Jail Inmates, 1995*. Washington, DC: U.S. Department of Justice, Office of Justice Programs.
Gitlin, Todd. 1995. *The Twilight of Common Dreams*. New York: Henry Holt.
Glasberg, Davita Silfen and Dan Skidmore. 1997. *Corporate Welfare Policy and the Welfare State: Bank Regulation and the Savings and Loan Bailout*. Hawthorne, NY: Aldine de Gruyter.
Goebel, Julius, Jr. 1976. *Felony and Misdemeanor: A Study in the History of Criminal Law*. Philadelphia: University of Pennsylvania Press.
Goldberg, Carey. 1997. "Geography and Class in Two Simpson Verdicts." *New York Times* (Feb. 7): A20.
Gooding-Williams, Robert, ed. 1993. *Reading Rodney King, Reading Urban Uprising*. New York: Routledge.
Gordon, Diana R. 1990. *The Justice Juggernaut: Fighting Street Crime, Controlling Citizens*. New Brunswick, NJ: Rutgers University Press.
Gordon, David M. 1996. *Fat and Mean: The Corporate Squeeze of Working Americans and the Myth of Managerial "Downsizing"*. New York: The Free Press.
Gottfredson, Denise C. 1985. "Youth Employment, Crime, and Schooling: A Longitudinal Study of a National Sample." *Developmental Psychology* 21:419–32.
Gottfredson, Don M. and Ronald V. Clarke. 1990. *Policy and Theory in Criminal Justice*. Brookfield, VT: Gower.
————. 1989. "Imprisonment and Unemployment: A Comment." *Journal of Quantitative Criminology* 5:187–92.
Gottfredson, Stephen D. and Ralph B. Taylor. 1987. "Attitudes of Correctional Policymakers and the Public," pp. 57–75 in S.D. Gottfredson and S. McConville (eds.) *America's Correctional Crisis: Prison Populations and Public Policy*. New York: Greenwood Press.
Grasmick, Harold G., Elizabeth Davenport, Mitchell B. Chamlin and Robert J. Bursik, Jr. 1992. "Protestant Fundamentalism and the Retributive Doctrine of Punishment." *Criminology* 30:21–46.

Greenberg, David F. 1977a. "The Dynamics of Oscillatory Punishment Processes." *Journal of Criminal Law and Criminology* 68:643–55.

————. 1977b. "The Correctional Effects of Corrections: A Survey of Evaluation Studies," pp. 11–48 in D.F. Greenberg (ed.) *Corrections and Punishment*. Beverly Hills: Sage.

————. 1980. "Penal Sanctions in Poland: A Test of Alternative Models." *Social Problems* 28:194–204.

————. 1983. "Donald Black's Sociology of Law: A Critique." *Law and Society Review*: 17:337–68.

————. 1989. "Unemployment and Imprisonment: A Comment." *Journal of Quantitative Criminology* 5:187–91.

————. 1990. "The Cost-Benefit Analysis of Imprisonment." *Social Justice* 17:49–75.

Greenberg, David F. and Ronald C. Kessler. 1982. "The Effect of Arrests on Crime: A Multivariate Panel Analysis." *Social Forces* 60:771–90.

Greenberg, David F., Ronald C. Kessler and Charles H. Logan. 1979. "A Panel Analysis of Crime Rates and Arrest Rates." *American Sociological Review* 44:843–50.

Greenhouse, Linda. 1996. "How Congress Curtailed the Courts' Jurisdiction." *New York Times* (Oct. 27): E5.

Greenwood, Peter. 1996. *Diverting Children from a Life of Crime: Measuring Costs and Benefits*. Santa Monica, CA: Rand.

Grogger, Jeffrey. 1992. "Arrests, Persistent Youth Joblessness, and Black/White Employment Differences," *Review of Economics and Statistics* 74:100–106.

———— 1995. "The Effect of Arrests on the Employment and Earnings of Young Men." *Quarterly Journal of Economics* 110:51–71.

Gross, Hyman. 1979. *A Theory of Criminal Justice*. New York: Oxford University Press.

de Haan, Willem. 1990. *The Politics of Redress: Crime, Punishment and Penal Abolition*. Boston: Unwin Hyman.

Hacker, Andrew. 1992. *Two Nations: Black and White, Separate, Hostile, Unequal*. New York: Scribner.

Hagan, John and Alberto Palloni. 1990. "The Social Reproduction of a Criminal Class in Working-Class London circa 1950–1980." *American Journal of Sociology* 96:265–99.

Hale, Chris. 1989. "Unemployment, Imprisonment, and the Stability of Punishment Hypotheses: Some Results Using Cointegration and Error Correction Models." *Journal of Quantitative Criminology* 5:169–86.

————. 1991. "Unemployment and Crime: Differencing Is No Substitute for Modeling." *Journal of Research in Crime and Delinquency* 28:426–29.

Hale, Chris and Dima Sabbagh. 1991. "Testing the Relationship between Unemployment and Crime: A Methodological Comment and Empirical Analysis Using Time Series Data from England and Wales." *Journal of Research in Crime and Delinquency* 28:400–17.

Harris, Louis. 1995. "Affirmative Action and the Voter." *New York Times* (July 31): A13.

Harris, Marvin. 1981. *America Now: The Anthropology of a Changing Culture*. New York: Simon and Schuster.

Head, Simon. 1996. "The New, Ruthless Economy." *The New York Review of Books* (Feb. 26):47–52.

Henderson, David R. 1997. "Canada's High Unemployment Rate Is No Mystery." *Wall Street Journal* (Feb. 7): A19.

Henig, Jeffrey R. 1994. *Rethinking School Choice*. Princeton, NJ: Princeton University Press.

Henkin, Josh. 1989. "The Meretricious Origins of Merit: Or, Why Jewish Males Oughtn't Be So Smug." *Tikkun* 4.1:53–7.

Herrnstein, Richard J. and Charles Murray. 1994. *The Bell Curve: Intelligence and Class Structure in American Life*. New York: The Free Press.

Hershey, Robert D., Jr. 1997. "Clinton Aides Say That Income Gap Narrows." *New York Times* (Feb. 11): D3.

Hewitt, Christopher. 1977. "The Effect of Political Democracy and Social Democracy on Equality in Industrial Societies: A Cross-National Comparison." *American Sociological Review* 42:450–64.

Higginbotham, A. Leon, Jr. 1998. "Breaking Thurgood Marshall's Promise." *New York Times Magazine* (Jan. 18):28–9.

Hindelang, Michael J., Christopher S. Dunn, Alison L. Aumick, and L. Paul Sutton, eds. 1975. *Sourcebook of Criminal Justice Statistics—1974*. U.S. Law Enforcement Assistance Administration, National Criminal Justice Information and Statistics Service. Washington, DC: Government Printing Office.

Hindelang, Michael J., Michael R. Gottfredson, and Timothy J. Flanagan, eds. 1981. *Sourcebook of Criminal Justice Statistics—1980*. U.S. Department of Justice, Bureau of Justice Statistics. Washington, DC: U.S. Government Printing Office.

Hinds, Michael deCourcy. 1991. "Minority Business Set back Sharply by Courts' Rulings." *New York Times* (Dec. 23): A1, A15.

Holmes, Steven A. 1996a. "Study Finds Rising Number of Black-White Marriages." *New York Times* July 4): A16.

———. 1996b. "In New Guide, U.S. Retreats on Contracts for Minorities." *New York Times* (May 23):A26.

Home Office. 1990. *Prison Statistics: England and Wales, 1989*. London: HMSO.

Horwitz, Allan V. 1990. *The Logic of Social Control*. New York: Plenum.

Howard, John A. 1780. *The State of the Prisons in England and Wales*. Warrington: W. Eyres.

Howard, O. O. 1866. *Report of the Assistant Commissioners of the Freedmen's Bureau*. Senate Executive doc. no. 27, 39th congress, 1st sess. (Senate Executive Documents, vol. 2, Serial 1238).

Hudson, Barbara A. 1993. *Penal Policy and Social Justice*. Toronto: University of Toronto Press.

Humphries, Drew and David F. Greenberg. 1981. "The Dialectics of Crime Control." In D.F. Greenberg (ed.) *Crime and Capitalism: Readings in Marxist Criminology*. Palo Alto: Mayfield.

Hunt, Alan. 1983. "Behavioural Sociology of Law: A Critique of Donald Black." *Journal of Law and Society* 10:19–33.

Ibrahim, Youssef M. 1996. "Welfare's Cozy Coat Eases Norwegian Cold." *New York Times* (Dec. 13): A1, A12.

Ignatieff, Michael. 1978. *A Just Measure of Pain: The Penitentiary in the Industrial Revolution, 1750–1850*. New York: Pantheon.

Interpol. 1992. *International Crime Statistics, 1989–1990*. Saint Cloud, France: Interpol.

Inverarity, James, Pat Lauderdale, and Barry C. Feld. 1983. *Law and Society: Sociological Perspectives on Criminal Law*. Boston: Little Brown.

Inverarity, James and L. M. Tedrow. 1987. "Unemployment, Crime and Imprisonment: A Pooled Cross Section and Time Series Analysis." Paper presented to the Society for the Study of Social Problems.

Jackman, Mary R. 1994. *The Velvet Glove: Paternalism and Conflict in Gender, Class and Race Relations*. Berkeley and Los Angeles: University of California Press.

Jackman, Mary R. and Robert W. Jackman. 1983. *Class Awareness in the United States*. Berkeley and Los Angeles: University of California Press.

Jackson, Pamela Irving. 1995. "Minority Group Threat, Crime, and the Mobilization of Law in France," pp. 341–59 in D.F. Hawkins (ed.) *Ethnicity, Race, and*

Crime: Perspectives across Time and Place. Albany: State University of New York.

Jacobs, David and Ronald E. Helms. 1996. "Toward a Political Model of Incarceration: A Time-Series Examination of Multiple Explanations for Prison Admission Rates." *American Journal of Sociology* 102:323–57.

Jacoby, Russell and Naomi Glauberman, eds.1995. *The Bell Curve Debate: History, Documents, Opinions.* New York: Times Books.

Jankovic, Ivan. 1977. "Labor Market and Imprisonment." *Crime and Social Justice* 8:17–31.

Jenkins, Richard L. and Waln K. Brown. 1988. *The Abandonment of Delinquent Behavior.* Westport, CT: Greenwood Press.

Jencks, Christopher. 1992. *Race, Poverty and the Underclass.* Cambridge, MA: Harvard University Press.

Junger, Marianne. 1988. "Racial Discrimination in the Netherlands." *Sociology and Social Research* 72:211–16.

Jones, Charisse. 1995. "Crack and Punishment: Is Race the Issue?". *New York Times* (Oct. 28): 1,10.

Juhn, Chinhu, Kevin M. Murphy, and Brooks Pierce. 1993. "Wage Inequality and the Rise in Returns to Skill," *Journal of Political Economy* 101:410–42.

Jurik, Nancy C. 1983. "The Economics of Female Recidivism: A Study of TARP Female Offenders." *Criminology* 21:603–22.

Kalmijn, Matthijs. 1993. "Trends in Black/White Intermarriage." *Social Forces* 72: 22–41.

Karmen, Andrew. 1996. "What's Driving New York's Crime Rates Down?" *Law Enforcement News* (Nov. 30):8–10.

Karoly, Lynn A. 1992. "Changes in the Distribution of Individual Earnings in the United States, 1967–1986." *Review of Economics and Statistics* 74:107–15.

———. 1993. "The Trend in Inequality among Families, Individuals, and Workers in the United States: A Twenty-five Year Perspective" pp. 1–97 in S. Danziger and P. Gottschalk (eds.) *Uneven Tides: Rising Inequality in America.* New York: Russell Sage Foundation.

Katz, Janet and William J. Chambliss. 1991. "Biology and Crime," pp. 245–71 in J.F. Sheley (ed.) *Criminology: A Contemporary Handbook.* Belmont, CA: Wadsworth.

Kemp, Alice Abel. 1994. *Women's Work: Degraded and Devalued.* Englewood Cliffs, NJ: Prentice-Hall.

Kick, Edward L. and Gary D. LaFree. 1985. "Development and the Social Context of Murder and Theft." *Comparative Social Research* 8:37–58.

Kilborn, Peter T. 1994. "Backlog of Cases Is Overwhelming Jobs-Bias Agency." *New York Times* (Nov. 25): A1.

———. 1995. "White Males and Management: Report Finds Prejudices Block Women and Minorities." *New York Times* (Mar. 17): A14.

Killias, Martin. 1986. "Power Concentration, Legitimation Crisis, and Penal Severity," pp. 95–117 in W.B. Groves and G. Newman (eds.) *Punishment and Privilege.* New York: Harrow and Heston.

Kleck, Gary. 1981. "Racial Discrimination in Criminal Sentencing: A Critical Evaluation of the Evidence on the Death Penalty." *American Sociological Review* 46:783–805.

Klein, Lawrence R., Brian Forst, and Victor Filatov. 1978. "The Deterrent Effect of Capital Punishment: An Assessment of Estimates," pp. 336–60 in A. Blumstein, J. Cohen, and D. Nagin (eds.) *Deterrence and Incapacitation: Estimating the Effects of Criminal Sanctions on Crime Rates.* Washington, DC: National Academy of Sciences.

Klein, S., J. Petersilia, and S. Turner. 1990. "Race and Imprisonment Decisions in California," *Science* 247:812–16.

Kluegel, James R. and Eliot R. Smith. 1986. *Beliefs about Inequality: Americans' Beliefs about What Is and What Ought to Be.* New York: Aldine de Gruyter.

Knepper, Paul. 1991. "A Brief History of Profiting from the Punishment of Crime." Paper presented to the American Society of Criminology.

Koon, Stacey, with Robert Deitz. 1992. *Presumed Guilty: The Tragedy of the Rodney King Affair.* Washington, DC: Regnery Gateway.

Kotlowitz, Alex. 1994. "Their Crimes Don't Make Them Adults." *New York Times* (Feb. 13):VI:40–41.

Krahn, Harvey, Timothy J. Hartnagel and John W. Gartrell. 1986. "Income Inequality and Homicide Rates: Cross-National Data and Criminological Theories." *Criminology* 24:269–95.

Kress, June B. 1994. "Homeless Fatigue Syndrome: The Backlash against the Crime of Homelessness in the 1990s." *Social Justice* 21:85–108.

Krugman, Paul R. 1992. "The Rich, the Right, and the Facts," *The American Prospect* 11 (Fall):19–31.

———. 1994. *The Age of Diminished Expectations.* Cambridge, MA: MIT Press.

Kunen, James S. 1995. "Teaching Prisoners a Lesson." *The New Yorker* (July 10):34–39.

Kuttner, Robert. 1996. *Everything for Sale: The Virtues and Limits of Markets.* New York: Alfred A. Knopf.

Lab, S. P. and J. T. Whitehead. 1990. "From 'Nothing Works' to 'The Appropriate Works': The Latest Stop on the Search for the Secular Grail." *Criminology* 28:405–17.

Laffargue, B. and T. Godefroy. 1989. "Economic Cycles and Punishment: Unemployment and Imprisonment." *Contemporary Crises* 13:371–404.

Landry, Bart. 1987. *The New Black Middle Class.* Berkeley and Los Angeles: University of California Press.

Langan, Patrick A. 1991. "America's Soaring Prison Population." *Science* 251:1568–73.

Langbein, John H. 1977. *Torture and the Law of Proof: Europe and England in the Ancien Regime.* Chicago: University of Chicago Press.

Laub, John H. and Robert J. Sampson. 1993. "The Long Term Effect of Punishment." Unpublished paper.

Lavin, David E. and David Hyllegard. 1996. *Changing the Odds: Open Admissions and the Life Chances of the Disadvantaged.* New Haven, CT: Yale University Press.

Lederman, Douglas. 1996a. "Split on Racial Preferences: Federal Courts Are Rejecting Affirmative Action, But Colleges Vow to Defend It," *Chronicle of Higher Education* (April 5):A25, A29.

———. 1996b. "College Leaders Plan Strategy to Defend Affirmative Action." *Chronicle of Higher Education* (May 31): A24.

Levin, Michael. 1989. "Affirmative Action vs. Jewish Men." *Tikkun* 4.1:50–3.

Levitt, Steven D. 1996. "The Effect of Prison Population Size on Crime Rates: Evidence from Prison Overcrowding Litigation." *Quarterly Journal of Economics* 111:319–51.

Levy, Frank and Richard J. Murnane. 1992. "U.S. Earnings Levels and Earnings Inequality: A Review of Recent Trends and Proposed Explanations." *Journal of Economic Literature* 30:1333–81.

Lewis, Anthony. 1995. "Is It a Zeal to Kill?" *New York Times* (Dec. 8): A31.

Lichter, Daniel T. and David J. Eggebeen. 1993. "Rich Kids, Poor Kids: Changing Income Inequality among American Children." *Social Forces* 71:761–80.

Lilly, J. Robert and Paul Knepper. 1993. "The Corrections-Commercial Complex." *Crime and Delinquency* 39:150–66.

Lipton, Douglas, Robert Martinson and Judith Wilks. 1975. *The Effectiveness of Correctional Treatment: A Survey of Treatment Evaluation Studies.* New York: Praeger.

Loftin, Colin and Robert H. Hill. 1974. "Regional Subculture and Homicide: An Examination of the Gastil-Hackney Thesis." *American Sociological Review* 39:714–24.

Lombroso, Cesare. 1871. *L'uomo bianco e l'uomo di colore: letture sull' origine e le varietà delle razze umane.* Padua: F.Sacceto.

———. 1876. *L'uomo delinquente.* Milan: Hoepli.

———. 1911. *Crime: Its Causes and Its Remedies.* Trans. Henry P. Horton. Boston: Little Brown.

Longmire, Dennis R. 1996. "America's Attitudes about the Ultimate Weapon," pp. 93–108 in T.J. Flanagan and D.R. Longmire (eds.) *Americans View Crime and Justice: A National Public Opinion Survey.* Thousand Oaks, CA: Sage.

Lord, C., L. Ross, and M. Lepper. 1979. "Biased Assimilation and Attitude Polarization: The Effects of Prior Theories on Subsequently Considered Evidence," *Journal of Personality and Social Psychology* 37:2098.

Lott, John R., Jr. 1990. "The Effect of Conviction on the Legitimate Income of Criminals." *Economic Letters* 34:381–5.

———. 1992. "An Attempt at Measuring the Total Monetary Penalty from Drug Convictions: The Importance of an Individual's Reputation." *Journal of Legal Studies* 21:159–87.

Lotz, R. and Robert M. Regoli. 1980. "Public Support for the Death Penalty." *Criminal Justice Review* 5:55–65.

Luker, Kristin. 1996. *Dubious Conceptions: The Politics of Teenage Pregnancy.* Berkeley and Los Angeles: University of California Press.

Lynch, Frederick R. 1989. *Invisible Victims: White Males and the Crisis of Affirmative Action.* New York: Greenwood Press.

Lynch, James P. 1988. "A Comparison of Prison Use in England, Canada, West Germany and the United States: A Limited Test of the Punitive Hypothesis." *Journal of Criminal Law and Criminology* 79:180–219.

Macfarlane, Alan. 1979. *The Origins of English Individualism: The Family, Property, and Social Transition.* New York: Cambridge University Press.

Maden, M. F. and D. F. Wrench. 1977. "Significant Findings in Child Abuse Research." *Victimology* 2:196–224.

Maguire, Kathleen and Ann L. Pastore, eds. 1996. *Sourcebook of Criminal Justice Statistics 1995.* U.S. Dept. of Justice, Bureau of Justice Statistics. Washington, DC: USGPO.

Martinson, Robert. 1974. "What Works? Questions and Answers about Prison Reform," *Public Interest* 10:22–54.

Marvell, Thomas B. and Carlisle E. Moody, Jr. 1994. "Prison Population Growth and Crime Reduction." *Journal of Quantitative Criminology* 10:109–40.

———. 1996. "Determinate Sentencing and Abolishing Parole: The Long-term Impacts on Prisons and Crime." *Criminology* 34:107–28.

Mauer, Marc. 1990. *Young Black Men and the Criminal Justice System: A Growing National Problem.* Washington, DC: The Sentencing Project.

———. 1995a. "The International Use of Incarceration." *Prison Journal* 75:113–23.

———. 1995b. *Americans Behind Bars: The International Use of Incarceration, 1992–1993.* Washington, DC: Sentencing Project.

Maume, David J., Jr. 1989. "Inequality and Metropolitan Rape Rates: A Routine Activity Approach." *Justice Quarterly* 6:513–27.

McAvoy, Paul W. 1976. *The Crisis of the Regulatory Commission*. New York: Norton.

McCorkle, R. C. 1993. "Research Note: Punish and Rehabilitate? Public Attitudes toward Six Common Crimes." *Crime and Delinquency* 39:240–52.

McCrate, Elaine. 1997. "Welfare and Women's Earnings." *Politics and Society* 25:417–42.

Mead, Lawrence A. 1992. *The New Politics of Poverty: The Nonworking Poor in America*. New York: Basic Books.

Melossi, Dario and Massimo Pavarini. 1980. *The Prison and the Factory*. London: Macmillan.

Messner, Steve F. 1980. "Income Inequality and Murder Rates: Some Cross-National Findings." *Comparative Social Research* 3:185–98.

———. 1982. "Societal Development, Social Equality and Homicide." *Social Forces* 61:225–240.

Michalowski, Raymond J. and Michael A. Pearson. 1990. "Punishment and Social Structure at the State Level: A Cross-Sectional Comparison of 1970 and 1980." *Journal of Research in Crime and Delinquency* 20:73–85.

Miller, Jerome. 1996. *Search and Destroy: African-American Males in the Criminal Justice System*. New York: Cambridge University Press.

Miller, Martin B. 1980. "Sinking Gradually into the Proletariat: The Emergence of the Penitentiary in the United States." *Crime and Social Justice* 14 (Winter):37–43.

Mishel, Robert and John Schmitt. 1996. "Cutting Wages by Cutting Welfare: The Impact of Reform on the Low-Wage Labor Market." Briefing Paper, Economic Policy Institute, Washington, DC.

Moffitt, Robert A. 1990. "The Distribution of Earnings and the Welfare State," pp. 201–30 in G. Burtless (ed.) *A Future of Lousy Jobs?* Washington, DC: Brookings Institution.

Muncie, John and Richard Sparks. 1991. "Expansion and Contraction in European Penal Systems." In J. Muncie and R. Sparks (eds.) *Imprisonment: European Perspectives*. New York: St. Martin's Press.

Murphy, William and Anthony M. DeStefano. 1996. "It's 'Open Season' to Snipe at Judges." *Newsday* (Feb. 27): A6.

Murray, Charles. 1984. *Losing Ground: American Social Policy, 1950–1980*. New York: Basic Books.

Myerson, Allen R. 1997. "As Federal Bias Cases Drop, Workers Take Up the Fight." *New York Times* (Jan. 12): A1, A14.

National Center for Children in Poverty. 1997. *One in Four: America's Youngest Poor*. New York: Columbia University School of Public Health.

National Center for Education Statistics. 1995. *The Condition of Education, 1995*. Washington, DC: U.S. Department of Education.

Nelkin, Dorothy and M. Susan Lindee. 1995. *The DNA Mystique: The Gene as a Cultural Icon*. New York: W. H. Freeman.

Nielson, Francois and Arthur S. Alderson. 1997. "The Kuznets Curve and the Great U-Turn: Income Inequality in U.S. Counties, 1970 to 1990." *American Sociological Review* 62:12–33.

Newman, Katherine. 1988. *Falling from Grace: The Experience of Downward Mobility in the American Middle Class*. New York: The Free Press.

New York Times. 1995. "Nearly 7% of Adult Black Men Were Inmates in '94, Study Says," (Dec. 4): A15.

Noble, Kenneth B. 1988. "Farm Workers Fault Lack of Enforcement of Sanitation Rules" (Oct. 4): A1, A18.

O'Brien, Robert M. 1996. "Police Productivity and Crime Rates: 1973–1992." *Criminology* 34:183–208.

O'Flaherty, Brendan. 1996. *Making Room: The Politics of Homelessness*. Cambridge, MA: Harvard University Press.

Ogletree, Charles J., Jr., Mary Prosser, Abbe Smith, William J. Talley, Jr. 1995. *Beyond the Rodney King Story: An Investigation of Police Misconduct in Minority Communities*. Boston: Northeastern University Press.

Orcutt, James D. and Rebecca Faison. 1981. "Sex-Role Attitude Change and Reporting of Rape Victimization, 1973–1985." *Sociological Quarterly* 29:589–604.

Ouimet, Marc and Pierre Tremblay. 1996. "A Normative Theory of the Relationship between Crime Rates and Imprisonment Rates: An Analysis of the Penal Behavior of U.S. States from 1972 to 1992." *Journal of Research in Crime and Delinquency* 33:109–25.

Ozawa, Martha N. 1995. "Antipoverty Effects of Public Income Transfers on Children." *Children and Youth Services Review* 17:43–59.

Pampel, Fred C., John B. Williamson and Robin Stryker. 1990. "Class Context and Pension Response to Demographic Structure in Advanced Industrial Democracies." *Social Problems* 37:535–47.

Parker, Robert Nash and Allan V. Horwitz. 1986. "Unemployment, Crime, and Imprisonment: A Panel Approach." *Criminology* 24:751–73.

Parmalee, Maurice. 1908. *The Principles of Anthropology and Sociology in their Relations to Primitive Procedure*. New York: Macmillan.

Passell, Peter. 1975. "The Deterrent Effect of the Death Penalty: A Statistical Test." *Stanford Law Review* 28:61–80.

Pear, Robert. 1990. "Courts are Undoing Efforts to Aid Minority Contractors." *New York Times* (July 16): A1.

Pearce, Frank. 1989. *The Radical Durkheim*. London: Unwin Hyman.

Perlstein, Gary R. and Thomas R. Phelps, eds. 1975. *Alternatives to Prison: Community-Based Corrections*. Pacific Palisades, CA: Goodyear.

Persell, Caroline Hodges. 1977. *Education and Inequality: A Theoretical and Empirical Synthesis*. New York: The Free Press.

Persson, Torsen and Guido Tabellini. 1994. "Is Inequality Harmful for Growth? Theory and Evidence." *American Economic Review* 48:600–21.

Peterson, Ruth D. and William C. Bailey. 1988b. "Forcible Rape, Poverty, and Economic Inequality in U.S. Metropolitan Communities." *Journal of Quantitative Criminology* 4:99–119.

Pettigrew, Thomas F. and Robert C. Green. 1976. "School Desegregation in Large Cities: A Critique of the 'White Flight' Thesis." *Harvard Education Review* 46:1–53.

Pezzin, Liliana E. 1995. "Earnings Prospects, Matching Effects, and the Decision to Terminate a Criminal Career." *Criminology* 11:29–50.

Phillips, Kevin. 1990. *The Politics of Rich and Poor: Wealth and the American Electorate in the Reagan Aftermath*. New York: Harper Perennial.

Pillsbury, Samuel H. 1989. "Understanding Penal Reform: The Dynamic of Change." *Journal of Criminal Law and Criminology* 80:726–80.

———. 1995. "Why Are We Ignored? The Peculiar Place of Experts in the Current Debate about Crime and Justice." *Criminal Law Bulletin* 31: 305–36.

Piven, Frances Fox and Richard A. Cloward. 1971. *Regulating the Poor: The Functions of Public Welfare*. New York: Pantheon Books.

Platt, Anthony M. 1969. *The Child Savers: The Invention of Delinquency*. Chicago: University of Chicago Press.

Polsky, Andrew J. 1991. *The Rise of the Therapeutic State*. Princeton, NJ: Princeton University Press.

Primus, Wendell, Kathryn Porter, Margery Ditto and Mitchell Kent. 1996. *The Safety Net Delivers*. Washington, DC: Center on Budget and Policy Priorities.

Quillian, Lincoln. 1996. "Group Threat and Regional Change in Attitudes toward African-Americans," *American Journal of Sociology* 102:816–60.

Quinney, Richard. 1977. *Class, State and Crime: On the Theory and Practice of Criminal Justice.* New York: David McKay.

Rainwater, Lee. 1995. "Poverty and the Income Package of Working Parents: The United States in Comparative Perspective." *Children and Youth Services Review* 17:11–41.

Reiss, Albert J., Jr. and Jeffrey A. Roth. 1993. *Understanding and Preventing Violence.* Washington, DC: National Academy Press.

Rich, Michael J., Robert L. Lineberry, and Herbert Jacob. 1982. "Police Policies and Urban Crime." In H. Jacob and R. L. Lineberry (eds.) *Crime and Governmental Responses in American Cities,* Washington, DC: National Institute of Justice.

Riley, P. J. and V. M. Rose. 1980. "Public vs. Elite Opinion on Correctional Reform: Implications for Social Policy." *Journal of Criminal Justice* 8:345–56.

Robison, James O. and George Smith. 1971. "The Effectiveness of Correctional Programs." *Journal of Research in Crime and Delinquency* 17:67–80.

Rokeach, Milton and Sandra J. Ball-Rokeach. 1989. "Stability and Change in American Value Priorities, 1968–81." *American Psychologist* 44:775–84.

Rosell, Christine. 1975–6. "School Desegregation and White Flight." *Political Science Quarterly* 90:675–95.

Rosen, Jeffrey. 1997. "One Angry Woman." *New Yorker* (24 Feb. and 3 Mar.3):54–64.

———. 1998. "Damage Control." *New Yorker* (23 Feb. and 2 Mar.):58–68.

Rosenfeld, Richard. 1986. "Urban Crime Rates: Effects of Inequality, Welfare Dependency, Region, and Race," pp. 116–30 in J.M. Byrne and R.J. Sampson (eds.) *The Social Ecology of Crime.* New York: Springer-Verlag.

Ross, Robert and Paul Gendreau. 1980. *Effective Correctional Treatment: A Survey of Treatment Evaluation Studies.* New York: Praeger.

Rossi, Peter H., Richard A. Berk, and Kenneth J. Lenihan. 1980. *Money, Work and Crime: Experimental Evidence.* New York: Academic Press.

Rossi, Peter H., Jon A. Simpson, and JoAnn L. Miller. 1985. "Beyond Crime Seriousness: Fitting the Punishment to the Crime." *Journal of Quantitative Criminology* 1:59–90.

Rothman, David J. 1971. *Discovery of the Asylum.* Boston: Little, Brown.

Rusche, Georg and Otto Kirchheimer. 1939. *Punishment and Social Structure.* New York: Columbia University Press.

Rushton, J. Philippe. 1990. "Race and Crime." *Canadian Journal of Criminology* 32:315–34.

———. 1995a. "Race and Crime: An International Dilemma." *Society* 32:37–41.

———. 1995b. *Race, Evolution and Behavior: A Life History Perspective.* New Brunswick, NJ: Transaction Publishers.

Sabol, William J. 1989. "The Dynamics of Unemployment and Imprisonment in England and Wales, 1946–1985." *Journal of Quantitative Criminology* 5:147–68.

Savelsberg, Joachim. 1994. "Knowledge, Domination, and Criminal Punishment." *American Journal of Sociology* 99:911–43.

Schlesinger, Philip. 1994. *Reporting Crime: The Media Politics of Criminal Justice.* New York: Oxford University Press.

Schuman, Howard, Charles Steeh, and Lawrence Bobo. 1985. *Racial Attitudes in America.* Cambridge, MA: Harvard University Press.

Scull, Andrew T. 1977. *Decarceration: Community Treatment and the Deviant—A Radical View.* Englewood Cliffs, NJ: Prentice-Hall.

Schwendinger, Herman and Julia Schwendinger. 1974. *Sociologists of the Chair: A Radical Analysis of the Formative Years of North American Sociology (1883–1922).* New York: Basic Books.

Sellin, J. Thorsten. 1976. *Slavery and the Penal System*. New York: Elsevier.

Service, Elmer R. 1975. *Origins of the State and Civilization: The Process of Cultural Evolution*. New York: W. W. Norton.

Sewell, William H. and Vimal P. Shah. 1967. "Socioeconomic Status, Intelligence, and the Attainment of Higher Education." *Sociology of Education* 40:1–23.

Shane-Dubow, Sandra, Alice P. Brown, and Erik Olsen. 1985. Sentencing Reform in the United States: History, Context, and Effect. Washington, DC: Government Printing Office.

Sheleff, Leon. 1975. "From Restitutive to Repressive Law." *Archive Européenes de Sociology* 16:6–45.

Shichor, David and Dale K. Sechrest, eds. 1996. *Three Strikes and You're Out: Vengeance as Public Policy*. Thousand Oaks, CA: Sage.

Shilts, Randy. 1982. *The Mayor of Castro Street*. New York: St. Martin's Press.

Sigelman, Lee and Susan Welch. 1991. *Black American's Views of Racial Inequality*. New York: Cambridge University Press.

Simeral, Isabel. 1916. *Reform Movements in Behalf of Children in England of the Early Nineteenth Century, and the Agents of Those Reforms*. New York: Columbia University Ph.D. diss.

Simon, Jonathan. "DON'T SHOOT ME, PLEASE, MR. STAGOLEE!: Violence, Discipline, and the Bodies of Young Black Men." Paper presented to New York University Law and Society Colloquium.

———. 1993. *Poor Discipline: Parole and the Social Control of the Underclass, 1890–1990*. Chicago: University of Chicago Press.

Simpson, Myles E. 1985. "Violent Crime, Income Inequality, and Regional Culture: Another Look." *Sociological Focus* 18:199–208.

Skolnick, Jerome. 1995. "A Durkheimian Moment: O.J. Simpson and the Collective Conscience." Paper presented to the American Society of Criminology.

Skolnick, Jerome and James J. Fyfe. 1993. *Above the Law: Police and the Excessive Use of Force*. New York: The Free Press.

Skovron, S. E., J. E. Scott, and F. T. Cullen. 1988. "Prison Crowding: Public Attitudes toward Strategies of Population Control." *Journal of Research in Crime and Delinquency* 25:150–69.

"A Small Ripple or a Large Wave? The Effect of Law on the Economic Progress of Minorities." 1996. *Researching Law: An ABF Update* 72:1,6.

Smith, T. W. 1990. "Social Inequality in Cross-National Perspective," pp.21–31 in J. W. Becker, J. A. Dais, P. Estes, and P. P. Mohler (eds.) *Attitudes to Inequality and the Role of Government*. Rijswijk, the Netherlands: Social en Cultural Planbureau.

Snell, Tracy L. 1995. *Correctional Populations in the United States, 1993*. NCJ-156241. Washington, DC: Bureau of Justice Statistics.

Sowell, Thomas. 1975. *Affirmative Action Reconsidered: Was It Necessary in Academia?*. Washington, DC: American Enterprise Institute for Public Policy Research.

Spalter-Roth, Roberta. 1994. "The Real Employment Opportunities of Women Participating in AFDC: What the Market Can Provide." *Social Justice* 21:60–70.

Spelman, William. 1994. *Criminal Incapacitation*. New York: Plenum.

Spierenberg, Petris Cornelis. 1984. *The Spectacle of Suffering, Executions, and the Evolution of Repression: From a Preindustrial Metropolis to the European Experience* New York: Cambridge University Press.

———. 1991. *The Prison Experience: Disciplinary Institutions and their Inmates in Early Modern Europe*. New Brunswick, NJ: Rutgers University Press.

Spilerman, Seymour. 1971. "The Causes of Racial Disturbances: Tests of an Explanation." *American Sociological Review* 36:427–42.

Spitzer, Steven. 1975. "Punishment and Social Organization: A Study of Durkheim's Theory of Penal Evolution." *Law and Society Review* 9:613–35.

Steel, Brent S. and Mary Ann E. Steger. 1988. "Crime: Due Process Liberalism Versus Law-and-Order Conservatism," pp. 74–110 in R. Tatalovich and B.W. Daynes (eds.) *Social Regulatory Policy: Moral Controversies in American Politics.* Boulder, CO: Westview Press.

Steele, Shelby. 1990. "A Negative Vote on Affirmative Action." *New York Times Magazine* (May 13):46–9, 73–9.

Stephan, James. 1994. *Capital Punishment 1993.* Washington, DC: Bureau of Justice Statistics.

Straus, Murray A. and Richard J. Gelles. 1990. *Physical Violence in American Families: Risk Factors and Adaptations to Violence in 8,145 Families.* New Brunswick, NJ: Transaction Publishers.

Straus, Murray A., Richard J. Gelles, and Susan Steinmetz. 1980. *Behind Closed Doors: Violence in the American Family.* New York: Anchor.

Strosnider, Kim. 1997. "Minority Law-School Enrollment Would Drop without Affirmative Action, Study Finds." *Chronicle of Higher Education* (Jan. 31): A28.

Sullivan, Andrew. 1995. "Let Affirmative Action Die." *New York Times* (July 23):A15.

Surette, Ray. 1992. *Media, Crime, and Criminal Justice: Images and Realities.* Pacific Grove, CA: Brooks/Cole.

Taylor, Ian, Paul Walton, and Jock Young. 1973. *The New Criminology: For a Social Theory of Deviance.* New York: Harper and Row.

Thornberry, Terence P. and R.L. Christenson. 1984. "Unemployment and Criminal Involvement: An Investigation of Reciprocal Causal Structures." *American Sociological Review* 49:398–411.

Tillman, Robert. 1987. "The Size of the 'Criminal Population': The Prevalence and Incidence of Adult Arrests," *Criminology* 25:561–80.

Tilly, Chris. 1996. "Workfare's Impact on the New York City Labor Foundation." Working Paper no. 92. Russell Sage Foundation, March 1996.

Tokar, Brian. 1992. "Regulatory Sabotage." *Z Magazine* (April):20–5.

Tonry, Michael. 1988. "Structured Sentencing," pp. 267–337 in M. Tonry and N. Morris (eds.)*Crime and Justice: A Review of Research,* vol. 10. Chicago: University of Chicago Press.

———. 1993. "Racial Disproportion in U.S. Prisons." *British Journal of Criminology*:

———. 1995. *Malign Neglect—Race, Crime, and Punishment in America.* New York: Oxford University Press.

———. 1997. "Ethnicity, Crime, and Immigration," pp. 231–59 in M. Tonry (ed.) *Ethnicity, Crime, and Immigration: Comparative and Cross-National Perspectives.* Chicago: University of Chicago Press.

Torbet, Patricia, Richard Gable, Hunter Hurst IV, Imogene Montgomery, Linda Szymanowski and Douglas Thome. 1996. *State Responses to Serious and Violent Juvenile Crime.* Washington, DC: Office of Juvenile Justice and Delinquency Prevention.

Treviño, A. Javier. 1996. *The Sociology of Law: Classical and Contemporary Perspectives.* New York: St. Martin's Press.

Twentieth Century Fund Task Force on Criminal Sentencing. 1976. *Fair and Certain Punishment.* New York: McGraw-Hill.

United Nations. 1995. *1993 Demographic Yearbook.* New York: Nations.

Unnithan, N. Prabha and Hugh P. Whitt. 1992. "Inequality, Economic Development and Lethal Violence: A Cross-Sectional Analysis of Suicide and Homicide." *International Journal of Comparative Sociology* 33:182–96.

Van den Haag, Ernest. 1975. *Punishing Criminals.* New York: Basic Books.

van Dijk, Jan J. M. and Pat Mayhew. 1992. *Criminal Victimization in the Industrialized World: Key Findings of the 1989 and 1992 International Crime Surveys.* The Netherlands: Ministry of Justice.

van Dijk, Jan J.M., Pat Mayhew, and Martin Killias. 1991. *Experiences of Crime across the World.* Boston: Kluwer.

van Duizend, Richard, L. Paul Sutton, and Charlotte A. Carter. 1984. *The Search Warrant Process: Preconceptions, Perceptions, Practices.* Williamsburg, VA: National Center for State Courts.

Verhovek, Sam Howe. 1997a. "Referendum in Houston Shows Complexity of Preferences Issues." *New York Times* (Nov. 6): A1, A26.

————. 1997b. "Judge Kills Texas Affirmative Action Plan." *New York Times* (Nov. 14): A33.

Vidmar, Neil and Phoebe Ellsworth. 1974. "Public Opinion and the Death Penalty." *Stanford Law Review* 26:1245–70.

Viteritti, Joseph P. 1973. *Police, Politics, and Pluralism in New York City: A Comparative Case Study.* Beverly Hills, CA: Sage.

von Hirsch, Andrew. 1976. *Doing Justice: The Choice of Punishments* New York: Hill and Wang.

————. 1985. *Past or Future Crimes: Deservedness and Dangerousness in the Sentencing of Criminals.* New Brunswick, NJ: Rutgers University Press.

Votey, Harold, Jr. 1991. "Employment, Age, Race, and Crime: A Labor-Theoretic Investigation." *Journal of Quantitative Criminology* 7:123–53.

Waldfogel, Joel. 1994a. "The Effect of Criminal Conviction on Income and the Trust 'Reposed in the Workmen.'" *Journal of Human Resources* 29:62–81.

————. 1994b. "Does Conviction Have a Persistent Effect on Income and Employment?" *International Review of Law and Economics* 14:103–9.

Walinsky, Adam. 1995. "The Crisis of Public Order." *The Atlantic Monthly* (July):39–44.

Wallace, Don. 1981. "The Political Economy of Incarceration Trends in Late U.S. Capitalism: 1971–1977." *Insurgent Sociologist* 10:59–66.

Warr, Mark. 1995. "The Polls—Poll Trends: Public Opinion on Crime and Punishment." *Public Opinion Quarterly* 59:296–310.

Warr, Mark and Mark Stafford. 1983."Public Goals of Punishment, and Publicly Preferred Penalties for Crimes." *Sociological Quarterly* 24:75–91.

Westergaard, John. 1995. *Who Gets What? The Hardening of Class Inequality in the Late Twentieth Century.* Cambridge, MA: Polity.

Wessel, David. 1997. "America's Wealth Is Being Distributed a Bit More Evenly, Fed survey Shows." *Wall Street Journal* (Jan. 24): A2.

Western, Bruce and Katherine Beckett. 1997. "How Unregulated Is the U.S. Labor Market? The Dynamics of Jobs and Jails, 1980–1995." Unpublished paper.

Whitehead, J. T. and S. P. Lab. 1989. "A Meta-Analysis of Juvenile Correctional Treatment." *Journal of Research in Crime and Delinquency* 26: 276–95.

Wilbanks, William. 1987. *The Myth of a Racist Criminal Justice System.* Monterey, CA: Brooks/Cole.

Wilkins, Leslie T. 1984. *Consumerist Criminology.* Totawa, NJ: Barnes and Noble.

Wilkins, Leslie T. and Ken Pease. 1987. "Public Demand for Punishment." *International Journal of Sociology and Social Policy* 7:16–29.

Williams, David. 1980. "The Role of Prisons in Tanzania: An Historical Perspective." *Crime and Social Justice* 13 (Summer):27–38.

Wicharraya, Tamasak. 1995. *Simple Theory, Hard Reality: The Impact of Sentencing Reforms on Courts, Prisons, and Crime.* Albany, NY: State University of New York Press.

Wilson, James Q. 1975. *Thinking about Crime.* New York: Basic Books.
————. 1981. "The Dead Hand of Regulation." *The Public Interest* 25:39–58.
Wilson, William Julius. 1987. *The Truly Disadvantaged: The Inner City, the Underclass, and Public Policy.* Chicago: University of Chicago Press.
Winnick, Andrew J. 1989. *Toward Two Societies: The Changing Distributions of Income and Wealth in the United States since 1960.* New York: Praeger.
Wolff, Edward N. 1995a. "How the Pie Is Sliced: America's Growing Concentration of Wealth." *The American Prospect* 22 (Summer):58–64.
————. 1995b. *Top Heavy: A Study of the Increasing Inequality of Wealth in America.* New York: The Twentieth Century Fund.
World Bank. 1994. *World Development Report 1994: Infrastructure for Development.* New York: Oxford University Press.
———— .1995. *World Tables, 1995.* Baltimore, MD: Johns Hopkins University.
Yates, Steven. 1994. *Civil Wrongs: What Went Wrong with Affirmative Action.* San Francisco: Institute for Contemporary Studies.
Yeager, Matthew G. 1979. "Unemployment and Imprisonment." *Journal of Criminology and Criminal Law* 70:586–88.
Young, Michael Dunlop. 1958. *The Rise of the Meritocracy, 1870–2033.* London: Thames and Young.
Young, Robert L. 1991. "Race, Conceptions of Crime and Justice, and Support for the Death Penalty." *Social Psychology Quarterly* 54:67–75.
Young, Warren and Mark Brown. 1993. "Cross-National Comparisons of Imprisonment," pp. 1–49 in M. Tonry (ed.) *Crime and Justice: A Review of Research*, vol. 17. Chicago: University of Chicago Press.
Zedlewski, Edwin W. 1985. "When Have We Punished Enough?" *Public Administration Review* 45:771–9.
————. 1987. *Making Confinement Decisions.* Washington, DC: U.S. Department of Justice, National Institute of Justice.
Zimring, Franklin E. and Gordon Hawkins. 1988. "The New Mathematics of Imprisonment." *Crime and Delinquency* 34:425–36.
———— 1995. *Incapacitation: Penal Confinement and the Restraint of Crime.* New York: Oxford University Press.

14

Back to the Future: A Reminder of the Importance of Sutherland in Thinking about White-collar Crime

*Kip Schlegel and
David Eitle*

Introduction

The concept of white-collar crime has come under renewed attack within the past decade, with calls to put an end to the term as we know it. The main stalking-horse of critics has been the role of such offender characteristics as social class, social status, respectability or prestige in explaining crime and responses to it. The fodder for such attacks has been both theoretical and empirical and can be divided into three main arguments: (1) the concept of white-collar crime offers no theoretical value in causal explanations of crime (Gottfredson and Hirschi 1990). Such a typology, built on factors such as social class, status, etc., merely confuses causation with social location and mixes explanation and definition; (2) research on sentencing white-collar offenders has produced mixed, if not benign findings on the relationship between sanction disparity and offender characteristics (e.g. Hagan, Nagel, and Albonetti 1980; Wheeler, Weisburd, and Bode 1982; Weisburd, Waring, and Wheeler 1990); and (3) the concept of white-collar crime, with its emphasis on status, class, and respectability, binds us to a framework based on offender characteristics, as opposed to a more useful framework based on offense characteristics (Shapiro 1990).

We contend that such calls to ignore, eliminate or liberate white-collar crime overstate their case. These criticisms dilute the concept of white-collar crime and trivialize what is still a powerful idea. They oversimplify the concept, at least as it was conveyed by its progenitor, by limiting its context, its characteristics, and its application. To varying degrees these criticisms fail for the following reasons: (1) they falsely dichotomize white-collar crime into concepts that emphasize either offense, or offender characteristics, as the central feature; (2) they dilute its contribution by focusing on the isolated issues of motivation, opportunity or social control, at the exclusion of a broader conceptualization of crime that includes motivation, opportunity structures, and social control responses taken together; and (3) they are based on biased data and narrow measures that do not sufficiently capture the complexity of white-collar crime.

Past research has turned the concept of white-collar crime into something it was never intended to be—that is, a typology with its own unique definition and etiology. Recent criticisms perpetuate this idea. When the term is reified in such a fashion we are forced into a particular framework and locked into answering such questions as: are white-collar criminals different from common criminals? or do those with wealth, status, power, etc., receive differential treatment compared to common criminals? However, the concept of white-collar crime should not be viewed as a typology, or as a discreet thing, but rather as a series of interactions, characterized by three central components. First, the behavior takes place in the context and course of an occupational role. That is to say, it is behavior that can only be understood in the context of the social organization of work. Second, actors possess the attributes of social class, status, respect, etc., which may arise from the occupational role, or be brought to bear on the performance of that role. Third, the interactions typically involve some form of organization. White-collar crime is not a "thing" to be explained and "proved," by the existence of any one of these components, but a context for behavior that includes all three components taken together. From this perspective, the value of Sutherland's contribution is twofold. First, it *expands* the parameters of the crime problem by urging us to consider broad issues related to the social organization of work and the role that social power plays in shaping opportunities for and responses to criminal behavior that takes place in that context. Second, it forces us to examine alternative social control mechanisms and reconsider both the meaning of crime and criminality and the administration of justice. Efforts to eliminate or restrict this notion either by restricting its meaning to isolated problems of motivation, opportunity or social response, or by limiting it to either offense or offender characteristics alone, ultimately miss the point and confine our efforts to understand crime. We address these ideas in more detail below.

A Brief Review

As Geis (1992) has noted, white-collar crime as a topic of criminology has had a short but checkered history. With some exceptions, including Sutherland's (1949) own research on the violations of law by the largest U.S. corporations, and the works of his students Donald Cressey (1953)[1] and Marshall Clinard (1952), much of the scholarly attention directed to this concept served as attempts to refine, recast, or clarify white-collar crime as a typology of crime. Scholars have offered alternative schemata, including, occupational crime, corporate crime, organizational crime, economic crime, with varying degrees of acceptance by others in the field. Empirical research during this period, again with some exceptions, tended toward case studies depicting the abuses of the powerful over the powerless and/or the degree to which the upper classes exercised control of the social control apparatus of the state to protect their interests.

The most significant development in white-collar crime research came in the early 1980s with a host of sentencing studies that compared the sanctions of white-collar offenders with those given to "common offenders." The first of these studies, by Hagan, Nagel and Albonetti (1980), compared the sentences of white-collar offenders with those of common offenders imposed in ten federal district courts. Contrary to expectations, their findings suggested that white-collar offenders, defined as those with a college education, received somewhat harsher sentences than those with less education convicted of common offenses. This research was followed by the findings from the Yale Project (Wheeler et al. 1982) which examined the sentences handed down for eight offenses that "virtually any American would regard as quintessential white-collar crimes" (9). These included securities offenses, bribery, bank embezzlement, antitrust, mail and wire fraud, tax fraud, false claims and statements, and credit and lending institution fraud. Their findings, based on 1,094 cases in ten federal courts, suggested that high status offenders received more severe punishments than their low status counterparts.

These findings were offset by other sentencing studies, which came to somewhat different conclusions. Benson and Walker's (1988) reanalysis of the Yale data from one district court found that high occupational status offenders were sanctioned no differently than low status offenders. Hagan and Parker (1985) expanded their sanctioning study of securities violators to include relational indicators of white-collar power, that is to say, class rather than status characteristics. They also included regulatory sanctions for securities offenses. Their findings suggested that class indicators affected the likelihood and severity of sanctioning, with managers sanctioned more readily and severely than employers. Similarly, Pontell and Tillman (1992) found that Medi-Cal fraud offenders were much less likely to receive incarceration than were persons arrested for grand theft in spite of the greater financial loss incurred by the frauds. These findings were mitigated somewhat when the administrative sanctions imposed in parallel proceedings were considered. We will have more to say about these studies shortly.

Much of the empirical research has been directed at the issue of disparity at the sentencing stage. Limited empirical data have also been used to support general claims about the nature and extent of white-collar offending and the degree to which any differences might exist between white-collar offenders and common offenders for etiological purposes. James Q. Wilson and Richard Hernstein (1985) excluded white-collar crimes in their theory on the grounds that white-collar offenses are not universally regarded as wrong, nor are they similarly ranked in terms of their seriousness. To the extent that the distinction between *mala in se* and *mala prohibita* offenses has any *real* meaning, their theory would pertain solely to the former.

Michael Gottfredson and Travis Hirschi (1990) argue that white-collar crime has limited utility in our understanding of crime generally. While it may remind us the crime is not restricted to those in the lower classes, the "typological approach inherent in the concept of white-collar crime was a mistake" (200). They note that the "value of any distinction must be determined by their usefulness in explaining, predicting or controlling the behavior of offenders, victims or officials of the criminal justice system" (185). However, they soon limit their discussion of white-collar crime to explanations for offender behavior. They argue that occupational theories of crime do not, in themselves, demonstrate the need for a special category of criminal, nor do they require distinct causes. Similarly, white-collar crime theories that focus on offender characteristics, such as wealth, high status, class, or respectability, have little value because in comparing high status offenders with low status offenders they "force a separate theory of criminal behavior by suggesting but not demonstrating that the causes of such behavior among the rich and powerful are different from the causes of such behavior among the poor and weak" (186). Such theories merely confuse social location of opportunity structures with causation and consequently contribute nothing to our explanation of offender behavior.

Gottfredson and Hirschi make the distinction between types of crimes and types of criminals, arguing that the "assumption that white-collar criminals differ from other criminals is simply the assumption, in another guise, that offenders specialize in particular crimes" (190); an argument they claim to be unsupported by research. To demonstrate their claim they cite data on offending in employee theft, embezzlement, fraud, and forgery. They argue that the data support their theory of criminality, which would predict similar patterns as those found in common crimes. That is to say, when opportunity is held constant, the order of magnitude and direction of white-collar offending compares to that of common crimes with respect to age, gender, and race. Furthermore, they argue that white-collar offenses are low rate offenses compared to common crimes, a trend predicted by their own theory of low self-control, since low self-control likely influences selection into the occupational structure. Simply put, there are fewer white-collar crimes because the rigors of stable employment generally preclude individuals with low self-control. The authors conclude by noting that the distinction between "crime in the streets and crime in the suite is an offense rather than an offender distinction, offenders in both cases are likely to share similar characteristics" (200). Different manifestations are a function of differential opportunities and situations, factors which themselves may be accounted for by low self-control.

Susan Shapiro (1990) has expanded on this general theme noting that white-collar crime has "become an imprisoning framework for contemporary scholarship." Labels attributed to these crimes, including white-collar crime, corporate crime, and occupational crime, ultimately "confuse acts with actors, norms with norm-breakers, the modus operandi with the operator" (347). Research on these concepts is not only of little value, but in her words, "impoverishes theory, distorts empirical inquiry, oversimplifies policy analysis, inflames muckraking instincts and obscures fascinating questions about the relationship between social organization and crime" (362). She offers to "liberate" the concept of white-collar crime by "disentangling the identification of the perpetrators with their misdeeds," focusing instead on shared characteristics of the offenses that comprise white-collar crime.

To do so she draws on the socio-legal concept of agency, loosely defining agency relationships as individuals or organizations acting on behalf of a principal. Principals transfer various powers (resources, property, etc.) to agents and delegate authority to them to perform tasks the principals are unwilling or unable to do themselves (348). Much of contemporary business is structured by such agency relationships, as demonstrated by the proliferation of attorneys and financial advisors, who not only represent clients in personal and fiduciary activities, but serve, along with other professionals, to administer and oversee collective interests represented in such diverse entities as labor unions, pension funds, charities, insurance, utility companies, and so forth. As she notes, the organization of agency relationships is unbalanced in favor of the agent. Expertise, information access and control, and geographical, temporal and spatial distances provide agents with control over resources and property that cannot be verified by principals.

According to Shapiro these relationships can be structured along a continuum of trust. As the scope of control between beneficiary and agent lessens, the role of trust increases. This notion is captured, according to Shapiro, in the legal concept of fiduciary trust (Finn 1977). Fiduciary trust differs from contract (the control structure governing most agency relationships) in the degree of discretion granted to agents to "exercise their particular brand of service," with fiduciary trust existing when the principal has *no* control over the agent's actions taken on his behalf (350). Shapiro then argues that these trust relationships constitute the majority of relationships found in white-collar crime, and that the violation and manipulation of the norms of trust (disclosure, disinterestedness, and role competence) represent the modus operandi of white-collar crime.

Shapiro documents the myriad ways fiduciaries exploit trust relationships—mainly through lying, self-dealing and incompetence. Structural properties of trust relationships facilitate crime by virtue of temporal and spatial distancing, the use and manipulation of symbolic proxies representing property (bank statements, contracts, mortgages, etc.), organizational embeddedness, and also by "furnishing mechanisms for minimizing the risk of detection and sanctioning" (353). The location of trust denies both principals and investigators access to the "loci of misconduct, by dispersing activities socially, organizationally, temporally, and geographically away from monitors, using such devices as hiding fiduciary activities behind organizational boundaries." These impedimenta extend to prosecution and punishment as well. For example, embedding trust relationships in organizations and networks conceal misconduct and diffuse culpability for their misdeeds to others.

Leniency in the treatment of white-collar offenders can be accounted for by the need to negotiate settlements in order to penetrate these structural obstacles, and by the limits and problems that arise in the choice of sanctions for trust abusers, as cited in the sanctioning problems associated with organizational offenders by Coffee (1981), Stone, (1975) and Wheeler et al. (1988).

Shapiro acknowledges that the concept of trust does not capture all events that have been subsumed under the rubric white-collar crime and that it is susceptible to charges of conceptual ambiguity. She claims, however, that the value of the term lies in its shift of focus away from offender characteristics of status, wealth, respect, etc., typically associated with white-collar crime. The relationship between the act and the social status of the actor is spurious at best. "The rewards of class and status enjoyed by many trustees comes from several sources, many of the trustees' own contrivance. Fiduciaries are well-paid for their expertise and their position of trust allows them to become even richer" (358).

> The concept of "white-collar crime" therefore encompasses a spurious relationship between role-specific norms and the characteristics of those who occupy these roles. Corporate, occupational, and upper status are related to the distribution of positions of trust, which, in turn, provide opportunities for abuse. But that correlation does not justify skipping the intermediate step and identifying the abuses with the status of the perpetrators. Indeed, the correlation between corporate, occupational or high status and abuse of trust is far from compelling. (358)

To demonstrate she cites her research on the sanctioning of securities violators, noting that "upper status offenders are less vulnerable to criminal prosecution, but must defend themselves frequently in civil and administrative proceedings...The data suggest that any apparent discrimination against lower status offenders in prosecutorial discretion is more readily explained by greater access to legal options than by social standing" (361–2).

This brief review of the literature is by no means exhaustive, but it does highlight the essence of recent criticisms about the usefulness of the term white-collar crime. Again, these criticisms can be roughly divided into the following claims: (1) the typology of white-collar crime is of little value to our understanding of crime because it offers no theoretical value in explanations of the causes of crime; (2) sentencing research demonstrates mixed findings with respect to offender-based characteristics; and (3) the concept of white-collar crime is trapped in offender-based characteristics of social status, respectability, and class that are misleading. White-collar crimes are better thought of in terms of characteristics of the offenses that reflect particular opportunity structures. Each of these positions discounts the value of white-collar crime on the grounds that the term overemphasizes offender-based characteristics. As we will argue, we believe these criticisms overstate their case and fundamentally stray from Sutherland's conception.

The Reification of an Idea

Scholars often attribute the problems of white-collar crime to Sutherland's inconsistency and apparent ambivalence in his own definition. Yet, in spite of his wavering definition, he was quite certain what the concept was intended to represent. He writes:

> The thesis of this book, stated positively, is that persons of the upper socioeconomic class engage in much criminal behavior; that this criminal behavior differs from the criminal behavior of the lower socioeconomic class principally in the administrative procedures which are used in dealing with the offenders, and that variations in administrative procedures are not significant from the point of view of causation of crime...These violations of law by persons in the upper socioeconomic class are, for convenience, called "white-collar crime." This concept is not intended to be definitive, but merely to call attention to crimes which are not included within the scope of criminology. White-collar crimes may be defined approximately as a crime committed by a person of respectability and high social status in the course of his occupation. (3)

From our perspective, the recent debates on the meaning and utility of white-collar crime have taken place in spite of Sutherland's conception rather than because of it. These debates are made all the more problematic by their different definitional starting points. Typically white-collar crime has been dichotomized, we believe wrongly, into positions emphasizing *either* offense characteristics such as fraud, deception, concealment, occupation and trust, *or* offender characteristics, such as social status, prestige, respectability, and so forth. Obviously, how one defines white-collar crime will ultimately shape the outcome. If one includes crimes that fit certain offense characteristics, then it is likely that important offender characteristics will go missing. On the other hand, if one includes offenses on the basis of offender characteristics, then offense characteristics get neglected. Both approaches are open to the criticism that they confuse explanation with definition. Surely the first question to be asked is, what are we trying to do? We begin our discussion with the premise that there are myriad ways to approach the general problem of crime, and the approach most certainly affects the significance of definition. One approach might be to search for causes. Another might be to examine the conditions under which certain events are likely to arise, take the form they do, grow or subside as they might, and just as importantly, are responded to in the fashion they are. If we are interested only in causation, then it is particularly important that the causal explanation be theoretically distinct from the definition.[2] However, if we are *also* interested in understanding how particular events arise, how they take place and evolve, then we would naturally want to incorporate all factors we suspect might be related to those interactions.

We make this rather obvious claim on the grounds that many of the problems with respect to white-collar crime are a product of treating white-collar crime as a "thing" separate and distinct from other types of crime. That is, it has come to be considered as a discreet event, or set of events, that can be measured in a fairly uniform fashion, preferably by a single indicator. As a discreet thing, white-collar crime requires a precise definition. Such occurances are commonplace in both the natural and social sciences. A good example of this is the concept of intelligence (Gould 1996). Though Binet recognized intelligence as an abstraction of general performance that could possibly be understood only through crude proxies that might be related to various aspects of reasoning, others turned intelligence into an innate object that could be measured with reliability and validity by reference to head shape or the use of a single numerical value. So it goes with the concept of white-collar crime. The abstract and mushy concept that was intended primarily to falsify existing theories of crime based on poverty was quickly affixed by others as a "thing," falling prey to Mill's warning that danger lurks in believing, "that whatever received a name must be an entity or being, having an independent existence of its own." White-collar crime was soon cast as separate and distinct from other kinds of crime, requiring its own unique definition, and in some respects, its own etiology. For the sake of parsimony perhaps, the concept became dichotomized, with scholars entrenched in camps based on offender and offense characteristics, with the intent to demonstrate the existence of this thing and to compare it to other typologies of crime to see how it "fits." Yet, white-collar crime, as it was originally conceived, was never intended to be a typology with its own definition and distinct etiology, delimited only by reference to the qualities of the offense, or the characteristics of the offender. Sutherland repeatedly discounted such attempts, whether they were based on attributes of poverty or wealth (1949).

If Sutherland did not intend white-collar crime to be a typology with its own unique definition, what did he mean by white-collar crime and why is it important? While we can only speculate on the former, we are quite certain that Sutherland saw more value in the concept than do Gottfredson and Hirschi. Our reading of his work suggests that white-collar crimes are best thought of, not as discreet objects, but rather as diverse interactions, fixed in particular spatio-temporal constraints, that involve individuals with high status, prestige, and respectability in the context and course of their legitimate occupational roles. This requires little justification. No one would deny that the powerful commit crimes. No one would deny that crimes take place in the context of occupations. No one would deny, we think, that there are powerful actors who commit crimes in the context of their legitimate occupation roles. Few would deny (with the possible exception, of course, of Gottfredson and Hirschi) that the study of these interactions serves no usefulness in understanding crime.

Sutherland used several different referents for the sources of power— social class, wealth, high status, prestige, and respectability. While we recognize that each of these referents is different and worthy of further discussion, we contend that what Sutherland meant by "white-collar" was a composite of these characteristics that produce social leverage, and that these characteristics apply to both the offender and to the offender's occupational role in the social organization of work. Social leverage can be simply defined as "positional advantage." One could easily choose power, yet this term carries its own sociological baggage that, for the purposes here, may only confuse matters. Simply put then, white-collar crimes are interactions involving individuals with social leverage in the course and performance of their occupational role. Social leverage may be derived from characteristics the individual brings to the occupational role (wealth, knowledge, charisma), or it may be derived from the occupational role itself.[3] Since they are crimes, they carry features similar to other crimes. Since they take place in occupational roles, they carry features similar to other criminal events taking place in the context of occupational roles, and features similar to noncriminal events that take place in the context of work. Since they involve leverage, they involve features similar to other crimes involving leverage, and features related to leverage in other noncriminal activities. As should be obvious by now, we have set up a very different sort of examination of the value of the concept of white-collar crime, since we are not so much interested in proving the existence of it, or simply comparing it to common crime, as we are in helping to clarify the conditions in which these interactions arise and are responded to. We contend that under Sutherland's perspective the central components to white-collar crime include leverage, occupation role, and organization. His aim was straightforward: (1) to call attention to these interactions and demonstrate their harm; (2) to demonstrate, by case study examples, the kinds of crimes that take place in the context of leverage, occupational role, and organization, and most importantly; (3) to call attention to the idea that these components account for both the structure of crime and differential implementation of the law. While each of these components may be more relevant to certain questions than to others, they are all relevant to these interactions and thus they are relevant to our general understanding of crime.

The bulk of Gottfredson and Hirschi's treatise is an attempt to demonstrate the precise point Sutherland so clearly made from the very beginning, and which, incidentally, they fail to acknowledge adequately. They differ, however, not simply in the general theory of crime they propose—Sutherland opted for differential association, Gottfredson and Hirschi, for low self-control—but in their willingness to consider the ways in which social leverage affect the application of their theories. Sutherland was careful to distinguish process and content in his theory. While the process of learning remained the same for all individuals, he clearly believed that economic and cultural factors shaped the content of learning. Thus:

> In both classes a person begins his career free from criminality, learns something about the legal code which prohibits certain kinds of behavior, and also learns in variant groups that other kinds of behavior which conflict with the general code may be practiced. Through contact with these variant cultures he learns the techniques, rationalizations and the specific drives and motives necessary for the successful accomplishments of crime. If he is reared in the lower socioeconomic class, he learns the techniques, rationalizations, and drives to be used in petty larceny, burglary, and robbery; while if he is reared in the upper socioeconomic class and engaged in an occupation of the kind characteristic of that class he learns the techniques, rationalizations, and drives to be used in frauds and false pretenses. The process of acquiring criminal behavior is identical in the two situations although the contents of the patterns which are transmitted in communication differ. (115)

While we may agree that the concept of white-collar crime was never intended to require a distinct motivation apart from that of common crime, we part ways with Gottfredson and Hirschi in their view that there is *no* value to these white-collar characteristics in causal explanations.[4] As long as the causal explanation is distinct from the definition, it is conceivable that some of the factors that contribute to common crime motivation are unique to common crimes, while some of the factors that contribute to the commission of white-collar offenses may be unique to white-collar crimes. Motivation may be largely attributable to factors independent of social context (as Gottfredson and Hirschi assert), or it may be constructed by factors both independent and dependent on the social context.[5] Thus, we are unwilling to give up the idea that crime is a complex behavior that entails many causal components, including the factors that may be found in white-collar crimes. More important, there are many challenges to the study of problems, not the greatest of which is the challenge of finding the "cause." Likewise, there are many subjects relevant to crime, such as the application of laws and the administration of sanctions, that are not particularly relevant to the problem of causation.[6] The claim that the subject is not relevant to causation does not mean that the subject is irrelevant to the study of crime. To the extent that we have qualms with the approaches taken by these critics, we are most troubled by the arrogance that only certain questions are important to study. To say then that the cause of criminality is low self-control, even if we are willing to suspend disbelief on this matter, tells us only so much about crime. We do not believe that crime can be neatly separated and studied under a microscope independent of the environment in which it occurs, nor do we believe that the crime and its environment can ever be fully understood without reference to the manner and mechanisms in which it is controlled.

The Limitations of White-collar Data

Independent from the questions of motivation, the concept of white-collar crime remains useful and important. If Sutherland contributed anything by the term it was surely his focus on the differential implementation of the law afforded in response to these crimes. Sutherland was critical of theories derived from biased criminal justice system data. This bias takes two forms.

Persons of the upper socioeconomic class are more powerful politically and financially and escape arrest and conviction to a greater extent than persons who lack such power. Wealthy persons can employ skilled attorneys and in other ways can influence the administration of justice in their own favor more effectively than can persons of the lower socioeconomic class. Even professional criminals, who have financial and political power, escape arrest and conviction more effectively than amateur and occasional criminals who have little financial or political power. This bias, while indubitable, is not of great importance from a theoretical point of view.

And, much more important is the bias involved in the administration of criminal justice under laws which apply exclusively to business and the professions and which therefore involve only the upper socioeconomic class. Persons who violate laws regarding restraint of trade, advertising, pure food and drugs, and similar business practices are not arrested by uniformed policemen, are not tried in criminal courts, and are not committed to prisons; their illegal behavior receives the attention of administrative commissions and of courts operating under civil or equity jurisdiction. For this reason such violations of law are not included in the criminal statistics nor are individual cases brought to the attention of the scholars who write the theories of criminal behavior. The sample of criminal behavior on which the theories are founded is biased as to socioeconomic status, since it excludes these business and professional men. The bias is quite certain as it would be if the scholars selected only red-haired criminals for study and reached the conclusion that redness of hair was the cause of crime.

In spite of Sutherland's observation, much of the research on white-collar crime continues to be plagued by these issues. Dangerous inferences are made from data that fail to capture the domain of white-collar crime. Two particular problems are worth citing. The first is to assume that offenses such as fraud, embezzlement, tax evasion, etc., fairly represent white-collar crime in all its dimensions—that is to say, in both offense *and* offender characteristics. Gottfredson and Hirschi fall prey to this error by assuming that their categories capture the essence of white-collar crime. Yet, research by Weisburd et al., provide convincing evidence to the contrary. Their inclusion of securities violations as well as other more complex business frauds demonstrate clearly that there are substantial differences in the nature of offending and in the characteristics of the offenders compared to the more simple frauds. In this respect, and from our perspective anyway, the offenses that represent the top of Weisburd et al.'s pryamid of white-collar crimes more readily capture what Sutherland meant by white-collar crime.

The second problem is more general and involves the limitations that are inherent in examining only those offenses represented in conviction data from the criminal courts. These types of studies run the risk of confounding our understanding the of white-collar crime process rather than improving it. Specifically, most of the sentencing studies cited earlier have attempted to examine how class or status influences the criminal sanctioning process (e.g., Wheeler et al. 1988; Wheeler, Weisburd, and Bode 1982; Weisburd et al. 1991; Benson and Walker 1988; Benson et al. 1992), particularly focusing on the sentencing of offenders convicted of acts the researchers define as white-collar offenses. By focusing on how *convicted offenders* in the criminal justice system are treated differently based upon offender characteristics such as class or status, they have truncated the population of acts and actors that represent the universe of white-collar crimes and offenders, so that what remains is a potentially biased and unrepresentative subset of acts and actors. Shapiro captures this problem nicely:

> The finding that upper status offenders and their collaborators are under represented among the ranks of "white-collar criminals" because other legal options divert them from the criminal process is precisely the problem that Sutherland identified fifty years ago in official crime statistics, which systematically underreport wrongdoing by corporations and persons of wealth. Just as this discovery impelled Sutherland to change the course of criminological inquiry a half-century ago, it should set off alarm bells today over the propensity of contemporary scholars to define and generalize about white-collar crime from highly selected samples of convicted upper status criminals whose wrongs are so egregious, whose positions so marginal, or whose tactics so inept that they were unable to take advantage of the rich array of opportunities to escape from the criminal justice system. (Shapiro 1990: 362)

While many of the authors of these studies note that their research may be biased by examining only convicted offenders, they nonetheless cast premature, if not dangerous, indictments of Sutherland's and others' propositions about the role of class position and status on the social response to socially harmful acts.

Fortunately, a few research endeavors have expanded their examination of how offender characteristics affect the social response to socially harmful acts by examining: (1) the relationship between offender characteristics and the likelihood that illegal acts will be adjudicated in the criminal justice system versus alternative systems of social control such as administrative or civil proceedings (i.e., Shapiro 1984, 1985, 1990; Hagan and Parker 1985); and (2) the relationship between offender characteristics and the sanction meted out to the offender, regardless of what legal system (criminal, civil, and/or administrative) the case is adjudicated in (Hagan and Parker 1985; Eitle 1996). These studies have found some important differences in how illegal actors are responded to and treated, depending primarily on their position in the social organization of work.

For example, in Shapiro's (1984) seminal study of the Securities and Exchange Commission's (SEC) enforcement capabilities, her analysis of more than 500 cases investigated by the SEC between 1948 and 1972 led her to conclude that there was a systematic bias in the enforcement of securities laws. She concluded that the use of certain detection strategies (and the failure to use other strategies) would likely uncover only certain offenses and certain offenders, and was not very capable of uncovering major violations at an early stage of commission:

> Many of the correlates of SEC detection strategies—types of violation, scope of the offense, characteristics of offenders, offense timing and duration, offense impact—are also related to the style, techniques, and scope of investigation (Shapiro 1984:135)...the social organization of illicit activities determines the way they are detected, and, therefore,...different strategies of intelligence catch different kinds of securities offenses (Shapiro 1984:167).

In her subsequent analysis of the SEC's decision making process to refer cases for criminal prosecution, Shapiro found that upper status offenders were less vulnerable to criminal prosecution, while being more likely to be defendants in civil and administrative proceedings than lower status offenders.[7] Despite a somewhat confusing discussion of how class and status affect the exercise of prosecutorial discretion, she acknowledges that the position of the actor in the organization of work affects both the opportunities to commit illegal acts and the social control responses to those acts.[8]

One study that focused on the role of the position of the actor in the workplace on both the likelihood of being a defendant in a criminal action and on the punishment that resulted was Hagan and Parker's (1985) study of white collar crime punishment.

Using data compiled from interviews with Ontario securities offense investigators, they predicted that class position[9] would be related both to the behaviors perpetrated and to the punishment of detected behaviors. They anticipated that employers (i.e., owners of the means of production, in positions of control in the legitimate economy) would be least likely to receive severe sentences and to even be responded to via the criminal justice system, with managers (non-owner but in authority positions in the legitimate economy), the petty bourgeoisie (owners with no authority in the legitimate economy) and workers (non-owner with no authority in either the legitimate or illegitimate economy) increasingly more likely to receive those stringent sanctions. They found that employers were indeed treated most leniently in securities matters, with managers treated most severely. Their explanation for the latter phenomenon is grounded in what they call a "Watergate" effect, or an institutional response to what Katz (1980) referred to as a social movement against white collar crime that gained momentum during the same rough period as the data analyzed by Hagan and Parker. They interpret this finding as supporting a structural explanation, arguing that the structural conditions of securities firms protect employers while leaving managers more vulnerable to criminal prosecution: "employers are in positions of power that allow them to be distanced from criminal events and that can obscure their involvement in them" (Hagan 1989:37).

Another relevant study is Eitle's (1996) examination of the effects of class position and organizational centrality on regulatory enforcement outcomes. Using recent data on formal actions taken against federal securities offenders, a logistical regression analysis was used to determine the likelihood of receiving a punitive versus a non-punitive sanction for defendants involved in securities offense legal actions. By combining the outcomes of civil, criminal, and administrative actions taken against a particular defendant, the question of whether the position of the actor in the organization of work influences the *overall* treatment of that actor is addressed, controlling for the possibility raised by Shapiro, Mann, and others that offenders who avoid a criminal trial might still be sanctioned punitively in alternative systems of social control. Examining both the position of the actor within the organization of work, and the position of the organization within the organizational field being regulated, Eitle found that both class position and organizational position influenced the likelihood of receiving a punitive sanction. Principals and workers not employed in the legitimate economy were both found to be significantly less likely to receive a punitive enforcement response than actors of other positions. Further, individuals affiliated with the largest firms were found to be *more* likely to receive a punitive sanction, but the effect was negligible for actors in the larger firms that were in positions of control (e.g., principals).

These studies, as a group, demonstrate the relevance of the position of the actor in the workplace as it pertains to the administration of justice. Additionally, they dramatically illustrate the problems that arise when one ignores the selection process that funnels out many actors in positions of power in organizations. No doubt such research paints a distorted picture of the relationship between class position and the social response.

The Role and Limitations of Trust

The data offered by Weisburd et al., Hagan and Parker, Shapiro, and Eitle all suggest a more complex relationship between the characteristics of social leverage and the administration of the law than found in the research by Gottfredson and Hirschi. Among the many issues not clearly understood by these findings is the potentially spurious relationship between sanctioning and offender characteristics. What do these characteristics of leverage actually represent? According to Shapiro, the concept of white-collar crime places too much attention on these notions, and cause conceptual mischief by obscuring more important features that have to do with modus operandi. While she acknowledges that offender characteristics may play a role in creating opportunities for wrongdoing, we are better off examining the characteristics of the deviant act, in particular the social organization of trust. To examine Shapiro's claim it is important to distinguish two questions. First, does the concept of trust fairly reflect white-collar crimes? Second, to what extent do characteristics of leverage play a role, if any, in the structure of trust relationships?

We agree with Shapiro that the concept of white-collar crime has been imprisoned by singular attention to offender-based characteristics. We also agree with her that much can be learned about crime by examining the structure of trust relationships. The propensity to focus on offender characteristics, however, does not lead us to the conclusion that notions of status, prestige, and respectability are somehow less important than the characteristics of the offense. Nor do we agree with her dictate that we will all be better off by following her lead and examine settings of trust, how fiduciaries define and enforce trust norms and the structural opportunities and patterns of misconduct that ensue (362). While notions of trust may stimulate our thinking in a number of important ways, we remain unconvinced that trust bottles the essence of what Sutherland referred to as white-collar crimes, or even that it is the most important ingredient in many of them. Furthermore, the notion of trust, as she describes it, raises as many conceptual problems as it solves.

Shapiro makes an important observation that much is to be gained by examining the structure of social relationships in the organization of work. The notion of agency—that certain actors act on behalf of others—is a compelling starting point. Shapiro's contribution to this notion, that agency relationships can be examined along a continuum of trust, is equally important in describing particular patterns of economic interaction. The adoption of the term, "fiduciary trust," is unfortunate in that it has a fixed and specific legal meaning with respect to relationships in which the principal has no say or power in the duties exercised by the trustee on his or her behalf. For example, if an individual establishes a trust on behalf of her children, with the condition that no money may be extracted from the trust until the children turn eighteen, the children may not pick up the phone and demand a check be cut, nor can they command the trust officer to invest their trust in securities as opposed to certificates of deposit. Thus, fiduciary trust is used to describe relationships at the far end of the trust spectrum, where the principal gives up all control of property or resources to the discretion of the agent. Yet, surely most economic relationships are not fiduciary relationships but rather agency relationships. Most white-collar crimes, we would argue, seldom involve relationships in which the principal, or the victim in this instance, has no control, whatsoever, over the actions of the agent. This is most evident in the recent reforms of the securities laws, particularly in efforts to increase control over brokers and dealers by supervisors, and more important, in providing access and information to investors regarding both their agents and the investments. No doubt these reforms are directed at balancing asymmetries, but these were never "fiduciary" in the strict sense of the term. Thus, it seems to us that most white-collar crimes consist of agency relationships as opposed to fiduciary relationships, where there are varying degrees of control and supervision by principals, officers, directors and supervisors in the course of one's duties. This distinction may appear subtle, yet it is significant with respect to Shapiro's argument. We agree that these relationships may be viewed along a continuum of trust—that is to say, some relationships, in some structures, markets, and organizations have varying degrees of direct control by the principals, and thus principals "trust" their agents in differing ways. But in granting this it turns the notion of trust into a different idea—one that takes on a broader sociological meaning that reflects conditions or expectations that adhere to particular roles or activities. When viewed from this perspective, trust no longer has specific applicability to white-collar crimes. Many forms of crime—some would argue that all forms of crime—can be considered as violations of trust. The obvious cases would involve child abuse and neglect or domestic assaults, where parents are entrusted with the duties of parenting, and spouses with the vows of marriage. It is not clear what conceptual clarity this notion thus provides. Nor does it offer much greater clarity by framing the concept as a violation of particular norms. The standards of full disclosure, selflessness, and diligence or care are surely not limited to trust relationships, but rather serve as the benchmarks for many, if not most civil relationships in business or elsewhere. Trust then becomes one of many possible expressions that may be used to describe norms of social interaction—honesty, integrity, compassion, civility, accountability, responsibility, to name but a few others.

Furthermore, as Shapiro acknowledges, even this broader conception of trust does not sufficiently explain or account for other events that typically fall under the rubric of white-collar— such as price-fixing, false insurance claims from doctors, most occupational health and safety violations, most pollution offenses, and most cases of injury resulting from corporate misconduct. In fact, most offenses that are characterized by diffused victimization would appear to fall outside of this concept, unless again, the term trust is broadly construed as synonymous with honesty. If these offenses, which most would recognize as white-collar offenses, are not fully captured by the concept of trust relationships, the concept strikes us as offering little in the way of liberation. If white-collar crime is analogous to conceptual imprisonment, then trust abuse is solitary confinement.

Finally, the social structure of trust relationships, like the social organization of work cannot be examined independent of the notions of leverage. Shapiro provides token acknowledgment to the idea that social class, status, privilege, etc., are differentially distributed in society and may well affect the structure of trust relationships. But we believe that more than token acknowledgment is needed here since this is no mere sociological annoyance. If, as John Hagan suggests, individuals, groups, and classes bring differing amounts of social capital in terms of wealth, education, and networks into their relationships that profoundly affect the social organization of work, then it seems unlikely that we could, or should, examine these trust relationships without regard to these concerns. Furthermore, Shapiro's suggestion that leverage emerges from the structure of trust strikes us as plausibly dubious. Her own description of the risk abatement strategies used to protect principals in agency relationships, which include checking references and examining past performances, indicate that reputation, status, and prestige may precede trust and ultimately define its role. This was, we think, precisely Sutherland's point. If we receive a cold call from the investment company, Fly by Night, we are likely to make inquiries into their history and practices. We may be highly skeptical of their investment opportunities and as a result make frequent calls to monitor their activities and review carefully statements of performance. On the other hand, if we receive a call from a "legitimate" investment company, that is to say, one that has a recognizable name, such as American Express Financial Services, then we are more willing to trust their sales pitch and believe their statements or explanations of performance. If both engage in some form of stock fraud we can readily agree that both violate norms of trust as Shapiro describes them. However, the reputation, status, respect, prestige, etc., that distinguish the two companies are likely to affect the opportunity structures for fraud, and as importantly, the social control reactions that result. As an investor, I may be less willing to accuse American Express of fraud, not because the duties and responsibilities of trust are any different but rather because American Express has "standing" or respectability in the investment community. I may seek redress through the company's channels as opposed to calling the police or the National Association of Securities Dealers or the Securities and Exchange Commission. Differences in leverage also account for the manner in which formal social responses are administered. If our complaint proceeds further, there is greater likelihood that our claim against American Express will be handled first through a civil or administrative remedy, and this decision is less likely to be a product of the structure of the trust relationships and more a function of the company's legitimacy in the social organization of investment services. While trust may play a role in this processing, we doubt that it is solely accountable by the structure of trust relationships. Rather, trust is likely to play a role as an indicator of the seriousness of the act, and typically seriousness is considered in the context of both the harm of the act and the intent of the actor. The harm of the act is the same in either instance. Perceptions about the intent of the actor are, however, strongly shaped by the associations and interpretations we bring to the actor's behavior. If the actor is American Express, (or an employee of American Express) we are simply less inclined to believe that they acted with the intent to purposefully part us from our investments. Thus, our conceptions of trust abuse are shaped in profound and important ways by the social leverage we grant actors by virtue of their legitimacy in the world of work.

The claim we wish to make here is quite simple. The structure of trust relationships, while important to examine, does not, in and of itself, account for the organization of opportunities for white-collar crime, nor does it account for the differences in social control responses. Other factors, independent of the notion of trust may also facilitate or impede these offenses. Other factors, including those that create social leverage, may also explain, rather than be explained by the structure of trust relationships. Sutherland's conception of white-collar crime includes both offense (guile, deceit, trust, etc.) and offender characteristics and accounts for both the structure of opportunities for crime and the social control responses we bring to bear on them. The question of what offenses constitute white-collar crime is irrelevant because white-collar crime does not convey a "thing," but a series of interactions that describe the emergence of crime and the responses we give to them. All facets of these interactions are worthy of study and none should be trivialized.

Expanding the Scope of White-collar Crime

As important as we believe the concept of white-collar crime is, it is ironic that most scholarly attention to it (this piece included) revolves around its meaning rather than its substance. As we have argued, this is in large part due to our desire to turn it into a "thing," and so our attention has been directed toward proving its form and demonstrating its existence. Under the guise of objective science, recent research has attempted to move the debate from theory to empiricism in order to test the constituent parts that make up white-collar crime. As useful as these approaches can be at times, there are at least two dangers to this methodology. One danger is the search for primacy. The other is the search for parsimony. The search for primacy is evident in our fixation on one particular component, such as trust, or in our attempt to determine which of several components explains the greatest variance. This approach is fundamentally flawed with respect to white-collar crime because the term takes its meaning as a composite of these factors working together, and because the factors themselves are interrelated in important ways. The search for parsimony is most evident in efforts to single out one particular feature of a component for study. For example, we contend that notions of social status, respectability, and prestige, are features of a broader concept of social power. We cannot assume to gain a complete understanding of social power by examining only social status, or only respectability. Furthermore, we must also question the degree to which any single measure of an idea such as social status, (e.g., the Duncan Economic Status scale), or level of education, can ever truly capture the complexity that this term represents. We are not implying that these indicators are not valid, or reliable, nor are we condemning research that focuses on one of these important components. Our charge, such as it is, is only relevant to assumptions that these components or indicators are solely sufficient to judge the worth of white-collar crime.

These claims raise an additional concern about the kinds of data we examine with respect to white-collar crime. We have already noted the unfortunate and misleading tendency to limit the scope of white-collar offenses to those found in the criminal courts. We have also noted that the picture of white-collar crime painted by these data is considerably different from that painted from crime statistics. These concerns strike a broader question about the emphasis placed on quantitative research to explain the phenomenon. This is not to say that such studies are unimportant. They are. Rather, the point here is to heed Sutherland's suggestion that much can be learned about white-collar crime through other kinds of research, including case studies, ethnographies, historical studies, and network analyses, that draw from a wide range of data. Such data might involve interviews, minutes, and memoranda from business meetings, autobiographies (a personal favorite of Sutherland's), business reports, job descriptions, codes of ethics, mission statements, operating procedures, etc., that shed light on both the organization and structure of work, as well as the structure and use of social power in the performance of those occupational roles.

It is also important that we heed Diane Vaughan's (1992) advice and study these ideas at both the macro and micro levels. Thus, it is important to ask, how might such things as social class and status differentially define or affect relationships in business and the structure of social control mechanisms, as well as, how might social class and status be exercised in particular relationships in particular instances in order to facilitate certain kinds of crimes, and control responses? In doing so, it is important that we be open to the likelihood that both offense and offender characteristics can tell us something about criminality. We may well hold to the idea that all crime is a product of a single theory of crime, be it low-self control or differential association, and, at the same time, this does not preclude us from asking important questions such as how such factors as the structure of economic systems, the organization of work, or the distribution of class and status might affect how offenders and nonoffenders interpret the world around them. These questions are not limited to white-collar crimes, of course, but they are the contexts of white-collar crime, and, if nothing else, the value of the concept lies in the reminder that such contexts do matter.

Finally, a major contribution of the concept of white-collar crime is the call to consider the different mechanisms used to administer justice. The questions raised above largely concern the structure of offending, but they are equally applicable to the structure of enforcement. Shapiro's study of the SEC is an excellent example of research in this direction. While her study focused primarily on how the structure of securities enforcement drives who gets caught and processed, it is also fruitful to examine how social power operates in the context of enforcement, not only with respect to violators, but to other enforcement agencies as well.

Conclusion

We have tried to argue here that the concept of white-collar crime is not limited to questions of causation; it is not limited to questions of sanctioning, nor is it limited only to opportunity structures. Therefore it is not "falsifiable," by reference to only one of these areas. White-collar crime is not limited solely to the criminal sanction, or to the civil or administrative remedies, and therefore it is not testable by reference to only one kind of data. White-collar crime is not limited to occupational structure and roles, organization, or social leverage, and therefore it is not sufficient to examine only one domain in order to demonstrate its utility. White-collar crime does not entail an event, but a series of complex interactions at multiple-levels that describe a context for particular kinds of behavior patterns. It is not the event but the interactions that make white-collar crime important and worthy of study. It is our premise that white-collar crime has taken on a meaning unintended. If researchers attended to the concept as Sutherland intended, indeed, had they paid heed to his warnings, many of the supposed "problems," would not be so considered. Instead, researchers have attributed causation when none was intended, defined the important characteristics central to his concept, included data he urged to ignore and ignored data he urged to include. While the research posited to date may say something about the utility of some concepts of white-collar crime, it says little about the concept as Sutherland considered it. Given this, it is premature to call for an end to the term. Not only is the jury still out, it really has yet to convene.

Notes

1. Cressey, however, did not consider his study of embezzlement to be a study of white-collar crime, but rather a test of differential association. See John Laub, *Criminology in the Making* (Boston, MA: Northeastern University Press, 1986).
2. While we recognize that Gottfredson and Hirschi argue for a generalist explanation of crime that denies the relevance of social location in explanation, we also recognize that alternative explanations have been forwarded that identify factors unique to the social location of the actors and acts that are still theoretically distinct from their definition (e.g., Wheeler 1990; Braithwaite 1990; Reed and Yaeger 1996).
3. Social psychologists have suggested that there are six major types of resources that are the sources of social power: (1) rewards; (2) coercive (i.e., the ability to harm or punish); (3) expert or informational (including expertise and trust); (4) information or persuasion; (5) personal (e.g., personal attractiveness of the actor); and (6) normative resources (e.g., authority) (French and Raven 1959; Podsakoff and Schriescheim 1985; Yukl and Falbe 1991; Wiggins, Wiggins and Vander Zanden 1994). Each of theses resources can be used to gain social leverage, and each of theses resources can be derived independent of the occupational role that an actor plays, although many of theses resources are associated or amplified by the resources commanded by one in a particular occupational role that an actor plays, although many of theses resources are associated or amplified by the resources commanded by one in a particular occupational role. Additionally, different resources can be used in conjunction with each other to increase the social leverage that an actor can use in an interaction, such as the use of authority, personal, and rewards together to affect a change in a situation.
4. We also agree with Weisburd et al., when they point out that certain white-collar offenses in their data (e.g., securities offenses) are vastly different in both offense and offender characteristics compared to the simple frauds examined by Gottfredson and Hirschi and appear to defy notions of low self-control. As they point out, such differences beg the questions, what then accounts for theses more complex offenses?
5. Nor do we find comfort with their own conclusion that the cause of white-collar crime, like all forms of crime, is low self-control. The point is not to delve into a discussion of the worth of the theory of low self-control. Our own condensed view of this theory is that any attempt to isolate a single cause of crime, while noble and heroic, is akin to efforts to account for a single cause of disease. In boiling strains and types to their least common denominator, one's theory runs the risk of becoming vacuous. So it goes with the notion of low self-control.
6. Perhaps Gottfreddson and Hirschi might agree here but it is not at all evident in their writings where white-collar crime is concerned.
7. Unfortunately, Shapiro's research design and analysis were not organized to answer the question of whether class position or status influenced the likelihood of an offender being a defendant in a criminal, civil, and/or administrative trial, since: (1) no adequate statistical controls were introduced to determine if the grouping of actors who share a similar class or status within a particular social control realm was due to other relevant factors (e.g., seriousness of the offense, type of offense); and (2) any finding could be distorted by historical changes that could influence the relationship between class position and legal arena of case ajudication (e.g., passage of legislation that provides more punitive sanctions in civil or administrative actions might encourage more use generally of civil and administrative actions).

8. We find her claims confusing to the extent that she appears to make the distinction between occupational position and class, as if the two ideas are unrelated. Yet, many sociological discussions of class turn to occupational position in the organization of work as indicators of class differences. See references to Hagan (1985) that follow.

9. Hagan and Parker reject a gradational notion of class as important in understanding crime and punishment. The definition is a *relational* conception of class: "it is not gradational status, but rather structural position in the social organization of work that makes such forms of organized crime possible" (Hagan and Parker 1985: 303). Rather than making inferences indirectly from titles or scales of occupational prestige, their conception of class position measures the location of individuals in position of ownership and authority (Hagan 1989: 4). Their notion of class has three primary dimensions: (1) position in the legitimate or illegitimate economic sector; (2) position relative to ownership of the means of production; and (3) authority in the workplace. Hagan and Parker assert that the power derived from being in positions of control of means of production in the legitimate economy not only provides for different opportunities to commit socially harmful acts, but also serves to influence the responses taken by the state against those actors who are detected by the state.

References

Benson, M. and E. Walker. 1988. "Sentencing the White-collar Offender." *American Sociological Review* 53: 294–302.

Braithwaite, J. 1992. "Poverty, Power and White-collar Crime: From Sutherland to the 1990s." In K. Schlegel and D. Weisburd (eds.) *White-collar Crime Reconsidered*. Boston, MA: Northeastern University Press.

Clinard, M. B. 1952. *The Black Market: A Study of White-collar Crime*. New York: Rinehart.

Coffee, J.C. 1981. "No Soul to Damn, No Body to Kick: An Unscandalized Inquiry into the Problem of Corporate Punishment." *Michigan Law Review* 79: 386–459.

Cressey, D. R. 1953. *Other People's Money: A Study in the Social Psychology of Embezzlement*. Glencoe, IL: Free Press.

Eitle, D. 1996. "Regulatory Justice: The Effects of Class Position and Organizational Centrality on Regulatory Enforcement Outcomes." Unpublished Ph.D. diss., Indiana University.

French, J. and B. Raven. 1959. "The Bases of Social Power." In D. Cartwright (ed.), *Studies in Social Power*. Ann Arbor: University of Michigan Press.

Finn, P.D. 1977. *Fiduciary Obligations*. Sydney, Australia: The Law Book Company.

Geis, G. 1990. "White-collar Crime: What Is It?" pp.31–52 in K. Schlegel and D. Weisburd (eds.) *White-collar Crime Reconsidered*. Boston: Northeastern University Press.

Gottfredson, M. and T. Hirschi. 1990. *A General Theory of Crime*. Stanford, CA: Stanford University Press.

Gould, S. J. 1996. *The Mismeasure of Man*, 2d ed. New York: W.W. Norton and Co.

Hagan, J. 1994. *Crime and Disrepute*. Thousand Oaks, CA: Pine Forge Press.

Hagan, J., I. Nagel, and C. Albonetti. 1980. "The Differential Sentencing of White-collar Offenders in Ten Federal District Courts." *American Sociological Review* 45: 802–20.

Hagan, J., and P. Parker. 1985. "White-collar Crime and Punishment: The Class Structure and Legal Sanctioning of Securities Violations." *American Sociological Review*, 56. 302–16.

Katz, J. 1980. "The Social Movement against White-collar Crime." In E. Bittner and S. Messinger (eds.) *Criminology Review Yearbook,* vol. 2. Beverly Hills: Sage.

Laub, J. 1986. *Criminology in the Making.* Boston: Northeastern University Press.

Podsakoff, P. and C. Schriesheim. 1985. "Field Studies of French and Raven's Bases of Power: Critique, Reanalysis, and Suggestions for Future Research." *Psychological Bulletin* 97: 387–411.

Reed, G. and P. Yeager. 1996. "Organizational Offending and Neoclassical Criminology: Challenging the Reach of a General Theory of Crime." *Criminology* 34: 357–82.

Shapiro, S. 1984. *Wayward Capitalists: Target of the Securities and Exchange Commission.* New Haven, CT: Yale University Press.

———. 1990. "Collaring the Crime, Not the Criminal: Reconsidering the Concept of White-collar Crime." *American Sociological Review* 55: 346–65.

Stone, C. D. 1985. *Where the Law Ends: The Social Control of Corporate Behavior.* New York: Harper and Row.

Sutherland, E. H. 1949. *White-collar Crime.* New York: Holt, Rinehart and Winston.

———. 1941. "Crime and Business." Annals of the American Academy of Political and Social Science 217: 112–8.

Vaughan, D. 1992. "The Macro-Micro Connection in White-collar Crime Theory." In K. Schlegel and D. Weisburd (eds.) *White-collar Crime Reconsidered.* Boston: Northeasten University Press.

Weisburd, D., S. Wheeler, E. Waring, and N. Bode. 1992. *Crimes of the Middle Classes.* New Haven, CT: Yale University Press.

Wheeler, S. 1992. "The Problem of White-collar Crime Motivation." In K. Schlegel and D. Weisburd (eds.) *White-collar Crime Reconsidered.* Boston: Northeastern University Press.

Wheeler, S., D. Weisburd, and N. Bode. 1982. "Sentencing the White-collar Offender: Rhetoric and Reality." *American Sociological Review* 47: 641–59.

Wheeler, S., D. Weisburd, E. Waring, and N. Bode. 1988. "White-collar Crimes and Criminals." *American Criminal Law Review* 25: 331–58.

Wiggins, J., B. Wiggins, and J. Vander Zanden. 1994. *Social Psychology.* New York: McGraw-Hill.

Wilson, J.Q. and R. Hernstein. 1985. *Crime and Human Nature*: The definitive study of the causes of crime. New York: Simon and Schuster.

Yukl, G. and C. Falbe. 1991. "Importance of Different Power Sources in Downward and Lateral Relations." *Journal of Applied Psychology* 76:416–23.

15

The Social Reaction to Treason within a Pluralistic Society: The Pollard Affair

Vered Vinitzky-Seroussi

Introduction

The American press called 1985 "the year of the spy," as one scandal followed another. In all, there were thirteen cases of American citizens who compromised classified documents for foreign governments (mainly to the Soviet Union).[1] In only one of these cases did U.S. secretary of defense Caspar Weinberger submit an affidavit to the presiding judge, in which he is purported to have written "it is difficult for me to conceive of a greater harm to national security than that caused by the defendant in view of the breadth, the critical importance to the United States and the high sensitivity of the information he sold to Israel" (Maclean 1987:8). That defendant was Jonathan Jay Pollard, who sold classified documents to Israel over a period of eighteen months from the summer of 1984 to the fall of 1985. As far as we know, the classified documents provided by Pollard consist of "...detailed analytical studies containing technical calculations, graphs and satellite photographs...highly classified message traffic and intelligence summaries...data on specific weapon systems...naval forces of a certain Middle Eastern country...a study on the lines of communication of a Middle Eastern country...." (Blitzer 1989:165), and so on.

Jonathan Jay Pollard, a U.S. citizen, was born in 1954 to a Jewish family in Texas. At the time of his arrest on 21 November 1985 he was a "watch officer for the Anti-Terrorist Alert Center (ATAC) in the Threat Analysis Division of the Naval Investigative Service of the United States Navy" (*United States v. Jonathan Pollard* 1992).

On 4 June 1986, Pollard pleaded guilty to the "charge of conspiracy to commit espionage, in violation of 18 U.S.C. 794 (c), carrying a maximum sentence of imprisonment for any term or for life, and a $250,000 fine" (DiGenova 1986:22). As part of the plea bargain reached, the prosecution was barred from asking for the maximum sentence. Nevertheless, on 4 March 1987, Jonathan Pollard was sentenced to life imprisonment.

This chapter analyzes the social reactions following the Pollard affair; its findings suggest the way in which a complex, pluralistic society copes with a threat to its moral boundaries. The study demonstrates the impact of various worldviews, priorities, and beliefs on the way in which different subcultures respond to deviant behavior. By understanding the logic behind the different social reactions to the affair, one can not only learn about the structure and values of various segments within society but also comprehend the extent of the threat inherent in the Pollard case.

Deviant Behavior within Modern Society: Treason

One of the approaches within the sociology of deviance posits that the importance of studying deviant behavior derives less from the behavior as such than from what might be learned about the social values and social structures that underlie it (Ben-Yehuda 1985). This perspective is rooted in labeling theory, which emphasizes societal reactions to crime and deviance. It implies that deviance is not a marginal phenomenon but a central one in understanding societies.

Deviant behavior has been long recognized as a relative phenomenon which depends on social, political, cultural, and historical circumstances (Ben-Yehuda 1985; Schur 1979; Schur 1971). Behavior categorized as deviant in one place or time may be acceptable, even encouraged, in another. It has been argued that deviance is often moralistic (e.g., Black 1983; Weisburd 1989). Moreover, deviant behavior may also be perceived as a form of heroism (Schafer 1974).

The substantial variability in definitions of deviant behavior is encouraged by the fact that society today is pluralistic. "Each segment of society has its own values, its own norms, and its own ideological orientation" (Quinney 1973:238). Nonetheless, wouldn't one expect that treason, "the oldest and the most strongly condemned wrongs, the *only* crime defined in the United States Constitution" (Nettler 1982:35), would provoke a more unified social reaction? After all, treason is a "breach of allegiance and of the faithful support a citizen owes to the sovereignty within which he lives" (Hurst 1983:1560). Considering that, at the heart of the definition of any crime or deviant behavior is the value it challenges, treason.threatens one of society's core values and necessities—loyalty—(Simmel 1950; Nettler1982) which is expected from every member of society (Roebuck and Weeber 1978:100).

Inevitably, the question that arises is, to whom precisely is loyalty owed? Simple societies are characterized by a strong sense of integration and community, a sense of center to which one owes loyalty. Pluralistic and complex societies, however, tend to lack a similar structure (Coser 1974:2). Thus, the question of loyalty becomes increasingly difficult in the American cultural context, which comprehends the concept of friendly countries to be cared about and helped. For many Americans, the boundaries between "us" and "them" are either blurry or nonexistent. Moreover, American society is composed of different subcultures with different priorities and beliefs: American citizens with an Irish background who organize fund raising for the Irish Republican Army (IRA), for instance, and the Jewish community which is very active in raising money and lobbying in Washington for Israel.

How can one expect loyalty when there are so many other affiliations and priorities? In fact, Douglas (1970) concludes that in a pluralistic society, the meaning of terms such as "loyalty" or "traitor" may become vague. Furthermore, "in a society of the complexity and diversity of the American one, there are available moral justifications for almost anything" (Lofland 1969:100). Nevertheless, people in the public sphere are most certainly expected to show complete loyalty (Coser 1974).

By punishing individuals who commit acts of treason, society seeks to clarify and sustain its moral and social boundaries. In this particular sense treason can be viewed as functional to social life. The traitor is the "perfect enemy" to society. By "driving" oneself away from the group, and by being punished for that move, the traitor helps to redefine and recreate the boundaries of a society. The deviant person gives "the rest of the community some sense of their own territorial identity" (Erikson 1966:196).

Redefinition and recreation of societal boundaries implies that there may have been a problem with those boundaries to begin with. Ben-Yehuda's study of the European witch craze (1985), and Erikson's study of the crime waves that swept Massachusetts Bay during the seventeenth century (1966), provide good illustrations. Ben-Yehuda states that "where the Church was strong or where progress was not marked (or both) hardly any witchcraze occurred" (1985:73). In the Pollard affair, a crime was committed, but the societal reaction that it precipitated indicated that there was a great concern about the state of the social and moral boundaries in contemporary America, at least among the administration in Washington.

In order to redefine boundaries, deviant behavior must be defined and viewed as opposed to society (Coser 1956). Once a person is classified as a "traitor," this definition becomes a "pivotal category" (Lofland 1969) or a "master status" (Becker 1963; Schur 1971:30). This new definition sets in motion a process of "retrospective interpretation" (Schur 1971); past events in the life of whoever is responsible for the crime are reevaluated according to the "new knowledge" that has been released. The past is reshaped to give the present a new meaning and sense of coherency. As we shall see, once Pollard is defined as a "traitor," his background and personality were redescribed to fit in perfectly with this new identity.

Reassurance and coherency are not the only needs that are met by defining the deviant as evil. Reducing Pollard to no more than a greedy mercenary obviates the need for society to cope with his ideological claims. If Pollard had been perceived as an intelligent, ideological actor, his actions could have implied greater substantial threat to society in terms of defining the exact nature of loyalty.

The fact that Pollard spied for Israel compounded the complications. Israel is considered an ally and friend of the United States. One might perhaps expect that the United States, although angry at the breach of trust committed by a friend, would nevertheless be less concerned about the actual damage caused. After all, it would have been much worse if the classified material had found its way to the Soviet Union or one of its allies. In the same year that former FBI analyst Larry Wu-Tai Chin was revealed to have been giving secrets to China for thirty years, and John A. Walker working for the Soviet Union for over seventeen years—and masterminding a family spy ring to boot—we might well be surprised that Pollard was the one to generate so much controversy and anger. That the Pollard case received so much public attention must be understood within a sociological perspective. Once the societal and moral boundaries are blurred, as in the case of relationships among friends, the perceived threat is much greater. In the Pollard case, American society had to cope not only with a citizen who compromised top secrets while claiming that he was not a traitor (Henderson 1988), but also with a country that breached a trust.

Most of the sociological literature discussing treason deals with the reasoning behind the crime (see, e.g., Hagan 1987; Nettler 1982; Bulloch 1966). This chapter is concerned with the public reaction to treason. Roebuck and Weeber state that "foreign and domestic spies received no support from any quarter in the United States" (1978:123–4), Cromer, however, concludes his study by saying that "even treason does not necessarily lead to...moral unity" (1985:70). Does the societal reaction to treason indeed create solidarity and integration? Although society does not support the traitor, the social reaction to treason does not appear to create greater societal cohesion and bonding. The fragmentary nature of a complex, pluralistic society means that, even under a threat (actual or symbolic) to national security, there is no longer anything that can unify us. This may have been what caused those involved in the affair (the Administration, for example) to be so concerned: even the reaction to treason cannot be counted on to create a strong cohesive force. If all segments of society condemned the act and justified the punishment, there would be no need to worry about the state of moral boundaries. The whole affair could be viewed as just an exceptional event caused by a lunatic. The disputes surrounding the act as well as the punishment imply that there was a problem with the boundaries and, more than anything else reflect the state of contemporary America. And this state is what generated the heat that followed the affair.

Methodology and Data Collection

Data for this study were collected from two Jewish-American newspapers and three non-Jewish-American newspapers. This choice makes it possible to contrast the reaction of the Jewish press to the affair with that of the non-Jewish press. Although the mass media cannot be said to fully represent public opinion, their views are one indicator as well as one of the common ways in which we measure public reactions.

The Jewish community and its press were deeply involved in the Pollard affair for two main reasons. The first has to do with the fact that "for American Jews...the subject that stirs ethnic identity is clearly the State of Israel and its perceived insecure position" (Halle 1984:275). Reactions to the Pollard case presented more than the usual involvement, since by engaging in espionage in the United States, Israel endangered its relationship with its major ally and supporter. The second reason has to do with the fact that Pollard is Jewish. As a result, the Jewish community felt that they faced a serious threat to their acceptance into American society, and of being accused of having a "double loyalty."

Since the Jewish community in the United States is not a monolithic entity, I selected two different newspapers which represent two different segments within this community: the *Jewish Week* and the *Jewish Press*. The *Jewish Week* represents secular Jewry and presents what one might call "mainstream-to-liberal" political views; the *Jewish Press* represents Orthodox Jewry and, in terms of issues which concern Israel, leans heavily to the right of the political spectrum. Moreover, given the fact that they are weekly[2] ethnic newspapers, the circulation[3] of the papers I selected is impressive.

To represent the non-Jewish press I selected three well-known and well-respected newspapers: the *New York Times*, the *Washington Post*, and the *Chicago Tribune*, which also have a very impressive circulation.[4]

The Pollard affair can be divided into three critical periods: (1) the arrest (November 1985); (2) the guilty plea (June 1986); and (3) the sentencing (March 1987). For two months after each of these critical periods, I analyzed everything that was published about the case in the above newspapers. Every theme mentioned was coded and put into specific category. Under "blame and responsibility," for example, I put all the persons, institutions, or nations to whom responsibility for the affair had been imputed. For this chapter I chose to discuss three of the total ten[5] issues or categories in detail: (1) Pollard—the man behind the affair; (2) blame and responsibility; and (3) reactions towards the punishment. The data set consists of 293 items. The distribution of the items according to where each was published is presented in table 15.1.

From table 15.1, we can see that most of the material comes from the non-Jewish press: 60 items come from the Jewish papers, compared to 233 items from the non-Jewish newspapers. This difference

TABLE 15.1
Number of News Items by Newspaper

Name of Newspaper	Number of Items
The Washington Post	92
The New York Times	90
Chicago Tribune	51
The Jewish Press	39
The Jewish Week	21

cannot be attributed to less interest by the Jewish press but to the fact that those papers are weekly papers, and so naturally one can expect fewer news items in them than from a daily newspaper.

Coding and counting the major themes enabled me to contrast the Jewish press and the non-Jewish press. The number of times a theme was mentioned was used as a rough measure of the significance of certain issue to a certain newspaper as well as to society. For example, placing the blame for the affair on the United States was a very popular theme in the Jewish press, while it was hardly mentioned in the non-Jewish American press.

Findings and Discussion

General Trends

In general, the findings reflect the different worldviews within various segments of American society, each of which had its own concerns about the Pollard affair. Thus, the concerns of the Jewish community do not necessarily overlap with those of the administration in Washington. The different reactions to the Pollard affair reflect this disparity.

One of the administration's problems was that the classified material had been transferred to a friendly nation. As mentioned earlier, at first glance, this seems paradoxical; one would expect greater concern if that material would had found its way to a country in the Eastern bloc. From the reactions provoked by the affair it seems that the administration's representatives were hurt as well as worried about the exposure of the material. Their fear, however, seemed to derive less from the actual damage caused than from the concern that an American citizen failing to distinguish between loyalty to his own country and loyalty to one of its allies. In other words, the boundaries between American society and its friends may have become blurred.

In a culture that consists of so many groups with so many priorities and beliefs as that of the United States, the issue of moral boundaries is a very important one. Today it may be a Jewish government employee who feels allegiance to Israel; tomorrow it may be an Irish-American who feels that the IRA may needs help. Furthermore, no excuses, and certainly not the possibility of having more than one loyalty could be shown to be acceptable.

The Jewish in America had other concerns. For this segment of American society a major threat is to be suspected of having a "double loyalty" to the United States and to Israel. Taken as a whole, the Jewish community is well incorporated in the social and political spheres in the United States. The more it is integrated into those institutions, the more it has to lose by being accused of privileging Israel over America. That Israel and the United States call each other friends and allies helps this community deal with both countries. American Jews can give donations to Israel, march in the "Israel Day Parade" in New York, and still be an integral part of American society. Something like the Pollard affair puts American Jews on the spot, makes them feel that they are being looked at with suspicion. This fear was actually voiced by Jews who worked for the administration and who stated that they felt betrayed by Israel, as if Israel was unethically asking them to choose between the two countries.

Hence, we might well expect the reaction of the Jewish community toward Pollard as presented by the newspapers to be strongly negative. However, this expectation was not met. Although the Jewish press does not encourage espionage on behalf of Israel it found its own way clear, if not to justify it, then at least to sympathetically understand it.

The rest of this chapter is devoted to three issues raised by the newspapers in the wake of the affair, issues which illustrate clearly the meaning of social reaction to treason in a pluralistic, complex society. The first illustrates how different subcultures described Jonathan Pollard, the man behind the affair; the second discusses the question of blame and responsibility; the third considers the way in which different segments within society responded to Pollard's punishment.

Jonathan Jay Pollard—The Man behind the Affair

Considering the previous discussion of how society treats its deviants, it should come as no surprise that, as soon as Pollard was arrested, his identity went through a metamorphosis.

The more different and bizarre the deviant is, the more the rest of us can reassure ourselves that this kind of behavior cannot happen to anyone else. In addition to such reassurance, cultures look for coherency; by reshaping the criminal's biography, by showing that "he was always like that," we are able to see that coherency.

Jonathan Pollard was portrayed by the non-Jewish American press as unreliable, as a liar and cheater: "Pollard...claimed frequently to be a colonel in the Israeli army and in the Mossad [the Israeli Secret Service]...that discrepancy indicated that he wasn't telling the truth...a guy who was full of air" (Pear 1985: B8). The Jewish press reacted in much the same way, describing Pollard as "a big mouth...loud and obnoxious" (Blitzer 1985a:46). He was also described as no more than a greedy mercenary. Almost inevitably, the composite description led to a more coherent and consistent perception of Pollard as a traitor. After all, what else could be expected from such a discredited individual?

That both the non-Jewish American press and the Jewish press described the man behind the affair so negatively implies that, beyond the differences between the subcultures that the papers reflect, coherency and reassurance are mutual needs. Moreover, each group could only lose by describing him otherwise. By displaying the man as a combination of greed and stupidity, no one needed to respond to his ideological claims. By ignoring those claims altogether, each segment could cope much better with the challenge to its boundaries.

Blame and Responsibility within a Pluralistic Society

The question of responsibility was a major theme in the Pollard affair. Two contrasting sociological approaches to the issue of responsibility exist. The first proposes that "responsibility for past actions can be fixed absolutely and independently of the method of reconstruction" (Scheff 1973:87). The second, which stems from the sociology of knowledge, suggests that "people go through their lives constructing reality" (Scheff 1973:103), and even responsibility can be "at least partly a product of social structure" (Scheff 1973: 88). The second approach furnishes a better insight into the process of determining responsibility in general and in the Pollard affair in particular.

Locating blame was intimately linked with the different concerns and interests of the parties involved in the Pollard affair and their relative power. By placing the blame in one direction we also display values and worldviews and mark moral boundaries. Placing the blame is a political process, too. "By placing blame people seek to create order, to reassert control over perceived threats, or to preserve existing social institutions" (Nelkin and Gilman 1988: 375–7). In analyzing a case of espionage within the Israeli establishment, Cromer shows that "rather than blaming the individual concerned, responsibility was placed on the shoulders of the founding fathers who supposedly nurtured him [the spy]" (1986:403). In the Israeli affair this type of blame served the interests of particular segments within the Israeli society, which used the affair to demonstrate their own moral superiority.

TABLE 15.2
Percentage of Blame by Type of Newspaper

Blame Ascribed:	Jewish Press		American Press	
	No.	%(*)	No.	%(*)
Pollard	10	25%	16	24%
Israel—Moral	2	5%	31	46%
Israel—Practical	8	20%	6	9%
United States	15	38%	6	9%
Media	4	10%	0	
Judge	1	2.5%	0	
U.S.-Israeli Relations			8	12%
N	40	100.5%	67	100%

*Percentages were calculated as the number of times blame was specifically ascribed, divided by the total number of times blame was ascribed. For example, if one type of newspaper ascribed blame twenty times, and ten of those times attributed it to Pollard, then Pollard was the target of blame in 50 percent of the cases.

Behind the imputation of responsibility often lies a certain logic which, more than anything else serves the blamer. The accounts used to justify certain attitudes are not arbitrary; rather, "they reflect the type of justification acceptable in a specific cultural matrix" (Ben-Yehuda 1985: 212). Even more so, those arguments reflect specific needs of a particular cultural and political matrix within society.

The above table displays the distribution of agents blamed for the Pollard affair according to type of press (Jewish versus non-Jewish).

As table 15.2 reveals, no blame for the affair was ever explicitly attributed to the Jewish community, although it could well have been expected, and although many articles mentioned the problem of "double loyalty." Either the act of one individual could not contaminate the entire community, or the indictment of the entire community could lay one open to the charge of anti-Semitism.

Ultimately, blaming Pollard serves all interests. "Blaming the individual for illness limits the responsibility of the larger society" (Nelkin and Gilman 1988: 371). Significant segments within American society wished to show that the problem lay with one specific person and not with society as a whole. By pointing the finger at Pollard and by showing how greedy, bizarre, and stupid he was, society limits its own responsibility for such incidents. The Jewish community also gains from describing Pollard in the same way. By displaying Pollard as a unique case of someone with emotional problems, a distorted sense of reality, and a lack of loyalty to his country, the Jewish community need not question itself and its ideology, which emphasizes the importance and the centrality of Israel in its life.

However, the findings show that, although Pollard was on the list of those accused, he was neither the sole nor even prime target. In both units the non-Jewish press and the Jewish press Pollard took only 25 percent of the total blame. This can be interpreted as indicating that although no one wanted to ignore Pollard's part in the affair, blaming him alone was not sufficient, neither for the American population nor for the Jewish one.

The most popular target for blame within the Jewish community was what we would call the victim, that is, the United States (38 percent— see table 15.2). An editorial published in the *Jewish Week* immediately after Pollard pleaded guilty states that "Israel was apparently *forced* to gather covertly information vital to its security, information it was probably entitled to receive" (editorial, 1986:24, emphasis added). A letter to the editor of the *Jewish Press* claims that "were our administration to accord the Israeli government access to America's secret files concerning Israel's enemies' activities,…and what else might affect Israel, the latter would not need to spy on the U.S.A." (Wahle 1985:48). America's blame derived also from its arms sales to Arab countries: "As long as the United States sells weapons to Arab countries, the State of Israel has an obligation to its citizens to find out by whatever means, everything about these U.S. weapons in Arab hands" (Barnett 1985:48).

Blame was also imputed to American agencies and individuals for the way in which the entire affair was handled. Under that category the media was a popular target. "Frequently…incidents are amplified and magnified by the press, creating a scandal that is out of all proportion to their importance. Such is the case with the Pollard affair" (Gersten 1986:12). Caspar Weinbeger, then secretary of defense, was also a target for the Jewish community's analysis. Weinberger was accused of maintaining a double standard when it comes to Israel (Friedman 1987), of exaggerating the importance of the case, and of being a traitor for not sharing information with Israel (Cooperberg 1987:56B).

Nor did the Jewish press spare Israel. Still, Israel was accused more on practical grounds than moral ones (20 percent for the former and 5 percent for the latter). Three types of practical criticism were leveled against Israel. The first concerned Pollard's personality: Israel was accused of stupidity in choosing him as its agent in the United States. A letter to the editor of the *Jewish Week* states: "I do blame Israel for engaging a clumsy, indiscreet amateur like Jonathan Pollard for carrying out this sensitive...mission" (Wahle 1985a:29). The second condemned Israel's recruitment of an American Jew, thereby endangering the Jewish community in the United States. "The decision by Israel to 'run' an American *Jewish* intelligence agent in Washington...a lot of people are saying that the Israelis are arrogant. They don't care about the American Jewish community" (Blitzer 1985:3; emphasis added). The third type of criticism focused on the financial and moral risks Israel took by spying on, and in, the United States. "Without American support in arms, there would be no Israel today...someone forgot to balance a gain gotten by transgression against the loss it involves" (Eisenstadt 1986:11).

In sum, the answers to the question of who should be blamed for the affair as provided by the Jewish press reflected its concerns and priorities. Their accounts reflect the fact that American Jews were concerned about being perceived as loyal and valuable members of this society, and about Israel's survival at the same time. As Ben-Yehuda noted, accounts do reflect the prevailing morality (1985). Blaming both Israel and the United States enabled the Jewish community to avoid contending with some problems that seem to threaten it, such as the chronic tension in their ideology and worldview concerning its relationship with its "homeland" and "Holy Land." It was easier to blame the media, Caspar Weinberger, and others. It would be inaccurate to claim that these issues were absent from the Jewish discourse that followed the affair; the Jewish community's love for both countries was clearly presented. However, it was displayed as something that should not cause any deviant or criminal behavior, since the act of treason had been explained away and justified in many other ways.

The non-Jewish press had a different agenda. It had to cope with a problem presented by a man who had committed an act of treason, with boundaries that needed redefinition, and with a nation that had breached a trust. Singling Pollard out for blame would not necessarily clarify the boundaries for all the segments that constitute the United States. Thus, Pollard was not the only one held responsible.

Interestingly enough, the list of accused included the United States, the victim itself (9 percent—see table 15.2). But this is no surprise when one understands the logic behind it. The United States was accused of being too soft when it came to Israel, encouraging Israel to feel she could do no wrong in the United States. "The Pollard operation was a direct outgrowth of the tight links between Jerusalem and the Reagan administration and the conviction here [in Israel] that Washington would forgive Israel any of its sins" (Broder 1987:5). The clear-cut message is that the United States should be harder on Israel (and on other countries as well) because otherwise people, as well as nations, will take advantage and cause harm. From the American point of view, the symbolic boundaries between the nations had become blurred.

At the top of the list of accused was Israel, blamed for the affair on practical (9 percent) and moral (46 percent) grounds. The practical grounds encompassed two types of arguments, the first regarding the notion that Israel had no need to spy on the United States since it was privy already to so much information. "Administration officials have said they are perplexed by the incident, noting that the United States already shares much of its most sensitive military information with the Israelis" (Shenon 1985:33). The second type of argument that was raised within the practical domain concentrated on the risk Israel had taken by spying in the United States. An article published after Pollard pleaded guilty asks whether "the Pollards in America, and their spymaster in Israel, have done more damage to their respective countries than any terrorist could dream of doing...Is there anybody in Jerusalem who asked 'is it worth it?'" (Safire 1986:31).

While the Jewish press underscored the practical problematics of Israel's espionage, the non-Jewish American press, and the administration, emphasized the moral issues and the compromise of friendship between countries. Secretary of State George Shultz declared, "I am deeply distressed about the Pollard case and I think it is very disheartening to find that Israel has been spying on the United States.... Perhaps it hurts especially when it's Israel" (Shipler 1987:12). The world may be cruel and cynical, and everybody may very well spy on everybody else; still, "That is no excuse...as for Israel, the Pollard affair... represents an act of breathtaking bad faith and ingratitude toward Israel's greatest benefactor.... To use an American citizen to steal American secrets is an atrocious breach of the American-Israeli relationship" (Krauthammer 1987:17). By the same token, there was a message to the general population that no matter what kind of relationship the United States has with its allies, transferring classified documents by unauthorized hands is an unacceptable act. If the press is any indication, what frightened the administration as well as American society, is the notion that American citizens could lose the ability to distinguish between loyalty to their country and loyalty to their country's friends.

The logic behind the blaming process in the Pollard affair reflects the problems and the concerns of American society, which must balance and confront different pressures. On one hand there is Pollard: blaming Pollard solely for the affair entails less responsibility as far as society is concerned and hence, one cannot use the case to redefine the social boundaries. On the other hand, blaming society for the affair may help it recreate its boundaries, but at the same time requires public admission of a problem. The solution that was found was perfect. Pollard was partially blamed for the affair, allowing different segments of the society to reassure their members that the problem was not crucial, since a deviant personality was at the core of the problem. The remaining responsibility was ascribed mainly to Israel. By dividing the blame for the affair in this fashion, American society did not have to declare that it had a problem with loyalty and boundaries, and at the same time it redefined them very clearly.

The Social Response to Pollard's Punishment

Considering that "the reaction may be stronger under these conditions [danger from within] because the 'enemy' from within,...not only puts into question the values and interest of the group, but also threatens its very unity" (Coser 1956:69), one might have expected Pollard's life sentence to be accepted and understood. Nevertheless, the reactions to Pollard's punishment were far from identical, enabling again different groups to express their perception of the whole affair and at the same time convey messages to members of society.

The fact that Walker, Chin, and Pollard received life term in prison means, basically, that it does not matter to whom one sells secrets; the punishment will be the same. The operation can go on for seventeen years (as in the Walker affair) or eighteen months (as in the Pollard case), the punishment will be the same. No acts of treachery are excusable. This theme was mentioned in the non-Jewish American press sixteen times but only once in the Jewish press.

At the beginning of the affair all the newspapers quoted then-president of the United States Ronald Reagan as saying that "the United States would not hesitate to root out and prosecute the spies of any nation, letting the 'chips fall where they may'" (Boyd 1985:1). The punishment gave formal support to that notion. After the sentencing, the *Washington Post* published an editorial which stated: "Jonathan Pollard got life imprisonment for spying for Israel. He deserved severe punishment. He took money for stealing quantities of major secrets over a period of eighteen months. To go easy because he was shoveling information to a country that is a friend would condone his compromising of specific secrets, of intelligence sources and methods of American Freedom of Action" (1987:22). Behind this message was the fear that only severe punishment of the defendant would make it clear to members of American society that boundaries exist even among friends. The prosecution in the Pollard case put it very clearly: "...a moderate sentence would not deter, and may even invite, similar unlawful conduct by others. If a less severe sentence were ruled out because the foreign nation involved is a U.S. ally, a potentially damaging signal would thereby be communicated to individuals, or foreign countries, contemplating espionage activities in the United States" (DiGenova 1986:49). That all the different spies received the same punishment, no matter what the circumstances, is more than just a matter of the criminal justice system; it is a redefinition of moral and social boundaries.

While the non-Jewish American press reiterated that the punishment was just and that the identity of the spying nation was immaterial, the Jewish press contended that it did matter to whom one sold secrets. Pollard's sentence was deemed, and dangerously resembled, revenge.

In support of the notion that the punishment was excessive (Halpern 1987) the Jewish community resorted to the issue of the threat to national security: "Helping Israel is not analogous to helping the Soviet Union, which poses a direct threat to the United States. Reports of the case do not suggest that Pollard's crime endangered American lives. And Israel has been a reliable custodian of U.S. secrets, some reportedly more sensitive than those Pollard passed" (Halpern 1987:56). Not surprisingly, this type of attitude was not popular in the non-Jewish American press, which emphasized how substantial the threat to U.S. national security was.

The non-Jewish American press and the administration sought to redefine boundaries that had been put into question. The Jewish community, on the other hand agreed that Pollard deserved punishment, but not the one meted out. The dispute, in fact, was not so much about the punishment *per se* but about the meaning of the punishment and the messages it conveyed. That meaning and those messages are, more than anything else, a reflection of different moral universes with different concerns and interests.

Concluding Remarks

The official societal reaction to Pollard was the criminalization of his acts. *Prima facie*, there was no argument that Pollard had committed a crime. However, the above findings illustrate that the social reaction to deviant behavior is determined not so much by an actual objective threat to the various parties involved, but by the different worldviews, priorities, and concerns that existed long before Pollard's actions took place, and will remain long after as well. This chapter illustrates how any reality can be constructed to conform with concerns and interests of the groups involved. The same damage or threat to the national security can be perceived as substantial or negligible according to the worldview behind each argument. The responsibility for the affair was demonstrated to suit the needs of the groups that felt threatened by the affair and its implications for their ideology and lifestyle. More than anything else, the social reaction to treason as presented here teaches us about different segments within society and how they deal with a challenge to their boundaries and existence.

The fact that the country involved was an ally of the United States provoked more concern than we would have expected, at least in the Administration in Washington. The major threat in the Pollard affair, in my opinion, was the fear that members of American society may have difficulty in distinguishing between loyalty to their country and to their country's friends in the world. If the boundaries between enemies need to be clarified, this case aroused a desperate need to redefine or even create the boundaries between friends.

The need to redefine moral, social, political as well as geographical boundaries can be understood by looking at the findings of the above study, by understanding the way in which the Pollard affair was perceived by the different segments of American society.

With these concerns in mind, one should not be surprised by the fact that the then-secretary of defense, Caspar Weinberger, felt the need to send the judge presiding in the Pollard case an affidavit in order to make sure that, at the very least, he would take the matter as seriously as possible. The feeling was that American society needed a clear-cut message that there were no excuses whatsoever for an act of treachery; that, with all due respect to the complex structure of this society, loyalty to the state should be above all challenges. This case, and especially Pollard's sentence, conveys a message to all potential traitors that society does not and will not tolerate any kind of espionage activities, regardless of the type of material, the country to which this material is delivered, or the ideology behind the act.

In this sense, this study illustrates that, although treason cannot integrate a pluralistic, complex society, the reaction to it can clarify bound-aries. Alas, such redefinition and clarification of boundaries cannot be perceived as the prefect remedy for those seeking societal cohesion. The findings may be frightening indeed, as they indicate that even trea-son can be understood, if not accepted.

Notes

A version of this paper was presented at the 1990 meetings of the American Socio-logical Association. I am grateful to Nachman Ben-Yehuda, David Weisburd, and Erich Goode for their helpful remarks and support. A postdoctoral fellowship from VATAT foundation at the Hebrew University is gratefully acknowledged.

1. Larry Wu-Tai Chin was charged with spying for China and faced two life terms in prison plus fines. He committed suicide in jail while awaiting sentencing. Jonathan Pollard was charged with selling classified documents to Israel and sentenced to life in prison. Anne Henderson Pollard (Pollard's wife) was charged with unauthorized possession of national defense information and sentenced to two-five years in prison (the sentences to run concurrently). John A. Walker, Jr., was charged with spying for the Soviet Union and sentenced to two life terms. Michael Walker was charged with providing classified documents to John Walker, his father, and sentenced to twenty-five years in prison. Arthur J. Walker was charged with delivering classified documents to John Walker, his brother, and sentenced to three life terms and forty years (the sentences to run concurrently). Jerry Whitworth was charged with passing classified documents to John Walker and sentenced to 365 years in prison. Edward L. Howard was charged with pass-ing intelligence information to the Soviet Union. Howard fled the country. Sharon M. Scranage was charged with passing intelligence information to her Ghanaian lover and sentenced to five years in prison and 1000 hours of community service. Richard M. Miller was charged with selling counterintelligence secrets to a So-viet émigrée lover and sentenced to two life terms. Karl F. Koecher was charged with spying for the Czechoslovakian intelligence service and sentenced to time served since his arrest, on condition that he was exchanged for a Soviet dissident. Thomas P. Cavanagh was charged with attempting to sell classified documents to Soviet agent and sentenced to life in prison. Ronald W. Pelton was charged with selling secrets to the Soviet Union and sentenced to life imprisonment.
2. *The Jewish Press* has a circulation of 130,000; the *Jewish Week's* circulation is 109,600.
3. The information about the *New York Times* and the *Jewish Press* came from The New York Publicity outlet, New York, 1988. The information about the *Wash-ington Post, Chicago Tribune,* and the *Jewish Week* came from Gale Directory of Publication, D. P. Boyden (ed.), Detroit, 1989 (see bibliography).
4. A circulation of 1,048,000 on weekdays, 815,000 on Saturdays and 1,616,000 on Sundays for the *New York Times*; 796,659 on weekdays, 753,762 on Satur-days, and 1,112,802 on Sundays for the *Washington Post*; 758,464 on week-days, 601,946 on Saturdays, and 1,126,293 on Sundays for the *Chicago Tribune.*
5. The ten categories/issues are: (1) Pollard—a description of the man behind the affair; (2) Israel—a description of the country behind the affair; (3) possible legitimation for espionage; (4) blame and responsibility; (5) how should the Jewish community react; (6) damage assessments; (7) does it matter to whom

one sells secrets; (8) reactions to the punishment; (9) the relationship between Israel and the United States; and (10) how to prevent recurrence.

References

Barber, Bernard. 1983. *The Logic and Limits of Trust*. New Brunswick, NJ: Rutgers University Press.

Barnett, Samuel and Thelma Barnett. 1985. "Why Israel Spy." *The Jewish Press* (13 Dec.):48.

Becker, Howard S. 1963. *Outsiders*. New York: The Free Press.

Ben-Yehuda, Nachman. 1985. *Deviance and Moral Boundaries*. Chicago: The University of Chicago Press.

———. 1986. "The Sociology of Moral Panics: Toward a New Synthesis." *The Sociological Quarterly* 27(4) :495–513.

Bergesen, Albert J. 1977. "Political Witch Hunts: The Sacred and the Subversive in Cross National Perspective." *American Sociological Review* 42:220–33.

Black, D. 1983. "Crime as Social Control." *American Sociological Review* 43:34–45.

Blitzer, Wolf. 1985. "Spy Case Dismays Jewish Federal Employees." *The Jewish Week* (20 Dec.):3.

———. 1985. "The Unlikely Spy." *The Jewish Week* (6 Dec.):46.

———. 1989. *Territory of Lies*. New York: Harper and Row.

Bovery, Margaret. 1963. *Treason in the Twentieth Century*. New York: G.P. Putnam Sons.

Boyd, Gerald M. 1985. "Reagan Voices Worry on Spies of Any Nation." *New York Times* (1 Dec.): A1.

Boyden, P.D., ed. 1989. *Gale Directory of Publications*. Detroit: Gale Research Inc.

Boyle, Andrew. 1979. *The Fourth Man*. New York: Bantam Books.

Broder, Jonathan. 1987. "Israel Finally Feels Impact of Pollard Spy Case." *Chicago Tribune* (8 Mar.): 5.

Bulloch, John. 1966. *Akin to Treason*. London: Arthur Barker.

Cohen, Stanley. 1972. *Folk Devils and Moral Panics*. London: MacGibbon and Kee.

Cooperberg, Gary M. 1987. "Open Letter to Jonathan Pollard." *Jewish Press* (27 Mar.):56B.

Coser, Lewis. 1956. *The Functions of Social Conflict*. New York: The Free Press.

———. 1974. *Greedy Institutions*. New York: The Free Press.

Cromer, Gerald. 1985. "The Beer Affair: Israeli Social Reaction to a Soviet Agent." *Crossroads* 15:55–75.

———. 1986. "Secularization is the Root of All Evil: The Response of Ultra Orthodox Judaism to Social Deviance." The Ninth International Congress for Jewish Science 2(3).

Dentler, Robert A. and Kai T. Erikson. 1959. "The Functions of Deviance in Groups." *Social Problems* 7(2): 98–107.

DiGenova, Joseph E. 1985. *United States of America v. Jonathan Jay Pollard*. United States District Court for the District of Columbia.

Douglas, Jack. 1970. "Deviance and Order in a Pluralistic Society." pp. 367–401 in J.C. MaKinney and E.A.Tiryakian (eds.)*Theoretical Sociology: Perspectives and Developments*. New York: Appleton-Century-Crofts.

Editorial. 1986. "Pollard in Perspective." *The Jewish Week* (13 Jun.):24.

Editorial. 1987. "And What about Israel?" *The Washington Post* (6 Mar.):22.

Editorial. 1987. "Reaction to the Pollard Affair." *The Jewish Press* (3 Apr.) :5, 54B.

Eisenstadt, Joseph. 1986. "The Pollard Affair." *The Jewish Week* (4 Jul.):11.

Erikson, Kai T. 1966. *Wayward Puritans*. New York: John Wiley and Sons.

Friedman, Silvia. 1987. "Why Did Israel Recruit Pollard? Did His Actions Hurt the U.S.?" *The Jewish Press*.

Garfinkel, Harold. 1956. "Conditions of Successful Degradation Ceremonies." *American Journal of Sociology* 61(5) :420–4.

Gersten, Chris. 1986. "Placing the Pollard Case in Perspective." *The Jewish Press* (18 Jul.):12.

Gusfield, J.R. 1963. *Symbolic Crusade: Status Politics and the American Movement*. Chicago: University of Illinois Press.

Hagan, Frank E. 1987. "Espionage as Political Crime?: A Typology of Spies." Paper presented at the American Society of Criminology, Montreal, November.

Halle, David. 1984. *American Working Man*. Chicago: University of Chicago Press.

Halpern, Seth A. 1987. "Why Pollard was Sentenced to Life." *The Jewish Press* (10 Apr.):55.

———. 1987a. "Pollard Sentence Too Harsh." *The Jewish Press* (17 Apr.):56.

Henderson, B.R. 1988. *Pollard: The Spy Story*. New York: Alpha Books.

Holsti, Ole R. 1969. *Content Analysis for the Social Sciences and Humanities*. Reading, MA: Addison-Wesley.

Hurst, James W. 1983. "Treason." in *Encyclopedia of Crime and Justice*, edited by S.H. Kadish. 4:1559–61

Kneece, Jack. [1986]1988. *Family Treason—The Walker Spy Case*. New York: Paper Jacks.

Krauthammer, Charles. 1987. "Pollard and the Jews." *Washington Post* (20 Mar.):17.

Lindey, Robert. 1979. *The Falcon and the Snow Man*. New York: Pocket Books.

Lofland, John. 1969. *Deviance and Identity*. Englewood Cliffs, NJ: Prentice-Hall.

Maclean, John N. 1987. "Navy Analyst Who Spied for Israel Gets Life Prison Sentence." *Chicago Tribune* (5 Mar.):8.

Nelkin, Dorothy and Sander I. Gilman. 1988. "Placing the Blame for Devastating Disease." *Social Research* 55(3) :361–78.

Nettler, Gwynn. 1982. *Lying, Cheating, Stealing*. Ohio: Anderson Publishers Co.

New York Publicity Outlet. 1988. New York.

Pear, Robert. 1985. "Analyst Told 10 Years Ago of Working for Israeli Intelligence." *New York Times* (27 Nov.): B8.

Quinney, Richard. 1973. "A Theory of Social Reality of Crime" in Harvey A. Farberman and Erich Good (eds.) *Social Reality*. Englewood Cliffs, NJ: Prentice-Hall.

Roebuck, Julian and Stanley C. Weeber. 1978. *Political Crime in the United States*. New York: Praeger.

Safire, William. 1986. "Rogues Rewarded." *New York Times* (6 Jun.): A31.

Schaffer, Stephen. 1974. *The Political Crime*. New York: The Free Press

Scheff, Thomas J. 1973. "Negotiation Reality: Notes on Power in the Assessment of Responsibility" pp. 87–103 in Harvey A. Farberman and Erich Goode (eds.) *Social Reality*. Englewood Cliffs, NJ: Prentice-Hall.

Schiffres, I.J. 1973. "Sedition, Subversive Activities, and Treason." *American Jurisprudence* 70:1–32.

Schur, Edvin M. 1971. *Labeling Deviance*. New York: Harper and Row.

Shenon, Philip. 1985. "Wife of Navy Analyst is Charged with Possessing Classified Data." *New York Times* (23 Nov): A1,33.

Shipler, David K. 1987. "Shultz 'Distressed' by Israel Spy Case." *New York Times* (12 Mar.):11.

Simmel, Georg. 1964. *Conflict and the Web of Group Affiliation*. New York: The Free Press.

Sutherland, Douglas. 1980. *The Great Betrayal*. Middlessex: Penguin Books.
United States of America v. Jonathan Jay Pollard. 959F. 2d 1011 D.C. cir. (1992).
Whale, Charlotte. 1985. "On Israel Spying." *The Jewish Press* (20 Dec.): 48.
————. 1985. "Israel's Right to Spy." *The Jewish Week* (13 Dec.): 29
West, Rebecca. 1964. *The New Meaning of Treason*. New York: Penguin Books.
Weisburd, David. 1989. *Jewish Settlers Violence*. University Park and London: Pennsylvania State University Press.
Young, George K. 1972. *Who is My Liege?* London: Gentry Books.

16

Technological and Other Changes: Boundary Crossings in the Control of Deviance

Bonnie Berry

Boundary crossings imply changes. The types of boundaries traditionally crossed over time in the social control of deviance are the stated purposes of control, definitions of deviance, the mechanisms of control, the composition and number of social control agents, the measured outcomes of control, and theory development and application. Time itself is a boundary; its passage denotes the evolutionary changes in the content of moral crusades and other social control agendas, which color social control practices and effects. Crime, as a legally defined behavior encompassed under the broader category of deviance, varies over time along these dimensions.

Boundaries are the conceptual walls that surround behaviors, organizations, and feelings (belief systems, values, perceptions) relevant to the social control of deviance. During a drug war, the public is instilled with the feeling that drug use is a crime and leads to crime, and the criminal justice system (as the organization) is charged with increasing arrests, convictions, and punishments (the behaviors of control). Considering the same "deviance," drug use, during nondrug war times, public perception might be that drug use is unhealthy behavior for the user and counseling by health and mental health professionals may be seen as the appropriate response.

Some of the boundaries in deviance and social control are tangible while others are not so evident. Concrete boundaries include laws; less tangible boundaries, which are influenced by and influence law, include public perceptions. Laws define deviant and nondeviant behavior and they prescribe the controls that will be applied when proscribed behaviors are discovered. Legal boundaries are crossed with the passage of laws that change definitions, change the formal responses to deviance, and possibly change the perception of deviant behavior.

We can imagine law as something that behaves (Black 1976). Law responds to calls for changes in societal and legal reaction to certain behaviors. These changes are initiated by political agendas and by social movements such as moral panics. Law is not only life-like in that it is reactive to social forces, it is the vehicle through which people who possess the power to impose social control do. In this way, law is dynamic since it is exercised by a changing set of individual social control actors with a changing set of agendas.

Social movements, variously termed moral panics (cf. Ben-Yehuda 1990) and moral crusades (cf. Becker 1963), change public perceptions about deviance as well as the activities of social control. These movements, illustrated by the drug war of the 1980s, the Temperance Movement, antipornography movements, and so on, are initiated by moral entrepreneurs whose directives are facilitated, legitimated, and strengthened by the mass media, religious leaders, politicians, and socially accredited experts (Becker 1963; Schur 1980; Cohen 1972; Goode 1989). The movement is then enacted by formal social control agents such as legislators and entire social control systems (mental health, criminal justice, etc.). While public attitudes, mass media, etc., in combination feed into the crusades, the great and singular force behind these movements is social power.

Probably the single best explanation for the phenomena of deviance and social control, in a state of flux or not, is power. And power is closely tied to a society's political and economic structure (Cohen 1974; Turk 1975; Schur 1969; Chambliss 1978; 1988; Quinney 1974). Specifically, an inequitable economic structure, which shapes the political and other social structures, ensures unwavering social stratification through social control (Ben-Yehuda 1990; Schur 1979; 1980; Turk 1979; Gusfield 1963; and Chambliss 1964).

In other words, deviance is socially constructed by moral entrepreneurs, legislators, political figures and other members of a society's controlling stratum who have the power to coerce and who are immune from retaliation (Gibbs 1967). Not all segments of society may agree on the definitions of deviance or the appropriate responses to deviance but consensus is not necessary in order to impose the will of the power elite (Cohen 1986a and 1986b). While definitions of deviance actually represent cultural and social conflict, the political symbols that control public opinion are manipulated by the socially powerful in a process of "deviantization" (Schur 1979; 1980).

Rather than suppressing or preventing deviance, this deviantization process escalates deviance by increasing the probability of primary and secondary deviance (Schur 1973; 1980; Lemert 1951). In his symbolic-interactionist view of crime as a product of criminal justice system behavior, Lemert (1967) proposes that the societal reaction to primary deviance leads to an "amplification spiral" (see also Lemert 1958). Lest one think that amplification is an unfortunate accident or unintended by-product of societal reaction, Ben-Yehuda (1990) goes so far as to say that, regardless of the purpose stated for public consumption, it is not the intention of moral panics to reduce deviance. That figures given what Turk (1979) and others have said about boundary maintenance and reduction of threat being prime interests of those with the power to determine deviance and social control. If the activities of the criminal justice and other social control systems are capable only of increasing deviance, radical nonintervention seems the more effective route to reducing deviance (Schur 1973). However, such a proposal presumes that the powerful are motivated to reduce deviance and control, which they may not be.

Let us now consider some of the bounded and interrelated variables of social control. Purposes, definitions, methods, and outcomes of social control change, and changes in one variable can cause changes in the other variables. Fluctuations in theoretical development could have the greatest impact on reducing socially harmful behavior, but theory has a peripheral influence on social control purposes, definitions, methods, and outcomes.

Definitions

Definitions of deviance are confined within boundaries which stretch and shrink. Over time, some definitions may broaden, allowing for a greater encompassing of behaviors defined deviant, as illustrated by drug-testing of certain occupations. Or the definitions may narrow, allowing for more restricted interpretations of deviant behavior and thereby fewer formal interventions to control behavior. In the third edition of the American Psychological Association Diagnostic and Statistical Manual, the clinical redefinition of homosexuality from a form of mental illness to an alternative lifestyle illustrates a narrowed definition (Teal 1971; Kitzinger 1987).

Some definitional boundaries change little over time, such as those surrounding elite and lower status crime. If definitions of elite deviance remain confined and static, the reason may be that elites do not want a heightened punitive response to a form of deviance for which they or their social peers could be identified. Wealth, through earned or unearned income, guarantees the power but not the expertise to define deviance. "Socially accredited experts" with social control-relevant educational degrees and occupational positions (notably in law, psychology, and medicine) along with the ruling elite, decide on the intricacies of savings and loan and other elite crimes as well as armed robbery and other lower status crimes (Cohen 1972: 9; Cohen 1985; Quinney 1974; 1985; Chambliss 1964; Gusfield 1963). In other words, the concept of power helps us to understand not only who can deviantize whom but also why the boundaries between elite and lower status deviance remain relatively firm.

While it is accepted that the elite are in a position to deviantize and that this power maintains political and economic power (Haskell and Yablonski 1983; Turk 1982), there is some disagreement about whether elite deviance is more stigmatized and controlled than it once was. Ben-Yehuda (1990) believes that there has been a change in moral boundaries, and cites the Watergate exposure as the catalyst. And with the advancements in technology allowing for greater paper trails, concealment of elite deviance may be more difficult. However, even if the capacity to discover elite deviance has increased, the criminal and internal organizational punishments continue to be unlikely and mild (cf. Berry 1994).

Compared to elite deviance, there may be more changes and more visible changes in the definition and control of lower status deviance. Under conservative social conditions, mainstream definitions cite the cause of deviance as some defect within the individual deviant. Moreover, definitions of deviance can take on rather pessimistic and severe attributes, such as habitual offender statutes and the "sex psychopath" statutes of decades ago (Hagan 1985). Labels such as these attribute serious deviancy traits to the labelees and encourage such harsh responses as lifelong confinement. Some definitions become more encompassing by becoming vague. The current drug war applies the widened category "drug-related offenders" to law violators who commit a truly drug-relevant crime such as selling drugs and to law violators who have used drugs. In other words, the relationship between drug use and law violation does not have to be close.

Application of this broad and ambiguous definition has widened the range of punishments to include compulsory drug-testing and drug treatment, electronic monitoring, intensive supervision programs, asset forfeiture, lengthier and mandatory prison sentences, and (if a death results from the offense) execution (Goode 1989; Clear and Cole 1990).

The relationship between changing definitions and social control responses is not always clear. With the advent of stated concern over drunk driving in the 1970s, drunk driving became a more serious offense in the eyes of the public and the criminal justice system, requiring more serious social control. Serious social control can mean additional punishment, even if the punishment is irrelevant to the specific form of deviance. Drunk driving offenders on electronic monitoring are drug tested in some programs even though they may have no history of drug use (Baumer and Mendelsohn 1990).

Methods of Social Control

First, let us distinguish between two methods, or channels if the reader prefers, of social control: (1) mechanisms of control and (2) agents of control. Mechanisms are the instruments of control, the technology and programs of control. They are the material objects (for example, electronic monitoring devices) and the behaviors that follow from policies and other calls for social control. Agents of control are the people who directly and indirectly impose control; they make up the systems, organizations, and individual actors who develop and administer control. Social control systems most obviously are mental health, criminal justice, medical, educational, and so on; but also include the economic and political systems since they determine policies and enact legislation. Organizations are smaller than systems. They comprise the police departments, mental health agencies, state departments of correction, and so on, that do the more "hands on" work of social control. For simplicity's sake, I will refer to all systems, organizations, and individuals as agents.

The number and composition of social control agents are related to the mechanisms of control since social control agents design the programs, apply the technology, and otherwise implement the policies. An example of available technology changing the number and composition of agents is the addition of private social control personnel and agencies to operate electronic monitoring programs.

Mechanisms of Control

The mechanisms of social control, as responses to definitions of deviance, are flexibly and variably bounded. They can vary in quantity, as when programs and policies call for a decrease or an increase in arrests, convictions, and sentence severity. They can also vary on the quality dimension, as when mechanisms of control become technologically advanced. Examples of quantitative and qualitative changes that cover the continuum of crime-control functions —from apprehension to correctional conditions—are DNA testing, innovations in drug-testing, faxing of fingerprints and other information, computerized decision making, and electronic monitoring. Qualitative and quantitative changes in technology can increase the discovery of primary deviance as well as secondary deviance, the latter occurring when violations of electronic monitoring conditions constitute a new and punishable offense (Berry 1985; 1986). Recently there has been a greater number of harsh, restrictive, and intrusive social control conditions applied (see Baumer and Mendelsohn 1990).[1]

Having said all of this, it is not always the case that changes in technology increase the scope or severity of control. For example, with advanced chemical treatment for psychological disturbances, U.S. society experienced a decrease in mental hospitalizations coinciding with the de-institutionalization movement of the 1950s and 1960s. In this case, however, one could argue that one type of control, hospitalization, was traded for another type of control, medication.

Agents of Control

Agents of social control are bounded by range of target (types of deviance controlled) and by function (type of controlling activity). For example, the criminal justice system manages crime, the mental health system manages mental illness, and child welfare agencies manage child abuse. The various agents are also charged with or limited to managing certain stages in the processing of deviance.

Agents vary in the degree to which they cross function and processing boundaries. For example, criminal justice and mental health overlap their resources and duties in determinations of competence to stand trial—"not guilty by reason of insanity," and "guilty but mentally ill"; adult criminal justice and juvenile justice agencies manage juvenile cases waived to the adult system; and welfare, family counseling, and public health agencies may be involved in child abuse cases. The various combinations of social control agencies and their degrees of interaction change over time depending upon the type of deviance of special interest in the current agenda (such as juvenile homicide) and the type of control (punitive, therapeutic, etc.) considered appropriate. Under some conditions, such as state mandates, the criminal justice, mental health, medical, educational, and other systems may work in concert. Under other conditions, as in the absence of an enforced mandate, they may not. They may agree or disagree about the composition and coverage of a definition of deviance; they may agree or disagree about the most appropriate response to deviance.

There are also changing interactions between formal control agents and more informal control agents such as the family. With the creation of the juvenile court system in the United States circa 1899, for example, parents "liberally" turned over their own children to juvenile court jurisdiction (Schultz 1973: 472).

Privatization and Methods

Changes in social control programs and technologies coincide with a trend toward privatization of social control agents. Changing mechanisms of control do not invariably require privatization; nevertheless, the social control systems in the United States and elsewhere (see Matthews 1989) have begun to utilize more private personnel and organizations to carry out the tasks of control. For example, approximately one-fourth of electronic monitoring providers are privately operated (Schmidt 1989; Renzema and Skelton 1990). And the variously termed "structured," "intensive," and "intermediate" supervision programs with their myriad drug testing, drug treatment, and other conditions are administered by private social control agencies and personnel. With privatization of crime control functions, there is a multidimensionality to social control agents: there are private and public prisons, private and public police, private and public pre-sentence investigation report preparers, private and public drug-testers, and private and public community corrections.

Some of these relationships between public and private agencies are contractual, such as those between a probation department and a private hospital for drug-testing or between the prosecutor's office and a private lab for DNA testing. But private and public control operations can be quite segregated, as when privately-owned and -operated prisons are distinct and autonomous from state-owned and -operated ones. Whether contractual or autonomous, there are more private agencies due to the perceived need for more prisons, more community corrections, and more police during the control-oriented 1980s.

Purposes and Outcomes

The stated purposes and the measured outcomes of social control change over time due to changing contents of concern brought forth by moral panics and by macro-level shifts in the politics and economics of a society. In a movement to change the perceptions and responses to deviance, topics of concerns can be refocused, deviance can be redefined, different methods of social control can be adopted, and the outcomes can be measured to support or refute the change in social control.

Before considering measures of effectiveness, let us consider the stated purposes versus the achieved purposes of social control. The intended effect of social control is presumably to reduce deviant behavior and follows from classicist reasoning that an increase in social control will decrease deviance. Steady accumulation of research has shown, however, that widened definitions and intensified responses either have no effect or increase apparent deviance. For example, the evidence strongly suggests that deterrence practices do not work (Gibbs 1975). Increasing the certainty of severe sentences does not result in specific or general prevention of crime. Moreover, widening the net of surveillance, undoubtedly intended to contain crime, has also failed to reduce crime (Cohen 1985). Nor does high-tech gadgetry ensure a reduction in deviance (Corbett and Marx 1991). Findings such as these beg the question of why the stated purpose of a social control movement is to reduce crime given what is known about the association between widened and intensified control and failed effects. I offer two possible answers. First, the association between controls and effects is not known, understood, or considered by those who design and implement social control programs. Second, the actual intended function may not be to reduce deviance. Along these lines, Zurcher et al. (1971; 1976) found in their studies of moral crusades against pornography that effectiveness, at least as measured by a reduction in pornography and its assumedly related deviant behavior, does not matter to the crusaders. Rather, in two antipornography campaigns, the crusaders emphasized a concern with values and lifestyle more than the specific steps to abolish pornography. And, as suggested earlier, if the actual intended func-

tion is to maintain unequal social stratification, such boundary maintenance can be accomplished through escalated social control.

Measurements of program success or failure are taken as assessments of social control effectiveness. However, measures such as program completion are questionable indicators of crime control success.
Successful parole completion is when no parole violations occur during the parole period. Similarly, in electronic monitoring programs, if
no program violations are confirmed during the monitoring period, then
the case is a success (Baumer and Mendelsohn 1990; Renzema and
Skelton 1990). Indeed, violations may have occurred during the monitoring period; but if no court action confirmed the violation during this
time, these cases are successes (Stover 1989). In short, measures of
program completion may be too limited to demonstrate any changes in
criminal behavior, future or present.

Spurious measures of success are rather obvious ways to disguise
the impact of social control on the actual quantity and quality of deviance. Addressing electronic monitoring, Corbett and Marx (1991) state
that social control agencies "ignore evidence of program failure if the
ideological 'spin' is right" (405). It is relatively easy to ignore program
failure, they further state, because of imprecise evaluation. Faulty measures of success and failure are permitted if not encouraged by the fallacy of explicit agendas. Regardless of how explicit, the agendas and
methods of social control may not change the level of deviance in a
society (Corbett and Marx 1991; Marx 1990; Berry 1987; 1990).

Theories

Trends in theoretical development have ranged from classicism to
neoclassicism, positivism, social psychology, Marxism, and many other
perspectives. Changes in the formal study of deviance reflect a society's
values (Gibbs 1989) and contemporary culture (Featherstone 1988).

Some deviance and social control theories are weakened over time,
some are strengthened, and some do not appear to grow stronger or
weaker but are nevertheless changed. A theory can be weakened, as
happened with deterrence theory, if met with a great deal of criticism in
the form of empirical refute or with loss of academic and political popularity (Gibbs 1975).

Certainly among the most influential of the approaches has been the
symbolic interactionist, transactional, and societal reaction perspectives that examine the "process of negotiations between the deviants

and the social environment" (Ben-Yehuda 1990:221). They became popular through shifts in the academic community to greater radicalism and social involvement and to a more positive, voluntaristic conceptualization of crime and criminals (Roshier 1989; see also Matza 1964; 1969; Becker 1964; Lemert 1967; Goffman 1968a; 1968b). Empirical support has strengthened some of the symbolic interactionist-inspired perspectives, notably labeling (Lemert 1951; Becker 1963; Schur 1971; 1979; Goode 1978; Dotter and Roebuck 1988). Secondary deviance has been confirmed by recidivism rates and a branching out of deviant activities following primary deviance.

Marxism, also a continuing, influential approach in explaining deviance and control, has gone through a number of renditions. "New criminology" (a form of Marxist criminology proposed in the early 1970s, sometimes called "radical criminology") and "left realism" have been especially useful to political analyses of crime (see Taylor, Walton, and Young 1973; Matthews 1987; Goode 1984a; Lea and Young 1984; Young 1986). A left-realist variation on the conflict theme is that crime comes about from individualistic and selfish attitudes on the part of offenders as well as from social conditions of relative deprivation. And, left realism purports that even though social control is managed by the ruling class, reforms in crime control programs are possible and worth pursuing (Lea and Young 1984; Lea and Young 1986; Matthews 1987).

Another relatively new perspective is Pepinsky and Quinney's (1991) peacemaking approach. The potential success of peacemaking lies in the theory's ability to offer sound scientific explanations for crime as well as to apply methods of crime reduction. Simple as it may seem, the explanations for crime, such as social disparity, provide the solutions. Part of the novelty of this theory is that both crime and punishment are considered socially harmful behavior. Both can be reduced by changing certain aspects of social institutions such as family socialization and economic disparity. Taking into account the synergism between crime and punishment and specific to criminal justice practices, peacemaking has encouraged penal abolition and other nonpunitive alternatives.

One of the disturbing trends theoretically is an inattention to causality questions. Young (1986) suggests that deviance and social control theory has degenerated to something called "administrative criminology," which is actually an atheoretical approach. It appears to be a predominant (non)perspective of social control practitioners, agenda setters, policymakers, and some academics. It focuses on technology and the use of control seemingly for control's sake, without an interest in understanding deviance, establishing causal generalizations, or effectively reducing deviant behavior. To the extent that "administrative criminology" is a theory, and I do not believe that anyone is arguing this, its inception may have been influenced by politically conservative policies and falsely measured success and failure rates of social controls.

Not ideologically uncontentious but certainly of some theoretical depth, are the situational or rational choice models. Their popularity in some criminological camps reflects the broader social control trends toward greater surveillance (Cohen 1985).

Theoretical development is an intellectual exercise confined largely to academics. Theories, old and new, are not considered for the most part by policymakers and have only an impure application in the realm of social control as a result.

Summary and Conclusions

In summary, boundaries surrounding the stated purposes of social control, the definitions of deviance, mechanisms and agents of control, the measured outcomes of control, and theoretical explanations change over time. When political forces wax conservative as they have in the United States in the 1980s, general trends are in the direction of widened social control purposes, enlarged definitions, and escalated applications of methods; while the expected and actually achieved outcomes, in the form of reduced deviant behavior, may shrink. Selective (in)attention to theory, absent research bases at the agenda-setting stage, and poor measurement practices would seem to guarantee ineffective control (Berry 1987; 1990).

Table 16.1 lists and describes the fluctuating parameters and fluctuating contents of the purposes, definitions, methods, outcomes, and theories of deviance and social control.

As to changing purposes, Ben-Yehuda (1990) and Cohen (1972) have shown that the specific content of social control concerns vary over time. A moral panic may introduce a new topic of concern or recycle an old one; the former being represented by new (at the time) juvenile reform movement in the late 1800s and early 1900s (Schultz 1973), the latter being represented by earlier and recent drug wars (Duster 1970; Akers 1992). Definitional boundaries, which are partly dependent upon changes in purposes and are the all-important catalyst for social control intervention, fluctuate (Lemert 1951; Becker 1963; 1964; Cohen

TABLE 16.1
Technological and Other Changes

Boundaries	Results and Changes	
	Fluctuating parameters	Fluctuating content
Purposes	Currently low expectations with (paradoxically) widened and deepened stated purposes of control; greater stated intentions to restrict social behavior	Emphasis on administration; the application of technology and other controls for their own sake
Definitions	Currently some widened definitions and increased reporting of targeted deviance leading to increased applications of control based upon the definitions	Recycled, for example, drug-"relevance"; harsh ("sex psychopath") or relaxed ("alternative life style")
Methods	Currently more and harsher controls; greater number of social control agencies	Technologically advanced and not advanced mechanisms; different implementers (e.g., private)
Outcomes	Maybe less than hoped-for, expected, and reported	May be different from the stated purpose; are unknown due to faulty measures
Theory	Perhaps less attended to then pre-1980s, a tendency toward the atheoretical, along with poor or absent research bases	Emphasis on the administrative, little general interest in causality, but a new comprehensive theory (peacemaking)

1974; 1986b; Gusfield 1963; and Turk 1975). As there can be "deviantization," there can also be a "normalizing" of deviance (Schur 1980). In other words, while a category of people or a behavior can at times be defined as deviant (Goode 1989), moral panics leading to such definitions can also become submerged, deteriorate, or disappear so that deviance is re-defined as nondeviance (Cohen 1972). But to bring about a shift in perception and response to deviance, normalizing deviance on a micro level is not sufficient: As with the movement to deviantize, macro-level changes in social perceptions must precede or occur simultaneously with deviance normalization.

As mentioned, methods of social control change in quantity and in quality. Considering methods and outcomes of control together, it is

FIGURE 16.1
Changes in the Purpose of Control and Their Effects

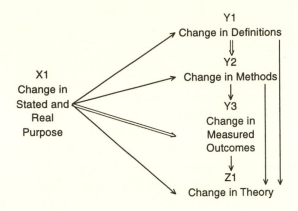

——— = does affect, in the directions indicated.
===== = could, but does not necessarily, affect the exogenous variable X1 and the endogenous variables Y1–Y3.

becoming well documented that more is not necessarily better (cf. Cohen 1985) and that technological advancements by no means guarantee deviance reduction (Corbett and Marx 1991). In fact, social control intervention, if it has any effect, is thought to do the opposite of its intended function (see Zurcher et al. 1971; 1976; Lemert 1967; 1958) to the point that nonintervention may be the most effective strategy (Schur 1973).[2]

Finally, theory evolves. Explanations can become more integrative of new and old research, they can fade into insignificance, and they can keep the main thrust of their argument but change the direction of particular propositions (see Roshier 1989). Importantly, if theoretical development is confined to academic exercise, it likely will have a limited impact on the other forces of social control (see figure 16.1).

Figure 16.1 shows how changes in these five variables influence each other. A change in stated purpose leads to changes in definitions, methods, and outcomes. A change in definitions changes methods and outcomes. A change in methods can influence outcomes, which is logical enough. But a change in methods can also affect definitions as when drug-testing enlarges and justifies definitions of drug-related offenses, and electronic monitoring creates the label of electronic-monitoring violator. A change in measured outcomes may or may not change the stated purposes of social control. Some measures of program outcome are of questionable validity; but as we have seen, success or failure may not have the importance to policymakers and program developers that might be assumed.

Changes in theory are connected loosely, precariously, or not at all to the purposes, definitions, methods, and outcomes. Changes in theory *could* (and should) influence purpose, definitions, methods, and outcomes. For that matter, changes in the process and practice of social control could change theory, as it does when, measurement issues aside, research on moral panics, labeling, inequitable application of controls, and so on are incorporated into theory.

In conclusion, the five forms of boundary crossings describe a general picture of changes in the social control of deviance. The bounded variables considered herein, while not universally conceptualized in the same way across time and across societies, address the integral components to this process: the definitions, the social control agents, the policies and programs, the technology, the measures of effectiveness, and (less so) theory. The parameters and content in table 16.1 and the direction and strength of the arrows in figure 16.1 may have been different in the past and may be different in the future from those examined in the present.

Notes

An earlier draft of this paper was presented at the Law and Society Meetings in Philadelphia 29 May 1992. The author wishes to express gratitude to Edwin M. Lemert for comments on an earlier draft.

1. Electronic monitoring has been established to be personally and socially intrusive (Berry 1985; 1986; Baumer and Mendelsohn 1990; 1992). That informed consent is required by many programs and that family members living with the monitoree complain indicate intrusiveness. When Baumer and Mendelsohn surveyed convicted offenders on EMHD (electronic monitored home detention) and on HD (home detention without electronic monitoring), they found far less satisfaction with the EMHD conditions by less willingness to recommend the program than HD respondents were. To establish that electronic monitoring is intrusive is not to say that it necessarily should not be. One of the stated purposes of electronic monitoring is to provide intermediate sanctioning between relatively unsupervised community corrections programs and incarceration. Intermediate sanctioning implies conditions harsher than something else, in this case, regular probation or some other less supervised community program.
2. I have mentioned that the social controllers themselves have little expectation of actual reduction of socially harmful behavior, as though the means justify the ends. We must also consider the public's reaction to changes in the control of

deviance. While technological and other changes increase the social control imposed upon particular targeted deviant groups, the general public has also experienced more controls in the forms of video surveillance of public places, weapons screening, drug-free workplace policies, and so on. I agree with Marx (1990) that, by and large, the public is passive and accepting when it is aware of enhanced social control practices, and that the public may perceive enhanced control to be "for it's own good." More to the point, Marx suggests that social expectations do not remain static; specifically, social expectations becomes less, as technologies for social intrusion become more powerful and as privacy becomes more restricted. So, social expectations too cross boundaries.

References

Akers, Ronald L. 1992. *Drugs, Alcohol, and Society*. Belmont, CA: Wadsworth Publishing Company.

Baumer, Terry L. and Robert I. Mendelsohn. 1990. *The Electronic Monitoring of Nonviolent Convicted Felons: An Experiment in Home Detention*. Washington, DC: National Institute of Justice.

Baumer, Terry L. Michael G. Maxfield, and Robert I. Mendelsohn. 1992. "A Comparative Analysis of Three Electronically Monitored Home Detention Programs." *Justice Quarterly* 10(1): 121–42.

Becker, Howard S. 1963. *Outsiders: Studies in the Sociology of Deviance*. New York: The Free Press.

———.1964. *The Other Side: Perspectives on Deviance*. New York: The Free Press.

Ben-Yehuda, Nachman. 1990. *The Politics and Morality of Deviance*. Albany, NY: State University of New York Press.

Berry, Bonnie. 1985. "Electronic Jails: A New Criminal Justice Concern." *Justice Quarterly* 2 (1): 1–22.

———. 1986. "More Questions and More Ideas on Electronic Monitoring." *Justice Quarterly* 3(3): 363–70.

———. "The Erosion of Effectiveness as a Criminal Justice Goal." Paper presented at the American Society of Criminology annual meetings, November 1987.

———. "Recent Trends Toward Increased Crime Control." Paper presented at the Academy for Criminal Justice Sciences annual meetings, March 1990.

———. 1994. "Discrepancies in the Control of Elite and Lower Status Deviance: A Theory of Multiple Control." Forthcoming in *Advances in Criminological Theory* (vol.6).

Black, Donald. 1976. *The Behavior of Law*. New York: Academic Press.

Chambliss, William J. 1964. "A Sociological Analysis of the Law of Vagrancy." *Social Problems* 12 (summer) : 46–67.

———. 1978. *On the Take: From Petty Crooks to Presidents*. Bloomington: Indiana University Press.

———. 1988. *Exploring Criminology*. New York: Macmillan Publishing.

Clear, Todd R. and George F. Cole. 1990. *American Corrections*. Pacific Grove, CA: Brooks/Cole Publishing Company.

Cohen, Stanley. 1972. *Folk Devils and Moral Panics*. London: MacGibbon and Kee.

———. 1974. "Criminology and the Sociology of Deviance in Britain." In P. Rock and M. McIntosh (eds.) *Deviance and Social Control*. London: Tavistock Publications.

———.1985.*Visions of Social Control*. Cambridge: Polity Press.

———. 1986a. "Bandits, Rebels or Criminals: African History and Western Criminology." *Africa: Journal of the International African Institute* 56(4): 468–83.

————.1986b. *Against Criminology*. New Brunswick, NJ: Transaction Publishers.

Corbett, Ronald and Gary T. Marx. 1991. "Critique: No Soul in the New Machine: Technofallacies in the Electronic Monitoring Movement." *Justice Quarterly* 8(3): 399–414.

Dotter, Daniel L. and Julian B. Roebuck. 1988. "The Labeling Approach Re-Examined: Interactionism and the Components of Deviance." *Deviant Behavior* 9: 19–32.

Duster, Troy. 1970. *The Legislation of Morality*. New York: The Free Press.

Featherstone, Mike. 1989. "In Pursuit of the Postmodern." *Theory, Culture and Society* 5(2-3): 195–215.

Gibbs, Jack P. 1967. "Definitions of Law and Empirical Questions." *Law and Society Review* 11: 429–46.

————. 1975. *Crime, Punishment and Deterrence*. New York: Elsevier.

————. 1981. *Norms, Deviance, and Social Control*. New York: Elsevier.

————. 1989. "Three Perennial Issues in the Sociology of Deviance." In Steven F. Messner, Marvin D. Krohn, and Allen E. Liska (eds.), *Theoretical Integration in the Study of Deviance and Crime: Problems and Prospects*. Albany, NY: State University of New Press.

Goffman, Erving. 1968a. *Stigma: Notes on the Management of Spoiled Identity*. Harmondsworth: Penguin.

————. 1968b. *Asylums*. Harmondsworth: Penguin.

Goode, Erich. 1978. *Deviant Behavior: The Interactionist Approach*. Englewood Cliffs, NJ: Prentice-Hall.

————. 1984. *Deviant Behavior*, 2d ed. Englewood Cliffs, NJ: Prentice-Hall.

————. 1989. *Drugs in American Society*, 3d ed. New York: Alfred A. Knopf.

Gusfield, Joseph R. 1963. *Symbolic Crusade: Status, Politics and the American Temperance Movement*. Chicago: University of Illinois Press.

Hagan, John. 1985. *Modern Criminology: Crime, Criminal Behavior, and its Control*. New York: McGraw-Hill, Inc.

Haskell, Martin R. and Lewis Yablonsky. 1983. *Criminology: Crime and Criminality*. Boston: Houghton Mifflin.

Kitzinger, Celia. 1987. *The Social Construction of Lesbianism*. London: Sage Books.

Lea, John and Jock Young. 1984. *What is to be Done about Law and Order?* New York: Penguin.

————. 1986. "A Realistic Approach to Law and Order," pp. 358–64 in Brian MacLean (ed.)*The Political Economy of Crime: Readings for a Critical Criminology*. Englewood Cliffs, NJ: Prentice-Hall.

Lemert, Edwin M. 1951. *Social Pathology: A Systematic Approach to the Theory of Sociopathic Behavior*. New York: McGraw Hill Book Company.

————. 1958. "The Behavior of the Systematic Check Forger." *Social Problems* 6: 141–8.

————. 1967. *Human Deviance, Social Problems and Social Control*. New York: Prentice-Hall.

Marx, Gary T. 1990. "Privacy and Technology." *The World and I* (Sept.): 523–41.

Matthews, Roger. 1987. "Taking Realistic Criminology Seriously." *Contemporary Crises* 11(4):371–401.

————, ed. 1989. *Privatizing Criminal Justice*. London: Sage Publications Ltd.

Matza, David. 1964. *Delinquency and Drift*. New York: John Wiley and Sons.

————. 1969. *Becoming Deviant*. Englewood Cliffs, NJ: Prentice-Hall.

Pepinsky, Harold E. and Richard Quinney, eds. 1991. *Criminology as Peacemaking*. Bloomington: Indiana University Press.

Quinney, Richard. 1974. *Critique of Legal Order*. Boston: Little, Brown and Company.

Renzema, Marc and David T. Skelton. 1990. "Use of Electronic Monitoring in the United States: 1989 Update," pp. 9–13 in *National Institute of Justice Reports* (Nov./Dec.) Washington DC: National Institute of Justice.

Roshier, Bob. 1989. *Controlling Crime: The Classical Perspective in Criminology.* Chicago: Lyceum Books, Inc.

Schmidt, Annesley K. 1989. "Electronic Monitoring of Offenders Increases." *National Institute of Justice Reports: Research in Action.* Washington, DC: National Institute of Justice.

Schultz, J. L. 1973. "The Cycle of Juvenile Court History." *Crime and Delinquency* 19: 457–76.

Schur, Edwin M. 1969. *Our Criminal Society.* New York: Spectrum Books.

———. 1971. *Labeling Deviant Behavior.* New York: Harper and Row.

———. 1973. *Radical Nonintervention.* Englewood Cliffs, NJ: Prentice-Hall.

———. 1979. *Interpreting Deviance.* New York: Harper and Row.

———. 1980. *The Politics of Deviance.* Englewood Cliffs, NJ: Prentice-Hall.

Stover, John. 1989. Personal communication. Bloomington, IN.

Taylor, I., P. Walton, and J. Young. 1973. *The New Criminology: For a Social Theory of Deviance.* London: Routledge and Kegan Paul.

Teal, D. 1971. *The Gay Militants.* New York: Stein and Day Publishers.

Turk, Austin T. 1975. *Political Criminality and Political Policing.* New York: MSS Modular Publishers.

———. 1979. "Analyzing Official Deviance: For Nonpartisan Conflict Analysis." *Criminology* 16(4): 459–76.

———. 1982. *Political Criminality.* Beverly Hills: Sage Publications.

Young, Jock. 1986.. "The Failure of Criminology: The Need for a Radical Realism," pp. 4–30 in Roger Matthews and Jock Young (eds.) *Confronting Crime.* London: Sage Publications.

Zurcher, Louis A., Jr., George R. Kirkpatrick, Robert G. Cushing, and Charles K. Bowman. 1971. "The Anti-Pornography Campaign: A Symbolic Crusade." *Social Problems* 19(2): 217–38.

Zurcher, Louis A., Jr. and George R. Kirkpatrick. 1976. *Citizens for Decency: Anti-Pornography Crusades as Status Defense.* Austin: University of Texas Press.

17

The Theoretical Development of "CPTED": Twenty-five Years of Responses to C. Ray Jeffery

Introduction

In 1971, when C. Ray Jeffery's *Crime Prevention through Environmental Design* was first published, it marked a significant turning point with regard to thinking about antisocial and illegal behavior. This work represented a major advance in criminological theory, in that the foundation was laid for the application of a unique perspective (the integrated systems perspective) to crime-related study. Despite his continued work since that time, and in spite of the evolution of his original ideas, many if not most criminologists have ignored the seminal contribution made by Jeffery's original and subsequent works.

According to Webster's Ninth New Collegiate Dictionary (1989:598), "ignore" generally means to refuse to take notice of or to reject as ungrounded. A synonym for ignore is "neglect" which generally means to give little attention or respect to or to disregard. It can also mean to leave undone or unattended to, especially through carelessness (Webster's 1989:791). Some of these definitions of "ignore" and "neglect" accurately characterize how academic criminologists have treated the recent work of C. Ray Jeffery regarding crime prevention through environmental design (CPTED). Some have refused to take notice of it, and others have rejected it outright. Many more have simply disregarded it and left it unattended. Although Jeffery's original work in this area is well known and has influenced academicians (Brantingham and Brantingham 1996), governmental agencies, architectural design, and

427

corporate and business initiatives related to crime prevention, his contribution to the evolution of CPTED theory and practice over the last twenty-five years has received minimal recognition in the field of criminology.

This chapter has several purposes, the first of which is to document reasons why Jeffery's work on CPTED has not influenced the field of criminology to a larger degree. It will trace the roots of CPTED, from which Jeffery's 1971 work arose; works which preceded Jeffery's, or developed independently of it, are discussed. The chapter then examines various reactions to Jeffery's original work, including governmental, architectural, academic, and corporate/business reactions. These reactions over the last twenty-five years are placed into a general context relating to the evolution of Jeffery's original work on CPTED. Jeffery's work has evolved into a more general notion of crime prevention, which includes both the *external* physical environment and the *internal* physical organism, as well as interactions between the two. Essentially, this chapter demonstrates that, while Jeffery has recognized and advocated the importance of studying both the environment and the organism which behaves in it, most of the literature related to CPTED over the last twenty-five years has not followed suit. Much of this subsequent work ignores the evolution of the CPTED concept as illustrated by Jeffery's more recent work, and neglects the internal, physical environment of individuals in doing so. On rare occasions, when the internal environment of the organism is taken into account, it is typically treated as nonphysical or "mental." Thus, most of the theoretical CPTED literature drifts away from the basic premise that crime prevention involves both the psychobiological aspects of human nature and the role of the external physical environment in human behavior (Jeffery 1996:1).

What is "CPTED"?

Crime prevention through environmental design is aimed at "identifying conditions of the physical and social environment that provide opportunities for or precipitate criminal acts...and the alteration of those conditions so that no crimes occur..." (Brantingham and Faust 1976: 289, 290, 292). Since it is aimed at preventing occurrences of criminality, CPTED is conceptually distinct and significantly different from the reactive (and largely failing) strategies employed by police, courts, and correctional facilities in the American criminal justice system (Wallis 1980).

A number of variations and refinements of the basic CPTED concept have been offered. Generally, CPTED "focuses on the settings in which crimes occur and on techniques for reducing vulnerability of the settings" (Taylor and Harrell 1996:1), because its central premise is that crime can be facilitated or inhibited by features of the physical environment (Clarke 1995a:2). According to Hough et al. (1980) CPTED is the "specific management, design, or manipulation of the immediate environment in which crimes occur in a systematic and permanent way" (in Bennett and Wright 1984). While CPTED generally involves changing the environment to reduce the opportunity for crime, it is aimed at other outcomes including reducing fear of crime, increasing the aesthetic quality of an environment, and increasing the quality of life for law-abiding citizens, especially by reducing the propensity of the physical environment to support criminal behavior (Clarke 1995a:8; Crowe 1991:1, 28–9, 40).

The underlying logic of designing a specific external environment in order to prevent crime makes sense for several reasons. For example, crime prevention efforts aimed at people through methods such as "general deterrence" and "special deterrence" (Packer 1968) are less sure to work, for the placement of people in the physical environment is temporary owing to their mobile nature—that is, they are not permanent fixtures of most environments for an extended period of time. Things such as buildings and other physical features of the environment are "relatively permanent" (Nasar and Fisher 1992:48–9). As a result, CPTED can produce effects on crime and perceptions of personal crime risks. Yet, the idea that CPTED only applies to the external physical environment is limited. To be more effective, CPTED should be applied both to external and internal environments, or to the environments of the place and the offender, respectively.

The term "environment" in standard CPTED definitions includes only the *external* environment of the place and not the *internal* environment of the offender. Del Carmen (1997) recently proposed a redefinition of the term "environment" to include both the macro (external) and the micro (internal) levels of analysis. It will become clear later in the chapter that Jeffery's concept of CPTED already has evolved into a crime prevention approach that encompasses both the external environment of the place *and* the internal environment of the offender.

Theoretical Development of CPTED

The first systematic discussions of CPTED in the scholarly literature did not occur until the 1960s and 1970s. Some of the earliest to write about CPTED were Wood, Jacobs, Angel, Newman, and Jeffery. The main ideas of these authors are discussed below.

Elizabeth Wood

According to Newman (1973:119), "one of the prime advocates of the importance of physical design considerations in achieving social objectives was Elizabeth Wood." Wood's (1961:4) belief was that managers of residential areas could never do enough to stop the damaging actions of even a small group of hostile or indifferent tenants. While Wood worked for the Chicago Housing Authority, she strove to make surrounding residential environments of lower class citizens more rich and fulfilling (Newman 1973:119). As she attempted to bring about design changes aimed at enhancing quality of life for residents and increasing the aesthetic qualities of the residential environment, she also developed a series of guidelines for improving security conditions of these environments (Newman 1973:122).

One of her design goals was to improve visibility of apartment units by residents; another was to create spaces where residents could gather, thereby increasing the potential for resident surveillability. As discussed by Newman (1973:122), "Miss Wood's concept of the social control of residential areas is predicated on the presence of and natural surveillance by residents. Areas that are out of view and unused are simply without control." As Jane Jacobs after her, Wood recognized that certain types of designs could translate into loss of opportunity for informal social control by residents (National Crime Prevention Institute 1986:119). Newman (1973:126) wrote that "Elizabeth Wood was perhaps the foremost practitioner of social design in the field of housing." Yet, given the fact that Wood's ideas were never widely put into practice, the validity of her ideas was never actually subjected to rigid empirical testing.

Jane Jacobs

Jacobs's work *The Death and Life of Great American Cities* really began the search for how both physical and social urban factors affected people and their interactions. Her's was among the earliest discussions of urban decay and its relationship to crime. Jeffery has often stated that it was Jane Jacobs who sparked the widespread interest in how environmental conditions could be related to crime prevention (e.g., see Jeffery and Zahm 1993:331–2). In fact, Jeffery reported that reading Jacobs's work caused him to "think about writing a book on crime prevention" (Jeffery, personal communication, 28 March 1996), which, of course, he later did. Jacobs hypothesized that urban residential crime could be prevented by reducing conditions of anonymity and isolation in those areas (Murray 1994:349).

Jacobs's work was "an indictment of postwar urban planning policies that gave precedence to the needs of the automobile at the expense of conditions fostering local community life" (Clarke 1995a:2). Jacobs (1961:31) felt that cities were custom-made for crime: the way they were designed and built meant that citizens would not be able to build or maintain informal social control networks necessary for effective self-policing. It was Jacobs's contention that crime flourished when people did not know and meaningfully interact with their neighbors, for they would thus be less likely to notice an outsider who may be a criminal surveying the environment for potential targets or victims.

Jacobs (1961) discussed the effects of street surveillance by neighbors, and claimed that high levels of natural surveillance created a safe environment. Jacobs stated that city streets often do not have the three primary qualities needed in order to make them safer: a clear demarcation between public and private space; diversity of street use; and fairly constant sidewalk use, which translated into "eyes on the street." Residential streets which promote multiple land uses promote natural and informal surveillance by pedestrians, and therefore, potentially increase residents' safety (National Crime Prevention Institute, 1986:118). To Jacobs, active streets served as deterrents to crime.

Jacobs's ideas about how the physical environment is related to the risk for crime are related to social control theory. This is not surprising given "another commonsense understanding about crime: one of our best protections against crime is to live in a community where neighbors watch out for each other and stand ready to call the police or to intervene directly where they spot a malefactor" (Murray 1994:349).

Schlomo Angel

Schlomo Angel (1968), in *Discouraging Crime through City Planning*, noted how citizens could take an active role in preventing crime, starting with a diagnosis of which environments afford the most opportunities for crime to occur. Angel thought that certain areas suffer from higher rates of crime than other areas because of the higher levels of opportunity that rational offenders could take advantage of. Offenders choose their specific targets through a decision-making process in which they weigh the effort and risk against potential payoffs. With more opportunity and a higher potential payoff, it is more likely that at least one successful target offering little risk will be found. Angel posited that deterrents to crime include high-intensity use of an area which provides large numbers of effective witnesses and low-intensity land use which decreases crime because of lower numbers of potential victims (Newman 1973:132). In between high- and low-intensity use, in periods of moderate use, criminal opportunities abound where there are not enough witnesses to deter crime (also see National Crime Prevention Institute 1986:119). Angel's ideas regarding changing the physical design of environments revolved around channeling pedestrian traffic and zoning businesses into areas where mass transit and parking facilities are near.

Oscar Newman

Each of these previous works, especially that of Jane Jacobs (Clarke 1995a:2), culminated in Oscar Newman's *Defensible Space*. Jeffery and Zahm (1993:332) wrote that: "Defensible space, more than any other crime prevention program, is an operationalization of the themes espoused by Jane Jacobs." In fact, Murray (1994:349) wrote that although Jacobs's work had a "great overall impact...its crime prevention implications were not much discussed until 1972," when Oscar Newman wrote his book (also see Newman 1973:119).

Newman's CPTED projects began in 1969 when the National Institute of Law Enforcement and Criminal Justice (NILECJ, now the National Institute of Justice) undertook a series of research projects to appraise the relationship between the physical environment and risk for criminal victimization (Wallis 1980:2). A result of these efforts was Oscar Newman's *Architectural Guidelines for Crime Prevention*, published in 1972, variously subtitled *Crime Prevention through Urban Design*, and *Architectural Design for Crime Prevention* (Jeffery and Zahm 1993:332).

Within two years of the original publication of *Defensible Space*, demonstration projects were initiated and, within one more year, the Law Enforcement Assistance Administration (LEAA) funded a multimillion dollar project to study crime in a commercial strip, a residential area, and a school. Eventually, public housing projects were designed based upon Newman's ideas. Newman's ideas may still be greatly influencing the design of public housing all over the world (Clarke 1992:6; also see Coleman 1985).

The term "defensible space" is used to describe a residential environment designed in order to allow and even encourage residents themselves to supervise and be seen by outsiders as responsible for their neighborhoods (Mayhew 1981:150; also see National Crime Prevention Institute, 1986:119). According to the National Crime Prevention Institute (1986:121) defensible space design changes strengthen two basic kinds of social behavior, territoriality and natural surveillance. The goal of the defensible space approach is "to release the latent sense of territoriality and community among inhabitants so as to allow these traits to be translated into inhabitants' assumption of responsibility for preserving a safe and well maintained living environment" (Newman 1976:4), and to increase the potential for residents to see and report likely offenders, thereby enabling residents to control the physical environments in which they reside. Newman's work was an attempt to reduce both crime and fear of crime in a specific type of environment, by means of reducing opportunity for crime and fostering positive social interaction among legitimate users (Taylor and Harrell 1996:3–4).

Areas low in defensible space are theoretically more vulnerable to crime, for, owing to the relatively large size of certain living areas compared to others, feelings of ownership and community spirit are not generated by residents, and they are less likely to be able to recognize outsiders as potential criminals. In small areas, defensible space increases the effectiveness of informal social control which makes crime less likely (Murray 1994:351).

C. Ray Jeffrey

The notion of CPTED came to the forefront of criminological thought with C. R. Jeffery's (1971) *Crime Prevention through Environmental Design*, a work written simultaneously and therefore without influence from Newman (National Crime Prevention Institute, 1986:120). According to the National Crime Prevention Institute (1986:120), Jeffery's book encouraged crime prevention strategies aimed at changes to the physical environment and increased citizen involvement and proactive policing. Jeffery contended that the way to prevent crime is to design the "total environment" in order to reduce opportunities for crime.

Jeffery's work was based on the precepts of experimental psychology represented in modern learning theory (Jeffery and Zahm 1993:329). Jeffery's CPTED concept arose out of his experiences with a rehabilitative project in Washington, DC that attempted to control the school environment of juveniles in the area. Rooted deeply in the psychological learning theory of B.F. Skinner, Jeffery's CPTED approach emphasized the role of the physical environment in the development of pleasurable and painful experiences for the offender that would have the capacity to alter behavioral outcomes. His original CPTED model was a stimulus-response (S-R) model positing that the organism learned from punishments and reinforcements in the environment. Jeffery "emphasized material rewards...and the use of the physical environment to control behavior" (Jeffery and Zahm 1993:330). The major idea here was that by removing the reinforcements for crime, it would not occur. Jeffery's 1971 book was an early argument for crime prevention which rejected the more popular crime control goals of revenge, just deserts, or retribution and deterrence, as well as punitive crime control strategies employed by the criminal justice system.

Because Jeffery's (1971) approach was largely founded on Skinner's behavioral learning theory (a S-R model), it is not surprising that no attention was paid to the individual organism in Jeffery's original model. Skinner was known for his criticisms of earlier "introspective" or "mentalistic" theories of behavior that are not empirically testable, not falsifiable and involve the logical error of circular reasoning (see Akers 1994:8). As a result, Skinner ignored the physical organism completely, since there was no way to know what was going on in the organism's brain or mind; he was content with merely observing and describing what he saw, rather than resorting to conjecture about what he could not see in the organism's brain or mind. Given that Jeffery attended Indiana University where B.F. Skinner was chair of the Psychology Department, and that Jeffery spent some time at Arizona State University, known as the "Fort Skinner of the West," it is to be expected that Jeffery's work was influenced by Skinner.

Jeffery's original work did not take into account either the mind or the brain of the organism. In the 1971 edition of his book, "Jeffery mentioned the biological basis of behavior and the role of the brain in behavior (171–2), but then dropped the concept from further discussion" (Jeffery and Zahm 1993: 330). Consequently, his first statement of the CPTED model in 1971 contained the flaw of the "empty organism." That is, the logical implication of Jeffery's original CPTED model was that the environment directly affected the behavior of the organism, without first entering the organism either physically or mentally.

Jeffery's 1977 second edition of *Crime Prevention through Environmental Design* involved a complete revision of the underlying theoretical approach for CPTED. While his 1971 edition was very limited in terms of its inclusion of material related to biology or the physical organism, the 1977 edition "included statements about human genetics and brain functioning from modern biology and psychobiology" (Jeffery and Zahm 1993:330). His empty organism approach was replaced by a new model commonly referred to as the "integrated systems model" of human behavior (e.g., see Jeffery 1990). This model utilizes systems logic rather than sequential logic. It denies or at least questions the logic of time-ordered causal reasoning, and instead posits continuous interactive effects of organisms and environments which have reciprocal influences on one another, among all levels of analysis, from cell to society (including genetics, the brain, the individual, the group, the community, and so forth).

According to Fishbein (personal communication, 28 March 1996), Jeffery was the first scholar in the field of criminology to fill the empty organism with knowledge he had learned from studying biology. Jeffery was preparing to develop a CPTED model aimed at modifying both the external environment and the internal environment of the offender.

Jeffery's 1977 work was based on a biological rather than a social ecology model, meaning that Jeffery's model of human behavior contained both a concrete physical environment and a concrete physical organism. This CPTED model does not focus on abstract sociological concepts such as social disorganization and social learning that tend to minimize the concrete physical environment in favor of the abstract social environment (Jeffery and Zahm 1993:326–9; Jeffery 1996:4). Jeffery's shift from a stimulus-response model of human behavior to an integrated systems approach was motivated by research into the role of the brain in human learning conducted by researchers outside the field of criminology such as Seligman and Hager (1972) in the early 1970s (Jeffery, personal communication, 28 March 1996). Jeffery's CPTED model has evolved into a general crime prevention model based on the integrated systems perspective. Thus, his model includes both the external environment of the place and the internal environment of the offender.

This CPTED model is much more fully developed in Jeffery's (1990) *Criminology: An Interdisciplinary Approach*, which puts forth an approach to crime prevention involving numerous academic disciplines including genetics and the brain sciences. The basic assumption of the CPTED approach of Jeffery, as it stood in the 1990 book, and as it stands today, is that:

> the response [i.e., behavioral adaptation] of the individual organism to the physical environment is a product of the brain; the brain in turn is a product of genetics and the environment. The environment never influences behavior directly, but *only through the brain*. Any model of crime prevention must include *both* the brain and the physical environment. (Jeffery and Zahm 1993:330; also see Jeffery 1996:4)

There are then two critical elements to crime prevention through environmental design: the place where the crime occurs *and* the person who commits the crime; thus, Jeffery (1990:418) asserts that we can successfully prevent crime by altering the organism and/or the external environment. Because the approach contained in Jeffery's CPTED model is today based on many fields, including scientific knowledge of modern brain sciences, a focus on only external environmental crime prevention is inadequate as it ignores another entire dimension of CPTED—that is, the internal environment.

Reactions to CPTED

A survey of various reactions to Jeffery's work on CPTED over the last twenty-five years demonstrates that, as his work has evolved into the general model of crime prevention which includes the external *and* internal environments, it has largely been ignored; for, as CPTED exists in government, architecture, academia, and corporate business, little if any consideration is given to the internal, physical environment of the offender. Rather, attention is given only to the external physical environment of the place. In academia particularly, CPTED has been developed only with regard to the external environment, which usually is not even treated as physical, but instead as some set of abstract social factors. When the internal environment of the offender or victim is taken into account, it is typically treated as nonphysical or "mental." This is a serious limitation of the current body of CPTED literature.

There are several factors which help to account for the fact that Jeffery's original work, as well as the evolution of his ideas, has been largely ignored or neglected by other criminologists. These factors are illustrated by examining various CPTED developments in government, architecture, corporate business, and academia. The following sections trace these reactions as they relate to the development of Jeffery's work, first providing evidence of the neglect of Jeffery's work, and then illustrating factors which may help understand how his work has been ignored.

Governmental/Architectural Reactions

In the 1970s, the National Institute of Law Enforcement and Criminal Justice (NILECJ), the research and development arm of the Law Enforcement Assistance Administration (LEAA), sponsored and conducted research on crime prevention. Their basic program would include target hardening measures—"such things as security locks, street lighting, residential security systems, and housing design" (LEAA newsletter, 1971, 1(6):7). Almost immediately thereafter, issues of the LEAA newsletter, a document distributed by NILECJ, contained detailed reports of crime prevention programs being implemented across the United States, including one in Washington, DC which included only the installation of high-intensity street lighting (LEAA newsletter, 1971, 1(7):3). According to Murray (1994:353), forty-one recorded street-lighting projects were undertaken up to 1977, with results showing that "occasional short-term improvements were ephemeral." Results of street lighting projects in Baltimore, Milwaukee, Tucson, Denver, and Minneapolis found that they did reduce perceptions of safety among residents (Murray 1994: 353), a stated goal of CPTED researchers. Although some of these street light projects preceded Jeffery's original work, his 1971 book would announce that this type of strategy clearly would not be sufficient for crime prevention. Nevertheless, when NILECJ allocated the majority of its $31-million budget for fiscal year 1973 on large-scale research projects aimed at goals such as reducing opportunities for crime, the main thrust of their efforts was on target hardening approaches such as increased building security, burglar alarms, and more street lighting and architectural design changes. Other LEAA newsletters were devoted to grants awarded for target hardening approaches, including one in Tyler, Texas which focused on "making burglary harder" (LEAA newsletter, 1973, 3(3):6).

Later editions of the LEAA newsletter (1973 3, 3(3):12) noted that LEAA earmarked $2 million for a defensible space project and would invite other federal agencies (Department of Housing and Urban Development, the National Science Foundation, the Department of Education and Welfare, and the Department of Transportation) to participate in founding a "Program for Crime Prevention through Environmental

Design" that would eventually initiate studies to be conducted by the Westinghouse Electric Corporation of Baltimore, Maryland. This program would focus on residential, school, and commercial environments, as discussed below, and although obviously borrowing Jeffery's title, it was based on Newman's ideas rather than Jeffery's (e.g., see Jeffery 1977:225).

According to Jeffery and Zahm (1993:332–3), under a grant from LEAA, the Westinghouse Electric Corporation designed a school crime prevention project in Broward County, Florida, a commercial crime prevention project in Portland, Oregon and a residential/mixed use crime prevention project in Hartford, Connecticut. These are the most well-known CPTED efforts (National Crime Prevention Institute 1986:124) incorporating *"physical, social, law enforcement, and management techniques to achieve its goal of reducing crime and the fear of crime"* (National Crime Prevention Institute 1986:24, citing Perce 1977:16–17). Crime prevention strategies aimed at these goals included controlling access, increasing surveillance, activity support, and reinforcement, or in other words, target hardening and defensible space. As discussed by Jeffery (1990:413), the Broward County school project "used Newman's concept of natural surveillance and an increased sense of responsibility on the part of students for crime prevention." The Portland commercial area project made changes "in outdoor lighting, emergency phones, landscaping, special bus shelters, security surveys, neighborhood watch programs, traffic patterns and one way-streets, and the amount of cash carried or kept in stores." In Hartford, "streets were closed or narrowed, some streets were made one-way streets, community anti-crime groups were formed, and police-community relations were improved" (also see National Crime Prevention Institute 1986:124-9).

Throughout the 1970s, until 1979 when LEAA was eliminated, Newman's book of crime prevention guidelines for public housing continued to be well received and projects based on it continued to be funded by governmental entities (LEAA newsletter, 1976, 6(2):8). For example, one of the defensible space designs Newman created was applied at two new housing developments—one in Indianapolis and another in Newark—with funding of $104,062 from NILECJ and $50,000 from the Department of Housing and Urban Development (HUD). This strategy was aimed at assigning different types of residents to the kinds of buildings they would best be able to control, subdividing buildings and corridors to promote a feeling of ownership by residents and increasing surveillability through design.

Other defensible space projects included the South Loop New Town Security Project, a residential development of mixed-income populations in Chicago (Jeffery and Zahm 1993:333) that "employed a broader orientation of Newman's philosophies developed by Richard Gardiner (1978)" under the concept of environmental security. Other programs spurred on by Newman included the Kansas City Lighting study, the Washington, DC burglary study conducted by Scarr, and the Boston residential crime study conducted by Reppetto (LEAA newsletter, 1974, 4, 3:19). Newman's defensible space approach was actually first tested at two public housing projects in New York City—Clason Point and Markham Gardens. The design changes at these areas established play areas, improved the appearance of the projects and also included installing better lighting, introducing fencing to divide areas into semi-private spaces and erecting barriers to channel pedestrian traffic (Murray 1994:352).

The first model developed by NILECJ which was aimed at modifying architectural design for entire neighborhoods was the Residential Neighborhood Crime Control project in Hartford, Connecticut (LEAA newsletter, 1974, 4(1):8) based on findings from studies (e.g., see Conklin 1975; Reppetto 1972) that suggested expanding the CPTED process to whole neighborhoods (National Crime Prevention Institute 1986:119–120). Under an Institute grant of almost $500,000, the Hartford Institute of Criminal and Social Justice developed and implemented a defensible space project in two Hartford neighborhoods, one a highly transient, apartment-dominated area and the other a family area containing mostly row houses—Asylum Hill and Clay Hill-Sand, respectively. In this project, streets were closed or narrowed in order to change traffic patterns, community groups were established or strengthened to increase a sense of "community" and police-community relations were strengthened (Murray, 1994:352; National Crime Prevention Institute, 1986:128).

Despite Newman's (1973:1) own assertions that this concept of defensible space was applicable beyond public housing units "to the residential settings of most income groups" such as the neighborhoods discussed above, the validity of his concept has been seriously challenged (e.g., see the multiple cites in Jeffery and Zahm, 1993). Murray (1994:352-3) called evidence of crime reduction through defensible space "ambiguous" and even wrote that "it did not reduce crime." In addition, in a test by Greenberg and Rohe (1984:45, 58) of two perspectives of the effects of the physical design of buildings, sites, and neighborhoods on crime (defensible space versus opportunity theory), far more support was generated for the opportunity model of crime than for the defensible space model. This was because the physical characteristics differentiating high- and low-crime neighborhoods reflected differential levels of opportunity and access, not latent territorial control on the part of the residents (Jeffery and Zahm 1993:333).

Despite these problems with Newman's argument, many crime prevention projects utilized Newman's concepts of environmental design rather than Jeffery's (Jeffery and Zahm 1993:332). Newman's notion of environmental design is based on:

> the development of coordinated design standards—for architecture, land use, street layout and street lighting—which improve security. Its goal is to create environments which reduce the opportunities for crime while encouraging people to use public space in ways that contribute to their safety and enhance their sense of community. (LEAA Newsletter, 1974, 4, 3:12–13)

Newman's notion of environmental design is more complex than simply redesigning space. It also includes redesigning residential environments so that residents use the areas and become willing to defend their "territory." Yet, it is limited to modifications of the *external* physical environment in order to produce changes in the *external* social environment, while completely neglecting the *internal* physical environment of the organism. For example, Newman advocated "reducing the size and height of blocks" in public housing and "reducing the number of dwellings sharing a single entrance and making public areas visible from dwellings" (Clarke 1995a:9, citing Coleman, 1985), as well as "enhanced lighting, the hiring of concierges and porters, and the installation of entry phones, fences and barriers" (Clarke 1995a:9, citing Wekerle and Whitzman 1995). Meanwhile, Jeffery's notion of environmental design has evolved into an integrated systems perspective, which focuses both on external *and* internal environments of individual organisms, as well as interactions between the two. Therefore, Jeffery's CPTED model is logically more complete than Newman's defensible space model.

Nevertheless, Newman's work continues to influence governmental and architectural decision making with regard to physical design changes (Jeffery and Zahm 1993:333–4). For example, many government-operated public housing projects, including the Outhwaite Homes Project in Cleveland, Ohio, and Renaissance Homes in Washington, DC, (Cisneros 1995), have recently adopted defensible space crime-prevention strategies. Also, neighborhoods in Atlanta, Georgia, Richmond, Virginia, and St. Louis, Missouri limit traffic and encourage resident associations, based on the principles of defensible space (Cisneros 1995). Other neighborhoods, such as Five Oaks in Dayton, Ohio, Miami Shores in Florida and an area of Bridgeport, Connecticut, have created neighborhood-wide defensible space strategies focusing primarily on limiting access to neighborhoods by outsiders so that residents will be more likely to recognize outsiders and to increase a sense of community among residents (Cisneros 1995). Other examples of Newman's continuing influence on government thinking with regard to CPTED and architectural design abound.

Such crime prevention programs, based particularly upon notions of social control and social surveillance (defensible space), ignore crucial differences such as genetic and brain differences between individual offenders (Jeffery 1996:5, 9). In the general context of the discipline of criminology, this is understandable, for ignoring differences in individual offenders is common in criminological theory. For example, Akers's (1996) social learning theory does not recognize that learning occurs in the brain, as opposed to Jeffery (1996:6) who posits that: "Learning occurs when an environmental stimulus enters the brain, changes the neural and biochemical structure of the brain, which in turn controls behavior." The human brain is a product of gene-environment interaction (Jeffery 1990). Because individuals are unique with regard to their genes (except for mono-zygotic twins), "no two individuals are alike and no two individuals will respond to environmental cues in the same way" (Jeffery 1996:7). No two individuals will learn the same things nor in the same way. According to Jeffery, this fact must be taken into account when we design crime prevention projects.

However, because the growth of scientific knowledge and technology related to biology since the 1970s (especially regarding the brain) has undergone extremely rapid change with slightly tested and often conflicting reports, it is not entirely clear how genetic and brain differences in offenders should be viewed. Moreover, taking into account individual differences in offenders would likely be much more expensive than other CPTED measures, such as defensible space. Doing so would also raise ethical, political, and legal issues regarding the use of biological knowledge and techniques, even in conjunction with other environmental approaches. These are possible reasons for Jeffery's theoretical advancement of CPTED being ignored.

In fact, not once during the entire 1970s did C. Ray Jeffery's name appear in any edition of the LEAA newsletter when CPTED was discussed. As noted by Murray (1994:583), Jeffery (1971) antedated Newman and "originated the acronym CPTED...which has remained a common label in the technical literature but (for obvious reasons) never grabbed the public imagination in the way that 'defensible space' did." Murray did not explain what those "obvious reasons" were, but Jeffery (personal communication, 20 September 1996) stated that he re-read his 1971 edition of *Crime Prevention through Environmental Design* in order to try to understand why "no one paid any attention to it," and he reasoned that it was because of his call for more research and the foundation of a crime-related research institute at a time when people were looking for practical applications for preventing crime. Jeffery's original work in 1971 contained no detailed recipes for crime prevention at a time when government leaders were looking for them and giving wide publicity to those they found (Jeffery personal communication, 20 September 1996; also see Jeffery and Zahm 1993:330). By contrast, other works related to CPTED, such as Newman's book in 1972, included specific suggestions for how to reduce crime—at least in public housing facilities—through such techniques as lowering building height, lowering the number of apartments sharing a common hallway, increasing lobby visibility, and altering entrance design and site layout to enhance surveillability (also see National Crime Prevention Institute, 1986:122–3 for other specific architectural guidelines based on Newman's defensible space approach to crime prevention). Such suggestions were promulgated by widely recognized publishing firms and in government documents. As a result, Jeffery (personal communication, 28 March 1996) has said that he could "only scream and holler for funding" while all the money went to defensible space research, to projects like those discussed above. Since Newman argued that physical environments could be designed in order to "encourage residents to assume the behavior necessary for deterring crime" (Wallis 1980:2), his work fit with a popular sentiment about people helping themselves. As noted by Newman (1973:1, italics added), "the physical mechanisms we have isolated as contributing to the creation of defensible space have the purpose of enabling inhabitants to themselves assume primary authority for insuring safe, well maintained residential areas." Ideas related to crime prevention are more likely to be well received when they include or revolve around provisions that allow citizens to play a meaningful role. This may be the same reason that community-oriented policing is so widely practiced in law enforcement today: it focuses on developing a partnership between the police and the community, where citizens take an active role in problem solving (e.g., see Fleissner and Heinzelmann 1996; Wrobleski and Hess 1993).

Even though the theoretical development of CPTED has been largely ignored, governmental agencies are still utilizing CPTED concepts and architectural design continues to reflect them. The fact that CPTED studies and programs are deeply rooted in the national government of the United States serves as evidence of this (e.g., see Crowe 1991:28). The National Crime Prevention Institute's CPTED studio and one- and two-week courses offered opportunities to organize workshops and classes related to CPTED for the corporate businessperson, planner, and designer. At lower levels of government, state-wide laws and city-wide ordinances aimed at crime prevention through environmental design are well known. For example, the state of Florida passed the "Safe Neighborhoods Act," discussed above, and the cities of Gainesville, Florida, and Kent, Ohio passed ordinances regarding changes at convenience stores aimed at reducing robberies (Crowe 1991:4; Jeffery 1990:415–6). In addition, virtually all law enforcement agencies in the United States of any decent size contain a crime prevention unit. These units often consult with businesses and builders in the design stages of various projects in order to assist with design strategies that will ultimately promote crime prevention and improve the quality of the built environment. Old buildings are frequently renovated or replaced; improvements of streets, walkways, courtyards, parks, and parking areas are made, not only to serve people during daytime working hours, but also to promote hotel, dining, and entertainment activities during evenings, weekends, and holidays. The interrelated objectives of increasing aesthetics and preventing crime are routinely promoted as critical aspects of these projects. "City governments are finding out that it is a lot cheaper to design crime prevention into the way things are done than to hire extra police, or to pay for extra protection than can make the community look like a fortress instead of a nice place to live" (Crowe 1991:27–8).

The focus of this CPTED activity by government agencies neglects half of the model developed by Jeffery—the internal physical environment of the offender. As a result, the CPTED model being used by government agencies is based on the assumption that all offenders are the *same*, rather than being unique. The development of CPTED by Jeffery would suggest that CPTED programs should take into account how individuals may react differently to environmental design changes.

Corporate/Business Reactions

Based on CPTED research into areas such as defensible space and target hardening, various businesses have sprung up across the United States which do little more than provide CPTED consultation. For example, according to Smith (1996), consultants specializing in parking lot design have espoused the use of CPTED for over twenty years. Additionally, professional alarm companies call residents living in neighborhoods where recent burglaries occurred in order to recommend design changes such as installing electric eyes, burglar alarms and other target hardening mechanisms (Robinson 1994). Almost every business utilizes some CPTED strategy, whether it be trimming the hedges near windows and doors to increase visibility or installing cameras to deter offenders from committing offenses. Such changes are rooted in common sense understandings about preventing crime (Crowe 1991:105; Murray 1994:349). In fact, when businesses refuse to participate in CPTED activities, police officials voice concern about the continued crimes committed against those businesses.

More specific and widespread examples of corporate CPTED activity are discussed by Crowe (1991:3–4): "The National Association of Convenience Food Stores highlighted CPTED as a feature panel in its 1987 convention in Toronto" resulting in "new store configurations that reportedly have increased *sales* as much as 33 percent and *decreased* security problems by 50 percent." Such activity has led to the establishment of crime prevention programs for national store chains such as 7-11, owned by Southland Corporation (Jeffery 1990:416). In addition, "The American Society for Industrial Security (ASIS) featured a CPTED session in its store security segment at the 1987 convention in Las Vegas," where "CPTED concepts in commercial, convenience and fast food stores were covered at length" (Crowe 1991:3-4). Crowe's CPTED strategies are suggested for numerous commercial establishments, as well as downtown streets and pedestrian areas, office and industrial systems, hallways and restrooms, malls and shopping centers, and convenience stores and branch banks.

Such strategies are being followed all over the United States and also around the world, including Canada, Japan, New Zealand, England, Australia, France, the Netherlands, and Germany, but under different names. For instance, Wekerle and Whitzman (1995) discussed examples of CPTED strategies being employed in transportation-linked spaces (e.g., public transportation and parking garages and parking lots,) commercial areas (e.g., central business districts, commercial streets in neighborhoods, shopping plazas, industrial areas) and residential areas (e.g., residential streets, alleys, high-rise residential areas, interior spaces in multi-unit housing, parks and university and college campuses). These CPTED initiatives are given a different name, the "Safe Cities" approach, which is focused on a "partnership between government and citizens...prevention of criminal behavior through environmental design, community development, education...social prevention...[and] urban safety as a catalyst for change" (Wekerle and Whitzman 1995:8) but are very similar to CPTED as it exists in the United States. Both approaches ignore the physical internal environment and assume that all offenders will react to external environmental design changes in the same manner.

Academic Reactions

Academic research in CPTED declined in the 1970s. This may be owing in part to the anti-police, courts, and corrections tone that flowed throughout the 1971 and 1977 editions of Jeffery's books:

> Deterrence and punishment are failures; treatment and rehabilitation are failures; the criminal justice system is a failure from police to courts to corrections...Nothing that we do today in the criminal justice system is a success. The public is not protected; the criminal is not protected. Police are totally ineffective except within a crime prevention framework. Courts are totally ineffective to handle the crime problem. Prisons brutalize and make hardened criminals out of those unfortunate to be put into them. The only way to handle the crime problem is to prevent it. (Jeffery 1977:9)

Jeffery's comments regarding the ineffectiveness of the reactive criminal justice system and his belief that the criminal justice system should be more proactive and concerned with primary crime prevention led the National Crime Prevention Institute (1986:18) to call C. Ray Jeffery a proponent of the "Contemporary School" of Criminology, which calls for proactive crime control strategies such as community policing. Jeffery's book was referred to as *the classic* presentation of this idea.

Citizens in the United States dislike government intervention and have "a strong ethos of individual responsibility that results in punishment being seen as the most appropriate response to law breaking" (Clarke 1995b:92, citing Bright, 1992). Thus, Jeffery's argument could be called bad timing, and the utilization of *only* Newman's ideas in crime prevention projects could be called a bad idea. This is because the discouraging results of tests of Newman's ideas, "combined with a new conservatism in the country which favored punitive responses to crime in the form of lengthy prison sentences for 'career criminals,' led to a loss of federal support for CPTED" (Clarke 1995a:3–4).

According to Clarke (1995a:3), the declining interest in CPTED research was also because *Newman's* ideas had been dismissed as "environmental determinism" and many thought he oversimplified the problem of crime by neglecting important social causes (e.g., poverty, unemployment, and racism). Moreover, CPTED studies were not proving to be very effective, and some scholars at the time began to question whether the causes of crime were beyond the control of CPTED (Clarke 1995a:4). Thus, relative to other crime prevention measures, such as situational crime prevention (Clarke 1980, 1983), CPTED support by governmental agencies declined:

> In Britain as well as in some other European countries, situational prevention has become an integral part of government policy. In the United States, comparatively less success has been enjoyed by CPTED because of the failure of some ambitious projects funded by the federal government and also...because CPTED, unlike situational prevention, has generally been confined to projects involving buildings and facilities. (Clarke 1992:6)

Examples of the failed CPTED projects discussed by Clarke include the Westinghouse CPTED projects discussed above, aimed at reducing crime in other types of physical environments. These were troublesome to implement and proved meager in terms of crime prevention (Murray 1994:354) because they attempted to extend the defensible space concept to inappropriate areas such as school and commercial sites where "'territorial' behavior is much less natural than in the residential context" (Clarke 1995b:97). According to Murray (1994:354): "In retrospect, it seems to have been a mistake to apply defensible space and territorial concepts in environments where a broader conception of CPTED would have been more appropriate." It seems very ironic now that it was Jeffery who has been arguing all along for a conception of CPTED that is *broader* than Newman's notion of defensible space. Changes to the external environment should be only a part of a larger crime control package in order to be effective (Murray 1994:354). This was Jeffery's argument in his 1971, 1977, and 1990 books.

These failing CPTED measures led Murray (1994:354) to claim that no strategies exist for altering the built environment which will reduce crime and the lesson is that it all depends on the specific situation. This lesson no doubt influenced the development of situational crime prevention (Clarke 1983), which is practiced by crime prevention units within central governments of Holland and Great Britain and semiautonomous governmental agencies in countries such as Sweden (Clarke 1995b:92).

The situational crime prevention model originated from lessons learned from research on correctional treatments by the British government's Home Office Research Unit that demonstrated the potential for designing out misbehavior by manipulating situational factors in the immediate environment of institutions (Clarke 1992:4–5; also see Clarke 1995b:94–6; Clarke and Cornish 1983). This research, combined with the "the action research model" in which researchers and practitioners work together to analyze and define problems, identify and implement possible solutions, and evaluate results (Clarke 1992:5), led to the development of the theory underlying situational crime prevention, as well as the standard methodology it uses (Clarke 1995b:91). According to Clarke, the concept of situational crime prevention was "soon influenced by two independent (Jeffery 1977), but nonetheless related strands of policy research in the United States"— defensible space (Newman 1972) and CPTED (Jeffery 1971)—"both of which had preceded situational prevention, but, because of the trans-Atlantic delay in the dissemination of ideas, had not been the spur to its development." Later, situational crime prevention was influenced by the notion of "problem-oriented policing" (e.g., Goldstein 1979), an approach aimed at identifying and solving the problems of particular communities rather than waiting for those problems to result in criminal behavior, which is viewed as a symptom of the underlying problems (e.g., see Wrobleski and Hess 1993).

According to Clarke (1992:3-4), situational crime prevention is aimed at eliminating opportunities for crime. It includes opportunity-reducing measures that are "directed at highly specific forms of crime...that involve the management, design, or manipulation of the immediate environment in as systematic and permanent way as possible...so as to increase the effort and risks of crime and reduce the rewards as perceived by a wide range of offenders." The approach was supported by studies of several related theories of crime, including the routine activity and opportunity perspectives (Clarke 1995b:91). Each of these theories will be discussed later in this chapter.

Clarke (1992:7) has written that situational crime prevention is broader than CPTED, because the former "encompasses the entire range of environments (and objects) involved in crime and because it encompasses legal and management as well as design solutions," while CPTED "tends to be focused on design of the built environment" (also see Fleissner and Heinzelmann 1996:1). This may be true in terms of how CPTED has been applied to physical design in a comprehensive, planned way (National Crime Prevention Institute 1986:123). Yet, Jeffery's CPTED model has evolved beyond these strategies to include both the external environment of the place *and* the internal environment of the offender. Clarke (1992:6) acknowledged that Jeffery's (1977) volume argued for a crime prevention approach that "took due account of both genetic predisposition and the physical environment." Therefore, Jeffery's theoretical concept of CPTED is actually broader than situational crime prevention, for Jeffery discusses crime prevention strategies that involve both the external environment of the place and the internal environment of the offender. Situational crime prevention only takes into account the nature of the external physical environment of the place (e.g., see Clarke 1992; 1995b:109) and makes inferences to the offender based on what must be going on in the offender's mind. Offenders are treated as a homogenous group of *rational* beings. The internal environment of the offender is treated as mental instead of physical.

Treating the internal environment of the offender as a mental environment is common in academic crime prevention theory even today. For example, Brantingham and Brantingham (1993) developed a "crime pattern theory" that accumulates theory and research from many diverse areas—all of which focus on the place of the criminal event in some manner or another and include CPTED and situational crime prevention. Brantingham and Brantingham's theory addresses the question of why offenders select some targets and avoid others. The target selection of offenders "depends on *mental templates* used to shape searches for targets or victims and to predefine the characteristics of a suitable target or suitable place for finding targets" (Brantingham and Brantingham 1993:269, italics added). For example, individual offenders create templates which are used by them to identify "good" or "bad" targets. Templates are used by both potential offenders and all people in society for legitimate purposes such as choosing where to eat, live, and shop because daily "functioning within the infinitely complex cue-emitting environment involves the development of cognitive images and cognitive maps and the use of these images" (Brantingham and Brantingham 1993:287). It is not made clear whether these templates are actually mentalistic phenomena or patterns of neurological processes, and such clarification is very important. As mentalistic phenomena, "mental templates" cannot be empirically verified except through verbal discussions with offenders. Verbal behavior is just that, behavior; it is not the internal thought processes that the researcher thinks he or she is studying. Both the verbal behavior and the thought process of offenders are under control of the brain, making even the thought process of offenders physical and not mental (Jeffery and Zahm 1993:337, 339). Although the existence of mentalistic templates cannot be empirically disproven, neither can it be empirically demonstrated. The notion of neurological templates consisting of coded and stored information in the brain at least holds greater promise for empirical study. Rapidly developing technology is making this a real possibility.

Jeffery (1990:413) has advocated replacing the "loose" and "fuzzy" variables, such as mental templates, that intervene between the environment and behavior in most CPTED literature with the physical organ of the brain in the offender. For those rare CPTED writers who even mention the offender, few are referring to this. Reliance by scholars such as Brantingham and Brantingham on the internal *mental* rather than the internal *physical* environment of the offender serves as further evidence that Jeffery's argument is not being tended to. Still, Brantingham and Brantingham have probably come the closest to realizing Jeffery's dream of a CPTED based both on the external physical environment of the place *and* the internal environment of the offender. Their reliance on "mental templates" is what separates their crime pattern theory from Jeffery's CPTED model. Yet, Brantingham and Brantingham's rationale for including mental templates in their model is partially valid. As argued by Brantingham and Brantingham (1996), criminologists are not yet able to take fully into account the internal physical environment of offenders. We have not gained the knowledge necessary to do so. As this knowledge grows, scholars in the field need to embrace it and integrate it into their theoretical models, as Jeffery has attempted to do. In addition, the Brantinghams' crime pattern theory was spurred by other theoretical perspectives that treated the internal environment of the offender as mental rather than physical. These perspectives include rational choice, opportunity and routine activity theories.

The development of these theories shifted attention away from Jeffery's CPTED model and have much in common; each assumes a "classical view of human nature based on free will, moral responsibility, and rational choice" (Jeffery and Zahm 1993:324). Because Jeffery holds that the concept of rationality is metaphysical and cannot be empirically tested for advancement of our scientific knowledge regarding crime prevention (Jeffery personal communication, 28 March 1996), the fact that CPTED projects have preceded on the assumption of a rational man clearly separates Jeffery from other scholars in the field.

Rational choice theory examines offender decision making and the factors that effect it such as assessments of risks, rewards and the morality of various behaviors (Clarke 1983:232). The balance between likely risks and rewards influences offenders' target selection. According to Brantingham and Brantingham (1984), the level of risk is one of the factors that makes a target "good" or "bad." Offenders plan to reduce the level of risk associated with committing criminal offenses through selecting the most suitable targets. Taylor and Harrell (1996:2) claimed that offenders often behave in a rational fashion, since they choose to commit crimes that require little effort, but which provide high rewards and pose low risks of painful consequences. Hickey (1991) and Wright and Rossi (1983) discussed how even violent criminals are selective in their choices of targets: serial killers rarely choose weight lifters or martial arts experts as victims. Other violent criminals rarely choose armed victims; they pose too much of a risk (Siegel 1995). The mere fact that victims are not chosen at random suggests a rational offender (Fattah 1993:244).

Of course, to conclude that offenders are rational based on their behaviors, and then to utilize the concept of rationality in order to explain the same behaviors, constitutes the logical error of circular reasoning (e.g., see Akers 1994:8). For instance, Jeffery and Zahm (1993:339) noted that the concept of choice "is neither empirical nor observable, and the investigator can only know when an individual has made a choice when he behaves in a given way. From the observed behavior, the investigator inputs a cause (such as rational choice or social control)." Jeffery and Zahm (1993:337) went on to note that because the heart of the rational choice model is focused on "an analysis of the thought or cognitive means by which individuals process information from the environment" (Jeffery and Zahm 1993:337), it is not possible to test the theory directly. Thoughts cannot be studied directly, they can only be verbalized by offenders. As explained above, verbal statements constitute verbal *behavior*, not the thought processes they are portrayed to represent by rational choice theorists. These problems with rational choice theory make interpretations of findings within such a framework questionable at best.

Opportunity theory holds that criminal behavior most often reflects offenders' exploitation of perceived opportunities. Opportunity theory can generally be understood in terms of the number of targets available for crime (Fattah 1993:248). Cook (1986) defined opportunity theory as "the interaction of victims and offenders in relation to targets," which are viewed by offenders as "opportunities" when they are "attractive because of a high payoff and little risk" (Jeffery and Zahm 1993:335). Of course, much environmental research can be interpreted using both rational choice and opportunity theory, for "rational" involves evaluation of opportunity (Cornish and Clarke 1986). The concept of opportunity is central to the rational choice perspective (Fattah 1993:248); the rational choice perspective views crime as a function of opportunity, where the opportunity structure is determined by contacts in the physical external environment (Fattah 1993:236, 239).

Interpretation of research findings with opportunity theory can be tautological, for they often translate into a statement such as "this victim was at higher risk because he or she or it offered a better or more suitable opportunity to the offender," where higher risks and better opportunity mean the same thing. This theory cannot *explain* why a particular offender thought the target was better or more suitable, nor what caused the offender to have criminal motivations in the first place and then act on them.

Routine activity theory (e.g., Cohen and Felson 1979; Cohen et al. 1980; Felson 1994, 1995; Kennedy and Baron 1993; Kennedy and Forde 1990a, 1990b; Massey et al. 1989; Maxfield 1987a, 1987b; Miethe et al. 1987; Roncek and Maier 1991; Sherman et al. 1989) suggests that crime results from the convergence of three elements in time and space: a presence of potential or motivated offenders; a presence of suitable targets; and an absence of capable guardians to prevent the criminal act. It assumes that "daily life systematically brings together or disperses offender and victim, parent and child, person and property, and so on," so that criminal activity is a natural by-product of legitimate activity. Specifically, as changes in society disperse peoples' activities away from households and families, opportunity for crime is increased, thereby increasing crime rates (Cohen and Felson 1979:588, 593). In the course of routine, normal, or patterned recreational or work activities, suitable targets become more discernable to offenders, thus increasing the likelihood of committing offenses.

Routine activity theory is widely held as a subset of a more general opportunity model (Cohen et al. 1981; Jeffery and Zahm 1993; Sampson and Wooldredge 1987), since "Routine activities theorists view street crime as a product of *opportunity* that arises in the ongoing activities that occur on the street," whereby the likelihood of being a victim of crime increases when the three elements noted above converge in time and space (Kennedy and Baron 1993:92, italics added). Routine activity theory is also related to rational choice theory (Miethe, Stafford, and Long 1987:193–4; also see Clarke et al. 1985; Cohen et al. 1981; Cohen et al. 1980). Motivated offenders rationally select suitable targets that lack guardianship. Massey, Krohn, and Bonati (1989:384–5) wrote that the notion that criminal victimization is not a random process is implicit within the routine activity approach, and thus potential offenders must pursue rational thought processes regarding the selection of targets. According to Felson (1987:120–1, italics added): "Routine activities patterns provide *choices* to individuals, including criminals, and set the stage for subsequent events determining the success of the offenders in carrying out the crime, or of the potential victim in avoiding victimization, however unwittingly" (see Felson 1983). Taylor and Harrell (1996:2, italics added) wrote that rational choice theory "suggests that crimes are most likely to occur when *potential offenders* come into contact with a *suitable crime target* where the chance of detection by others are thought to be low or the criminal, if detected, will be able to exit without being identified or apprehended." Questions of the offender, such as "How visible, attractive, or vulnerable do targets appear?" assume a rational offender (Taylor and Harrell 1996:2).

These main theoretical perspectives of rational choice, opportunity theory, and routine activity have shifted attention away from the theoretical argument of Jeffery. Rather than arguing for a primary crime prevention model aimed at identifying conditions both in the external environment of the place *and* in the internal environment of the offender, CPTED research based on rational choice, opportunity, or routine activity theory (e.g., crime pattern theory) leads to crime prevention projects aimed at reducing *opportunities* for *rational* offenders through increasing surveillance, deterrence, target hardening and removal, access control, and so forth. Instead of leading to complete CPTED projects, they have led to situational crime prevention projects related to CPTED which assume a rational offender who seeks to maximize utility, benefit, or pleasure and to minimize cost or loss of pain.

Only recently has an academic interest in CPTED been rekindled. With growing evidence that crime may not be displaced with the implementation of CPTED projects and that a diffusion of benefits to other forms of crimes may exist (see Clarke 1995a: 6; 1995b:122–32), there may be promise that in the future CPTED will remain a popular crime prevention strategy. Given the apparent concentration of crime in some locations—the "hot spots" of crime (Robinson 1997a; Sherman et al.1989; Spring and Block 1988)—CPTED strategies aimed at those locations might provide big pay-offs in terms of crime prevention results.

Unfortunately for the field of criminology, the notion of CPTED that exists today still largely ignores Jeffery's ideas. For example, Fleissner and Heinzelmann (1996) discussed the basic principles of CPTED: they mentioned designing and managing the physical environment of buildings, residential neighborhoods, and businesses through target hardening, surveillance, and territorial reinforcement. In addition, Crowe's (1991:3) *Crime Prevention through Environmental Design: Applications of Architectural Design and Space Management Concepts* utilizes the "Three D" approach based on the three dimensions of human space (Designation, Definition, and Design) to describe useful CPTED strategies that can be used in various environments, including commercial, residential, and school environments. Neither book includes statements regarding any "environment" except for the external physical environment and how it can be altered to prevent criminal behavior. Neither book follows the development of Jeffery's work closely enough to include strategies for "designing" the internal environment of the offender in order to prevent criminal behavior. Moreover, Clarke recently presented a paper entitled "CPTED and Situational Prevention in Public Housing" to the technical assistance workshop on CPTED organized for the U.S. Department of Housing and Urban Development by SPARTA Consulting Corporation in which he (1995a:2) rightfully wrote: "No account of CPTED in public housing can neglect Oscar Newman's contribution"; yet, Jeffery's CPTED model is not given its due weight. The result is not surprising. Although, to the author's knowledge, Jeffery has not concentrated specifically on crime in public housing, his general model points out limitations to current CPTED projects at housing complexes based largely on defensible space or situational crime prevention strategies. Crime prevention projects being used at public housing projects around the United States generally do not take into account how the physical external environment affects the physical internal environments (i.e., brains) of the people living there. Living in public housing projects in conditions of poverty might translate into increased exposure to toxic chemicals and violence and decreased levels of exercise and nutrition (Jeffery 1996). No amount of defensible space or situational crime prevention will overcome the effects that such factors have on human behavior.

Defensible space and situational crime prevention, both rooted in popular theoretical traditions of social control and rational choice, are more celebrated than Jeffery's CPTED model because the field of criminology, like any other discipline, tends to resist change. For example, between Jeffery's original 1971 edition of *Crime Prevention through Environmental Design*, and his revised 1977 edition, he took on the challenge of teaching himself the "new biology." The information he needed to revise his theoretical model regarding the role of the physical organism (e.g., the brain as it relates to human learning) was simply not being pursued in the field of criminology (Jeffery personal communication, 28 March 1996).

As Jeffery's ideas have evolved and he has written about the role of the human brain in learning behavior generally, including criminal, delinquent, and maladaptive behaviors in particular, his pleas for attention to the "new biology" have largely fallen on deaf ears in the field of criminology. For example, in Ronald Akers's *Criminological Theory: Introduction and Evaluation* (1996), a chapter is devoted to his "social learning theory," which does not discuss the role of the brain in human learning. Without such a discussion, any explanation of a learning theory of crime is logically incomplete. Instead, Akers founds his theory on earlier mentalistic, introspective, non-disprovable statements of learning that include no discussion of the role of the physical organism. His treatment of social learning theory, as well as academia's treatment of CPTED, illustrates what some have called "disciplinary myopia" (Faust personal communication, 29 October 1996), a term that refers to scholars' being unable to see outside of their own areas of specialty. Generally, social learning theorists do not take into account individual differences that could explain different learning capacities. The result is that scholars who are well-equipped with only the tools of their discipline have continued conducting studies with regard only to the knowledge being generated in their own fields.

This situation occurs with regard to crime prevention studies as well. For instance, works related to crime prevention have been published in the disciplines of geography (Davidson 1981; Georges-Abeyie and Harries 1980; Harries 1980; Herbert 1982; Smith 1986), sociology (Smith 1986), ecology (Byrne and Sampson 1986) and urban planning (Wekerle and Whitzman 1995), to name only a few. Each of these disciplines may contribute something important to crime prevention, but Jeffery stands out in his efforts to utilize meaningfully the tools of all relevant academic disciplines, through an interdisciplinary approach, in order to understand and prevent crime.

Biological disciplines (e.g., behavioral genetics, brain sciences) are included in Jeffery's interdisciplinary model of CPTED. In fact, some credit Jeffery with being the father of "biological criminology" (Fishbein personal communication, 28 March 1996), prompting Jeffery to state "I guess that makes me the illegitimate son of Lombroso" (Jeffery personal communication, 28 March 1996), referring to Cesare Lombroso, who is considered by many to be the father of positivistic criminology. According to Jeffery, arguments and debates about biology have followed him and when president of the American Society of Criminology, he was "raked over the coals as a neo-Lombrosian" (Jeffery personal communication, 28 March 1996).

Yet, with a true understanding of the integrated systems perspective and its implications for crime-related study, one realizes that biological factors of physical organisms are simply *important* factors in the constellation of factors that play a role in the etiology of human behavior. They are not the *only* factors or even the *only important* factors. Acknowledging the role of the internal environment of the physical organism (i.e., genetics and the brain) in human behavior is logical, and doing so does not lead to reductionism or biological determinism. Nevertheless, these charges have been levied against the theoretical argument of C. Ray Jeffery as his original CPTED model has developed into a more general notion of crime prevention. That the theoretical development of Jeffery's ideas has been largely ignored, partly because his recent research has focused on the biological aspects of human behavior and their implications for crime prevention, is not surprising. This also must be put into the general context of criminology: overall, the field has dismissed biological factors as unimportant for understanding human behavior. According to Raine (1993: xvii), biology is ignored in most criminology textbooks.

Hope for the Future?

Many CPTED studies have been completed by students of Jeffery. Although it would be difficult to provide a complete list, some of these include Hunter's (1988) study of convenience store robberies, studies of burglaries by Cromwell et al. (1991) and Robinson (1994, 1995,

1997a, 1997b; Robinson and Robinson 1997), Robinson's (1995) study of crimes at highway interchange activity areas, del Carmen's and Stretesky's (1997) study of crime in parking lots, Cunningham's (1996) study of blue light trails on a university campus and Kelley's (1997) study of neurological assessment of juvenile offenders. Of these studies, only the ones by Cromwell et al. and Kelley dealt directly with offenders, and only Kelley's delved into the biological aspects of human behavior. Kelley's study focused on the internal *physical* environment of the offender, as it assessed neurological dysfunctions in juvenile offenders, and discovered interrelationships with external environmental factors.

Generally, Jeffery's students recognize the physical internal environment of the offender and avoid making mentalistic assumptions about offenders, thus reflecting Jeffery's CPTED theory. Jeffery is seeking crime prevention programs involving the individual offender level as well as the external environmental level, since criminal behavior is a product of both. The numerous examples of CPTED strategies that exist today (e.g., see National Crime Prevention Institute, 1986:129) do not take into account both the environment of the place and the offender. In terms of crime prevention, CPTED projects today attempt to influence the motivations of offenders, increase the potential for risk to the offender and reduce or alter opportunities, and treat offenders as if they are all the same. The fact that no two individuals are alike in terms of genetics, the brain, and learning experiences, suggests that factors unique to individual offenders should also be built into a complete model of crime prevention. That is, CPTED should be expanded to include both the external environment of the place *and* the internal environment of the offender. According to Jeffery (personal communication, 28 March 1996), this would entail testing for brain damage, nutritional defects, heavy metal contamination, neurological problems, and might lead to alteration of nutritional factors, environmental pollutants, drug treatment and so forth. The result would be crime prevention research and policy which would be interdisciplinary in nature and based on an organism-environment interaction model of behavior (Jeffery 1990:418). Until this occurs, CPTED in practice cannot and will not reflect Jeffery's CPTED in theory.

Conclusion

This chapter examined various reactions to C. Ray Jeffery's CPTED and found evidence that CPTED in government, architecture, academia, and corporate businesses is not meaningfully related to Jeffery's model. Part of why his CPTED model has been ignored is straightforward and easy to understand: Jeffery's works included no detailed recipes for crime prevention, while Newman's did. Newman's works on defensible space were supported by the government in part because they involved citizen participation, while Jeffery's works criticized the criminal justice system and called for more academic research into the relationship between the internal physical environment and human behavior. Because Jeffery's model would entail examining biological factors, the field of criminology has resisted it, owing in part to the unwelcome niche of biology in the field, and in part to the field's resistance to change. How to specifically include individual genetic and brain differences into a CPTED model is unclear, because the growth of knowledge regarding the brain and genetics has been in a state of rapid change with untested and often conflicting reports. Accepting individual differences would also raise uncomfortable ethical, political, and legal issues. The highly supported Newman model has been criticized for neglecting other important factors and found to be insufficient for preventing crime, leading to a loss of interest in CPTED until very recently. Unfortunately, the crime prevention through environmental design that is popular today is rooted deeply in the theoretical perspectives of rational choice, opportunity, and routine activity theories. Thus, crime pattern theory and situational crime prevention treat the internal environment of the offender as mental rather than physical. This stands as a major barrier to scientific study in the field of criminology.

Despite these facts, the term CPTED is still credited to Jeffery today even though, as it exists in the government, architecture, academia, and corporate businesses, it does not resemble Jeffery's evolved model. This prompted Jeffery to write:

> It may be time to drop the term in referring to the Jeffery model, as the term has applied to many different models of crime prevention including Newman's model...[and Crowe's model]. The term *crime prevention* may be more accurate and more descriptive of the concepts included in the 1971 and 1977" books. (Jeffery and Zahm 1993:330–1)

Since Jeffery's CPTED model does include both the external environment of the place *and* the internal environment of the offender, perhaps "crime prevention" is a better term for it. This is especially true, given peoples' reluctance to use the term CPTED for anything other than defensible space, target hardening, and altering buildings and other external environments. Nevertheless, CPTED could still be an accurate term, if changing either or both of the environments was taken to mean crime prevention through environmental design (del Carmen 1997). As it is though, Jeffery's work in the area of crime prevention has been ignored in government, architecture, academia, and corporate businesses. Jeffery has developed his original notion of CPTED into a more general theoretical framework of crime prevention. It is hoped that this notion will soon emerge as a guiding beacon for academic criminologists and crime prevention policymakers. Otherwise, crime prevention through environmental design programs will continue to show ephemeral results owing to their narrow focus on external environmental factors.

Note

An earlier version of this chapter was presented to the annual meeting of the American Society of Criminology, Chicago, Illinois, November 1996. The author would like to thank C. Ray Jeffery, Paul and Patricia Brantingham, Fred Faust, Diane Zahm, Paul Cromwell and the anonymous reviewers for their helpful comments regarding this paper.

References

Akers, R. 1994. *Criminological Theory: Introduction and Evaluation.* Los Angeles: Roxbury.

Angel, S. 1968. *Discouraging Crime through City Planning.* Berkeley and Los Angeles: University of California.

Bennett, T. and R. Wright. 1984. *Burglars on Burglary: Prevention and the Offender.* Brookfield, VT: Gower Publishing.

Box, S., C. Hale and G. Andrews.1988. "Explaining Fear of Crime." *British Journal of Criminology* 28:340–56.

Brantingham, P. J. and P. L. Brantingham. 1984. *Patterns in Crime.* New York: MacMillan.

———. 1996. "The Theory of CPTED." Paper presented to the annual meeting of the American Society of Criminology, Chicago.

Brantingham, P. J. and F. L. Faust.1976. "A Conceptual Model of Crime Prevention." *Crime and Delinquency* 7:284-95.

Brantingham, P. L. and P. J. Brantingham.1993. "Environment, Routine, and Situation: Toward a Pattern Theory of Crime." In R.V. Clarke and M. Felson (eds.) *Routine Activity and Rational Choice: Advances in Criminological Theory* (vol. 5). New Brunswick, NJ: Transaction Publishers.

Bright, J.1992. *Crime Prevention in America: A British Perspective.* Chicago: University of Illinois at Chicago, Office of International Criminal Justice.

Byrne, J. M. and R. J. Sampson.1986. *The Social Ecology of Crime.* New York: Springer-Verlag.

Cisneros, H. G.1995. *Defensible Space: Deterring Crime and Building Community.* Washington, DC: Department of Housing and Urban Development.

Clarke, R. V.1980. *Situational Crime Prevention: Theory and Practice*. Albany, NY: Harrow and Heston.

―――. 1983. *Situational Crime Prevention: Its Theoretical Basis and Practical Scope*, vol. 4 of *Crime and Justice: An Annual Review of Research*. Chicago: University of Chicago Press.

―――. 1992. *Situational Crime Prevention: Successful Case Studies*. Albany, NY: Harrow and Heston.

―――. 1995a. "CPTED and Situational Crime Prevention in Public Housing." Paper presented to the Technical Assistance Workshop on CPTED organized by the U.S. Department of Housing and Urban Development by SPARTA Consulting Corporation.

―――. 1995b. "Situational Crime Prevention." In M. Tonry and D. Farrington (eds.) *Building a Safer Society: Strategic Approaches to Crime Prevention*, vol. 19 of *Crime and Justice*. Chicago: University of Chicago Press.

Clarke, R. V. and D. B. Cornish.1985. "Modeling Offenders' Decisions: A Framework for Research and Policy." *Crime and Justice: An Annual Review of Research* 6:147–85.

Cohen, L. E. and M. Felson.1979. "Social Change and Crime Rate Trends: A Routine Activity Approach." *American Sociological Review* 44:588–608.

Cohen, L. E., M. Felson, and K. C. Land.1980. "Property Crime Rates in the United States: A Macrodynamic Analysis, 1947–1977; with ex-ante forecasts for the mid-1980s." *American Journal of Sociology* 86:90–118.

Cohen, L. E., J. Kluegel, and K. C. Land.1981. "Social Inequality and Predatory Criminal Victimization: An Exposition and a Test of a Formal Theory." *American Sociological Review* 46:505–24.

Coleman, A. 1985. *Utopia on Trial: Vision and Reality in Planned Housing*. London: Hilary Shipman.

Conklin, J.1975. *The Impact of Crime*. New York: Macmillan.

Cornish, D. and R. Clarke.1986. *The Reasoning Criminal: Rational Choice Perspectives on Offending*. The Hague: Springer-Verlag.

Cromwell, P. F., J. N. Olson, and D. W. Avary 1991. *Breaking and Entering: An Ethnographic Analysis of Burglary*. Newbury Park, CA: Sage.

Crowe, T. D.1991. *Crime Prevention through Environmental Design: Applications of Architectural Design and Space Management Concepts*. Boston: Butterworth-Heinemann.

Crowe, T. D. and D. L. Zahm. 1994. "Crime Prevention through Environmental Design." *Land Development* Fall:22–7.

Cunningham, S.1996. "The Blue Light Emergency Automated Communications Network: A Spatial and Temporal Analysis." Ph.D. diss., The Florida State University School of Criminology and Criminal Justice.

Davidson, R. N.1981.*Crime and Environment*. London: Billing and Sons.

del Carmen, A.1997. "An Analysis of the Theoretical, Empirical, and Policy Development of Crime Prevention through Environmental Design in the United States during the Nineteenth and Twentieth Centuries Employing the Conceptual Orientation of Interactive Systems." Ph.D diss., The Florida State University, School of Criminology and Criminal Justice.

del Carmen, A. and P. Stretesky. 1997. "Campus Crime: An Environmental Assessment." *Journal of Security Administration*, forthcoming.

Fattah, E. A.1993. "The Rational Choice/Opportunity Perspectives as a Vehicle for Integrating Criminological and Victiminological Theories." In R.V. Clarke and M. Felson (eds.) *Routine Activity and Rational Choice: Advances in Criminological Theory* (vol. 5). New Brunswick, NJ: Transaction Publishers.

Felson, M.1987. "Routine Activities and Crime Prevention in the Developing Metropolis." *Criminology* 25(4):911–31.

———. 1994. *Crime and Everyday Life: Insights and Implications for Society*. Thousand Oaks, CA: Pine Forge Press.

———. 1995. "Those Who Discourage Crime." In J. E. Eck and D. Weisburd (eds.) *Crime and Place*. Monsey, NY: Criminal Justice Press.

Fleissner, D. and F. Heinzelmann.1996. "Crime Prevention through Environmental Design and Community Policing." National Institute of Justice Research in Action, August.

Gardiner, R. A.1978. *Design for Safe Neighborhoods*. Washington, DC: U.S. Department of Justice.

Georges-Abeyie, D. E. and K. D. Harries. 1980. *Crime: A Spatial Perspective*. New York: Columbia University Press.

Greenberg, S. and M. W. Rohe. 1984. "Neighborhood Design and Crime." *Journal of the American Planning Association* 50:48–61.

Harries, K. D. 1980. *Crime and the Environment*. Springfield, IL: Charles C. Thomas.

Healy, R. J.1968. *Design for Security*. New York: John Wiley and Sons.

Herbert, D.1982. *The Geography of Urban Crime*. Burnt Mill, Harlow, Essex, England: Longman Group Limited.

Hunter, A.1978. "Symbols of Incivility." Paper presented to the annual meeting of the American Society of Criminology, Dallas.

Hunter, R. D. 1988. "Environmental Characteristics of Convenience Store Robbery in the State of Florida." Paper presented to the annual meeting of the American Society of Criminology, Chicago.

Jacobs, J. 1961. *The Life and Death of Great American Cities*. New York: Random House.

Jeffery, C. R. 1971. *Crime Prevention through Environmental Design*. Beverly Hills, CA: Sage.

———. 1977. *Crime Prevention through Environmental Design*. Beverly Hills, CA: Sage.

———. 1990. *Criminology: An Interdisciplinary Approach*. Englewood Cliffs, NJ: Prentice-Hall.

———. 1996. "Mental Health and Crime Prevention: A Public Health Model." Paper presented to the International Crime Prevention Practitioners Conference, Vancouver.

Jeffery, C. R. and D. L. Zahm.1993. "Crime Prevention through Environmental Design, Opportunity Theory, and Rational Choice Models." In R.V. Clarke and M. Felson (eds.) *Routine Activity and Rational Choice: Advances in Criminological Theory* (vol. 5). New Brunswick, NJ: Transaction Publishers.

Kelley, T.1997. "An Integrated Systems Approach to Screening for Brain Dysfunction in Delinquent Offenders." Master's Thesis. The Florida State University School of Criminology and Criminal Justice.

Kennedy, L. W. and S. W. Baron.1993. "Routine Activities and a Subculture of Violence: A Study of Violence on the Street." *Journal of Research in Crime and Delinquency* 30(1):88-112.

Kennedy, L. W. and D. R. Forde. 1990a. "Risky Lifestyles and Dangerous Results: Routine Activities and Exposure to Crime." *Sociology and Social Research: An International Journal* 74(4):208–11.

———. 1990b. "Routine Activities and Crime: An Analysis of Victimization in Canada." *Criminology* 28(1):137–52.

Massey, J. L., M.D. Krohn, and L. M. Bonati.1989. "Property Crime and the Routine

Activities of Individuals." *Journal of Research in Crime and Delinquency* 26(4):378–400.

Maxfield, M.G.1987a. "Household Composition, Routine Activity, and Victimization: A Comparative Analysis." *Journal of Quantitative Criminology* 3(4):301–20.

———. 1987b. "Lifestyle and Routine Activity Theories of Crime: Empirical Studies of Victimization, Delinquency, and Offender Decision Making." *Journal of Quantitative Criminology* 3(4):275–82.

Mayhew, P.1981. "Crime in Public View: Surveillance and Crime Prevention." In P. J. Brantingham and P. L. Brantingham (eds.) *Environmental Criminology*. Beverly Hills, CA: Sage.

Mayhew, P., R.V. Clarke, A. Sturman, and J. Hough. 1976. *Crime as Opportunity*. Home Office Research Study No. 34, Her Majesty's Stationary Office.

Miethe, T. D., M. C. Stafford, and J. S. Long.1987. "Social Differentiation in Criminal Victimization: A Test of Routine Activities/Lifestyle Theories." *American Sociological Review* 52:184–94.

Murray, C.1994. "The Physical Environment." In J. Q. Wilson and J. Petersilia (eds.) *Crime* San Francisco, CA: Institute for Contemporary Studies.

Nasar, J. L. and B. Fisher.1992. "Design for Vulnerability: Cues and Reactions to Fear of Crime." *Sociological and Social Research* 76(2):48–57.

National Crime Prevention Institute. 1986. *Understanding Crime Prevention*. Louisville, KY: National Crime Prevention Institute, School of Justice Administration, University of Louisville.

Newman, O. 1972. *Defensible Space: People and Design in the Violent City*. New York: Macmillan.

———. 1973a. *A Design Guide for Improving Residential Security*. Washington, DC: U.S. Department of Housing and Urban Development.

———. 1973b. *Architectural Design for Crime Prevention*. Washington, DC : U.S. Department of Justice.

———. 1976. *Design Guidelines for Creating Defensible Space*. National Institute of Law Enforcement and Criminal Justice. Washington, DC: U.S. Government Printing Office.

Packer, H. L.1968. *The Limits of the Criminal Sanction*. Stanford, CA: Stanford University Press.

Perce, E. 1977. The CPTED concept. Nation's Cities. Rockville, MD: National League of Cities.

Raine, A.1993. *The Psychopathology of Crime: Criminal Behavior as a Clinical Disorder*. San Diego, CA: Academic Press.

Rainwater, L.1966. "Fear and the Home-as-Haven in the Lower Class." *Journal of the American Institute of Planners* 1:23–7.

Reppetto, T. A.1974. *Residential Crime*. Cambridge: Ballinger.

Robinson, D. M.1995. "Environmental Characteristics Associated with Criminal Victimization in Interstate Highway Interchange Activity Areas." Ph.D diss., The Florida State University School of Criminology and Criminal Justice.

Robinson, M. B.1994. "Environmental Characteristics of Burglaries in Private Apartment Complexes Predominantly Occupied by University Students, Zone 7, Tallahassee, Florida, 1993." Master's Thesis: The Florida State University School of Criminology and Criminal Justice.

———. 1995. "Once Bitten, but Not Twice Bitten: Student Apartment Burglary 'Cool Spots.'" Paper presented to the annual conference of the Southern Criminal Justice Association, Gatlinburg, Tennessee.

———. 1997a. "Burglary Re-victimization: The Time Period of Heightened Risk." *British Journal of Criminology* 38(1):76–85.

————. 1997b. "Lifestyles, Routine Activities, and Residential Burglary Victimization." Ph.D. diss. The Florida State University School of Criminology and Criminal Justice.

Robinson, M. B., M. Gertz, and F. L. Faust. 1995. A Look at the Relationship between High Aesthetics/Low Incivilities, Criminal Victimizations and Perceptions of Risk. Unpublished paper.

Robinson, M. B. and C. Robinson.1997b. Environmental Characteristics Associated with Residential Burglaries of Student Apartment Complexes." *Environment and Behavior* 29(5):657–75.

Roncek, D. W. and P. A. Maier. 1991. "Bars, Blocks, and Crimes Revisited: Linking the Theory of Routine Activities to the Empiricism of 'Hot Spots.'" *Criminology* 29(4):725–53.

Scarr, H. A.1972. *Patterns of Burglary.* U.S. Department of Justice, Law Enforcement Assistance Administration. Washington, DC: U.S. Government Printing Office.

Seligman, M. E. P. and J. L. Hager.1972. *Biological Boundaries of Learning.* New York: Appleton-Century-Crofts.

Sherman, L. W., P. R. Gartin and M. E. Buerger. 1989. "Hot Spots of Predatory Crime: Routine Activities and the Criminology of Place." *Criminology* 27(1):27–55.

Siegel, L. J. 1995. *Criminology.* St. Paul, MN: West.

Smith, M. S.1996. *Crime Prevention through Environmental Design in Parking Facilities.* National Institute of Justice Research in Brief. Washington, DC: U.S. Department of Justice.

Smith, S. J.1986. *Crime, Space, and Society.* Cambridge: Cambridge University Press.

Spring, J. V. and C. R. Block.1988. "Finding Crime Hot Spots: Experiments in the Identification of High Crime Areas." Paper presented to the annual meeting of the Midwest Sociological Association.

Taylor, R. B. and A. V. Harrell.1996. *Physical Environment and Crime.* National Institute of Justice Research Report. Washington, DC: U.S. Department of Justice.

Wallis, A.1980. *Crime Prevention through Environmental Design: An Operational Handbook.* Washington, DC: U.S. Department of Justice, National Institute of Justice.

Warr, M.1990. "Dangerous Situations: Social Context and Fear of Victimization." *Social Forces* 68:891–907.

Wekerle, G. R. and C. Whitzman.1995. *Safe Cities: Guidelines for Planning Design, and Management.* New York: Van Nostrand Reinhold.

Wood, E.1961. *Housing Design: A Social Theory.* New York: Citizens' Housing and Planning Counsel of New York.

Wrobleski, H. M. and K. M. Hess. 1993. *Introduction to Law Enforcement and Criminal Justice.* St. Paul, MN: West.

18

Justifiable Homicide by Civilians

John M. MacDonald and
Abraham N. Tennenbaum

Introduction

Approximately 3.5 percent of the homicides in the United States are defined as "justifiable," meaning they were intentional homicides in special circumstances where the killer was not deemed responsible for the killing. "Justifiable homicide" refers to two different classes of homicide: justifiable homicide by police officers, and justifiable homicide by civilians. This chapter considers a neglected subtype of homicide, justifiable homicide by civilians.[1]

There is little uniformity in the literature defining justifiable homicides. The topic of justifiable homicide by civilians has also been called "excusable homicide," "self-defense homicide," and "civilian legal defensive homicide." These terms have been used interchangeably with varying definitions.

For the sake of simplicity, the term "justifiable civilian homicide" (JCH) will be used for justifiable homicides by civilians. The term "police homicide" will be used in this research for cases of justifiable homicides by police. Non-justifiable homicides will be called "criminal homicide."

With a few exceptions, most researchers avoid the subject of justifiable homicides. For example, Riedel, Zahn, and Mock (1985) investigated the nature and patterns of American homicides between the years 1968–78 using FBI data and local police agency information. They did not examine, however, police homicides or JCH. Riedel et al. noted that justifiable homicides are treated differently by the FBI, and they therefore avoided the subject (see Tennebaum 1993). Also, when Block and Block (1976, 1985, 1987, 1992) investigated homicides in Chicago over the last twenty-five years, they did not examine police homicides or justifiable citizen homicides.

Most available studies deal with JCH in one of two contexts. The first are JCH's as a subset of the gun-control debate. Usually, pro-gun writers[2] claim that the frequency of JCH is higher than the official number. In contrast, anti-gun writers try to minimize the number of JCH (see for example Kates 1991; Kellermann and Reay 1986; Kleck 1991). In both cases, however, the JCH issue is supplementary to other questions.[3] In the second context, some researchers deal with JCH as one type of homicide among many others they deal with. This is often the case when there is a spatial analysis of homicides and the researcher classifies the homicides according to circumstances. Usually, they devote negligible effort to JCH (See, for example, Brearley [1932] 1969:62–64; Wolfgang 1975; Lundsgaarde 1977:161–166).

Altogether, only four articles were found that deal exclusively with the subject of JCH. Of these four, two deal with JCH and police homicides together (Griswold and Massey 1985; Challener, Adelson, and Rushforth 1987), and a third claims to deal with JCH but actually deals with a much broader class of homicides (Copland 1984).

As a result there are no articles available that answer even simple questions. How many people kill justifiably each year? Men or women? Who are the victims? Which weapons are used? What are the circumstances?

Importance of Issue

Why is it important at all to investigate justifiable homicides by civilians given that they comprise only 1.65 percent of homicides? We think the answer to this question is that the study of JCH may generate data and conclusions directly relevant to the issue of gun control, and will help us better understand a form of homicide not previously discussed. We return to these issues at the end of this chapter.

Definitions

For our purpose, justifiable homicides can be defined as homicides which are not prohibited by the law. Specifically, this study emphasizes only justifiable homicides by civilians which fit our "classic model"— cases where we have a malicious immediate aggressor, a specific victim, and the use of deadly force is determined to be reasonable.[4]

This study is meant to emphasize the mainstream of JCH. In other words, the focus is not on excusable or non-prosecutable homicides, but on those cases where society justifies the use of deadly force where there is no question whether or not the homicide was justifiable. While excusable or non-prosecutable homicides are sometimes similar to justifiable homicides they are not the focus of this study.

Prior Literature

Previous empirical research regarding justifiable homicides by civilians is almost nonexistent. Therefore, we review and summarize the few studies on homicides which have implications for JCH.

Brearley's ([1932]1969) arguments in the past for reliable data on homicides are still relevant today. His study of homicides used data from the Division of Vital Statistics for two years (1920 and 1925), as well as state of South Carolina authorities and newspaper articles.[5]

Specifically, with regard to justifiable homicides, Brearley mentioned (1969:64) four jurisdictions where justifiable homicides (by police and civilians) accounted for 20–30 percent of the homicides (Washington, DC; Detroit; Cook County; and Chicago). However, Brearley does not distinguish between justifiable homicides by police and by civilians. In addition, his estimates of justifiable homicides are much higher than today's numbers, which may be explained by the evidence suggesting a reduction in the number of police homicides over that past two decades (Sherman and Cohn 1976).

Also, Wolfgang investigated all the homicides that occurred in the city of Philadelphia between 1 January 1948 and 31 December 1952, using police files. Overall, there were 625 homicides in this period. Five hundred eighty-eight (94 percent) were criminal homicides and 37 were non-criminal. Twenty-three of the 37 were accidental deaths and 14 homicides were by police officers. Wolfgang, used the designation "justifiable homicides" for police killings only. There were fourteen cases of police homicides (all justifiable) and eight cases of self-defense which all ended in acquittal (1975:301). Wolfgang specifically states (1975:243, note 1) that JCH are not included in his book.

Since these early analyses, only four studies specifically dealt with JCH. First, Copeland (1984) studied JCH in metro Dade County from 1957 to 1982. He identified 151 cases of JCH over these years, approximately 2.5 percent of the total homicide number. The majority of the victims were black, and 41 percent were between twenty-one and thirty years old. Overall, 86 percent were under forty. The majority of the cases (56 percent) happened in a home or in a store. Approximately 76 percent of JCHs were carried out with a handgun, 11 percent with a shotgun and 7 percent with a rifle. Overall, 95 percent of the homicides were committed with guns. After 1975, data available on the prior arrest record of some of the victims found that 53 percent of them had prior arrests (N=77).

In a second study, Griswold and Massey (1985) investigated all the JCH and police homicides in Dade County for the years 1957–1980. Their main focus was to look at the common features and differences between these two kinds of justifiable homicides. They found that criminal suspects were killed more frequently by the police than by civilians. Blacks were overwhelmingly represented in the victim populations, 71.4 percent of the civilian cases and 53.9 of the police cases. Most police homicides occurred in public buildings and outdoors, while 80 percent of JCHs were in private apartments or homes.

A third study by, Challener, Adelson, and Rushforth (1987), investigated justifiable homicides by police and civilians which occurred during a quarter century (1958–1982) in Cuyahoga County, Ohio. Coroner's office data were employed.[6] Overall, the coroner's office investigated and certified 5725 homicides, of which 642 (11.2 percent) were ruled "justifiable." The study found that victims of JCH were overwhelmingly urban residents aged fifteen and above, with a higher homicide rate for non-whites. The great majority of the victims (87 percent) were slain by single civilians of their same race; one-fourth of the assailants were women.

The authors also found some differences between justifiable homicides by civilians and police homicides. On average, those who were slain by police were younger, more often unmarried, and less likely to be under the influence of alcohol. Most JCH by civilians occurred during or immediately following a quarrel, whereas police homicides were in cases of self-defense where the victims were committing a crime or resisting arrest. In addition, most JCH occurred in buildings or apartments, while most police homicides occurred in public places such as roads and parks.

There were difference between the Dade County and Cuyahoga County sample in the proportion which were JCH versus police homicides. Civilians killed justifiably almost three and half times more than police in Cuyahoga (Challener et al. 1987); whereas, in Dade County police homicides occurred at a higher rate than JCH. Also, in the Cuyahoga sample a lot of the victims knew their assailants (Challener et al. 1987), and the homicide occurred after a quarrel. In Dade County most of the JCH happened during a robbery or burglary.

Despite these differences, there are similarities. First, the victim population in both samples were overwhelmingly young black males. Second, most of the JCH cases happened in homes, apartments, or business places.

The fourth study, conducted by Alvarez (1992), analyzed the Comparative Homicide File[7] for the years 1976–1986. Alvarez found that blacks were overwhelmingly represented as victims of both police homicides and JCH, and that where criminal homicide rates were high so were JCH rates.

Summary

Overall, the findings from these four studies suggest that victims of JCH are commonly urban residents and overwhelming young black males (Copeland 1984; Griswold and Massey 1985; Challener et al. 1987; Alvarez 1992). Also, the four studies suggest there is an association between JCH and place of incident (typically JCH in private residences) and are typically the result of a gun shot. Despite these facts, it is clear that many simple questions remain unanswered.

Methods

Data

The data set used for the research is the justifiable civilian homicides cases in the Supplementary Homicide Report (SHR). The SHR is part of the general Uniform Crime Report system (UCR). Law enforcement agencies that report criminal homicides on the basic UCR forms are requested to submit a SHR for each month (Uniform Crime Report Hand Book, 1984). The SHRs are not submitted by agencies for months in which no homicides were reported to police.[8]

The data sources for this research are SHR data files for the years 1976–1990.[9] While the data cover twenty-five years, we refer more extensively to the data from the last fifteen years (1976–1990). This is because the offender data, which includes everything known about the people who killed justifiably, were collected from that time on. We excluded data post-1990 because during this time period several states passed legislation permitting citizens to carry concealed firearms. The passage of these laws may have had their own separate affect on justifiable citizen homicides (see Lott and Mustard 1997). Therefore, for purposes of our analysis we thought it would be advantageous to exclude this possible confounding factor.

Validity

There are questions about the validity of the SHR data that need to be addressed. First, some homicides are not reported to the police at all, perhaps including some justifiable homicides. Second, it is possible that some data do not actually reach the FBI. Either the police agency did not report them, or they disappeared somewhere between the local agency and the FBI headquarters. Third, some homicides that are reported to the police have incorrect details. This can happen because of a simple mistake, or because not enough evidence was available to the police at the time of the investigation.

In response, however, there is general agreement that most homicides find their way into a reporting system (Riedel 1990:175; Blackman 1986:1). This is even more correct concerning justifiable homicides, in which the killer is generally a law-abiding citizen. Therefore, reporting problems should not be significant. With regard to the second question, Riedel (1990) and Loftin (1986) generally find a high level of agreement between police data and SHR in addition to few problems with the classification of justifiable homicides.[10]

With regard to issues of reliability regarding race, gender, etc., in the case of justifiable homicide the data have an advantage that the assailant is present when the police arrive (many times he calls the police himself) and fewer data are missing.[11] For instance, in justifiable homicide cases the killer is usually present and cooperates with police, so the level of ambiguity is reduced significantly.

Also, some scholars criticize the FBI classification of justifiable homicides by civilians (Kates 1991; Blackman 1986; Kleck 1991). For instance, Kleck (1991) suggests the definition of "justifiable homicide" in the SHR omits "pure self-defense homicides." These are the cases which are not a result of a felony attempt (other than the assault itself), but a result of self-defense against pure aggression (see Tennenbaum 1993).

Consequently, there are known problems with the SHR as with every data set dealing with homicides.[12] Despite these and other limitations, the SHR is the richest data set available today. With awareness of the limitations in mind, it can be used to generate important and insightful knowledge.

Specific Research Questions

The two questions of interest are: (1)How are JCH different from criminal homicides?; and (2) Are JCH more correlated to some subtypes of criminal homicide than to other subtypes? These questions will be explored primarily through the examination of seven factors.

Factors

Gender

As a universal rule, females are much less likely to be murderers (see Copland 1984).[13] Therefore, we expect fewer female perpetrators in JCH cases.

Race

Official data indicate that blacks are disproportionately represented among both homicide offenders and victims (see Copland 1984; Griswold and Massey 1985; BJS 1996). Therefore, we predict blacks to be overrepresented among those killed in JCH.

Age

The age group of the felons killed in JCH is expected to be concentrated between seventeen and thirty. This is based on the fact that crime is known to be committed by young males in most known societies (Gottfredson and Hirschi 1990). Robbers and burglars, who form a significant part of the felons killed by civilians, are usually in this age group (Blumstein, Cohen and Farrington 1988).

Relationship

The assumption is that a large percentage of JCH will happen among strangers. This percentage will be higher than the stranger percentage in standard criminal homicides.

Weapon

We also predict that the number of justifiable homicides by gun (especially a handgun) will be much higher than criminal homicides. This may be due to the fact that the perpetrator of the JCH (see Copland 1984)[14] is physically weaker than the assailant and may have no practical choice other than firearms.

Also, using firearms for self-defense has much more lethal consequences than the use of other weapons.[15] It seems reasonable, therefore, that if a person uses a gun for self-defensive purposes the results will be more lethal. In addition, justifiable homicides by the police will involve guns because this is their standard instrument of defense in life-threatening situations.

City and Region

Evidence suggest that violent crime rates vary by the level of population and region of the country (McCall, Land, Cohen 1992). As a result, we expect that JCH will be concentrated predominately in the inner city and southern regions of the country.

TABLE 18.1
Gender of Those Involved in Criminal and Justifiable Citizen Homicides
(1976–1990)

Criminal Homicides

Victims	Number	%of all	%of known
Male	222398	76.1	76.2
Female	69331	23.7	23.7
Total	291729	99.9	—
Known Offenders			
Male	208502	65.3	86.5
Female	32478	10.1	13.4
Total known	240980	75.5	—

Justifiable Citizen Homicides

Offenders	Number	%of all	%of known
Male	3782	76.3	84.6
Female	688	13.9	15.3
Total	4470	90.2	—
Known Victims			
Male	4800	98.0	98.0
Female	100	2.0	2.0
Total Known	4900	100.0	100.0

FIGURE 18.1
Age Distribution of Offenders and Felons
(By Percentage for Each Age Group)

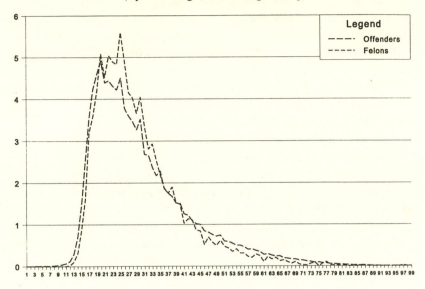

FIGURE 18.2
Age Distribution of Victims and Perpetrators
(By Percentage for Each Age Group)

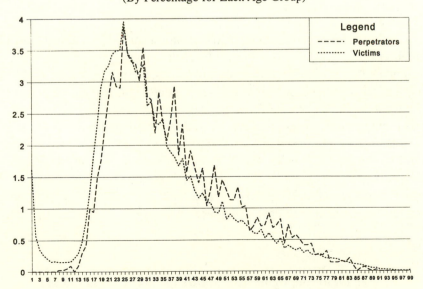

Subtypes of Criminal Homicides

Homicide is one of the few crimes which is defined by its *outcome* instead of the *process* that led to this outcome. This suggests that homicides would be defined better by using categories that are created considering the processes involved, instead of the outcome (Zahn and Sagi 1987:396).

With this in mind, we will examine whether JCH is correlated with some subtypes of homicide, especially with felony-homicide.[16] An additional analysis will be conducted examining the total numbers of JCH and the total numbers of other subtypes of homicide over time (each month). Because we are dealing with the total number, the problem of outliers is not critical (still, outlier possibilities will be examined). However, a correlation between the number of JCH in following months is expected (first-order auto-correlation), so it will have to be fixed (Pindyck and Rubinfeld 1991:138; Neter, Wasserman and Kutmer 1989:488). This fixing may destroy the usefulness of the R-square test for comparing the different regressions, so other ways of comparing the coefficients will be employed.

Results

Gender

Table 18.1 shows the gender distribution for offenders and victims of both criminal homicides and JCH. In each category, the percentage is calculated for the known and the unknown cases. Approximately 65 percent of all criminal homicides were committed by males and 10 percent by females. In 24 percent of the cases the gender of the offender/offenders is unknown. If we take into account only the cases where the offender's gender is known, the percentage is approximately 87 percent for males, and 13 percent for females. For JCH, the percentage of people killed are about 98 percent (victims) for males and 2 percent for females (where the offender gender is known). The results demonstrate congruence between offenders in criminal homicides and those killed (victims) in JCH.

Age

With regard to age, figure 18.1 shows the age distribution of criminal homicide offenders and victims of JCH (felons). Each point repre-

TABLE 18.2
Race of Those Involved in Criminal and Justifiable Citizen Homicides
(1976–1990)

Criminal Homicides

Victims	Number	%of all	%of known
White	154844	53.0	53.4
Black	129361	44.3	44.6
Other	5587	1.9	1.9
Total Known	289792	99.8	

Offenders			
White	118225	36.5	48.6
Black	116051	35.8	47.7
Other	4321	1.3	3.7
Total Known	243028	75.6	

Justifiable Citizen Homicides

Offenders	Number	%of all	%of known
White	2383	48.1	54.1
Black	1922	38.8	43.6
Other	96	1.7	2.1
Total Known	4401	88.6	

Victims			
White	1929	39.3	39.6
Black	2882	58.8	59.2
Other	54	1.1	1.1
Total Known	4865	99.2	

sents the percentage in this age of the general population. From this graph one can see the great similarity between the age distributions of these two groups.

In addition, figure 18.2 shows the age distribution of offenders in JCH (perpetrators) and victims of criminal homicides. Figure 18.1 shows the age of offenders of criminal homicides starts only in the early teens, peaks in the early twenties and then declines sharply. In contrast, figure 18.2 shows the age of the JCH offenders (perpetrators) peaks in the late twenties and then declines less sharply. Overall, the age variable shows the offenders in JCH (perpetrators) are similar to the victims of criminal homicide, and the victims of JCH (felons) are similar to the offenders in criminal homicides, as predicted.

Race

In the SHR, four races are available: white, black, Asian, and Indians.[17] Table 18.2 summarizes all of the information about the races of offenders and victims in criminal homicides and JCH.[18] More than half (53 percent) of the victims of criminal homicides and 54 percent of the offenders in JCH are white. A smaller proportion (44.8 percent) of the victims of criminal homicides and offenders in JCH (43.6 percent) are black. It seems that the same percentage of "would-be victims," either white or black, commit JCH rather than being killed themselves.

This similarity does not exist concerning criminal homicide offenders and victims of JCH. Of the offenders in criminal homicides, 48.6 percent are whites, but only 39.6 percent of JCH victims are white. Also, only 47.5 percent of the offenders in criminal homicides are black but they comprise 59.2 percent of the victims of JCH. The data show that more blacks than whites are killed in justifiable homicides than are represented in official arrest data.

In addition, the data for whites and blacks only is summarized in table 18.3 (whites kill whites, whites kill blacks, blacks kill blacks, blacks kill whites). The data show there is a large number of justifiable cases where whites kill blacks. In contrast, more blacks kill whites than whites kill blacks in criminal homicides.

Weapon

There are also some differences in weapons used by offenders and perpetrators. Table 18.4 summarizes the weapon distribution for criminal homicides and justifiable citizen homicides. Almost 70 percent of JCHs were committed with handguns (68.2 percent), compared to 47.8 percent of criminal homicides. Combining all firearms, close to 87 percent of JCHs were committed with firearms, compared to about 64 percent of criminal homicides, demonstrating that firearms are more common in justifiable homicides.

Relationship

Table 18.5 includes the data for relationship. The relationship variable in the SHR is coded as the relationship between the victim and the offender. We constructed five subgroups (spouse, other-family, acquaintance, stranger, and unknown) of relationships out of the fifteen groups in the SHR. The data demonstrate that stranger-related justifiable homicides are the most common category with approximately 60 percent of cases involving strangers; whereas, in criminal homicides they most

TABLE 18.3
Race Distribution of Criminal and Justifiable Citizen Homicides (1976–1990)

Criminal Homicides

Offender	Victim	Total	% Of All	% Of Known
White	White	92750	33.09	45.61
Black	White	12586	4.49	6.18
White	Black	6337	2.26	3.12
Black	Black	86516	30.87	42.54
Other/Unknown	Other/Unknown	82231	29.28	—

Justifiable Citizen Homicides

Offender	Victim	Total	% Of All	% Of Known
White	White	1532	31.75	35.84
Black	White	123	2.55	2.88
White	Black	746	15.46	17.45
Black	Black	1747	36.20	40.86
Other/Unknown	Other/Unknown	678	14.05	—

TABLE 18.4
Weapons Used in Criminal and Justifiable Citizen Homicides (1976–1990)

Weapon	JCH % Known	Criminal % Known
Handgun	68.2	47.4
Knife	10.4	19.7
Shotgun	10.3	7.5
Rifle	5.6	4.8
Firearm	2.3	3.9
Blunt Object	1.5	5.7
Personal Weapon	1.2	6.4
Other	.32	3.3
Other-gun	.08	.16
Strangulation	.08	1.8
Asphyxiation	.06	.57
Fire	.02	.88

N.B.: Includes only incidents in which the weapon was known.

frequently involved acquaintances. These findings indicate that cases of justifiable homicides are more likely to involve strangers compared to criminal homicides. [19]

Table 18.6 shows the distribution of the subcircumstances variable. Not surprisingly, 63.4 percent are a "felon killed in commission of a crime" and 26.3 percent are cases of "felon attacked civilian" which

TABLE 18.5
Relationship for Criminal and Justifiable Citizen Homicides, 1976–1990
(Grouped into five main categories)

Relationship	Total Criminal	% of All	Total Justifiable	% of All
Spouse	34889	10.9	250	5.0
Family	23765	7.4	185	3.7
Acquaintance	112252	35.1	1075	21.7
Stranger	56348	17.6	3004	60.6
Unknown	91670	28.7	437	8.8

TABLE 18.6
Subcircumstances Distribution (1976–1990)

Subcircumstances	Total	Percent
Attacked Police Officer	69	1.3
Attacked Fellow Police Officer	8	.16
Attacked Civilian	1305	26.3
Attempted Flight From Crime	100	2.0
Killed In Commission Of Crime	3141	63.4
Resisted Arrest	18	.36
Unknown	310	6.2

seem to be cases of self-defense. Further crosstab analyses indicate that approximately 75.9 percent of justifiable homicides where the felony is a stranger occurred during the commission of a crime, as opposed to only 37.1 percent of cases where the perpetrator knew the felon. However, the reliability of this variable is questionable because the categories appear to overlap. Yet, the analyses do suggest that stranger on stranger attacks during the commission of a crime are associated with a higher percentage of justifiable homicides than cases of self-defense where the parties involved are acquaintances or family.

City and Region

The population size seems to be a significant factor. Table 18.7 summarizes the distribution of criminal homicides and JCH for different sizes of cities and counties. It includes the total number, the average yearly population in each police agency's jurisdiction,[20] the criminal homicides and JCH rates per 100,000 people over fifteen years,[21]the

TABLE 18.7
Criminal and Justifiable Citizen Homicides by City and County Size

Size Description	Crim-Rate	Just-Rate	% Crim	% Just	Expected	Crim-Ratio	Just-Ratio
All Cities 1,000,000 +	365.024	10.830	22.38	39.57	8.12	2.755	4.871
Cities 500,000–999,999	296.545	4.150	12.99	10.84	5.81	2.238	1.867
Cities 250,000–499,999	249.655	5.076	10.36	12.55	5.50	1.884	2.283
Cities 100,000–249,999	163.901	2.404	9.29	8.12	7.51	1.237	1.081
Cities 50,000–99,999	95.323	1.484	6.95	6.45	9.66	0.719	0.667
Cities 25,000–49,999	74.826	0.790	5.87	3.69	10.40	0.565	0.355
Cities 10,000–24,999	59.339	0.556	5.30	2.96	11.84	0.448	0.250
Cities 2,500–9,999	67.221	0.524	3.56	1.65	7.02	0.507	0.236
Cities under 2,500	128.222	0.686	0.64	0.20	0.66	0.968	0.309
Non-SMSA counties 100,00+	231.963	5.122	0.22	0.29	0.12	1.751	2.304
Non-SMSA counties 25,000–99,999	74.852	0.680	3.09	1.67	5.47	0.565	0.306
Non-SMSA counties 10,000–24,999	74.021	0.640	3.57	1.84	6.38	0.559	0.288
Non-SMSA counties under 10,000	170.319	1.052	3.21	1.18	2.50	1.285	0.473
State Police	0.000	0.000	0.00	0.00	0.00	0.000	0.000
SMSA counties 100,000+	100.616	1.582	7.27	6.82	9.58	0.759	0.712
SMSA counties 25,000–99,999	62.670	0.471	3.60	1.61	7.61	0.473	0.212
SMSA counties 10,000–24,999	76.333	0.419	0.87	0.29	1.52	0.576	0.188
SMSA counties under 10,000	367.749	2.018	0.81	0.27	0.29	2.775	0.908

Crim-Rate—Number of Criminal Homicides per 100,000 (1976-1990)
Just-Rate—Number of Justifiable Citizen Homicides per 100,000 (1976-1990)
%Crim—Percentage of Criminal Homicides in each group
%Just—Percentage of Justifiable Citizen Homicides in each group
Expected—Expected Percentage based on the assumption that homicides (criminal and justifiable) are distributed with no connection to population size
Crime-Ratio—Ratio between the actual and expected percentage of criminal homicides
Just-Ratio—Ratio between the actual and expected percentage of justifiable citizen homicides

TABLE 18.8
Criminal and Justifiable Citizen Homicides by Region

Region	%Crim	%Just	Expected	Crim-Ratio	Just-Ratio
New England	2.83	1.18	5.34	0.52	0.22
Mid-Atlantic	7.01	3.85	12.26	0.57	0.31
East N. Central	11.80	12.09	17.12	0.68	0.70
West N. Central	5.07	3.64	7.52	0.67	0.48
South Atlantic	24.72	21.68	18.62	1.32	1.16
East S. Central	8.44	8.13	6.52	1.29	1.24
West S. Central	17.61	16.98	11.38	1.54	1.49
Mountain	5.23	3.95	5.79	0.90	0.68
Pacific	17.25	28.47	15.42	1.11	1.84

%Crim—Percent of criminal homicides out of all criminal homicides
%Just—Percent of justifiable homicides out of all justifiable homicides
N.B.—data excludes six largest cities in the United States

expected percentage of homicides,[22] and the ratio between the actual and expected percentages.[23]

As can be seen, criminal homicides in general and justifiable homicides in particular are a phenomenon of the big city. There are only six cities above one million people in the United States: Chicago, Detroit, Houston, Philadelphia, Los Angeles, and New York. However, these six cities are responsible (inside their borders only, not including suburbs) for approximately 22 percent of all the criminal homicides and 40 percent of all the JCH.

Table 18.8 shows the criminal homicides and JCH distribution for different regions in the United States. It seems that the three regions of the South[24] have higher rates of criminal homicides and JCH.[25]

The Discriminant Function

In addition to the descriptive analyses we attempt through discriminate methods to organize all of the variables in the SHR into one framework in an effort to quantify their relative importance.[26]

After calculating the coefficients, we use them to predict the group membership of future cases. Each case gets a "score," or a "discriminant function" which is based on the linear combination of the variables with the calculated coefficients. A way to measure the success of this procedure is to operate it on cases where the group membership is already known and to compare the predicted results to the actual ones.

TABLE 18.9
Discriminate Procedure Results

Variable	Wilks' Lambda	F	Significance	Coefficents	Correlation
STRANGER	0.97190	5255.	0.0000	0.63160	0.65891
WHIKBLA	0.98558	2659.	0.0000	0.39245	0.46865
DIFFAGE	0.99135	1586.	0.0000	0.34498	0.36202
VICMALE	0.99429	1045.	0.0000	0.19863	0.29378
VICFEMAL	0.99429	1045.	0.0000		−0.29378
OFFAGE	0.99451	1003.	0.0000	0.23324	0.28787
ACQUAITA	0.99591	746.5	0.0000	−0.05603	−0.24834
HANDGUN	0.99597	735.6	0.0000	0.03446	0.24651
C1000000	0.99638	659.8	0.0000	0.12923	0.23346
MSA	0.99734	484.1	0.0000	0.05532	0.19999
EASTNORT	0.99821	326.7	0.0000	0.14429	0.16430
KNIFE	0.99833	303.3	0.0000	−0.10162	−0.15830
VBLACK	0.99835	300.7	0.0000	0.15889	0.15760
VICAGE	0.99848	277.3	0.0000		−0.15135
WIFE	0.99856	262.5	0.0000	−0.06322	−0.14821
VWHITE	0.99854	265.9	0.0000	−0.14140	−0.14726
PACIFIC	0.99864	247.1	0.0000	−0.19260	0.14287
PERSONAL	0.99871	234.4	0.0000	−0.03392	−0.13915
VICCHILD	0.99898	184.8	0.0000	−0.13074	−0.12355
WHIKWHI	0.99915	154.5	0.0000	0.24853	−0.11299

Description of Variables
ACQUAITA—Victim acquaintance of offender
C1000000—A city with one millon and over
DIFFAGE—Offender age minus victim age
EASTNORT—East North region
HANDGUN—Committed with hand gun
KNIFE—Committed with a knife
MSA—Not a suburb of an SMSA
. OFFAGE—Offender age
PACIFIC—Pacific region
PERSONAL—Committed by beating, kicking, etc.
STRANGER—Victim stranger to offender
VBLACK—Victim is black
VICAGE—Victim age
VICCHILD—Victim is child (under 13)
VICFEMAL—Victim is female
VICMALE—Victim is male
VWHITE—Victim white
WHIKBLA—WHIte kill BLAck
WHIKWHI—WHIte Kill WHIte
WIFE—Victim wife of offender

TABLE 18.10
Regression Results (cross-section) with JCH as Dependent Variable

Variable	Coeff	T-Coeff	Constant	T-Constant	R^2	Log
Robbery	.1619	11.54	1.96	3.69	.52	−344.59
Argument	.0066	9.91	.88	1.28	.44	−353.77
Suspect Felony	.1852	8.12	4.25	8.58	.34	−363.66
Burglary	1.087	6.99	2.66	3.77	.28	−369.58
Argument-Money	.4145	6.70	3.25	4.93	.26	−371.03
Police Killed	.5942	6.42	3.07	4.39	.25	−372.41
Gangland Killing	.1060	5.97	5.95	13.18	.22	−374.57
Non-Felony	.0898	5.41	4.01	6.11	.19	−377.15
Drugs	.1180	5.21	5.07	9.40	.18	−377.99
Lover's Triangle	.3392	3.81	4.62	6.55	.10	−383.52
Unknown	.0270	3.57	5.32	8.92	.09	−384.30
Alcohol Related	.0385	.64	6.33	9.39	.00	−390.29

N.B—Each line represents one regression where the dependent variable is JCH and the only independent variable appears on the line.

The degree to which the prediction improves the results compared to chance alone is seen as the procedure's "success" or goodness of fit.[27]

Concerning our case, we classified each case as "justifiable" or "criminal," and used all the other variables to calculate the "discriminant function." Because discriminant analysis can use only numerical or dichotomous variables, categorical variables were transformed into dichotomous ones. Some variables such as "weapon" and "relationship" had values which resulted in new variables (93 in all). After running the model with all the variables, a reduced model was employed that included the twenty variables which contributed the most to the discriminant function.

Table 18.9 summarizes the results for the twenty most influential variables. WILKS' LAMBDA (or the U statistic) measures the mean differences among the different groups (JCH and criminal homicides in our case).[28] The coefficients were used to calculate the "score" for each case by multiplying them by the variable value.[29] The column "correlation" measures the pooled within-group correlations between the discriminating variables and the discriminant function, or the measure of the predicative level of each variable.

The findings indicate that the most influential variable is "stranger," followed by "whikbla" (white kill black) and third "diffage" (the difference in age between the offender and the victim).[30] Furthermore, the analyses suggest that the likelihood of a case being classified as JCH is increased if the killer is a stranger to his victim, the victim is black and the killer is white, the killer is older and the victim younger, the victim is male, a handgun was used, the incident was in an SMSA center or in a big city, and it was in an East North Central or Pacific state. In contrast, if the victim is female, acquaintance or a wife, a knife or hands were used, or the victim is a child (under thirteen), the likelihood of the case being justifiable is reduced.

Yet, due to the fact that JCH is a relatively rare event, the prediction accuracy of these methods are modest and the coefficient estimates are therefore marginal. Regardless, it is apparent from the findings that justifiable citizen homicides have similar patterns to many criminal homicides. Therefore, the distinction between justifiable citizen homicides and some types of criminal homicides from a conceptual standpoint may be unnecessary.

Circumstances and Subcircumstances

Previously, we used the "circumstances" variable to compare characteristics of JCH cases with criminal homicides. In this section we address the connection between JCH and other subtypes of criminal homicides. Because the "circumstances" variable includes a lot of exotic and rare values such as "sniper attack," "hunting accident," etc., only circumstances which account for at least 1 percent of all homicides were included. Two aspects of the correlation were investigated; space and time. For the spatial analysis a linear region model was used in which the dependent variable is the rate of JCH and the independent variable is the rate of another subtype of homicide. For this analysis, only police agencies with at least five cases of JCH were chosen (a total of 125 agencies). Table 18.10 summarizes the results.

The results indicate that the variable, "robbery" (robbery-homicide) is the most correlated with JCH (R-square = 0.52). Next most highly correlated variables were "argother" (other arguments), and "susfelon" (suspect felony). These results support the idea that JCH are correlated with some subtypes of criminal homicides, especially to robbery homicides.

With regard to the time analysis employed, a similar linear regression was employed where the dependent variable was the total number of JCH each month and the independent variable is the total number of other subtypes of homicides.[31]

TABLE 18.11
Regression Results (time) with JCH Rate as Dependent Variable

Variable	Log	Improvement
Robbery	−622.82	11.83
Suspect Felony	−622.07	13.34
Police Killed	−620.83	15.82
Non-Felony	−627.68	2.11
Alcohol	−624.55	8.37
Lover's Triangle	−625.57	6.34
Argument	−628.37	0.73
Drugs	−628.65	0.18
Burglary	−627.87	1.74
Argument-Money	−626.76	3.96
Juvenile Gang Killing	−625.12	7.24
Unknown	−628.72	0.03
Gangland Killing	−626.52	4.44

The log-likelihood of chance is −628.738

N.B: The R-square of this model is not relevant due to autocorrelation and cannot be used to estimate the correlation. Therefore, it was excluded from the table.

As was discussed earlier, some questions arose about the robbery classification accuracy in the SHR (Loftin 1986; Maxfield 1988). Therefore, the results of this analysis have to be taken cautiously. However, the findings suggest that JCHs are more correlated with some subtypes of criminal homicides (especially robbery) than with other subtypes (see table 18.11.[32]

Conclusions

Usually, criminals do not attack and kill innocent people for no reason.[33] Also, it is easier to define a homicide as an "evil murder," when it is the result of another felony. Therefore, cases are more likely to be defined as "justifiable" if the "would-be victim" succeeds in killing the "would-be offender."

The findings from this study support this conclusion. The majority of the JCH were cases where the perpetrators and the victims were strangers (60.6 percent). In these incidents, most often, the victim was killed while committing a felony. Homicides for pure self-defense reasons between relatives or acquaintances were less common. This is due to the fact that such cases were less likely to be termed justifiable because the "blame" of the participants was not as clear.

Although robbery homicides represent only 9.4 percent of all homicides, they are more connected with JCH than other subtypes of homicides. This correlation is strong over both time and space. Justifiable citizen homicides are more common in big cities than in small cities and suburbs. This corresponds to the fact that most robbery homicides occur in big cities. This distinction appears to be more important than regional differences.

It also appears that there are some similarities between perpetrators of JCH and the offender population. For instance, males commit both more criminal homicides and JCH than females. Young people are more likely to commit both criminal and justifiable homicides than elderly people.

These findings also support the notion that homicides are the result of different factors that occur in time and place. Justifiable citizen homicides appear unique because the "would-be victim" succeeds in killing the "would-be offender." Yet, factors such as availability of an adequate weapon, mental state of the killer, or physical capability which help explain JCH, have a similar influence on criminal homicides.

Also, our findings show that those who commit JCH are generally white males with an average age of 37.5 who use handguns. White males of this age generally are not considered to be from a weak segment of society and, therefore, the evidence suggests a strong defendant in cases of JCH.

The findings clearly show that firearms and especially handguns are the main instruments for these killings. Approximately 87 percent of all JCH are carried out with firearms, considerably higher than cases of criminal homicides.

Concerning the race variable, a disproportionate number of JCH cases involved white perpetrators killing blacks. When we compare it, however, to the interracial robbery homicides number, the race variable is consistent with official data.

Justifiable citizen homicides are also more correlated to robbery homicides than to any other type. The support for this conclusion is apparent from the fact that the subcircumstance variable indicates that in the majority of JCH, the victim is killed while committing a felony, suggesting that self-defense from a stranger is the predominate cause behind such killings.

Policy Recommendations and Future Research

When we began this analysis of JCHs and criminal homicides, we observed that there were two major reasons for conducting this research: (1) the insights it could give us into the way homicide research should be conducted; and (2) the suggestions it could lead us to for the establishment of policy recommendations to control JCHs. Now that we have completed our analysis of JCHs using the supplemental homicide reports, we offer observations on each of these justifications for the research.

Our research, like the early work of Marvin Wolfgang (1955) has demonstrated that homicide events are complex. This is true for JCHs and criminal homicides. Yet, the data that we routinely have available to us for the analysis of homicides cannot capture this complexity, especially with regard to the patterns of interaction between the participants in these events. We are left with data systems that are essentially static snapshots of exceedingly complex and dynamic events. Therefore, we think our research reinforces the need to include a developmental dimension. By that, we mean data should be collected and analyzed to facilitate an understanding of how individuals who begin an event without the desire for a homicide to occur end up in a situation that results in a death. Years ago, Leslie Wilkens offered some thoughts on this by referring to what he called a deviation amplifying mechanism (Wilkens 1965). He suggested that as individuals participate in various interactions, choices are made that may lead towards greater probabilities of deviance, including violence. While this is a helpful heuristic for thinking about criminal events and homicides, it does not address the critical question which is why those paths leading towards more dangerous situations and eventually death are taken. Homicide research in the future needs not only to be able to describe the interactions and the choices within these interactions, but to help us understand why certain individuals in specific situations take the path that leads towards death. This is especially true in the study of JCHs that do not involve an offender/victim. These JCHs offer an important subarea within the study of homicides. These are events that society has deemed justifiable, but where the available data do not help us understand the nature of the events that produce such outcomes.

This leads us to our consideration of the policy issues raised by JCHs. Like criminal homicides, JCHs overwhelmingly involve the use of a handgun. Therefore, this research supports the notion that the society's ability to control the access to lethal weapons could be an important element in reducing death. Strategies such as gun registration, requirement for gun locks, smart guns, improved education and training for gun owners, locking of guns within residences, etc., may all play a part in reducing homicides, and justifiable civilian homicides. At the same time it is also clear that there is a policy dilemma for those justifiable citizen homicides where the victim was in fact perpetrating a crime, and the offender defended himself with lethal force. It is not clear that society desires to control these events, evidence for which is the recent passage of "right to carry" laws in a number of states (Lott and Mustard 1997). However, for other justifiable civilian homicides where the motivation for the taking of the life is not the avoidance of a crime, there may be a social value in seeking to control these events. These appear to be primarily domestic events where a weapon is present and the victim is a contributor to the violence that results in death. These subset of homicides may, therefore, be preventable. To the extent that our interpretation of these events is correct, then efforts to intervene in domestic violence cases more effectively than current police department practices could have a long-range effect on reducing this subset of justifiable civilian homicides. Altogether, this research supports policies that seek to restrict access to lethal weapons and to improve police response to domestic violence incidents before they escalate into homicides.

Notes

1. The statistic 3.5 percent is calculated from the Supplementary Homicide Report (SHR) for the years 1976–1990, which have a total of 296, 920 victims (the SHR will be described and analyzed later). This number refers to police homicides and justifiable homicides by civilians together. Police homicides account for 1.85 percent (5481 victims), and justifiable homicides by civilians account for 1.65 percent (49000) of total homicides.
2. The terms pro-gun or anti-gun are not used in any way to evaluate the merits of specific studies or researchers. Instead, they are an easy way (even though not always correct) to classify research on the subject.
3. It was claimed that Congress has spent more time on the subject of gun control than on all other crime-related measures combined (Bruce-Briggs 1976:37). It is surprising, therefore, that more was not done about JCH, despite its relevancy to the debate.
4. We will omit euthanasia, abortion, killing innocent person to save others, etc. These are very rare and involve issues that go well beyond the legal taking of life.
5. The reliability of theses sources is therefore questionable.
6. The Coroner himself did not change from 1936 (at least until 1982), so the data are fairly consistent.

7. The Comparative Homicide File is a publicly used computer file organized by Kirk R. Williams and Murray A. Strauss from the family research Laboratory in the University of New Hampshire. It includes part of the FBI Supplementary Homicide Reports data, and parts of the Census data, as well as various environmental variables (Strauss and Williams 1988).

8. The form is incidents-oriented; i.e., if more than one murder occurred during the same incident, only one form will be filled out. Every record includes one event with details on the victims and offenders (if known) including age, race, gender, weapon, circumstances, and relationship. The SHR system has been revised more than once over the years, so not every statistic appears in all yearly reports. The "circumstances" variable was added in the year 1963, and one of its values, "justifiable homicide" was added in 1966 (Wilson 1992). Until 1976 data were collected on victims only, but in 1976 the system was revised again, and data on offenders started to be collected (Riedel 1990:178).

9. For the years 1976–1990, the SHR data as processed by the ICPSR from the original SHR master tapes provided by the FBI will be used. The most substantial procedure of the ICPSR was the transfer of the data to an SPSSX format.

10. The ratio between the total number of murder cases as reported by police departments and the SHR was between 0.97 and 1.07.

11. Kleck (1991:116, 469–72) suggests that many homicides ultimately ruled noncriminal by prosecutors or judges are reported to the FBI as criminal homicides, because that is how the initial police investigation treated them. This may be, but it can also go in the opposite direction. Some offenders convince the police and the local prosecutor that the killing was justifiable when it as not. It can also happen that innocent people are convicted and guilty people are acquitted.

12. Rand (1992) tried to match all the cases from the SHR to death certificates in the United States for one month (July 1986). While the agreement of the total number (1,783 and 1,855) was good (96 percent), only around 67 percent matched in the basic details (age, race, gender, weapon, relationship). Rand could find no clear explanation to this huge discrepancy.

13. A comprehensive discussion on this subject can be found in Daly and Wilson (1988:137–156).

14. It has been found that male victims of violent crime are more likely than female victims to be attacked by persons with weapons (Reiss and Roth 1993:262).

15. Use of a gun for self-defense has been found to be more efficient (in the sense of preventing crime) than other weapons (see Cook 1991:57–8; Kates 1990:23–4; Kleck 1988; Kleck and DeLone 1993).

16. Because the classification of the homicide's circumstance in the SHR has thirty values, some of them will have too few cases to measure. To avoid this, another decision rule will be made. Only circumstances that are at least 1 percent of the total homicides will be calculated.

17. The official complete definitions of Indian and Asian in the SHR is: Indian—American Indian or Alaskan native; Asian—Asian or Pacific islander.

18. The number of homicides among races other than white and black is small and accounts for less than 2 percent of the total homicide victims. As a result, we deal primarily with white and black subjects.

19. Spouse includes also boyfriend, girlfriend, ex-spouse, and common-law husband/wife. Acquaintance includes employee, employer, neighbor, friend, homosexual relationship, and other-known to victim.

20. The SHR includes the population for each agency for the year. However, many agencies do not report on homicides for each year because they do not have a homicide every year. The average population was calculated by combining the population for each given year and dividing it by the number of years.

21. Because of the small number of JHC, a fifteen-year period seems to be more appropriate than one year. However, the yearly rate for criminal homicides and JCH can be easily calculated by dividing this rate by fifteen.

22. The expected percentage is based on the assumption that homicides (criminal and justifiable) are distributed randomly with no connection to the city/county population size. In such a case, we will expect a state or a city which has X percentage of the population in the United States, to have the same X percentage of the criminal homicides and JCH. The number X is the "expected" percentage.

23. The actual percentage is the percentage of criminal homicides and JCH from the total in the United States.

24. Of course, there is a big debate over the question of what exactly are "the southern states." Loftin and Hill (1974) defined the South simply as the states that participates in the Confederacy. Gastil (1975) uses a different and more complicated classification. In the SHR, the classification follows the Census (Bureau of the Census 1992). This classification includes nine regions: New England states (ME, VT, NH, CT, RI, MA); Middle Atlantic (NY, PA, NJ); East North Central (OH, IN, IL, MI, WI); West North Central (ND, SD, MN, IA, NE, KS, MO); South Atlantic (DE, MD, WV, VA, NC, SC, GA, FL); East South Central (KY, TN, AL, MS); West South Central (AR, OK, LA, TX); Mountain (MT, ID, WY, CO, UT, NV, AZ, NM); Pacific (WA, OR, CA, AK,HI).

25. However, we showed before that Criminal homicides and JCH appear much more in the big cities. Only one of the big cities (Houston) is in the south. To control for it, the data were also analyzed without the six cities. The results indicated that the differences between the South and all the other regions increase. The reduction is clear in the Middle Atlantic States after excluding New York and Philadelphia.

    In addition, we also conducted analyses on SMSA's and found that justifiable homicides were clustered in the centers of SMSA as opposed to the suburbs.

26. In general, discriminant analysis is a statistical technique that uses linear combinations of variables to distinguish between two or more categories of cases. It is done by finding the linear combination of variables that separate "best" the groups we want to investigate. These variables can be chosen by stepwise methods or predefined by theory. In the case of two groups, discriminant analysis is similar to logistic regression, which is more popular today. It used to be claimed that discriminant analysis is somehow more efficient than logistic regression (Efron 1975) but in general, both of theses methods generate similar results (Kao and McCAbe 1991; O'Gorman and Woolson 1991). One technical advantage of discriminant analysis is the ability to test easily the fit of the classification. Thoughtful consideration, however, has to be given to the big size of our data set. In general, discriminant analysis consumes much less computer time and resource (Brenn and Arnesen 1985).

27. For more information on discriminant analysis see Tatsuoka (1970), SPSS Advanced Statistic User Guide (1990: 1–42), and SPSS-X Users's Guide (3d ed., 1990 455–80). The actual procedure was done by SPSS version 4.

28. The value 1 would appear when the groups' means are the same. The higher the value of this statistic, the less the variable can be used as a discriminator.

    The F statistic measures the null hypothesis that the means of the groups are equal. In cases of two groups only (like ours), it is actually the square of the t value from the usual two-sample t-test. Our sample is extremely large so the F for all the variables will likely be significant, but the F size differs from variable to variable.

29. The values of the coefficients are automatically standardized even though the

variables are originally measured in different units. Two variables (VICFEMALE and VICAGE) are not included in the coefficients column. This is because they are linear combinations of other variables. These coefficients should be viewed with caution because some of the variables are highly correlated. VWHITE (victim white) and WHIKWHI (white kill white) are, for example, highly correlated. As a result, it is a mistake to interpret their coefficients separately.

30. Additional analyses of discriminate procedure predictions were also employed. One model used only the variables concerning the gender, age, and race of the persons involved, and if the victim was a stranger to the offender. A second model included only the top twenty variables, and a third model used all the ninety-three variables. While there is improvement from the reduced to the full model, the improvement was modest. In the full model, for instance, predicted only 9.06 percent of the justifiable cases correctly. While this is a significant improvement over chance (approximately four times more than chance), it is still rather modest. Also, additional analyses adjusting the probability of prediction from the 0.5 level to a lower level improved the prediction accuracy of justifiable homicides but we reduced the accuracy in classification accuracy. For more on this topic see SPSS Advanced Statistics User's Guide (1990).

31. Most models using time data are auto-correlated and therefore violate the autoregressive assumption. This was the case in our model as well, so a first-order auto-correlation regression model was done with the same variables. The basic model is: $Y_t = B_0 + B_1 * X_t + \varepsilon_v$

where $\varepsilon_t = \rho * U_{t-1} + z_v$. B_0 is the intercept, B_i is the coefficient and X_t is the independent variable. If our assumptions are met, z_t is the well-behaved (nonautocorrelated) residual in the regression model and $\rho < 1$. It can be shown that if we calculate ρ, then we can calculate unbiased coefficients B_0 and each B_1 (Pindyck and Rubinfeld 1991: 138; Neter, Wasserman, and Kutmer 1989:488).

32. It is more clear in the space analysis than in the time analysis. This is in general the case when cross-section analysis is compared to time analysis. The reason seems to be the fact that the variability is much higher over cross-section than on time. In our case, different cities will vary more in their homicide rate than will different months.

33. Recent research suggests that the number of innocent bystanders has increased lately (Sherman, Steele, Laufersweiler, Hoffer and Julian 1989).

References

Alvarez, A. 1992. "Trends and Patterns of Justifiable Homicide: A Comparative Analysis." *Violence and Victims* 7(4): 347-356.

Blackman, P. H. and R.E. Gardiner. 1986. "Flaws in the Current and Proposed Uniform Crime Reporting Programs Regarding Homicide and Weapons Use in Violent Crime." Paper presented at the annual meeting of the American Society of Criminology, Atlanta, Georgia.

Block, C. R. 1987. *Homicide in Chicago*. Chicago: Loyola University of Chicago. Urban Insights Series.

———. 1993. *The Meaning and Measurement of Victim Precipitation*. Paper presented at the Homicide Research Group annual meeting. FBI Academy in Quantico, Virginia, June.

———. 1985. "Race/Ethnicity and Patterns of Chicago Homicide: 1965 to 1981." *Crime & Delinquency* 31: 104–116.

Block, C. R. and R. Block. 1991. "Beginning with Wolfgang: An Agenda for Homicide Research." *Journal of Crime and Justice* 14 (2): 31–70.

Block, R. 1976. "Homicide in Chicago: A Nine-Year Study (1965–1973)." *Journal of Criminal Law and Criminology* 66: 496–510.

Block, R. and C.R. Block. 1991. "Beginning with Wolfgang: An Agenda for Homicide Research." Paper presented at the annual meeting of the American Society of Criminology, San Francisco, California, November.

———. 1992. "Homicide Syndromes and Vulnerability: Violence in Chicago Community Areas over Twenty-five Years." *Studies on Crime and Crime Prevention* 1(1): 61–87.

Blumstein, A., J. Cohen, and D.P. Farrington. 1988. "Criminal Career Research: Its Value for Criminology." *Criminology* 26(1): 1–35.

Brearley H. C. [1932] 1969. *Homicide in the United States*. Montclair, NJ: Patterson Smith.

Brenn, T. and E. Arnesen. 1985. "Selecting Risk Factors: A Comparison of Discriminant Analysis, Logistic Regression and Cox's Regression Model using Data from the Tromso Heart Study." *Statistics in Medicine* 4: 413–423.

Bureau of the Census. 1992. *1990 Census of Population Characteristics, United States (CP-1-1)*. Washington, DC: U.S. Department of Commerce.

———. 1991. *State and Metropolitan Area Data Book 1991: A Statistical Abstract Supplement*. Washington, DC: U.S. Department of Commerce.

Bureau of Justice Statistics. 1988. *Report to the Nation on Crime and Justice: Second Edition*. Washington, DC: Government Printing Office.

Challener, R. C., L. Adelson, and N.B. Rushforth. 1987. "Justifiable Homicide: A Study of the Application of Nonculpable Deadly Force in Cuyahoga County (Cleveland), Ohio, 1958–1982." *Journal Of Forensic Sciences* 32(5): 1389–1402.

Cook, P. J. 1991. "The Technology of Personal Violence," pp. 1–71 in Michael Tonry (Ed.), *Crime and Justice: A Review of Research,* vol. 14. Chicago: The University of Chicago Press.

Copeland, A. R. 1984. "The Right to Keep and Bear Arms: A Study of Civilian Homicides Committed against Those Involved in Criminal Acts in Metropolitan Dade County from between 1957 to 1982." *Journal of Forensic Sciences* 29(2): 584–590.

Daly, M., and M. Wilson. 1988. *Homicide*. New York: Aldine de Gruyter.

Federal Bureau of Investigation. 1984. *Uniform Crime Report Hand Book*. Washington, DC: U.S. Department of Justice, Federal Bureau of Investigation.

Gastil, R. D. 1975. *Cultural Regions of the United States*. Seattle: University of Washingtion Press.

Gottfredson, M., and T. Hirshi. 1990. *A General Theory of Ccrime*. Stanford, CA: Stanford University Press.

Griswold, D. B. and C. R. Massey. 1985. "Police and Citizen Killings of Criminal Suspects: A Comparative Analysis." *American Journal of Police* 4 (1): 1–19.

Kates, D. B. J. 1990. *Guns, Murders, and the Constitution: A Realistic Assessment of Gun Control*. San Francisco, CA: Pacific Research Institute for Public Policy.

———. 1991. "The Value of Civilian Handgun Possession as a Deterrent to Crime or a Defense against Crime." *American Journal of Criminal Law* 18(2):113–167.

Kellermann, A. and D.T. Reay. 1986. "Protection or Peril? An Analysis of Firearm-Related Death in the Home." *The New England Journal of Medicine* 314 (June): 1557–1560.

Kleck, G. 1988. "Crime Control through the Private Use of Armed Force". *Social Problems* 35(1): 1–21.

———. 1991. *Point Blank: Guns and Violence in America*. New York: Aldine de Gruyter.

Kleck, G. and M.A. DeLone. 1993. "Victim Resistance and Offender Weapon Effects in Robbery." *Journal of Quantitative Criminology* 9(1): 55–81.

Loftin, C. 1986. "The Validity of Robbery-Murder Classifications in Baltimore." *Violence and Victims* 1(3): 191–204.

Lott, J. R. and D.B. Mustard. 1997. "Crime, Deterrence, and the Right to Carry Concealed Handguns." *Journal of Legal Studies* 26(1): 1–68.

Lundsgaarde, H. P. 1977. *Murder in Space City: A Cultural Analysis of Houston Homicide Patterns*. New York: Oxford University Press.

Maxfield, M. G. 1989. "Circumstances in Supplementary Homicide Reports: Variety and Validity." *Criminology* 27(4): 671–698.

McCall, P. L., K.C. Land, and L.E. Cohen. 1992. "Violent Criminal Behavior: Is There a General and Continuing Influence of the South?" *Social Science Research* 21(3): 286–310.

Moore, A. A. and A.N. Tennenbaum. 1992. "Is There an Exceptional Sex Ratio of Spousal Homicides in the United States? A Reply to Wilson and Daly." Manuscript submitted for publication.

Neter, J., W. Wasserman, and M.H. Kutner. 1989. *Applied Linear Regression Models.* Irwin: Boston.

Pindyck, R. S. and D.L. Rubinfeld. 1991. *Econometric Models and Economic Forecasts*, 3d ed. New York: McGraw-Hill, Inc.

Polsby, D. D. 1986. "Reflections on Violence, Guns, and the Defensive Use of Lethal Force." *Law and Contemporary Problems* 49(1): 89–111.

Rand, M. R. 1992. "The Study of Homicide Caseflow: Creating a Comprehensive Homicide Dataset." Paper presented in the 1992 meeting of the American Society of Criminology, New Orleans, Louisiana.

Reiss, A. J. and J.A. Roth. 1993. *Understanding and Preventing Violence*. Washington, DC: National Academy Press.

Riedel, M. 1990. "Nationwide Homicide Data Sets: An Evaluation of the Uniform Crime Reports and the National Center for Health Statistics Data," pp. 175–205 in D. Mackenzie Layton, P. J. Baunach, and R. R. Roberg (eds.), *Measuring Crime: Large-scale, Long-range Efforts*. Albany, NY: State University of New York Press.

Riedel, M., M.A. Zahn, and L. Felson-Mock. 1985. *The Nature and Patterns of American Homicide*. Washington, DC: National Institute of Justice.

Sherman, L. W., and E.G. Cohn, with P.R. Gartin, E.E. Hamilton, and D.P. Rogan. 1986. *Citizens Killed by Big City Police, 1970–1984*. Washington, DC: Crime Control Institute.

Sherman, L.W., L. Steele, D.I. Laufersweiler, N. Hoffer, and S.A. Julian. 1989. "Stray Bullets and 'Mushrooms': Random Shootings of Bystander in Four Cities, 1977–1988." *Journal of Quantitative Criminology* 5 (4): 297–316.

SPSS Inc. 1990. *SPSS Advanced Statistics User's Guide*. Chicago, IL: SPSS Inc.

———. 1988. *SPSS-X User's Guide.*2d ed. Chicago, IL: SPSS Inc.

Tatsuoka, M. M. 1970. *Discriminant Analysis: The Study of Group Differences*. Champaign, IL: Institute for Personality and Ability Testing.

Tennenbaum, A. N. 1993. *Justifiable Homicides by Civilians in the United States, 1976–1990: An Exploratory Analysis*. Ph.D. diss. University of Maryland, College Park.

Tennenbaum, A. N. and A.A. Moore. 1993. "Technological Development as a Solution of the Gun Debate." *The Futurist* 27(5): 20–23.

Uniform Crime Reporting Section. 1988. "National Incident-Based Reporting System." vol. 1, *Data Collection Guidelines*. Washington, DC: Federal Bureau of Investigation, U.S. Department of Justice.

———. 1992. "National Incident-Based Reporting System." vol. 2, *Data Submission Specifications*. Washington, DC: Federal Bureau of Investigation, U.S. Department of Justice.

Wilkens, L. W. 1965. *Social Policy, Action and Research*. London: Tavistock Publishing.

Wilson, H. J. 1992. Letter to Abraham N. Tennenbaum by the chief of the UCR program. Washington, DC, December 30.

Wilson, M. I. and M. Daly. 1992. "Who Kills Whom in Spouse Killings? On the Exceptional Sex Ratio of Spousal Homicides in the United States." *Criminology* 30(2): 189–215.

Wolfgang, M. E. [1958] 1975. *Patterns in Criminal Homicide*. Montclair, NJ: Patterson Smith.

Zahn, M. and P.C. Sagi. 1987. "Stranger Homicides in Nine American Cities." *Journal of Criminal Law and Criminology* 78(2): 377–397.

19

The Most-Cited Scholars and Works in Criminological Theory

Richard A. Wright and Jason Rourke

In recent years, numerous articles have identified some of the most-cited scholars and works in criminology and criminal justice (see Cohn and Farrington 1990, 1994a, 1994b, 1996; Wright 1995, 1996; Wright and Cohn 1996; Wright and Soma 1996). So far, these studies have examined general criminology and criminal justice journals (Cohn and Farrington 1990, 1994a, 1994b, 1996) or introductory textbooks (Wright 1995, 1996; Wright and Cohn 1996; Wright and Soma 1996): no attempt has been made to analyze the most-cited scholars and works in particular specialties within criminology and criminal justice. Here we extend citation research to the analysis of scholars and works in one important specialization: criminological theory.

Through an examination of eight recent advanced textbooks specifically devoted to criminological theory and six volumes of *Advances in Criminological Theory*, we identify the fifty most-cited scholars and the twenty-seven most-cited works. These lists of the most-cited scholars and works in criminological theory are compared to similar lists appearing in recent studies of general criminology and criminal justice journals and textbooks. We conclude with some thoughts about the importance of conducting citation research in criminological theory, along with other specialty areas in criminology and criminal justice.

Existing Literature

Citation studies in criminology and criminal justice can be traced to Cole (1975), Wolfgang, Figlio, and Thornberry (1978), and Shichor

(1980). Cole (1975) examined the most-cited scholars in 533 articles dealing with general social deviance topics (including mental illness and suicide) published in four *journals—American Journal of Sociology, American Sociological Review, Social Forces,* and *Social Problems—from* 1950 to 1973. In particular, Cole (1975) studied Robert K. Merton's position among these scholars, concentrating on the citations to Merton's (1938) renowned article "Social Structure and Anomie." He found that these citations were strongly affected by the publication of major studies inspired by Merton (1938), notably Cohen (1955) *Delinquent Boys: The Culture of the Gang* and Cloward and Ohlin's (1960) *Delinquency and Opportunity: A Theory of Delinquent Gangs.* Citations to Merton's article rose immediately following the publication of these works, but fell shortly thereafter.

Subsequent studies specifically analyzed the citation patterns to scholars and works in large numbers of criminological publications. Most noteworthy is Wolfgang, Figlio, and Thornberry's (1978) *Evaluating Criminology,* a monumental examination of the citation patterns in all known scholarly journal articles and research books dealing with crime-related topics published from 1945 to 1972. Because Wolfgang, Figlio, and Thornberry (1978) ignored textbooks, Shichor (1980) soon followed with an analysis of the most-cited scholars in twenty introductory criminology textbooks appearing from 1976 to 1980.

Recent citation studies in criminology and criminal justice have been done by Cohn and Farrington (1990, 1994a, 1994b, 1996) and Wright and his associates (Wright 1995, 1996; Wright and Cohn 1996; Wright and Soma 1996). Cohn and Farrington (1990, 1994a, 1994b, 1996) have identified the most-cited scholars and works in journals. For example, from an analysis of three American criminology journals (*Criminology, Journal of Quantitative Criminology,* and *Journal of Research in Crime and Delinquency*) and three American criminal justice journals (*Criminal Justice and Behavior, Journal of Criminal Justice,* and *Justice quarterly*) published from 1986 to 1990, Cohn and Farrington (1994b) ranked the forty-seven most-cited scholars. Similarly, Cohn and Farrington (1996) ranked the fifty-three most-cited scholars in the annual *Crime and Justice: A Review of Research* (volumes 1 to 17), and the seventy-five most-cited criminology/criminal justice works in the Social Science Citation Index (SSCI), from 1979 to 1993.

Wright and his associates (Wright 1995, 1996; Wright and Cohn 1996; Wright and Soma 1996) extended the recent study of the most-cited scholars to criminology and criminal justice textbooks. For example, in an analysis of fifty-three introductory criminology textbooks published from 1963 to 1968, 1976 to 1980, and 1989 to 1993, Wright and Soma (1996) reported the sixty-five most-cited scholars over thirty-one years. Similar studies of textbooks published from 1989 to 1993 identified: (1) the forty-seven most-cited scholars in twenty-three introductory criminology textbooks (Wright 1995); (2) the twenty-two most-cited scholars in sixteen introductory criminal justice textbooks (Wright and Cohn 1996); and (3) the sixteen most-cited scholars in thirty-nine introductory criminology and criminal justice textbooks (Wright 1996).

Citation studies have been criticized for a number of reasons. For example, it is often noted that these studies do not distinguish between positive and negative evaluations of cited works (Cohn and Farrington 1994a, 1994b). Still, Cole's (1975) analysis of social deviance articles shows that the vast majority of citations to Merton (1938) elicited either a positive or a neutral response; only 6 percent of the citations were critical of Merton's arguments. The consensus among citation researchers throughout the social sciences is that authors and works are seldom cited for the purposes of criticism (Chapman 1989; Cohn and Farrington 1994a, 1994b; Garfield 1979).

Studies that rely on the SSCI (e.g., Cohn and Farrington 1996) have some special problems. For example, the SSCI indexes only a few of the many journals published in criminology and criminal justice: citations in non-indexed journals are missing in these studies. Perhaps worse, the SSCI lists only first authors of works; publications with multiple authors are routinely tabulated incorrectly in studies that use the SSCI database.

More to the point of this chapter, recent citation studies have had a general focus, attempting to report the "most influential" (Cohn and Farrington 1994a) scholars and works throughout criminology and criminal justice. Although this research has helped discern broad, discipline-wide trends and developments—including the changing fortunes of methodological approaches and theoretical perspectives (see Cohn and Farrington 1994b, 1996; Wright and Soma 1996)—citation analysts have not examined the most-cited scholars and works in particular specializations within criminology and criminal justice. While some experts on the police, courts, corrections, women and crime, or critical criminology may have little regard for broad studies that identify the most-cited scholars and works throughout criminology and criminal justice, they probably would express far more interest in narrow studies that examine the citation patterns within their specialty.

This study begins the process of channeling citation research toward specialty areas in criminology and criminal justice through an examination of the most-cited scholars and works in criminological theory. By focusing our analysis only on publications specifically devoted to theoretical issues and concerns, we identify the fifty most-cited scholars and the twenty-seven most-cited works in criminological theory. We then compare our findings to more general studies that report the most-cited scholars and works throughout criminology and criminal justice journals and textbooks.

Research Design

We began our study by analyzing the citation patterns in the first six volumes of the annual *Advances in Criminological Theory*, appearing from 1988 to 1995. Because the publication history of this annual is still fairly short, we supplemented these data by examining the citations in several advanced textbooks dealing with criminological theory, appearing from 1986 to 1995. Altogether, we analyzed eighty-one publications, including seventy-three essays from *Advances in Criminological Theory* and eight textbooks.

At the time of our study, the annual *Advances in Criminological Theory* was the only periodical in criminology/criminal justice specifically devoted to theoretical issues. (A new journal—Theoretical Criminology—began publication in 1997.) We originally envisioned our study as a complementary piece to Cohn and Farrington's (1996) citation analysis of the annual *Crime and Justice: A Review of Research*. While the choice of *Crime and Justice* may have inadvertently skewed Cohn and Farrington's (1996) list of most-cited scholars toward those who conduct practitioner-oriented, quantitative research, our selection of *Advances in Criminological Theory intentionally* biased our findings toward identifying the most-cited scholars and works specializing in criminological theory.

Cohn and Farrington (1996) had a long publication history (from 1979 to 1993) of seventeen volumes of *Crime and Justice* available for analysis; however, we were limited to only six volumes of *Advances in Criminological Theory*. We became concerned that a number of special topic volumes—including volume 5, *Routine Activity and Rational Choice* (Clarke and Felson 1993) and volume 6, *The Legacy of Anomie Theory* (Adler and Laufer 1995)—might distort our findings in favor of scholars and works associated with particular perspectives. To guard against this possibility, we supplemented our study of *Advances in Criminological Theory* with an analysis of eight advanced textbooks specifically covering criminological theory.

Although Vold's (1958) *Theoretical Criminology* once stood alone as the only textbook devoted solely to the topic, in recent years numerous advanced texts have appeared on criminological theory (Wright and Rogers 1996). We analyzed the most recent editions of all eight textbooks published in the last decade (since 1986) dealing principally with criminological theory (see Wright and Rogers 1996), including Akers (1994), Curran and Renzetti (1994), Einstadter and Henry (1995), Gibbons (1994), Lilly, Cullen, and Ball (1995), Martin, Mutchnick, and Austin (1990), Vold and Bernard (1986), and Williams and McShane (1994).[1] We then pooled the citation data from *Advances in Criminological Theory* and these textbooks.

In recent analyses of the most-cited scholars and works in journals (see Cohn and Farrington 1994a, 1994b, 1996; Wright and Carroll 1994), citations were tallied from references at the ends of articles. Because two of the books (Curren and Renzetti 1994; Vold and Bernard 1986) included in this study exclusively incorporate references in footnotes, we had to use a far more cumbersome and time-consuming means to count citations: in our study, each mention of a scholar/work—in the text or in a substantive footnote—accompanied by a reference was counted as a citation.

In prior citation studies, self-citations have been a problem for researchers. Some analysts always exclude these citations from their counts (see Cohn and Farrington 1994a, 1994b, 1996); others routinely include self-citations (see Wright 1995, 1996; Wright and Cohn 1996; Wright and Soma 1996). Neither approach is entirely satisfactory; excluding self-citations risks underestimating the influence of prolific authors, responsible for a number of books, book chapters, and articles examined in a study (in effect, these scholars are ranked against others based on fewer publications). Including self-citations risks overestimating the influence of scholars who are fond of citing their own work.

In this study, we developed a formula to adjust for self-citations. "C_2" (the adjusted number of citations) was calculated as follows:

$$C_2 = C_1 + \frac{C_1}{P_1} (P_2),$$

where "C_1" is the total number of citations to a scholar in publications not written by the scholar, "P_1" is the total number of publications not written by a scholar that cite his/her work, and "P_2" is the total number of publications written by a scholar that contain self-citations. For all the publications that cite a scholar, this formula adjusts for self-citations by projecting the average number of citations the scholar receives in works that he/she did not write into the works that he/she wrote.[2] To control for self-citations in publications of different lengths (articles and books), we separately calculated adjusted citation scores for the essays in *Advances in Criminological Theory* and for the textbooks.

Although we calculated adjusted citation scores for each scholar who wrote at least one work examined in our study that contained a self-citation, the adjusted scores were only used to rank scholars when these estimates were lower than the actual counts that included self-citations. It should be noted that the adjusted citation scores prevented scholars from being ranked in our study if they extensively cite themselves in a handful of publications, but are seldom cited elsewhere.

Following Cohn and Farrington (1996), we used both incidence and prevalence measures to rank the most-cited scholars and works. Incidence is the total number of times that scholars/works were cited in the eighty-one publications that we examined; prevalence is the total number of publications that cite a scholar/work. Most previous citations studies (Cohn and Farrington 1990, 1994a, 1994b; Wright 1995, 1996; Wright and Cohn 1996; Wright and Soma 1996) rank scholars mostly by incidence of citations, not prevalence (but see Cohn and Farrington 1996). When citation studies ignore prevalence measures, they risk overestimating the influence of scholars who are heavily cited, but only in a handful of publications.

In particular, prevalence measures were used to compile our list of the most-cited works in criminological theory. We implemented a simple procedure to offset the influence of ten "citation outliers," or works that are repeatedly cited in a few publications, but nowhere else. To appear on our list, a work had to be cited at least thirty times (incidence) in at least ten publications (prevalence). The self-citation adjustment formula was also applied to the most-cited works in our study.

Findings

Table 19.1 reports the fifty most-cited scholars in the eighty-one criminological theory publications that we examined. The table ranks these scholars by incidence of citations (again, the total number of citations that each received) and by prevalence of citations (the total num-

TABLE 19.1
The Fifty Most-Cited Scholars in Criminological Theory

Ranks[a]	Scholar	Incidence of Citations[b]/ Prevalence of Citations[c]
1/1	Travis Hirschi	499/52(53)
2/3	Edwin H. Sutherland	298/38
3/37	Richard Quinney	272/16
4/5	Robert K. Merton	259(388)/29(30)
5/2	Michael R. Gottfredson	237(241)/43(44)
6/4	Donald R. Cressey	216(228)/33(34)
7/38	Thomas J. Bernard	207/16(18)
8/–	George B. Vold	189/13(14)
9/8	Richard A. Cloward	174/26
10/16	Ronald V. Clarke	164(168)/23(25)
11/22	Ronald L. Akers	157(227)/22(23)
12/9	Albert K. Cohen	154/26
13/–	Jock Young	151/13
14/–	William J. Chambliss	137/13
15/6	Lloyd E. Ohlin	134/29
16/13	John Braithwaite	132/24(25)
17/–	Cesare Beccaria	124/9
18/14	Derek B. Cornish	114(126)/24(25)
19/23	Émile Durkheim	114/22
20/39	Howard S. Becker	113/16
21/7	Delbert S. Elliott	112/27
22/40	John L. Hagan	112(124)/16(17)
23/24	Gresham M. Sykes	109/21
24/–	Walter C. Reckless	109/13
25/17	Marvin D. Krohn	108/23
26/–	Robert Agnew	108(138)/13(14)
27/10	Marvin E. Wolfgang	102/26
28/28	Clifford R. Shaw	100/18
29/41	Sarnoff A. Mednick	99/16
30/11	James Q. Wilson	96/26
31/12	David Matza	96/25
32/26	Jack P. Gibbs	92/19
33/18	Richard J. Herrnstein	90/23
34/–	Erving Goffman	89/7
35/25	Marcus Felson	86(89)/20(21)
36/–	C. Ray Jeffery	86(101)/10(12)
37/27	Marshall B. Clinard	83/19
38/32	Francis T. Cullen	81(94)/17(18)

TABLE 19.1 (continued)

Ranks[a]	Scholar	Incidence of Citations[b]/ Prevalence of Citations[c]
39/–	Raymond Paternoster	80/11(13)
40/–	Austin T. Turk	78(84)/10(12)
41/29	James F. Short	77/18
42/15	Lawrence E. Cohen	76/24
43/19	Albert J. Reiss, Jr.	76/23
44/–	Paul Walton	73/10
45/44	Edwin M. Lemert	72/15
46/–	Ian Taylor	72/10
47/33	Henry D. McKay	69/17
48/34	Gilbert Geis	68(70)/17(18)
49/42	Ruth Rosner Kornhauser	67/16
50/45	Thorsten J. Sellin	66/15
–/20	David P. Farrington	63(92)/23(24)
–/21	Michael J. Hindelang	56/23
–/30	Suzanne S. Ageton	56/18
–/31	Albert Bandura	53/18
–/35	Steven F. Messner	56/17(18)
–/36	Allen E. Liska	36/17
–/43	Charles R. Tittle	56/16(17)
–/46	David Huizinga	60/15
–/47	Gary F. Jensen	41(45)/15(17)
–/48	Robert J. Sampson	39(77)/15(16)[d]

[a] The first rank is by the total number of citations to the scholar (incidence); the second is by the total number of publications citing the scholar (prevalence). In cases of ties in incidence of citations, ranks were determined by the prevalence of citations (and vice versa).

[B] When incidence scores were adjusted because of self-citations, the unadjusted scores (that include self-citations) are reported in parentheses.

[c] The first prevalence score excludes publications with self-citations; the second score (in parentheses) includes these publications. Prevalence rankings were based on the scores that *excluded* self-citations.

[d] For the prevalence rankings, five scholars tied for fifty-first place, with citations in fourteen publications: Robert J. Bursik, Jr., Don C. Gibbons, Sheldon Glueck, David F. Greenberg, and Terence P. Thornberry.

ber of publications that cited each scholar at least once). In incidence, Travis Hirschi ranked first with 499 citations, an impressive 201 citations ahead of Edwin H. Sutherland in second place. Hirschi also finished first in prevalence, with a total of 52 of the 81 publications (or 59.8 percent) citing him at least once.

Six scholars—Richard A. Cloward, Donald R. Cressey, Michael R. Gottfredson, Travis Hirschi, Robert K. Merton, and Edwin H. Sutherland—ranked among the top ten both in incidence and prevalence of citations. Although Thomas J. Bernard, Ronald V. Clarke, Richard Quinney and George B. Vold ranked among the top ten scholars in incidence of citations, they were replaced by Albert K. Cohen, Delbert S. Elliott, Lloyd E. Ohlin, and Marvin E. Wolfgang among the top ten in prevalence of citations.

Scanning through the rest of table 19.1, some similarity is apparent between the incidence and prevalence measures; altogether, thirty-one scholars who rated among the most-cited in incidence also were among the most-cited in prevalence. A simple correlation calculated on the two sets of names shows a strong relationship (r = .78). When shifting from incidence to prevalence measures, Suzanne S. Ageton, Albert Bandura, David P. Farrington, Michael J. Hindelang, David Huizinga, Gary F. Jensen, Allen E. Liska, Steven F. Messner, Robert J. Sampson, and Charles R. Tittle replaced Robert Agnew, Cesare Beccaria, William J. Chambliss, Erving Goffman, C. Ray Jeffery, Raymond Paternoster, Walter C. Reckless, Ian Taylor, Austin T. Turk, George B. Vold, Paul Walton, and Jock Young among the most-cited scholars.

A close examination of table 19.1 shows the advantage of ranking the most-cited scholars by incidence and by prevalence of citations. Many scholars ranked similarly in incidence and prevalence (cf., John Braithwaite, Richard A. Cloward, Donald R. Cressey, Michael R. Gottfredson, Travis Hirschi, Robert K. Merton, Edwin H. Sutherland, and Gresham M. Sykes). Still, several scholars (cf., Cesare Beccaria, Thomas J. Bernard, William J. Chambliss, Richard Quinney, George B. Vold, and Jock Young) ranked much higher in incidence than in prevalence, while a number of others (cf., Delbert S. Elliott, David P. Farrington, Michael J. Hindelang, David Matza, James Q. Wilson, and Marvin E. Wolfgang) ranked far higher in prevalence than in incidence. If this were a conventional citation study, that primarily emphasized the measurement of the incidence of citations to the exclusion of prevalence, the influence of the former scholars would be exaggerated, while the contributions of the latter would be underestimated.

Further inspection of table 19.1 shows that the most-cited scholars in criminological theory are characterized by much diversity in perspectives and generations, but by little cultural diversity. Scholars closely associated with various disciplinary and theoretical orientations include Richard J. Herrnstein, C. Ray Jeffery, and Sarnoff A. Mednick for biological theory; William J. Chambliss, Richard Quinney, George B. Vold, and Jock Young for conflict perspectives; John Braithwaite and Delbert S. Elliott for integrated approaches; Howard S. Becker, Erving Goffinan, and Edwin M. Lemert for labeling/social reaction perspectives; Albert Bandura and David P. Farrington for psychology; Ronald V. Clarke and Derek B. Cornish for rational choice; Lawrence E. Cohen and Marcus Felson for routine activity; Émile Durkheim, Travis Hirschi, Walter C. Reckless, and Albert J. Reiss, Jr. for social control; Henry D. McKay and Clifford R. Shaw for social disorganization; Ronald L. Akers, Donald R. Cressey, and Edwin H. Sutherland for social learning; and Robert Agnew, Richard A. Cloward, Albert K. Cohen, Robert K. Merton, and Lloyd E. Ohlin for strain perspectives. Different generations and even centuries are represented in table 19.1; for example, Cesare Beccaria published *On Crimes and Punishments* in 1764, and Émile Durkheim wrote in the late nineteenth- and early twentieth centuries. Altogether, fourteen scholars in table 19.1 are now deceased: Beccaria, Donald R. Cressey, Durkheim, Erving Goffman, Richard J. Herrnstein, Michael J. Hindelang, Ruth Rosner Kornhauser, Edwin M. Lemert, Henry D. McKay, Walter C. Reckless, Thorsten J. Sellin, Clifford R. Shaw, Edwin H. Sutherland, and George B. Vold.

Much less cultural diversity is found among the most-cited criminological theorists. Most are Americans or residents of the United States (the exceptions are Derek B. Cornish, David P. Farrington, and Jock Young in England, John Braithwaite and Paul Walton in Australia, Ian Taylor in Canada, Cesare Beccaria in Italy, and Émile Durkheim in France). There is almost no gender diversity in table 19.1; the only women are Suzanne S. Ageton and Ruth Rosner Kornhauser.

When comparing the most-cited criminological theorists to recent studies of citations in criminology and criminal justice textbooks (Wright 1995, 1996; Wright and Cohn 1996; Wright and Soma 1996) and journals (Cohn and Farrington 1990, 1994a, 1994b, 1996), some interesting patterns emerge.[3] A close association exists between the most-cited criminological theorists and the most-cited scholars in recent criminology textbooks: there are thirty-three matches of names in our study and Wright's (1995) analysis of the forty-seven most-cited scholars in criminology textbooks (r = .68). Less similarity appears between the most-cited criminological theorists and scholars who are heavily cited in recent leading criminology journals: a fairly weak association (r = .37) exists between the fifty most-cited criminological theorists and Cohn and Farrington's (1994b) list of the twenty-five most-cited scholars in

Criminology, Journal of Quantitative Criminology, and *Journal of Research in Crime and Delinquency* (fourteen of the same names appear on the lists). These conclusions seem to support Wright's (1993, 1995) assessment that criminology textbooks extensively cover theoretical issues, while leading journals have a different, more quantitative slant.[4]

Table 19.2 reports the most-cited works in the eighty-one publications that we examined. Again, to compile this list, we required works to be cited a minimum of thirty times (incidence) in at least ten publications (prevalence). Altogether, twenty-seven works met this criterion. Table 19.2 ranks these works by incidence and by prevalence.

It is interesting to note that most of the heavily cited works in criminological theory are books: the exceptions are five journal articles (Cohen and Felson 1979; Colvin and Pauly 1983; Merton 1938; Reiss 1951; Sykes and Matza 1958). Other recent studies of the most-cited works in criminology/criminal justice also show that books are much more extensively cited that other types of publications (e.g., articles, research notes, and book chapters). For example, in Cohn and Farrington's (1996) analysis of the most-cited works in the crime and justice journals indexed in SSCI from 1986 to 1993, twenty-five of the twenty-seven most cited works were books.[5] In criminology/criminal justice scholarship, books clearly have a better chance of garnering substantial citations than other types of publications.

The same general features noted about the most-cited criminological theorists also apply to the most-cited works in criminological theory. Again, Travis Hirschi appears at the top of the rankings for both incidence and prevalence, for *Causes of Delinquency* (1969). Once more, much theoretical and generational diversity can be observed in the works and the authors appearing in table 19.2, but less international and gender diversity. As examples of particularly venerable works, consider that Émile Durkheim's *The Division of Labor in Society* ([1893] 1984) and Robert K. Merton's "Social Structure and Anomie" (1938) are still heavily cited in their original forms.[6] Revised works spanning decades that appear in table 19.2 include Merton (1968; see Merton 1949), Shaw and McKay (1969; see Shaw and McKay 1942), Sutherland (1983; see Sutherland 1949), Sutherland, Cressey, and Luckenbill (1992; see Sutherland 1924), and Vold and Bernard (1986; see Vold 1958).

Table 19.2 permits a comparison of the most-cited works in criminological theory by incidence and prevalence measures. Publications that are frequently cited in many places (high incidence and high preva-

TABLE 19.2
The Twenty-seven Most-Cited Works in Criminological Theory

Ranks[a]	Work	Incidence of Citations[b]/ Prevalence of Citations[c]
1/1	Travis Hirschi (1969), *Causes of Delinquency*	231/35
2/18	George B. Vold and Thomas J. Bernard (1986), *Theoretical Criminology*	180/13(14)[d]
3/2	Edwin H. Sutherland, Donald R. Cressey, and David F. Luckenbill (1992), *Principles of Criminology*	150/32[d]
4/5	Robert K. Merton (1968), *Social Theory and Social Structure*	137(159)/23(24)[d]
5/3	Michael R. Gorrfredson and Travis Hirschi (1990), *A General Theory of Crime*	132/31
6/4	Richard A. Cloward and Lloyd E. Ohlin (1960), *Delinquency and Opportunity: A Theory of Delinquent Gangs*	125/26
7/8	Albert K. Cohen (1955), *Delinquent Boys: The Culture of the Gang*	91/21
8/16	Howard S. Becker (1973), *Outsiders: Studies in the Sociology of Deviance*	88/14[d]
9/6	James Q. Wilson and Richard J. Herrnstein (1985), *Crime and Human Nature*	79/22
10/24	Ian Taylor, Paul Walton, and Jock Young (1973), *The New Criminology: For a Social Theory of Deviance*	70/10
11/7	Derek B. Cornish and Ronald V. Clarke (1986), *The Reasoning Criminal: Rational Choice Perspectives on Offending*	68/22(24)
12/13	Ronald L. Akers (1985), *Deviant Behavior: A Social Learning Approach*	68(81)/15(16)[d]
13/12	Ruth Rosner Kornhauser (1978), *Social Sources of Delinquency: An Appraisal of Analytic Models*	67/16
14/14	John Braithwaite (1989), *Crime, Shame, and Reintegration*	64/15
15/15	Clifford R. Shaw and Henry D. McKay (1969), *Juvenile Delinquency and Urban Areas*	58/15[d]
16/25	William J. Chambliss and Robert B. Seidman (1982), *Law, Order, and Power*	54/10[d]
17/11	Robert K. Merton (1938), "Social Structure and Anomie"	52(56)/17(18)

TABLE 19.2 (continued)

Ranks[a]	Scholar	Incidence of Citations[b]/ Prevalence of Citations[c]
18/26	Mark Colvin and John Pauly (1983), "A Critique of Criminology: Toward an Integrated Strucutral-Marxist Theory of Delinquency Production"	48/10
19/9	Lawrence E. Cohen and Marcus Felson (1979), "Social Change and Crime Rate Trends: A Routine Activity Approach"	44/19(20)
20/20	Edwin H. Sutherland (1983), *White Collar Crime: The Uncut Version*	43/12[d]
21/19	Albert J. Reiss, Jr. (1951), "Delinquency as the Failure of Personal and Social Controls"	41/13
22/21	David Matza (1964), *Delinquency and Drift*	38/12
23/22	F. Ivan Nye (1958), *Family Relationships and Delinquent Behavior*	36/12
24/23	Delbert S. Elliott, David Huizinga, and Suzanne S. Ageton (1985), *Explaining Delinquency and Drug Use*	36/11
25/10	Gresham M. Sykes and David Matza (1957), "Techniques of Neutralization: A Theory of Delinquency"	33/18
26/27	Edwin M. Lemert (1972), *Human Deviance Social Problems, and Social Control*	33/10[d]
27/17	Émile Durkheim ([1893] 1984), *The Division of Labor in Society*	30/14

[a] The first rank is by the total number of citations to the work (incidence); the second is by the total number of publications citing the work (prevalence). In cases of ties in incidence of citations, ranks were determined by prevalence of citations (and vice versa).

[b] When incidence scores were adjusted because of self-citations, the unadjusted scores (that include self-citations) are reported in parentheses.

[c] The first prevalence score excludes publications with self-citations; the second score (in parentheses) includes these publications. Prevalence rankings were based on the scores that *excluded* self-citations.

[d] Reports the total citations to all editions of books in multiple editions. These books are listed in table 19.2 and in the References by most recent edition.

lence)—including Cloward and Ohlin (1960), Cohen (1955), Gottfredson and Hirschi (1990), Hirschi (1969), Merton (1968), and Sutherland, Cressey, and Luckenbill (1992)—have had a deep and a broad impact on recent criminological theory. These are stellar works that are extensively discussed *and* cited in many places. Works that are frequently cited, but in fewer places (higher incidence, lower prevalence)—e.g., Becker (1973), Chambliss and Seidman (1982), Colvin and Pauly (1983), Taylor, Walton, and Young (1973), and Vold and Bernard (1986)—have had a deep but narrow impact on recent scholarship. It is interesting to note that all of these works endorse conflict perspectives that are often critical of conventional theoretical approaches; these publications seem to have a somewhat limited, but loyal following. Finally, works that are typically cited only once or twice, but in many different places (lower incidence, higher prevalence), include Cohen and Felson (1979), Durkheim ([1893] 1984), Merton (1938), and Sykes and Matza (1958). These publications appear to have the enviable status of the "standard citation": in effect, they are so well-known in criminological theory that they "need no introduction" (and require little discussion).

By comparing tables 19.1 and 19.2, it is clear that some theorists are heavily cited mostly because of one work: Ruth Rosner Kornhauser for *Social Sources of Delinquency: An Appraisal of Analytic Models* (1978), Lloyd E. Ohlin for *Delinquency and Opportunity: A Theory of Delinquent Gangs* (Cloward and Ohlin 1960), Ian Taylor and Paul Walton for *The New Criminology: For a Social Theory of Deviance* (Taylor, Walton, and Young 1973), George B. Vold for *Theoretical Criminology* (Vold and Bernard 1986), and James Q. Wilson and Richard J. Herrnstein for *Crime and Human Nature* (1985). The opposite extremes are Robert Agnew, John L. Hagan, Richard Quinney, and Marvin E. Wolfgang, who are extensively cited despite having no work listed in table 19.2. Interestingly, Michael R. Gottfredson, Travis Hirschi, and Edwin H. Sutherland each garner over 100 citations *apart* from those received for their most-cited works.

Finally, there is a fairly weak relationship (r = .32) between the twenty-seven most-cited works in criminological theory and Cohn and Farrington's (1996) list of the fifty-four most-cited publications in the crime and justice periodicals included in the SSCI from 1986 to 1995.[7] Altogether, thirteen matches appear: Akers (1985), Becker (1973), Cloward and Ohlin (1960), Cohen (1955), Cohen and Felson (1979), Elliott, Huizinga, and Ageton (1985), Hirschi (1969), Lemert (1972), Matza (1964), Shaw and McKay (1969), Sutherland, Cressey, and Luckenbill (1992), Sykes and Matza (1957), and Wilson and Herrnstein (1985).[8] Apparently, important works in criminological theory sometimes do not have a wider impact on general scholarship in criminology and criminal justice.

Summary and Discussion

Recently, numerous studies have reported the most-cited scholars and works in criminology and criminal justice journals and textbooks. Up to this point, these studies have had a general orientation, attempting to list the "most influential" (Cohn and Farrington 1994a) scholars and works throughout criminology and criminal justice. We believe that a fruitful new research direction involves the examination of the most-cited scholars and works in particular specializations within criminology and criminal justice. Our study begins this research agenda by reporting the most-cited scholars and works in criminological theory.

We analyzed the citations in eighty-one publications appearing from 1986 to 1995, including seventy-three essays from the first six volumes of *Advances in Criminological Theory*, and eight advanced textbooks dealing specifically with criminological theory. From these publications, we identified the fifty most-cited scholars and the twenty-seven most-cited works, using both incidence and prevalence measures. We compared our lists of the most-cited scholars and works in criminological theory to other lists from general studies of citation patterns in journals and in introductory textbooks: we found more similarity between the citations in criminological theory and introductory criminology textbooks than with the journal data.

There is one important caveat to our research: lists of the most-cited scholars and works are no more representative of a discipline or a specialty than the publications that researchers choose to analyze. For example, one reason that Cohn and Farrington (1990, 1994a, 1994b, 1996) typically find so many quantitative researchers among the most-cited criminologists and criminal justicians is that they analyze mostly quantitative-oriented journals (e.g., *Criminology, Journal of Quantitative Criminology*, and *Journal of Research in Crime and Delinquency*; see Cohn and Farrington 1994b). If we included different types of publications in our research design—for example, books proposing original theories instead of textbooks for advanced courses in criminological theory—our results would certainly be different.

We believe that reporting the most-cited scholars and works in criminological theory is important for several reasons. First, the comparisons of our findings with citation studies of leading criminology journals suggest that a number of quantitative researchers may have little awareness of some of the authors and works that have credibility and influence in criminological theory. We hope that our study will alert scholars *outside* criminological theory about some of the most important contributors and contributions *inside* this specialty.

Specialists in criminological theory can gain some critical insight by our analysis of the most-cited scholars and works in their area. In particular, our study suggests that while criminological theorists have been sufficiently attentive to the advances made by scholars from different perspectives and generations, they tend to overlook the important theoretical contributions made by international and especially women scholars. For example, feminist perspectives on crime and justice have blossomed in recent years: there are now clearly articulated liberal, radical, socialist, Marxist, and postmodern theoretical positions in feminist criminology (for example, see Beirne and Messerschmidt 1995; Gelsthorpe and Morris 1990; Jagger and Rothenberg 1984). The citation patterns in the theoretical publications that we examined suggest that some criminological theorists may not be familiar with these developments.

We also believe that our lists of the most-cited scholars and especially the most-cited works will prove helpful to specialists for library acquisition purposes and as they prepare reading lists for their courses. Our inventory of the twenty-seven most-cited works is a particularly useful resource for assessing the collections in university libraries: criminology/criminal justice faculty who either teach theory courses or who are responsible for library acquisitions should see that these works— along with the annual *Advances in Criminological Theory* and the new journal *Theoretical Criminology*—are ordered by campus librarians.

It should be kept in mind that extensive citation sometimes helps the career advancement of academics (see Cohn and Farrington 1994a, 1994b). Scholars on the job market who are searching for a position at a top-ranked criminal justice program, or those seeking promotion (especially to the rank of "full professor"), can receive a crucial boost by appearing on a list of most-cited scholars. In earlier studies of leading criminology/criminal justice journals (see Cohn and Farrington 1990, 1994a, 1994b, 1996), quantitative researchers largely appeared on most-cited lists; as a result, these are the scholars who have reaped career advantages from previous studies. We hope that our analysis of the most-cited scholars and works in criminological theory will extend these benefits to prominent theorists.

Finally, it is important for citation research to move beyond general studies of the citation patterns throughout criminology and criminal justice to more specific analyses of the most-cited scholars and works in specialty areas. Besides criminological theory, other specialties that seem ripe for citation analysis include law enforcement, legal studies and the sociology of law, corrections, women and criminal justice, and critical criminology. We offer our study of publications in criminological theory as an example to prospective researchers, showing how to conduct citation analyses in other specialty areas in criminology and criminal justice.

Notes

1. Only textbooks published in the United States were included in the analysis. Anthologies/readers dealing with criminological theory (e.g., Jacoby 1994; Williams and McShane 1993) and theory textbooks covering related topics—including juvenile delinquency (Shoemaker 1996) and social deviance (Pfohl 1994)—were excluded from the study.
2. To take one hypothetical example, say that Professor X cites himself/herself 150 times in ten publications, and is cited 30 additional times in fifteen other publications. The adjusted citation score (50) probably better estimates his/her impact on scholarship than either the extreme number of total citations when self-citations are counted (180), or the modest number of citations received in the publications that he/she did not write.
3. These comparisons must be based on incidence measures, since previous studies of the most-cited scholars in criminology/criminal justice have largely measured incidence of citations to the exclusion of prevalence.
4. These conclusions may be a product of the leading journals that Cohn and Farrington (1994b) chose for their study. Had they analyzed other prominent criminology journals—especially *Journal of Criminal Law and Criminology* and *Law and Society Review—their* findings may have changed.
5. The exceptions are two articles: Becker (1968) and Loeber and Dishion (1983). The former is a path-breaking application of economic theory to the etiology of crime; the latter is an important comparison and evaluation of numerous instruments designed to predict male delinquency.
6. Although Durkheim ([1893] 1984) is a translated work, from the French original.
7. This comparison is limited to journals because to date, no study has analyzed the most-cited works in criminology/criminal justice textbooks (see Shichor 1982; Wright 1995, 1996; Wright and Cohn 1996; Wright and Soina 1996).
8. In cases of multiple editions, these works are listed by their most recent publication date.

References

Adler, Freda, and William S. Laufer, eds. 1995. *The Legacy of Anomie Theory: Advances in Criminological Theory* (vol. 6). New Brunswick, NJ: Transaction Publishers.

Akers, Ronald L. 1985. *Deviant Behavior: A Social Learning Approach.* 3d ed. Belmont, CA: Wadsworth.

———. 1994. *Criminological Theories: Introduction and Evaluation.* Los Angeles: Roxbury.

Beccaria, Cesare. [1764]1963. *On Crimes and Punishments*. Indianapolis, IN: Bobbs-Merrill.

Becker, Gary S. 1968. "Crime and Punishment: An Economic Approach." *Journal of Political Economy* 76: 169–217.

———. 1973. *Outsiders: Studies in the Sociology of Deviance*. Rev. ed. New York: The Free Press.

Beirne, Piers and James Messerschmidt. 1995. *Criminology*. 2d ed. Fort Worth, TX: Harcourt Brace.

Braithwaite, John. 1989. *Crime, Shame, and Reintegration*. New York: Cambridge University Press.

Chambliss, William J. and Robert B. Seidman. 1982. *Law, Order, and Power*. 2d ed. Reading, MA: Addison-Wesley.

Chapman, Antony J. 1989. "Assessing Research: Citation-Count Shortcomings." *The Psychologist* 2:336–44.

Clarke, Ronald V., and Marcus Felson, eds. 1993. *Routine Activity and Rational Choice: Advances in Criminological Theory* (vol. 5). New Brunswick, NJ: Transaction Publishers.

Cloward, Richard A. and Lloyd E. Ohlin. 1960. *Delinquency and Opportunity: A Theory of Delinquent Gangs*. New York: The Free Press.

Cohen, Albert K. 1955. *Delinquent Boys: The Culture of the Gang*. New York: The Free Press.

Cohen, Lawrence E. and Marcus Felson. 1979. "Social Change and Crime Rate Trends: A Routine Activity Approach." *American Sociological Review* 44:588–608.

Cohn, Ellen G. and David P. Farrington. 1990. "Differences between British and American Criminology: An Analysis of Citations." *British Journal of Criminology* 30:467–82.

———. 1994a. "Who Are the Most Influential Criminologists in the English-speaking World?" *British Journal of Criminology* 34:204–25.

———. 1994b. "Who Are the Most-Cited Scholars in Major American Criminology and Criminal Justice Journals?" *Journal of Criminal Justice* 22:517–34.

———. 1996. "Crime and Justice and the Criminology and Criminal Justice Literature," pp. 265–300 in M. Tonry and N. Morris (eds.) *Crime and Justice: A Review of Research* (vol. 20). Chicago: University of Chicago Press.

Cole, Stephen. 1975. "The Growth of Scientific Knowledge: Theories of Deviance as a Case Study," pp. 175–230 in Lewis A. Coser (ed.) *The Idea of Social Structure*. New York: Harcourt Brace Jovanovich.

Colvin, Mark, and John Pauly. 1983. "A Critique of Criminology: Toward an Integrated Structural-Marxist Theory of Delinquency Production." *American Journal of Sociology* 89:513–51

Cornish, Derek B., and Ronald V. Clarke, eds. 1986. *The Reasoning Criminal: Rational Choice Perspectives on Offending*. New York: Springer-Verlag.

Curran, Daniel J., and Claire M. Renzetti. 1994. *Theories of Crime*. Boston: Allyn and Bacon.

Durkheim, Émile. [1893]1984. *The Division of Labor in Society*. New York: The Free Press.

Einstadter, Werner and Stuart Henry. 1995. *Criminological Theory: An Analysis of Its Underlying Assumptions*. Fort Worth, TX: Harcourt Brace.

Elliott, Delbert S., David Huizinga, and Suzanne S. Ageton. 1985. *Explaining Delinquency and Drug Use*. Beverly Hills, CA: Sage.

Garfield, E. 1979. "Is Citation Analysis a Legitimate Evaluation Tool?" *Scientometrics* 1:359–75.

Geisthorpe, Loraine and Allison Morris, eds. 1990. *Feminist Perspectives in Criminology*. Milton Keynes, England: Open University Press.

Gibbons, Don C. 1994. *Talking about Crime and Criminals: Problems and Issues in Theory Development in Criminology.* Englewood Cliffs, NJ: Prentice-Hall.

Gottfredson, Michael R. and Travis Hirschi. 1990. *A General Theory of Crime.* Stanford: Stanford University Press.

Hirschi, Travis. 1969. *Causes of Delinquency.* Berkeley and Los Angeles: University of California Press.

Jacoby, Joseph, ed. 1994. *Classics of Criminology.* 2d ed. Prospect Heights, IL: Waveland.

Jagger, Alison N., and Paula Rothenberg, eds. 1984. *Feminist Frameworks.* New York: McGraw-Hill.

Kornhauser, Ruth Rosner. 1978. *Social Sources of Delinquency: An Appraisal of Analytic Models.* Chicago: University of Chicago Press.

Lemert, Edwin M. 1972. *Human Deviance, Social Problems,and Social Control.* 2d ed. Englewood Cliffs, NJ: Prentice-Hall.

Lilly, J. Robert, Francis T. Cullen, and Richard A. Ball. 1995. *Criminological Theory: Context and Consequences.* 2d ed. Thousand Oaks, CA: Sage.

Loeber, Rolf and Thomas Dishion. 1983. "Early Predictors of Made Delinquency: A Review." *Psychological Bulletin* 94: 68–99.

Martin, Randy, Robert J. Mutchnick, and W. Timothy Austin. 1990. *Criminological Thought: Pioneers Past and Present.* New York: Macmillan.

Matza, David. 1964. *Delinquency and Drift.* New York: Wiley.

Merton, Robert K. 1938. "Social Structure and Anomie." *American Sociological Review* 3:672-82.

———. 1949. *Social Theory and Social Structure.* Glencoe, IL: Free Press.

———. 1968. *Social Theory and Social Structure.* 3d ed. New York: The Free Press.

Nye, F. Ivan. 1958. *Family Relationships and Delinquent Behavior.* New York: Wiley.

Pfohl, Steven J. 1994. *Images of Deviance and Social Control: A Sociological History.* 2d ed. New York: McGraw-Hill.

Reiss, Albert J., Jr. 1951. "Delinquency as the Failure of Personal and Social Controls." *American Sociological Review* 16:196–207.

Shaw, Clifford R. and Henry D. McKay. 1942. *Juvenile Delinquency and Urban Areas.* Chicago: University of Chicago Press.

———. 1969. *Juvenile Delinquency and Urban Areas.* Rev. ed. Chicago: University of Chicago Press.

Shichor, David. 1982. "An Analysis of Citations in Introductory Criminology Textbooks: A Research Note." *Journal of Criminal Justice* 10:231–7.

Shoemaker, Donald J. 1996. *Theories of Delinquency: An Examination of Explanations of Delinquent Behavior.* 3d ed. New York: Oxford University Press.

Sutherland, Edwin H. 1924. *Criminology.* Philadelphia: Lippincott.

———. 1949. *White Collar Crime.* New York: Dryden.

———. 1983. *White Collar Crime: The Uncut Version.* New Haven, CT: Yale University Press.

Sutherland, Edwin H., Donald R. Cressey and David F. Luckenbill. 1992. *Principles of Criminology.* 11th ed. Dix Hills, NY: General Hall.

Sykes, Gresham N. and David Matza. 1957. "Techniques of Neutralization: A Theory of Delinquency." *American Sociological Review* 22: 664–70.

Taylor, Ian, Paul Walton and Jock Young. 1973. *The New Criminology: For a Social Theory of Deviance.* London: Routledge and Kegan Paul.

Vold, George B. 1958. *Theoretical Criminology.* New York: Oxford University Press.

Vold, George B. and Thomas J. Bernard. 1986. *Theoretical Criminology.* 3d ed. New York: Oxford University Press.

Williams, Frank P., III, and Marilyn D. McShane, eds. 1993. *Criminology Theory: Selected Classic Readings.* Cincinnati: Anderson.

Williams, Frank P., III, and Marilyn D. McShane. 1994. *Criminological Theory.* 2nd ed. Englewood Cliffs, NJ: Prentice-Hall.

Wilson, James Q. and Richard J. Herrnstein. 1985. *Crime and Human Nature.* New York: Simon and Schuster.

Wolfgang, Marvin E., Robert N. Figho, and Terrence P. Thornberry. 1978. *Evaluating Criminology.* New York: Elsevier.

Wright, Richard A. 1993. "The Two Criminologies: The Divergent Woridviews of Textbooks and Journals." *The Criminologist* 18(3): 1, 8, 10.

———. 1995. "The Most-Cited Scholars in Criminology: A Comparison of Textbooks and Journals." *Journal of Criminal Justice* 23:303–11.

———. 1996. "The Most-Cited Scholars in Criminology and Criminal Justice Textbooks, 1989 to 1993." *The Justice Professional* 10: 199–213.

Wright, Richard A. and Kelly Carroll. 1994. "From Vanguard to Vanished: The Declining Influence of Criminology Textbooks on Scholarship." *Journal of Criminal Justice* 22:559–67.

Wright, Richard A. and Ellen G. Cohn. 1996. "The Most-Cited Scholars in Criminal Justice Textbooks, 1989 to 1993." *Journal of Criminal Justice* 24: 459–67.

Wright, Richard A. and Colette Soma. 1996. "The Most-Cited Scholars in Criminology Textbooks, 1963 to 1968, 1976 to 1980, and 1989 to 1993." *Journal of Crime and Justice* 19:45–60.

Wright, Richard A. and Joseph W. Rogers. 1996. "An Introduction to Teaching Criminology: Resources and Issues," pp. 1–33 in Richard A. Wright (ed.)*Teaching Criminology: Resources and Issues.* Washington, DC: American Sociological Association.

Author Index

Anderson, P.R. and L.T. Winfree
Supreme Court decisions basis from criminalists testimony, 83
Angel, Schlomo
Discouraging Crime through City planning, 431–32

Bauman, Zygmunt
Modernity and the Holocaust, 72
critique on genocide, 78
Beccaria, C.
on proportional punishment, 249
Ben-Yehuda, Nachman
on changing of social control concerns, 419–20
on deviant reduction, 411
on redefining societal boundaries, 391–92
Bernard, Thomas J.
on juvenile justice court model, 151
Bernstein, Basil
on verbal control of infants, 236
Bishop, Donna, Charles E. Frazier, and J.C. Henretta
on separate juvenile justice system, 150
Black, Donald
on punishment and societal inequality, 287
Block, R. and W.G. Skogen
stranger victimization findings, 42
Blumstein, A.
on ethnic imprisonment disporportionality, 201
Blumstein, A., J. Cohen, S.E. Martin, and M. Tonry
on abolishment of parole release, 203
Bortner, Margaret A.
on public safety and juvenile waivers, 149
remanded juveniles as most dangerous, 147–48

Brantingham, P.L., and P.J. Brantingham
crime pattern theory, 448–49
Brearley, H.C.
data relevance today, 465
Browne, A.
When Battered Women Kill, 38
Butts, J., H. Snyder, T. Finnegan, A. Aughenbaugh, N. Tierney, R. Poole, M. Sickmund, and E. Pole
Juvenile Court Statistics, 144

Cavan, S.
un-serious settings, 39–40
Center for Disease Control
medical treatment of violence, 8
Chancer, Lynn and Pamela Donovan
on moral outrage on crime, 320
Chiricos, T.G. and C. Crawford
on ethnicity of prisoners, 202–3
Chruchfield, R.D., G.S. Bridges, and S.R. Pritchford
on ethnic imprisonment disporportionality, 201
Clarke, R.V. and M. Felson
routine activity theory and stranger violence, 35
Clarke, R.V.
on CPTED and social causes, 446–48
Cohen, L.E. and M. Felson
private vs. public space and violence, 35
Cohen, Stanley
on changing of social control concerns, 419–20
Colborn, T.
genetic systems destruction, 10
Cook, P.J.
guns superiority over other types of threats, 42
Cooley, C.H.
primary stranger relationships, 31

513

Subject Index